D0420241

used in most introductory textbooks, namely 〜です・〜ます forms.

We have tried to give some indication of the various styles of Japanese speech and guidance on how to find a Japanese word that does not at first seem to be included by breaking it down into meaningful elements or by changing its form – see **How to use this Dictionary**.

One important feature of the Japanese-English section is that we have given some of the most common verbs in their 〜ます, 〜て and 〜ない forms. These entries are cross-referenced and will provide support in learning the relations between forms which are vital for understanding the grammar of Japanese and making progress with the language.

Another feature of this dictionary is that it avoids romanized Japanese. It is not usually the practice to teach Japanese seriously using roman script so we have given the translations and examples in syllabic scripts and an alternative using Chinese characters where this is appropriate. This helps learners to master the scripts quickly, learn Japanese word-order patterns, and avoid reliance on romanized forms which can lead to errors – especially in pronunciation. The syllabic scripts are easily learned and we have given a reference chart to help during early stages of script learning. We have kept to the government list of approved characters in the English to Japanese section examples. In the Japanese to English section we have kept some non-standard forms as they are likely to be encountered by people in Japan. Remember that kanji are not compulsory in many situations. Space prevents this dictionary including

About this dictionary

To get the most out of the information contained in this dictionary please see **How to use this Dictionary**.

In the Japanese to English section, we have given a wide range of Japanese words with English equivalents and suggestions as to how to understand and translate them. We have tried to be simple and straightforward and have therefore not included all possible meanings. Our guide for selection was usefulness not only to students but also to those visiting or working in Japan who will encounter a wide range of vocabulary, including culturally specific items needing explanation rather than just a translation.

In the English to Japanese section, the English words are followed by either translations or a suggested method of conveying English uses in Japanese. This section is mostly aimed at those studying the language formally. Such people often have to write short essays and diaries or make short presentations as part of their course and need to supplement their textbooks with other sources of Japanese. We have not tried to give all possible ways of expressing the English and our guideline for inclusion or exclusion was whether it seemed likely that users could manipulate the word or expression in the contexts in which they are most likely to need it. This will not produce perfect solutions to the problem of moving between two very different languages but it is better to try something and then find out why it is not right in a particular case than to not try at all. We have (after much consideration) been consistent in giving examples in the forms

The Oxford Japanese Minidictionary

Contributors and acknowledgements

Chief editors

Jonathan Bunt
with
Gillian Hall
Japan Centre North West – University of Manchester

Editors and Contributors

Miyoko Yamashita
Ayako Somers
Yukiko Shaw
Motoi Kitamura
Yumi Tozuka
Nobumi Kitamura

and many other family, friends and visitors to the Japan Centre who the editors would like to thank for their patience and their valiant attempts to answer impossible questions.

Special thanks to Suzuko Anai.

Thanks also to colleagues from the BATJ (British Association for the Teaching of Japanese) for their interest and support.

Contents

Proprietary terms

This dictionary includes some words which are, or are asserted to be, proprietary names or trade marks. Their inclusion does not imply that they have acquired for legal purposes a non-proprietary or general significance, nor is any other judgement implied concerning their legal status. In cases where the editor has some evidence that a word is used as a proprietary name or trade mark, this is indicated by the symbol ®, but no judgement concerning the legal status of such words is made or implied thereby.

The Oxford Japanese Minidictionary

Edited by

Jonathan Bunt
and
Gillian Hall

OXFORD

UNIVERSITY PRESS

Great Clarendon Street, Oxford OX2 6DP

Oxford University Press is a department of the University of Oxford.
It furthers the University's objective of excellence in research, scholarship,
and education by publishing worldwide in

Oxford New York

Auckland Cape Town Dar es Salaam Hong Kong Karachi Kuala Lumpur
Madrid Melbourne Mexico City Nairobi New Delhi Shanghai Taipei Toronto

With offices in
Argentina Austria Brazil Chile Czech Republic France Greece
Guatemala Hungary Italy Japan South Korea Poland Portuga
Singapore Switzerland Thailand Turkey Ukraine Vietnam

Oxford is a registered trade mark of Oxford University Press
in the UK and in certain other countries

Published in the United States
by Oxford University Press Inc., New York

© Jonathan Bunt 2000, 2001

The moral rights of the authors have been asserted

Database right Oxford University Press (maker)

First published as The Oxford Starter Japanese Dictionary, 2000
The Oxford Japanese Minidictionary first published 2001

All rights reserved. No part of this publication may be reproduced,
stored in a retrieval system, or transmitted, in any form or by any means,
without the prior permission in writing of Oxford University Press,
or as expressly permitted by law, or under terms agreed with the appropriate
reprographics rights organization. Enquiries concerning reproduction
outside the scope of the above should be sent to the Rights Department,
Oxford University Press, at the address above

You must not circulate this book in any other binding or cover
and you must impose this same condition on any acquirer

British Library Cataloguing in Publication Data

Data available

Library of Congress Cataloging in Publication Data

Data available

ISBN-13: 978-0-19-860366-5
ISBN-10: 0-19-860366-5

10 9 8 7 6

Typeset by Graphicraft Limited, Hong Kong
Printed and bound in Italy by
Legoprint S.p.A.

type 1 n it's a type of fish さかなの いっしゅです。・ 魚の 一種です。; this type of person この ような ひと・この ような 人; that type of book その ような ほん・そのような本; he's not my type かれは わたしの タイプではありません。・彼は 私の タイプではありません。 **2** vb タイプする

typewriter n タイプライター

typical adj てんけいてき(な)・典型的(な)

typist n タイピスト

tyre n (British English) タイヤ

Uu

ugly adj みにくい・醜い

umbrella n かさ・傘

unbelievable adj しんじられない・信じられない

uncle n (one's own) おじ; (someone else's) おじさん

uncomfortable adj ふゆかい(な)・不愉快(な); (describing shoes) きつい; (describing a seat) すわりごこちがわるい・座り心地が 悪い

unconscious adj いしきふめい(の)・意識不明(の)

under prep 〜の した・〜の 下; to hide under the bed ベッドの したに かくれる・ベッドの 下に 隠れる; I found the newspaper under it それの したで しんぶんを みつけました。・それの 下で 新聞を 見つけました。; (less than) 〜いか・〜以下; a wage of under three pounds an hour さんポンドいかの じきゅう・三ポンド以下の 時給; children under five ごさいいかの こども・五歳以下の 子供

underground n (British English) ちかてつ・地下鉄

underline vb かせんを ひく・下線を 引く

underneath 1 *adv* した ・ 下; I want to see what's underneath したに なにが あるか みたいです。・ 下に 何が あるか 見たいです。**2** *prep* 〜の したに ・ 〜の 下に; underneath the building たてものの したに ・ 建物 の 下に

underpants *n* パンツ

understand *vb* わかる・分かる; I can't understand what they're saying かれらが なにを いっているか わかりません。・彼らが 何を 言っているか 分かりません。; to make oneself understood つうじる・通じる

understanding *adj* おもいやりの ある ・ 思いやりの ある

underwater *adv* すいちゅうで ・ 水中で

underwear *n* したぎ ・ 下着

undo *vb* もとに もどす ・ 元に 戻す; (clothing) はずす ・ 外す; to undo a button ボタンを はずす ・ ボタンを 外す

undress *vb* ふくを ぬぐ ・ 服を 脱ぐ

uneasy *adj* ふあん(な) ・ 不安(な)

unemployed *adj* unemployed person しつぎょうしゃ ・ 失業者

unemployment *n* しつぎょう ・ 失業; unemployment rate しつぎょうりつ ・ 失業率; unemployment benefit しつぎょうてあて ・ 失業手当

unfair *adj* ふこうへい(な) ・ 不公平(な)

unfortunately *adv* ざんねんながら ・ 残念ながら

unfriendly *adj* (describing a person) ふしんせつ(な) ・ 不親切(な); (describing a place) ふんいきが わるい ・ 雰囲気が 悪い

ungrateful *adj* おんしらず(の) ・ 恩知らず(の)

unhappy *adj* (sad) かなしい ・ 悲しい; (not satisfied) ふまんが ある ・ 不満が ある

unhealthy *adj* (describing a way of life, food, conditions) けんこうに わるい ・ 健康に 悪い; (describing a person) びょうじゃく(な) ・ 病弱(な).

uniform *n* せいふく・制服

union *n* trade union くみあい・組合

unique *adj* どくとく(な)・独特(な)

United Kingdom *n* えいこく・英国！イギリス is also used for the UK

United States (of America) *n* アメリカがっしゅうこく・アメリカ合衆国！アメリカ is more generally used. べいこく・米国 is often used in newspapers.

universe *n* うちゅう・宇宙

university *n* だいがく・大学

unkind *adj* ふしんせつ(な)・不親切(な)

unknown *adj* しられていない・知られていない

unless *conj* I'm not going out unless it stops raining あめがやまなければ、でかけません。・雨が やまなければ、出かけません。; she can't work unless she buys a car かのじょは くるまを かわなければ、しごとが できません。・彼女は 車を 買わなければ、仕事が できません。

unlock *vb* かぎを あける・鍵を 開ける

unlucky *adj* (person) うんが わるい・運が 悪い; you were unlucky うんが わるかったです。・運が 悪かったです。; (object, number) えんぎが わるい・縁起が 悪い

unpack *vb* にもつを ほどく・荷物を 解く

unsuitable *adj* (clothes) ばちがい(の)・場違い(の); (person) ふてきとう(な)・不適当(な)

untidy *adj* (room) ちらかった・散らかった; (in how one looks) だらしが ない・だらしが ない; untidy handwriting じが きたない・字が きたない

until 1 *prep* use particle まで; I'm staying in a hotel until Thursday もくようびまで ホテルに とまります。・木曜日まで ホテルに 泊まります。; until now いままで・今まで; I'm going to wait until after Christmas クリスマスのあとまで まちます。・クリスマスの 後まで 待ちます。; she won't get an answer until next week かのじょは らいしゅうまでこたえを もらいません。・彼女は

来週まで 答えを もらいません。 **2** *conj* verb in dictionary form + まで; I'll wait until I go home うちに かえるまで まちます。・ 家に 帰るまで 待ちます。・ we'll be here until they come かれらが くるまで ここに います。・ 彼らが 来るまで ここに います。・ please don't look until it's ready できあがるまで みないでください。・ 出来上がるまで で 見ないで ください。

unusual *adj* (rare) めずらしい・珍しい; (different, out of the ordinary) かわった・変わった

up ! Often up occurs in combinations with verbs, for example: blow up, give up, own up, etc. To find the correct translations for this type of verb, look up the separate dictionary entries at blow, give, own etc. **1** *prep* This is not used as a preposition in Japanese; she ran up the stairs かのじょは かいだんを はしってのぼりました。・ 彼女は 階段を 走って 登りました。 **2** *adv* This is not used as an adverb in Japanese; up in the sky そらに・ 空に; up on (top of) the chest of drawers たんすのうえ・たんすの 上; to go up あがる・上がる; to go up to Scotland スコットランドにいく・スコットランドに 行く **3** *adj* (out of bed) to be up おきている・起きている; to be up all night ひとばんじゅう おきている・一晩中 起きている; (increase in amount) ふえる・増える; to be up by 20% にじゅうパーセント ふえる・二十パーセント 増える; (increase in level) あがる・上がる **4** up to (well enough) I'm not up to it できません。; (until) use particle まで; up to now いままで・ 今まで; up to 2010 にせんじゅうねんまで・ 二千十年まで

upset 1 *adj* to be upset; (annoyed) いらいらしている; (crying) ないている・泣いている; to get upset (annoyed) いらいらする; (cry) なく・泣く **2** *vb* (to make someone unhappy) to make someone cry だれかを なかせる・誰かを 泣かせる; (to annoy) いらいらさせる

upside down *adv* さかさま・逆さま

upstairs *adv* うえの かい・上の 階 In a two storey building or house use にかい; to go upstairs うえの かいに いく・上の 階に 行く; to bring the boxes upstairs うえの

かいにはこを もって いく・上の 階に 箱を 持って 行く

urgent adj きんきゅう(な)・緊急(な)

us pron わたしたち・私達 This can often be left out when it is obvious; they know us かれらは わたしたちを しっています。・彼らは 私達を 知っています。; he's seen us かれは わたしたちを みました。・彼は 私達を 見ました。; please help us! たすけてください。・助けてください。; please don't bother us! じゃまを しないでください。・邪魔を しないでください。; please don't show it to us! みせないでください。・見せないでください。; he did it for us かれは わたしたちの ために しました。・彼は 私達の ために しました。

USA n アメリカがっしゅうこく・アメリカ合衆国 ! アメリカ is more generally used. べいこく・米国 is often used in newspapers.

use 1 vb (to make use of) つかう・使う; I use the car to go to work くるまを つかって しごとに いきます。・車を 使って 仕事に 行きます。; he uses this room as an office かれは この へやを オフィスと して つかっています。・彼は この 部屋を オフィスと して 使っています。; what is it used for? なにに つかいますか。・何に 使いますか。; to use a different word ちがう ことばを つかう・違う 言葉を 使う; (to operate on) this car uses unleaded petrol この くるまは むえんガソリンで はしります。・この 車は 無鉛ガソリンで 走ります。; (to take advantage of) to use someone だれかを りようする・誰かを 利用する **2** n to make use of a room へやを つかう・部屋を 使う; to have the use of a car くるまが つかえる・車が 使える; (when talking about what is useful) to be of use やくに たつ・役に 立つ; to be no use やくに たたない・役に 立たない; what's the use of complaining? もんくを いっても しかたが ありません。・文句を 言っても 仕方が ありません。; **use up** to use up all the money おかねを ぜんぶ つかって しまう・お金を 全部 使って しまう

used 1 *vb* I used to read books a lot まえは よく ほんを よんでいました。・前は よく 本を 読んでいました。; you used not to smoke まえは たばこを すっていません でした。・前は たばこを 吸っていませんでした。; there used to be a castle here まえは ここに おしろが あ りました。・前は ここに お城が ありました。**2** *adj* な れている・慣れている; I'm used to life in Japan にほんの せいかつに なれています。・日本の 生活に 慣れていま す。; he's not used to living on his own かれは ひとりぐ らしに なれていません。・彼は 一人暮らしに 慣れて いません。; to get used to a new job あたらしい しごとに なれる・新しい 仕事に 慣れる

useful *adj* べんり(な)・便利(な)

useless *adj* (*not working, having no use*) つかえない・使え ない; (*having no point or purpose*) むいみ(な)・無意味 (な); it's useless complaining もんくを いうのは むいみ です。・文句を 言うのは 無意味です。; (*not good at*) にがて(な)・苦手(な); I'm useless at chemistry かがくが にがてです。・化学が 苦手です。

usually *adv* ふつうは・普通は

Vv

vacant *adj* あいている・空いている

vacation *n* (*US English*) りょこう・旅行; to take a vacation りょこうに いく・旅行に 行く

vacuum *vb* to vacuum a room へやに そうじきを かける ・部屋に 掃除機を 掛ける

vacuum cleaner *n* そうじき・掃除機

vague *adj* あいまい(な)

vain *adj* うぬぼれた

valid *adj* ゆうこう(な)・有効(な)

valley n たに・谷

valuable adj (very useful) きちょう(な)・貴重(な); (worth a lot of money) こうか(な)・高価(な)

van n バン

vandalize vb はかいする・破壊する

vanilla n バニラ

various adj いろいろ(な)・色々(な); there are various ways of saying this いろいろな いいかたが あります。・色々な 言い方が あります。

vary vb it varies from town to town まちに よって ちがいます。・町に よって 違います。

vase n かびん・花瓶

vegetable n やさい・野菜

vegetarian n さいしょくしゅぎしゃ・菜食主義者

vein n じょうみゃく・静脈

velvet n ベルベット

versus prep たい・対

very 1 adv とても; (with a negative) あまり + negative; I don't know him very well かれを あまり しりません。・彼を あまり 知りません。; to eat very little あまり たべない・あまり 食べない; you haven't said very much あまり いっていません。・あまり 言っていません。; I like him very much かれが とても すきです。・彼が とても 好きです。; for the very first time はじめて・初めて; they called the very next day かれらは つぎの ひ、でんわを しました。・彼らは 次の 日、電話を しました。 **2** adj at the very beginning はじめに・始めに; to sit at the very front いちばんまえに すわる・一番前に 座る; to stay to the very end さいごまで いる・最後まで いる

vest n (British English) (a piece of underwear) アンダーシャツ; (US English) (a waistcoat) チョッキ

vet n じゅうい・獣医

via prep 〜けいゆ・〜経由; we came via Hong Kong ホンコンけいゆで きました。・ホンコン経由で 来ました。

vicious adj (violent) もうれつ(な)・猛烈(な)・(nasty, meant to hurt) ざんこく(な)・残酷(な); vicious dog もうけん・猛犬

victory n しょうり・勝利; to win a victory しょうりする・勝利する

video 1 n (a recorded film, programme, event) ビデオ; ▶ video cassette, video recorder **2** vb (to record) ろくがする・録画する; (to film) to video a wedding けっこんしきの ビデオを とる・結婚式の ビデオを 撮る

video camera n ビデオカメラ

video cassette n ビデオカセット

video game n ビデオゲーム

video recorder n ビデオレコーダー

view n けしき・景色; you're blocking my view! じゃまです。・邪魔です。; (an opinion, an attitude) いけん・意見

village n むら・村

vinegar n す・酢

vineyard n ぶどうえん・ぶどう園

violent adj らんぼう(な)・乱暴(な)

violin n バイオリン

Virgo n おとめざ・乙女座

visit 1 vb (a place) いく・行く; to visit someone (to call on) たずねる・訪ねる; (to stay with) とまりに いく・泊りに行く **2** n (a call) ほうもん・訪問; (a stay) たいざい・滞在; to pay someone a visit だれかを たずねる・誰かを訪ねる

visitor n (a guest) おきゃくさん・お客さん; to have visitors おきゃくさんが いる・お客さんが いる; (a tourist) かんこうきゃく・観光客

vocabulary n ごい・語彙

voice n こえ・声; to have a good voice いい こえを もつ・いい 声を 持つ; to speak in a low voice ひくい こえで はなす・低い 声で 話す; in a loud voice おおごえで・大声で

volleyball n バレーボール

vomit vb はく・吐く

vote vb とうひょうする・投票する

....

Ww

....

wages n きゅうりょう・給料

waist n ウエスト

waistcoat n (British English) チョッキ

wait vb まつ・待つ; to wait for someone だれかを まつ・誰かを 待つ; I'm waiting to use the phone でんわを つかうのをまっています。・電話を 使うのを 待っています。; to wait for someone to go home だれかが かえるのをまつ・誰かが 帰るのを 待つ; let's have a beer while we're waiting for them かれらを まっている あいだに ビールをのみましょう。・彼らを 待っている 間に ビールを飲みましょう。; I can't wait to meet them かれらに あえるのをたのしみに しています。・彼らに 会えるのを 楽しみに しています。; **wait up** to wait up for someone だれかのかえりを まつ・誰かの 帰りを 待つ

waiter n ウェーター

waiting room n まちあいしつ・待合室

waitress n ウエートレス

wake vb to wake someone だれかを おこす・誰かを起こす; **wake up** めが さめる・目が 覚める

Wales n ウェールズ

walk 1 vb あるく・歩く; (for pleasure) さんぽする・散歩する; let's walk to the pool プールまで あるきましょう。・プールまで 歩きましょう。; to walk down the streetみちをあるく・道を 歩く; to walk the dog いぬを さんぽにつれて いく・犬を 散歩に 連れて 行く **2** n さん

ぽ・散歩; to go for a walk さんぽする・散歩する; it's five minutes' walk from here ここから あるいて ごふんです。・ここから 歩いて 五分です。; **walk around** あるきまわる・歩き回る; to walk around town まちを あるきまわる・町を 歩き回る; to walk around the lake みずうみ のまわりを あるく・湖の 周りを 歩く; **walk back** to walk back home あるいて かえる・歩いて 帰る; **walk round** あるきまわる・歩き回る; to walk round the park こうえんを あるきまわる・公園を 歩き回る

walkman® n ウォークマン

wall n かべ・壁

wallet n さいふ・財布

wallpaper n かべがみ・壁紙

walnut n くるみ

wander vb ぶらぶら あるく・ぶらぶら 歩く; to wander around town まちを ぶらぶら あるく・町を ぶらぶら 歩く

want vb (to want something) ほしい・欲しい not a verb in Japanese; I want a new camera あたらしい カメラが ほしいです。・新しい カメラが 欲しいです。; I don't want it ほしくないです。・欲しくないです。; do you want some coffee? コーヒーは いかがですか。; (to want to do...) Use the pre ます form of the verb + たい; I want to go out でかけたいです。・出かけたいです。; I don't want to go home かえりたくないです。・帰りたくないです。; I wanted to go to Japan にほんに いきたかったです。・日本に 行きたかったです。; I want to play あそびたいです。・遊びたいです。; the children want to eat it こどもたちは たべたがっています。・子供達は 食べたがっています。; (to want someone else to do...) use the ～て form of the verb + ほしい; I want you to read this これを よんでほしいです。・これを 読んで 欲しいです。; do you want me to come with you? いっしょに いって ほしいですか。・一緒に 行って 欲しいですか。; (to need) いる・要る; I don't want this anymore これは もう いりません。・これは もう 要りません。

war n せんそう・戦争

wardrobe n ようふくだんす・洋服だんす

warm 1 adj あたたかい・温かい; (air temperature) あたたかい・暖かい; I'm very warm あたたかいです。・暖かいです。; the classroom is warm きょうしつは あたたかいです。・教室は 暖かいです。; to get warm あたたかくなる・暖かく なる **2** vb to warm the plates さらを あたためる・皿を 温める; to warm the room へやを あたためる・部屋を 暖める; **warm up** (to get warm) あたたかくなる・暖かく なる; (for a sporting event) ウォーミングアップする; (to make warm) あたためる・温める

warn vb けいこくする・警告する; to warn someone about the danger だれかに きけんを けいこくする・誰かに 危険を 警告する; to warn someone to be careful だれかに きをつける ように ちゅういする・誰かに 気を 付けるように 注意する

wash vb (to clean) あらう・洗う; to wash one's face かおを あらう・顔を 洗う; to wash one's clothes せんたくする・洗濯する; **wash up** (British English) (to do the dishes) しょっきを あらう・食器を 洗う; (US English) (to clean oneself) かおを あらう・顔を 洗う

washbasin (British English), **wash-hand basin** n せんめんき・洗面器

washing n せんたく・洗濯; to do the washing せんたくする・洗濯する

washing machine n せんたくき・洗濯機

washing-up n (British English) しょっきあらい・食器洗い; to do the washing-up しょっきを あらう・食器を 洗う

wasp n すずめばち・雀蜂

waste 1 vb むだに する・無駄に する; to waste one's time じかんを むだに する・時間を 無駄に する; to waste electricity でんきを むだに つかう・電気を 無駄に 使う **2** n むだ・無駄; that's a waste of money それは おかねの むだです。・それは お金の 無駄です; it's a waste of time じかんの むだです。・ 時間の 無駄です。; it's a waste of time going there あそこに いくのは じかんの むだです。・ あそこに 行くのは 時間の 無駄です。

watch 1 n (to look at) みる ・ 見る; to watch television テレビを みる ・ テレビを 見る; I feel I'm being watched みられているように かんじます。・ 見られている ように 感じます。; (to pay attention to) きを つける ・ 気を つける; please watch what you're doing きを つけてください。・ 気を つけてください。; please watch you don't fall ころばないように きを つけてください。・ 転ばない ように 気を つけてください。 **2** n とけい ・ 時計; **watch out** きをつける ・ 気を つける

water 1 n (cold) みず ・ 水; (hot) おゆ ・ お湯; drinking water のみみず ・ 飲み水 **2** vb みずを やる ・ 水を やる

waterfall n たき ・ 滝

water-skiing n すいじょうスキー ・ 水上スキー

wave 1 vb てを ふる ・ 手を 振る **2** n (sea) なみ ・ 波; (radio) でんぱ ・ 電波

way 1 n (a means, a method) ほうほう ・ 方法; it's a way of earning money おかねを かせぐ ほうほうです。・ お金を 稼ぐ 方法です。; he does it the wrong way かれの やりかたは まちがっています。・ 彼の やり方は 間違っています。; (how one does something) やりかた ・ やり方 the suffix 〜かた can also be added to the pre ます form of the verb in specific cases; I prefer to do it my way じぶんの やりかたが いいです。・ 自分の やり方が いいです。; I like the way she speaks かのじょの はなしかたが すきです。・ 彼女の 話し方が 好きです。; (a route, a road) みち ・ 道; I can't remember the way to the station えきまでの みちを おぼえていません。・ 駅までの 道を 覚えていません。; on the way とちゅう ・ 途中; on the way to Hiroshima ひろしまに いく とちゅうで ・ 広島に 行く 途中で; where's the way out? でぐちは どこですか。・ 出口は どこですか。; to lose one's way みちに まよう ・ 道に 迷う; (a direction) which way are you going? どちらに いきますか。・ どちらに 行きますか。; they went that way かれら

はあちらに いきました。・彼らは あちらに 行きました。; please come this way こちらへ きてください。・こちらへ 来てください。; (*someone's route*) in the way じゃま; to get out of the way どく・退く; (*when talking about distances*) it's a long way from here ここから とおいです。・ここから 遠いです。; to go all the way to Japan にほんまで いく・日本まで 行く; if I had my way... できれば。。。 **2 by the way** ところで; What's his name, by the way? ところで、かれの なまえは なんですか。・ところで 彼の 名前は 何ですか。

we *pron* Note that if the subject of the sentence is obvious, it can often be left out. わたしたち・私達; we saw her yesterday きのう かのじょを みました。・昨日 彼女を 見ました。; we all make mistakes だれでも まちがえます。・誰でも 間違えます。

weak *adj* よわい・弱い; he has a weak heart かれは しんぞうの ちょうしが わるいです。・彼は 心臓の 調子が 悪いです。; (*not good or able*) にがて・苦手; he is weak at languages かれは ごがくが にがてです。・彼は 語学が 苦手です。; (*easily damaged*) こわれやすい・壊れやすい; (*having very little power*) ちからの ない・力の ない; (*describing tea or coffee*) うすい・薄い

wealthy *adj* ゆうふく(な)・裕福(な)

wear *vb* (*shirts, dresses*) きる・着る; (*hats*) かぶる; (*shoes, trousers, skirts, socks*) はく; (*makeup*) つける; (*spectacles*) かける; to be wearing a kimono きものを きている・着物を 着ている; to wear boots ブーツを はく; (*to put on*) きる・着る other verbs may be used depending on which item of clothing is being worn. See above; what will you wear? なにを きますか。・何を 着ますか。; I've got nothing to wear なにも きる ものが ありません。・何も 着る 物が ありません。; (*to damage*) つかいふるす・使い古す; **wear out** つかいふるす・使い古す; to wear one's shoes out くつを つかいふるす・靴を 使い古す; to wear someone out だれかを つかれさせる・誰かを 疲れさせる

weather *n* てんき・天気; what's the weather like? てんきは どうですか。・天気は どうですか。; the weather is bad てんきが わるいです。・ 天気が 悪いです。; the weather is nice てんきが いいです。・ 天気が いいです。; the weather is hot あついです。・ 暑いです。

weather forecast n てんきよほう・ 天気予報

wedding n けっこんしき・ 結婚式

Wednesday n すいようび・ 水曜日

week n one week いっしゅうかん・ 一週間; in two weeks' time にしゅうかんご(に)・ 二週間後(に)

weekend n しゅうまつ・ 週末

weigh vb おもさを はかる・ 重さを 計る; what do you weigh? たいじゅうは なんキロですか。・ 体重は 何キロですか。; to weigh oneself たいじゅうを はかる・ 体重を 計る

weight n (body) たいじゅう・ 体重; (object) おもさ・ 重さ; to lose weight たいじゅうを へらす・ 体重を 減らす

weird adj きみょう(な)・ 奇妙(な)

welcome vb to welcome someone だれかを かんげいする・ 誰かを 歓迎する; (when receiving people) (to your house) いらっしゃい; (in a formal situation) ようこそ; welcome to Japan にほんへ ようこそ・ 日本へ ようこそ; (when acknowledging thanks) 'thanks'—'you're welcome' 「どうも ありがとう。」「どう いたしまして。」 3 n かんげい・ 歓迎

well 1 adv (when talking about a skill) じょうずに・ 上手に; he can speak English well かれは えいごが じょうずに はなせます。・ 彼は 英語が 上手に 話せます。; to go well うまくいく; the test went well テストは うまく いきました。; it is well paid きゅうりょうが いいです。・ 給料が いいです。; he's not eating well かれは ちゃんと たべていません。・ 彼は ちゃんと 食べていません。 2 adj I feel well げんきです。・ 元気です。; to get well げんきに なる・ 元気に なる 3 as well use particle も 4 as well as ～の ほかに・ ～の 外に

well-known adj ゆうめい(な)・ 有名(な)

west 1 *n* にし・西; in the west of Japan にしにほんに・西日本に 2 *adv* to go west にしに いく・西に 行く 3 *adj* にし・西; to work in west London にしロンドンで はたらく・西ロンドンで 働く

West Indies *n* にしインドしょとう・西インド諸島

wet 1 *adj* (*damp*) ぬれている・濡れている; your hair is wet かみが ぬれています。・髪が 濡れています。; to get wet ぬれる・濡れる; she got her feet wet かのじょは あしが ぬれました。・彼女は 足が 濡れました。; (*when talking about weather*) in wet weather あめが ふっている とき・雨が 降っている とき; a wet day あめの ひ・雨の 日 2 *vb* ぬらす・濡らす

what 1 *pron* (*used in questions*) なに・何 *in some cases this is pronounced* なに; what's that box? あの はこは なんですか。・あの 箱は 何ですか。; what's the Japanese for 'boring'? にほんごで boring は なんですか。・日本語で boring は 何ですか。; what is she like? かのじょは どんな ひとですか。・彼女は どんな 人ですか。; what's her phone number? かのじょの でんわばんごうは なんばんですか。・彼女の 電話番号は 何番ですか。; what time is it? なんじですか。・何時ですか。; what day of the week? なんようびですか。・何曜日ですか。; (*used as a relative pronoun*) please do what you want すきな ように してください。・好きな ように してください。 2 *det* do you know what train to take? どの でんしゃに のれば いいか わかりますか。・どの 電車に 乗れば いいか 分かりますか。; what a great idea! すばらしい アイディアですね。 3 *exc* へえ 4 what if what if I don't get there on time? まに あわなければ どう しますか。・間に 合わなければ どう しますか。; what if it rains? あめが ふれば どう しますか。・雨が 降れば どう しますか。

whatever *pron* (*when anything is possible*) please ask whatever you want なんでも きいてください。・何でも 聞いてください。; (*when it doesn't matter*) use the ～て form of the verb + も; whatever they do, it won't change anything かれらが なにを しても かわりません。・彼らが 何を しても 変わりません。

wheat *n* むぎ・麦

wheel *n* ホイール

wheelchair *n* くるまいす・車椅子

when 1 *adv* (*generally*) いつ; when did she go? かのじょは いつ いきましたか。・彼女は いつ 行きましたか。; when is your birthday? たんじょうびは いつですか。・誕生日は いつですか。; (*what time*) なんじ・何時; I don't know when the film starts えいがが なんじに はじまるか わかりません。・映画が 何時に 始まるか 分かりません。 なん *can be added to other time counters when referring to a day or date.* ▶なんにち ▶なんようび ▶なんがつ ▶なんねん **2** *conj* 〜とき; I was asleep when the phone rang でんわが なった とき、ねていました。・電話が 鳴った とき、寝ていました。; when I was a student がくせいのとき・学生の とき; when I'm 18 I can get married じゅうはっさいに なったら けっこんが できます。・十八才になったら 結婚が できます。 **3** *pron* (*used as a relative pronoun*) 〜とき; in the days when there was no TV テレビが なかった ときに

where 1 *adv* どこ; where are you going? どこに いきますか。・どこに 行きますか。; where do they work? かれらは どこで はたらいていますか。・彼らは どこで 働いていますか。; Do you know where I is? かれが どこに いるか しっていますか。・彼が どこに いるか 知っていますか。; Do you know where we're going? どこに いくか わかりますか。・どこに 行くか わかりますか。; the village where we live わたしたちが すんでいる むら・私達が 住んでいる 村 **2** *conj* that's where the accident happened じこが あったのは あそこです。・事故が あったのは あそこです。; I'll leave the key where you can see it すぐ わかる ところに かぎを おいて おきます。・すぐ 分かる 所に カギを 置いて おきます。

whether *conj* 〜かどうか〜; I don't know whether or not to go there そこに いくか どうか わかりません。・そこ に 行くか どうか わかりません。

which 1 *pron* the house which I saw yesterday きのう みた いえ・昨日 見た 家 **2** *det* which one? どれですか。; which fruit do you like best? どの くだものが いちばんすきですか。・どの 果物が 一番好きですか。; tell me which film you'd like to see どの えいがを みたいか おしえてください。・どの 映画を 見たいか 教えてください。

while *conj* 〜あいだ・〜間; I had a party while my parents were in Spain りょうしんが スペインに いっている あいだ、パーティーを しました。・両親が スペインに 行っている 間、パーティーを しました。Note that ながら may also be added to the pre ます form of the verb to indicate that two action were taking place simultaneously; she ate while watching TV かのじょは テレビを みながら たべました。・彼女は テレビを 見ながら 食べました。

whisper *vb* ささやく

whistle 1 *vb* くちぶえを ふく・口笛を 吹く **2** *n* ふえ・笛

white *adj* しろい・白い

who *pron* (used in questions) だれ・誰; who told you? だれが いいましたか。・誰が 言いましたか。; who did you invite? だれを しょうたいしましたか。・誰を 招待しましたか。; who did he buy the book for? かれは だれに ほんを かいましたか。・彼は 誰に 本を 買いましたか。; (used as a relative pronoun) my friend who lives in Paris パリに すんでいる ともだち・パリに 住んでいる 友達; those who can't come by car くるまで こられない ひと・車で 来られない 人; a friend who I see at school がっこうの ともだち・学校の 友達

whole 1 *n* ぜんぶ・全部; the whole of Tokyo とうきょうの ぜんぶ・東京の 全部; the whole of the country ぜんこく・全国 **2** *adj* a whole day まる いちにち・まる 一日; the whole day いちにちじゅう・一日中; three whole weeks まる さんしゅうかん・まる 三週間

whom *pron* (used in questions) だれに・誰に; whom did you meet? だれに あいましたか。・誰に 会いましたか。;

(*used as a relative pronoun*) the person to whom I spoke on the phone でんわで はなした ひと・電話で 話した 人

whose 1 *pron* (*used in questions*) だれの・誰の; whose is the dog? いぬは だれの ですか。・犬は 誰の ですか。 (*used as a relative pronoun*) the person whose bike was stolen じてんしゃを ぬすまれた ひと・自転車を 盗まれた 人 **2** *det* whose car is that? それは だれの くるまですか。・それは 誰の 車ですか。 whose pen did you borrow? だれの ペンを かりましたか。・誰の ペンを 借りました か。

why 1 *adv* (*used in questions*) どうして; why did you do that? どうして それを しましたか。; why aren't they coming? かれらは どうして きませんか。・彼らは どうして 来 ませんか。; (*when making suggestions*) why don't we eat out tonight? こんばん がいしょくしませんか。・今晩 外食 しませんか。 **2** *conj* that's why I don't like him だから かれ が すきではありません。・だから 彼が 好きではあり ません。

wide *adj* (*in size*) ひろい・広い; a wide garden ひろい にわ・広い 庭; the room is ten metres wide この へやの はばは じゅうメートルです。この部屋の 幅は 十メートルで す。; (*in range*) there is a wide range いろいろ あります。・ 色々 あります。

width *n* はば・幅

wife *n* (*one's own*) つま・妻; (*someone else's*) おくさん・ 奥さん

wild *adj* (*describing animals, birds*) やせい(の)・野生(の)

wildlife *n* やせいどうぶつ・野生動物

will *vb* ! There is no specific future tense in Japanese. Use the non-past tense; (*when talking about the future*) it will be sunny tomorrow あしたは 晴れます。・明日は 晴れます。; what will we do? なにを しますか。・何を しますか。; (*when talking about intentions*) I'll wait for you at the airport くうこうで まちます。・空港で 待ちます。; we won't be here long ここに ながく いません。・ここに 長く いま せん。; (*in invitations and requests*) will you have some coffee?

コーヒーは いかがですか。; will you close the door? ドア
をしめてください。・ドアを 閉めてください。; (when
making assumptions) they won't understand かれらは わか
らないでしょう。・彼らは 分からないでしょう。; (in
short questions and answers) Use particle ね; you'll come again,
won't you? また きますね。・また 来ますね。; that will be
cheaper, won't it? それは もっと やすいですね。・それ
は もっと 安いですね。

win *vb* かつ・勝つ

wind *n* かぜ・風

window *n* まど・窓

windsurfing *n* ウィンドサーフィン

windy *adj* it's windy かぜが つよいです。・風が 強いです。

wine *n* ワイン

wing *n* (of a bird) はね・羽; (of an aeroplane) つばさ・翼

winter *n* ふゆ・冬; in winter ふゆに・冬に

wipe *vb* ふく; to wipe one's feet あしを ふく・足を 拭く;
to wipe one's nose はなを かむ・鼻を かむ

wise *adj* かしこい・賢い

wish 1 *n* ねがう・希望; to make a wish ねがいごとを
する・願い事を する; (in greetings) please give me best
wishes to your family ごかぞくに よろしく おつたえくだ
さい。・ご家族に よろしく お伝え ください。! Not
used in Japanese letters. Usually a general greeting such as
はいけい is used at the beginning of a formal letter and it is
finished with けいぐ **2** *vb* (expressing what one would like)
she wished she hadn't lied かのじょは うそを つかなけれ
ばよかったと おもいました。・彼女は 嘘を つかな
ければよかったと 思いました。; (in greetings) to wish
someone a happy birthday 「おたんじょうび おめでとう」
という・「お誕生日 おめでとう」と 言う

with *prep* use particle と; to go on holiday with friends ともだ
ちとりょこうする・友達と 旅行する; I'm living with my
parents りょうしんと すんでいます。・両親と 住んで
います。; (when describing) a girl with black hair くろい か

みの おんなの こ・黒い 髪の 女の 子; the boy with the long legs あしが ながい おとこの こ・足が 長い 男の 子; my clothes were covered with mud ふくは どろ だらけ でした。・服は 泥 だらけ でした。; she's married with two children かのじょは けっこんして こどもが ふたり います。・彼女は 結婚して 子供が 二人 います。

without *prep* 〜なしで; I went out without my wallet さいふ なしで でかけました。・財布なしで 出かけました。; (*without ...ing*) use the verb in the 〜ない form + で; we got in without paying はらわないで はいれました。・払わない で 入れました。; I went to school without eating breakfast あさごはんを たべないで がっこうに いきました。・ 朝ご飯を 食べないで 学校に 行きました。

wolf *n* おおかみ

woman *n* おんなの ひと・女の 人; a single woman どく しんの おんなの ひと・独身の 女の 人

wonder *vb* (*to ask oneself*) I was wondering why she's late か のじょが なぜ おくれているのかなと おもっていまし た。・彼女が なぜ 遅れているのかなと 思っていまし た。; I wonder whether he's coming かれが くるか どうか わかりません。・彼が 来るか どうか 分かりません。; (*in polite requests*) I wonder if you could help me? ちょっと おねがい できますか。・ちょっと お願い できますか。

wonderful *adj* すばらしい

wood *n* (*timber*) き・木; made of wood きで つくられてい る・木で 作られている; (*a small forest*) はやし・林

wool *n* ウール

word *n* ことば・言葉; what's the Japanese word for 'breakfast'? にほんごで breakfast は なんですか。・ 日本 語で breakfast は 何ですか。; in other words いいかえると ・ 言い換えると

work 1 *vb* (*to have or do a job*) はたらく・働く; to work at home いえで はたらく・家で 働く; to work as a doctor いしゃとして はたらく・医者として 働く; (*to operate properly*) the TV isn't working properly テレビの ちょうし

が わるいです。・ テレビの 調子が 悪いです。; (to be successful) (if it's an idea, a trick, a plan) うまく いく; (if it's a medicine, a treatment) きく; (to use, to operate) そうさする・ 操作する; do you know how to work the computer? コンピューターの つかいかたが わかります か。・ コンピューターの 使い方が 分かりますか。 **2** *n* しごと・ 仕事; I've got work to do しごとが あります。・ 仕事が あります。; I am out of work しつぎょうちゅうで す。・ 失業中です。; it's hard work learning Japanese にほ んごを ならうのは たいへんです。・ 日本語を 習うの は 大変です。; (for building, for repairs) こうじ・ 工事; there are road works at the moment いま どうろは こうじ ちゅうです。・ 今 道路は 工事中です。; (by an artist, a musician) さくひん・ 作品; **work out** (to find) みつける・ 見つける; to work out the answer こたえを みつける・ 答えを 見つける; (to understand) わかる・ 分かる; (with figures) けいさんする・ 計算する; (to go well) うまく いく; (to take exercise) うんどうする・ 運動する; **work up** to get worked up おこる・ 怒る

worker *n* (in a factory) じゅうぎょういん・ 従業員; (in a bank) ぎんこういん・ 銀行員; (in a company) かいしゃいん ん・ 会社員; (for local government) こうむいん・ 公務員

world *n* せかい・ 世界; all over the world せかいじゅう・ 世界中; the biggest city in the world せかいで いちばん おおきいまち・ 世界で 一番 大きい 町

World Cup *n* ワールドカップ

worm *n* みみず

worried *adj* しんぱいしている・ 心配している; to be worried about someone だれかの ことを しんぱいしてい る・ 誰かの ことを 心配している

worry *vb* (to be worried) しんぱいしている・ 心配してい る; there's nothing to worry about しんぱいする ことは ありません。・ 心配する ことは ありません。; (to make someone worried) しんぱいさせる・ 心配させる; that's worrying me それが しんぱいです。・ それが 心配です。

worse adj もっと わるい・もっと 悪い; this book is worse than the others この ほん は ほかより わるいです。・この 本 は 他より 悪いです。; she's worse than me at sports スポーツは かのじょの ほうが へたです。・スポーツは 彼女の 方が 下手です。; the weather is going to get worse てんきが もっと わるくなります。・天気が もっと 悪く なります。; he's getting worse (in health) かれの ぐあいが もっと わるく なっています。・彼の 具合が もっと 悪く なっています。

worst 1 n いちばんわるい・一番悪い **2** adj いちばんひどい・一番酷い; the worst hotel in town この まちで いちばんひどい ホテル・この 町で 一番酷い ホテル; the worst thing to do would be to tell him いちばんひどいのは かれに いう ことです。・一番酷いのは 彼に 言う ことです。

worth adj it's worth £100 ひゃくポンドの かちが あります。・百ポンドの 価値が あります。; it's not worth doing it やる かちが ありません。・やる 価値が ありません。

would vb (when talking about hypothetical rather than real situations) if I had more money, I would buy a car もっと おかねがあれば、くるまをかいます。・もっと お金が あれば、車を 買います。; we would have missed the train if we hadn't go a taxi タクシーに のらなければ、でんしゃ にまに あいませんでした。・タクシーに 乗らなければ、電車に 間に 合いませんでした。; (in reported speech) I thought you'd forget わすれると おもいました。・忘れると 思いました。; we were sure she would like it きっとかのじょは すきだと おもいました。・きっと 彼女は 好きだと 思いました。; (when making an assumption) it would have been about midday たぶん じゅうにじ ごろ でした。・多分 十二時 ごろでした。; (to be prepared to) he wouldn't listen to me かれは わたしの いうことを きこうとしませんでした。・彼は 私の 言う ことを 聞こうとしませんでした。; (when talking about one's wishes) I'd like a beer ビールが ほしいです。・ビールが 欲しい

です。; we would like to stay another night もう ひとばん とまりたいです。・ もう 一晩 泊まりたいです。; (when asking, offering or advising) would you turn the TV off? テレビ をけしてください。・ テレビ を 消してください。; would you excuse me for a moment? ちょっと しつれいします。・ ちょっと 失礼します。; would you like something to eat? なにか たべませんか。・ 何か 食べませんか。; you would do well to check たしかめた ほうが いいです。・ 確かめた 方が いいです。

wrap *vb* つつむ・包む; to wrap (up) a present プレゼント をつつむ・プレゼント を 包む

wrestling *n* レスリング

wrist *n* てくび・手首

write *vb* かく・書く; to write to someone, to write someone (US English) だれかに てがみを かく・誰かに 手紙を 書く; to write an essay さくぶんを かく ・作文を 書く; to write a cheque こぎってを かく・小切手を 書く; to write a message メッセージを かく・メッセージを 書く; **write back** へんじを かく・返事を 書く; **write down** かきとめる・書き留める

writing *n* じ・字; your writing is good じが じょうずです。・字が 上手です。

wrong *adj* (not as it should be) there's something wrong なにかが へんです。・何かが 変です。; what's wrong? どうしましたか。; (not proper or suitable) ちがう・違う; I took the wrong key ちがう かぎを とりました。・違う 鍵を 取りました。; to go the wrong way ちがう みちを とおる・違う 道を 通る; (not correct) that's wrong ちがいます。・違います。; it was a wrong number まちがい でんわでした。・間違い 電話でした。; to be wrong (if it's a person) まちがっている・間違っている; (not honest, not good) it's wrong to steal things ものを ぬすむのは わるい ことです。・物を 盗むのは 悪い ことです。; she hasn't done anything wrong かのじょは わるい ことを しませんでした。・彼女は 悪い ことを しませんでした。

Xx

X-ray 1 n (photo) レントゲンしゃしん・レントゲン写真
2 vb レントゲンを とる・レントゲンを 撮る

Yy

yacht n ヨット

yard n (when measuring) ヤード ! Note that a yard 0.9144 m;
(US English) (a garden) にわ・庭

yawn vb あくびする

year n (when talking about time) ねん・年; last year きょね
ん・去年; two years ago にねんまえ・二年前; to work all
year round いちねんじゅうはたらく・一年中 働く;
he's lived there for five years かれは そこに ごねんかん
すんでいます。・彼は そこに 五年間 住んでいます。;
that'll take years! それは すうねんかん かかります。・
それは 数年間 かかります。; (when talking about age)
〜さい・〜才; I am 15 years old じゅうごさいです。・
十五才です。; a four-year old girl よんさいの おんなの こ
・四才の 女の 子; (in a school system) first year, year one ≈
いちねん・一年; I am in the second year, I am in year two
にねんせいです。・二年生です。; a first year いちねん
せい・一年生

yell 1 vb さけぶ・叫ぶ; to yell at someone だれかに さけ
ぶ・誰かに 叫ぶ **2** n さけび・叫び

yellow adj きいろい・黄色い; to go yellow きいろく なる
・黄色く なる

yes adv はい Note that when a question is asked in the negative and the answer would be "yes" in English, it would be いいえ in Japanese to mean "that is incorrect" e.g.; "Didn't you know that?" "Yes, I did"「それを しりませんでしたか。」「いいえ、しっていました。」; 'are you coming with us?'—'yes I am'「いっしょに いきますか。」「はい、いきます。」・「一緒に 行きますか。」「はい、行きます。」

yesterday adv きのう・昨日

yet 1 adv (with negatives) まだ; not yet まだ I haven't eaten yet まだ たべていません。・まだ 食べていません。; (with positives) もう; have they eaten yet? かれらは もう たべましたか。・彼らは もう 食べましたか。; have you read this yet? これを もう よみましたか。・これを もう 読みましたか。 **2** conj しかし

yogurt n ヨーグルト

you pron ! There are various words for 'you' in Japanese, of which the most common is あなた however whenever possible the person's name should be used rather than this.

young 1 adj わかい・若い; a young lady わかい おんなの ひと・若い 女の 人; young people わかもの・若者; she is a year younger than me かのじょは わたしより いっさい とししたです。・彼女は 私より 一才 年下です。; a younger brother ▶ **brother** a younger sister ▶ **sister** to look young わかく みえる・若く 見える **2** n (of an animal) こ・子

your det ! There are various words for 'your' in Japanese, of which the most common is あなたの however whenever possible the person's name + の should be used rather than this.

yours pron ! There are various words for 'yours' in Japanese, of which the most common is あなたの however whenever possible the person's name + の should be used rather than this.

yourself pron Not used as a reflexive pronoun in Japanese; you'll enjoy yourself たのしみます。・楽しみます。; did you hurt yourself? けがを しましたか。・ 怪我を しましたか。; *(when used for emphasis)* you did it yourself じぶんで しました。・ 自分で しました。

yourselves *pron* Not used as a reflexive pronoun in Japanese; you'll enjoy yourselves たのしみます。・ 楽しみます。; did you hurt yourselves? けがを しましたか。・ 怪我を しましたか。; *(when used for emphasis)* are you going to do it yourselves? じぶんたちで しますか。・ 自分達で しますか。

youth *n (a young man)* しょうねん・ 少年; *(young people)* わかもの・ 若者

youth club *n* せいしょうねんクラブ・ 青少年クラブ

youth hostel *n* ユースホステル

Zz

zap *vb (to destroy)* さくじょする・ 削除する

zebra *n* しまうま・ しま馬

zebra crossing *n (British English)* おうだんほどう・ 横断歩道

zero *num* ゼロ the alternative word れい is also used.

zip *(British English)*, **zipper** *(US English)* *n* チャック; to undo a zip チャックをはずす・ チャックを 外す

zip code *n (US English)* ゆうびんばんごう・ 郵便番号

zodiac *n* じゅうにきゅうず・ 十二宮図

zone *n* ちたい・ 地帯

zoo *n* どうぶつえん・ 動物園

Hiragana Chart

Note that Japanese words in this and other dictionaries are arranged according to this chart from left to right and top to bottom. The Japanese equivalent of 'from A to Z' is 'from あ to ん'. In dictionary order the K and G and S and Z etc. will not be separated i.e. the next word after かい (floor) is がい (damage).

'a' line		'i' line		'u' line '		'e' line		'o' line	
あ	a	い	i	う	u	え	e	お	o
か	ka	き	ki	く	ku	け	ke	こ	ko
が	ga	ぎ	gi	ぐ	gu	げ	ge	ご	go
さ	sa	し	shi	す	su	せ	se	そ	so
ざ	za	じ	ji	ず	zu	ぜ	ze	ぞ	zo
た	ta	ち	chi	つ	tsu	て	te	と	to
だ	da	ぢ	ji	づ	zu	で	de	ど	do
な	na	に	ni	ぬ	nu	ね	ne	の	no
は	ha	ひ	hi	ふ	fu	へ	he	ほ	ho
ば	ba	び	bi	ぶ	bu	べ	be	ぼ	bo
ぱ	pa	ぴ	pi	ぷ	pu	ぺ	pe	ぽ	po
ま	ma	み	mi	む	mu	め	me	も	mo
や	ya			ゆ	yu			よ	yo

ら	ra	り	ri	る	ru	れ	re	ろ	ro
わ	wa							を	o/wo
ん	n								

Hiragana symbol plus small や、ゆ or よ

きゃ	kya	きゅ	kyu	きょ	kyo
ぎゃ	gya	ぎゅ	gyu	ぎょ	gyo
しゃ	sha	しゅ	shu	しょ	sho
じゃ	ja	じゅ	ju	じょ	jo
ちゃ	cha	ちゅ	chu	ちょ	cho
にゃ	nya	にゅ	nyu	にょ	nyo
ひゃ	hya	ひゅ	hyu	ひょ	hyo
びゃ	bya	びゅ	byu	びょ	byo
ぴゃ	pya	ぴゅ	pyu	ぴょ	pyo
りゃ	rya	りゅ	ryu	りょ	ryo

Pronunciation Guide

Vowels: Long vowels:

'a' as in cat
'i' as in sheep
'u' as in boot
'e' as in bed   えい is pronounced as a long え
'o' as in dog   おう is pronounced as a long お

Small つ

A small つ has an effect similar to doubling the following consonant. For example in the word ちょっと, the と following the small つ is pronounced in a similar manner to the double t in 'hot toddy'.

Note that は is read 'ha' when it is part of a word, but when used as the topic particle it is pronounced 'wa'.

Similarly, へ is pronounced 'he' when it is part of a word but 'e' when it is used as a particle showing the direction of travel.

Katakana chart

'a' line		'i' line		'u' line		'e' line		'o' line	
ア	a	イ	i	ウ	u	エ	e	オ	o
カ	ka	キ	ki	ク	ku	ケ	ke	コ	ko
ガ	ga	ギ	gi	グ	gu	ゲ	ge	ゴ	go
サ	sa	シ	shi	ス	su	セ	se	ソ	so
ザ	za	ジ	ji	ズ	zu	ゼ	ze	ゾ	zo
タ	ta	チ	chi	ツ	tsu	テ	te	ト	to
ダ	da	ヂ	ji	ヅ	zu	デ	de	ド	do
ナ	na	ニ	ni	ヌ	nu	ネ	ne	ノ	no
ハ	ha	ヒ	hi	フ	fu	ヘ	he	ホ	ho
バ	ba	ビ	bi	ブ	bu	ベ	be	ボ	bo

パ	pa	ビ	pi	プ	pu	ペ	pe	ポ	po
マ	ma	ミ	mi	ム	mu	メ	me	モ	mo
ヤ	ya			ユ	yu			ヨ	yo
ラ	ra	リ	ri	ル	ru	レ	re	ロ	ro
ワ	wa							ヲ	o/wo
ン	n								

Katakana symbol plus small ヤ、ユ or ヨ

キャ	kya	キュ	kyu	キョ	kyo
ギャ	gya	ギュ	gyu	ギョ	gyo
シャ	sha	シュ	shu	ショ	sho
ジャ	ja	ジュ	ju	ジョ	jo
チャ	cha	チュ	chu	チョ	cho
ニャ	nya	ニュ	nyu	ニョ	nyo
ヒャ	hya	ヒュ	hyu	ヒョ	hyo
ビャ	bya	ビュ	byu	ビョ	byo
ピャ	pya	ピュ	pyu	ピョ	pyo
リャ	rya	リュ	ryu	リョ	ryo

Note that in katakana, long vowels are usually written by putting a — after the sound as in the case of コーヒー (coffee) or ヒーター (heater). As katakana is used to indicate the pronunciation of foreign words there are other possible combinations not included in the chart.

Verb tables

Abbreviations for verb forms

plain non-past	pl. n-pst
plain negative	pl. neg.
conjunctive	conj.
plain past	pl. pst
potential	poten.
passive	pass.
volitional	volit.
causative	caus.
causative passive	caus. pass.
conditional (if)	cond. (if)
conditional (when)	cond. (when)
imperative	imp.

Japanese verbs are divided into three groups for conjugation purposes:

Group 1

A form appearing in the chart does not necessarily mean it is in common use

Verb ending	る	ぶ	む	す	う	つ	く	ぐ	ぬ
meaning	to take	to call	to read	to speak	to say	to wait	to write	to swim	to die
pl. n-pst	とる	よぶ	よむ	はなす	いう	まつ	かく	およぐ	しぬ
～ない pl. neg	とら ない	よば ない	よま ない	はなさ ない	いわ ない	また ない	かか ない	およが ない	しな ない
～て conj.	とって	よんで	よんで	はなして	いって	まって	かいて	およいで	しんで
～た pl. pst	とった	よんだ	よんだ	はなした	いった	まった	かいた	およいだ	しんだ
pre ～ます	とり	よび	よみ	はなし	いい	まち	かき	およぎ	しに
poten.	とれる	よべる	よめる	はなせる	いえる	まてる	かける	およげる	しねる

Group 1 continued

	とる	よぶ	よむ	はなす	いう	まつ	かく	およぐ	しぬ
pass.	とられる	よばれる	よまれる	はなされる	いわれる	またれる	かかれる	およがれる	しなれる
volit.	とろう	よぼう	よもう	はなそう	いおう	まとう	かこう	およごう	しのう
caus.	とらせる	よばせる	よませる	はなさせる	いわせる	またせる	かかせる	およがせる	しなせる
caus. pass.	とらせられる	よばせられる	よませられる	はなさせられる	いわせられる	またせられる	かかせられる	およがせられる	しなせられる
cond. (if)	とれば	よべば	よめば	はなせば	いえば	まてば	かけば	およげば	しねば
cond. (when)	とったら	よんだら	よんだら	はなしたら	いったら	まったら	かいたら	およいだら	しんだら
imp.	とれ	よべ	よめ	はなせ	いえ	まて	かけ	およげ	しね

There is one slight irregularity in group 1, the verb いく・行く to go

pl. n-pst	~ない pl. neg.	~て conj.	~た pl. pst	pre ~ます	poten.	caus.	pass.	caus. pass.	volit.	imp.	cond. (if)	cond. (when)
いく	いか ない	いって	いった	いき ます	いける	いか せる	いか れる	いか せら れる	い こう	いけ	い けば	いっ たら

Group 2

Form

Note that group 2 verbs are the vast majority of those with a dictionary form ending in '-eru' = ~える, ~ける, ~せる, ~てる, ~ねる, ~へる, ~める, ~れる, or '-iru' ~いる, ~きる, ~しる, ~ちる, ~にる, ~みる, ~ひる, ~りる.

Note that when a group 1 verb is conjugated into a passive, causative or potential and then has a form ending in '-eru' = ~える, ~ける, ~せる, ~てる, ~ねる, ~へる, ~める, ~れる it becomes treated as a group 2 verb for any subsequent transformations.

meaning	to eat	to go out, to leave to answer the phone	to wear	to borrow
pl. n-pst	たべる	でる	きる	かりる
～ない pl. neg.	たべない	でない	きない	かりない
～て conj.	たべて	でて	きて	かりて
た pl. pst	たべた	でた	きた	かりた
pre ～ます	たべ	で	き	かり
poten.	たべられる	でられる	きられる	かりられる
pass.	たべられる	でられる	きられる	かりられる
volit.	たべよう	でよう	きよう	かりよう
caus.	たべさせる	でさせる	きさせる	かりさせる
caus. pass.	たべさせられる		きせられる	かりさせられる
cond. (if)	たべれば	でれば	きれば	かりれば
cond. (when)	たべたら	でたら	きたら	かりたら
imp.	たべろ	でろ	きろ	かりろ

Common group 1 verbs that end in 'iru' or 'eru'. NOTE that some of these have the same dictionary form as a group 2 verb with a different meaning i.e. きる・切る 'to cut' (group 1) and きる・着る 'to wear' (group 2) but the negative and some other forms will be different. i.e. きらない・切らない = not cut, きない・着ない = not wear

verb	meaning
きる・切る	to cut
ける・蹴る	to kick
しる・知る	to know
かえる・帰る	to return, to go home
はいる・入る	to enter
はしる・走る	to run
へる・減る	to reduce, to decline
しゃべる・喋る	to chat

An example of a group 1 verb that has a dictionary form ending in 'iru'
きる・切る = to cut

pl. n-pst	~ない pl. neg.	~て conj.	~た pl. pst	pre ~ます	poten.	pass.	caus.	caus. pass.	volit.	imp.	cond. (if)	cond. (when)
きる・切る	きら ない	き って	き った	き り	きれる	きら れる	きら せる	きら せられる	き ろう	きれ	き れば	き ったら

Group 3

meaning	pl. n-pst	~ない pl. neg.	~て conj.	~た pl. pst	pre ~ます	poten.	pass.	caus.	caus. pass.	volit.	imp.	cond. (if)	cond. (when)
to do (see する)	する	しない	して	した	し	でき る	さ れる	さ せる	さ せられる	しよう	しろ	すれば	したら
to come	くる	こない	きて	きた	き	こら れる	こら れる	こさ せる	こさ せられる	こよう	こい	くれば	きたら

Chinese character look-up information but as many users will also be studying the use of Chinese characters, we have given some information relating to them throughout the main entries and notes. In particular, we have given as main entries in the Japanese to English section a very wide range of suffixes and prefixes which will allow careful users to find the meanings of a vastly greater number of words than are here as headword entries. For information on how to do this see **How to use this Dictionary**.

We hope that in addition to being a practical tool and reference for learners that this dictionary will prove *interesting*! The value of browsing and curiosity as part of language learning is all too often forgotten and teachers and learners tend to stick to self-contained textbooks. We would like to think that anyone who is interested in Japanese can find something of interest and value by dipping into this book. Japanese is a fascinating language and it is the interest and enjoyment of our students that has led us to want to produce a much-needed resource for them.

Japanese Script

Japanese is usually written using a combination of scripts. It can be written horizontally from left to right よこがき・横書き or, more traditionally, in vertical columns from right to left たてがき・縦書き. Vertical writing tends to be used for books, newspapers, formal letters and essays.

There are two series of phonetic symbols or かな of 46 sounds each which can be combined to write the sounds of the language, and Chinese characters or かんじ・漢字 which carry meaning and may have more than one way of being pronounced depending on the context. See the entries on おんよみ and くんよみ for more about the use of Chinese characters. The characters used in books and newspapers are largely limited to those in the official list produced for schools and those which can be used for personal names. The characters for schoolchildren to be taught are called じょうようかんじ・常用漢字 which means 'characters for everyday use'. There are 1945 of them.

In a sentence such as 'I am going to London tomorrow' the Japanese will feature かたかな・片仮名 for the place name, ひらがな・平仮名 for the grammatical particles and the ending on the verb and かんじ・漢字 for the words 'tomorrow' and 'I' as well as the stem of the verb 'to go'. わたしはあした ロンドンへ いきます。・ 私は明日ロンドンへ行きます。

The main use of かたかな is to write words of foreign origin and it is used for the names of non-Japanese people and places. By convention the names of Chinese and Korean people and places are

often left in characters and a pronunciation indicated in ふりがな・振り仮名 (see below). かたかな is also used for onomatopoeia, some adverbs and as a kind of italic script for emphasis. It is common for the pronunciation of (possibly) unfamiliar characters to be indicated by small script above or to the side. This is called ふりがな ルビ or よみがな and can be in either ひらがな or かたかな. This also appears in textbooks to help learners with new かんじ readings.

This dictionary uses either ひらがな or かたかな for the headwords in the Japanese to English section and the translations in the English to Japanese section as appropriate. Where かんじ would normally be employed we have given a 'standard' script form immediately after the かな version. There is some flexibility about whether or not to use かんじ for a particular word or just ひらがな. We have tried to give something approximating standard usage and so we have some characters not in the government lists where we judge them to be in common use and we have left some words without characters even though the characters are common if it felt stylistically better in a given case.

We advise beginners not to attempt to copy out the more complicated kanji until they are more confident with Japanese writing. A word written in legible hiragana is much better than a badly copied kanji which will be difficult for the intended reader to understand.

How to use this dictionary

Japanese into English side

There are a lot more words in this dictionary than it may at first appear!

The following section gives advice on what to do if the word you want does not seem to be present.

Japanese verbs and certain adjectives can have a variety of endings. If the form of a word in front of you does not seem to be in the dictionary try and identify what kind of word it is. Verbs are often at the end of sentences and will have some hiragana characters after the Chinese characters (if they are used) i.e. いきます・行きます. Adjectives may also be detectable by their 'tail' of hiragana characters after the Chinese character/s i.e. あたらしい・新しい. The notes on verbs and adjectives give tables showing possible endings which can help you identify an unknown word. For convenience a table is given below with some of the most common inflectional endings and ideas on how to convert them back to a form that can be looked up.

Also note that it is common practice in Japanese textbooks for beginners where words are spaced, any particles are added to words without a space separating them. The same is true of です・でした and する and related forms して・した etc. Make sure you are not trying to look up a form of a word that is the word itself plus a particle or one of these words!

If the word you want to look up has one of the following endings try to change it as indicated in the table below and look up the new form and the ending as separate items. This is not guaranteed but should give you a very good chance of finding the

word you want. If the word does not seem to have one of these endings see the note on prefixes and suffixes below.

ending	how to change it back to a form you can look up	Example from	Example to
〜かった	remove ending and add い	さむかった	さむい
〜くない	remove ending and add い	おおきくない	おおきい
〜くなかった	remove ending and add い	おいしくなかった	おいしい
〜た 〜て	remove ending and add る	たべた・ たべて	たべる
〜った 〜った	remove ending and add る or う	あった・ あって	ある・ あう
〜んだ 〜んで	remove ending and add む or ぶ or ぬ there is only one verb with the latter ending	よんだ・ あそんだ・ あそんで・ しんで	よむ・ あそぶ しぬ
〜いた 〜いて	remove ending and add く	きいた・ きいて	きく
〜いだ 〜いだ	remove ending and add ぐ	およいだ・ およいで	およぐ

ending	how to change it back to a form you can look up	Example from	Example to
〜した 〜して	remove ending and add す	はなした・ はなして	はなす
〜たい	remove ending and add る or change the last syllable before the ending from '-i' to '-u' i.e. り to る or き to く etc.	みたい・ やりたい・ あいたい・ ききたい	みる・ やる・ あう・ きく
〜たくない	as above	みたくない	みる
〜ます	remove ending and add る or change the last syllable before the ending from '-i' to '-u' i.e. り to る or き to く etc.	たべます・ おきます・ とります・ ききます	たべる・ おきる・ とる・ きく
〜ません	as above	とりません	とる
〜ました	as above	ききました	きく
〜ましょう	as above	いきまし ょう	いく

ending	how to change it back to a form you can look up	Example from	Example to
～ない	remove ending and add る or change the last syllable before the ending from '-a' to '-u' i.e. ら to る or か to く etc.	たべない・おわらない・いかない	たべる・おわる・いく
～なかった	as above	とらなかった みなかった	とる みる
～ら	always follows either ～た or ～だ so find the appropriate form of that ending in the chart	きいたら	きく
initial word followed by する、しない、した、したい、します、しません、しましょう、したら、すれば	look up the initial word and then the relevant part of する in the verb note. Note that the elements in front of these forms are usually nouns written with Chinese characters	べんきょうすれば けんきゅうした	べんきょうけんきゅう

ending	how to change it back to a form you can look up	Example from	Example to
〜なければ なりません	as for 〜ない or 〜くない	かかなければ なりません	かく
〜なければ ならなかった	as for 〜ない or 〜くない	いかなければ ならなかった	いく
〜ければ	remove ending and add い	たかければ	たかい
〜えば or other endings with -eba such as 〜せば or 〜てば	remove the ば and add る or remove the ば and change the preceding '-e' to '-u' i.e. せ to す	とれれば・みせれば・はなせば	とる・みせる・はなす
〜くて	remove ending and add い	あたらしくて	あたらしい

Exercise

Try to find the basic forms of the following and their meaning from the chart above using only the main entries. Use the notes on verbs or adjectives only to check!

あつかった　おいしくない　みた　よまない

いきたい　けんぶつしました　かえらなければな らなかった

Prefixes and Suffixes

If a word is not in the dictionary try separating the first one or two symbols and looking it/them up to see if it/they is/are a common prefix element. You can also try looking at the final few syllables and trying the same thing to check for suffixes.

Exercise

Try to find the following words' meanings and the elements of which they are composed

prefix

ふてきとう　ごあいさつ　おしろ

suffix

がくせいむき　せんせいらしい　えきちょう

A Note on Verb Forms

There are two common styles of Japanese verbs and textbooks for beginners tend to use the polite (as opposed to plain) style as this is the normal way of talking to people other than friends and family. The plain style tends to be introduced at a later stage but is important for the learning of grammar and in a wide range of constructions. Because the polite style of a verb is not a basic 'word' but a form of the plain or dictionary 'word' we have followed usual dictionary practice and given verb entries in what is often called the dictionary form. The same applies in the English to Japanese section. However, as beginners tend to use the polite style we have kept examples in that form. We have also selected some of the most common verbs in beginners' textbooks and given them as main entries in their so-called 〜ます form and conjunctive or 〜て form in the

Japanese-English section. This will allow you to look up a verb in these forms so even if you have not yet studied the relation of plain and polite style verbs or learned the formation of conjunctives you can find a cross-reference to the dictionary form where a translation and conjugation information will be found. The verb entries have numbers referring to the conjugation patterns and symbols to show if they are transitive or intransitive and reference can be made to the notes and tables situated between the Japanese-English and English-Japanese sections. The table above will also assist you to find a dictionary form of a verb.

Try to find the dictionary form and meaning of the following polite style verbs

たべます　みます　おきます　おわります

Try to find the dictionary form and meaning of the verbs from the following conjunctive forms

のんで　いって　まって　およいで

For further information see the notes on **plain and polite style** and **verbs**

English into Japanese side

The English into Japanese side of the dictionary attempts to give full guidance on how to write and speak correctly in Japanese. Plenty of examples are given to demonstrate not only the translation of words into Japanese but also their usage in Japanese sentences. You will find additional information on grammatical points, such as the use of words in certain contexts, in the grammatical notes that occur within the entries on certain words. These notes are designed to help you produce correct

Japanese in areas where mistakes are frequently made due to Japanese usage being different from English.

If you are unable to translate an English word into Japanese because you cannot find it in the wordlist, try to use another word with the same or a similar meaning, or choose another form of wording which will enable you to find what you're looking for. For instance, if you want to translate the adjective *complex* but cannot find it in the dictionary, you could try *complicated* as an alternative, which gives ふくざつ (な)・複雑 (な) as the Japanese equivalent.

A very useful feature of this dictionary are the usage notes which cover sets of related words based on topics such as *family*, *dates*, and *nationalities etc.* You will find these in the centre of the dictionary.

Structure of Japanese-English entries

headword in Japanese syllabic script

MASU forms of common verbs cross-referenced

alternative script for headword to show use of Chinese characters (kanji) where appropriate

the TE, NAI and MASU forms of common verbs are given to assist beginners

TE forms of common verbs as headwords and cross referenced

commonly used particles apart from the transitive/intransitive marker are shown

うまい *adj* (of food) delicious; (of ability) skillful ! *in the sense 'delicious' this word is generally only used by men.*

うります ▶ うる

うる・売る *vb 1* ⓣ うって・うらない・うります *to sell*

うるさい・煩い・五月蝿い *adj* noisy; annoying ! *as an exclamation it means 'shut up'*

うって ▶ うる ▶ うつ

いく・行く *vb 1* ⓘ いって・いかない・いきます *to go* ! *following the ～て form of a verb it can add the sense of an ongoing process or direction of movement of the subject*

いくじ・育児 *n* – *bringing up children*

いっち・一致 *n* agreement *2 vb 3* ⓘ にいっち する *to agree*

usage notes

verb conjugation group clearly shown (see p. 597)

transitive or intransitive nature of verb shown by the appropriate particle in a circle

notes on contexts and meanings

explanation where no exact equivalent exists

any changes in form are shown

Structure of English-Japanese entries

headwork ···· **able** *adj* to be able to... use the ···· information on
how to
translate into
Japanese

example
translations in
kana and
repeated in
standard
Japanese script
(kanjikana-
majiri)

potential form of the verb or the
dictionary form of the verb +
ことが できる; to be able to swim
およげる・泳げる; I am able to
read hiragana ひらがなを よむ
ことが できます。・ ひらがな
を読む ことが できます。

associated
elements which
are present in
some
circumstances
appear in
brackets

ambitious *adj* やしんてき(な)・
野心的(な)

translations
written in
Japanese
syllabic script

alternative
script version
of the
translations to
show use of
Chinese
characters
(kanji) where
appropriate

feel *vb* かんじる・ 感じる
! *Japanese is very different to English
when describing feelings, it is often
best to translate with an adjective +
です* when referring to yourself;
*(referring to an emotion, an
impression or a physical feeling)*;
I feel lonely さびしいです。・
寂しいです。; it feels cold さむい
です。・ 寒いです。; I feel tired つかれました。
・ 疲れました。; it feels nice きも
ちいいです。・ 気持ち いいで
す。; *(to touch)* さわる・ 触る; to
feel like... use the pre ます form of
the verb + たい for yourself and the
pre ます form of the verb + たがる
for others; I feel like eating pizza ピ
ザが たべたいです。・ ピザが
食べたいです。; I don't feel like it
したくないです。

potentially
misleading
translations are
clarified and
suggestions
made

Abbreviations

adjective	adj
adjectival noun	adj n
adverb	adv
auxiliary verb	aux vb
conjunction	conj
determiner	det
noun	n
number	num
preposition	prep
pronoun	pron
reflexive pronoun	ref pron
relative pronoun	rel pron
verb	vb
prefix	prf
exclamation	exc
particle	pt
suffix	suf

あア

ああ *adv* such; that

ああいう *attributive* that kind; like that

ああして *adv* like that; in that way

あい・愛 1 *n* love **2** *vb* 3 ㊝ **あいする** to love

あいかわらず・相変わらず *adv* the same as ever

あいさつ・挨拶 1 *n* greetings; a brief speech **2** *vb* 3 ㊦ **に あいさつする** to greet

あいじょう・愛情 *n* affection

あいず・合図 1 *n* signal **2** *vb* 3 ㊦ **に あいず (を)する** to signal

アイスクリーム *n* ice cream

あいだ・間 *n* a space; a while; between; during

あいだがら・間柄 *n* relationship

あいづち・相づち *n* – noises and words used to show someone that you are listening to what is being said (rather like 'uh-huh' etc. in English)

あいて・相手 *n* the other person; opponent; partner

あいて ▶ あく

アイデア *n* idea

あいにく *adv* unfortunately

あいまい(な) *adj* vague

あいます ▶ あう

アイロン *n* iron; **アイロンを かける** to iron

あう・会う・遭う *vb* 1 ㊦ **に と あって・あわない・あいます** to meet; to encounter

あう・合う *vb* 1 ㊦ **と に あって・あわない・あいます** to fit; to be right; to be correct

あお・青 *n* blue

あおい・青い *adj* blue ❗ *refers to both the blue of the sky and the green of vegetation and traffic lights*

あおぐ・仰ぐ *vb 1 を* to look up (at)

あおぐ・扇ぐ *vb 1 を* to fan

あおじろい・青白い *adj* pale

あおぞら・青空 *n* blue skies

あか・垢 *n* scum; dirt

あか・赤 *n* red

あかい・赤い *adj* red

あかちゃん・赤ちゃん *n* baby

あかり・明かり *n* light

あがり・上がり *n* rise ▶ **おあがり**

あがる・上がる *vb 1 か* あがって・あがらない・ あがって to rise; to stop (rain); to become nervous; to enter (a house)

あかるい・明るい *adj* bright; cheerful

あかんぼう・赤ん坊 *n* baby

あき・秋 *n* autumn; fall

あき・空き *prf* empty

あきち・空き地 *n* disused plot of land

あきあき(する)・飽き飽き(する) *vb 3 か* に to be fed up

あきます ▶ **あく**

あきらか・明らか **1** *adj* あきらか(な) clear **2** *adv* あきらかに clearly

あきらめる・諦める *vb 2 を* to abandon

あきる・飽きる *vb 2* to be tired of

あきれる・呆れる *vb 2 か* に to be astonished; to be appalled

あく・開く *vb 1* ㋕ あいて・あかない・あきます
to open; to be open

あく・空く *vb 1* ㋕ あいて・あかない・あきます to be
empty

あくしゅ・握手 **1** *n* handshake **2** *vb 3* ㋕ あくしゅ する
to shake hands

アクセサリー *n* – fashion accessories and especially jewellery

アクセント *n* accent (emphasis)

あくび・欠伸 **1** *n* yawn **2** *vb 3* ㋕ あくびをする to yawn

あくま・悪魔 *n* the devil

あくまでも *adv* persistently

あくるひ・明くる日 *n* the next day

あけがた・明け方 *n* daybreak

あけて ▶ あける

あげて ▶ あげる

あけまして おめでとう ございます *phrase* Happy New
Year!

あけます ▶ あける

あげます ▶ あげる

あけて ▶ あける

あげて ▶ あげる

あける・開ける *vb 2* ㋾ あけて・あけない・あけま
す to open

あける・明ける *vb 2* ㋕ to dawn

あげる・上げる *vb 2* ㋾ あげて・あげない・あげます
to give; to raise **!** when following the 〜て form of a verb it
indicates that the action of that verb is being done for someone
else and is to their benefit; みて あげます I will show you;
みてあげる I'll look at it for you

あこがれ・憧れ *n* yearning

あこがれる・憧れる *vb 2* ㋾ に to yearn for

あさ・朝 *n* morning

あざ *n* bruise; birthmark

あさい・浅い *adj* shallow

あさって・明後日 *n* the day after tomorrow

あさねぼう・朝寝坊 1 *n* oversleeping **2** *vb* **3** 加 あさねぼうする to sleep late

あざやか(な)・鮮やか(な) *adj* vivid; fresh

あし・足 *n* leg; foot

あじ・味 *n* flavour; 〜の あじがする to taste of ...

アジア *n* Asia

あしあと・足跡 *n* footprint

あしおと・足音 *n* footsteps

あした・明日 *n* tomorrow

あしもと・足元 *n* – literally 'the area around the feet' it can be translated as 'footing' or 'around you' depending on the context

あじわう・味わう *vb 1* を to taste; to experience

あずかる・預かる *vb 1* を to take charge of ❗ used when something of someone else's is taken to be looked after in some way such as by a cloakroom or a bank ▶ おあずかり

あずける・預ける *vb 2* を to entrust; to leave ❗ used when something is given to be looked after in some way such as a jacket to a cloakroom or children to a nursery

あせ・汗 *n* sweat; あせを かく to sweat

あせる・焦る *vb 1* 加 to be in a hurry

あそこ *n* there; over there; that place

あそび・遊び *n* play; game

あそびに いく・遊びに行く *vb 1* 加 に to (go and) visit

あそびに くる・遊びに来る *vb 3* 加 に to (come and) visit

あそびます ▶ あそぶ

あそぶ・遊ぶ vb 1 🄰 **とあそんで・あそばない・ あそびます** to play; to be with (friends)

あたえる・与える vb 2 🄴 to give; to cause; to provide

あたし n – a version of **わたし** used by some girls and young women

あたたか(な) ▶ **あたたかい**

あたたかい・暖かい・温かい adj warm ! the first Chinese character is used when referring to the weather and air temperature while the second is used for warm to the touch

あたたまる・暖まる・温まる vb 1 🄰 to get warm; to get hot – see the note to **あたたかい**

あたためる・温める・暖める vb 2 🄴 to warm; to heat – see the note to **あたたかい**

あたま・頭 n head

あたらしい・新しい adj new

あたり・辺り n area; surroundings

あたり・当たり n a hit – literally 'being on target' it is used of someone's answer to a question to mean 'you're right'

あたりまえ(な・の)・当たり前(な・の) adj as you would expect; natural; reasonable

あたる・当たる vb 1 🄰 to hit; to be right; to win

あちこち ▶ **あちらこちら**

あちら n that place; over there; in that direction ! not near either the speaker or listener

あちらこちら n here and there

あつい・暑い・熱い adj hot ! the first Chinese character is used for weather and air temperature while the second is used for things hot to the touch

あつい・厚い adj thick

あつかい・扱い n handling

あつかう・扱う vb 1 🄴 **と** to handle; to deal with

あつかましい・厚かましい adj cheeky

あっち ▶ あちら

あって ▶ あう ▶ ある

あっとうてき(な)・圧倒的(な) *adj* overwhelming

あつまり・集まり *n* collection; meeting

あつまる・集まる *vb 1* ㉗ に to be gathered

あつめる・集める *vb 2* ㉛ to gather; to attract

あて・宛・宛て *suf* addressed to

あてじ・当て字 *n* – Chinese characters borrowed to write a Japanese word and whose usual pronunciations (in Japanese use) or original meanings are disregarded or altered

あてな・宛名 *n* address

あてはまる・当てはまる *vb 1* ㉗ に to apply to; to fulfil

あてはめる・当てはめる *vb 2* ㉛ to adapt; to apply

あてる・当てる *vb 2* ㉛ to hit; to win; to guess

あと・後 *n* back; after; remainder

あと・跡 *n* remains

あな・穴 *n* a hole; a cave

アナウンサー *n* TV or radio presenter

あなた *n* you ❗ *the word is not equivalent to 'you' in English as Japanese people prefer to use a person's name or title (when necessary) and it can be rude to use* **あなた**. *Also used by women to call their husbands*

あに・兄 *n* one's own older brother

あね・姉 *n* one's own older sister

あの *attributive* that; the ❗ *refers to a person, place or thing distant from speaker and listener or which is previously known to both of them. It must be followed by a noun.*

あのね *interjection* I say

あのう *interjection* – indicates hesitation in speaking and so can be used as 'excuse me' or just 'er... er ... er .... um ...'

アパート *n* apartment; (small) block of apartments

あばれる・暴れる *vb 2* ㋑ to behave violently; to run riot

あびる・浴びる *vb 2* ㋓ to bathe; シャワーを あびる to have a shower

あぶない・危ない *adj* dangerous

あぶら・油 *n* oil

あぶら・脂 *n* fat

あぶらっぽい・油っぽい *adj* oily

アフリカ *n* Africa

あふれる・溢れる *vb 2* ㋑ to overflow

あまい・甘い *adj* sweet; lenient

あまえる・甘える *vb 2* に – to rely on someone's being nice or to play up to someone

あまぐ・雨具 *n* rainwear

アマチュア *n* amateur

あまど・雨戸 *n* shutters

あまやかす・甘やかす *vb 1* ㋓ to spoil (a child)

あまり・余り **1** *n* remainder **2** *adv* too; very; (with negative) not very; not much; not often **3** *suf* more than

あまる・余る *vb 1* ㋑ to be left; to be more than required

あみもの・編み物 *n* knitwear; knitting

あむ・編む *vb 1* ㋓ to knit

あめ・雨 *n* rain

あめ・飴 *n* candy

アメリカ *n* America

あやしい・怪しい *adj* suspicious

あやまり・誤り *n* mistake; misunderstanding

あやまる・謝る *vb 1* ㋓ に to apologise

あら *interjection* – used by women to express surprise

あらい・粗い・荒い *adj* rough

あらいます ▶ あらう

あらう・洗う *vb 1* 㑹 あらって・あらわない・あらいます to wash

あらし・嵐 *n* storm

あらすじ・粗筋 *n* plot (of a story)

あらそう・争う *vb 1* 㑹 と to dispute; to compete

あらた(な)・新た(な) **1** *adj* new **2** *adv* あらたに anew; once again

あらためて・改めて *adv* again; anew

あらためる・改める *vb 2* 㑹 to change; to renew; to correct

あらって ▶ あらう

あらっぽい・粗っぽい・荒っぽい *adj* rough

あらゆる *attributive* every

あらわす・現す *vb 1* 㑹 to appear

あらわす・表す *vb 1* 㑹 to show; to express

あらわす・著す *vb 1* 㑹 to write

あらわれ・現れ *n* sign; expression

あらわれる・現れる *vb 2* 㑹 to appear; to show up

ありがたい *adj* grateful; thankful

ありがとう・有り難う *phrase* ! used in a variety of forms of the full phrase どうも ありがとう ございます to mean 'thank you (very much)'

あります ▶ ある

ある・或 *attributive* a certain; a

ある・在る・有る *vb 1* 㑹 にあって・ない・あります to be; to have; to happen

あるいて ▶ あるく

あるいは *conj* or; either

あるきます ▶ あるく

あるく・歩く *vb 1* 㑹 あるいて・あるかない・あるきます to walk

アルバイト 1 *n* part time job **2** *vb 3* ㉖ **アルバイト(を)する** to do a part time job – *and refers to a job which is not permanent but which can be full time such as a student holiday job*

アルバム *n* photo album

あれ *interjection* – used to express surprise

あれ *n* that; that thing; it ! *used to refer to something distant from both speaker and listener or something that is previously known to both of them*

あれこれ *adv* this and that

あれる・荒れる *vb 2* ㉑ to be rough

アレルギー *n* allergy

あわ・泡 *n* bubble; foam

あわい・淡い *adj* pale; faint

あわせる・合わせる *vb 2* ㊦ to join together; to fit in with; to adjust; to mix

あわただしい・慌ただしい *adj* hurried; flustered

あわてる・慌てる *vb 2* ㉑ to hurry; to be flustered

あわれ・哀れ *n* pity

あん・案 *n* plan

あんい(な)・安易(な) *adj* relaxed

あんがい・案外 1 *adv* **あんがい** unexpectedly **2** *adj* **あんがい(な)** unexpected

あんき・暗記 1 *n* rote learning **2** *vb 3* ㊦ **あんきする** to memorise

アンケート *n* questionnaire; survey

あんしん・安心 1 *n* peace of mind **2** *vb 3* ㉑ **あんしんする** to feel relieved; to feel safe **3** *adj* **あんしん(な)** reassuring; safe

あんぜん・安全 1 *n* safety **2** *adj* **あんぜん(な)** safe

あんてい・安定 1 *n* stability **2** *vb 3* ㉑ **あんていする** to be stable

あんな *adj* that; like that

あんない・案内 1 *n* information **2** *vb* 3 を あんないする
to guide; to show around; to show the way

あんなに *adv* like that; in that way

あんまり ▶ あまり

いイ

い・胃 *n* stomach

い・位 *suf* position

いい・良い *adj* good ! *the past and negative forms are made
from the alternative form* よい

いいえ *interjection* no

いいかげん(な)・いい加減(な) *adj* – *the literal
meaning is that the quantity of something is just right but it is
more common as an idiom meaning that something is
'inadequate' in some way and when applied to people's actions
and behaviour the translation and meaning will vary greatly
depending on the context and the expectation of the person
judging;* このしごとは けっこう いいかげんです this job
has not been done properly; いいかげんに しなさい That's
Enough!

いいだす・言い出す *vb* 1 を to propose

いいつける・言いつける *vb* 2 を to tell someone (to do
something)

いいます ▶ いう

いいわけ・言い訳 *n* excuse

いいん・委員 *n* committee member

いう・言う *vb* 1 を と いって・いわない・いいます
to say; これは にほんごで なんといいますか what do

you call this in Japanese?; かれが 「ぼく やめる」 と いいました He said "I quit!"; かれは やめると いいました he said that he would quit ▶ という

いえ・家 *n* house

いか・以下 *suf* less than; under

いがい・以外 *suf* apart from

いがい(な)・意外(な) *adj* unexpected

いかが *adv* how; how about; えいがを みるのは いかがで すか how about seeing a film?; コーヒーは いかがですか would you like some coffee?; しごとは いかがですか how is work?

いがく・医学 *n* medical science

いかす・活かす *vb 1* ㊦ to make active use of

いかり・怒り *n* anger

いき・行き *n* outward journey

いき・息 *n* breath

いぎ・意義 *n* significance

いぎ・異議 *n* objection

いきいき (と) *adv* vividly

いきおい・勢い *n* vigour

いきなり *adv* unexpectedly

いきます▶いく

いきもの・生き物 *n* living creatures

いきる・生きる *vb 2* ㊦ to live

いく・行く *vb 1* ㊦ いって・いかない・いきます to go
▌ following the 〜て form of a verb it can add the sense of an ongoing process or direction of movement of the subject

いくじ・育児 *n* – bringing up children

いくつ *adv* how many; (お)いくつですか how old are you?

いくつか *n* some

いくぶん・幾分 *adv* a little

いくら adv how much; いくら べんきょうしても なかなか むずかしいです no matter how much I study it's still difficult; いくらですか how much is it?

いけ・池 n pond

いけない adj bad ! following the 〜て form of a verb and は it means something should not be done

いけばな・生け花 n flower arrangement

いけません a politer version of いけない

いけん・意見 n opinion

いご・以後 n and suf since

いこう・以降 n and suf since

イコール n equals

いさましい・勇ましい adj brave

いし・石 n stone

いし・医師 n doctor

いし・意志 n will

いし・意思 n intention

いじ・維持 1 n maintenance 2 vb 3 ⊛ いじする to maintain

いしき・意識 n consciousness

いじめ n bullying

いじめる vb 2 ⊛ to bully

いしゃ・医者 n doctor

いじょう・以上 n the foregoing ! often used in the form いじょうです to end an announcement

いじょう・異常 1 n abnormality 2 adj いじょう(な) exceptional 3 adv いじょうに exceptionally

いじわる・意地悪 1 n malice 2 adj いじわる(な) malicious

いす・椅子 n chair

いずみ・泉 n (natural) spring

いずれ adv one day; いずれに しても in any event

いせき・遺跡 n remains

いぜん・以前 n before; once

いぜん・依然 n as it was before

いそいで ▶ いそぐ

いそがしい・忙しい adj busy

いそぎます ▶ いそぐ

いそぐ・急ぐ vb 1 ㊥ いそいで・いそがない・いそ
ぎます to hurry

いた・板 n board; skis

いたい・痛い adj painful

いだい(な)・偉大(な) adj grand

いだく・抱く vb 1 ㊧ to hold

いたす・致す vb 1 ㊧ – a humble equivalent of する

いたずら 1 n pranks; vandalism 2 n 3 ㊥ いたずら(を)する
to play pranks; to deliberately behave badly

いただいて ▶ いただく

いただきます phrase – used before eating it is somewhat
similar to the Christian grace 'for what we are about to receive
may the Lord make us truly thankful' but literally a form of the
humble verb 'to receive' without any religious meaning
▶ いただく

いただく・頂く vb 1 ㊧ いただいて・いただかない・
いただきます to take; to receive; to eat; to drink

いたみ・痛み n pain

いたむ・痛む vb 1 ㊥ いたんで・いたまない・いた
みます to hurt

いち・一 n one

いち・市 n market

いち・位置 n position

いちいち・一々 adv in detail; one by one

いちおう・一応 *adv* for the time being; just in case

いちご・苺 *n* strawberry

いちじ・一時 *adv* for a while; once; one o'clock

いちど・一度 *n* once

いちどに・一度に *adv* at one time

いちば・市場 *n* market

いちぶ・一部 **1** *n* part **2** *adv* partly

いちりゅう・一流 *n* first class

いつ *adv* when

いつか・五日・5日 *n* the fifth day of the month; five days

いつか *n* someday; sometime

いっか・一家 *n* family

いっさくじつ・一昨日 *n* the day before yesterday

いっさくねん・一昨年 *n* the year before last

いっしゅ・一種 *n* kind (of)

いっしゅうかん・一週間 *n* one week

いっしゅん・一瞬 *n* an instant; for a moment

いっしょ・一緒 *n* together; with

いっしょう・一生 *n* life

いっしょうけんめい・一生懸命 **1** *adj* いっしょうけんめい(な) hard working **2** *adv* いっしょうけんめい(に) as hard as possible; to the best of one's ability

いっしょに・一緒に *adv* together; at the same time

いっせいに・一斉に *adv* simultaneously

いっそう・一層 *adv* all the more

いったい・一体 *adv* – literally meaning '(as) one body' it is most common with questions indicating surprise or threat as in English 'what on earth ...?'.

いったん・一旦 *adv* once

いっち・一致 **1** *n* agreement **2** *vb 3 ㉑* に いっち する to agree

いつつ・五つ *n* five

いって ▶ いく ▶ いう

いってい(の)・一定 (の) *adj* fixed

いっていらっしゃい *phrase* – literally meaning 'go and come back' this phrase is used to people leaving the home (or other place if they are expected to return there) ▶ いってきます

いってきます *phrase* – literally '(I will) go and come back' this phrase is used by people leaving the home (or other place if they expect to return there)

いってまいります *phrase* – a more polite version of いってきます

いつでも *adv* always; anytime

いつのまにか・いつの 間にか *adv* before (I) really noticed

いっぱい **1** *adj* いっぱい(の・な) crowded; full **2** *adv* lots of; until the end of

いっぱい・一杯 *counter* a cup of; a glass of; a bowl of; いっぱいする to have a drink

いっぱん(に)・一般 (に) *adv* generally

いっぽう・一方 **1** *n* one side; one end; more and more **2** *conj* on the other hand; しけんが むずかしく なる いっぽう です the exams get more and more difficult

いつまでも *adv* always

いつも *adv* always; as usual

いて ▶ いる

いてん・移転 **1** *n* transfer **2** *vb 3 ㉑* に いてんする to move (to)

いでんし・遺伝子 *n* gene

いと・糸 *n* thread

いど・井戸 *n* a well

いどう・移動 1 *n* movement **2** *vb 3* ㋕ に いどう する
to move

いとこ *n* cousin

いない・以内 *suf* within

いなか・田舎 *n* – the basic meaning is 'country' as opposed to 'urban' but it can carry connotations of backwardness and a lack of sophistication. Sometimes used of urban areas smaller than Tokyo and Osaka. Can be used to mean 'home town' especially in the phrase; いなかに かえる go home

いぬ・犬 *n* dog

いね・稲 *n* rice plant

いねむり・居眠り 1 *n* doze **2** *vb 3* ㋕ いねむり (を) する
to doze off

いのち・命 *n* life

いのり・祈り *n* prayer

いのる・祈る *vb 1* ㋔ を to pray

いばる・威張る *vb 1* ㋕ to boast; to be proud

いはん・違反 1 *n* violation **2** *vb 3* を いはん する
to break (a rule)

いふく・衣服 *n* clothing

いま・今 1 *n* now; at the moment **2** *adv* right away

いま・居間 *n* living room

います ▶ いる

いまに・今に *adv* soon

いまにも・今にも *adv* at any moment

いみ・意味 1 *n* meaning; sense **2** *vb 3* ㋕ いみ する
to mean

イメージ *n* image

いもうと・妹 *n* one's own younger sister

いもうとさん・妹さん *n* someone else's younger sister

いや(な)・嫌(な) *adj* unpleasant; annoying; disgusting

いや *interjection* – contradicts a previous statement and so can be translated as either 'yes' or 'no' depending on whether it refers to a positive or a negative statement

いやがる・嫌がる *vb 1* Ⓔ to dislike (doing something); to be unwilling (to do something)

いよいよ *adv* even more; at last

いらい・以来 *suf* since

いらい・依頼 1 *n* request **2** *vb 3* Ⓔ いらいする to request

いらいら(する) *vb 3* Ⓝ to get annoyed

いらっしゃい *phrase* – used to mean 'welcome' or 'come in' and carries a nuance of 'thank you for coming'

いらっしゃいませ *phrase* – used to welcome customers and meaning 'welcome' or 'may I help you?' depending on the context

いらっしゃる *vb 1* Ⓝ いらっしって・いらっしゃらない・いらっしゃいます to go; to come; to be ! *honorific equivalent of* いく, くる *and* いる

いりぐち・入り口 *n* entrance

いりょう・医療 *n* medical treatment

いる・居る *vb 2* Ⓝ いて・いない・います (*of people or animals*) to be; to exist; (*of a place*) to live; to be; (*of a family member*) to have; いもうとと あにが います I have a younger sister and an elder brother ! *after the* 〜て *form of a verb it indicates continuous action or continuing or completed states.*

いる・要る *vb 1* Ⓝ いって・いらない・いります to be necessary; to want

いる・炒る・煎る *vb 1* Ⓔ to roast

いれて ▶ **いれる** ▶ **〜て**

いれます ▶ **いれる**

いれもの・入れ物 *n* container

いれる・入れる *vb 2* Ⓔ いれて・いれない・いれます to put in; to let in; to turn on (a switch)

いろ・色 *n* colour

いろいろ(な)・色々(な) *adj* various; all sorts of

いわ・岩 *n* rock

いわい・祝い *n* celebration; a present

いわう・祝う *vb 1* を to celebrate

いわば・言わば *adv* so to speak

いわゆる・ *attributive* so-called

いん・員 *suf* member

いんかん・印鑑 *n –* an official name stamp that functions as a signature on documents

インク *n* ink

いんさつ・印刷 **1** *n* printing **2** *vb 3* を いんさつ する to print

いんしょう・印象 *n* impression; いんしょうを あたえる to give an impression

いんたいする・引退する *vb 3* か を to retire

インタビュー *n* interview

インテリ *n* intellectual

いんよう・引用 *n* quotation

いんりょく・引力 *n* gravity

- -

うウ

- -

ウイスキー *n* whiskey; whisky

ウール *n* wool

ううん *interjection* no ! *informal equivalent of* いいえ

うえ・上 *n* on; over; above; top; older

ウェートレス *n* waitress

うえき・植木 *n* – trees, plants and pots in a garden

うえきや・植木屋 *n* – a person or business growing trees and plants for gardens

うえる・植える *vb 2* を to plant

うえる・飢える *vb 2* が to starve

うお・魚 *n* fish

うがい **1** *n* gargling **2** *vb 3* が うがいする to gargle

うかがう・伺う *vb 1* を うかがって・うかがわない・うかがいます to visit; to ask; to be told ! *this is a humble equivalent of the verbs* たずねる *and* いう

うかぶ・浮かぶ *vb 1* が to float; to occur

うかべる・浮かべる *vb 2* を to float; to occur

うかる・受かる *vb 1* が に to pass (an exam)

うく・浮く *vb 1* が to float up

うけいれる・受け入れる *vb 2* を to accept

うけたまわる・承る *vb 1* を to hear; to know; to be told; to take an order

うけつけ・受け付け *n* reception

うけつける・受け付ける *vb 2* を to accept

うけて ▶ うける

うけとめる・受け止める *vb 2* を to catch; to react

うけとり・受け取り *n* receipt; receiving

うけとる・受け取る *vb 1* を to receive

うけます ▶ うける

うけもつ・受け持つ *vb 1* を to be in charge of

うける・受ける *vb 2* を うけて・うけない・うけます to receive; (of an exam) to take; (of harmful effects) to suffer

うごかす・動かす *vb 1* を to move

うごく・動く *vb 1* が to move

うごき・動き *n* movement

うさぎ・兎 *n* rabbit

うし・牛 *n* cow

うしなう・失う *vb 1* Ⓔ to lose

うしろ・後ろ *n* behind; back; rear

うすい・薄い *adj* thin; (*of drinks*) weak; (*of colours*) pale

うすぐらい・薄暗い *adj* dim

うすめる・薄める *vb 2* Ⓔ to dilute

うそ・嘘 *n* lie; うそを つく to (tell a) lie ❗ *as an exclamation it indicates surprise and is similar to 'you must be joking!'*

うそつき *n* liar

うた・歌 *n* song

うたいます ▶ うたう

うたう・歌う *vb 1* Ⓔ うたって・うたわない・うたいます to sing

うたがい・疑い *n* suspicion

うたがう・疑う *vb 1* Ⓔ to suspect; to doubt

うたって ▶ うたう

うち・家 *n* house; home; family ❗ *sometimes translatable 'we' or 'us' when talking about a company or a family etc.*; うちの いぬ our dog

うち・内 *n* while; during; in; (*of a number of items*) from ❗ *following the 〜ない form of a verb it conveys the meaning of 'before'*; あめが ふらない うちに かえりましょう・雨が降らない うちに 帰りましょう let's go home before it rains

うちあわせ・打ち合わせ *n* arrangement

うちあわせる・打ち合わせる *vb 2* Ⓔ to arrange

うちけす・打ち消す *vb 1* Ⓔ to deny

うちゅう・宇宙 *n* the universe; space

うちわ・団扇 *n* hand-held fan

うつ・打つ *vb 1* Ⓔ to hit; to type

うつ・撃つ *vb 1* (を) to shoot

うっかり(と) *adv* carelessly

うつくしい・美しい *adj* beautiful

うつす・移す *vb 1* (を) to transfer

うつす・写す *vb 1* (を) to copy

うつす・映す *vb 1* (を) to reflect

うったえる・訴える *vb 2* (を) to sue; to complain

うって ▶ うる ▶ うつ

うつる・移る *vb 1* (か) to move; (of a cold etc.) to be contagious

うつる・写る *vb 1* (か) (of a photograph) to come out (well); (of something in a photograph) to be in

うつる・映る *vb 1* (か) to be reflected

うつわ・器 *n* container

うで・腕 *n* arm; うでを みがく to practise

うでどけい・腕時計 *n* (wrist) watch

うてん・雨天 *n* rainy weather

うどん *n* – a kind of thick, white noodle

うながす・促す *vb 1* (を) に to urge

うなぎ・鰻 *n* eel

うなずく *vb 1* (か) to nod

うなる・唸る *vb 1* (か) to groan

うばう・奪う *vb 1* (を) to steal

うま・馬 *n* horse

うまい *adj* (of food) delicious; (of ability) skillful **!** *in the sense 'delicious' this word is generally only used by men.*

うまれ・生まれ *n* birth

うまれつき(の)・生まれつき(の) *adj* (of talent etc.) natural

うまれて ▶ うまれる

うまれます ▶ うまれる

うまれる・生まれる *vb 2* ㋑ うまれて・うまれない・
　うまれます to be born

うみ・海 *n* sea

うむ・産む・生む *vb 1* ㋾ to give birth to; to produce

うめ・梅 *n* plum

うめぼし・梅干し *n* – salty pickled plum

うめる・埋める *vb 2* ㋾ to bury; to make up (for); to fill in
　(the gaps)

うやまう・敬う *vb 1* ㋾ to respect

うら・裏 *n* back; behind

うらがえし・裏返し *n* inside out

うらがえす・裏返す *vb 1* ㋾ to turn inside out

うらぎる・裏切る *vb 1* ㋾ to betray

うらない・占い *n* fortune telling

うらないし・占い師 *n* fortune-teller

うらなう・占う *vb 1* ㋾ to tell someone's fortune

うらみ・恨み *n* ill will; grudge

うらむ・恨む *vb 1* ㋾ to resent

うらやましい・羨ましい *adj* envious; enviable

うらやむ・羨む *vb 1* ㋾ to envy

うりあげ・売り上げ *n* sales

うりきれ・売り切れ *n* sold out

うりきれる・売り切れる *vb 2* ㋑ to be sold out

うりだし・売り出し *n* sale

うりだす・売り出す *vb 1* ㋾ to put on sale

うりば・売り場 *n and suf* department

うります ▶ うる

うる・売る *vb 1* ㋾ うって・うらない・うります to sell

うるさい・煩い・五月蝿い *adj* noisy; annoying ❗ *as an exclamation it means 'shut up'*

うれしい・嬉しい *adj* glad; happy

うれゆき・売れ行き *n* sales

うれる・売れる *vb 2* ㉚ to be sold

うろうろ(する) *vb 3* ㉚ to loiter

うわき・浮気 1 *n* affair **2** *vb 3* ㉚ うわきする to have an affair

うわぎ・上着 *n* – clothing for the upper body, especially in the sense of a coat or jacket

うわさ・噂 *n* rumour

うわまわる・上回る *vb 1* ㉜ to exceed

うん *interjection* yes; ok ❗ *informal equivalent of* はい

うん・運 *n* fate; うんが いい lucky; うんが わるい unlucky

うんえい・運営 1 *n* management **2** *vb 3* ㉜ うんえいする to manage

うんが・運河 *n* canal

うんざり(する) *vb 3* ㉚ に to be fed up

うんちん・運賃 *n* fare

うんてん・運転 1 *n* driving **2** *vb 3* ㉚㉜ うんてんする to drive

うんてんしゅ・運転手 *n* driver

うんてんめんきょ・運転免許 *n* driving licence

うんと *adv* very; hard

うんどう・運動 1 *n* exercise; movement **2** *vb 3* ㉚ うんどうする to exercise; to move

うんどうかい・運動会 *n* – a sports competition

うんどうじょう・運動場 *n* playground; playing field; sports ground

え エ

え・絵 *n* picture

えいえん・永遠 *n* eternity

えいが・映画 *n* movie; film

えいきゅう・永久 **1** *adj* えいきゅう(の) eternal **2** *adv* えいきゅうに for ever

えいきょう・影響 **1** *n* influence **2** *vb 3* か に えいきょうする to have an influence

えいぎょう・営業 **1** *n* business **2** *vb 3* か えいぎょうする to do business

えいご・英語 *n* English (language)

えいこく・英国 *n* the United Kingdom

えいせい・衛生 *n* hygiene

えいせい・衛星 *n* satellite

えいぶん・英文 *n* – written in English

えいよう・栄養 *n* nutrition

えいわ・英和 *n and suf* English and Japanese language

えいわじてん・英和辞典 *n* English-Japanese dictionary

ええ *interjection* yes ! *a less formal equivalent of* はい

ええと *interjection* – a noise indicating hesitation or consideration

えがお・笑顔 *n* smiling face

えがく・描く *vb 1* を to draw; to paint

えき・駅 *n* station

えき・液 *suf* liquid

えきたい・液体 *n* liquid

えさ・餌 *n* feed (for animals)

エスカレーター *n* escalator

えだ・枝 *n* branch (of a tree)

エネルギー *n* energy

えはがき *n* picture post card

えほん・絵本 *n* – an illustrated book for children

えらい・偉い *adj* wonderful; praiseworthy; important

えらぶ・選ぶ *vb 1* Ⓔ to choose

えり・襟 *n* collar

える・得る *vb 2* Ⓔ to get; to obtain

エレベーター *n* elevator

えん・円 *n and suf* yen

えん・縁 *n* relationship

えんかい・宴会 *n* – a formal party where food and drink are served

えんき・延期 **1** *n* postponement **2** *vb 3* Ⓔ えんきする to postpone

えんぎ・演技 *n* performance

えんぎ・縁起 *n* omen

えんげい・園芸 *n* gardening; horticulture

えんげき・演劇 *n* drama; play

えんしゅう・円周 *n* circumference

えんしゅう・演習 *n* practice

えんじょ・援助 **1** *n* assistance **2** *vb 3* Ⓔ えんじょする to assist

エンジニア *n* engineer

エンジン *n* engine

えんぜつ・演説 **1** *n* speech **2** *vb 3* Ⓔ えんぜつする to deliver a speech

えんそう・**演奏 1** *n* performance **2** *vb* **3** を えんそうする
to perform

えんそく・**遠足** *n* outing; trip

えんちょう・**延長 1** *n* extension **2** *vb* **3** を えんちょう
する to extend

えんとつ・**煙突** *n* chimney

えんぴつ・**鉛筆** *n* pencil

えんりょ・**遠慮 1** *n* restraint **2** *vb* **3** を か えんりょする
to refrain from **!** *often used with the sense of taking other
people's feelings or situations into consideration and acting
accordingly rather than just doing what you yourself feel like*

お オ

O ! *note that the direct object particle is written with the* ひらがな
character を *or (very occasionally) the* かたかな *character* ヲ
▶ を

お *prf* **!** *when put in front of certain nouns it makes them polite. It
can also used to refer to items which are connected with a
person to whom respect should be shown*

おあがり（ください）・お上がり（ください） *phrase*
– *literally meaning 'please step up' it means 'please come in'
and is said to someone entering a house by stepping up from
ground level or* げんかん *Also used to mean 'please eat'*

おあずかり します・お預かり します *phrase* –
*meaning 'I|we will take charge of' it is used when receiving
something of someone else's to be looked after in some way
such as at a cloakroom or in a bank*

おい・**甥** *n* nephew

おいかける・**追いかける** *vb* 2 を to chase

おいこす・**追い越す** *vb* 1 を to overtake

おいしい *adj* delicious

おいつく・追い付く *vb 1* を に to catch up

おいて ▶ おく

おいで・お出で to come; to go; to be; (ちょっと) おいで come here! ! *a noun which forms an honorific equivalent of the verbs* いく、くる *and* いる *when used with* に なる *or* です

オイル *n* oil

おう・王 *n* king

おう・追う *vb 1* を to follow

おうえん・応援 **1** *n* support; cheering **2** *vb 3* を おうえん する to support; to cheer

おうじる・応じる *vb 2* か に to respond

おうせつ・応接 **1** *n* entertaining guests **2** *vb 3* を おうせ つする to entertain guests

おうたい・応対 **1** *n* attending to (guests) **2** *vb 3* を おうた いする to deal with (guests etc.)

おうだん・横断 **1** *n* crossing **2** *vb 3* を おうだんする to go across

おうふく・往復 **1** *n* return (ticket) **2** *vb 3* か おうふくする to make a return journey

おうべい・欧米 *n* Europe and America

おうよう・応用 **1** *n* application **2** *vb 3* を おうようする to put to use

おえる・終える *vb 2* を to finish

おお・大 *prf* – used to add the meaning of 'great' to a following noun such as あめ ▶ おおあめ

おおあめ・大雨 *n* heavy rain

おおい・多い *adj* numerous

おおいに *adv* greatly

おおう・覆う *vb 1* を to cover

おおき(な) *adj* big

おおきい・大きい *adj* large

オーエル *n* – *female clerical worker* ❗ *usually written with the capital roman letters OL which stand for 'office lady'*

オーケストラ *n* orchestra

おおげさ・大袈裟 1 *n* exaggeration **2** *adj* おおげさ(な) exaggerated **3** *adv* おおげさに exaggeratedly

おおざっぱ 1 *adj* おおざっぱ(な) approximate **2** *adv* おおざっぱに roughly

おおぜい・大勢 *adv* in great numbers

おおどおり・大通り *n* main street

オートバイ *n* motor bike

オートマチック(な) *adj* automatic

オープン 1 *n* opening **2** *vb* **3** ⑰ ⑯ オープン する to open

オーバー *n* overcoat

おおや・大家 *n* – *the owner of a rental property and so often translatable as either 'landlord' or 'landlady' as appropriate*

おおやけに・公に *n* in public

おおやさん・大家さん ▶おおや

おおよそ・大凡 *adv* approximately

おか・丘 *n* hill

おかあさん・お母さん *n* mother

おかえり(なさい) *phrase* welcome home; welcome back

おかげ *n* – *used in the form* の おかげ で *to mean 'thanks to ...' usually in a positive sense*

おかげさまで・お蔭様で *phrase* – *means 'Yes, thanks to you, all is well' as a polite response to enquiries about health etc. and so often translatable as 'fine, thank you'*

おかし・お菓子 *n* confectionery

おかしい *adj* funny; peculiar

おかず *n* – *dishes eaten with rice as part of a meal*

おかね・お金 *n* money

おかまいなく・お構いなく *phrase – a polite phrase used in response to an offer etc. meaning 'please don't trouble yourself on my behalf'*

おがむ・拝む *vb 1* ㊛ to worship

おかわり・お代わり *n* second helping of food

おき・沖 *n* open sea

おき・置き *suf* every other ....; at intervals of ....; いちにちおき every other day

おきて ▶ おきる

おぎなう・補う *vb 1* ㊛ to make up for

おきのどく・お気の毒 *phrase – used in response to bad news affecting others with the sense of 'I'm very sorry to hear that'*

おきます ▶ おきる ▶ おく

おきる・起きる *vb 2* ㊝ おきて・おきない・おきます to get up

おく・置く *vb 1* ㊛ において・おかない・おきます to put ! when attached to the 〜て form of a verb it adds the meaning that the action of that verb has been done in preparation for some future need or left 'as it as'

おく・億 *n and suf* ▶ unit of 100,000,000

おく・奥 *n* the inner part

おくがい・屋外 *n* outdoors

おくさま・奥様 *n* someone else's wife ! *a very polite term also used to address a female customer*

おくさん・奥さん *n* someone else's wife ! *a polite term also used to address a female customer*

おくじょう・屋上 *n* rooftop

おくりがな・送り仮名 *n – the part of a Japanese word written in hiragana following a Chinese character stem. The word* おおきい *'big' is normally written* 大きい *and the* き *and* い *are okurigana*

おくりもの・贈り物 *n* present

おくる・送る *vb 1* を to send; to see off

おくる・贈る *vb 1* を to give a (present etc.)

おくれて ▶ おくれる

おくれます ▶ おくれる

おくれる・遅れる *vb 2* か おくれて・おくれない・おくれます to be late

おげんきですか・お元気ですか *phrase* how are you?

おこさま・お子様 *n* child **!** *a very polite way of referring to someone else's child*

おこさん・お子さん *n* child **!** *a polite way of referring to someone else's child*

おこして ▶ おこす

おこします ▶ おこす

おこす・起こす *vb 1* を おこして・おこさない・おこします to wake someone up

おこたる・怠る *vb 1* を to neglect

おこなう・行う *vb 1* を to do; to hold (an exam etc.)

おこる・起こる *vb 1* か to take place

おこる・怒る *vb 1* に to lose one's temper

おごる・奢る *vb 1* を to treat someone (to food or drinks)

おさえる・押さえる・抑える *vb 2* を to hold down; to suppress

おさきに・お先に *phrase – used when leaving work etc. before other people and translatable as 'see you' or 'goodbye'*

おさけ・お酒 *n* Japanese sake (rice wine); alcoholic drink in general

おさない・幼い *adj* very young

おさまる・治まる *vb 1* か to calm down

おさまる・納まる *vb 1* か to be paid

おさまる・収まる *vb 1* か to fit; to be kept in

おさめる・治める *vb 2* を to rule

おさめる・納める *vb 2* を to pay; to put back

おさめる・収める *vb 2* を to put away

おじ・叔父・伯父 おじさん

おしい・惜しい *adj* precious; regrettable ! as an exclamation it means 'good try!' or 'nearly right'

おじいさん・お祖父さん *n* grandfather

おじいさん・お爺さん *n* – general term of address and reference for older men

おしいれ・押し入れ *n* – a built-in storage closet used to store things like futons and bedding and to hang clothes

おしえ ▶ おしえる

おしえます ▶ おしえる

おしえる・教える *vb 2* を に おしえて・おしえない・おしえます to teach; to tell (the way etc.)

おじぎ・お辞儀 **1** *n* bow **2** *vb 3* ㋾ おじぎ (を) する to bow

おじさん・小父さん *n* – general term of address and reference for middle aged men

おじさん・叔父さん・伯父さん *n* uncle ! if the brother is older than your father or mother 伯父さん, is used, if younger 叔父さん

おしまい・お終い *n* the end

おしゃれ・お洒落 *n* smartly dressed person

おしゃべり・お喋り **1** *n* a talkative person **2** *vb 3* ㋾ おしゃべりする to chatter

おじゃまします *phrase* – a polite phrase derived from a verb 'to interrupt', 'to visit' and used when entering a room or someone's house ▶ じゃま

おじょうさん・お嬢さん *n* – a polite term for someone else's daughter or a young girl in general

おす・押す *vb 1* を to push

おすまい・お住まい・お住い *n* (your) house; おすまいはどこですか where do you live?

おせわになりました・お世話になりました *phrase* – said to someone to show the feeling that they have been of assistance, especially in the context of work. It's direct translation would be 'you have looked after me, (thank you)' but often left untranslated as there is no real English equivalent in many situations

おせん・汚染 *n* pollution

おそい・遅い *adj* late

おそらく・恐らく *adv* probably; possibly

おそれいりますが・恐れ入りますが *phrase* – used when excusing yourself for interrupting or when asking questions and so translatable as 'excuse me but ...'. More polite than すみません

おそれる・恐れる *vb 2 ㊙* to be frightened

おそろしい・恐ろしい *adj* frightening

おそわる・教わる *vb 1 ㊙* に to be taught

おだいじに・お大事に *phrase* – used to people who are ill or appear tired it means 'please take care of your health'

おたがいさま・お互い様 *phrase* in the same circumstances

おだやか・穏やか 1 *adj* おだやか (な) calm **2** *adv* おだやかに calmly

おちつく・落ち着く *vb 1 ㊙* to calm down

おちゃ・お茶 *n* tea; おちゃを いれる to make tea ! used for Japanese tea and especially green tea as opposed to こうちゃ

おちる・落ちる *vb 2 ㊙* to fall; しけんに おちました・試験に落ちました (I) have failed the exam

おっしゃる *vb 1 ㊙* to say ! this is an honorific equivalent of いう

おっと・夫 *n* one's own husband –

おつまみ *n – side dishes and snacks eaten with alcoholic drinks*

おてあらい・お手洗い *n* toilet

おでかけ・お出掛け *n* going out; **おでかけ ですか・お出掛け ですか** are you going out?

おてすう・お手数 *n* trouble; **おてすうですが** I'm sorry to trouble you but would you mind (doing something for me)?

おてつだいさん・お手伝いさん *n* maid

おと・音 *n* sound; noise; **おとが した・音がした** there was a noise

おとうさん・お父さん *n* father

おとうと・弟 *n* younger brother

おとうとさん・弟さん *n* someone else's younger brother

おどかす・脅かす *vb 1* Ⓔ to threaten

おとこ・男 *n* man

おとこのこ・男の子 *n* boy

おとこのひと・男の人 *n* man

おとしもの・落とし物 *n* lost property

おとす・落とす *vb 1* Ⓔ to drop

おとずれる・訪れる *vb 2* Ⓝ to visit

おととい・一昨日 *n* the day before yesterday

おととし・一昨年 *n* the year before last

おとな・大人 *n* adult

おとなしい *adj* quiet

おどり・踊り *n* dance ! *usually refers to Japanese traditional dancing*

おとる・劣る *vb 1* Ⓝ to be inferior

おどる・踊る *vb 1* Ⓝ **おどって・おどらない・おどります** to dance

おとろえる・衰える *vb 2* Ⓝ to weaken

おどろかす・驚かす *vb 1* 乞 to startle

おどろく・驚く *vb 1* 加 に to be startled

おなか *n* stomach

おなじ・同じ *adj* same **!** *note that there is no change in form when used in front of a noun*

おなじく・同じく *adv* similarly

おに・鬼 *n* – the giant monster of Japanese folk tales which is often translated as 'ogre'

おにいさん・お兄さん *n* older brother **!** *also used as a general term for a young man*

おねえさん・お姉さん *n* older sister **!** *also used as a general term for a young woman*

おねがい・お願い **1** *n* a request **2** *vb 3* 乞 に おねがいする to ask **!** *usually used as a set phrase in the form* おねがいします *meaning 'please' and indicating that a favour has been asked*

おのおの・各々 *n* each

おば・叔母・伯母 *n* aunt **!** *if an older sibling of the parent* 伯母 *is used, if a younger* 叔母

おばあさん・お祖母さん *n* grandmother

おばあさん・お婆さん *n* – a general term for an older woman

おばさん・叔母さん・伯母さん *n* aunt **!** *if an older sibling of the parent* 伯母さん *is used, if a younger* 叔母さん

おばさん・小母さん *n* – a general term for a mature woman

おはよう *phrase* good morning **!** *usually as a set expression* おはようございます

おび・帯 *n* – the wrap around "belt" on a Japanese きもの

おひる・お昼 *n* lunch (time)

オフィス *n* office

おふくろ *n* – a man's way of referring to his mother

おぼえる・覚える *vb 2* **を** to learn; to memorise

おぼれる・溺れる *vb 2* **が** to drown

おまいり・お参り **1** *n* – a visit to a temple or shrine for prayer, especially at the family graves **2** *vb 3* **が** **に** おまいり **!** to visit a shrine

おまえ・お前 *n* you **!** this is a term used by superior males to inferior status individuals. While common in the workplace hierarchy it is best avoided by non-Japanese.

おまたせ(しました)・お待たせ(しました) *phrase* sorry to have kept you waiting

おまちください・お待ちください *phrase* please wait

おまちどおさま *phrase* sorry to have kept you waiting

おまわりさん・お巡りさん *n* police officer

おみあい・お見合い *n* – an arranged introduction to a potential marriage partner

おみあいけっこん・お見合い結婚 *n* arranged marriage

おむつ *n* nappy; diaper

おめでたい *adj* joyous

おめでとう *phrase* congratulations! **!** usually in the form おめでとうございます

おめにかかる・お目に掛かる *vb 1* **を** **に** to meet with **!** humble equivalent of あう

おもい・重い *adj* heavy

おもいがけない・思い掛けない *adj* unexpected

おもいきって・思い切って *adv* resolutely

おもいきり・思い切り **1** *n* decisiveness **2** *adv* – gives the idea that something is done with energy, to the best of one's ability or as much as possible

おもいこむ・思い込む *vb 1* **と** to assume

おもいだす・思い出す *vb 1* **を** to remember

おもいつく・思い付く *vb 1* **を** to think of (an idea etc.)

おもいで・思い出 *n* recollection

おもいます ▶ おもう

おもう・思う *vb 1 ㉟* と おもって・おもわない・
おもいます to think; to hope; to intend

おもしろい・面白い *adj* interesting; amusing

おもたい・重たい *adj* heavy

おもちゃ・玩具 *n* toy

おもって ▶ おもう

おもて・表 *n* surface; front

おもな・主な *adj* main

おもに・主に *adv* mainly

おもむき・趣 *n* intention; appearance

おもむく・赴く *vb 1 ㉟* に – used to mean to go いく
especially in the sense of being sent on a posting from work

おもわず・思わず *adv* inadvertently

おや・親 *n* parent

おやじ・親父 *n* father ! *a rough term used by men to refer to
their own father*

おやすみ・お休み *n* good night ! *usually as a fixed phrase*
おやすみなさい ▶ やすみ

おやつ *n* snack

おやゆび・親指 *n* thumb

およいで ▶ およぐ

およぎます ▶ およぐ

およぐ・泳ぐ *vb 1 ㉟* に およいで・およがない・
およぎます to swim

およそ *adv* about

および・及び *conj* and

およぼす・及ぼす *vb 1 ㉟* to exercise; to exert

おり・折り *n* occasion

おり・檻 *n* cage

おりがみ・折り紙 *n – the traditional Japanese craft of folding paper to create models*

おりて ▶ おりる

おります ▶ おりる ▶ おる

おりもの・織物 *n* fabric

おりる・降りる・下りる *vb 2* ㋐ おりて・おりない・おります to get off (a vehicle); to go down (stairs etc.)

おる・折る *vb 1* ㋺ to fold; ほねを おる to break a bone

おる・居る *vb 1* ㋐ に to be ! *humble equivalent of* いる

おる・織る *vb 1* ㋺ to weave

おれ・俺 *n* I ! *an informal word used by men*

おれい・お礼 *n* thanks; reward; fee; おれいを いう to say thank you

おれる・折れる *vb 2* ㋐ to break

オレンジ *n* orange

オレンジいろ・オレンジ色 *n* orange

おろす・降ろす・下ろす *vb 1* ㋺ to drop; to set down (a passenger); to lower; to withdraw (money from the bank)

おろす・卸す *vb 1* ㋺ to sell (wholesale)

おわって ▶ おわる

おわり・終わり *n* end

おわります ▶ おわる

おわる・終わる *vb 1* ㋺ おわって・おわらない・おわります to finish

おん・恩 *n* obligation; おんを かえす・恩を返す to repay a favour

おん・音 *n* sound

おんがく・音楽 *n* music

おんけい・恩恵 *n* favour
おんしつ・温室 *n* greenhouse
おんしらず・恩知らず *phrase* ungrateful
おんせん・温泉 *n* – a hot mineral spring used for bathing for health benefits or a resort based on such a spring
おんだん・温暖 *n* mild (climate)
おんちゅう・御中 *n* – a formal title used after the name of a company when addressing a letter without using an individual's name
おんど・温度 *n* temperature
おんな・女 *n* woman **!** *Impolite. Use* おんなのひと
おんなの・女の *adj* female
おんなのこ・女の子 *n* girl
おんなのひと・女の人 *n* woman
おんよみ・音読み *n* – the pronunciation assigned to a Chinese character かんじ which is predominantly used when 2 or more characters are combined to form a word
オンライン *adjectival n* on line (computer network)

か カ

か *pt* **!** marks questions, choice, or uncertainty
か・蚊 *n* mosquito
か・課 *suf* section
か・日 *suf* day
が **1** *pt* **2** *conj* but, however
カー *n* car
カーテン *n* curtain
カード *n* card

カーブ *n* curve

カーペット *n* carpet; rug

かい・会 *n and suf* meeting

かい *pt* (! *an informal version of* か *used by men*)

かい・貝 *n* shellfish

かい・回 *counter* times

かい・階 *counter* floor

がい・害 *n* damage

がい・外 *suf* outside

かいいん・会員 *n* member

かいが・絵画 *n* painting

かいかい・開会 1 *n* opening **2** *vb* **3** (爲) (办) かいかいする to open

かいかいしき・開会式 *n* opening ceremony

かいがい・海外 *n* overseas

かいかく・改革 1 *n* reorganisation **2** *vb* **3** (爲) かいかくする to reform

かいかん・会館 *n* ▶ *a public building for meetings and functions*

かいがん・海岸 *n* coast; beach

かいぎ・会議 *n* meeting

かいけい・会計 *n* accounting

かいけいし・会計士 *n* accountant

かいけつ・解決 1 *n* solution **2** *vb* **3** (爲) かいけつする to solve

かいけん・会見 1 *n* meeting; interview **2** *vb* **3** (办) とかいけんする to have an interview

かいご・介護 1 *n* nursing **2** *vb* **3** (爲) かいごする to nurse

かいごう・会合 1 *n* assembly **2** *vb* **3** (办) かいごうする to assemble

がいこう・外交 *n* diplomacy

がいこく・外国 *n* abroad

がいこくじん・外国人 *n* foreigner

かいさつ・改札 *n* ticket inspection

かいさつぐち・改札口 *n* – the ticket barrier forming the entrance and exit points to stations

かいさん・解散 1 *n* dissolution **2** *vb* 3 ㊌ ㊒ かいさんする to break up

かいし・開始 1 *n* start **2** *vb* 3 ㊒ かいしする to start

かいしゃ・会社 *n* company ❗ often used in the sense of (place of) 'work'

かいしゃく・解釈 1 *n* interpretation **2** *vb* 3 ㊒ かいしゃくする to interpret

かいじゅう・怪獣 *n* monster

がいしゅつ する・外出する *vb* 3 ㊌ to go out

かいしょ・楷書 *n* – printed style Japanese characters as opposed to the handwritten forms. Often used in the sense of 'please write in block capitals''

かいじょう・会場 *n* meeting place

かいすいよく・海水浴 *n* bathing in the sea

かいすう・回数 *n* number of times

かいすうけん・回数券 *n* – book of tickets for several journeys on public transport

かいせい・改正 1 *n* revision **2** *vb* 3 ㊒ かいせいする to amend

かいせい・快晴 *n* fine weather

かいせつ・解説 1 *n* commentary **2** *vb* 3 ㊌ ㊒ かいせつ する to analyse

かいぜん・改善 1 *n* improvement **2** *vb* 3 ㊌ かいぜんする to improve

かいだん・階段 *n* stairs; steps

かいだん・会談 1 *n* conference **2** *vb* **3** ㉝ かいだんする
to have discussions

かいて ▶ かく

かいてき (な)・快適 (な) *adj* pleasant

かいてん・回転 1 *n* rotation **2** *vb* **3** ㉝ かいてんする
to revolve

ガイド *n* guide

かいとう・回答 *n* response

かいとう・解答 1 *n* answer **2** *vb* **3** ㉢ かいとうする
to solve

がいとう・街頭 *n* streets

がいとう・街灯 *n* street light

かいとうようし・解答用紙 *n* answer paper (for an
exam)

かいはつ・開発 1 *n* development **2** *vb* **3** ㉢ かいはつする
to develop

がいぶ・外部 *n* exterior

かいふく・回復 1 *n* recovery **2** *vb* **3** ㉢ かいふくする
to recover

かいほう・開放 1 *n* opening **2** *vb* **3** ㉢ かいほうする
to open

かいほう・解放 1 *n* liberation **2** *vb* **3** ㉢ かいほうする
to release

かいます ▶ かう

かいもの・買物 1 *n* shopping **2** *vb* **3** ㉝ かいもの (を)す
る to go shopping; to shop

かいよう・海洋 *n* the seas

がいらいご・外来語 *n* – words of foreign origin used in
Japanese and specifically those words predominantly from
western languages and written in the **かたかな** script

がいろん・概論 *n* outline

かいわ・会話 **1** *n* conversation **2** *vb 3* ㉚ かいわする
to talk with

かう・買う *vb 1* ㉚ かって・かわない・かいます
to buy

かう・飼う *vb 1* ㉘ to keep (an animal)

かえす・返す *vb 1* ㉘ to return

かえす・帰す *vb 1* ㉘ to send home

かえって・却って *adv* on the contrary

かえって ▶ かえる

かえて ▶ かえる

かえり・帰り *n* journey back; homecoming

かえります ▶ かえる

かえる・変える・代える・換える・替える *vb 2*
㉚ ㉘ かえて・かえない・かえます to change

かえる・帰る *vb 1* ㉚ に かえって・かえらない・かえ
ります to return; to go home; to come home

かえる・返る *vb 1* ㉘ に かえって・かえらない・
かえります to be returned

かお・顔 *n* face

かおく・家屋 *n* house

かおり・香り *n* scent

がか・画家 *n* artist

かかえる・抱える *vb 2* ㉘ to hold (in one's arms)

かかく・価格 *n* cost

かがく・科学 *n* science

かがく・化学 *n* chemistry

かかって ▶ かかる

かがみ・鏡 *n* mirror

かがやく・輝く *vb 1* ㉘ to shine; to sparkle

かかり・係り *suf* in charge of

かかりのひと・係りの人 *n* the person in charge (of ...)

かかります ▶ かかる

かかる・掛かる *vb 1 ㉝* かかって・かからない・
　かかります to take (time or money); to be telephoned; to hang;
　to be locked

かかわる・係わる *vb 1* に ㉝ to have to do with

かぎ・鍵 *n* key; lock; かぎを かける to lock; かぎが かかる
　to be locked

かきとめ・書留 *n* registered post

かきとり・書き取り *n* dictation

かきね・垣根 *n* fence

かきます ▶ かく

かぎり・限り *suf – sometimes used as a noun meaning
'limits' but often attached to verbs to give the meaning of 'as far
as' or 'as long as'. With a negative verb it can often be translated
'unless'.*

かぎる・限る *vb 1㉝* に to be limited

かく・核 *prf* nuclear

かく・書く *vb 1㉠* かいて・かかない・かきます to write

かく・描く *vb 1㉠* かいて・かかない・かきます to
draw; to paint

かく・欠く *vb 1㉠* to lack

かく・掻く *vb 1㉠* to scratch

かく・格 *n* rank

かく・各 *prf* each

かぐ・家具 *n* furniture

かぐ・嗅ぐ *vb 1㉠* to smell; to sniff

がく・学 *n* learning

かくう(の)・架空(の) *adj* fictional

かくご・覚悟 **1** *n* readiness; resolution **2** *vb 3㉠* かくご
　する to be resigned to; to be ready for

かくじ・各自　*n* each person

かくじつ（な）・確実な　*adj* definite; reliable

がくしゃ・学者　*n* academic

がくしゅう・学習　**1** *n* studying　**2** *vb* **3** を がくしゅうする to study

かくす・隠す　*vb* **1** を to hide something

がくせい・学生　*n* student

かくだい・拡大　**1** *n* magnification　**2** *vb* **3** を かくだいする to enlarge

かくち・各地　*n* each place

かくちょう・拡張　**1** *n* extension　**2** *vb* **3** を かくちょうする to widen

かくど・角度　*n* angle

かくにん・確認　**1** *n* confirmation　**2** *vb* **3** を かくにんする to confirm

がくねん・学年　*n* school year

がくぶ・学部　*n* faculty

かくべつ・格別　**1** *adj* かくべつの exceptional　**2** *adv* かくべつに particularly

かくめい・革命　*n* revolution

かくりつ・確率　*n* probability

がくりょく・学力　*n* academic ability

かくれる・隠れる　*vb* **2** を to be hidden

かげ・影　*n* shadow

かげ・陰　*n* shade

かけざん・掛け算　**1** *n* multiplication　**2** *vb* **3** を かけざんをする to multiply

かけつ（する）・可決（する）　*vb* **3** を to approve (a motion)

かけて ▶ かける

かけます ▶ かける

かける・掛ける・懸ける *vb 2* ㊉ かけて・かけない・かけます to take (time, money); to put over; to hang; to lock; to telephone; to multiply by; to be wearing (glasses)

かける・駆ける *vb 2* ㊀ to run

かける・欠ける *vb 2* ㊀ to be lacking; to be chipped

かげん・加減 *n* condition

かこ・過去 *n* past

かご・籠 *n* basket

かこう・火口 *n* crater

かこう・下降 1 *n* descent **2** *vb 3* ㊉㊀ かこうする to go down

かこう・加工 1 *n* process **2** *vb 3* ㊉ かこうする to process

かこけい・過去形 *n* – the past tense of verbs, in this dictionary we have usually referred to the ～た form

かこむ・囲む *vb 1* ㊉ to surround

かさ・傘 *n* umbrella

かさい・火災 *n* fire

かさなる・重なる *vb 1* ㊀ かさなって・かさならない・かさなります to be piled up; to happen at the same time

かさねる・重ねる *vb 2* ㊉ to pile up

かざりもの・飾り物 *n* decoration; ornament

かざる・飾る *vb 1* ㊉ to decorate; to display

かざん・火山 *n* volcano

かし・菓子 *n* confectionery; snacks

かじ・火事 *n* fire

かじ・家事 *n* housework

かしこい・賢い *adj* clever

かしこまりました・畏まりました *phrase* ▶ used in the sense of 'certainly' to show not only understanding but that an order or request will be acted upon

かしだす・貸し出す *vb 1* Ⓔ to lend; to rent out

かしつ・過失 *n* a blunder

かして ▶ かす

かします ▶ かす

かしや・貸し家 *n* house for rent

かしゅ・歌手 *n* singer

かしょ・個所 *suf* place

かじょう(の)・過剰(の) *adj* excessive

かじる *vb 1* Ⓔ to chew

かす・貸す *vb 1* Ⓔ かして・かさない・かします
　　to lend; to rent

かず・数 *n* number; quantity

ガス *n* gas

かぜ・風 *n* wind

かぜ・風邪 *n* a cold; かぜを ひく to catch a cold

かぜい・課税 *n* taxation

かせん・下線 *n* underline

かせぐ・稼ぐ *vb 1* Ⓔ to earn money

カセット *n* cassette

かぞえて ▶ かぞえる

かぞえます ▶ かぞえる

かぞえる・数える *vb 2* Ⓔ かぞえて・かぞえない・
　　かぞえます to count

かそく・加速 1 *n* acceleration **2** *vb 3* Ⓝ かそくする
　　to accelerate

かぞく・家族 *n* family

かそくど・加速度 *n* acceleration

ガソリン *n* petrol; gasoline

ガソリンスタンド *n* petrol station; gasoline station

かた・方 *n* person

かた・肩 *n* shoulder

かた・型 *n* style; mould

かた・方 *suf – when added to the pre 〜ます form of a verb it means 'way of ...ing'*

かたい・固い・堅い・硬い *adj* hard; stiff

がたい・難い *suf – when added to the pre 〜ます form of a verb it means 'difficult to ...'*

かたがた・方々 *n* people

かたかな・片仮名 *n – the script primarily used to write words of foreign origin and which functions as a kind of italic*

かたち・形 *n* form; shape

かたづく・片付く *vb 1 ㊢* かたづいて・かたづかない・かたづきます *(of a room)* to be tidy

かたづけて ▶ かたづける

かたづけます ▶ かたづける

かたづける・片付ける *vb 2 ㊢* かたづけて・かたづけない・かたづけます to tidy up

かたまり・塊 *n – bits which are stuck together, a lump*

かたまる・固まる *vb 1 ㊢* to harden

かたみち・片道 *n* one-way (ticket)

かたむく・傾く *vb 1 ㊢* to incline

かたよる・片寄る・偏る *vb 1 ㊢* to be prejudiced (in favour of)

かたる・語る *vb 1 ㊢* to tell

かち・価値 *n* value

かち・勝ち *n* victory

がち *suf !* added to the pre ます form of a verb it adds the meaning of 'tends to ...'

かつ・勝つ *vb 1 に㊢* かって・かたない・かちます to win

がつ・月 *suf* month

がっか・学科 *n* university or school department

がっかい・学会 *n* academic conference

がっかり(する) *vb 3* か に to be disappointed

かっき・活気 *n* vigour

がっき・楽器 *n* (musical) instrument

がっき・学期 *n* semester; term

かつぐ・担ぐ *vb 1* を to carry (on the shoulders)

かっこ・括弧 *n* brackets

かっこう・格好 *n* appearance; かっこういい of nice appearance; stylish; かっこうわるい not stylish; not attractive

がっこう・学校 *n* school

かつじ・活字 *n* print

がっしょうだん・合唱団 *n* choir

かって・勝手 *n* kitchen

かって ▶ かう ▶ かつ

かってに・勝手に *adv* without asking permission; selfishly

かつどう・活動 **1** *n* activity **2** *vb 3* に かつどうする to work actively

かつやく・活躍 **1** *n* activity **2** *vb 3* か に かつやくする to play an active role

かつよう・活用 **1** *n* utilisation; conjugation **2** *vb 3* を か かつようする to make use of; to conjugate (verbs)

かつりょく・活力 *n* vitality

かてい・仮定 **1** *n* assumption **2** *vb 3* を かていする to assume

かてい・家庭 *n* household

かてい・過程 *n* process

かてい・課程 *n* curriculum

かど・角 *n* corner

かな・仮名 n ! *the Japanese syllabic scripts* **ひらがな** *and* **かたかな** *as opposed to Chinese characters or* **かんじ**

かない・家内 n one's own wife

かなしい・悲しい adj sad

かなしむ・悲しむ vb 1 ⓔ to be sad about

かなづかい・仮名遣い n – the way of using **かな** in the writing of Japanese

かなづち・金槌 n hammer

かならず・必ず adv definitely

かならずしも・必ずしも adv (preceding a negative) not necessarily

かなり adv considerably

かね・金 n money ▶ **おかね**

かね・鐘 n bell

かねない ▶ かねる

かねつ(する)・加熱(する) vb 3 ⓔ to heat

かねもち・金持ち n a rich person

かねる・兼ねる vb 2 ⓔ to serve as (both of) two things at the same time

かねる suf – attached to the pre ～ます form of a verb it adds the meaning of being unable to do to a preceding verb and is thus often translated as 'cannot' and indicates a refusal of a request. Although the meaning is negative the form is positive and even native-speakers can get it wrong! The negative form **かねない** it is used for the meaning 'I wouldn't put it past (somebody) to do that'.

かのう(な)・可能(な) adj possible

かのうせい・可能性 n possibility; **かのうせいが こい** it is very likely

カバー 1 n cover **2** vb 3 ⓔ **カバーする** to cover

かばん・鞄 n bag

かはんすう・過半数 *n* majority

かび *n* mould

かびん・花瓶 *n* vase

かぶ・株 *n* stocks

かぶしき・株式 *n* shares

かぶしきがいしゃ・株式会社 *n* corporation

かぶせる・被せる *vb 2* ⊛ to cover

かぶる・被る *vb 1* ⊛ to put on; to be wearing (a hat)

かべ・壁 *n* wall

かま・釜 *n* ▶ *large pot for cooking rice*

かまいません *phrase – deriving from* かまう *this phrase is used to mean 'it doesn't matter' and in the question form* かまいませんか *to mean 'would you mind if ...?'*

かまう・構う *vb 1* ⊛ to mind

がまん・我慢 **1** *n* endurance **2** *vb 3* ⊛ がまんする to put up with

がまんづよい・我慢強い *adj* patient

かみ・髪 *n* hair (on head)

かみ・紙 *n* paper

かみ・神 *n* god

かみ・上 *prf* upper (part); first (part)

かみくず・紙屑 *n* waste paper

かみさま・神様 *n* God

かみそり・剃刀 *n* shaver; razor

かみなり・雷 *n* thunder

かみのけ・髪の毛 *n* hair (on the head)

かむ・噛む *vb 1* to bite; to chew

ガム *n* chewing gum

ガムテープ *n* sticky tape

カメラ *n* camera

かもく・科目・課目 *n* objective

かもしれません ▶ かもしれない

かもしれない *phrase* probably; perhaps

かもつ・貨物 *n* freight

かゆい・痒い *adj* itchy

かよう・通う *vb 1* ⑳ に to commute; to travel; to attend

かよう・歌謡 *n* song

から・殻 *n* shell

から *pt* because; from

がら・柄 *n* pattern; design; nature

から(の)・空(の) *adj* empty

カラー *n* colour

からい・辛い *adj* spicy

カラオケ *n* – singing to the accompaniment of a backing tape especially at bars

からかう *vb 1* ⑳ to tease

ガラス *n* glass

からだ・体 *n* body

からっぽ *adj* empty

かりて ▶ かりる

かりに・仮に *adv* temporarily; supposing

かります ▶ かりる

かりる・借りる *vb 2* ⑳ に かりて・かりない・かります to borrow; to rent; to hire

かる・刈る *vb 1* ⑳ to cut

がる *suf* – when added to the stem of adjectives of emotion or sensation it indicates that the state is not that of the speaker or writer but refers to some other person.

かるい・軽い *adj* light

かるた・カルタ *n – traditional Japanese playing cards featuring poems or proverbs*

カルテ *n* medical record

かれ・彼 *n* he

カレー *n* curry

かれし・彼氏 *n* boyfriend

かれら・彼ら *n* they

かれる・枯れる *vb 2 ㋕* to wither

カレンダー *n* calendar

かろう・過労 *n* overwork

かろうじて・辛うじて *adv* only just

カロリー *n* calorie

かわ・川・河 *n* river

かわ・皮 *n* skin

かわ・革 *n* leather

がわ・側 *suf* side

かわいい・可愛い *adj* cute

かわいがる・可愛がる *vb 1 ㋕* to love (grandchildren or pets etc.)

かわいそう・可哀想 1 *adj* かわいそう(な) pitiful **2** *adv* かわいそうに sadly ! *often used in the sense 'oh that's terrible (news)!' or 'what a pity!'*

かわいらしい ▶ かわいい

かわかす・乾かす *vb 1 ㋕* to dry

かわく・渇く *vb 1 ㋕* のどが かわく to be thirsty

かわく・乾く *vb 1 ㋕* to get dry

かわす・交わす *vb 1 ㋕* to exchange

かわせ・為替 *n* exchange (rate)

かわって ▶ かわる

かわり(に)・代わり(に) *n* instead of

かわり・変わり・替わり *n* change

かわります ► かわる

かわる・変わる *vb 1 ㋐* かわって・かわらない・かわります to change

かわる・代わる *vb 1 ㋐* かわって・かわらない・かわります to replace

かわるがわる(に) *adv* in turn

かん・缶 *n* can (of ...); tin (of ...)

かん・間 *suf* – adds the sense of duration to time words

かん・巻 *counter* volume

かん・勘 *n* intuition

がん・癌 *n* cancer

かんえい(じてん)・漢英(辞典) *n* ! a dictionary of かんじ characters with explanations in English ► かんわ

かんがえ・考え *n* idea; way of thinking

かんがえて ► かんがえる

かんがえます ► かんがえる

かんがえる・考える *vb 2 ㋒* かんがえて・かんがえない・かんがえます to think about; to expect

がんか・眼科 *n* opthalmologist

かんかく・感覚 *n* sense(s)

かんかく・間隔 *n* interval; かんかくを おく leave space (between)

かんき・換気 **1** *n* ventilation **2** *vb 3 ㋒* かんきする to ventilate

かんきせん・換気扇 *n* extractor fan

かんきゃく・観客 *n* spectators

かんきょう・環境 *n* environment; surroundings

かんきょうおせん・環境汚染 *n* pollution

かんけい・関係 *n* relationship; connection

かんげい・歓迎 1 *n* welcome **2** *vb* **3** 鈴 かんげいする
to welcome

かんげいかい・歓迎会 *n* – a formal welcome party

かんけいない・関係ない *adj* unconnected **!** as a phrase
it can mean 'that's nothing to do with it' or 'it's none of your
business'

かんげき・感激 1 *n* deep emotion **2** *vb* **3** 鈴 にかんげき
する to be moved

かんご・看護 *n* nursing

かんご・漢語 *n* – words written with Chinese characters

がんこ(な)・頑固な *adj* stubborn

かんこう・観光 1 *n* sightseeing **2** *vb* **3** 鈴 かんこうする
to sightsee

かんこうきゃく・観光客 *n* tourist

かんこく・勧告 *n* advice

かんこく・韓国 *n* South Korea

かんごふ・看護婦 *n* nurse

かんさい・関西 *n* – the region of Japan around Osaka,
Kyoto and Kobe

かんさつ・観察 1 *n* observation **2** *vb* **3** 鈴 かんさつする
to observe

かんじ・漢字 *n* Chinese characters

かんじ・感じ *n* feeling

がんじつ・元日 *n* new year's day

かんしゃ・感謝 1 *n* gratitude **2** *vb* **3** 鈴 にかんしゃする
to be grateful; to thank

かんじゃ・患者 *n* patient (at a hospital etc.)

かんしゅう・観衆 *n* audience; spectators

かんしょう・干渉 1 *n* interference **2** *vb* **3** 鈴 にかんし
ょうする to interfere

かんしょう・鑑賞 **1** *n* appreciation **2** *vb 3* 🅔 かんしょうする to enjoy

かんじょう・感情 *n* emotions

かんじょう・勘定 *n* the bill

かんじる・感じる *vb 2* 🅔 to feel; to sense

かんしん・感心 **1** *n* admiration **2** *adj* かんしん(な) admirable **3** *vb 3* に かんしんする to be impressed

かんしん・関心 *n* concern

かん(する)・関(する) *vb 3* 🅐 に to be concerned (with)

かんずる・感ずる *vb 3* 🅔 to feel

かんせい・完成 **1** *n* completion **2** *vb 3* 🅔 かんせいする to complete

かんせつ・間接 **1** *adj* かんせつ(の)indirect **2** *adv* かんせつに indirectly

かんぜん・完全 **1** *adj* かんぜん(な)complete **2** *adv* かんぜんに fully

かんそう・乾燥 **1** *n* drying **2** *vb 3* 🅔 かんそうする to dry

かんそう・感想 *n* impression

かんそく・観測 **1** *n* observation **2** *vb 3* 🅔 かんそくする to observe; to predict

かんたん・簡単 **1** *adj* かんたん(な)easy **2** *adv* かんたんに easily

かんちょう・官庁 *n* government agency

かんちがい・勘違い *n* misunderstanding

かんづめ・缶詰 *n* tinned goods; canned goods

かんでんち・乾電池 *n* battery

かんとう・関東 *n* (❗ the area around Tokyo)

かんどう・感動 **1** *n* deep emotion **2** *vb 3* 🅐 に かんどうする to be moved

かんとく・監督 1 *n* directing; director **2** *vb 3* ㊫ かんとく
する to direct (a film)

カンニング 1 *n* cheating **2** *vb* ㋕ カンニングする
to cheat

かんねん・観念 1 *n* idea; sense **2** *vb 3* ㋕ かんねんする
to be resigned (to one's fate)

かんぱい・乾杯 1 *n* toast **2** *vb 3* ㋕ かんぱいする to
drink a toast **!** *as a phrase it is used like English 'cheers' before
drinking*

がんばって ▶ がんばる – *on its own or in the form* がんばっ
てください *it is an expression meaning 'do your best'*

がんばります ▶ がんばる – *an expression meaning 'I'll try'
or 'I'll do my best'*

がんばる・頑張る *vb 1* ㋕ がんばって・がんばらない
・がんばります to do one's best

かんばん・看板 *n* sign

かんぺき・完璧 1 *adj* かんぺき(な) perfect **2** *adv* かん
ぺきに perfectly

かんべん・勘弁 1 *n* pardon **2** *vb 3* ㊫ かんべんする
to pardon

かんむり・冠 *n* crown; the top part of a Chinese character

かんり・管理 1 *n* management **2** *vb 3* ㊫ かんりする
to control; to manage

かんりょう・完了 1 *n* completion **2** *vb 3* ㊫ かんりょう
する to complete

かんりょう・官僚 *n* bureaucracy

かんれん(する)・関連(する) *vb 3* ㋕ to be connected

かんわ (じてん)・漢和 (辞典) *n* – a dictionary of かん
じ *characters with their meanings and readings (designed for
the use of native-speakers of Japanese)* ▶ かんえい

きキ

- き・木 *n* tree
- き・気 *n* ▸ *variously translatable as 'mood', 'mind', 'spirits'*; きにいる to like; きを つける to be careful; きを つけ てください please be careful; きに する to worry; きに なる to feel bothered by; きが つく to notice
- き・機 *suf* machine
- きあつ・気圧 *n* air pressure
- きいろ・黄色 *n* yellow
- きいろい・黄色い *adj* yellow
- ぎいん・議員 *n* assembly member; member of parliament; member of congress
- きえる・消える *vb 2* ⑰ きえて・きえない・きえます (*of a light*) to go out; to disappear
- きおく・記憶 *n* memory
- きおん・気温 *n* (air) temperature
- きかい・機会 *n* opportunity
- きかい・機械 *n* machine
- ぎかい・議会 *n* assembly; parliament; congress
- きがえ・着替え **1** *n* change of clothes **2** *vb 3* ⑯ に きがえ (を)する to change clothes
- きがえる・着替える *vb 2* ⑯ に きがえて・きがえな い・きがえます to change (clothes)
- きかん・期間 *n* period of time
- きかん・機関 *n* institution
- きき・危機 *n* crisis
- ききとり・聞き取り *n* listening

きます ▶ きく

きぎょう・企業 n business

ききん・飢饉 n famine

きく・聞く・聴く vb 1 を にきいて・きかない・
ききます to hear; to ask; to listen

きく・効く vb 1 か にきいて・きかない・ききます
to work (to have an effect)

きぐ・器具 n appliance

きけん・危険 1 n danger 2 adj きけん(な) dangerous

きげん・期限 n time limit

きげん・機嫌 n mood

きこう・気候 n climate

きごう・記号 n symbol

きこえる・聞こえる vb 2 か きこえて・きこえない・
きこえます (to be able) to hear

きざむ・刻む vb 1 を to carve

きし・岸 n coast; shore; (river) bank

きじ・記事 n article (in the press)

きじ・生地 n cloth; material

ぎし・技師 n engineer

ぎしき・儀式 n ceremony

きしゃ・貴社 n – polite way of referring to someone's
company

きしゃ・記者 n journalist

きしゃ・汽車 n steam locomotive

ぎじゅつ・技術 n technique

きじゅん・基準 n standard

きしょうする・起床する vb 3 か to get up

きず・傷・疵 n injury; damage; きずをつける to injure;
to damage

きすう・奇数 *n* odd number

既製 *as prefixing element* ready made

きせつ・季節 *n* season

きせる・着せる *vb 2* を・きせて・きせない・きせます
to dress (somebody)

きそ・基礎 *n* foundation

きそく・規則 *n* regulation

きた・北 *n* north

ギター *n* guitar

きたい・期待 1 *n* expectation **2** *vb 3* を **きたいする** to
expect

きたい・気体 *n* gas

きたく(する)・帰宅(する) *vb 3* を to go home

きたない・汚い *adj* dirty; untidy

きち・基地 *n* base

きちょう(な)・貴重な *adj* valuable

きちょうひん・貴重品 *n* valuables

きちんと *adv* neatly; properly

きつい *adj* severe; (*shoes, clothes*) tight

きっかけ *n* chance

きづく・気付く *vb 1* に **きづいて・きづかない・**
きづきます to notice

きっさてん・喫茶店 *n* coffee shop

ぎっしり *adv* tightly

きって・切手 *n* stamp

きって ▶ **きる**

きっと *adv* definitely

きっぷ・切符 *n* ticket

きて ▶ **きる** ▶ **くる**

きにゅう・記入 **1** *n* (text) entry **2** *vb 3* Ⓢ きにゅうする
to fill in

きぬ・絹 *n* silk

きねん・記念 **1** *n* anniversary **2** *vb 3* Ⓢ きねんする
to commemorate

きねんび・記念日 *n* anniversary

きのう・昨日 *n* yesterday

きのう・機能 *n* function

きのどく・気の毒 *phrase – used in the sense of 'I'm very
sorry to hear it'!' when expressing sympathy or condolences*

きばん・基盤 *n* base

きびしい・厳しい *adj* strict

きふ・寄付 *n* donation

きぶん・気分 *n* mood

きぼう・希望 **1** *n* hope **2** *vb 3* Ⓢ きぼうする to hope for

きほん・基本 *n* basis

きほんてき・基本的 **1** *adj* きほんてき(な)
fundamental **2** *adv* きほんてきに fundamentally

きます ▶ くる ▶ きる

きまり・決まり *n* rule

きまる・決まる *vb 1* Ⓘ きまって・きまらない・
きまります to be decided

きみ・君 *n* you

きみ・気味 *n* feeling; きみが わるい eerie

ぎみ・気味 *suf* – added to nouns like かぜ meaning 'a cold'
to give compounds like かぜぎみ 'having a touch of cold'

きみょう・奇妙 **1** *adj* きみょうな strange **2** *adv* きみょ
うに strangely

ぎむ・義務 *n* duty

きめる・決める *vb 2* Ⓢ きめて・きめない・きめます
to decide

きもち・気持ち n feeling; **きもちいい** pleasant; **きもちわるい** unpleasant

きもの・着物 n – used to mean clothes in general and the traditional Japanese women's kimono in particular

ぎもん・疑問 n doubt

きゃく・客 n customer

ぎゃく・逆 1 n opposite **2** adj **ぎゃくの** opposite **3** adv **ぎゃくに** on the contrary; in reverse

きゃくせき・客席 n seat; passenger seat

きゃくま・客間 n drawing room ! the room in a Japanese house which is used for entertaining guests

キャッチ 1 n catch **2** vb 3 ⊛ **キャッチする** to hear

ギャング n gang

キャンプ 1 n camp **2** vb 3 ⑦ **キャンプする** to camp

きゅう・九 n nine

きゅう・急 1 adj **きゅう(な)** sudden **2** adv **きゅうに** suddenly

きゅう・旧 prf former (state)

きゅうか・休暇 n holiday; break

きゅうがく・休学 1 n absence (from school or university) **2** vb 3 ⊛ **きゅうがくする** to take a year off (from school or university)

きゅうきゅうしゃ・救急車 n ambulance

きゅうぎょう・休業 n holiday (for a business or shop)

きゅうけい・休憩 1 n break **2** vb 3 ⊛ **きゅうけいする** to take a break

きゅうげき・急激 1 adj **きゅうげきな** drastic **2** adv **きゅうげきに** suddenly

きゅうこう・急行 n express (train)

きゅうこう・休講 n cancellation of lecture/s

きゅうじつ・休日 n holiday (for a business or restaurant)

きゅうしゅう・吸収 **1** *n* absorption **2** *vb* **3** を きゅうし ゅうする to absorb

きゅうじょ・救助 **1** *n* rescue **2** *vb* **3** を きゅうじょする to rescue

きゅうしょく・給食 *n* school meals

きゅうそく・休息 **1** *n* rest **2** *vb* **3** きゅうそくする to rest

きゅうそく(な)・急速な *adj* rapid

きゅうに・急に ▶きゅう

ぎゅうにゅう・牛乳 *n* milk

きゅうよ・給与 *n* wage

きゅうよう・休養 *n* rest

きゅうよう・急用 *n* urgent business

きゅうりょう・給料 *n* salary

きよい・清い *adj* pure

きよう・器用 **1** *adv* きように skillfully **2** *adj* きような adroit

きょう・今日 *n* today

ぎょう・行 *n* line

きょういく・教育 **1** *n* education **2** *vb* **3** を きょういく する to educate

きょういん・教員 *n* teacher

きょうかする・強化する *vb* **3** を to strengthen

きょうかい・境界 *n* boundary

きょうかい・教会 *n* church

きょうかしょ・教科書 *n* textbook

きょうぎ・競技 *n* contest

ぎょうぎ・行儀 *n* manners

きょうきゅう・供給 **1** *n* supply **2** *vb* **3** を きょうきゅ うする to supply

きょうさんしゅぎ・共産主義 *n* communism

きょうし・教師 *n* teacher

ぎょうじ・行事 *n* event

きょうしつ・教室 *n* classroom

きょうじゅ・教授 *n* professor

きょうしゅく・恐縮 – in the expressions きょうしゅく ですが and きょうしゅくしますが *it means 'sorry to trouble you' or 'I'm sorry to interrupt but ...'*

きょうせい(する)・強制(する) *vb 3* 🈁 to compel

きょうせいてき(な)・強制的(な) *adj* compulsory

ぎょうせい・行政 *n* administration

きょうそう・競争 **1** *n* competition **2** *vb 3* 🈁 と きょう そうする to compete

きょうだい・兄弟 *n* brothers **!** *often meaning 'brothers and sisters'*

きょうちょう・強調 **1** *n* emphasis **2** *vb 3* 🈁 きょうち ょうする to emphasise

きょうつう(の)・共通(の) *adj* (in) common

きょうどう・共同 **1** *n* collaboration **2** *vb 3* 🈁 きょうど うする to share

きょうふ・恐怖 *n* fear

きょうみ・興味 *n* interest

きょうよう・教養 *n* education

きょうりょく・協力 **1** *n* cooperation **2** *vb 3* 🈁 きょうり ょくする to cooperate

きょうりょく(な)・強力(な) *adj* powerful

ぎょうれつ・行列 *n* procession

きょか・許可 *n* pemission

ぎょぎょう・漁業 *n* fishing industry

きょく・曲 *n* tune; song

きょく・局 *suf* office; store

きょくせん・曲線 *n* curve

きょだい(な)・巨大(な) *adj* enormous

きょねん・去年 *n* last year

きょひ・拒否 **1** *n* refusal **2** *vb 3* 圏 きょひする to refuse

きょり・距離 *n* distance

きらい(な)・嫌い(な) *adj* hated; disliked

きらう・嫌う *vb 1* 圏 ⑰ to dislike; to hate

きらく・気楽 **1** *adj* きらく(な) comfortable and relaxed **2** *adv* きらくに freely

きり・霧 *n* fog; mist

ぎり・義理 *n* obligation ❗ *Used with the sense of a favour/favor being owed. Also used with family words in the form* ぎりの〜 *to mean '- in law'.*

きり *suf* only

きります▶きる

きりつ(する)・起立(する) *vb 3* ⑰ to stand up

きりつ・規律 *n* rules

きる・切る *vb 1* 圏 きって・きらない・きります to cut

きる・着る *vb 2* 圏 きて・きない・きます to put on; to be wearing

きれい・奇麗 **1** *adj* きれい(な) pretty; clean; tidy **2** *adv* きれいに tidily

きれる・切れる *vb 2* ⑰ to be cut

キロ *n* kilogram; kilometre

きろく・記録 *n* record

キログラム *n* kilogram

キロメートル *n* kilometre

ぎろん・議論 **1** *n* argument **2** *vb 3* 圏 ぎろんする to argue

きん・金 *n* gold

きん・菌 ▶ばいきん

ぎん・銀 *n* silver

きんえん・禁煙 *n* no smoking

きんがく・金額 *n* amount (of money)

きんきゅう(の)・緊急(の) *adj* urgent

きんぎょ・金魚 *n* goldfish

きんこう・近郊 *n* suburbs

ぎんこう・銀行 *n* bank

きんし・禁止 **1** *n* prohibition **2** *vb* **3** ㊂ きんしする to forbid

きんじょ・近所 *n* neighbourhood

きんせん・金銭 *n* money

きんぞく・金属 *n* metal

きんだい・近代 **1** *n* the modern age **2** *adj* きんだいの modern

きんだいてき(な)・近代的な *adj* modern

きんちょう・緊張 **1** *n* tension **2** *vb* **3** ㊂ きんちょうする to feel nervous

きんにく・筋肉 *n* muscle

きんべん(な)・勤勉(な) *adj* diligent

きんゆう・金融 *n* finance

きんようび・金曜日 *n* Friday

きんろうかんしゃのひ・勤労感謝の日 *n* – Labor Thanksgiving Day (November 23) – a Japanese public holiday

くク

く・九 *n* nine

ぐあい・具合 *n* condition

くいき・区域 *n* zone

くう・食う *vb 1* ㊂ to eat

くうき・空気 *n* air

くうこう・空港 *n* airport

ぐうすう・偶数 *n* even number

ぐうぜん・偶然 **1** *adj* ぐうぜん(の) (by) chance **2** *adv* ぐうぜんに by chance; by coincidence

くうそう・空想 **1** *n* fantasy **2** *vb* **3** ㊝ くうそうする to imagine

くうちゅう(の)・空中(の) *adj* mid-air

クーラー *n* air conditioning

くかん・区間 *n* section

くぎ・釘 *n* nail

くぎる・区切る *vb 1* ㊝ to divide (off)

くさ・草 *n* grass

くさい・臭い *adj* bad smelling

くさり・鎖 *n* chain

くさる・腐る *vb 1* ㊝ to rot

くし *n* comb

くしゃみ **1** *n* sneeze **2** *vb 3* ㊙ くしゃみを する to sneeze

くじょう・苦情 *n* complaint

くしん・苦心 **1** *n* effort **2** *vb 3* ㊙ くしんする to take pains (over)

くず・屑 *n* waste

くすぐったい *adj* ticklish; it tickles!

くすぐる *vb 1* ㊝ to tickle

くずす・崩す *vb 1* ㊝ to break down

くすり・薬 *n* medicine; chemicals

くずれる・崩れる *vb 2* ㊙ to break down

くせ・癖 *n* habit; くせに in spite of

くだ・管 *n* pipe

ぐたいてき・具体的 **1** *adj* ぐたいてき(な) concrete **2** *adv* ぐたいてきに concretely

くだく・砕く *vb 1* 🈯 to pulverise

くだける・砕ける *vb 2* 🈁 to be crushed

ください・下さい – added to the 〜て *form of a verb it means 'please (do)' and when following an object marked with* を *it means 'please give me'. Following the ending* 〜ないで *it means 'please don't (do)'*

くださる・下さる *vb 1* 🈯 to give ! *honorific verb which often follows the* 〜て *form of another verb to show that an action has been done for the benefit of speaker by someone of higher status.*

くたびれる *vb 2* 🈁 to become tired

くだもの・果物 *n* fruit

くだらない *adj* worthless

くだり・下り *n* descent

くだりざか・下り坂 *n* downward slope

くだる・下る *vb 1* 🈁 to descend

くち・口 *n* mouth

ぐち・愚痴 *n* complaint

くちびる・唇 *n* lip

くちべに・口紅 *n* lipstick

くつ・靴 *n* shoes

くつう・苦痛 *n* pain

くつした・靴下 *n* socks

くっつく *vb 1* 🈁 to be stuck

くっつける *vb 2* 🈯 to stick

ぐっすり *adv* deeply (asleep)

くどい *adj* insistent; tedious

くとうてん・句読点 *n* – Japanese punctuation marks.
▶くてん▶とうてん

くに・国 *n* country ! *used not only in the sense of 'nation' but of also of the place where your family home is situated.*

Japanese people talk of くに in the sense of 'home country' when referring to non-Japanese and in the sense of 'home region' when referring to other Japanese

くばる・配る *vb 1* Ⓔ to distribute

くび・首 *n* neck; (くびに なる) to be fired

くふう・工夫 **1** *n* trick; method **2** *vb 3* Ⓔ くふうする to devise

くべつ・区別 **1** *n* distinction **2** *vb 3* Ⓔ くべつする to distinguish (between)

くみ・組み *n* group ! *as a suffix it can mean (school) class*

くみあい・組合 *n* trade union; labor union

くみあわせ・組み合わせ *n* combination

くみたてる・組み立てる *vb 2* Ⓔ to assemble

くむ・組む *vb 1* Ⓔ to cross (arms or legs)

くむ・汲む・酌む *vb 1* Ⓔ to scoop

くも・雲 *n* cloud

くも・蜘蛛 *n* spider

くもり・曇り *n* cloudy weather

くもる・曇る *vb 1* Ⓣ to cloud over

くやしい・悔しい *adj* mortifying; regrettable

くやむ・悔やむ *vb 1* Ⓔ to feel vexed by

くらい・暗い *adj* dark

くらい・位 ▶ ぐらい

ぐらい *n* approximately; about

くらし・暮らし *n* way of living

クラシック *n* classical music

くらす・暮らす *vb 1* Ⓣ to live

グラス *n* glass (for drinking)

クラブ *n* club

グラフ *n* graph

くらべる・比べる *vb 2* 🛇 to compare

グラム *n* gram(me)

クリーニング *n* dry cleaning

クリーニングや・クリーニング屋 *n* dry cleaner

クリーム *n* cream

くりかえす・繰り返す *vb 1* 🛇 to repeat

クリスマス *n* Christmas

くる・来る *vb 3* 🕪 きて・こない・きます to come

くるう・狂う *vb 1* 🕪 to go mad

グループ *n* group

くるしい・苦しい *adj* painful

くるしむ・苦しむ *vb 1* 🕪 to suffer

くるしめる・苦しめる *vb 2* 🛇 to cause suffering

くるま・車 *n* car; vehicle

くるまいす・車椅子 *n* wheelchair

くるむ・包む *vb 1* 🛇 to wrap

くれ・暮れ *n* end of the year

グレー **1** *n* grey **2** *adj* グレー（の）grey

くれぐれも *adv* please; sincerely ❗ *used to indicate sincerity in formal requests*

クレジットカード *n* credit card

くれます▶くれる

くれる *vb 2* 🛇 くれて・くれない・くれます to give; to be given ❗ *meaning 'given to the speaker' it is often added to the ～て form of a preceding verb to indicate that the action was done for the speaker's benefit by somebody else* ▶あげる

くれる・暮れる *vb 2* 🕪 to draw to a close

くろ・黒 *n* black

くろい・黒い *adj* black

くろう・**苦労 1** *n* difficulty **2** *vb* **3** ㋕ くろうする to work hard

くろうと・**玄人** *n* specialist

くわえる・**加える** *vb* 2 ㋓ to add

くわえる *vb* 2 ㋓ to hold (in the mouth)

くわしい・**詳しい** *adj* detailed; knowledgeable

くわわる・**加わる** *vb* 1 ㋕ に to join

くん・**訓** ▶ くんよみ

くん・**君** *suf* – added to family names of males to form a title. Commonly used in schools by a teacher as a way of addressing boys or in companies by bosses to address junior staff. It is sometimes used with women's names in large companies. Also used between male friends.

ぐん・**群** *n* county

ぐん・**軍** *n* army

ぐんたい・**軍隊** *n* troops

くんよみ・**訓読み** *n* – the reading assigned to a かんじ character in Japanese usage (typically as a noun or root of a word) ▶ おんよみ

くんれん・**訓練 1** *n* training **2** *vb* **3** ㋕ くんれんする to practise

....

け ケ

....

け・**毛** *n* hair; wool

け・**家** *suf* family

げ・**下** *n* lowest grade

げ・**気** *suf* – added to adjective stems it means 'seemingly ...'

けい・**計** *n* total; plan

げい・芸 *n* skill

けいい・敬意 *n* respect

けいい・経緯 *n* circumstances

けいえい・経営 **1** *n* management **2** *vb* **3** ㋾ けいえいする to manage

けいえいしゃ・経営者 *n* manager

けいかく・計画 **1** *n* plan **2** *vb* **3** ㋾ けいかくする to plan

けいかん・警官 *n* police officer

けいき・景気 *n* – the climate for doing business or the 'general economic situation'.

けいぐ・敬具 *n* – a word used to end a formal letter and so roughly equivalent to 'yours sincerely' and similar phrases ▶はいけい

けいけん・経験 **1** *n* experience **2** *vb* **3** ㋾ けいけんする to experience

けいこ・稽古 **1** *n* practice **2** *vb* **3** ㋾ けいこする to practice

けいご・敬語 *n* – polite forms of language used to indicate respect

けいこう・傾向 *n* tendency

けいこう・蛍光 *prf* florescent

けいこく・警告 **1** *n* warning **2** *vb* **3** ㋾ けいこくする to warn

けいざい・経済 *n* (the) economy

けいざいがく・経済学 *n* economics (academic subject)

けいさつ・警察 *n* police

けいさつかん・警察官 *n* police officer

けいさん・計算 **1** *n* calculation **2** *vb* **3** ㋾ けいさんする to calculate

けいさんき・計算機 *n* calculator

けいじ・刑事 *n* detective

けいじ(する)・掲示する (する) *vb 3* Ⓔ to put up a notice

けいじばん・掲示板 *n* notice board

けいしき・形式 *n* formality

けいしきてき・形式的 **1** *adj* けいしきてき(な) superficial **2** *adv* けいしきてきに as a formality

げいじゅつ・芸術 *n* the arts

けいぞく・継続 **1** *n* continuation **2** *vb 3* Ⓔ Ⓚ けいぞくする to continue

けいたい(する)・携帯(する) *vb 3* Ⓔ to carry around

けいたいでんわ・携帯電話 *n* mobile phone

けいと・毛糸 *n* wool

けいとう・系統 *n* system; lineage

けいとうてき・系統的 **1** *adj* けいとうてき(な) systematic **2** *adv* けいとうてきに systematically

げいのうかい・芸能界 *n* show business world

げいのうじん・芸能人 *n* show business personality

けいば・競馬 *n* horse racing

けいばじょう・競馬場 *n* horse race track

けいひ・経費 *n* expenses

けいび・警備 **1** *n* defence **2** *vb 3* Ⓔ けいびする to guard

けいべつ・軽蔑 **1** *n* contempt **2** *vb 3* Ⓔ けいべつする to look down on (somebody)

けいやく・契約 *n* contract

けいゆ・経由 *suf* via

けいようし・形容詞 *n* adjective

けいようどうし・形容動詞 *n* ▸ *a part of speech often called* な *adjectives*

けいれき・経歴 *n* career history

けいろうのひ・敬老の日 *n* – Respect for the Aged Day (September 15) – a Japanese public holiday

ケーキ n (western style) cake

ケーキや・ケーキ屋 n (western style) cake shop

ケース n case

ゲーム n game

けが・怪我 **1** n injury **2** vb 3 ㉑ に けが(を)する to be injured

げか・外科 n surgery

けがわ・毛皮 n fur

げき・劇 n drama

げきじょう・劇場 n theatre

げこう・下校 **1** n leaving school **2** vb 3 ㉑ げこうする to go home from school

けさ・今朝 n this morning

けしき・景色 n scenery

けしゴム・消しゴム n eraser

げしゃ(する)・下車(する) vb 3 ㉑ to get off (a train or bus); to get out of (a vehicle)

げじゅん・下旬 n – the last ten days of the month which can often be translated as 'towards the end of the month'

けしょう・化粧 **1** n makeup **2** vb 3 ㉑ けしょう(を)する to put on makeup

けしょうひん・化粧品 n cosmetics

けす・消す vb 1 ㊀ to put out; to turn off

げすい・下水 n sewage

けずる・削る vb 1 ㊀ to shave bits off; to sharpen

けた・桁 suf – when attached to a number it indicates how many digits there are

げた・下駄 n – Japanese traditional wooden shoes

けち(な) adj mean

けつあつ・血圧 n blood pressure

けつえき・血液 *n* blood

けっか・結果 *n* result

けっかん・欠陥 *n* defect

げっきゅう・月給 *n* monthly salary

けっきょく・結局 *adv* in the end

けっこう(な)・結構(な) *adj n* good **!** *sometimes used to express 'quite/very' with adjectives. When used in the expression* けっこうです *it shows refusal of an invitation or (when accompanied by appropriate gesture or context) acceptance. The phrase* (いいえ) もう けっこうです *means 'I have had sufficient'.*

けっこん・結婚 **1** *n* marriage **2** *vb* **3** と けっこんする to marry

けっこんしき・結婚式 *n* wedding ceremony

けっさく・傑作 *n* masterpiece

けっして・決して *adv* (with negative) utterly (not)

けっしん・決心 **1** *n* decision **2** *vb* **3** を けっしんする to resolve (to do)

けっせき・欠席 **1** *n* absence **2** *vb* **3** を けっせきする to be absent (from school etc.)

けってい・決定 **1** *n* decision **2** *vb* **3** が に けっていする to decide

けってん・欠点 *n* weak point; minus point

げつまつ・月末 *n* the end of the month

げつようび・月曜日 *n* Monday

けつろん・結論 *n* conclusion

けはい・気配 *n* indication

げひん(な)・下品(な) *adj* vulgar

けむい・煙い *adj* smoky

けむり・煙 *n* smoke

げり・下痢 *n* diarrhoea

ける・蹴る *vb 1* ㊟ to kick

けれど(も) *conj* however; but

けわしい・険しい *adj* steep

けん・件 *n* incident

けん・県 *n* – Japan is divided into administrative regions which are called 'prefectures' in English and are similar to 'states' or 'counties'

けん・券 *n* ticket

けん・軒 *counter* houses

げん・現 *prf* current

げんいん・原因 *n* cause

けんお・嫌悪 *n* hatred

けんか・喧嘩 **1** *n* quarrel; fight **2** *vb 3* と けんかする to argue; to fight

けんかい・見解 *n* opinion

げんかい・限界 *n* limit

けんがく・見学 **1** *n* educational visit **2** *vb 3* ㊟ けんがくする to visit (for the purpose of learning about)

げんかん・玄関 *n* – the entrance to a Japanese house which is a small hallway where shoes are left before stepping up into the house itself. The word is also used in the sense of 'front door'

げんき・元気 **1** *n* energy **2** *adj* げんき(な) energetic; healthy **3** *adv* げんきに spiritedly; (お)げんきですか How are you?; げんきです I'm fine

けんきゅう・研究 **1** *n* research **2** *vb 3* ㊟ の けんきゅう(を)する to research

けんきゅうしゃ・研究者 *n* researcher

けんきゅうせい・研究生 *n* research student

けんきょ・謙虚 **1** *n* modesty **2** *adj* けんきょ(な) modest

げんきん・現金 *n* cash

げんご・言語 *n* language/s

げんごがく・言語学 *n* linguistics

けんこう・健康 *n* health

けんこうてき・健康的 **1** *adj* けんこうてき(な)
healthy **2** *adv* けんこうてきに healthily

げんこうようし・原稿用紙 *n* – squared writing paper
used for writing Japanese vertically

けんこくきねんび・建国記念日 *n* – National
Foundation Day (February 11) – a Japanese public holiday

けんさ・検査 **1** *n* inspection **2** *vb* **3** ㊚ けんさする to test

げんざい・現在 **1** *n* (at the) present time **2** *adj* げんざいの
present

げんし・原子 *n* atom

げんしばくだん・原子爆弾 *n* atomic bomb

げんしりょくはつでんしょ・原子力発電所 *n*
nuclear power station

げんしてき(な)・原始的(な) *adj* primitive

けんじつ・堅実 **1** *adj* けんじつ(な) steady **2** *adv* けん
じつに steadily

げんじつ・現実 **1** *n* reality **2** *adj* げんじつの real

げんじつてき・げんじつてき **1** *adj* げんじつてき
(な) realistic **2** *adv* げんじつてきに realistically

けんしゅう・研修 **1** *n* training **2** *vb* **3** ㊚ **の** けんしゅう
をする to study

けんしゅうせい・研修生 *n* trainee

げんじゅう・厳重 **1** *adj* げんじゅう(な) strict **2** *adv* げ
んじゅうに strictly

げんしょう・現象 *n* phenomenon

げんじょう・現状 *n* current situation

げんしりょく・原子力 *n* nuclear power

げんしろ・原子炉 *n* nuclear reactor

けんせつ・建設 **1** *n* construction **2** *vb 3* **を** けんせつする
to build

げんぞう・現像 **1** *n* developing (of pictures) **2** *vb 3* **を** げん
ぞうする to develop (photographs)

げんそく・原則 *n* principle; (げんそくとして) generally

けんそん・謙遜 **1** *n* humility **2** *adj* けんそん(な) modest
3 *vb 3* **か** に けんそんする to behave humbly towards

げんだい・現代 **1** *n* the present day **2** *adj* げんだいの
contemporary

けんちく・建築 **1** *n* construction; architecture **2** *vb 3* **を**
けんちくする to construct

けんちくし・建築士 *n* architect

けんちょう・県庁 *n* – the office of Japanese prefectural
government and figuratively 'local government' ▶ けん

げんど・限度 *n* limit

けんとう・見当 *n* estimate; けんとうを つける to guess;
けんとうが つかない I have no idea

けんとう・検討 **1** *n* investigation **2** *vb 3* **を** けんとうする
to investigate

げんに・現に *adv* actually

げんば・現場 *n* scene (of an event)

げんばく・原爆 *n* nuclear explosion

けんびきょう・顕微鏡 *n* microscope

けんぶつ・見物 **1** *n* sightseeing **2** *vb 3* **を** けんぶつする
to sightsee

けんぽう・憲法 *n* constitution

けんぽうきねんび・憲法記念日 *n* – Constitution
Memorial Day (March 3rd) – a Japanese public holiday

けんめい・懸命 **1** *adj* けんめい(な) diligent **2** *adv* けん
めいに hard

けんり・権利 *n* right/s

げんり・原理 *n* principle

けんりつ・県立 *prf* – established by the prefectural government ▶ けん

げんりょう・原料 *n* natural resources

こコ

こ・子 *n* child

こ・小 *prf* small

こ・個 *counter* – used for counting small, rounded things such as pieces of fruit

こ・粉 *n* flour; powder

ご・五 *n* five

ご・語 *n* word

ご・語 *suf* – added to the name of a country to indicate the language spoken there or attached to the names of languages

ご・後 *suf* after

ご・碁 *n* – a Japanese board game

ご・御 *prf* – added to certain words made up of Chinese characters (sometimes those with some connection to a respected person) it shows politeness

こい・濃い *adj* thick; (of colours) dark; (of drinks) strong

こい・恋 **1** *n* love **2** *vb* 3 ⓔ に こい(を)する to be in love with

こい・鯉 *n* carp

ごい・語彙 *n* vocabulary

こいしい・恋しい *adj* dear

こいびと・恋人 *n* boyfriend; girlfriend

こう *adv* this way; like this; こうすると if this is done then ...; こうして in this way ▶ こういう

こう・高 *prf* high

こう・校 *suf* school

こう・港 *suf* harbour

ごう・号 *suf* – added to numbers to mean 'issue number ...' of a magazine

こうい・行為 *n* behaviour

ごうい・合意 **1** *n* agreement **2** *vb 3 ㉞* に ごういする to agree

こういう *attributive* this kind of

こういん・工員 *n* factory worker

ごういん・強引 **1** *adj* ごういん(な) pushy **2** *adv* ごういんに forcibly

こううん・幸運 *n* good luck

こうえん・公園 *n* park; playground

こうえん・講演 *n* lecture; performance

こうか・効果 *n* effect

こうか・硬貨 *n* coin

こうか(な)・高価(な) *adj* expensive

ごうか(な)・豪華(な) *adj* magnificent

こうかい・後悔 **1** *n* regret **2** *vb 3 ㉞* こうかいする to regret

こうがい・郊外 *n* suburbs

こうがい・公害 *n* pollution; environmental damage

こうがく・工学 *n* engineering

ごうかく・合格 **1** *n* pass (in an exam) **2** *vb 3 ㉞* に ごうかくする to pass an exam

こうかてき・効果的 **1** *adj* こうかてき(な) effective **2** *adv* こうかてきに effectively

こうかん・交換 **1** *n* exchange **2** *vb 3* 左 こうかんする
to exchange

こうき・後期 *n* second half of the year; second semester

こうぎ・講義 *n* lecture

こうぎ・抗議 **1** *n* protest **2** *vb 3* 自 こうぎする to protest

こうきゅう(な)・高級 (な) *adj* high-quality

こうきょう・公共 *n* (the) public

こうぎょう・工業 *n* industry

こうくうがいしゃ・航空会社 *n* airline

こうくうけん・航空券 *n* plane ticket

こうくうびん・航空便 *n* airmail

こうけい・光景 *n* scene

こうげい・工芸 *n* craft

ごうけい・合計 *n* total

こうげき・攻撃 **1** *n* attack **2** *vb 3* 左 こうげきする
to attack

こうけん・貢献 **1** *n* contribution; donation **2** *vb 3* 左 に
こうけんする to contribute; to donate

こうこう・高校 *n* senior high school

こうこう・孝行 *n and adj* (な) – being obedient to one's
parents and behaving in a dutiful manner towards them

こうこがく・考古学 *n* archaeology

こうこく・広告 **1** *n* advertisement (in newspaper etc.);
advertising **2** *vb 3* 左 こうこくする to advertise

こうさ・交差 **1** *n* intersection **2** *vb 3* 自 と こうさする
to intersect

こうさい・交際 **1** *n* acquaintance (with) **2** *vb 3* 自 と こう
さいする to associate with

こうさてん・交差点 *n* crossroads

こうし・講師 *n* lecturer

こうじ・工事 **1** *n* construction work **2** *vb* **3** ㉚ こうじする
to be worked on

こうしき・公式 **1** *adj* こうしきの formal; official **2** *adv*
こうしきに officially; formally

こうしきてき・公式的 **1** *adj* こうしきてき(な) official
2 *adv* こうしきてき(に) officially

こうじちゅう・工事中 *n* under construction; under repair

こうじつ・口実 *n* excuse

こうして *adv* like this; in this way

こうしゃ・後者 *n* the latter

こうしゃ・校舎 *n* school building

こうしゅう・公衆 **1** *n* the public **2** *adj* こうしゅうの
public

こうしゅうでんわ・公衆電話 *n* public telephone

こうしゅうべんじょ・公衆便所 *n* public toilet

こうじょう・工場 *n* factory

こうすい・香水 *n* perfume

こうずい・洪水 *n* flood

こうせい・公正 **1** *n* justice **2** *adj* こうせいの fair **3** *adv*
こうせいに fairly

こうせい・構成 **1** *n* structure **2** *vb* **3** ㉚ こうせいする
to make up

こうせき・功績 *n* achievement

こうせん・光線 *n* beam of light

こうそうビル・高層ビル *n* high rise building

こうぞう・構造 *n* structure; construction

こうそくどうろ・高速道路 *n* expressway

こうたい・交代・交替 **1** *n* alternation; (factory) shift
2 *vb* **3** ㉚ こうたいする to take turns; to swap

こうち・耕地 *n* arable land

こうちゃ・紅茶 *n* tea **!** *this refers to black tea (with or without milk) in contrast to Japanese teas such as green tea* ▶おちゃ

こうつう・交通 *n* transport; traffic

こうつうあんぜん・交通安全 *n* road safety

こうつういはん・交通違反 *n* traffic offence

こうつうきかん・交通機関 *n* transportation system

こうつうじゅうたい・交通渋滞 *n* traffic jam

こうつうひ・交通費 *n* travel expenses

こうてい・校庭 *n* school grounds

こうてい・肯定 **1** *n* affirmation **2** *vb* **3** ⓔ こうていする to affirm

こうど・高度 **1** *n* altitude **2** *adj* こうど(な) high level

こうとう(な)・高等(な) *adj* advanced

こうどう・行動 **1** *n* behaviour **2** *vb* **3** ⓚ こうどうする to behave

こうどう・講堂 *n* auditorium

ごうとう・強盗 *n* robbery; robber

こうとうがっこう・高等学校 *n* senior high school

こうどく・購読 **1** *n* subscription **2** *vb* **3** ⓔ に こうどく する to subscribe

こうにゅう・購入 **1** *n* purchase **2** *vb* **3** ⓔ こうにゅうす る to purchase

こうはい・後輩 *n* – a junior person (in comparison to a specific senior) in either an educational establishment or the workplace ▶せんぱい

こうはん・後半 *n* second half (of a match etc.)

こうばん・交番 *n* – a 'police box' (substation) where police officers are stationed

こうひょう・公表 **1** *n* (official) announcement **2** *vb* **3** ⓔ こうひょうする to announce

こうふく・幸福 *n* happiness

こうぶつ・鉱物 *n* mineral

こうふん・興奮 **1** *n* excitement **2** *vb 3 ㉚* こうふんする to be excited

こうへい・公平 **1** *n* fairness **2** *adj* こうへい(な) fair **3** *adv* こうへいに fairly

こうほしゃ・候補者 *n* candidate

こうむいん・公務員 *n* – this term refers to people working for national or local government

こうもく・項目 *n* item

こうよう・紅葉 *n* – the period or phenomenon of the leaves changing colour in autumn|fall. One of the tourist season highlights in Japan.

こうりつ(の)・公立 (の) *adj n* public

こうりつ・効率 *n* efficiency

ごうりてき・合理的 **1** *adj* ごうりてき(な) reasonable **2** *adv* ごうりてきに rationally

こうりゅう・交流 *n* interchange (between countries)

ごうりゅう(する)・合流(する) *vb 3 ㉚* to merge

こうりょ・考慮 **1** *n* consideration **2** *vb 3 ㉚* こうりょする to consider

こうりょく・効力 *n* こうりょくの ある valid; こうりょくのない invalid

こえ・声 *n* (people) voice; (birds and animals) cry

こえる・超える *vb 2 ㉚* to exceed

こえる・越える *vb 2 ㉚* to go over

ごえんりょなく・ご遠慮なく *phrase* – used to urge people to accept something or do something and meaning something like 'please don't hesitate' or 'please feel free to ...'

コース *n* course

コーチ *n* coach

コート *n* coat

コード *n* electrical wire

コーヒー *n* coffee

こおり・氷 *n* ice

こおる・凍る *vb 1* ㊉ to freeze

ゴール *n* goal

ごかい・誤解 1 *n* misunderstanding **2** *vb 3* ㋫ ごかいする to misinterpret

ごがく・語学 *n* (the study of) languages

こがす・焦がす *vb 1* ㋫ to burn

こがた (の)・小型 (の) *adj n* small sized

こぎって・小切手 *n* cheque

こきゅう・呼吸 1 *n* breathing **2** *vb 3* ㋫㋬ こきゅうする to breathe

こきょう・故郷 *n* home (town)

こぐ・漕ぐ *vb 1* ㋫ to pedal; to row

ごく・極 *adv* extremely

こくご・国語 *n* the Japanese language; Japanese classes in Japanese school

こくごじてん・国語辞典 *n* Japanese-Japanese dictionary

こくさい・国際 *prf* international

こくさいか・国際化 *n* internationalisation

こくさいこうりゅう・国際交流 *n* international relations

こくさいてき・国際的 1 *adj* こくさいてき(な) international **2** *adv* こくさいてきに internationally

こくせき・国籍 *n* nationality

こくばん・黒板 *n* blackboard

こくふく(する)・克服(する) *vb 3* ㋫ to conquer

こくみん・国民 *n* citizens of a country

こくみんのきゅうじつ・国民の休日 *n* – Nation's day (May 4) – a Japanese public holiday

こくもつ・穀物　n cereal (crops)

こくりつ・国立　prf national

こくりつこうえん・国立公園　n national park

こくれん・国連　n the United Nations

ごくろうさま (でした)・ご苦労様 (でした)
phrase – used to thank someone for their work and used to someone who is leaving the workplace in place of 'thank you' and 'goodbye'. Not used to superiors

こげる・焦げる　vb 2 ㊉ to be burnt

ここ　n here

ごご・午後　n afternoon; p.m.

ここのか・九日　n the ninth day of the month; nine days

ここのつ・九つ　n nine

こころ・心　n heart; mind

こころあたり・心当たり　n こころあたりが ある to have an idea of; こころあたりが ない to have no idea of

こころえる・心得る　vb 2 ㊉ to be aware of

こころみる・試みる　vb 1 ㊉ と to attempt

こころよい・快い　adj pleasant

ございます・御座います　*phrase* – following the particle で it is used as an honorific equivalent of です and it is used on its own as an equivalent of ある and いる as well as in certain everyday expressions.

ござる・御座る　vb 1 ㊉ ございます・ございません – an honorific substitute for です. ある and いる ▶ ございます note that there is no 〜て form and no plain negative for this verb

こし・腰　n lower back; hips; こしが いたい (to have) backache; こしを かけてください please sit down

こしかけ・腰掛け　n seat

こしかける・腰掛ける　vb 2 ㊉ に to sit down

ごじゅうおん・五十音 *n* – the chart of the かな syllabic scripts which is used as the Japanese equivalent of 'alphabetic' order in lists and dictionaries (such as this one) etc.

こしょう・故障 1 *n* breakdown **2** *vb 3* ㊉ こしょうする to be not working

こしょう・胡椒 *n* pepper

こしらえる・拵える *vb 2* ㊉ to make

こじん・個人 *n* individual

こじんてき・個人的 1 *adj* こじんてき (な) personal **2** *adv* こじんてきに personally

こす・越す *vb 1* ㊉ to go over

こす・超す *vb 1* ㊉ to exceed

こする・擦る *vb 1* ㊉ to rub

こせき・戸籍 *n* – the family register kept by local government which records births, marriages and deaths. A certified copy of the family register is used to prove identity.

こぜに・小銭 *n* small change

ごぜん・午前 *n* (in the) morning

ごぜんちゅう・午前中 *n* morning; during the morning

ごぞんじ・ご存知 *phrase* – usually in the form ごぞんじ ですか this is a polite equivalent of しる and means 'do you know?'

こたい・固体 1 *n* solid **2** *adj* こたいの solid

こたえ・答え *n* answer

こたえる・答える *vb 2* ㊉ に こたえて・こたえない ・こたえます to answer

ごちそう・ご馳走 1 *n* treat **2** *vb 3* ㊉ に ごちそうする to treat **!** usually used for meals and other entertainments

ごちそうさま・ご馳走様 *phrase* – most commonly in the form ごちそうさまでした which is the phrase said at the conclusion of a meal and as a way of thanking someone for entertainment or a treat

こちら *n* here; this direction; this person; this thing

こちらこそ *phrase* – used to respond to expressions of thanks with the sense of 'not at all' and meaning that on the contrary it is you who should be expressing thanks

こっか・国家 *n* nation

こっかい・国会 *n* the (Japanese) parliament

こづかい・小遣い *n* pocket money

こっきょう・国境 *n* (international) border

コック *n* chef

こっせつ・骨折 **1** *n* break; fracture **2** *vb 3* を こっせつする to break (a bone)

こっそり(と) *adv* secretly

こっち *n* – a less formal version of こちら

こづつみ・小包 *n* parcel; package

コップ *n* glass (for drinking)

こてん・古典 *n* – while meaning 'classics' in a general sense it often refers to the major works of classical Japanese literature

こてんてき(な)・古典的(な) *adj* classical

こと・事 *n* thing; matter; incident; 〜ことが ある have done ...; 〜ことが できる can ...; 〜ことに なる to be scheduled to ...; 〜ことに する decide to ... ! when it occurs as a modifying phrase in the forms listed above it is attached to a verb which will determine the translation.

こと・琴 *n* – a traditional Japanese stringed musical instrument

ごと *suf* every other

ことし・今年 *n* this year

ことづけ・言付け *n* message left in someone's absence

ことづて・言づて・言伝 *n* message

ことなる・異なる *vb 1* を to be different

ことに・殊に *adv* especially

ことば・言葉 *n* word/s; language

ことばづかい・言葉づかい *n* choice of words

こども・子ども・子供 *n* child; children

こどもたち・子供たち・子供達 *n* children

こどものひ・子供の日 *n* – Children's Day (May 5) – a Japanese public holiday

ことわざ・諺 *n* proverb

ことわる・断る *vb 1* ㉟ to refuse ! in the form ことわって おく it means 'get permission in advance'.

こな・粉 *n* flour; powder

こない・来ない ▶ くる

この *attributive* this

このあいだ *phrase* recently; the other day; last time

このごろ *phrase* recently

このたび・この度 *phrase* this time; last time

このつぎ・この次 *phrase* next (time)

このまえ・この前 *phrase* previously

このましい・好ましい *adj* desirable

このまま *phrase* as it is (now)

このみ・好み *n* taste

このむ・好む *vb 1* ㉟ to like

ごはん・ご飯・御飯 *n* (cooked) rice; meal

コピー**1** *n* (photo)copy **2** *vb 3* ㉟ コピーする to (photo)copy

コピーき・コピー機 *n* photocopier

ごぶさた・ご無沙汰 *n* – used in the form ごぶさた しています which means '(sorry) I have not written/been in contact for a long time'

こぼす・零す *vb 1* ㉟ to spill

こぼれる・零れる *vb 2* ㉜ to be spilled

こまかい・細かい *adj* very small; (of money) small change; detailed

こまる・困る vb 1 ⑰ こまって・こまらない・こまります to be in an awkward situation ❗ in the form こまったね it means either 'that's terrible, what are you going to do?' or 'what shall I do?'

ごみ・ゴミ n rubbish; garbage

ごみばこ・ごみ箱 n rubbish bin; garbage can

コミュニケーション n communication

こむ・込む・混む vb 1 ⑰ こんで・こまない・こみます to be crowded; みちが こんでいる the traffic is heavy

ゴム n rubber

こむぎ・小麦 n wheat

こむぎこ・小麦粉 n flour

こめ・米 n (uncooked) rice

ごめん・御免 phrase – informal equivalent of ごめんなさい

ごめんください・御免下さい phrase – used on entry to the げんかん of a house and equivalent to 'excuse me is there anyone at home?'. Also used to attract the attention of a clerk in a shop if nobody seems to be around.

ごめんなさい・御免なさい phrase – meaning 'sorry' it is used as both an apology and as a refusal of a request

こや・小屋 n hut; shed

こゆび・小指 n little finger

こよう・雇用 1 n employment **2** vb 3 ⑧ こようする to employ

こらえる・堪える vb 2 ⑧ to endure

ごらく・娯楽 n entertainment

ごらん・ご覧・御覧 phrase – in the form ごらんに なる this is an honorific equivalent of みる. Note that ごらん can substitute for みる following a 〜て form with the meaning 'try'. Following ちょっと or followed by ください or なさい it means 'please look' or 'look'

これ n this; it

これから *phrase* (from) now

これで *phrase* with this

これでいい *phrase* this/that will do

コレクション *n* collection

ころ *n* time ❗ *often attached to words and phrases about time to mean 'the time when ...', 'about' or ' time to|for ...'*

ころがす・転がす *vb 1* Ⓣ to roll (something)

ころがる・転がる *vb 1* Ⓘ to roll

ころす・殺す *vb 1* Ⓣ to kill

ころぶ・転ぶ *vb 1* Ⓘ to fall

こわい・恐い・怖い *adj* frightened; frightening

こわす・壊す *vb 1* Ⓣ to break

こわれる・壊れる *vb 2* Ⓘ こわれて・こわれない・こわれます to be broken

こん・紺 *n* navy blue

こん・今 *prf* this

こんかい・今回 *n* this time; next time

コンクール *n* contest

コンクリート *n* concrete

こんげつ・今月 *n* this month

こんご・今後 *n and adv* from now on

こんごう・混合 **1** *n* mixture **2** *vb 3* Ⓣ こんごうする to mix

コンサート *n* concert

こんざつ・混雑 **1** *n* congestion **2** *vb 3* Ⓘ こんざつする to be crowded

こんしゅう・今週 *n* this week

コンタクト *n* contact; contact lens; コンタクトを つける to put in contact lenses; コンタクトを する to wear contact lenses

こんだて・献立 *n* menu

こんど・今度 *n* this time; next time

こんな *attributive* this; like this

こんなに *adv* like this; to this extent

こんなん・困難 **1** *n* difficulty **2** *adj* こんなん(な) difficulty

こんにち・今日 *n* today; the present

こんにちは・今日は *phrase* hello

こんばんは・今晩は *phrase* good evening

コンピューター *n* computer

こんぽんてき(な)・根本的(な) **1** *adj* basic **2** *adv* こんぽんてきに fundamentally

こんやく・婚約 **1** *n* engagement **2** *vb* **3** と こんやく する to get engaged

こんやくゆびわ・婚約指輪 *n* engagement

こんらん・混乱 **1** *n* confusion **2** *vb* **3** こんらんする to be in confusion

さサ

さ・差 *n* difference

さ *suf* – added to adjective stems to produce a noun i.e. ながい 'long' and ながさ 'length'

さ *pt* – used at the end of sentences or phrases in colloquial speech to add emphasis

さあ *interjection* – used when commencing something and translatable as 'well' or 'now'

サークル *n* club

サービス 1 *n* service; service; given as a free gift **2** *vb 3* を か
サービスする to give away for free; to serve

さい・際 *n* occasion

さい・再 *prf* again

さい・最 *prf* most

さい・才・歳 *counter* years old

さい・祭 *suf* festival

さいかい・再開 **1** *n* reopening **2** *vb 3* を さいかいする
to reopen

ざいがく・在学 **1** *n* attending school/college **2** *vb 3* か に
ざいがくする to attend school

さいきん・最近 **1** *n* recently **2** *adv* recently **3** *adj* さいき
んの recent

さいきん・細菌 *n* microscopic organisms

さいご・最後 **1** *n* (the) last **2** *adj* さいごの last **3** *adv* さい
ごに finally

ざいこ・在庫 **1** *n* (in) stock **2** *vb 3* か ざいこする to be in
stock

さいこう・最高 *n* (the) best; さいこうです brilliant!

さいさん・再三 *adv* again and again

ざいさん・財産 *n* property; fortune

さいじつ・祭日 *n* national holiday (celebrating something)

さいしゅう・最終 *n* final

さいしょ・最初 **1** *n* (the) first **2** *adj* さいしょ(の)first **3** *adv*
さいしょに firstly

さいしょう・最小 *n* minimum

さいしょくしゅぎ・菜食主義 *n* – another way of saying
'vegetarian' ベジタリアン

さいしょくしゅぎしゃ・菜食主義者 *n* (a) vegetarian
▶さいしょくしゅぎ

サイズ *n* size

さいそく・催促 **1** *n* reminder (bill) **2** *vb* 3 🈁 さいそくする to demand (repayment)

さいだい・最大 *n* maximum

さいちゅう・最中 *n* in the middle of

さいて▶さく

さいてい・最低 *n* (the) lowest; さいていだ that's horrible!

さいてん・採点 **1** *n* marking **2** *vb* 3 🈁 さいてんする to mark

さいなん・災難 *n* disaster

さいのう・才能 *n* talent

さいばん・裁判 *n* trial; court

さいばんかん・裁判官 *n* judge

さいばんしょ・裁判所 *n* court; courthouse

さいふ・財布 *n* wallet; purse

さいほう・裁縫 *n* needlework

さいぼう・細胞 *n* cell

ざいもく・材木 *n* timber

さいよう・採用 **1** *n* adoption; employment **2** *vb* 3 🈁 さいようする to adopt; to employ

ざいりょう・材料 *n* materials; ingredients

さいわい・幸い **1** *adj* さいわい（な）happy **2** *adv* さいわい（に）fortunately

サイン **1** *n* signature; autograph; sign **2** *vb* 3 🈎 🈁 に サインする to sign

さお・竿 *n* pole

さか・坂 *n* slope

さかい・境 *n* boundary

さかさ・逆さ *n etc.* – an alternative form of さかさま

さかさま・逆さま **1** *n* disorder **2** *adj* さかさま(の) upside down; reversed **3** *adv* さかさまに wrong way up

さがす・探す・捜す *vb 1* Ⓔ to look for; to search

さかな・魚 *n* fish

さかな・肴 *n – small dishes of food to accompany drinks* ▶おつまみ

さかなや・魚屋 *n* fishmonger

さかのぼる・遡る *vb 1* Ⓚ に to date back to

さかば・酒場 *n* bar

さからう・逆らう *vb 1* Ⓚ に to go against

さがる・下がる *vb 1* Ⓚ to go down; to step back

さかり・盛り *n* the height (of)

さがります ▶さがる

さき・先 *n* tip (of something); future; ahead

さぎ・詐欺 *n* fraud

さきに *adv* in advance; ahead ▶おさきに

さきほど・先ほど *n* just now

さきます ▶さく

さぎょう・作業 **1** *n* work **2** *vb 3* Ⓚ さぎょうする to work

さく・柵 *n* fence

さく・咲く *vb 1* Ⓚ さいて・さかない・さきます to bloom

さく・裂く *vb 1* Ⓔ to tear

さく・昨 *prf* last

さくいん・索引 *n* index

さくじつ・昨日 *n* yesterday

さくしゃ・作者 *n* author

さくじょ(する)・削除(する) *vb 3* Ⓔ to delete

さくせい・作成 **1** *n* production (of a document) **2** *vb 3* ⓦ
さくせいする to put together (a document)

さくひん・作品 *n* work (of art); piece (of work)

さくぶん・作文 *n* (piece of) writing; essay

さくもつ・作物 *n* crops

さくら・桜 *n* cherry tree; cherry blossom

さぐる・探る *vb 1* to search for; to sound out

さけ・酒 *n* sake (rice wine); alcoholic drink

さけ・鮭 *n* salmon

さげて ▶ さげる

さけぶ・叫ぶ *vb 1* ⓚ ⓦ と to shout; to cry out

さける・裂ける *vb 2* ⓚ to rip

さける・避ける *vb 2* ⓦ to avoid

さげる・下げる *vb 2* ⓦ さげて・さげない・さげます
to lower; to wear (hanging items); to clear away (dishes and
plates)

ささえる・支える *vb 2* ⓦ to support

ささやく *vb 1* ⓚ に to whisper

さしあげる・差し上げる *vb 2* ⓦ to give ! respectful
equivalent of あげる

ざしき・座敷 *n* – a traditional Japanese style room usually
used for entertaining and floored with たたみ mats

さしず・指図 *n* orders

さしだす・差し出す *vb 1* ⓦ to hold out; to present

さしつかえ・差し支え *n* – it often means 'interference' or
'difficulty' but can also be translated as 'bland' or 'inoffensive' in
negatives and refers to not causing difficulty or trouble

さしひく・差し引く *vb 1* ⓦ to deduct

さしみ・刺し身・刺身 *n* – thin slices of raw fish and
meat

さす・指す *vb 1* ⓦ to point (to)

さす・刺す *vb 1* 🅠 to stab; to sting

さす *vb 1* 🅠 to put up (an umbrella)

さす *suf* – a spoken equivalent of the させる *suffix* used for forming the causative of a verb

さすが (に) *adv* – indicates that something has happened as expected and often translatable as 'truly' or 'indeed'

ざせき・座席 *n* seat

させる *vb 2* 🅠 させて・させない・させます – this is the causative form of する and a suffix for verbs indicating causation

さそう・誘う *vb 1* 🅠 to invite

さつ・札 *n* (bank) note

さつ・冊 *counter* book ❗ used for counting books and magazines

さつえい・撮影 **1** *n* filming; taking photographs **2** *vb 3* 🅠 さつえいする to photograph; to film

ざつおん・雑音 *n* interference (static noise)

さっか・作家 *n* writer

さっき *adv* a little while ago; some time ago

さっきょく・作曲 **1** *n* noun **2** *vb 3* 🅠 さっきょくする to compose

さっきょくか・作曲家 *n* composer

さっさと *adv* quickly

ざっし・雑誌 *n* magazine

さつじん・殺人 *n* murder; murderer

さっする・察する *vb 3* 🅠 to guess

さっそく・早速 *adv* straight away

ざっと *adv* briefly; roughly

さっぱり *adv* (with negatives) (not) at all

さっぱり(する) *vb 3* 🅟 to feel refreshed

さて interjection – used to mark a change of topic and translatable as 'well' or 'next'

さとう・砂糖 n sugar

さばく・砂漠 n desert

さび・錆 n rust

さびしい・寂しい adj lonely; sad

さびる・錆びる vb 2 ㉘ to rust

ざぶとん・座布団 n – a large flat cushion used for sitting on and placed on the floor of rooms with **たたみ** mats

さべつ・差別 1 n discrimination **2** vb 3 さべつする to discriminate

さほう・作法 n manners

さま・様 suf – a more polite equivalent for **さん** and attached to names of clients and customers to show politeness and used after a person's name when addressing a letter. Also used in certain idioms with the original meaning of 'seeming to be ...' or 'appearance'

さまざま・様々 1 adj さまざま(な) various **2** adj さまざまに variously

さます・冷ます vb 1 ㉘ to cool (something)

さます・覚ます vb 1 ㉘ めを さます to wake up

さまたげる・妨げる vb 2 ㉘ to obstruct

さむい・寒い adj cold

さめる・冷める vb 2 ㉘ to cool

さめる・覚める vb 2 ㉘ めが さめる to wake up

さゆう・左右 1 n right and left **2** vb 3 ㉘ さゆうする to influence

さようなら phrase goodbye

さら・皿 n dish; plate

さらいげつ・再来月 n the month after next

さらいしゅう・再来週 n the week after next

さらいねん・再来年 *n* the year after next

さらう *vb 1* ㊎ to kidnap

サラダ *n* salad

さらに・更に *adv* further; even more

サラリーマン *n* – an employee of one of the large Japanese corporations (or a white collar worker in general)

される *vb 2* ㊆ されて・されない・されます – *this is the passive form of* する

さる・去る *vb 1* ㊎ to leave

さる・猿 *n* monkey

さわがしい・騒がしい *adj* noisy

さわぎ・騒ぎ *n* uproar

さわぐ・騒ぐ *vb 1* ㊎ to make a noise

さわやか(な)・爽やか(な) *adj* refreshing

さわる・触る *vb 1* ㊎ に to touch

さん・三 *n* three

さん・山 *suf* mountain

さん・産 *suf* made in

さん *suf* – added to surnames it is an equivalent of English titles such as 'Mr', 'Mrs' and 'Ms' but is used far more extensively. It can sometimes be added to given names and job titles.

さんか・参加 1 *n* participation **2** *vb 3* ㊆ に さんかする to participate

さんかく・三角 *n* triangle

さんぎょう・産業 *n* industry

さんこう・参考 *n* reference

ざんこく・残酷 1 *adj* ざんこく(な) cruel **2** *adv* ざんこくに cruelly

さんしょう(する)・参照(する) *vb 3* ㊎ to refer to

し シ

し *pt* and (when giving a list of reasons)

し・四 *n* four

し・市 *suf* city

し・死 *n* death

し・詩 *n* poem

し・氏 *suf* Mr

し・史 *suf* history

じ・字 *n* – this can be either a letter (of the alphabet), a character of Japanese or other script or someone's 'handwriting'

じ・時 *suf* o'clock; time

じ・寺 *suf* temple

しあい・試合 **1** *n* match **2** *vb 3* ㉟ しあい(を)する to play (against)

しあげる・仕上げる *vb 2* ㉒ to finish something

しあさって *n* in three days time

しあわせ・幸せ **1** *n* happiness **2** *adj* しあわせ(な) happy **3** *adv* しあわせに happily

シーズン *n* season

シーツ *n* sheet

シートベルト *n* seatbelt

ジーパン *n* jeans

じえいぎょう・自営業 *n* self employment

じえいたい・自衛隊 *n* the Japanese self defence forces

ジェット *prf* jet

しえん・支援 **1** *n* support **2** *vb 3* ㊧ しえんする
to support

しお・塩 *n* salt

しお・潮 *n* tide

しおからい・塩辛い *adj* salty

しか・鹿 *n* deer

しか・歯科 *n* dentistry

しか *pt* only; nothing to do but … **!** *requires a negative*; わたし
はにせんえんしか ない I have only two thousand yen

しかい・視界 *n* (field of) vision

しがい・市街 *n* streets

しかいしゃ・司会者 *n* master of ceremonies

しかく・四角 **1** *n* square **2** *adj* しかく(な) square
▶ しかくい

しかく・資格 *n* qualification

しかくい・四角い *adj* square

しかし *conj* however; but

しかしながら *conj* however

しかた・仕方 *n* way of doing (it)

しかた(が)ない・仕方がない *phrase* it can't be helped;
there's nothing to be done (about it); there's no point (doing it)
! *following the* 〜て *form of a verb it adds the meaning 'be
dying to (do)'*

しかたなく *adv* reluctantly

じかに・直に *adv* directly

しかも *conj* besides; never the less

しかる・叱る *vb 1* ㊧ to tell off

じかん・時間 **1** *n* time **2** *counter* hours

じかんめ・時間目 *suf* period (of the school timetable)

じかんわり・時間割 *n* timetable

しき・式 *n* ceremony ❗ *as a suffix it can also mean 'style'*
▶わしき ▶ようしき

しき・四季 *n* the four seasons

じき・時期 *n* period

しきち・敷地 *n* site

じきに・直に *adv* soon; readily

しきゅう・至急 **1** *adv* urgently **2** *adj* しきゅうの urgent

しきゅう・支給 **1** *n* provision **2** *vb 3* ⊛ に しきゅうする to provide

しきゅう・子宮 *n* womb

じきゅう・時給 *n* hourly payment

しきりに *adv* frequently; constantly

しきる・仕切る *vb 1* ⊛ to partition

しきん・資金 *n* fund

しく・敷く *vb 1* ⊛ to spread; to lay ❗ *used of futons in the sense of 'prepare the bed'*

しげき・刺激 **1** *n* stimulus **2** *vb 3* ⊛ しげきする to stimulate

しける・湿気る *vb 1* ⓝ to be damp

しけん・試験 *n* examination; test

しげん・資源 *n* resources

じけん・事件 *n* incident; case; matter

じこ・事故 *n* accident

じこ・自己 *prf* self

しこうさくご・試行錯誤 *n* trial and error

じごうじとく・自業自得 *n* one's just desserts

じこしょうかい・自己紹介 *n* self introduction

じこくひょう・時刻表 *n* (transport) timetable

じごく・地獄 *n* hell

しごと・仕事 *n* work; job

しごと・仕事 **1** *n* work; job **2** *vb* 3 ㉟ しごとをする
to work

じさ・時差 *n* time zone difference

じさつ・自殺 **1** *n* suicide **2** *vb* 3 ㉟ じさつする to commit
suicide

しじ・支持 **1** *n* support **2** *vb* 3 ㉜ しじする to support

しじ・指示 **1** *n* instructions **2** *vb* 3 ㉜ しじする to give
instructions (that ..)

じじつ・事実 *n* the facts; reality

じしゃく・磁石 *n* magnet

じしゅ・自主 *prf* voluntary; independent

ししゅう・刺繍 *n* embroidery

しじゅう・始終 *adv* often; frequently

じしゅう・自習 **1** *n* self-study **2** *vb* 3 ㉟ じしゅうする
to study unsupervised

ししゅつ・支出 *n* expenditure

じしょ・辞書 *n* dictionary ▶ **dictionary**

しじょう・市場 *n* market

じじょう・事情 *n* situation; circumstances

じしょく・辞職 **1** *n* resignation **2** *vb* 3 ㉟ じしょくする
to resign from a job

じじょでん・自叙伝 *n* autobiography

ししん・指針 *n* guidelines

しじん・詩人 *n* poet

じしん・自信 *n* self confidence

じしん・地震 *n* earthquake

じしん・自身 *n* – used as a suffix to the preceding noun to
add the sense of 'self' and so variously translatable as 'himself',
'herself', 'myself', 'themselves' etc.

しずか・静か **1** *adj* しずか(な) quiet **2** *adv* しずかに
quietly

システム *n* system

しずまる・静まる・鎮まる *vb 1* ㋘ to grow quiet; to subside

しずむ・沈む *vb 1* ㋘ to sink

しせつ・施設 *n* facilities

しぜん・自然 **1** *n* nature **2** *adj* しぜん(な) natural **3** *adv* しぜんに naturally

じぜんに・事前に *adv* in advance

じぜん・慈善 *n* charity

しそう・思想 *n* thought

じぞう・地蔵 *n* – a Buddhist guardian of children and travellers or statues of him. Usually in the form じぞうさま. These statues are found in temples and all over Japan at the roadside and on paths

じそく・時速 *n* speed (per hour)

しそん・子孫 *n* descendents

した・下 *n* under; below; down; lower; younger

した・舌 *n* tongue

した ▶ する

したい・死体 *n* dead body

しだい・次第 **1** *suf* it depends on; かれしだい です it's up to him **2** *adv* しだいに gradually

じたい・事態 *n* situation

じだい・時代 *n and suf* age; period

じだいげき・時代劇 *n* historical dramas

したう・慕う *vb 1* ㋫ to adore; to miss

したうけ・下請け *n* subcontract; subcontractor

したがう・従う *vb 1* に to obey

したがえる・従える *vb 2* ㋫ to be accompanied by

したがき・下書き *n* draft (of a piece of writing)

したがって *adv* therefore; 〜にしたがって in accordance with

したぎ・下着 *n* underwear

したく・支度 1 *n* preparation **2** *vb 3* ㊌ したく（を）する to prepare

じたく・自宅 *n* (one's own) home; house

したごころ・下心 *n* hidden motive

したしい・親しい *adj* intimate; close

したまち・下町 *n* – the older residential parts of a city or 'downtown'

しち・七 *n* seven

しちがつ・7月・七月 *n* July

しつ・質 *n* quality

しつ・室 *n* and *suf* room

じつ・実 *n* the truth ▶ じつは

じつ・日 *suf* day

しっかり（と） *adv* firmly; しっかり している reliable

じっかん・実感 1 *n* realisation **2** *vb 3* ㊥ じっかんする to realise

しっき・湿気 ▶ しっけ

しつぎょう・失業 1 *n* unemployment **2** *vb 3* ㊌ しつぎょうする to become unemployed

しつぎょうしゃ・失業者 *n* unemployed person/people

しつぎょうてあて・失業手当 *n* unemployment benefit

じつぎょうか・実業家 *n* businessman; businesswoman

じっくり（と） *adv* carefully; thoroughly

しつけ・躾 1 *n* discipline **2** *vb 3* ㊁ しつけ（を）する to teach discipline (to)

しっけ・湿気 *n* dampness; humidity

じっけん・実験 1 *n* experiment **2** *vb 3* ㊥ じっけんする to experiment

じつげん・実現 **1** *n* realization **2** *vb 3* を 加 じつげんす
る to realize; to come true

じっけんだい・実験台 *n* (experimental) guinea pig

しつこい *adj* persistent

じっこう・実行 **1** *n* execution **2** *vb 3* を じっこうする
to carry out

じっさい・実際 **1** *n* fact **2** *adj* じっさいの actual **3** *adv*
じっさい(に) actually; じっさいは actually

じっさいてき(な) *adj* practical

じっし・実施 **1** *n* carrying out **2** *vb 3* を じっしする
to implement

じっしゅう・実習 **1** *n* practice; practical element of a
course **2** *vb 3* を じっしゅうする to practise

しっしん・湿疹 *n* (a) rash

じっせき・実績 *n* results

しって ▶ しる

しっと・嫉妬 **1** *n* jealousy **2** *vb 3* を に しっとする to be
jealous

しつど・湿度 *n* humidity

じっと **1** *adv* intently **2** *vb 3* 加 じっとする to remain still

じつに・実に *adv* very

じつは・実は *adv* actually

しっぱい・失敗 **1** *n* failure **2** *vb 3* 加 に しっぱいする
to fail

しっぴつ・執筆 **1** *n* writing **2** *vb 3* を しっぴつする
to write

しっぴつしゃ・執筆者 *n* writer

じつぶつ・実物 *n* the real thing

しっぽ・尻尾 *n* tail

しつぼう・失望 **1** *n* disappointment **2** *vb 3* 加 に しつぼ
うする to be disappointed

しつもん・質問 1 n question **2** vb 3 を に しつもんする
to ask questions

じつよう・実用 n practical use

じつようてき(な)・実用的(な) adj practical

じつりょく・実力 n capability

しつれい・失礼 1 n impoliteness **2** adj しつれい(な)
rude **3** vb 3 ㉛ しつれいする to be rude; to leave **!** there are
idiomatic uses of this word given under the next two entries

しつれいします・失礼します phrase (I'm) leaving;
excuse me (for interrupting) **!** used when entering a room or
interrupting a conversation and when about to leave as a polite
way of saying 'goodbye'

しつれいしました・失礼しました phrase excuse me
(I'm sorry) **!** used to apologise and also when leaving a room as
a polite way of saying 'goodbye'

して ▶ する

してい・指定 1 n designation **2** vb 3 を していする
to designate

していけん・指定券 n reservation ticket

していせき・指定席 n reserved seat

してきする・指摘する vb 3 を to point out

してん・支店 n and suf branch (of a bank or store)

じてん・辞典 n dictionary

じてんしゃ・自転車 n bicycle

しどう・指導 1 n guidance **2** vb 3 を しどうする
to instruct

じどう・児童 prf child

じどうし・自動詞 n – verbs which do not have a direct
object. For explanations of this important concept in Japanese
grammar In this dictionary じどうし is marked with the
symbol ㉛ in the entry and the opposite type of verb (transitive)
たどうし is marked with the symbol を

しどうしゃ・指導者 *n* leader

じどうしゃ・自動車 *n* car

しな・品 *n* article; goods

しない ▶ する

しなもの・品物 *n* goods

しぬ・死ぬ *vb 1 ㋐* to die

しはい・支配 **1** *n* rule **2** *vb 3* ㋐ しはいする to rule

しばい・芝居 *n* (a) play

しはいにん・支配人 *n* manager

しばしば *adv* often

しばふ・芝生 *n* lawn

しはらい・支払い *n* payment

しはらう・支払う *vb 1* ㋐ to pay

しばらく・暫く *adv* for a while; しばらくですね
　I haven't seen you for a while! ▶ ひさしぶり

しばる・縛る *vb 1* ㋐ to bind

じばん・地盤 *n* ground

じびいんこうか・耳鼻咽喉科 *n* ear, nose and throat
　doctor

じびか・耳鼻科 ▶ じびいんこうか

しびれる *vb 2* ㋐ to be numb; to have pins and needles

しぶき *n* splash

しぶしぶ *adv* unwillingly

じぶん・自分 *n* oneself

しへい・紙幣 *n* paper money

しぼう・死亡 **1** *n* death **2** *vb 3* ㋐ しぼうする to die

しぼう・脂肪 *n* fat

しぼう・志望 **1** *n* desire **2** *vb 3* ㋐ しぼうする to want

しぼむ・萎む *vb 1* ㋐ to wither

しぼる・絞る *vb 1* ⑭ to wring out; to squeeze

しほん・資本 *n* capital (sum of money)

しほんしゅぎ・資本主義 *n* capitalism

しま・島 *n* island

しま・縞 **1** *n* stripe **2** *adj* しまの(ある) striped

しまい・終い *n* (the) end **!** often found in the form おしまい

しまい・姉妹 *n* sisters **!** often used for 'twinning' as in しまいとし・姉妹都市 'sister city'/'twin town' and しまいこう・姉妹校 'sister school'

しまう *vb 1* ⑭ to put away **!** following the 〜て form of a verb it adds the meaning of something being completely finished or being regretable in some way.

しまう *vb 1* ⑭ to shut; to close

じまく・字幕 *n* subtitles

しましょう ▶ する

します ▶ する

しません ▶ する

しませんか ▶ する

しまって ▶ しまる

しまった *exc* oh no!

しまります ▶ しまる

しまる・閉まる *vb 1* ⑭ しまって・しまらない・しまります to be shut

じまん・自慢 **1** *n* boasting **2** *vb 3* ⑭ じまんする to boast

じみ(な)・地味(な) *adj* plain

しみじみ(と) *adv* deeply

しみん・市民 *n* citizen; inhabitant (of a city)

じむ・事務 *n* office work

じむいん・事務員 *n* clerk

じむきょく・事務局 *n* secretariat

じむしつ・事務室　*n* office (room)

じむしょ・事務所　*n* office

しめい・氏名　*n* full name

しめきり・締め切り　*n* deadline

しめす・示す　*vb 1* ⑧ to indicate

しめて ▶ しめる

しめます ▶ しめる

しめる・閉める　*vb 2* ⑧ しめて・しめない・しめます
　to shut

しめる・締める　*vb 2* ⑧ to fasten

しめる・占める　*vb 2* ⑧ to occupy

しめる・湿る　*vb 1* ⑩ to get damp

じめん・地面　*n* ground

しも・霜　*n* frost

しも・下　*prf* lower; second

しも　*pt* (not) necessarily

しゃ・者　*suf* person

しゃ・車　*suf* vehicle

しゃ・社　*suf* company

じゃ – *reduced form of* では *used in the formation of some
　negative sentences. See the entries for* じゃありません *and*
　じゃない *below.*

じゃあ　*conj* well (then) ❗ *used as an informal way of saying
　'goodbye', especially in the form* じゃあ、またね *or simply*
　じゃあ

じゃありません – *negative form of* です *and variously
　translatable as 'am not', 'is not', or 'are not'*

じゃありませんでした – *past form of* じゃありません
　and translatable as 'was not' or 'were not'

ジャーナリスト　*n* journalist

しゃかい・社会　*n* society

しゃかいかがく・**社会科学** *n* social science

しゃかいしゅぎ・**社会主義** *n* socialism

しゃがむ **vb 1** ㉚ to squat

じゃく・**弱** *suf* less than

じゃぐち・**蛇口** *n* tap; faucet

じゃくてん・**弱点** *n* weak point

しゃこ・**車庫** *n* garage (for storing car)

しゃしょう・**車掌** *n* ticket collector (buses and trains)

しゃしん・**写真** *n* photograph

ジャズ *n* jazz

しゃせい・**写生 1** *n* sketch **2 vb 3** ㉚ しゃせいする
to sketch

しゃせつ・**社説** *n* (newspaper) editorial

しゃたく・**社宅** *n* – housing provided by a company for
workers to live in

シャツ *n* shirt

じゃっかん・**若干** *n* a few

しゃっきん・**借金 1** *n* loan **2 vb 3** ㉚ しゃっきんする
to take out a loan

しゃっくり **1** *n* hiccup **2 vb 3** ㉚ しゃっくりする to hiccup

しゃない・**社内** *n* within the company

しゃない・**車内** *n* inside (of a vehicle)

じゃない – plain equivalent of じゃありません

じゃなかった – past form of じゃない

しゃぶる **vb 1** ㉚ to suck

しゃべる・**喋る** **vb 1** ㉚ to chat; to speak

じゃま・**邪魔 1** *n* hindrance; obstruction **2** *adj* じゃま(な)
obstructive **3 vb 3** ㉚ じゃま(を)する to hinder; to visit

じゃまもの・**邪魔物** *n* nuisance

しゃみせん・三味線 *n* – a traditional Japanese stringed musical instrument

しゃめん・斜面 *n* slope

じゃり・砂利 *n* gravel

しゃりん・車輪 *n* wheel

しゃれ・洒落 *n* joke

ジャム *n* jam

シャワー *n* shower; シャワーを あびる to take a shower

シャンプー *n* shampoo

しゅ・手 *suf* person

しゅ・酒 *suf* alcoholic drink

しゅう・週 *n and suf* week

しゅう・州 *n and suf* state ❗ often used to translate the English words 'state', 'province' or 'county'

しゅう・集 *suf* collection

じゆう・自由 **1** *n* freedom **2** *adj* じゆう(な) free **3** *adv* じゆうに freely

じゅう・十 *n* ten

じゅう・銃 *n* gun

じゅう・中 *suf* throughout

じゅう・重 *suf* fold

しゅうい・周囲 *n* circumference

しゅうかい・集会 *n* gathering

しゅうかく・収穫 **1** *n* harvest **2** *vb* 3 ㊥ しゅうかくする to harvest

しゅうかん・週間 *counter* week

しゅうかん・習慣 *n* custom

しゅうぎいん・衆議院 *n* house of representatives

しゅうぎいんぎいん・衆議院議員 *n* member of the house of representatives

じゅうきょ・住居 *n* residence

しゅうきょう・宗教 *n* religion

じゅうぎょういん・従業員 *n* employee

しゅうきん・集金 **1** *n* collecting money **2** *vb* **3** を しゅうきんする to collect money

しゅうげき・襲撃 **1** *n* assault **2** *vb* **3** を しゅうげきする to attack

しゅうごう・集合 **1** *n* gathering **2** *vb* **3** を しゅうごうする to gather

しゅうし・収支 *n* income and expenditure

しゅうし・終始 *adv* from beginning to end

しゅうし・修士 *n* Master's degree

しゅうじ・習字 *n* (Japanese) calligraphy

じゅうし (する)・重視(する) *vb* **3** を to consider important

じゅうじつ・充実 **1** *n* fulfillment **2** *vb* **3** が じゅうじつする to be fulfilling

しゅうしゅう・収集 **1** *n* collection **2** *vb* **3** を しゅうしゅうする to collect

じゅうしょ・住所 *n* address

しゅうしょく・就職 **1** *n* finding a job **2** *vb* **3** に しゅうしょくする to get a job

しゅうしょくかつどう・就職活動 *n* looking for a job

じゅうじろ・十字路 *n* crossroads

ジュース *n* soft drink(s)

しゅうせい・修正 **1** *n* modification **2** *vb* **3** を しゅうせいする to amend

しゅうぜん・修繕 **1** *n* repair **2** *vb* **3** を しゅうぜんする to repair

じゅうたい・渋滞 **1** *n* traffic jam **2** *vb* **3** が じゅうたいする to be congested

じゅうたい・重態・重体 *n* in a serious condition

じゅうだい(な)・重大(な) *adj* serious

じゅうたく・住宅 *n* house; housing

しゅうだん・集団 *n* group

じゅうたん・絨毯 *n* carpet; rug

しゅうちゅう・集中 **1** *n* concentration **2** *vb 3* ㉑ に しゅうちゅうする to concentrate

しゅうてん・終点 *n* terminus

じゅうなんせい・柔軟性 *n* flexibility

しゅうにゅう・収入 *n* income

しゅうにん・就任 **1** *n* taking up a post **2** *vb 3* ㉑ しゅうにんする to take office

しゅうのう・収納 *n* storage

じゅうびょう・重病 *n* serious illness

しゅうぶんのひ・秋分の日 *n* – Autumnal Equinox Day – a Japanese public holiday

じゅうぶん・十分 **1** *n* enough **2** *adv* thoroughly **3** *adj* じゅうぶん(な) adequate

しゅうへん・周辺 *n* vicinity

しゅうまつ・週末 *n* weekend

じゅうみん・住民 *n* resident

じゅうみんぜい・住民税 note – tax paid to local government by all residents of a town, village or city

じゅうやく・重役 *n* executive

しゅうよう・収容 **1** *n* capacity **2** *vb 3* ㉓ しゅうようする to accommodate

じゅうよう(な)・重要(な) *adj* important

じゅうらい・従来 *n* until now

しゅうり・修理 **1** *n* repair **2** *vb 3* ㉓ しゅうりする to repair

しゅうりょう・終了 1 *n* close **2** *vb 3* か を しゅうりょうする to finish

じゅうりょう・重量 *n* weight

しゅうりょうしょう・修了証 *n* certificate (of completing a course)

しゅうりょうしょうしょ・修了証書 *n* – alternative form of しゅうりょうしょう

じゅうりょく・重力 *n* gravity

しゅかんてき・主観的 1 *adj* しゅかんてき(な) subjective **2** *adv* しゅかんてきに subjectively

しゅぎ・主義 *suf* – similar to the English suffix '-ism' as in 'patriotism' etc.

じゅぎょう・授業 *n* class

じゅく・塾 *n* – a supplementary 'cram' school attended by children after (or even before!) normal school hours. Usually providing supplementary teaching towards school or university entrance examinations but some じゅく provide special subjects not covered at school such as abacus or calligraphy or just 'top up' teaching of the same materials as the ordinary school syllabus.

じゅくご・熟語 *n* – words or idiomatic phrases made up several elements, especially in the sense of compound use of Chinese characters and translatable as 'kanji compounds'

しゅくじつ・祝日 *n* – a national holiday celebrating something

しゅくしょう・縮小 1 *n* reduction **2** *vb 3* を か しゅくしょうする to reduce

しゅくだい・宿題 1 *n* homework **2** *vb 3* か しゅくだい (を)する to do homework

じゅけん・受験 1 *n* (entrance) examination **2** *vb 3* を じゅけんする to take an examination

じゅけんしゃ・受験者 *n* examination candidate

じゅけんせい・受験生 *n* examination candidate (student)

じゅけんべんきょう・受験勉強 *n* studying in preparation for an exam

じゅけんりょう・受験料 *n* examination fee

しゅざい・取材 1 *n* gathering materials **2** *vb 3* を しゅざいする to research (a story); to cover (an event)

しゅざいきしゃ・取材記者 *n* reporter

しゅし・趣旨 *n* gist; purpose

しゅじゅつ・手術 *n* operation

しゅしょう・首相 *n and suf* Prime Minister

しゅじん・主人 *n* (one's own) husband **!** *also used about the 'owner' of a shop, restaurant or bar and translatable as 'proprietor'*

しゅじんこう・主人公 *n* the leading role

しゅだん・手段 *n* means

しゅちょう・主張 1 *n* insistence **2** *vb 3* を しゅちょうする to insist

しゅっきん・出勤 1 *n* coming/going to work **2** *vb 3* を に しゅっきんする to go/come to work

しゅっけつ・出血 1 *n* bleeding **2** *vb 3* ㉟ しゅっけつする to bleed

しゅっさん・出産 *n* childbirth

しゅつじょう・出場 1 *n* participation **2** *vb 3* ㉟ しゅつじょうする to take part

しゅっしん・出身 *n and suf* place of birth; graduate of

しゅっせ・出世 1 *n* success (in life) **2** *vb 3* ㉟ しゅっせする to be successful (in life)

しゅっせき・出席 1 *n* attendance **2** *vb 3* ㉟ に しゅっせきする to attend

しゅっちょう・出張 1 *n* business trip **2** *vb 3* ㉟ しゅっちょうする to go on a business trip

しゅっぱつ・出発 1 *n* departure **2** *vb 3* ㉟ しゅっぱつする to depart

しゅっぱん・出版 1 n publishing **2** vb 3 ㊀ しゅっぱんする to publish

しゅっぱんしゃ・出版社 n publisher (company)

しゅっぴ・出費 n expenditure

しゅっぴん(する)・出品(する) vb 3 ㊀ to exhibit

しゅと・首都 n capital (city)

しゅのう・首脳 n leader/s

しゅび・守備 1 n defence **2** vb 3 ㊀ しゅびする to defend

しゅふ・主婦 n housewife **!** used to refer to married women generally even if they work

しゅみ・趣味 n hobby; taste

じゅみょう・寿命 n life expectancy

じゅもく・樹木 n trees

しゅやく・主役 n leading role

しゅよう(な)・主要(な) adj main

しゅよう・腫瘍 n tumour

じゅよう・需要 n demand

しゅるい・種類 n kind (of)

じゅわき・受話器 n (telephone) receiver

じゅん・順 suf (in) order

しゅんかん・瞬間 n moment

じゅんかん・循環 n circulation

じゅんさ・巡査 n police officer

じゅんじょ・順序 n order; じゅんじょのある orderly; じゅんじょがたたない disorderly

じゅんじょう(な)・純情(な) adj naive

じゅんすい(な)・純粋(な) adj pure

じゅんちょう・順調 1 adj じゅんちょう(な) going well **2** adv じゅんちょうに smoothly

じゅんばん・順番 n turn; じゅんばんに in turn

じゅんび・準備 1 *n* preparation **2** *vb* **3** 悉 **じゅんび(を)する** to prepare

しゅんぶんのひ・春分の日 *n* – Vernal Equinox Day – a Japanese public holiday

しょ・初 *prf* first

しょ・諸 *prf* various

しょ・書 *suf* written item

しょ・所 *suf* place

じょ・所 *suf* place

じょ・女 *prf and suf* woman

しよう・使用 1 *n* use **2** *vb* **3** 悉 **しようする** to use

しよう・仕様 ▶ しょがない

しよう・▶する

しょう・小 *prf* small

しょう・賞 *n and suf* prize

しょう・章 *n and suf* chapter

しょう・省 *suf* ministry

じょう・上 *n* the best

じょう・上 *prf* upper

じょう・上 *suf* concerning

じょう・情 *n* emotion

じょう・場 *suf* place

じょう・畳 *suf* – the counter for たたみ mats when used as an indication of the floor area of a house or apartment. Each piece of matting is approximately 90 x 180 cm

じょう・状 *suf* letter

しょうか・消火 1 *n* fire fighting **2** *vb* **3** 悉 **しょうかする** to extinguish

しょうか・消化 1 *n* digestion **2** *vb* **3** 悉 **しょうかする** to digest

しょうかい・紹介 1 *n* introduction **2** *vb* 3 ㊒ しょうか いする to introduce

しょうかき・消化器 *n* fire extinguisher

しょうがい・障害 *n* obstacle

しょうがい・生涯 *n* throughout one's life

しょうがいじ・障害児 *n* disabled child

しょうがいしゃ・障害者 *n* disabled person

しょうがいがくしゅう・生涯学習 *n* continuing education

しょうがくきん・奨学金 *n* scholarship

しょうがくせい・小学生 *n* elementary school student

しょうがつ・正月 *n* new year

しょうがっこう・小学校 *n* elementary school

しょうがない *phrase* there's no choice; it can't be helped; it's hopeless

しょうぎ・将棋 *n* – a Japanese board game with some similarities to chess

じょうき・蒸気 *n* steam

じょうき (の)・上記 (の) *adj* the above **!** *formal phrase for letters similar to 'the aforesaid' and 'the above-mentioned'*

じょうぎ・定規 *n* (a) ruler

じょうきゃく・乗客 *n* passenger

じょうきゅう・上級 *n and prf* advanced (level)

しょうぎょう・商業 1 *n* commerce **2** *adj* しょうぎょう の commercial

じょうきょう・上京 1 *n* going/coming to Tokyo **2** *vb* 3 ㊑ じょうきょうする to go/come to Tokyo

じょうきょう・状況 *n* situation

しょうきょくてき・消極的 1 *adj* しょうきょくてき (な) negative **2** *adv* しょうきょくてきに unenthusiastically

しょうきん・賞金 *n* prize money

じょうげ・上下 **1** *n* top and bottom; upper and lower **2** *vb 3* じょうげする to fluctuate; to vary

じょうけん・条件 *n* condition

しょうこ・証拠 *n* proof

しょうご・正午 *n* noon

しょうこうかいぎしょ・商工会議所 *n* chamber of commerce

しょうさい・詳細 *n* the details

しょうじ・障子 *n* – sliding paper screen doors

じょうし・上司 *n* – someone who is higher in authority than you at work so translatable as 'boss', 'management' or 'my superiors' etc. depending on the situation

しょうじき・正直 **1** *adj* しょうじき(な) honest **2** *adv* しょうじきに honestly

じょうしき・常識 *n* common sense

しょうしゃ・商社 *n* trading company

じょうしゃ・乗車 **1** *n* boarding (a vehicle) **2** *vb 3* ㋕ にじょうしゃする to get on/into (a vehicle)

じょうしゃけん・乗車券 *n* ticket (bus or train)

じょうじゅん・上旬 *n* the first ten days of the month

しょうじょ・少女 *n* girl

しょうしょう・少々 *adv* a little

しょうしょう(お)まち(ください)・少々(お)待ち(ください) *phrase* please wait a moment

しょうじる・生じる *vb 3* ㋕ to occur; to come about

しょうしん・昇進 **1** *n* promotion **2** *vb 3* ㋕ しょうしんする to be promoted

じょうず・上手 **1** *adj* じょうず(な) skillful; good at ... **2** *adv* じょうずに skillfully; well

しょうすう・少数 *n* small number; minority

しょうすうみんぞく・少数民族 *n* ethnic minority

しょうせつ・小説 *n* novel

しょうたい・招待 **1** *n* invitation **2** *vb* **3** 🄖 しょうたいする to invite

じょうたい・状態 *n* condition; state

しょうたいじょう・招待状 *n* (letter of) invitation

じょうたつ・上達 **1** *n* improvement **2** *vb* **3** 🄖 じょうたつする to make progress

じょうだん・冗談 *n* joke; じょうだんを いう to tell a joke

しょうち(する)・承知(する) *vb* **3** 🄖 to be aware; to consent; (ご)しょうちの ように as you know; しょうちの とおり as you know

じょうちょ・情緒 *n* emotions

じょうちょてき・情緒的 **1** *adj* じょうちょてき(な) emotional **2** *adv* じょうちょてきに emotionally

しょうちょう・象徴 *n* symbol

しょうてん・商店 *n* store

しょうてん・焦点 *n* focus; しょうてんを あわせる to focus

しょうてんがい・商店街 *n* shopping area/centre

じょうとう(な)・上等(な) *adj* high quality

しょうどく・消毒 **1** *n* sterilisation **2** *vb* **3** 🄖 しょうどくする to sterilize

しょうとつ・衝突 **1** *n* collision **2** *vb* **3** 🄖 に しょうとつする to collide

しょうにん・商人 *n* person in business

しょうにん・承認 **1** *n* approval **2** *vb* **3** 🄖 しょうにんする to approve

じょうねつ・情熱 *n* passion

じょうねつてき・情熱的 **1** *adj* じょうねつてき(な) enthusiastic **2** *adv* じょうねつてきに enthusiastically

しょうねん・少年 *n* boy

しょうはい・勝敗 *n* victory and defeat

しょうばい・商売 **1** *n* trade **2** *vb 3* か しょうばい(を)する to do business

じょうはつ・蒸発 **1** *n* evaporation **2** *vb 3* か じょうはつする to evaporate

しょうひ・消費 **1** *n* consumption **2** *vb 3* を しょうひする to consume

しょうひしゃ・消費者 *n* consumer

しょうひぜい・消費税 **1** *n* 'consumption tax' – *a tax levied on goods and services by central government*

しょうひん・商品 *n* goods

じょうひん(な)・上品(な) *adj* elegant; refined

しょうぶ・勝負 **1** *n* match **2** *vb 3* か しょうぶする have a game

じょうぶ(な)・丈夫(な) *adj* sturdy; strong

しょうべん・小便 **1** *n* urine **2** *vb 3* か しょうべんする to urinate

しょうぼうしゃ・消防車 *n* fire engine

しょうぼうしょ・消防署 *n* fire station

じょうほう・情報 *n* information

じょうほうこうがく・情報工学 *n* information technology

しょうみ・正味 **1** *adv* fully; nett

しょうめい・証明 **1** *n* proof **2** *vb 3* を しょうめいする to prove

しょうめい・照明 *n* lighting

しょうめん・正面 *n* front

しょうめんしょうとつ・正面衝突 *n* head on collision

しょうもう・消耗 **1** *n* using up **2** *vb 3* を しょうもうする to exhaust

じょうやく・条約 *n* treaty

しょうゆ・醤油 *n* soy sauce

しょうらい・将来 *n* (the) future

じょうりく・上陸 **1** *n* landing (from a boat) **2** *vb 3* か じょうりくする to land

しょうりゃく・省略 **1** *n* shortening **2** *vb 3* を しょうりゃくする to abridge

しょうわ・昭和 *n* – era name for 1926 to 1989 and used for dates during that period

じょおう・女王 *n* queen

しょきゅう・初級 *n and prf* beginners (level)

ジョギング **1** *n* jogging **2** *vb 3* か ジョギングする to jog

しょく・職 *n* occupation

しょくいん・職員 *n* staff

しょくいんかいぎ・職員会議 *n* staff meeting; teachers' meeting

しょくいんしつ・職員室 *n* staff room; teachers' room

しょくぎょう・職業 *n* occupation

しょくじ・食事 **1** *n* meal **2** *vb 3* か しょくじ する to have a meal

しょくたく・食卓 *n* dining table

しょくどう・食堂 *n* canteen; dining room

しょくにん・職人 *n* craftsman

しょくば・職場 *n* workplace

しょくパン・食パン *n* loaf of bread

しょくひん・食品 *n* foods

しょくぶつ・植物 *n* plants

しょくもつ・食物 *n* food

しょくよく・食欲 *n* appetite

しょくりょう・食糧 *n* foodstuffs

しょくりょうひん・食料品 *n* groceries

しょさい・書斎 *n* study (room)

しょじ・所持 1 *n* possession **2** *vb 3* ㊊ **しょじする**
to have

じょし・女子 *n* woman; female **!** *often occurs as a prefix to add the meaning 'women's' or girls' especially in the names of schools, colleges and universities*

じょし・助詞 *n* – *part of speech usually called particle or postposition which expresses grammatical relations. Also sometimes called* てにをは. *For further information on these words and their uses*

じょしゅ・助手 *n* assistant

しょじゅん・初旬 *n* – *the first ten days of the month and translatable as 'at the beginning of the month'*

じょじょに・徐々に *adv* gradually

じょせい・女性 *n* woman; women

しょせき・書籍 *n* books

しょち・処置 1 *n* measures **2** *vb 3* ㊊ **しょちする** to deal with

しょっき・食器 *n* – *plates, bowls and utensils for eating*;
しょっきをあらう to wash the dishes

ショック *n* shock

しょっちゅう *adv* constantly; often

ショップ *n* shop

しょてん・書店 *n* bookstore

しょどう・書道 *n* traditional Japanese calligraphy

しょとく・所得 *n* income

しょとくぜい・所得税 *n* income tax

しょぶん・処分 1 *n* disposal; punishment **2** *vb 3* ㊊ **しょぶんする** to dispose of; to punish

しょめい・署名 1 *n* signature **2** *vb 3* ㊁ **に しょめいする** to sign

しょもつ・書物 *n* books

しょゆう・所有 **1** *n* possession **2** *vb 3* 🈯 しょゆうする
to own

じょゆう・女優 *n* actress

しょゆうしゃ・所有者 *n* owner

しょり・処理 **1** *n* treatment **2** *vb 3* 🈯 しょりする to deal
with

しょるい・書類 *n* documents

しらが・白髪 *n* white (grey) hairs

しらせ・知らせ *n* notification; news

しらせる・知らせる *vb 2* 🈯 to inform

しらべ・調べ *n* investigation

しらべる・調べる *vb 2* 🈯 to investigate; to look up

しり・尻 *n* (person's) bottom

しりあい・知り合い *n* acquaintance

シリーズ *n* series

しりつ・私立 *prf* – established privately (as opposed to by
prefectural or national government)

しりょう・資料 *n* data; materials

しります ▶ しる

しる・知る *vb 1* 🈯 to know

しる・汁 *n* soup; juice

しるし・印 *n* sign

しろ・白 *n* white

しろ・城 *n* castle

しろい・白い *adj* white

しろうと・素人 *n* (an) amateur

しろくろ・白黒 *n* black and white

しわ・皺 *n* wrinkles; creases

しん・芯 *n* core; (pencil) lead

しん・新 *prf* new

じん・人 *suf* – added to country names it means person from that country

しんがく・進学 **1** *n* advancing to the next level of education **2** *vb* 3 ㉓ しんがくする to advance to the next educational level

しんかんせん・新幹線 *n* – the high speed 'bullet train' express linking many of Japan's cities

しんくう・真空 *n* vacuum

しんけい・神経 *n* nerve

しんけいしつ(な)・神経質(な) *adj* nervous

しんけん・真剣 **1** *adj* しんけん(な) serious **2** *adv* しんけんに seriously

しんこう・進行 **1** *n* advance **2** *vb* 3 ㉓ しんこうする to advance

しんこう・信仰 **1** *n* (religious) faith **2** *vb* 3 ㉓ しんこうする to believe (in)

しんごう・信号 *n* traffic lights; traffic signals

じんこう・人口 *n* population

じんこう・人工 *prf* artificial; man-made

しんこく・深刻 **1** *adj* しんこく(な) serious **2** *adv* しんこくに seriously

しんさつ・診察 **1** *n* medical examination **2** *vb* 3 ㉓ しんさつする to examine

じんじ・人事 *prf* personnel

しんじゃ・信者 *n* (religious) believer

じんじゃ・神社 *n* a Shinto shrine

しんじゅ・真珠 *n* pearl

じんしゅ・人種 *n* race

じんしゅさべつ・人種差別 *n* racial discrimination

しんじる・信じる *vb* 2 ㉓ to believe

しんせい・申請 **1** *n* application **2** *vb* 3 ㊡ しんせいする
to apply (for)

じんせい・人生 *n* (a person's) life

しんせき・親戚 *n* relatives

しんせつ・親切 **1** *adj* しんせつ(な) kind **2** *adv* しんせ
つに kindly

しんせん(な)・新鮮(な) *adj* fresh

しんぞう・心臓 *n* heart

じんぞう・人造 *prf* artificial

しんたい・身体 *n* the body

しんだい・寝台 *n* bed

しんだん・診断 **1** *n* diagnosis **2** *vb* 3 ㊡ しんだんする
to diagnose

しんちょう・身長 *n* (person's) height

しんちょう・慎重 **1** *adj* しんちょう(な) careful **2** *adv*
しんちょうに carefully

しんど・震度 *n* – indicates the scale of an earthquake on the
Japanese scale (not the Richter scale) and is therefore followed
by a number from 1 (weakest) to 8

しんとう・神道 *n* – a Japanese religion

しんどう・振動 **1** *n* vibration **2** *vb* 3 ㊢ しんどうする
to shake

しんどう・震動 *n* earth tremor

しんにゅう・侵入 **1** *n* raid **2** *vb* 3 ㊢ しんにゅうする
to invade

しんねん・新年 *n* new year; しんねん あけまして おめ
でとう ございます Happy New Year!

しんぱい・心配 **1** *n* worry **2** *vb* 3 ㊡ しんぱいする
to worry

しんぱん・審判 *n* referee

しんぴてき(な)・神秘的(な) *adj* mysterious

しんぷ・新婦 *n* bride

しんぷ・神父 *n and suf* – used to mean 'father' for Catholic priests

じんぶつ・人物 *n* person

しんぶん・新聞 *n* newspaper

じんぶんかがく・人文科学 *n* the humanities

しんぽ・進歩 **1** *n* progress **2** *vb* **3** ⑦ しんぽする to make progress

しんぼう・辛抱 *n* patience

じんめい・人命 *n* (human) life

しんや・深夜 *prf* in the middle of the night

しんゆう・親友 *n* close friend

しんよう・信用 **1** *n* trust **2** *vb* **3** ⑥ しんようする to rely on

しんらい・信頼 **1** *n* trust **2** *vb* **3** ⑥ しんらいする to trust

しんり・心理 *n* state of mind

しんり・真理 *n* truth

しんりがく・心理学 *n* psychology

しんりゃく・侵略 **1** *n* (military) aggression **2** *vb* **3** ⑥ しんりゃくする to invade

しんりん・森林 *n* forest(s)

しんるい・親類 *n* relative

じんるい・人類 *n* humanity

しんろ・進路 *n* course

しんろう・新郎 *n* bridegroom

しんわ・神話 *n* myth

すス

す・巣 *n* nest

す・酢 *n* vinegar

すいえい・水泳 **1** *n* swimming

すいか・西瓜 *n* water melon

すいさん・水産 *prf* fisheries

すいじ・炊事 **1** *n* cooking **2** *vb 3* ⓗ すいじする to cook

すいじゅん・水準 *n* standard

すいせん・推薦 **1** *n* recommendation **2** *vb 3* ⓦ すいせん
　する to recommend

すいせんじょう・推薦状 *n* a reference (for a job etc.)

すいそ・水素 *n* hydrogen

すいそく・推測 **1** *n* guess **2** *vb 3* ⓦ すいそくする
　to guess

すいちょく・垂直 **1** *adj* すいちょく(な) vertical **2** *adv*
　すいちょくに vertically

スイッチ *n* switch; スイッチを いれる to turn on

すいて ▶ すく

すいてい・推定 **1** *n* estimate **2** *vb 3* ⓦ すいていする
　to estimate

すいてき・水滴 *n* drop of water

すいでん・水田 *n* paddy field

すいとう・水筒 *n* water bottle

すいどう・水道 *n* water supply

ずいひつ・随筆 *n* essay (article)

すいぶん・水分 *n* water

ずいぶん・随分 *adv* very

すいへい(な)・水平(な) *adj* level

すいへいせん・水平線 *n* horizon

すいます▶すう

すいみん・睡眠 *n* sleep

すいみんぶそく・睡眠不足 *n* lack of sleep

すいめん・水面 *n* surface (of the water)

すいようび・水曜日 *n* Wednesday

すう・吸う *vb 1* ⓔ すって・すわない・すいます
　to smoke; to take in (air or liquid)

すう・数 *prf* several

すうがく・数学 *n* mathematics

すうじ・数字 *n* numbers

ずうずうしい・図々しい *adj* cheeky

スーツ *n* suit

スーツケース *n* suitcase

ずうっと *adv* continuously

スーパー *n* supermarket

スープ *n* soup

すえ・末 *n* end

すえっこ・末っ子 *n* youngest child

すえる・据える *vb 2* ⓔ to place

すがた・姿 *n* shape; figure (of)

スカート *n* skirt

スカーフ *n* scarf

ずかん・図鑑 *n* illustrated book; reference work

すき(な)・好き(な) **1** *adj* favourite/favorite; すきなよう
にする do as one pleases **!** *although an adjective in Japanese it
is often best translated using a verb such as 'to like';* テニスが
すきです (I) like tennis

すぎ・杉 *n* cedar

すぎ・過ぎ *suf* – adds the meaning of 'after' or 'more than' to nouns and (following the pre ～ます form) it adds the meaning of 'done to excess' to verbs; **ろくじすぎ** after six o'clock; **たべすぎ** overeating

スキー 1 *n* skis; skiing **2** *vb 3* ⑩ **スキーをする** to ski

すききらい・好き嫌い *n* likes and dislikes; **すききらいが ある** to be fussy

すきずき・好き好き *n* personal taste

すきとおる・透き通る *vb 1* ⑩ to be transparent

すきま・隙間 *n* a gap

すきまかぜ・隙間風 *n* a draft

すぎる・過ぎる *vb 2* ⑩ to be more than; to pass through ❗ added to verbs and adjectives to make compounds with the meaning '... too much'

すく・空く *vb 1* ⑩ **すいて すかない すきます** to not be crowded; to be empty; **おなかが すいている** to be hungry

すぐ・直ぐ *adv* immediately; soon; as soon as

すくう・救う *vb 1* ⑧ to save

すくない・少ない *adj* few

すくなくとも・少なくとも *adv* at least

すぐれる・優れる *vb 2* ⑩ to excel

スケート 1 *n* ice skating **2** *vb 3* ⑩ **スケートをする** to ice skate

スケートぐつ・スケート靴 *n* ice skates

スケジュール *n* schedule; plans

すごい・凄い *adj* tremendous; brilliant

すこし・少し *adv* a few; some; a short time; a little bit of

すこしも・少しも *adv* (with negative) (not) at all

すごす・過ごす *vb 1* ⑧ to pass; (of time) to spend

すじ・筋 *n* muscle; stripe; logic; reason; **すじが とおった** logical

すずしい・涼しい *adj* (pleasantly) cool

すすむ・進む *vb 1 ㊥* to make progress; to advance

すすめる・進める *vb 2 ㊦* to proceed with

すすめる・勧める・薦める *vb 2 ㊦* to advise; to recommend

スター *n* star

スタート *n* start

スタイル *n* style

スタジアム *n* stadium

スタジオ *n* studio

スタンド *n* desk light; stands

ずつ *suf* each

ずつう・頭痛 *n* headache

すっかり *adv* completely; perfectly

すっきり(した) *adjectival phrase* refreshing; clear

すっきり(する) *vb 3 ㊥* to feel refreshed

すって ▶ すう

すっと *adv* gently; quietly

ずっと *adv* directly; for a long time

すっぱい・酸っぱい *adj* sour

ステージ *n* stage (for performances)

すてき(な) *adj* lovely; nice

すでに・既に *adv* already

すてる・捨てる・棄てる *vb 2 ㊦* to throw away

ストーブ *n ~ a* free-standing room heater

ストッキング *n* stockings; tights

ストップ **1** *n* stop **2** *vb 3 ㊦* ストップする to stop

ストレス *n* stress

すな・砂 *n* sand

すなお・素直 **1** adj obedient **2** adv すなおに obediently

すなわち・即ち conj that is to say

ずのう・頭脳 suf brain

すばやい・素早い adj very quick

すばらしい・素晴らしい adj wonderful

スピーカー n speaker/s

スピーチ **1** n speech **2** vb 3 ㉚ スピーチ(を)する to make a speech

スピード n speed

ずひょう・図表 n chart

スプーン n spoon

スペース n space

すべて・全て n all (of them)

すべる・滑る vb 1 ㉚ to slip; to ski

スポーツ **1** n sport **2** vb 3 ㉚ スポーツ(を)する to do sport

ズボン n trousers

スマート(な) adj slim

すまい・住まい n home

すませる・済ませる vb 2 ㊉ to finish; to manage

すまない・済まない adj unpardonable **!** used as an informal apology for causing trouble to somebody
▶すみません

すみ・墨 n ink

すみ・炭 n charcoal

すみ・隅 n corner

すみます ▶ すむ

すみません phrase excuse me; sorry

すむ・住む *vb 1 ㊕* にすんで すまない すみます
to live (in)

すむ・済む *vb 1 ㊕* to be finished; to get through

すむ・澄む *vb 1 ㊕* to become clear

すもう・相撲 *n* sumo wrestling

ずらり(と) *adv* in a line

すり *n* pickpocket

スリッパ *n* slippers

する *vb 3 ㊂* して・しない・します！ *although the
principle meaning of this verb is 'to do' it has many uses and can
be translated as 'to play', "to put on', 'to cost', 'to decide to' and
'to be' as well as appearing in various constructions where it will
not be translated as a verb. It is used to transform nouns into
verbs. Try looking up the word|s with which it occurs. For more
on* する

ずるい *adj* unfair; sly

すると *conj* in that case; just at that moment

するどい・鋭い *adj* sharp

ずれ *n* discrepancy; lag

すれちがう・擦れ違う *vb 1 ㊕* to pass someone or
something coming from the opposite direction

すれる・擦れる *vb 2 ㊕* to rub

ずれる *vb 2 ㊕* to be out of place/position

すわって ▶ すわる

すわります ▶ すわる

すわる・座る *vb 1 ㊕* すわって・すわらない・すわり
ますto sit

すんで ▶ すむ

すんぽう・寸法 *n* measurements

せ セ

せ・背 *n* back; せが たかい tall

せい・背 *n* (person's) height

せい・性 *n and prf* gender

せい・性 *suf* character; nature

せい・姓 *n* surname

せい・所為 *n* (somebody's) fault

せい・製 *suf* made in ...; made of ...; made from ...

ぜい・税 *prf and suf* element tax

せいかく・性格 *n* character

せいかく・正確 **1** *adj* せいかく（な) accurate **2** *adv* せいかくに accurately

せいかつ・生活 *n* life (style)

ぜいかん・税関 *n* customs

せいき・世紀 *n and suf* century

せいきゅう・請求 **1** *n* demand; claim **2** *vb 3* を せいきゅうする to demand; to claim

せいきゅうしょ・請求書 *n* bill

ぜいきん・税金 *n* tax

せいけつ（な)・清潔（な) *adj* clean

せいげん・制限 **1** *n* restriction **2** *vb 3* を せいげんする to restrict

せいこう・成功 **1** *n* success **2** *vb 3* が せいこうする to succeed

せいさく・製作 **1** *n* manufacturing **2** *vb 3* を せいさくする to manufacture

せいさく・制作 **1** *n* production **2** *vb 3* 🐾 せいさくする
to produce

せいさく・政策 *n* policy

せいさん・生産 **1** *n* output **2** *vb 3* 🐾 せいさんする
to produce

せいじ・政治 *n* politics

せいじか・政治家 *n* politician

せいしき・正式 **1** *adj* せいしき (な) official **2** *adv* せい
しきに formally

せいしつ・性質 *n* nature; character

せいしょ・聖書 *n* (the) bible

せいしょうねん・青少年 *n* youth; young people

せいしん・精神 *n* spirit; mind

せいじん・成人 *n* adult **!** *adulthood begins at 20 in Japan*

せいじんしき・成人式 *n* – *ceremony marking coming of
age at 20*

せいしんてき・精神的 **1** *adj* せいしんてき (な) mental
2 *adv* せいしんてきに mentally

せいじんのひ・成人の日 *n* – *Coming of Age Day
(January 15) – a Japanese public holiday*

せいぜい・精々 *adv* at most; as much as possible

せいせき・成績 *n* (school or exam) results

せいせきひょう・成績表 *n* – *school report*

せいそう (する)・清掃 (する) *vb 3* 🐾 to clean

せいそうしゃ・清掃車 *n* garbage truck

せいぞう・製造 **1** *n* manufacture **2** *vb 3* 🐾 せいぞうする
to manufacture

せいぞん・生存 **1** *n* survival **2** *vb 3* 🐾 せいぞんする
to exist

せいぞんしゃ・生存者 *n* survivor

ぜいたく・贅沢 **1** *n* luxury **2** *adj* ぜいたく(な) luxurious
3 *adv* ぜいたくに luxuriously

せいちょう・成長 **1** *n* growth **2** *vb* ㋕ せいちょうする
to grow

せいてん・晴天 *n* fine weather

せいと・生徒 *n* school student

せいど・制度 *n* system

せいとう・政党 *n* political party

せいねん・青年 *n* young man; youth

せいねんがっぴ・生年月日 *n* date of birth

せいのう・性能 *n* performance

せいび・整備 **1** *n* maintenance **2** *vb* **3** ㋓ せいびする
to maintain; to repair

せいひん・製品 *n* article

せいふ・政府 *n* government

せいふく・制服 *n* uniform

せいぶつ・生物 *n* living thing

せいぶつがく・生物学 *n* biology (as a subject)

せいぶん・成分 *n* ingredients

せいべつ・性別 *n* distinction by gender

せいぼ・歳暮 ▶おせいぼ

せいめい・生命 *n* life

せいめい・姓名 *n* full name

せいもん・正門 *n* main entrance

せいよう・西洋 *prf* Western (style)

せいり・整理 **1** *n* putting in order **2** *vb* **3** ㋓ せいりする
to put in order

せいり・生理 *n* physiology; (menstrual) period

せいりつ・成立 **1** *n* formation **2** *vb* **3** ㋕ せいりつする
to come into existence

せいれき・西暦 *n* (western calendar) date ❗ *although the western calendar is also in widespread use, Japan still uses its own calendar system based on the ruling emperor and the number of years of his reign*

セーター *n* jumper/sweater

セール *n* sale

せおう・背負う *vb 1* 🅰 to carry (on the back)

せかい・世界 *n* world

せき・席 *n* seat

せき・咳 *n* cough; せきが でる to cough

せき・隻 *counter* ships

せきたん・石炭 *n* coal

せきどう・赤道 *n* equator

せきにん・責任 *n* responsibility

せきゆ・石油 *n* oil

せけん・世間 *n* the world

せけんばなし・世間話 *n* small talk

せじ・世辞 ▶ おせじ

せたい・世帯 *n* household

せだい・世代 *n* generation

せつ・説 *suf* explanation

せっかく・折角 1 *adv* specially **2** *adj* せっかくの valuable

せっきょくてき・積極的 1 *adj* せっきょくてき(な) positive **2** *adv* せっきょくてきに positively

せっきん・接近 1 *n* approach **2** *vb 3* 🅷 せっきんする to approach

セックス 1 *n* sex **2** *vb 3* 🅷 と セックス(を)する to have sex

せっけい・設計 1 *n* plan **2** *vb 3* 🅰 せっけいする to design

せっけん・石鹸 *n* soap

せっしょく・接触 1 *n* contact **2** *vb 3* かと せっしょく する to touch

せっする・接する *vb 3* かと to touch; to be in contact

せっせと *adv* hard

せつぞく・接続 1 *n* connection **2** *vb 3* か を せつぞくする to connect

ぜったい(に)・絶対(に) *adv* definitely; (*with negative*) absolutely (not)

セット *n* set

せっとく・説得 1 *n* persuasion **2** *vb 3* を せっとくする to persuade

せつび・設備 *n* equipment; facilities

せつめい・説明 1 *n* explanation **2** *vb 3* を せつめいする to explain

せつめいしょ・説明書 *n* instruction manual

ぜつめつ・絶滅 1 *n* extinction **2** *vb 3* か ぜつめつする to be extinct

せつやく・節約 1 *n* economisation **2** *vb 3* を せつやくする to economise

せつりつ・設立 1 *n* foundation **2** *vb 3* を せつりつする to found

せともの・瀬戸物 *n* porcelain; china

せなか・背中 *n* (person's) back

ぜひ・是非 1 *n* the rights and wrongs **2** *adv* without fail; definitely; no matter what

せびろ・背広 *n* suit (clothing)

せまい・狭い *adj* narrow; cramped ! used to mean 'small' when describing a room/house

せまる・迫る *vb 1* か to draw near ! often used with a sense of 'time pressing' and in the passive form it can mean 'to be under pressure'

せみ *n* cicada

ゼミ *n* seminar

せめて *adv* at least

せめる・責める *vb 2* ㉜ to blame

せめる・攻める *vb 2* ㉜ to attack

セメント *n* cement

ゼリー *n* jelly

せりふ・台詞 *n* lines (of a script)

ゼロ *n* zero

せろん・世論 *n* public opinion

せわ・世話 **1** *n* care **2** *vb 3* ㉜ せわする to look after
▶おせわに なりました

せん・千 *n, prf and suf* thousand

せん・線 *n and suf* line; railway line

せん・栓 *n* stopper; plug; cork

せん・戦 *suf* war

ぜん・善 *n* good

ぜん・全 *prf* all

ぜん・前 *prf* former

ぜん・前 *suf* before

ぜんいん・全員 *n* all (the members); everyone

せんきょ・選挙 **1** *n* election **2** *vb 3* ㉜ せんきょ(を)する
to elect

ぜんご・前後 *n* before and after; front and rear

ぜんご・前後 *suf* about

せんこう・専攻 **1** *n* subject (of study) **2** *vb 3* ㉜ せんこう
する to major (in)

ぜんこく・全国 *n and prf* nationwide

せんざい・洗剤 *n* detergent

せんじつ・先日 *n* the other day; a few days ago

せんしゃ・戦車 *n* tank

ぜんしゃ・前者 *n* the former

せんしゅ・選手 *n* – this word can be used on its own to mean a sportsman or sportswoman and is thus translated as 'player' or 'athlete' or other terms depending on the sport. Since it can also be plural in meaning another possible translation is 'team'. Also added as a suffix to individual family names as a title to address and refer to sportsmen and sportswomen.

せんしゅう・先週 *n* last week

ぜんしん・前進 1 *n* advance **2** *vb* **3** ㉞ ぜんしんする to advance

ぜんしん・全身 *n* the whole body; all over (the body)

せんす・扇子 *n* (folding) fan

センス *n* sense (of fashion etc.); (good) taste (in)

せんすい・潜水 *n and prf* underwater

せんすいかん・潜水艦 *n* submarine

せんせい・先生 *n and suf* – on its own the word is used to mean 'teacher' and 'doctor' and it is used as a way of addressing and referring to teachers, professors, doctors, politicians and lawyers either directly or as a title attached to a family name.

ぜんぜん・全然 *adv* (with negative) not at all; (with positive) completely

せんぞ・先祖 *n* ancestors

せんそう・戦争 *n* war

センター *n and suf* centre (as an institutional name)

ぜんたい・全体 *n* (the) whole

せんたく・洗濯 1 *n* (the) washing **2** *vb* **3** ㉛ せんたくする to wash (clothes)

せんたく・選択 1 *n* selection **2** *vb* **3** ㉛ せんたくする to choose

せんたくき・洗濯機 *n* washing machine

せんたくもの・洗濯物 *n* (the) washing; せんたくもの を ほす to hang the washing to dry

センチ *n* centimetre/s

センチメートル ▶ センチ

せんでん・宣伝 1 *n* advertisement; publicity **2** *vb 3* を せん でんする to advertise

せんてんてき・先天的 1 *adj* せんてんてき(な) innate **2** *adv* せんてんてきに naturally

せんとう・先頭 *n* head; lead

せんとう・銭湯 *n* – a public bath house often found in older residential areas of Japanese towns

せんぬき・栓抜き・栓抜 *n* bottle opener; corkscrew

せんぱい・先輩 *n* – a junior person in relation to a senior in either an educational establishment or the workplace. It is used alone to address people or can be attached to names as a title of address and reference ▶ こうはい

ぜんはん・前半 *n* first half (of a match etc.)

ぜんぱんてき・全般的 1 *adj* ぜんぱんてき(な) overall **2** *adv* ぜんぱんてきに generally

ぜんぶ・全部 *n* all; everything

せんぷうき・扇風機 *n* electric fan

せんめん・洗面 1 *n* washing (the face) **2** *vb 3* を せんめん (を)する to wash the face

せんめんじょ・洗面所 *n* washroom **!** *a place where there is a sink for washing the face and hands*

せんもん・専門 *n* academic subject; major

せんもんか・専門家 *n* specialist

ぜんりゃく・前略 *phrase* – used to open an informal letter and meaning something like 'this is just a quick note to say ...'

せんりょう・占領 1 *n* occupation **2** *vb 3* を せんりょう する to occupy

せんりょく・戦力 *n* military power

ぜんりょく・全力 *n* all one's strength; ぜんりょくを
つくす to try as hard as possible

せんろ・線路 *n* railway (track)

....

そ ソ

....

そ ▶ そう

ぞ *pt* – used to add emphasis to a statement, especially one
expressing intention. Used by males

ぞい・沿い *suf* – means 'running parallel to' some kind of line
of things such as a street or a river and translatable as ' along
the ...' or 'running along the ...'

そう *adv* that way; like that ▶ そういう ! very common in the
form そうです or informally just as そう (sometimes repeated
for emphasis) which is used to show agreement with a question
and translatable as 'that's right'. In the form そうですね it
indicates a hesitation in answering and can be translated as
'well' or 'let me see'. Take care to distinguish this from the noun
phrase そうです which is mentioned two entries below. In the
form そうですか or そうか it is used to indicate that new
information has been received by the listener and can be
thought of as roughly similar to 'really?', 'is that so?' or 'is that
right?'

そう・総 *prf* all; general

そう *n* – used in the form そうです or そうだ at the end of a
statement|sentence it means 'apparently' or 'it's said that ...' or 'I
heard that ...'; かいぎは あしただ そうです apparently the
meeting is tomorrow

ぞう・象 *n* elephant

そうい・相違 1 *n* difference **2** *vb 3* ㉚ そういする to differ

そういえば・そう言えば *phrase* by the way; speaking of which

そうおん・騒音 *n* (unpleasant) loud noise

ぞうか・増加 1 *n* increase **2** *vb 3* 例 を ぞうかする to increase

そうきん・送金 1 *n* money transfer **2** *vb 3* 例 そうきんする to send money

ぞうきん・雑巾 *n* cloth (for cleaning)

ぞうげん・増減 1 *n* fluctuation **2** *vb 3* 例 ぞうげんする to fluctuate

そうこ・倉庫 *n* warehouse; store room

そうご (の)・相互 (の) *n* (used as adjective) mutual

そうさ・操作 1 *n* operation (of a machine etc.) **2** *vb 3* 例 そうさする to operate

そうさ・捜査 1 *n* (criminal) investigation **2** *vb 3* 例 そうさする to investigate

そうさく・創作 1 *n* creation (of something) **2** *vb 3* 例 そうさくする to create

そうじ・掃除 1 *n* cleaning **2** *vb 3* 例 そうじする to clean

そうじき・掃除機 *n* vacuum cleaner; そうじきをかける to vacuum

そうしき・葬式 *n* funeral

そうして 1 *conj* and then **2** *adv* that way; like that

そうじゅう・操縦 1 *n* operation of controls (of plane or ship) **2** *vb 3* 例 そうじゅうする to pilot; to fly

そうじゅうし・操縦士 *n* pilot

そうすると▶そう

そうぞう・想像 1 *n* imagination **2** *vb 3* 例 そうぞうする to imagine

そうぞう・創造 1 *n* creation **2** *vb 3* 例 そうぞうする to create

そうぞうりょく・想像力 *n* imagination

そうぞうりょく・創造力 *n* creativity

そうぞうしい・騒々しい *adj* noisy

ぞうだい・増大 **1** *n* increase **2** *vb 3* ⓚ ぞうだいする
to increase

そうだん・相談 **1** *n* discussion **2** *vb 3* ⓦ そうだんする
to consult; to discuss

そうち・装置 *n* equipment; device

そうとう・相当 **1** *adv* considerably; quite **2** *adj* そうとう
(な)・そうとう(の) considerable

そうとう・相当 *suf* worth; equivalent to

そうば・相場 *n* exchange rate

そうべつかい・送別会 *n* – a formal farewell party

ぞうり・草履 *n* – flat sandals worn with きもの or for
*nipping out of a house (which means putting on and removing
footwear of some kind)*

そうりだいじん・総理大臣 *n* Prime Minister

そうりょう・送料 *n* postage (cost)

そく・足 *counter* pairs of (shoes or socks)

ぞく(する)・属(する) *vb 3* ⓚ to belong to; to be attached
to

ぞくぞく(と)・続々(と) *adv* one after another

そくたつ・速達 *n* express delivery (post)

そくてい・測定 **1** *n* measurement **2** *vb 3* ⓦ そくていする
to measure

そくど・速度 *n* speed

そくばく・束縛 **1** *n* restriction **2** *vb 3* ⓦ そくばくする
to restrict

そくりょう・測量 **1** *n* survey **2** *vb 3* ⓦ そくりょうする
to survey

そくりょうぎし・測量技師 *n* surveyor

そくりょく・速力 *n* speed

そこ *n* there; that

そこ・底 *n* bottom (of the sea etc.)

そこで *conj* so; therefore

そこなう・損なう *vb 1* 🅚 – on it's own the verb means 'to impair' and it is common as a suffix element on the pre **〜そう** form of verbs to add the meaning 'fail to (do)'

そしき・組織 *n* organisation; system

そしきてき・組織的 1 *adj* そしきてき(な) systematic **2** *adv* そしきてきに methodically

そしつ・素質 *n* qualities

そして *conj* and; and then

そせん・祖先 *n* ancestors

そそぐ・注ぐ *vb 1* 🅚 to pour

そそっかしい *adj* careless

そだち・育ち *suf* brought up in

そだつ・育つ *vb 1* 🅝 to grow up; to be brought up

そだって・育って ▶そだつ

そだてる・育てる *vb 2* 🅚 to bring up (children); to grow (vegetables)

そちら *n* over there; that one; that way; you

そっち *n* – informal version of そちら

そつぎょう・卒業 1 *n* graduation **2** *vb 3* 🅚 そつぎょうする to graduate

そっくり 1 *adj* そっくり(な)・そっくり(の) exactly like **2** *adv* entirely

そっちょく・率直 1 *adj* そっちょく(な) frank **2** *adv* そっちょくに candidly

そっと *adv* quietly; gently

そで・袖 *n* sleeve

そと・外 *n* outside; outdoors

そなえる・備える *vb 2* ⊛ に to prepare; to install

その *attributive* that; it ❢ meaning 'close to the listener' it is also often used to refer to something previously mentioned

そのうえ・その上 *conj* moreover

そのうち(に)・その内(に) *adv* soon; before long

そのころ *n* (about) then

そのとおり・その通り *phrase* you are right!

そのほか・その外・その他 *n* the rest

そのまえ(に)・その前(に) *adv* before that; in front of (it)

そのまま *phrase* as it is; straightaway

そば *n* side; beside; near

そば *n* – thin buckwheat noodles

そふ・祖父 *n* grandfather

ソファー *n* sofa; armchair

ソフト *n and adj n* software; soft

そぼ・祖母 *n* grandmother

そまつ・粗末 **1** *adj* そまつ(な) poor (quality); simple **2** *adv* そまつに roughly

そむく・背く *vb 1* ⊛ to disobey; to disregard

そら・空 *n* sky

そる・剃る *vb 1* ⊛ to shave

それ *n* that; it ❢ meaning 'close to the listener' it is also often used to refer to something previously mentioned

それから *conj* after that; since then

それぞれ *adv* each; respectively

それで *adv* and then; therefore

それでは *conj* in that case; well ❢ sometimes used informally to say 'I'm leaving', 'that's all' or 'let's go'

それでも *conj* but; even so

それと *conj* and; plus

それとも *conj* or

それなのに *conj* even so

それなら *conj* in that case

それに *conj* and; what's more

それほど *n* that many/much; so many/much

そろう・揃う *vb 1 ㋑* to be gathered; to be complete (as a group or set)

そろえる・揃える *vb 2 ㋒* to put in order; to arrange

そろそろ *adv* soon; almost ❗ *often used as an abbreviated form of* そろそろ しつれい します *meaning 'I must be going'*

そろばん・算盤 *n* abacus

そん・損 *n* disadvantage; loss

そん・損 1 *n* loss; disadvantage **2** *vb 3 ㋒* そんする to lose

そんがい・損害 *n* damage

そんけい・尊敬 1 *n* respect **2** *vb 3 ㋒* そんけいする to respect

そんけいご・尊敬語 *n* – respect language used towards older people and to be polite and deferential in general

そんざい・存在 1 *n* existence **2** *vb 3 ㋑* そんざいする to exist

ぞんざい 1 *adj* ぞんざい(な) rough **2** *adv* ぞんざいに roughly

ぞんじる・存じる *vb 3 ㋒* – humble equivalent of verbs しる and わかる and thus translatable as 'to know' or 'to think' ▶ごぞんじ

そんちょう・尊重 1 *n* respect **2** *vb 3 ㋒* そんちょうする to respect

そんな *attributive* such; like that

そんなに *adv* such; so much; (not all) that

た タ

た・田 *n* paddy field

た・他 *n* (the) other/s

だ – plain form of です and translatable as 'am', 'is' or 'are'

たい・対 *suf and prf* – placed between two two sets of numbers or two people|teams it means 'versus' or '(as opposed) to'. As a prefix it means 'concerning ...' or 'towards ...'

たい *suf* – added to the pre ～ます form of a verb it adds the meaning 'want to'

だい・大 *n* (a) large (one)

だい・台 *n* stand

だい・台 *counter* – used for large items such as vehicles, machines and (large) electrical goods

だい・題 *n* title

だい・第 *prf* – indicates ordinal numbers such as だいいち・第一 'the first' or だいさん・第三 'the third'

だい・代 *suf* – a bill (for gas, electricity, water or telephone)

たいいく・体育 *n* – this term covers physical education and sports as school and college subjects and sports and training more generally

たいいくかん・体育館 *n* sports hall; gymnasium

たいいくのひ・体育の日 *n* – Health and Sports Day (October 10) – a Japanese public holiday

だいいち・第一 **1** *n* the first; the most important **2** *adv* だいいち(に) first of all

だいいちじせかいたいせん・第一次世界大戦 *n* the first world war

たいいん・退院 **1** *n* coming out of hospital **2** *vb* 3 ㉗ たいいんする to leave hospital

たいおん・体温　*n* (body) temperature

たいおんけい・体温計　*n* thermometer (for the body)

たいかい・大会　*n* contest; convention

たいがく・退学　**1** *n* withdrawing from school/college **2** *vb* **3** ㉘ たいがくする to withdraw from school or college

だいがく・大学　*n* university

だいがくいん・大学院　*n* – this word is used in place of だいがく 'university' when referring to post-graduate work and study

たいがくしょぶん・退学処分　*n* expulsion from school/college

たいき・大気　*n* (the) atmosphere

だいきん・代金　*n* payment; amount

だいく・大工　*n* carpenter

たいくつ・退屈　**1** *adj* たいくつ(な) boring **2** *vb* **3** ㉘ たいくつする to be bored

たいけい・体系　*n* system

たいけいてき・体系的　**1** *adj* たいけいてき(な) systematic **2** *adv* たいけいてきに systematically

たいこ・太鼓　*n* – a traditional Japanese drum and the playing of Japanese drums as a style of music

たいざい・滞在　**1** *n* stay **2** *vb* **3** ㉘ に たいざいする to stay

たいざいきかん・滞在期間　*n* length of stay

たいさく・対策　*n* measures; countermeasures

たいし・大使　*n* ambassador

たいしかん・大使館　*n* embassy

だいじ・大事　**1** *adj* だいじ(な) important **2** *vb* **3** ㉜ だいじにする to treat well; to treat carefully

たいした・大した　*phrase* (as adj) (with positive) quite a ...; (with negative) not much of a ...

たいして・大して *adv* not very; not much

たいして・対して *phrase* – in the form 〜にたいして this is used to express ideas like 'towards', 'regarding' and 'about'. It can also be used to mean 'as opposed to' and 'in contrast to' when a contrast is stated

たいじゅう・体重 *n* body weight

たいじゅうけい・体重計 *n* – scales for measuring body weight

たいしょう・対象 *n* object; subject

たいしょう・対照 **1** *n* contrast **2** *vb 3* を と たいしょう する to compare; to contrast

だいしょう・大小 large and small; size

だいじょうぶ (な)・大丈夫 (な) *adj* OK; all right; safe

たいしょく・退職 **1** *n* retirement; resignation **2** *vb 3* の たいしょくする to retire; to resign

だいじん・大臣 *n* and *suf* (government) minister

たいする・対する *vb 3* の に to be against ▶ たいして

たいせい・体制 *n* system

たいせき・体積 *n* volume

たいせつ・大切 **1** *adj* たいせつ (な) important **2** *adv* たいせつに carefully

たいせん・大戦 *n* – used to mean a great war and especially to refer to the first and second world wars ▶ だいいちじせかいたいせん ▶ だいにじせかいたいせん

たいそう・体操 *n* gymnastics

だいそう・大層 *adv* greatly

だいたい・大体 **1** *n* general idea (of) **2** *adv* approximately; generally

たいてい・大抵 **1** *n* most (of) **2** *adv* generally

たいど・態度 *n* attitude

だいとうりょう・大統領 *n* President

だいどころ・台所 *n* kitchen

だいにじせかいたいせん・第二次世界大戦 *n* the second world war

たいはん・大半 *n* the greater part (of)

だいひょう・代表 *n* (a) representative

タイプ *n* type (of person)

タイプ 1 *n* typing **2** *vb 3* Ⓐ **タイプする** to type

だいぶ・大分 *adv* considerably; mostly

たいふう・台風 *n* typhoon

だいぶぶん・大部分 1 *n* most (of) **2** *adv* mostly

たいへん・大変 1 *adj* **たいへん(な)** hard; awful **2** *adv* very; extremely; **たいへんです** 'oh no'! ! *often used to describe something which might be translated as 'serious' or 'difficult'. Also used to show sympathy as in 'oh no, how awful!'*

たいほ・逮捕 1 *n* arrest **2** *vb 3* Ⓐ **たいほする** to arrest

タイマー *n* timer

タイミング *n* timing

だいめい・題名 *n* title

ダイヤ *n* timetable (for public transport); diamond

ダイヤル 1 *n* dial **2** *vb 3* Ⓐ **に ダイヤルする** to dial

たいよう・太陽 *n* the sun

たいら(な)・平ら(な) *adj* flat; level

だいり・代理 *n* representative; agent

だいりてん・代理店 *n* agency

たいりく・大陸 *n* continent

たいりつ・対立 1 *n* conflict **2** *vb 3* Ⓝ **に たいりつする** to be opposed

たいりょく・体力 *n* strength

たえず・絶えず *adv* continually

たえる・耐える *vb 2* Ⓝ **に** to endure

だえんけい・楕円形 *n* oval

たおす・倒す *vb 1* ㊊ to knock down

タオル *n* towel

たおれる・倒れる *vb 2* ㋩ to fall down

だが *conj* however

たかい・高い *adj* high; expensive

たがい・互い *n* each other ▶ おたがいに

たかめる・高める *vb 2* ㊊ to raise

たがやす・耕す *vb 1* ㊊ to plough

たから・宝 *n* treasure

たからくじ・宝くじ *n* lottery

だから *conj* therefore; so

だからこそ *phrase* therefore

たがる *suf* – added to the pre 〜ます of a verb to give the meaning 'wants to' when referring to people other than oneself ▶ たい ▶ がる

たき・滝 *n* waterfall

たきます ▶ たく

だきょう・妥協 **1** *n* compromise **2** *vb 3* ㋩ だきょうする to compromise

たく・炊く *vb 1* ㊊ to cook (rice)

だく・抱く *vb 1* ㊊ to hug

だくおんふ・濁音符 *n* – the two marks placed beside かな characters which change the pronunciation from 'ka' か to 'ga' が etc.

たくさん・沢山 *adv* a lot of

タクシー *n* taxi

たけ・竹 *n* bamboo

だけ *suf* only; just; できるだけ as much as possible

だげき・打撃 *n* (a) blow

だけど *conj* however

だけれども ▶ だけど

たしか・確か **1** *adv* perhaps **2** *adj* たしか(な) definite **3** *adv* たしかに definitely

たしかめる・確かめる *vb 2* 🉀 to confirm

だして ▶ だす

だします ▶ だす

たしょう・多少 **1** *n* large and small **2** *adv* some; a bit

たす・足す *vb 1* 🉀 to add

だす・出す *vb 1* 🉀 to hold out; to take out (of); to hand in; to put out; to send; to give out; to publish ❗ *commonly added to the pre ～ます form of verbs to add the meaning 'start to' or to indicating the direction of action as outwards*

たすう・多数 *n* a large number; majority

たすうけつ・多数決 *n* majority decision

たすかる・助かる *vb 1* 🄗 to be helped; to be rescued

たすける・助ける *vb 2* 🉀 to help; to rescue

たずねる・訪ねる *vb 2* 🉀 to visit

たずねる・尋ねる *vb 2* 🉀 to ask

ただ **1** *n* free of charge **2** *adv* only **3** *adj* ただの the only; merely **4** *conj* however

ただいま *adv* just now ❗ *also as a greeting phrase used when returning to the home or workplace having been away for a while. It is usually met with the response* おかえりなさい *and is translatable as either 'I'm home!' or 'I'm back!' depending on the context*

たたかい・戦い *n* battle; struggle

たたかう・戦う *vb 1* 🄗 と to fight; to struggle (against)

たたく・叩く *vb 1* 🉀 to hit; to beat

ただし・但し *conj* however

ただしい・正しい *adj* correct

ただちに・直ちに *adv* at once

たたみ・畳 *n* – flooring mats that are used inside Japanese homes and made from straw and rushes woven together

たたむ・畳む *vb 1* を to fold

たち・達 *suf* – added to words referring to people to make them specifically plural i.e. こども means 'child' or 'children' but こどもたち means 'children'

たちあがる・立ち上がる *vb 1* か to stand up

たちどまる・立ち止まる *vb 1* か to stop (and stand still)

たちば・立場 *n* standpoint; position

たちます ▶ たつ

たちまち *adv* swiftly

たちよる・立ち寄る *vb 1* か to drop in (at|on)

たつ・立つ *vb 1* か たって・たたない・たちます to stand; to rise

たつ・経つ *vb 1* か to pass

たつ・発つ *vb 1* か to depart

たつ・絶つ *vb 1* を to cut off

たっする・達する *vb 3* か に to reach (achieve)

たった *adv* only

だった – the past of だ which is a plain equivalent of です. Translatable as 'was' or 'were'.

だったら *conj* if that's the case ! added to nouns and な adjectives to form a conditional

たって ▶ たつ

だって *phrase* – an informal version of でも which is used to mean 'even' or give a sense of 'every' when giving examples and to emphasise negatives. Also used to mean 'but' or 'because' when explaining and making excuses.

たっぷり *adv* fully; lots of ! added to nouns to give the meaning 'plenty of'

たて・縦 *n* – the word means 'vertical plane' as opposed to
よこ 'horizontal plane' and is used both to mean 'vertical' and to
give length when talking of measurements and thus translatable
as 'long'

たて *suf* – adds the meaning of just (having been done) to a
preceding verb in the pre 〜ます form

たてがき・縦書き *n* – vertical writing (of Japanese) as used
in (formal) letters, books and newspapers

たてまえ・建前 *n* – what is said and done to be superficially
polite and agreable as opposed to what is really thought and
felt. ▶ ほんね

たてもの・建物 *n* (a) building

たてる・立てる・建てる *vb 2* Ⓖ to build; to put up;
to raise

だとう(な)・妥当(な) *adj* appropriate

たとえ *adv* even if

たとえ・例え *n* example; analogy

たとえば・例えば *adv* for example

たとえる *vb 2* Ⓖ に to compare

たな・棚 *n* shelf

たに・谷 *n* valley

たにん・他人 *n* other people

たね・種 *n* seed

たのしい・楽しい *adj* enjoyable

たのしみ・楽しみ *n* pleasure; たのしみに している
to be looking forward to ...

たのしみます ▶ たのしむ

たのしむ・楽しむ *vb 1* Ⓖ たのしんで・たのしまない
・たのしみます to look forward to

たのしんで・楽しんで ▶ たのしむ

たのみ・頼み *n* (a) request

たのみます ▶ たのむ

たのむ・頼む *vb 1* ⊛ たのんで・たのまない・たの
　みます to ask (something as a favour); to order

たのもしい・頼もしい *adj* reliable

たば・束 *counter* bunch (of)

たばこ・煙草 *n* cigarette; tobacco

たび・旅 *n* journey; travel

たび・度 *n* every time (something happens); occasion

たび・足袋 *n* – a kind of traditional Japanese footwear
　something like a sock with a sole

たびたび・度々 *adv* many times; repeatedly

ダブる *vb 1* ⑰ to overlap; to be double ❗ often used in the sense
　of something being done twice and thus unnecessarily

たぶん・多分 *adv* perhaps; possibly; probably

たべて ▶ たべる

たべます ▶ たべる

たべもの・食べ物 *n* food

たべる・食べる *vb 2* ⊛ たべて・たべない・たべます
　to eat

たま・球 *n* ball ❗ used in the sense of 'globe' or 'globular' it is
　also written 玉

たま・弾 *n* bullet

たま(に・の) ▶ たまに

たまご・卵 *n* egg

だます *vb 1* ⊛ to trick; to deceive

たまたま *adv* by chance

たまに *adv* occasionally

たまりません ▶ たまらない

たまらない *adj* unbearable ❗ as an auxiliary following the
　～て form of the verb it adds the meaning 'unbearably' or

'unrestrainedly' and can suggest eagerness to do something.
It is translatable as *'be dying to (do something)'*

たまる・溜まる *vb 1* ㋑ to be accumulated

たまる・貯まる *vb 1* ㋑ to be saved up

だまる・黙る *vb 1* ㋑ to say nothing

ダム *n* dam

ため・為 *n* for the sake of; for the purpose of; because of

だめ(な)・駄目(な) *adj* useless; forbidden; broken; だめに
なる to be ruined ❗だめ(だ) can mean *'No!'* or that something
is forbidden or otherwise *'wrong'* or not as it should be

ためいき・溜め息 *n* sigh

ためし・試し **1** *n* trial **2** *adv* ためしに experimentally

ためす・試す *vb 1* ㋦ to try out

ために ▶ ため

ためらう *vb 1* ㋑ ㋦ to hesitate

ためる・貯める *vb 2* ㋦ to amass (money)

ためる・溜める *vb 2* ㋦ to store up

たもつ・保つ *vb 1* to maintain; to preserve

たより・便り *n* – means news of/from someone and is often
translatable as *'letter'*

たより・頼り *n* dependability; たよりに なる reliable;
たよりにならない unreliable

たよる・頼る *vb 1* に to rely (on)

たら *suf* – created by adding ら to the past form of verb or
adjective it can indicate meanings *'if'* and *'when'* and is used in
a number of expressions such as ～たら どうですか
meaning *'how about (doing ...)?'* or *'why don't you ...'*.

だらけ *suf* – adds the sense of *'being covered with'* or *'being full
of'* with a negative nuance

だらしない *adj* untidy; slovenly

たり *suf* – usually appearing as an ending on the pre 〜ます stem of a pair of verbs (or more) and followed by **する** it indicates that the actions were simultaneous, in succession or just part of all those that took place and translatable as 'and so on' or 'and things like that'. These forms can also express opposites.

たりる・足りる *vb 2 ㊉* to be sufficient

だるい *adj* dull; listless

たれる・垂れる *vb 2 ㊉* to be dangling; to hang down

だれ・誰 *n* who

だれか・誰か *n* someone; anyone

だれも・誰も *phrase (with a negative)* no one

タレント *n* star (entertainer)

だろう – plain form of でしょう *often translatable as 'I suppose' and also used to get confirmation from the listener that what is being said is correct so translatable as 'isn't it?', 'aren't they?', 'haven't they?', 'didn't he?' etc.*

だん・段 *step* step

だん・団 *suf* group

たんい・単位 *n* unit; credit unit at university or college

だんかい・段階 *n* stage

たんき(な)・短気(な) *adj* short tempered

たんき・短期 *n* a short period of time

たんきかん・短期間 *n* a short period of time

たんきだいがく・短期大学 ▶たんだい

たんご・単語 *n* word

だんし・男子 *n* boy; male

たんじゅん・単純 1 *adj* たんじゅん(な) simple **2** *adv* たんじゅんに simply

たんしょ・短所 *n* weak point

たんじょう・誕生 *n* birth

たんじょうび・誕生日 *n* birthday; たんじょうび おめでとう Happy Birthday!

たんしんふにん・単身赴任 *n* – a posting to a workplace in another city or country which entails living away from the family

たんす *n* chest of drawers; wardrobe

ダンス 1 *n* dancing; dance **2** *vb 3 ㉗* ダンス(を)する to dance

たんすい・淡水 *n* fresh water

だんせい・男性 *n* man; male

だんせいてき(な)・男性的(な) *adj* male

たんそ・炭素 *n* carbon

たんだい・短大 *n* – an abbreviation of たんきだいがく a junior college where the courses last for 2 years

だんたい・団体 *n* group

だんたいりょこう・団体旅行 *n* a group tour; package holiday

だんだん・段々 *adv* gradually

だんち・団地 *n* – an estate of apartment housing in public ownership

たんちょう(な)・単調(な) *adj* monotonous

だんてい・断定 1 *n* decision **2** *vb 3 ㉗* だんていする to decide

たんとう・担当 1 *n* (person) in charge; responsibility (for) **2** *vb 3 ㉗* たんとうする to be in charge of

たんとうしゃ・担当者 *n* person in charge

だんな・旦那 *n* (one's own) husband

だんなさん・旦那さん *n* (someone else's) husband

たんなる・単なる *phrase* nothing more than

たんに・単に *adv* simply

たんぱくしつ・蛋白質 *n* protein

たんぺん・短編 *n* short story

たんぺんしゅう・短編集 *n* collection (book) of short stories

たんぼ・田んぼ・田圃 *n* rice paddy

だんぼう・暖房 *n* heater

だんりょく(せい)・弾力(性) *n* elasticity

ちチ

ち・血 *n* blood

ち・地 *n* (the) ground

ちあん・治安 *n* – this word means 'safety' with reference to issues of law and order and crime; ちあんが いい safe; ちあんが わるい unsafe

ちい・地位 *n* position; standing

ちいき・地域 *n* area

ちいさい・小さい *adj* small

ちいさな・小さな *adj* small

チーズ *n* cheese

チーム *n* team

チームワーク *n* teamwork

ちえ・知恵 *n* intelligence; sense

ちか・地下 *n* underground

ちかい・近い *adj* close

ちがい・違い *n* difference

ちがいない・違いない *adj* certain; definite ❗ *usually in the form* 〜に ちがいない

ちがいます・違います *phrase – means 'No!' or 'Wrong!'*
▶ちがう

ちかう・誓う *vb 1 ⓔ* to swear (promise)

ちがう・違う *vb 1 ⓝ* to be different; to be wrong

ちかく・近く 1 *n* neighbourhood **2** *adv* almost; soon ! *the translation will vary depending on the context but 'around', 'local' and 'close to' are possible renderings and if no reference point is supplied it means 'around here'.*

ちかごろ(の)・近頃(の) *n* recently

ちかづく・近づく *vb 1 ⓝ* to approach; to draw near

ちかづける・近づける *vb 2 ⓔ* to bring nearer

ちがって ▶ちがう

ちかてつ・地下鉄 *n – an underground railway so variously translatable as 'subway', 'metro', 'underground' etc.*

ちかよる・近寄る *vb 1 ⓝ* to get near (to)

ちから・力 *n* power; strength; ability; ちからを いれる to make an effort

ちからづよい・力強い *adj* powerful

ちきゅう・地球 *n* the earth (world)

ちきゅうおんだんか・地球温暖化 *n* global warming

ちぎる・契る *vb 1 ⓔ* to swear (promise)

ちぎる・千切る *vb 1 ⓔ* to tear into pieces

ちく・地区 *n* area

ちくいち・逐一 *adv* in detail

ちくさん・畜産 *n* farming (animals)

ちくしょう・畜生 *n – a (somewhat) vulgar expression of annoyance and disappointment used in situations where many English speakers would probably swear*

ちこく(する)・遅刻(する) *vb 3 ⓝ* to be late

ちこくしゃ・遅刻者 *n* latecomer

ちじ・知事 *n* governor (of a state or prefecture)

ちしき・知識 *n* knowledge

ちしつ・地質 *n* geology (of)

ちしつがく・地質学 *n* geology (subject)

ちじん・知人 *n* acquaintance

ちず・地図 *n* map

ちせい・知性 *n* intelligence

ちせいてき(な)・知性的(な) *adj* intelligent

ちたい・地帯 *n* zone

ちち・父 *n* (one's own) father

ちちおや・父親 *n* (one's own) father

ちぢむ・縮む *vb 1 ⑰* to shrink

ちぢめる・縮める *vb 2 ⑱* to shrink (something)

ちぢれる・縮れる *vb 2 ⑰* to become curled (hair)

ちつじょ・秩序 *n* order

ちっそ・窒素 *n* nitrogen

ちっとも *adv* (with negative) utterly (not)

チップ *n* tip; gratuity

ちてき(な)・知的(な) *adj* intellectual

ちてん・地点 *n* place; spot

ちのう・知能 *n* intelligence

ちへいせん・地平線 *n* horizon

ちほう・地方 *n* district; region ❗ *often used with a sense of 'rural' or 'local' to describe areas both geographically distant from a centre and for 'local' government or businesses and organisations having a regional focus.*

ちめい・地名 *n* (place) name

ちめいてき(な)・致命的(な) *adj* fatal

ちゃ・茶 *n* tea

ちゃいろ・茶色 **1** *n* brown **2** *adj* ちゃいろの brown

ちゃいろい・茶色い *adj* brown

ちゃく・着 *suf* arrival

ちゃく・着 *counter* suits; dresses

ちゃくじつ・着実 **1** *adj* ちゃくじつ（な）steady **2** *adv* ちゃくじつに steadily

ちゃくしゅ・着手 **1** *n* commencement **2** *vb 3* ㋕ ちゃくしゅする to commence

ちゃくせき（する）・着席（する）*vb 3* ㋕ to sit down

ちゃくちゃく（と）・着々（と）*adv* steadily

ちゃくばらい・着払い *n* payment on delivery

ちゃくりく・着陸 **1** *n* (of a plane) landing **2** *vb 3* ㋕ ちゃくりくする (of a plane) to land

ちゃのま・茶の間 *n* living room

ちゃのゆ・茶の湯 *n* tea ceremony ▶ さどう

ちゃぶだい・卓袱台 *n* – a small low table used for traditional Japanese dining

チャレンジ **1** *n* (a) challenge; try **2** *vb 3* ㋕ に チャレンジ する to attempt

ちゃわん・茶碗 *n* bowl for rice; (tea) cup

ちゃん *suf* – attached to names to give an informal or affectionate form of reference. Used especially with children's and girls' names.

ちゃんと *adv* properly

ちゃんとした *adj* proper

チャンネル *n* TV channel

ちゅう・中 *n* medium

ちゅう・中 *suf* in the middle (of)

ちゅうい・注意 **1** *n* warning; care; attention **2** *vb 3* ちゅういする to take care; to warn; to tell off

ちゅういぶかい・注意深い *adj* cautious

ちゅうおう・中央 *n* (the) centre

ちゅうがく・中学 ▶ ちゅうがっこう

ちゅうがくせい・中学生 *n* – student at a middle school or junior high school

ちゅうがっこう・中学校 *n* – a middle school or junior high school (ages 12 to 15)

ちゅうかん・中間 *n* midway

ちゅうこ・中古 *adj* second-hand

ちゅうこしゃ・中古車 *n* second-hand car

ちゅうこひん・中古品 *n* second-hand item

ちゅうこく・忠告 1 *n* advice **2** *vb 3* を にちゅうこくする to advise

ちゅうごく・中国 *n* China ! beware of confusion with an area of Japan called ちゅうごくちほう and sometimes referred to by this name

ちゅうごくご・中国語 *n* Chinese (language)

ちゅうし・中止 ちゅうしに なる to be called off **2** *vb 3* を ちゅうしする to call off

ちゅうしゃ・注射 1 *n* injection **2** *vb 3* を ちゅうしゃする to inject

ちゅうしゃ・駐車 1 *n* parking **2** *vb 3* か ちゅうしゃする to park

ちゅうしゃじょう・駐車場 *n* car-park

ちゅうじゅん・中旬 *n* the middle ten days of the month

ちゅうしょうてき(な)・抽象的(な) *adj* abstract

ちゅうしょく・昼食 *n* lunch

ちゅうしん・中心 *n* centre

ちゅうだん・中断 1 *n* interruption **2** *vb 3* か を ちゅうだんする to be interrupted; to interrupt

ちゅうと・中途 *n* midway

ちゅうとう・中東 *n* the Middle East

ちゅうねん・中年 *n* middle age

ちゅうもく・注目 1 *n* attention **2** *vb 3* か を にちゅうもくする to pay attention (to)

ちゅうもん・注文 1 *n* order (goods or food) **2** *vb* **3** ⊛ ちゅうもんする to order (goods or food)

ちょう・蝶 *n* butterfly

ちょう・長 *suf* – added to nouns to denote someone in charge and so translatable as 'head ...'.or 'chief ...'

ちょう・兆 *n* – 'trillion' (U.S) or 'billion' (U.K)

ちょう・町 *suf* – used with place names it denotes either a town or an area of a city

ちょう・庁 *suf* – government agency

ちょうか・超過 1 *n* excess **2** *vb* **3** ⊛ ちょうかする to exceed

ちょうかん・長官 *n* director

ちょうき・長期 *n and prf* – used alone to mean 'a long period of time' and translatable as 'long term ...' in compounds

ちょうこく・彫刻 *n* sculpture; carving

ちょうさ・調査 1 *n* survey **2** *vb3* ⊛ ちょうさする to carry out a survey

ちょうし・調子 *n* condition; manner; health; ちょうしがいい in good condition; working well; ちょうしがわるい in poor condition; not working properly

ちょうしょ・長所 *n* strong point; merit

ちょうじょ・長女 *n* eldest daughter ! can be used even if there is only one daughter

ちょうじょう・頂上 *n* summit

ちょうせい・調整 1 *n* adjustment **2** *vb 3* ⊛ ちょうせいする to adjust

ちょうせつ・調節 1 *n* adjustment; control **2** *vb 3* ⊛ ちょうせつする to control; to adjust

ちょうだい・頂戴 – used as an informal version of ください meaning '(please) give me' or '(please) do ... for me'. Also used as a humble verb in the form ちょうだいする which means 'to receive' or 'to have (food and drink)'

ちょうてん・頂点 *n* peak

ちょうど *adv* exactly; just

ちょうなん・長男 *n* the eldest son ❗ can be used even if there is only one son

ちょうみりょう・調味料 *n* seasoning

ちょうめ・丁目 *suf* – a numbered area of a Japanese town used as a subdivision in addresses

ちょうり・調理 *n* cooking

ちょうりし・調理師 *n* chef

ちょうりほう・調理法 *n* cooking instructions

チョーク *n* chalk

ちょきん・貯金 **1** *n* savings **2** *vb 3* Ⓔ **ちょきんする** to save

ちょくご・直後 *n* immediately after

ちょくせつ・直接 **1** *adv* directly; immediately **2** *adj* ちょくせつの immediate; direct

ちょくせつてき・直接的 **1** *adj* ちょくせつてき(な) direct **2** *adv* ちょくせつてきに directly

ちょくせん・直線 *n* straight line

ちょくぜん・直前 *n and suf* immediately before

ちょくつう・直通 *prf* through (train); direct (dial)

ちょくめん(する)・直面（する） *vb 3* Ⓔ に to face

ちょくやく・直訳 *n* literal translation

ちょこ・猪口 *n* – a small cup used for drinking さけ

チョコレート *n* chocolate

ちょしゃ・著者 *n* author

ちょっかく・直角 *n* right angle

ちょっけい・直径 *n* diameter

ちょっと *adv* slightly; just a little; somewhat; ちょっとまってください please wait a moment ❗ often used to make expressions softer in tone and not always requiring translation.

Another common use of the word is as a way of expressing hesitation, doubt or disapproval. Depending on the context the word itself can be a clear refusal of a request in the sense of 'I'm sorry but ..'

ちらかす・散らかす *vb 1* ㊥ to scatter; to make a mess

ちらかる・散らかる *vb 1* ㋺ to be scattered; to be untidy

ちらす・散らす *vb 1* ㊥ to scatter

ちり *n* dust; dirt

ちり・地理 *n* geography

ちりがく・地理学 *n* geography (subject)

ちりがみ・ちり紙 *n* tissue (paper)

ちりとり・ちり取り *n* dustpan

ちりょう・治療 1 *n* medical treatment **2** *vb 3* ㊥ **ちりょうする** to treat

ちる・散る *vb 1* ㋺ to fall (leaves etc.); to scatter

ちんぎん・賃金 *n* wages

ちんつうざい・鎮痛剤 *n* painkiller

しんぼつ・沈没 1 *n* sinking **2** *vb 3* ㋺ **ちんぼつする** to sink

ちんもく・沈黙 *n* silence

ちんれつ・陳列 1 *n* display **2** *vb 3* ㊥ **ちんれつする** to exhibit

つツ

つい *adv* just; carelessly; by mistake

ついか・追加 1 *n* supplement **2** *vb 3* ㊥ **ついかする** to add

ついたち・一日 *n* the first day of the month

ついて ▶ **つく**

～について about (concerning); per

ついで・序で ついでの とき whenever it is convenient
▶ついでに

ついで・次いで *adv* next

ついでに・序でに *adv* on the way; while (doing something else)

ついに・終に・遂に *adv* at last

ついやす・費やす *vb 1* 窗 に to spend

ついらく・墜落 1 *n* (aeroplane) crash **2** *vb 3* か ついらくする to crash (aeroplane or helicopter)

つう・通 *counter* – used for letters and documents

つうか(する)・通過(する) *vb 3* か to pass through

つうか・通貨 *n* currency

つうがく・通学 1 *n* travelling to school **2** *vb 3* か つうがくする to go to school

つうきん・通勤 1 *n* travelling to work **2** *vb 3* か つうきんする to commute

つうきんじかん・通勤時間 *n* commuting time

つうきんでんしゃ・通勤電車 *n* commuter train

つうこう・通行 1 *n* traffic; passage **2** *vb 3* か つうこうする to pass (along)

つうこうどめ・通行止め *n* no through road

つうこうにん・通行人 *n* passer-by

つうじて・通じて – a form of つうじる used in certain expressions with the sense of 'through' or 'by'

つうじる・通じる *vb 2* か to make (oneself) understood; to get through (on the telephone); to be connected (by); to be well informed (about)

つうしん・通信 1 *n* communication; correspondence **2** *vb 3* か つうしんする to communicate

つうしんきょういく・通信教育 *n* correspondence course

つうしんはんばい・通信販売 *n* mail order (selling)

つうち・通知 **1** *n* notification **2** *vb 3* 🈂 つうちする
to notify

つうちひょう・通知表 *n* (school) report card

つうちょう・通帳 *n* bank book; pass book

つうやく・通訳 **1** *n* interpreting; interpreter **2** *vb 3* 🈂
つうやくする to interpret

つうやくしゃ・通訳者 *n* interpreter

つうよう(する)・通用(する) *vb 3* 🈶 to be valid

つうろ・通路 *n* aisle; passage

つえ・杖 *n* walking stick

つかい・使い *n* errand

・づかい *suf* – adds the meaning 'use'

つかいかけ(の)・使い掛け(の) *adj* partly used

つかいかた・使い方 *n* way of using

つかいすて (の)・使い捨て(の) *adj* disposable

つかいます ▶ つかう

つかいみち・使い道 *n* use

つかう・使う・遣う *vb 1* 🈂 つかって・つかわない
・つかいます to use; to spend

つかって ▶ つかう

つかまえる・捕まえる *vb 2* 🈂 to catch; to arrest

つかまる・捕まる *vb 1* 🈶 to be caught; to be arrested

つかむ・掴む *vb 1* 🈂 to grab; to take hold of; to grip

つかれ・疲れ *n* tiredness

つかれて ▶ つかれる

つかれます ▶ つかれる

つかれる・疲れる *vb 2* 🈶 to get tired; to be tired

つき・月 *n* month; moon

つき・付き *suf* with

つぎ・次 *n* next; つぎから つぎへ one after another

つきあい・付き合い *n* acquaintance

つきあう・付き合う *vb 1* ㊾ と to associate with **!** *often used in the form* つきあっている *to mean 'to be going out with', 'to have a relationship with'*

つきあたり・突き当たり *n* end

つきあたる・突き当たる *vb 1* ㊾ to run into

つぎつぎ・次々 *adv* one after another

つきひ・月日 *n* time

つきそい・付き添い *n* (being in) attendance; (being in) accompaniment

つきそう・付き添う *vb 1* ㊾ に to attend; to accompany

つきとめる・突き止める *vb 2* ㊧ to find out

つきます ▶ つく

つく・着く *vb 1* ㊾ to arrive; to reach

つく・付く *vb 1* ㊾ to be stuck (to); to be attached; to be included; to be with; to be stained (with/by)

つく・就く *vb 1* に to take (a job)

つく・吐く *vb 1* ㊧ to tell (a lie)

つく・点く *vb 1* ㊾ to light; to catch fire; to come on

つく・突く *vb 1* ㊧ to poke

つぐ・注ぐ *vb 1* ㊧ to pour

つぐ・次ぐ *vb 1* ㊾ に to be next

つくえ・机 *n* desk

つくす・尽くす *vb 1* ㊧ to use up

つくって ▶ つくる

つくり・造り・作り *n* construction

つくり・旁 *n* – the right hand part of a かんじ *character*

つくる・作る *vb 1* ⓦ つくって・つくらない・つくります to make; to form; to grow

つくる・造る *vb 1* ⓦ to build; to create

つけ *suf* – used to show an attempt to recall something and so translatable as 'wasn't it ...?', 'haven't we...?' or 'what was it again?'. Very commonly with the sense of '(what) did you say?' or '(where) did you say (it was)?' etc. Related to particle か

つけて ▶ つける

つけもの・漬物 *n* – traditional Japanese pickled vegetables served as a side dish with a main meal

つける・付ける *vb 2* ⓦ つけて・つけない・つけます to attach; to install; to spread (butter etc.); てんを つける to mark (homework etc.)

つける・着ける *vb 2* ⓦ to put on; to wear

つける・点ける *vb 2* ⓦ (a light or machine) to turn on; (a fire) to light

つごう・都合 *n* convenience; circumstances; つごうが いい convenient; つごうが つく to be convenient; つごうを つける to manage to ! the phrase つごうが わるい is used to refuse requests and may be translatable as 'I'm very sorry but I am unable to ... at that time'

つじつま・辻褄 つじつまが あう to be consistent; つじつまが あわない to be inconsistent

つたえる・伝える *vb 2* ⓦ to tell; to transmit

つたわる・伝わる *vb 1* ⓚ to be transmitted

つち・土 *n* soil

つつ *suf* – attached to the pre ～ます form of a verb it adds the meaning 'while' or 'continuing to'

つづき・続き *n* continuation

つづく・続く *vb 1* ⓚ to continue ! added to the pre ～ます form of a verb as a suffix to mean 'continuing to ...'

つづける・続ける *vb 2* ⓦ to continue ! added to the pre ～ます form of a verb as a suffix to mean 'to continue to ...'

つっこむ・突っ込む *vb 1* を to thrust (into)

つつしむ・慎む *vb 1* を to be careful **!** *has a range of uses which generally mean 'to exercise self-control'*

つつみ・包み ▶こづつみ

つつむ・包む *vb 1* を to wrap

って *suf* – an abbreviated from of ～と いった *meaning '(somebody) said (that) ...'*

つとめ・勤め *n* work; duties

つとめさき・勤め先 *n* place of work

つとめる・勤める *vb 2* を に to work (for) **!** *implies long term work*

つとめる・努める *vb 2* か に to try hard to...

つな・綱 *n* rope

つながり・繋がり *n* connection; context

つながる・繋がる *vb 1* か to be connected

つなぐ・繋ぐ *vb 1* を to connect; join

つなげる・繋げる ▶つなぐ

つなみ・津波 *n* tidal wave

つねに・常に *adv* always

つばさ・翼 *n* wing

つぶ・粒 *n* grain (of)

つぶす・潰す *vb 1* を to crush; じかんを つぶす to kill time

つぶる *vb 1* を to shut (eyes)

つぶれる・潰れる *vb 2* か to be crushed

つま・妻 *n* (one's own) wife

つまずく・躓く *vb 1* か to trip; to stumble

つまらない *adj* bored; boring; worthless **!** *used in the set expression* つまらないものですが *when giving a gift and translatable as 'it's just a little something'*

つまり・詰まり *conj* in other words

つまる・詰まる *vb 1 ㊥* to be blocked; to be stuffed full of

つみ・罪 *n* guilt; sin; offence

つむ・積む *vb 1 ㊦* to pile up; to load

つめ・爪 *n* nail; claw

つめたい・冷たい *adj* cool; cold

つめる・詰める *vb 2 ㊦* to pack (in)

つもり *n* intention **!** added to forms of the verb to make
sentences with meanings like 'intend to ...' and 'plan to ...'.

つもる・積もる *vb 1 ㊥* to be piled up

つや・艶 *n* shine; lustre

つゆ・露 *n* dew

つゆ・梅雨 *n* – the Japanese rainy season (June-July)

つゆ *n* – sauce for dipping noodles or soup

つよい・強い *adj* strong

つよき・強気 **1** *adj* つよき(な) brave; aggressive **2** *adv*
つよきに bravely; aggressively

つよまる・強まる *vb 1 ㊥* to become strong(er)

つよめる・強める *vb 2 ㊦* to strengthen

つらい・辛い *adj* hard; bitter

づらい・辛い *suf* – when added to the pre ～ます form of a
verb it adds the meaning 'hard to ...'

つり・釣り *n* fishing; change ▶ おつり

つりあう・釣り合う *vb 1 ㊥* to be balanced; to be in
proportion

つる・釣る *vb 1 ㊦* to catch (a fish)

つる・吊る *vb 1 ㊦* to hang

つる・鶴 *n* crane (bird)

つるす・吊るす *vb 1 ㊦* to hang

つれて *adv* ～につれて as; in accordance with

つれ・連れ *n* companion

つれて・連れて ▶つれる

つれていく・連れて行く・連れていく *vb 1* 🅔
to take (a person)

つれてくる・連れてくる・連れて来る *vb 3* 🅔
to bring (a person)

つれる *vb 2* 🅔 to take/bring (a person) ▶つれていく
▶つれてくる

....

てテ

....

て・手 *n* hand; way (of doing); てが かかる to take time;
てが とどく to reach; ても あしも でない to be helpless;
てを うつ to take steps (to sort out); てを だす to hold out
the hand to begin; てを ぬく to cut corners

て・手 *suf* – added to pre ～ます form some verbs to indicate
'person who does ...' i.e. ききて listener

～て *suf* – a form of the verb or adjective allowing other words to
be added and supplementary meanings created

で *pt* (location of an action) at; in; on; (method or means) by; with;
(cause or reason) because of; by; (describing materials used)
from; with; (describing a limited time or space or group) in;
(describing prices or quantities of things or people) for; by
❗ particles show the grammatical functions of words and the
context will determine an appropriate English translation which
may vary considerably for the same particle in different uses.
The above are a few of the more common possibilities.

で – the ～て form of です/だ which is used to join sentences
together and can be translated as 'and' or 'is ... and' among
other things.

であい・出会い *n* meeting; encounter

であう・出会う vb 1 ⓐ と to meet; to encounter

てあて・手当て n allowance

てあらい・手洗い n toilet

である a version of です used in writing and formal speech situations

てい・低 prf low

ていあん・提案 n proposal

ていいん・定員 n (full) capacity

ていか・低下 1 n decline **2** vb **3** ⓐ ていかする to decline

ていか・定価 n (retail) price

ていき・定期 n fixed period of time; ▶ていきけん

ていきけん・定期券 n season ticket for bus or train

ていきゅうび・定休日 n – the day or days which a shop or restaurant is closed on a regular basis and translatable as 'closed on ...'

ていきょう・提供 1 n ! although translatable as 'offer' it is most commonly used to describe sponsors or advertisers and translatable as 'support' or 'sponsorship' **2** vb **3** ⓐ ていきょうする to provide

ていこう・抵抗 1 n resistance **2** vb **3** ⓐ ていこうする to oppose

ていし・停止 1 n stop; suspension **2** vb **3** ⓐ ていしする to stop; to suspend

ていしゃ(する)・停車(する) vb **3** ⓐ to stop

ていしゃえき・停車駅 n (train) stop

ていしゅつ・提出 1 n submission (of) **2** vb **3** ⓐ ていしゅつする to hand in

ティシュ(ペーパー) n tissue (paper)

ていしょく・定食 n – a set menu in a restaurant

ていでん・停電 1 n power cut **2** vb **3** ⓐ ていでんする to be cut off (electric power)

ていど・程度 *n* extent; degree

ていねい・丁寧 1 *adj* ていねい（な）polite; careful; kind **2** *adv* ていねいに politely; carefully; kindly

ていねいご・丁寧語 *n* – polite speech forms used in Japanese

ていねん・定年 *n* retirement age

でいり・出入り *n* coming and going (in and out)

でいりぐち・出入り口 *n* entrance and exit

ていりゅうじょう・停留場 *n* bus stop

ていれ・手入れ 1 *n* care **2** *vb 3* ⑧ ていれ（を）する to care for; to repair

データ *n* data

データベース *n* database

デート 1 *n* a date **2** *vb 3* ⑰ とデートする to have a date; to go out with

テープ *n* tape

テーブル *n* table

テープレコーダー *n* tape recorder

テーマ *n* theme

でかけて ▶ でかける

でかける・出かける・出掛ける *vb 2* ⑰ でかけて・でかけない・でかけます to go out

でかけます ▶ でかける

てがみ・手紙 *n* letter

てがる・手軽 1 *adj* てがる（な）easy **2** *adv* てがるに easily

てき・敵 *n* enemy

てき・的 *suf* – added to some nouns it produces an adjective or adverb (depending on the particle used) with the meaning 'being ...' , 'of the character of' or '...like'. Similar to English endings -al and -ally in words like 'political/politically' and 'educational/educationally'.

でき・出来 *n* workmanship; finish

できあがり・出来上がり *n* completion

できあがる・出来上がる *vb 1 ㋟* to be completed

てきかく・的確 **1** *adj* てきかく(な) accurate **2** *adv* てきかくに precisely

できごと・出来事 *n* event; happening

テキスト *n* textbook

てきする・敵する *vb 3 ㋟* に to be suitable (for)

てきせつ・適切 **1** *adj* てきせつ(な) appropriate; suitable **2** *adv* てきせつに appropriately

できたて・出来立て *phrase* just made

できて ▶ できる

てきとう・適当 **1** *adj* てきとう(な) suitable **2** *adv* てきとうに suitably ❗ *sometimes used in the sense of 'not making an effort' or 'taking it easy'*

できます ▶ できる

てきよう・適用 **1** *n* application **2** *vb 3 ㋠* てきようする to apply

できる・出来る *vb 2 ㋟* できて・できない・できます to be able to; to be possible; to be made (of)from); to appear; to be formed ❗ *can be used in the expression 〜ことが できる after the dictionary form of a verb to mean 'can ...' which is an alternative to the potential form of the verb*

できるだけ・出来るだけ *phrase* as much as possible; as well as possible; as ... as possible

できれば・出来れば *phrase* if possible

でぐち・出口 *n* exit

てくび・手首 *n* wrist

てこ・梃子 *n* lever

てごたえ・手応え *n* response; effect

でこぼこ(な)・凸凹(な) *adj* uneven; bumpy

てごろ(な)・手ごろ(な) *adj* handy; reasonable (price)

デザート *n* dessert

デザイナー *n* designer

デザイナー ようひん・デザイナー 用品 *n* designer goods

デザイン *n* design

デジタル(な) *adj* digital

てじゅん・手順 *n* plan; order

でしょう *phrase* – often translatable as 'I suppose' this is a polite form of だろう and can be used to get confirmation from the listener that what is being said is correct so also translatable as 'isn't it?', 'aren't they?', 'weren't you?', 'hasn't it?' etc.

です – added to statements which do not have a verb or い adjective it means 'is', 'am' and 'are'. Also used after い adjectives to sound more polite. The plain form is だ and the negative is either では ありません or じゃ ありません. The plain negative form is じゃ ない. Past form is でした and plain form past is だった.

てすう・手数 *n* trouble ▶ おてすう

ですが *conj* however; but

ですから *conj* because; since

テスト *n* test

でたらめ 1 *n* nonsense **2** *adv* でたらめに haphazardly **3** *adj* でたらめ(な) unreliable

てちょう・手帳 *n* notebook ❗ *can be used of personal organisers or diaries*

てつ・鉄 *n* iron

てつがく・哲学 *n* philosophy

てっきょう・鉄橋 *n* bridge (for railway)

てつだい・手伝い *n* help; helper

てつだいます ▶ てつだう

てつだう・手伝う *vb 1* ⓒ てつだって・てつだわない・てつだいます to help

てつづき・手続き *n* procedures **!** *used of form filling and administrative work*

てってい(する)・徹底 (する) *vb 3* ⓝ to be thorough

てっていてき・徹底的 1 *adj* てっていてき(な) thorough **2** *adv* てっていてきに thoroughly

てつどう・鉄道 *n* railway

てっぱん・鉄板 *n* metal plate

てっぽう・鉄砲 *n* gun

てつや・徹夜 1 *n* staying up all night **2** *vb 3* ⓝ てつやする to stay up all night

でて ▶ でる

テニス *n* tennis; テニスする to play tennis

テニスコート *n* tennis court

てぬき・手抜き *n* cutting corners

てぬぐい・手拭い *n* – a towel for wiping the hands

ては – a ～て form followed by particle は. Also used to mark the condition under which a following statement holds and so meaning 'if ...is the case then ....'. Very commonly the particles are being used to highlight a topic and carry the sense of 'as for ...' or 'in the case of ...'. There is sometimes a comparison (explicit or implicit) with something else. When followed by いけない or だめ it carries the meaning '... is wrong' and is translatable as 'must not ..' or 'should not ..'

では – a combination of particles used to make the negative forms of です and so part of a structure equivalent to 'isn't', 'aren't' or 'am not' in the present and 'wasn't' or 'weren't' in the past. Also used to mark the condition under which a following statement holds and so meaning 'if ...is the case then ....'. Very commonly the particles are being used to highlight a topic and carry a sense of 'as for ...' or 'in the case of ...'. There is sometimes a comparison (explicit or implicit) with something else. This follows from a word or phrase marked with particle で

being further marked as a topic with particle は . *Following some nouns such as country names it could be translated as 'in'. When followed by* いけない *or* だめ *it carries the meaning '... is wrong' and is translatable as 'must not ..' or 'should not ..'. Also used at the start of sentences as a conjunction meaning 'well', 'next' etc.*

デパート *n* department store

てぶくろ・手袋 *n* gloves

てほん・手本 *n* example

てま・手間 *n* time; trouble

てまえ・手前 *n* (just in) front; (just) before

でまえ・出前 *n* (restaurant food) delivery service

でます ▶ でる

でむかえ・出迎え *n* meeting (somebody)

でむかえる・出迎える *vb 2* ⊛ to meet (somebody at the station etc.)

ても *suf – representing the* 〜て *form of a verb and the particle* も *and translatable as 'even if ...'.* ▶ も

でも だれでも anybody; everyone; どこでも anywhere; everywhere; なんでも anything; everything; いつでも anytime！ *as a suffix it is a form of* ても *above. but more likely to be found as a combination of particles* で *and* も *translatable as 'even (in the case that ...)' . This usage is from a word or phrase marked with particle* で *being further marked as a topic with particle* も. *Also used with the meaning 'or something (else)' when making suggestions. When following words used to form questions such as 'who?', 'where?' and 'what?' it gives the meaning 'any...'.* ▶ で ▶ も

デモ *n* demonstration

デモンストレーション *n* demonstration

てら・寺 *n* (Buddhist) temple

てらす・照らす *vb 1* ⊛ to illuminate; to shine (a torch)

てる・照る *vb 1* ㉓ to shine

でる・出る *vb 2 ㋑* でて・でない・でます to leave; to go out (of); to appear; to come out; to take part (in); to protrude; to graduate (from)

テレビ *n* television

テレビばんぐみ・テレビ番組 *n* television programme

テレホンカード *n* telephone card

てれる・照れる *vb 2 ㋑* to be shy

てん・点 *n* mark; point; てんをつける to mark (homework etc.)

てん・店 *suf* shop

てんいん・店員 *n* – a member of the staff of a shop. Translatable as 'clerk' or 'sales assistant'.

でんか・殿下 *suf* – title and form of address for the Japanese Imperial family meaning 'your imperial||royal highness'

でんかせいひん・電化製品 *n* electrical goods

てんかぶつ・添加物 *n* additive

てんかい・展開 **1** *n* development **2** *vb 3 ㋑* を てんかい する to develop

てんき・天気 *n* weather

でんき・電気 *n* electricity

でんき・伝記 *n* biography

でんきスタンド・電気スタント *n* desk light

でんきゅう・電球 *n* light bulb

てんきよほう・天気予報 *n* weather forecast

てんきん・転勤 **1** *n* transfer **2** *vb 3 ㋑* てんきんする to be transferred ! refers to the system operated by a company, school board or other organisation of moving staff around to different branches, departments and||or jobs

てんけいてき・典型的 **1** *adj* てんけいてき（な）typical **2** *adv* てんけいてきに typically

でんげん・電源 *n* power point; power (switch)

てんこう・天候 *n* weather

てんごく・天国 *n* heaven

でんごん・伝言 *n* message

てんさい・天才 *n* genius

でんし・電子 *prf* electronic

てんじ・点字 *n* Braille

でんしじしょ・電子辞書 *n* electronic dictionary

でんしてちょう・電子手帳 *n* electronic organiser

でんしメール・電子メール *n* e-mail

でんしレンジ・電子レンジ *n* microwave oven

でんしゃ・電車 *n* train

てんじょう・天井 *n* ceiling

てんすう・点数 *n* marks (in a test)

でんせん(する)・伝染 (する) *vb 3* ⑰ to be infectious

でんせんびょう・伝染病 *n* infectious disease

てんたいかんそく・天体観測 *n* astronomy

でんち・電池 *n* battery

てんちょう・店長 *n* manager (of a shop or bank)

てんてん(と)・転々 (と) *adv* from place to place

てんてん・点々 – as an adverb in the form てんてんと it means 'here and there' but is also used to describe the marks used to form voiced syllables in かな script. These are the marks placed beside a kana character to transform the pronunciation from 'ka' か to 'ga' が etc. The proper term for these marks is だくおんふ

テント *n* tent

でんとう・伝統 *n* tradition

でんとうてき(な)・伝統的(な) *adj* traditional

てんねん・天然 *suf* natural

てんのう・天皇 *n* (Japanese) emperor

てんのうたんじょうび・天皇誕生日 *n* – The Emperor's Birthday (December 23) – a Japanese public holiday

てんのうへいか・天皇陛下 *n* – a form of words equivalent to 'His Imperial Majesty, the Emperor (of Japan)'

てんぽ・店舗 *n* shops

テンポ *n* tempo

でんぽう・電報 *n* telegram

てんらんかい・展覧会 *n* exhibition

でんりょく・電力 *n* electric power

でんわ・電話 *n* telephone

でんわちょう・電話帳 *n* telephone directory

でんわばんごう・電話番号 *n* telephone number

と ト

と *pt* – this particle has numerous uses. It can link two nouns and be translatable as '... and ...' or follow a noun referring to a person to mean 'with ...'. Sometimes used in expressions of comparison and so variously translatable as '(different) from', '(same) as' etc. It's use is compulsory with some verbs such as けっこん（する） 'to marry' and optional (but very common) with others such as はなす 'to speak' to express the meaning 'with'. Used in the verb 'to think' 〜と おもう meaning '(I) think that ...' and with to say' in the idiom 〜と いう meaning '... said that ...' or 'called ...' ▶という▶おもう▶いう The particle can also show that a preceding phrase is a quotation. Sometimes used with the verb なる in the sense of 'become'. Also used with certain adverbs, especially onomatopoeic expressions. Following the dictionary or 〜ます form of a verb it makes a conditional.

と・戸 *n* door

ど・度 *suf* (number of) times; degrees (of angle or temperature)

ドア *n* door

とい・問い *n* question

といあわせ・問い合わせ **1** *n* enquiries **2** *vb* **3** ㉟ に といあわせ(を)する to enquire

といあわせる・問い合わせる *vb* 2 ㉟ に to enquire

ドイツ *n* Germany

という *phrase* – used following a noun or noun phrase to mean 'called ...' or 'something like ...' and in the expression ということ to mean 'apparently'

といって *conj* however

というのは *conj* because ...

トイレ *n* toilet

トイレットペーパー *n* toilet paper

といわんばかり *phrase* as if to say

とう・塔 *n* tower

とう・頭 *counter* large animals

とう・等 *suf* grade

とう・島 *suf* island

どう・銅 *n* copper

どう *adv* how; what; どうですか how are you?; how is it (going)?; どうでしたか how was it?; どうしますか what shall (I/we) do?; どうしたんですか what's the matter?; どう おもいますか what do you think (about ...)?; どう なります か what will happen?! *when followed by a 〜て form and the particle* も *it means* 'even if ....' *or* 'no matter how much one ...'

どういう *phrase* what kind of ..; how; why; どういうふうに in what way ...?; どういう いみ ですか what does it mean?

どういたしまして *phrase* you're welcome ! *a polite response to expressions of thanks such as* どうも ありがと う ございます

とういつ・統一 1 n unity **2** vb 3 ㉧ とういつする
to make the same

どうか adv – can be used in the sense of 'please ...' and when following a phrase ending with the particle **か** it means 'whether or not ...'. It is also used idiomatically with a sense of something being not quite right.

とうかん(する)・投函(する) vb 3 ㉧ **か** to post (a letter)

とうき・陶器 n pottery

どうき・動機 n motivation

どうきゅう・同級 n same class/grade

どうきゅうせい・同級生 n classmate

どうぐ・道具 n tools; implements

とうげ・峠 n (mountain) pass

とうけい・統計 n statistics

とうこう・登校 1 n going to school **2** vb 3 ㉩ とうこうする to go to school

どうさ・動作 n movements

とうじ・当時 n at that time

どうし・動詞 n verb

どうし・同士 suf – shows that the people referred to are sharing a set of circumstances or are members of the same group with similar status such as **ともだちどうし** '(among) friends' or **なかまどうし** 'colleagues'.

どうじ・同時 1 n at the same time **2** adv (〜と)どうじに simultaneously

どうしたんですか ▶ どう

とうじつ・当日 n that day; the day of the ...

どうじつうやく・同時通訳 n simultaneous interpreting

どうして adv why; how

どうしても adv however; no matter what ... **!** also be used to give the meaning '(I) can't help ...' and to emphasise wanting

something 'no matter what'. Has a general sense of insistence and/or necessity.

とうじょう・登場 1 *n* appearance **2** *vb 3* ⓚ とうじょうする to appear

とうじょう・搭乗 1 *n* boarding (ship or plane) **2** *vb 3* ⓔ ⓚ とうじょうする to board (ship or plane)

どうじょう・道場 *n* – a place for the practice of martial arts like じゅうどう and からて

とうじょうけん・搭乗券 *n* boarding card (ticket)

とうじょうじんぶつ・登場人物 *n* character (in a film or book etc.)

どうせ *adv* after all; anyhow; anyway **!** carries a negative or pessimistic nuance

どうせい・同棲 1 *n* living together **2** *vb 3* ⓚ どうせいする to live together

どうせいあい・同性愛 *n* homosexuality

どうせいあいしゃ・同性愛者 *n* a homosexual

とうぜん・当然 1 *adj* とうぜん（な） natural; reasonable **2** *adv* naturally

どうぞ *adv* please; of course

どうぞよろしく *phrase* – an abbreviated form of どうぞよろしく おねがい します which is used to express the speaker's hopes for a future successful relationship of some kind and carries a sense of 'thank you in advance for ...' or 'please think well of me'. Very difficult to translate as there is no real English equivalent.

とうちゃく・到着 1 *n* arrival **2** *vb 3* ⓚ とうちゃくする to arrive

とうてい・到底 *adv* utterly

とうとう *adv* finally; after all

どうとく・道徳 *n* morality **!** Japanese schools teach 'moral education' どうとくきょういく which is similar to social ethics

どうとくてき・道徳的 1 adj どうとくてき(な) moral
2 adv どうとくてきに morally

とうなん・盗難 n theft **!** Japanese use covers a broad sense of 'theft' and can be translated with the most appropriate term from the English 'robbery', 'burglary' and 'theft'

どうにか adv somehow (or other); どうにかなる (it) will be ok; どうにか する do (it) somehow or other

どうにゅう・導入 1 n introduction (of something) **2** vb 3 ㊝ に どうにゅうする to introduce (something)

とうばん・当番 n – used in the sense of 'turn' when there is a list of duties to be performed

とうひょう・投票 1 n vote; voting **2** vb 3 ㉗ とうひょう する to vote

どうぶつ・動物 n animal

どうぶつえん・動物園 n zoo

とうめい(な)・透明(な) adj transparent

どうも adv – the basic meaning is 'somehow' but it is often used as an abbreviation of polite phrases where it acts something like 'very'. This means that depending on the context the word can mean 'hello' and 'thank you' as well as 'sorry'. When used with negative statements and comments it is translatable as 'apparently' or 'somehow or other ...'; どうも ありがとう (ございます) thank you (very much); どうも すみません (でした) I'm sorry to have troubled you

どうやら adv somehow; apparently

とうゆ・灯油 n – kerosene or paraffin oil used in many Japanese homes for the mobile room heaters

とうよう・東洋 n Asia; Orient

どうよう・同様 1 adv どうよう(に) similarly **2** adj どうよう(な) the same as

どうりょう・同僚 n colleague

どうろ・道路 n road

どうろこうじ・道路工事 n road-works

とうろく・登録 1 *n* registration **2** *vb* **3** を に とうろくする to register

とうろん・討論 1 *n* debate **2** *vb* **3** を とうろんする to debate

どうわ・童話 *n* – Japanese traditional stories for children. Translatable as 'nursery stories' or 'fairy tales'

とお・十 *n* ten

とおい・遠い *adj* distant; far from

とおか・十日 *n* the tenth (day of a month); ten days

とおかん・十日間・10日間 *n* ten days

とおく・遠く *n* a long way away

とおす・通す *vb* **1** を to let pass; through (someone or someone's connections)

とおり・通り *n* – used to mean 'road' especially in naming large and famous roads. Used after other nouns (sometimes connected with の and sometimes not) and the past or dictionary forms of verbs it signifies 'as' or 'like' or 'according to' or 'in the manner of'; いつも の とおり as usual; せつめい の とおり following the explanation/instructions; そのとおり that's (you're) right!; わたしが するとおりにして ください Please do (it) as I do

どおり ▶ とおり

とおりかかる・通りかかる *vb* **1** か to pass by

とおりすぎる・通り過ぎる *vb* **2** か to go past

とおる・通る *vb* **1** か to pass; to go through

とか *pts* and; etc. ! as well as when giving examples it is sometimes used when trying to remember something and added to uncertain statements with the meaning 'or something like that'

とかい・都会 *n* large city; とかい の urban

とかく *adv* tend to ...

とかす・溶かす *vb* **1** を to dissolve (something)

どかす・退かす *vb* **1** を to move (something out of the way)

とき・時 *n* time **!** *often used following another noun linked with* の *or following the plain forms of verbs or adjectives to mean 'when' or 'while';* こどもの とき *when (I was) a child;* さむい とき *when it is cold;* はしるとき *while running;* わからな いとき *when you don't understand*

ときおり・時折 *adv* occasionally

ときどき・時々 *adv* occasionally

どきどき(する) *vb* 3 ㋩ – *the basic meaning is to have the heart beat faster with excitement or fear etc. and so translatable as '(my) heart was pounding' etc. or 'to be excited', 'to be anxious' etc. depending on the context.*

ときには・時には *adv* sometimes

とく・得 *n* (a) benefit; profit

とく・溶く *vb* 1 ㋐ to dissolve

とく・解く *vb* 1 ㋐ to untie; to solve

とぐ・砥ぐ *vb* 1 ㋐ – *the basic meaning is 'to sharpen' but it is also used to describe washing rice grains prior to cooking to remove the powdery residue and ensure soft, white cooked rice*

どく・毒 *n* poison

どく・退く *vb* 1 ㋩ to get out of the way **!** *used in the form* どいて(ください) *it is translatable as '(please) get out of the way'*

とくい・得意 *n* – *means 'something someone is good at' and so is translatable as 'speciality' or 'strong point'*

どくしゃ・読者 *n* reader

とくしゅ(な)・特殊(な) *adj* TV or press special

どくしょ・読書 **1** *n* reading **2** *vb* 3 ㋩ どくしょする to read (as a hobby)

とくしょく・特色 *n* characteristic

どくしん・独身 *n* single (not married)

とくちょう・特徴 *n* characteristic

とくちょう・特長 *n* (someone's) strong point

とくてい(する)・特定(する) vb 3 を to specify

とくてい(の)・特定(の) adj specific

どくとく(な・の)・独特(な・の) adj unique

とくに・特に adv especially; in particular

とくばい・特売 1 n sale 2 vb 3 を とくばいする to put on sale

とくばいひん・特売品 n sale item/s

とくべつ・特別 1 adj とくべつ(な)special 2 adv とくべつに especially

どくりつ・独立 1 n independence 2 vb 3 か どくりつする to become independent

とけい・時計 n clock; watch

とけこむ・溶け込む vb 1 に to dissolve; to fit in with

とくめい・匿名 n anonymity; とくめいで anonymously

とける・溶ける vb 2 か to melt; to dissolve

とける・解ける vb 2 か to come undone; to be solved

どける・退ける vb 2 を to move (something out of the way)

とこ・床 n とこにつく to go to bed

どこ n where

どこか 1 n somewhere 2 adv something; a little bit

どこで ▶ どこ

どこでも ▶ どこも

どこに where?; where to?

どこへ where (to)

どこまで how far; to what extent

どこまでも adv endlessly

どこも adv (with positive) everywhere; (with negative) nowhere

とこのま・床の間 *n* – the alcove in a traditional Japanese room where hanging scrolls, ornaments and flowers are often displayed

とこや・床屋 *n* barber

ところ・所 *n* place; point **!** added to the past tense of a verb and followed by です・でした it indicates point in time and is translatable as 'have|had just (done)' or 'when ...'. Added to a dictionary form of a verb and followed by です・でした it indicates that an action is just about to occur or has just started and is translatable as 'be just about to ...' See also ところが and ところで

ところが *conj* however; well **!** when following a past tense it carries the meaning of 'however'

どころか *pt* on the contrary (to preceding statement) ...; not only ... but also ...

ところで *conj* by the way **!** following a past tense it conveys a meaning of 'even if' or 'however much'. See also ところでは

ところでは *phrase* – following a past tense means 'as far as (I know etc.)' or 'according to ...'.

ところどころ(に)・所々(に) *adv* here and there

とざん・登山 1 *n* mountain climbing **2** *vb 3 ㉚* とざんする to go mountain climbing

とし・年 *n* year; age

とし・都市 *n* city

としうえ・年上 *n* (person) who is older

としたら *phrase* supposing (that) ...

としつき・年月 *n* years

として *phrase* as (a ...); not even a ...

としては *phrase* for (a ...)

としても *phrase* even if

としとった・年取った *adj* old

どしゃぶり・どしゃ降り *n* heavy downpour

としょ・図書 *n* books

としょかん・図書館 *n* library

としより・年寄り *n* old person; old people

とじる・閉じる *vb 2* Ⓔ to close (the eyes)

としん・都心 *n* the centre of a city

とすると *phrase* assuming (that) ...

とすれば *phrase* supposing (that) ...

とそう・塗装 *n* paint

どそく・土足 *n* – refers to shoes that are worn outside (in contrast to slippers which can be worn inside a house or other building). Often seen in entrances and hallways in the phrase どそくきんし which can be translated as 'no shoes' or 'please remove your shoes'

どそくきんし・土足禁止 ▶どそく

とだな・戸棚 *n* closet; cupboard

とたん(に)・途端(に) *suf* just as ...

とち・土地 *n* land

とちゅう・途中 *n* in the middle of (doing); on the way to

どちら *n* where; which; who

どちらも *phrase* both; even

とっきゅう・特急 *n* express (train)

とくに・特に *adv* specially; especially

とつぜん・突然 **1** *adj* とつぜん(の・な) sudden **2** *adv* suddenly

どっち *n* where; which ▶どちら

どっちでも *phrase* both; even ▶どちらでも

どっちも ▶どちらも

とって・取っ手 *n* handle

とって – used in the pattern 〜にとって to mean 'as for' or 'to' when giving an opinion or judgement; にほんにとって for Japan; かいしゃにとって to/for the company

とって ▶ とる
トップ *n* top
とても *adv* very; extremely; completely
とどく・届く *vb 1* ㋕ to arrive (be delivered); to reach
とどける・届ける *vb 2* ㋾ to deliver (something to ...); to report
ととのう・整う *vb 1* ㋕ to be ready
ととのえる・整える *vb 2* ㋾ to get (something) ready
どなた *n* who; どなたさま ですか who is it (are you) please? **!** *a more polite equivalent of* だれ
となり・隣 *n* next to; neighbour(ing)
となりさん・隣さん *n* a neighbour
どなる・怒鳴る *vb 1* ㋕ to shout
となれば ▶ とすれば
とにかく *adv* anyway
どの *attributive* which; what; who **!** *used in the pattern* どの... も *it means 'any ..' or 'every ...'*
どの・殿 *suf – sometimes added to family names in the address or opening line of a letter (from an official organisation) and so translatable as 'Mr', 'Mrs', Miss, 'Ms' or 'esquire'*
どのくらい *phrase* how much; how many; how long
とばす・飛ばす *vb 1* ㋾ to (make) fly; to skip (omit); to splash; to drive (at high speed)
とびこむ・飛び込む *vb 1* ㋕ to dive into; to jump into
とびだす・飛び出す *vb 1* ㋕ to rush out
とびら・扉 *n* door **!** *usually refers to a sliding or automatic door*
とぶ・飛ぶ *vb 1* ㋕ to fly
とぶ・跳ぶ *vb 1* ㋕ to jump
どぶ・溝 *n* ditch; drain
どぼく・土木 *suf* (civil) engineering

とぼしい・乏しい *adj* short of; lacking

トマト *n* tomato

とまって ▶ とまる

とまどう・戸惑う *vb 1 か* to be at a loss (to know what to do)

とまり・泊り *n* staying overnight

とまります ▶ とまる

とまる・止まる *vb 1 か* とまって・とまらない・とまります to stop; to be parked

とまる・泊まる *vb 1 か* to stay (overnight)

とめて ▶ とめる

とめます ▶ とめる

とめる・止める *vb 2 を* とめて・とめない・とめます to stop; to park

とめる・泊める *vb 2 を* to put somebody up (overnight)

とめる・留める *vb 2 を* to fasten; to fix

とも all; both; at the (least/most/latest etc.); of course ! *this is a combination of particles* と *and* も

とも・友 *n* friend

ともかく *adv* anyway; regardless (of)

ともだち・友達 *n* friend

ともなう・伴う *vb 1 か* to take; to bring; to be accompanied (by)

ともに・共に *adv* together with; as well as ! *usually in the form* 〜とともに

ともばたらき・共働き *n* – a couple who are both working

どようび・土曜日 *n* Saturday

とら・虎 *n* tiger

ドライクリーニング *n* dry cleaning

ドライバー *n* screwdriver; driver

ドライブ 1 *n* driving; (a) drive **2** *vb 3* ㊡ **ドライブする** to go for a drive

とらえる・捕らえる *vb 2* ㊤ to arrest; to catch

トラック *n* truck

トラブル *n* trouble

ドラマ *n* drama

ドラム *n* drum/s

トランプ *n* (playing) cards

とり・鳥 *n* bird; chicken

とりあえず *adv* for the time being

とりあげる・取り上げる *vb 2* ㊤ to pick up; to adopt; to take away

とりあつかい・取り扱い *n* treatment

とりあつかう・取り扱う *vb 1* ㊤ to handle; to deal with

とりあわせ・取り合わせ *n* combination; assortment

とりい・鳥居 *n* – the red gateway which marks the entrance to a Shinto shrine

とりいれる・取り入れる *vb 2* ㊤ to take in; to adopt

とりかえ・取り替え *n* exchange; replacement

とりかえす・取り替えす *vb 1* ㊤ to get (something) back

とりかえる・取り替える *vb 2* ㊤ to exchange; to replace

とりくむ・取り組む *vb 1* ㊡ に to get to grips with

とりけす・取り消す *vb 1* ㊤ to cancel

とりしまり・取り締まり *n* crackdown

とりしまりやく・取締役 *n* company director

とりしまる・取り締まる *vb 1* ㊤ to crack down on

とりだす・取り出す *vb 1* ㊤ to take (something) out (of)

とりつける・取り付ける *vb 2* ㊤ to install

とりにく・鳥肉 *n* chicken (meat)

とりのぞく・取り除く *vb 1* を to remove

とりひき・取り引き *n* trading

とりもどす・取り戻す *vb 1* を to get (something) back

どりょく・努力 **1** *n* effort **2** *vb 3* の どりょくする
to make an effort

とる・取る *vb 1* を とって・とらない・とります
to take; to get; to steal; to have; to occupy

とる・採る *vb 1* を to pick; to employ

とる・撮る *vb 1* を to take (a picture)

とる・捕る *vb 1* を to catch

どれ *n* which **!** when followed by も or でも it means 'whichever'
or (with a negative) 'all'

トレーニング *n* training

ドレス *n* dress

どれでも whichever; any ▶ どれ

どれも ▶ どれ

とれる・取れる *vb 2* の to come off

とれる・捕れる *vb 2* の to be caught

どろ・泥 *n* mud

どろぼう・泥棒 *n* thief; burglar

トン *n* metric tonne

とんでもない *adj* terrible

とんとん とんとんです to be (break) even

どんどん *adv* quickly

どんな *attributive* what (kind of) **!** when followed by a noun and
も or でも it means 'however', 'no matter what' or 'any', 'every'

どんなに *adv* how; how much; no matter how; however

トンネル *n* tunnel

どんぶり・丼 *n* – a bowl for rice somewhat larger than the
usual ちゃわん and by extension any meal served in such a
bowl with rice under the meat, fish or vegetables

な ナ

な・名 _n_ name

な _pt_ – used after the dictionary form of a verb it acts as a strong negative imperative 'don't ...'. Sometimes used after a verb in the pre ～ます form as an abbreviation of なさい which produces an a polite imperative 'do ...' which is often used by teachers to students and parents to children

な _pt_ – used by men when expressing emotion and also as an alternative to particle ね

なあ _pt_ – an alternative form of particle な above

ない・無い – used in the formation of the plain negative of です which is ではない and variously translatable as 'am not', 'is not', 'are not'. Also for the negative of ある to mean 'not existing' and translatable as 'don't have' or 'is|are' missing' in addition to the translations given above.

～ない _suf_ – indicates the negative form of a verb or an adjective

ない・内 _suf_ within

ないか・内科 _n_ internal medicine

ないしょ・内緒 _n_ secret

ないせん・内線 _n_ (telephone) extension ! often used in the sense of 'it's an internal call'

ないせんばんごう・内線番号 _n_ (telephone) extension number

ないで _suf_ – Used to form an expression similar to 'please do not ...'. In this use it is often followed by ください Also used to mean 'without doing ...'. In this usage it is usually followed by another verb

ナイフ _n_ knife

ないぶ・内部 _n_ interior

ないよう・内容 *n* contents

ナイロン *n* nylon

なお・尚 *adv* **1** *adv* (*in positive sentences*) still (more); (*in negative sentences*) even (less) **2** *conj* furthermore

なおす・直す *vb 1* 🖐 to repair; to adjust; to correct; to translate (into) **!** *as a suffix attached to the pre* ～ます *form of other verbs it indicates that the action is done again so often equivalent to the 're' element of 'redone', 'reconsider' etc.*

なおす・治す *vb 1* 🖐 to cure; to heal

なおる・直る *vb 1* 🖐 to be repaired; to be corrected

なおる・治る *vb 1* 🖐 to get better (after illness or injury)

なか・中 *n* inside; in; into; middle; among

なか・仲 *n* relations; なかが いい to be friendly with ...; なかが わるい to be on bad terms with ...

なが・長 *suf* long

ながい・長い *adj* long

ながく(する)・長く(する) *vb 3* 🖐 to make something long(er)

ながさ・長さ *n* length

ながし・流し *n* (kitchen) sink

ながす・流す *vb 1* 🖐 to run (water); to flush (a toilet); to empty (a bath); to wash away

なかなおり・仲直り 1 *n* reconciliation **2** *vb 3* と なか なおりする to make up

なかなか *adv* (*with positives*) quite; very; (*with negatives*) (not) easily

なかば・半ば 1 *n* middle **2** *adv* partly

ながびく・長引く *vb 1* 🖐 to drag on

なかま・仲間 *n* friend (at work)

なかみ・中身 *n* contents; ingredients

ながめ・眺め *n* view

ながめる・眺める *vb 2* 🅔 to look; to watch

なかよく・仲良く 1 *adv* happily **2** *vb 3* 🅐 **と なかよく する** to get on well with (someone)

なかよし・仲良し *n* friend

ながら *suf* – following the pre 〜ます form of a verb it adds the meaning 'while ... 〜ing' and shows that two actions take place simultaneously. Also used with adjectives and nouns in the sense of 'although ...' and in certain fixed expressions.

ながれ・流れ *n* flow

ながれる・流れる *vb 2* 🅔 to flow; to be washed away

なく・泣く *vb 1* 🅐 to cry

なく・鳴く *vb 1* 🅐 to call ❗ used for the noises made by birds and animals and so variously translatable as 'sing', 'roar', 'screech' etc. depending on the animal concerned

なぐさめる・慰める *vb 2* 🅔 to console

なくす・無くす *vb 1* 🅔 to lose (something)

なくす・亡くす *vb 1* 🅔 to lose (a relative or friend by death)

なくて *suf* – the 〜て form of ない and the 〜ない form of verbs which is used in the expression 'don't have to ...'. In this use it is followed by もいい. Also used as an emphatic negative form of ない たべなくても いい you don't have to eat

なくなる *vb 1* 🅐 to run out; to disappear; to be missing

なくなる・亡くなる *vb 1* 🅐 to die

なぐる・殴る *vb 1* 🅔 to hit (violently)

なげる・投げる *vb 2* 🅔 to throw

なければ *suf and conj* if not (then ...)

なければいけない *suf* must

なければならない *suf* must

なさい *suf* – used after the pre 〜ます form of a verb to form a polite imperative and translatable as 'do ... please' or 'please ...'

なさけない・情けない *adj* shameful; deplorable

なさる *vb 1* を ▶ honorific equivalent of する

なし・無し *n* nothing ! *used as a more emphatic form of* ない *in the sense of 'without...'.*

なし・梨 *n* Japanese pear

なしとげる・成し遂げる *vb 2* を to accomplish

なじむ・馴染む *vb 1* か に to get used to

なす・為す *vb 1* を to do

なぜ *adv* why

なぜなら(ば) *conj* the reason is ...

なぞ・謎 *n* mystery

なだらか(な) *adj* gentle

なだれ・雪崩 *n* avalanche

なつ・夏 *n* summer

なつかしい・懐かしい *adj* – the meaning is similar to 'nostalgic' or 'longed for ...' so that it can be translated by '... reminds me of (something good)' but the specific memory is not stated and must be inferred. Sometimes translatable as 'I remember ... well' or 'I have a lot of (good) memories of ...'

なって ▶ なる

なっとく・納得 **1** *n* understanding **2** *vb 3* か なっとくする to be convinced; なっとくさせる to persuade (someone)

なでる・撫でる *vb 2* を to stroke

など・等 *pt* such as; something like ...

なな・七 *n* seven

ななつ・七つ *n* seven

ななめ・斜め **1** *adj* ななめ(な) slanted; diagonal **2** *adv* ななめに diagonally

なに・何 *n* what

なにか・何か *interrogative* something; anything

なにしろ *adv* at any rate

なになに・何々 *n* something or other **!** *used by teachers to mean any word which could fill the blank in example sentences*

なにぶん・何分 *adv* anyway

なにも・何も *adv* nothing

なにより・何より *adv* better than (anything)

なのか・七日・7日 *n* seven days; the seventh (day of the month)

なべ・鍋 *n* pot; pan

なま・生 *prf and n* raw; live; draft/draught (beer)

なまいき・生意気 1 *adj* なまいき(な) cheeky **2** *adv* なまいきに cheekily

なまえ・名前 *n* name ▶ おなまえ

なまけもの・怠け者 *n* lazy person

なまける・怠ける *vb 2* ⊗⑰ to be lazy; to neglect

なまなましい・生々しい *adj* vivid

なまぬるい・生ぬるい *adj* tepid

なまほうそう・生放送 *n* live (broadcast)

なまり・鉛 *n* lead

なまり・訛り *n* accent

なみ・波 *n* wave

なみ・並 *n and suf* ordinary; the same as

なみだ・涙 *n* tear(s)

なめらか・滑らか 1 *adj* なめらか(な) smooth **2** *adv* なめらかに smoothly

なやみ・悩み *n* problem; (a) worry

なやむ・悩む *vb 1* ⑰ to worry (about); to be troubled (by)

なら *suf* if; when it comes to ....; supposing ... **!** *a way of making conditional sentences.*

ならば ▶ なら

ならう・習う *vb 1* ⊗ に to learn; to study

ならす・鳴らす *vb 1* を to ring (a bell); to sound (a horn)

ならない – *the negative form of* なる *and used in a number of idiomatic structures. When following a positive* 〜て *form plus particle* は *it means 'must not ...' and when following a negative such as* なければ *or* なくては *it means 'must'. When following a* 〜て *form it can mean 'can't help (doing) ...'*

ならぶ・並ぶ *vb 1* ⑩ to stand in a line

ならべる・並べる *vb 2* を to line (something) up; to display; to arrange

なり *pt* – *used after a verb it means 'as soon as ...' and used in the pattern* **A**なり ... **B**なり *it means 'either ... or ...'*

なる・成る *vb 1* ⑩ なって ならない なります to become; to consist of ▎ *following the dictionary or potential form of a verb in the form ...* ように なる *it means 'to become able to ...'. Following the* 〜く *form of an adjective it means 'to get ...', 'to become ...'. Used to form honorific verb forms in the pattern* お ...に なる.

なる・鳴る *vb 1* ⑩ to ring

なるべく *adv* as ... as possible; if possible

なるほど *adv* I see; indeed

なれる・慣れる *vb 2* に to get used to

なわ・縄 *n* rope

なん・何 *n and prf* what; how (many); how (much) ▎ *See the notes on counters for how to ask 'how many ...?' This is an alternative form of* なに

なんか ▶ なにか ▶ など – *sometimes used to express doubt and hesitation*

なんきょく・南極 *n* South Pole

なんじ・何時 *phrase* what time?

なんせい・南西 *n* south-west

なんだか・何だか *n* somehow; somewhat

なんて *adv* how; what

なんて *suf* like; such (as)

なんで・何で *adv* why

なんでも・何でも *adv* anything; everything; whatever
❗ *followed by a negative it means 'nothing'*

なんと *phrase* what; how

なんとう・南東 *n* south-east

なんとか *adv* somehow; anyhow; somehow or other ▶ なんとか する ▶ なんとか なる

なんとかして ▶ なんとか ▶ なんとか(する)

なんとか(する) *vb 3 ㉚* to do ... somehow or other; to manage to do

なんとか(なる) *vb 3 ㉚* it will sort itself out; it will be ok in the end

なんとなく *adv* somehow (or other); in some way (or other); more or less

なんとも ▶ なにとも

なんにち・何日 *phrase* what is the date?; how many days?

なんにん・何人 *phrase* how many people?

なんぶ・南部 *n* the south; the southern part

なんべい・南米 *n* South America

なんみん・難民 *n* refugee

なんぼく・南北 *n* North and South

に *pt* in; into; on; onto; to; toward; from; by; at; for; in order to; and ❗ *used in a variety of grammatical structures and idiomatically with certain verbs. Translations will depend on the words being used. Note that with verbs of giving and receiving it can be translated as either 'to' or 'from' depending on the verb.*

に・ニ *n* two

にあう・似合う *vb 1* ㋑ to suit

にいさん・兄さん ▶おにいさん

にえる・煮える *vb 2* ㋺ to be cooked

におい・匂い *n* smell; 〜の においが する to smell of ...

にがい・苦い *adj* bitter

にかかわらず *suf* regardless

にがす・逃がす *vb 1* ㋑ to let escape

にがて・苦手 *n* weak point; dislike ! *It is often translatable as 'not be very good at ...'*

にぎやか・賑やか **1** *adj* にぎやか(な) lively; noisy; busy **2** *adv* にぎやかに noisily; cheerfully

にぎる・握る *vb 1* ㋑ to grip

にぎわう・賑わう *vb 1* ㋑ to be busy and noisy

にく・肉 *n and suf* meat ! *can also be used to refer to muscles or body fat*

にくい・憎い *adj* hateful

にくい・難い *suf* difficult to ...

にくたい・肉体 *n* (the) body

にくたいろうどう・肉体労働 *n* physical labour

にくむ・憎む *vb 1* ㋑ to hate

にくらしい・憎らしい *adj* hateful

にくや・肉屋 *n* butcher; butcher's shop

にげる・逃げる *vb 2* ㋺ to run away; to escape

にこにこ(する) *vb 3* ㋩ to smile

にごり・濁り *n* – the basic meaning of the word is that a liquid is not 'clear' but it is also used to describe changes in sound such as those when the two marks ″ placed beside かな characters change the pronunciation from 'ka' か to 'ga' が etc.

にごる・濁る *vb 1* ㋑ to be cloudy (liquid) ▶ にごり

にし・西 *n* west

にじ・虹 *n* rainbow

にせ(の) *adj* fake

にせい・二世 *n* – meaning second generation it is especially used to describe people of Japanese ancestry who were born and now live in other countries. Can be translated as 'Japanese American', 'Japanese Canadian', 'Japanese Australian' etc.

にせもの・偽物 *n* (a) fake item

にち・日 *prf* Japan

にち・日 *suf* day/s

にちえい・日英 *n* Japan and the UK; Japanese and English (languages)

にちじ・日時 *n* date and time

にちじょう・日常 *suf* everyday

にちじょうかいわ・日常会話 *n* everyday conversation

にちじょうせいかつ・日常生活 *n* everyday life

にちべい・日米 *n* Japan and the USA

にちようび・日曜日 *n* Sunday

にちようひん・日用品 *n* daily necessities

〜について *phrase* about; regarding; にほんに ついて はなす talk about Japan

にっか・日課 *n* daily task

にっき・日記 *n* diary

にづくり・荷造り **1** *n* packing **2** *vb 3* ㉠ にづくり(を)する to pack (for a holiday etc.)

にっけい・日系 *n and prf* – used in front of words indicating nationality it means 'of Japanese origin' and so can be translated 'Japanese American', 'Japanese Brazilian' etc.

にっこう・日光 *n* sunlight

にっちゅう・日中 *n* Japan and China

にってい・日程 *n* schedule

にっぽん・日本 *n and prf* – an older and less common version of ▶ にほん

には ▶ に

にぶい・鈍い *adj* dull

にほん・日本 *n and prf* Japan

にほんご・日本語 *n* Japanese (language)

にほんじん・日本人 *n* Japanese (person/people)

にほんりょうり・日本料理 *n* Japanese food

にもかかわらず *suf* in spite of ...; although

にもつ・荷物 *n* baggage; luggage

ニュアンス *n* nuance

にゅういん・入院 **1** *n* going into hospital **2** *vb 3* か にゅういんする to go into hospital; にゅういん している to be in hospital

にゅうがく・入学 **1** *n* entering school/college **2** *vb 3* か にゅうがくする to enter (school/college)

にゅうがくしけん・入学試験 *n* entrance examination (for a university or school)

にゅうしゃ・入社 **1** *n* entering a company **2** *vb 3* か にゅうしゃする to join a company

にゅうじょう・入場 **1** *n* admission **2** *vb 3* か にゅうじょうする to gain admission

にゅうじょうけん・入場券 *n* admission ticket

にゅうじょうりょう・入場料 *n* entrance fee

ニュース *n* news

にょうぼう・女房 *n* (one's own) wife

〜によって *phrase* by

〜による(と) *phrase* according to

にらむ・睨む *vb 1* を to glare (at)

にる・煮る *vb 2* を to boil; to simmer

にる・似る *vb 2* に to resemble

にわ・庭 *n* garden

にわいじり・庭弄り *n* gardening

にわし・庭師 *n* gardener

にわかあめ・にわか雨 *n* shower (of rain)

にわかに・俄かに *adv* suddenly

にわとり・鶏 *n* chicken

にん・人 *counter* people

にんき・人気 *n* popularity; にんきが ある popular; にんきがない unpopular

にんぎょう・人形 *n* doll; toy figurine

にんげん・人間 *n* human

にんしん・妊娠 **1** *n* pregnancy **2** *vb* 3 ㉓ にんしんする to get pregnant; にんしん している to be pregnant

にんじん・人参 *n* carrot

にんずう・人数 *n* number (of people)

にんにく *n* garlic

ぬヌ

ぬいぐるみ *n* child's soft toy

ぬいで ▶ぬぐ

ぬう・縫う *vb 1* ㉓ to sew

ぬぎます ▶ぬぐ

ぬく・抜く *vb 1* ㉓ to pull out; to outrun

ぬぐ・脱ぐ *vb 1* ㉓ ぬいで・ぬがない・ぬぎます to take off (clothing or footwear)

ぬける・抜ける *vb 2* ㉗ to come out; to be missing

ぬすむ・盗む　*vb 1* を to steal

ぬの・布　*n* cloth

ぬま・沼　*n* marsh

ぬらす・濡らす　*vb 1* を to make wet

ぬる・塗る　*vb 1* を to apply (paint etc.); to spread (butter etc.)

ぬるい・温い　*adj* lukewarm

ぬれる・濡れる　*vb 2* が to get wet

. . . .

ねネ

ね　*pt* – used at the end of phrases and sentences to seek confirmation or agreement and to add emphasis or express surprise. In the first instance it is somewhat similar to English tag questions such as 'isn't it?', 'don't you?', 'haven't they?' etc. and can sometimes be translated in that way.

ね・根　*n* root

ね・値　*n* price

ねあがり・値上がり　**1** *n* price rise　**2** *vb 3* が ねあがり する to increase in price

ねえ ▶ ね

ねえさん ▶**noun** おねえさん

ネガ　*n* (photographic) negatives

ねがい・願い　*n* request; wish ▶ おねがい

ねがう・願う　*vb 1* を to wish for ...

ネクタイ　*n* necktie

ねこ・猫　*n* cat

ねじ・ネジ　*n* screw

ねじれる　*vb 2* が to be twisted

ねじる　*vb 1* ⊛ to twist

ねずみ　*n* mouse; rat

ねだん・値段　*n* price

ねつ・熱　*n* fever; heat

ねつい・熱意　*n* eagerness

ネックレス　*n* necklace

ねっしん・熱心　**1** *adj* ねっしん(な) eager　**2** *adv* ねっしんに eagerly

ねっする・熱する　*vb 3* ⊛ to heat

ねったい・熱帯　*prf* tropical

ねぼう・寝坊　**1** *n* oversleeping　**2** *vb 3* ㋕ ねぼうする to sleep in

ねまき・寝間着・寝巻　*n* nightclothes; pyjamas

ねまわし・根回し　*n* – the process in Japanese companies of consulting people widely prior to formal approaches being made in order to gain agreement or consensus and so translatable as 'laying the groundwork'. Also used as a verb in the form ねまわし(を)する

ねむい・眠い　*adj* sleepy

ねむれる・眠れる　*vb 2* ㋕ to be able to sleep

ねむる・眠る　*vb 1* ㋕ to sleep

ねらい・狙い　*n* aim

ねらう・狙う　*vb 1* ⊛ to aim for/at

ねる・寝る　*vb 2* ㋕ to sleep; to go to bed

ねん・年　*prf and suf* year

ねんがじょう・年賀状　*n* – a card sent for January 1st wishing people well in the new year

ねんかん・年間　*counter* year(s)

ねんじゅう・年中　*n* throughout the year

ねんせい・年生　*suf* – following a number it indicates which year of a school a student is in

ねんだい・年代 *n* – the basic meaning is 'generation' although sometimes 'age' is a better translation. It is also added to numbers to express time 70 **ねんだい** *'the 70s'*

ねんど・年度 *suf* year

ねんりょう・燃料 *n* fuel

ねんれい・年齢 *n* age

の ノ

の *pt* – there are a number of uses of this particle. One of its most common uses is to connect nouns to show a relationship of some kind. In this use it can be thought of as similar to the apostrophe + s in the sense of 'belonging to' i.e. **わたしの ほん** *'my book'*. However the range of relationships expressed in Japanese is much wider and the meaning 'about' is also common i.e. **くるまの ほん** *'a book about cars'*. Used at the end of sentences, especially by women it can indicate a question.

のう・脳 *n* (the) brain

のうか・農家 *n* farmer; farmhouse

のうぎょう・農業 *n* farming

のうさんぶつ・農産物 *n* agricultural produce

のうじょう・農場 *n* farm

のうそん・農村 *n* farming village/community

のうち・農地 *n* agricultural land

のうど・濃度 *n* concentration (of)

ノウハウ *n* know how

のうみそ・脳みそ *n* brains

のうみん・農民 *n* farmers

のうやく・農薬 *n* agricultural chemicals

のうりつ・能率 *n* efficiency

のうりつてき・能率的 **1** *adj* のうりつてき(な)
efficient **2** *adv* のうりつてきに efficiently

のうりょく・能力 *n* ability

ノート *n* notebook; note

のがれる・逃れる *vb 2 ㊗* to escape

のがす・逃す *vb 1 ㊗* to lose (an opportunity etc.)

のこす・残す *vb 1 ㊗* to leave

のこり・残り *n* remainder

のこる・残る *vb 1 ㊗* to remain

のせる・載せる *vb 2 ㊗* to put on/in; to load

のせる・乗せる *vb 2 ㊗* to give (someone) a lift

のぞく・除く *vb 1 ㊗* to remove; to exclude

のぞく・覗く *vb 1 ㊗* to peep

のぞましい・望ましい *adj* desirable

のぞみ・望み *n* hope; chance (of)

のぞむ・望む *vb 1 ㊗* to hope for; to want

のぞむ・臨む *vb 1 ㊗* に to face; to overlook

のち・後 *n* after

のちほど・後程 *adv* later

ノック **1** *n* knock; knocking **2** *vb 3 ㊗* ノックする to knock
(on the door)

のって ▶ のる

ので *pt* because

のです – particle の and です. often used at the end of a
sentence with some emphasis in explanations especially where
personal sentiment is involved. Also used to ask questions in the
form のですか and contracted in casual speech to 〜んです

のど・喉 *n* throat

のばす・伸ばす *vb 1* ㊑ to lengthen; to stretch; to let (hair) grow

のばす・延ばす *vb 1* ㊑ to extend; to postpone

のびる・伸びる *vb 2* ㊐ to grow; to lengthen; to improve

のびる・延びる *vb 2* ㊐ to be extended; to be postponed

のべる・述べる *vb 2* ㊑ to state

のぼって ▶ のぼる

のぼり・上り *n* ascent ! used in the form のぼりでんしゃ *to describe trains travelling in the direction of a major city (especially Tokyo) which is the terminus of the line*

のぼります ▶ のぼる

のぼる・上る・昇る *vb 1* ㊐ to go up; to rise

のぼる・登る *vb 1* に のぼって のぼらない のぼります to climb

のみこむ・飲み込む *vb 1* ㊑ to swallow

のみます ▶ のむ

のむ・飲む *vb 1* ㊑ のんで・のまない・のみます to drink; to take (medicine); to eat (soup)

のり *n* glue

のり・海苔 *n* – an edible seaweed prepared in dry sheets and often used to wrap rice balls and sushi

のりおくれる・乗り遅れる *vb 2* ㊐ to miss (train, plane etc.)

のりかえ・乗り換え *n* change (of train etc.)

のりかえる・乗り換える *vb 2* ㊐ to change (train etc.)

のりこえる・乗り越える *vb 2* ㊑ to climb over; to overcome

のりこす・乗り越す *vb 1* ㊑ to miss (getting off at) the right station

のりそこなう・乗り損なう *vb 1* ㊑ to miss (train, plane etc.)

のりば・乗り場 *n* – a place to get on and off transport such as buses and taxis

のります ▸ のる

のる・乗る *vb 1 ⑰* にのって・のらない・のります
to ride; to take (transport); to get on (transport)

のる・載る *vb 1 ⑰* に to be on; to be in

のろい・鈍い *adj* slow

のろのろ **1** *adv* のろのろ(と) slowly **2** *vb 3 ⑰* のろのろする to be slow

のんき・呑気 **1** *adj* のんき(な) easy going **2** *adv* のんきに care free

のんで ▸ のむ

のんびり **1** *adv* のんびり(と) relaxed **2** *vb 3 ⑰* のんびりする to be care free; to relax

はハ

は *pt* – pronounced わ There are a number of uses of this particle. The most common is as a marker for the topic about which a comment is made. It marks the subject of a comment but NOT necessarily the grammatical subject

は・歯 *n* tooth; teeth

は・葉 *n* leaf

ば・場 *n* place; occasion

〜ば *suf* – indicates the conditional form of verbs and adjectives

バー *n* bar

ばあい・場合 *n* occasion; time; case

パーセント *n* percentage; percent

パーティー *n* party; パーティーする to have a party; パーティーをひらく to hold a party

パート *n* part-time job

ハードウェア *n* (computer) hardware

バーベキュー *n* barbeque

はい *interjection* – *while the basic meaning is 'yes' it is also used to confirm a statement and can mean 'no' in response to negative questions etc. Also used as* あいづち *to indicate that someone is listening and not necessarily carrying any sense of agreement*

はい・灰 *n* ash

はい・肺 *n* lungs

はい・杯 *counter* cups of; bowls of

ばい・杯 ▶はい

ぱい・杯 ▶はい

ばい・倍 *n and suf* – *as a noun it means 'double' but as a suffix on a number it means '～ times (that amount)'*

はいいろ・灰色 *n* grey

はいいろ(の)・灰色 (の) *adj* grey

ばいう・梅雨 *n* the rainy season

はいきガス・排気ガス *n* exhaust fumes

はいきょ・廃虚 *n* ruin; abandoned building

ばいきん・ばい菌 *n* germs; bacteria

ハイキング **1** *n* hiking **2** *vb 3* ㉠ ハイキングする to go hiking

はいけい・拝啓 *phrase* – *used as the opening of a formal letter and equivalent to 'Dear Sir or Madam'*

はいけん(する)・拝見(する) *vb 3* ㉠ to see ! *humble equivalent of* みる

はいざら・灰皿 *n* ashtray

はいし(する)・廃止(する) *vb 3* ㉠ to abolish

はいしゃ・歯医者 *n* dentist

ばいしょう・賠償 *n* compensation

ばいしょうきん・賠償金 ▶ばいしょう

はいたつ・配達 **1** n delivery **2** vb **3** ⊛ はいたつする to deliver

はいって ▶はいる

はいて ▶はく

ハイテク n high technology **!** *can be used as an adjective with* な

ばいてん・売店 n small shop; kiosk

バイト n part time job; バイト(を)する to do a part-time/short term job

バイバイ *phrase* bye bye

ばいばい・売買 **1** n buying and selling **2** vb **3** ばいばいする to buy and sell

ハイヒール n high heels

パイプ n pipe **!** *sometimes used to describe 'connections' with people or companies*

はいゆう・俳優 n actor

ハイライト n highlights

はいります ▶はいる

はいりょ・配慮 **1** n consideration; attention **2** vb **3** ⊛ はいりょする to consider; to give attention to

バイリンガル n bilingual

はいる・入る vb **1** ⑰ に はいって・はいらない・はいります to enter; to come in; to go in; to join; to be contained; to get in (bath)

パイロット n pilot

はう vb **1** ⑰ to crawl

ハウス n greenhouse

はえ・蝿 n fly

はえる・生える vb **2** ⑰ to grow

はか・墓 n grave

ばか・馬鹿 **1** *n* an idiot **2** *adj* ばか(な) stupid; 〜を ばか にする to make fun of ! *this word carries more or less strength of feeling depending on the tone of voice. It can be used in teasing amongst friends but also be sufficiently offensive to cause a fight! It will thus vary greatly in translation!*

はがき・葉書 *n* postcard

はかせ・博士 *n and suf* Doctor (PhD)

ばかばかしい *adj* stupid

ばからしい・馬鹿らしい *adj* stupid

はかり・秤 *n* (kitchen or laboratory) scales

ばかり *suf* – has a variety of meanings including 'just', 'only' and 'approximately'. It can also mean 'do nothing but ...', 'do ... continuously' and following the 〜た form it means 'have just ...'.

はかる・計る・測る *vb* 1 を to measure

はかる・図る *vb* 1 を to attempt (to)

はきけ・吐き気 *n* nausea

はきます ▶ はく

はく・履く *vb* 1 を はいて・はかない・はきます to wear; to put on

はく・吐く *vb* 1 を to vomit; to spit

はく・掃く *vb* 1 を to sweep

はく・泊 *counter* nights' stay

ぱく・泊 ▶ はく

はくし・博士 *suf* doctor of ... (PhD)

はくしゅ・拍手 **1** *n* applause **2** *vb* 3 か はくしゅする to applaud

ばくぜん(と)・漠然(と) *adv* vaguely

ばくだい(な)・莫大(な) *adj* enormous

ばくだん・爆弾 *n* bomb

ばくはつ・爆発 **1** *n* explosion **2** *vb* 3 か ばくはつする to explode

はくぶつかん・博物館 *n* museum

はぐるま・歯車 *n* gear

はげしい・激しい *adj* intense; violent

バケツ *n* bucket

はげます・励ます *vb 1* ⓦ to encourage

はこ・箱 *n* box

はこぶ・運ぶ *vb 1* ⓦ to carry; to transport; to go (well/badly)

はさまる・挟まる *vb 1* ⓗ to get something caught in (a door etc.)

はさみ *n* scissors

はさむ・挟む *vb 1* ⓦ to place (in/between); to insert

はさん・破産 **1** *n* bankruptcy **2** *vb 3* はさんする to go bankrupt

はし・橋 *n* bridge

はし・箸 *n* chopsticks

はし・端 *n* edge; end; corner

はじ・恥 *n* shame; embarrassment; disgrace; 〜に はじを かける to embarrass

はしご *n* ladder

はしって ▶ はしる

はじまって ▶ はじまる

はじまり・始まり *n* beginning

はじまります ▶ はじまる

はじまる・始まる *vb 1* ⓗ に はじまって・はじまらない・はじまります to begin

はじめ・初め *n* beginning

はじめて・初めて **1** *n* (the) first time **2** *adv* first

はじめに・初めに *conj* firstly; at the beginning

はじめは・始めは *phrase* at first

はじめまして・始めまして *phrase* how do you do

はじめます ▶ はじめる

はじめる・始める *vb 2* Ⓐ はじめて・はじめない・
　はじめます to start ▮ added to the pre ～ます form of other
　verbs to express 'begin to ...'

パジャマ *n* pyjamas; nightdress

ばしょ・場所 *n* place; space (in a room)

はしら・柱 *n* pillar

はしります ▶ はしる

はしる・走る *vb 1* Ⓝ はしって・はしらない・はし
　ります to run; to travel (at high speed)

はず *n* – used after the plain forms of verbs and adjectives the
　basic meaning is 'expectation' and when following positive
　statements it conveys the idea of 'should ...', 'it is expected that
　...'. When following negative statements it is translatable as 'not
　expected' etc.

バス *n* bus

パス **1** *n* pass **2** *vb 3* Ⓐ Ⓝ パスする to pass

はずかしい・恥ずかしい *adj* embarrassing; embarrassed;
　shy; ashamed; shameful

バスケットボール *n* basketball

はずす・外す *vb 1* Ⓐ to take off; to remove; to undo; to leave

パスポート *n* passport

はずれる・外れる *vb 2* Ⓝ to be loose; to be wrong; to be
　undone

はた・旗 *n* flag

はだ・肌 *n* skin

バター *n* butter

パターン *n* pattern

はだか・裸 *n and adj* nakedness; naked

はたけ・畑 *n* (cultivated) field

はだし(で)・裸足(で) *n and adj* barefoot

はたち・二十歳・20歳 *n* twenty years old **!** *In Japan this is the age at which young people become adults*

はたらいて ▶ はたらく

はたらき・働き *n and prf* work

はたらきます ▶ はたらく

はたらきもの・働き者 *n* hard worker

はたらく・働く *vb 1 ㋕* はたらいて・はたらかない・はたらきます to work

はち・八・8 *n* eight

はち・蜂 *n* bee; wasp

はち・鉢 *n* (flower) pot

はちがつ・八月・8月 *n* August

はちみつ・蜂蜜 *n* honey

パチンコ *n* – a game related to pinball played by many Japanese

はつ・初 *prf* (the) first

はつ・発 *suf* departing at/from

ばつ *n* – has several meanings amongst which are 'incorrect answer', 'punishment' and a cross or X symbol.

はつおん・発音 1 *n* pronunciation **2** *vb 3 ㋰* はつおんする to pronounce

はつか・二十日・20日 *n* the twentieth day of the month; twenty days

はっきり（と）1 *adv* clearly **2** *vb 3 ㋰* はっきり（と）する to be clear

ばっきん・罰金 *n* (a) fine

バック 1 *n* background **2** *vb 3 ㋕* バックする to reverse

バッグ *n* bag

パックりょこう・パック旅行 *n* package holiday

バックアップ 1 *n* backup **2** *vb 3 ㋕ ㋰* バックアップする to back up

はっけん・発見 **1** n discovery **2** vb 3 を はっけんする
to discover

ばっさい・伐採 **1** n timber felling **2** vb 3 を ばっさいする
to fell

はっしゃ・発車 **1** n departure **2** vb 3 ㉟ を はっしゃする
to depart

ばっする・罰する vb 3 を to punish

はっせい・発生 **1** n occurrence **2** vb 3 ㉟ はっせいする
to occur

はっそう・発想 n way of thinking

はったつ・発達 **1** n development **2** vb 3 ㉟ はったつする
to develop

ばっちり phrase just right!

バッテリー n (car) battery

はってん・発展 **1** n development **2** vb 3 ㉟ を はってん
する to develop

はつでんしょ・発電所 n (electricity) power station

バット n bat

ぱっと・パッと adv suddenly

はつばい・発売 **1** n sale **2** vb 3 を はつばいする to put
on sale; はつばいちゅう now on sale!

はっぴょう・発表 **1** n announcement; presentation **2** vb
3 を はっぴょうする to announce; to present

はつめい・発明 **1** n invention **2** vb 3 を はつめいする
to invent

はつもうで・初詣 n – the first visit to a shrine or temple of
the year (often just after midnight on January 1st and a major part
of the new year celebration for many Japanese people)

はて・果て n (extreme) end

はで(な)・派手(な) adj brightly coloured; showy

パトカー n police car

バドミントン n badminton

はな・花 *n* flower

はな・鼻 *n* nose

はなし・話 *n* talk; subject (of/for a talk)

はなしあい・話し合い *n* talks

はなしあう・話し合う *vb 1 か* と to discuss

はなしかける・話し掛ける *vb 2 か* に to speak to

はなしちゅう・話し中 *phrase* (the telephone is) engaged

はなして ▶ はなす

はなします ▶ はなす

はなす・話す *vb 1 か* に と はなして・はなさない・
　はなします to talk; to speak

はなす・放す *vb 1 を* to release

はなす・離す *vb 1 を* to separate

はなぢ・鼻血 *n* nosebleed

バナナ *n* banana

はなはだしい・甚だしい *adj* serious

はなび・花火 *n* fireworks

はなみ・花見 *n* – going to see the blossoms of the plum tree
　うめ and (especially) the cherry tree さくら as an occasion
　for picnics and partying.

はなやか(な)・華やか(な) *adj* splendid

はなよめ(さん)・花嫁(さん) *n* bride

はなれる・離れる *vb 2 か* を to be separated

はね・羽 *n* wing; feather

はねる・跳ねる *vb 2 か* to jump up; to splash

はねる *vb 2 を* to run over; くるまに はねられる to be run
　over by a car

はは・母 *n* (one's own) mother

はば・幅 *n* width

パパ *n* dad

はばおや・母親 *n* mother

はばひろい・幅広い *adj* wide

はぶく・省く *vb 1* ㋾ to reduce; to leave out

バブル *n* bubble **!** in the form バブルけいざい・バブル経済
it is used to describe an economic boom and subsequent
collapse, and specifically that of the 1990s in Japan of which the
good times are referred to as the バブルじだい・バブル時代

はへん・破片 *n* fragment

はま・浜 *n* beach

はまべ・浜辺 *n* beach

はみがき・歯磨き *n* toothpaste; cleaning the teeth; はみが
きする to clean the teeth

はみがきこ・歯磨き粉 *n* toothpaste

はめる *vb 2* ㋾ to put on (a ring or gloves); to wear (a ring or
gloves)

ばめん・場面 *n* scene

はやい・早い・速い *adj* early; fast

はやおき・早起き **1** *n* getting up early **2** *vb 3* ㋕ はやお
きする to get up early

はやさ・速さ *n* speed

はやし・林 *n* woods

はやる・流行る *vb 1* ㋕ to be prevalent; to be in fashion;
かぜがはやっている a cold is going around

はら・原 *n* plain

はら・腹 *n* belly; はらが たつ to get angry

ばら・薔薇 *n* rose

はらいます ▶ はらう

はらいもどす・払い戻す *vb 1* ㋾ to refund

はらう・払う *vb 1* ㋾ はらって・はらわない・はら
います to pay

はらって ▶ はらう

ばらばら 1 *n* scattered **2** *vb* 3 ⑰ ばらばら(に)なる to be scattered

バランス *n* balance

はり・針 *n* needle; hand (of a clock)

はりがね・針金 *n* wire

はりきる・張り切る *vb* 1 ⑰ to be full of energy

はる・春 *n* spring

はる・張る *vb* 1 ⑰ ⑧ to stretch

はる・貼る *vb* 1 ⑧ to stick

はるか・遥か 1 *adv* far away **2** はるかに by far

はれ・晴れ *n* clear skies

はれる・晴れる *vb* 2 ⑰ to be fine (weather)

はん・班 *n* and *suf* group

はん・半 *suf* half; half past

はん・反 *prf* anti-

ばん・晩 *n* evening; night

ばん・番 *n* turn ! *as a suffix it means 'number' and is used to make the ordinal numbers rather like the small letters attached to numbers in English 1st, 2nd, 3rd, 4th, etc.*

バン *n* van

パン *n* bread

はんい・範囲 *n* scope

はんえい・反映 1 *n* reflection **2** *vb* 3 ⑰ ⑧ はんえいする to be reflected

はんえい・繁栄 1 *n* prosperity **2** *vb* 3 ⑰ はんえいする to prosper

ハンガー *n* (coat) hanger

はんがく・半額 *n* half price

ハンカチ *n* handkerchief

パンク 1 *n* puncture **2** *vb* 3 ⑰ パンクする to be punctured

ばんぐみ・番組 *n* (television or radio) programme

はんけい・半径 *n* radius

はんこ・判子 *n* – a carved stamp with a person's surname which is often used in place of a signature on official documents

はんこう・犯行 *n* crime

はんこう・反抗 1 *n* opposition **2** *vb 3* ㋕ に はんこうする to resist

ばんごう・番号 *n* number

はんざい・犯罪 *n* crime

ばんざい・万歳 *n* – literally 'ten thousand years' it is used in the same way as English 'hip hip hooray' or 'three cheers'

ハンサム(な) *adj* handsome

はんじ・判事 *n* judge

ばんじ・万事 *n* everything

はんせい・反省 1 *n* thinking over **2** *vb 3* ㋔ はんせいする to reflect (on)

ばんせん・番線 *suf* platform number

はんそで・半袖 *prf* short-sleeved

はんたい・反対 1 *n* opposition **2** *vb 3* ㋕ に はんたいする to be against

はんだくおん・半濁音 *n* – the 'p' sound in Japanese which is represented by the small circle next to かな symbols to indicate a change in pronunciation i.e. from ひ 'hi' to ぴ 'pi'

はんだん・判断 1 *n* judgement **2** *vb 3* ㋔ はんだんする to judge; to decide

ばんち・番地 *n and suf* – follows a number as a subdivision of a Japanese address which is similar to a 'block' in the USA or Canada

パンチ 1 *n* punch **2** *vb 3* ㋔ に パンチする to punch

パンツ *n* underpants; knickers; shorts

バント *n* a bunt; a drudge

バンド *n* strap; bracelet; (pop) band

はんとう・半島 *n and suf* peninsula

はんとし・半年 *n* a six month period

ハンドバッグ *n* handbag

ハンドル *n* steering wheel

はんにん・犯人 *n* criminal

はんのう・反応 **1** *n* reaction **2** *vb* **3** ㉗ はんのうする
　　to react

はんばい・販売 **1** *n* sales **2** *vb* **3** ㉘ はんばいする to sell

はんばいき・販売機 *n* vending machine

はんぱつ・反発 **1** *n* opposition **2** *vb* **3** ㉗ に はんぱつする
　　to rebel

はんぶん・半分 *n* half

ばんめ・番め・番目 *suf* – added to numbers to give
　　position in a sequence like the ordinal numbers 1st, 2nd, 3rd, 4th, etc.

ひヒ

ひ・日 *n* day; the sun

ひ・火 *n* fire; たばこに ひを つける to light a cigarette

ひ・灯 *n* the lights (of a town or building)

ひ・非 *prf* – a negative prefix similar to English 'un-' and 'non-'

ひ・費 *suf* expenses

ピアス *n* earring

ひあたり・日当たり *n* sunlight; ひあたりの いい へや
　　a sunny room

ピアノ *n* piano; ピアノを ひく play the piano

ヒーター *n* heater

ビール *n* beer

ひえる・冷える *vb 2 ㊦* to get cold; to be chilled

ひがい・被害 *n* damage

ひがいしゃ・被害者 *n* victim

ひかえめ・控え目 **1** *adj* ひかえめ(な) moderate **2** *adv* ひかえめに moderately

ひがえり・日帰り *n* one day trip

ひがえりりょこう・日帰り旅行 ▶ ひがえり

ひかく(する)・比較(する) *vb 3 ㊥* と to compare

ひかくてき・比較的 **1** *adj* ひかくてき(な) comparative **2** *adv* ひかくてきに comparatively

ひかげ・日陰 *n* shade

ひがし・東 *n* east

ぴかぴか(と) *adv* – the basic meaning is 'shining' or 'glittering' but it can be used to mean 'brand new' or 'clean', the latter especially in the form ぴかぴかに なる

ひかり・光 *n* light

ひかる・光る *vb 1 ㊦* to shine

ひき・匹 *counter* smaller animals and fish

びき ▶ ひき

ぴき ▶ ひき

ひきいる・率いる *vb 2 ㊥* to lead (a group of people)

ひきうける・引き受ける *vb 2 ㊥* to undertake

ひきおこす・引き起こす *vb 1 ㊥* to cause

ひきかえす・引き換えす *vb 1 ㊦* to turn around and go back

ひきがね・引き金 *n* trigger

ひきざん・引き算 **1** *n* subtraction **2** *vb 3 ㊥* ひきざんする to subtract

ひきだし・引き出し *n* drawer

ひきだす・引き出す *vb 1* ㉟ to withdraw (money from a bank)

ひきょう(な)・卑怯(な) *adj* cowardly; unfair

ひきよせる・引き寄せる *vb 2* ㉟ to draw (something) closer

ひきわけ・引き分け *n* a draw

ひきわたす・引き渡す *vb 1* ㉟ to hand over

ひく・引く *vb 1* ㉟ ひいて・ひかない・ひきます to pull; to attract; to draw; to catch (a cold); to look up (in a dictionary)

ひく・弾く *vb 1* ㉟ ひいて・ひかない・ひきます to play (an instrument with the fingers or plectrum)

ひく・轢く *vb 1* ㉟ to run over (with a vehicle)

ひくい・低い *adj* low; せが ひくい short

ピクニック *n* picnic

ひげ・髭 *adj* moustache; beard

ひげき・悲劇 *n* tragedy

ひこう・飛行 *n* flight

ひこうき・飛行機 *n* aeroplane

ひこうじょう・飛行場 *n* airport

ひざ・膝 *n* knee; lap

ビザ *n* visa

ピザ *n* pizza

ひざし・日差し・陽射し *n* sunlight

ひさしぶり・久し振り *phrase* it's been a long time (since we last had contact); long time no see

ひさん(な)・悲惨(な) *adj* terrible

ひじ・肘 *n* elbow

ビジネス *n* business

ビジネスウーマン *n* businesswoman

ビジネスマン *n* businessman

びじゅつ・美術 *n* art

ひしょ・秘書 *n* secretary

ひじょう・非常 *n* emergency

ひじょうに・非常に *adv* extremely

ひじょうきん・非常勤 *prf* part-time

ひじょうぐち・非常口 *n* emergency exit

ひじょうしき・非常識 *n* lacking in common sense

ビスケット *n* biscuit

ピストル *n* pistol

びせいぶつ・微生物 *n* micro-organism

ひたい・額 *n* forehead

ひたすら *adv* whole-heartedly

ビタミン *n* vitamin

ひだり・左 *n* left

ひだりがわ・左側 *n* left hand side

ひだりきき・左利き *n* left handed (person)

ひだりて・左手 *n* left hand

ひっかかる・引っかかる *vb 1㋑* to get caught

ひっかける・引っかける *vb 2㋔* to catch

ひっきりなし *adv* constantly; incessantly

びっくり(する) *vb 3㋩* to be surprised; to be shocked

ひっくりかえす・引っくり返す *vb 1㋔* to overturn

ひっくりかえる・引っくり返る *vb 1㋑* to be overturned

ひづけ・日付 *n* date

ひっこし・引越し *n* moving house

ひっこす・引っ越す *vb 1㋩* to move house

ひっし・必死 **1** *n* desperation **2** *adv* ひっしに desperately

ひっし・必至 *n* inevitable

ひつじ・羊 *n* sheep

ひっしゃ・筆者 *n* author

ひっしゅうかもく・必修課目 *n* compulsory subject (of study)

ひつじゅひん・必需品 *n* necessities

ぴったり(に) *adv* exactly

ひっぱる・引っ張る *vb 1* 🈴 to pull

ひつよう・必要 **1** *n* necessity **2** *adj* ひつよう(な) necessary

ひてい・否定 **1** *n* denial; negative **2** *vb 3* 🈴 ひていする to deny

ビデオ *n and prf* video

ビデオプレヤー *n* video player

ビデオレコーダー *n* video recorder

ひと・人 *n* person; people

ひと・一 *prf* one

ひどい・酷い *adj* terrible

ひとがら・人柄 *n* personality

ひとこと・一言 *n* a few words

ひとごみ・人込み *n* a crowd

ひとしい・等しい *adj* equal

ひとつ・一つ *n* one

ひとつめ・一つ目 *n* (the) first

ひとで・人手 *n* (people to) help

ひととおり・一通り **1** *adv* briefly **2** *adj* ひととおりの general

ひとどおり・人通り *n* pedestrian traffic

ひとびと・人々 *n* people

ひとまず・一先ず *adv* first; for a while

ひとやすみ ・ 一休み *n* a break

ひとり ・ 一人 ・ 独り *n* one person; on one's own

ひとりあたり ・ 一人当たり *n* per person

ひとりぐらし ・ 一人暮らし *n* living alone; ひとりぐらし(を)する to live alone

ひとりっこ ・ 一人っ子 *n* only child

ひとりで ・ 一人で *phrase* by oneself ❗ translations will vary with context i.e. 'by myself', 'by herself' etc.

ひとりでに ・ 独りでに *adv* automatically

ひとりひとり(に) ・ 一人一人(に) *adv* one by one; one after another; in single file

ひとりむすこ ・ 一人息子 *n* only son

ひとりむすめ ・ 一人娘 *n* only daughter

ひなた ・ 日向 *n* sunny place; ひなたぼっこを する to sunbathe

ひなん ・ 非難 **1** *n* criticism **2** *vb 3* を ひなんする to criticise

ひなん ・ 避難 **1** *n* shelter **2** *vb 3* に ひなんする to take refuge

ビニールぶくろ ・ ビニール袋 *n* plastic bag; carrier bag

ひにく ・ 皮肉 *n* sarcasm; irony

ひにち ・ 日にち *n* days

ひにん ・ 避妊 *n* contraception

びねつ ・ 微熱 *n* a slight temperature

ひねる ・ 捻る *vb 1* を to twist

ひのいり ・ 日の入り *n* sunset

ひので ・ 火の手 *n* flames

ひので ・ 日の出 *n* sunrise

ひのまる ・ 日の丸 *n* – the Japanese flag which shows a round red sun on a white background

ひはん・批判 1 *n* criticism 2 *vb* 3 (を) ひはんする
to criticise

ひび・日々 *n* days

ひび *n* crack; fracture

ひびき・響き *n* sound

ひびく・響く *vb 1* (⾃) to sound; to echo

ひひょう・批評 1 *n* critical commentary 2 *vb* 3 (を) ひひょ
うする to review

ひふ・皮膚 *n* skin

ひふか・皮膚科 *n* dermatology

ひま・暇 *n* free time; ひまですか are you free?

ひみつ・秘密 1 *n* secret 2 *adj* ひみつ(な) secret

びみょう(な)・微妙(な) *adj* subtle

ひめい・悲鳴 *n* scream; ひめいを あげる to scream

ひも・紐 *n* string

ひゃく・百 *n* hundred

びゃく・百 ▶ ひゃく

ぴゃく・百 ▶ ひゃく

ひやけ・日焼け 1 *n* suntan; sunburn 2 *vb 3* (⾃) ひやけする
to get suntanned; to get sunburnt

ひやす・冷やす *vb 1* (を) to chill

ひゃっかじてん・百科事典・百科辞典 *n*
encyclopaedia

ひよう・費用 *n* expenses

ひょう・表 *n and suf* chart; table

ひょう・票 *n* vote

びょう・秒 *n* seconds

びょう・鋲 *n* tack

びょう・病 *suf* illness

びよういん・美容院 *n* beauty salon

びょういん・病院 *n* hospital **!** *often translatable as* 'doctor's surgery' *or* 'the doctor' *as it describes the premises where a doctor has a consulting room as well as large hospitals*

ひょうか・評価 **1** *n* evaluation **2** *vb 3* Ⓢ ひょうかする to evaluate

びょうき・病気 *n* illness; びょうきに なる to become ill; びょうきが なおる to get well

ひょうげん・表現 **1** *n* expression **2** *vb 3* Ⓢ ひょうげん する to express

ひょうし・拍子 *n* rhythm

ひょうしき・標識 *n* mark

びょうしつ・美容室 *n* (women's) hairdresser

びょうしゃ・描写 **1** *n* description **2** *vb 3* Ⓢ びょうしゃ する to describe

ひょうじゅん・標準 *n* criterion; standard

ひょうじょう・表情 *n* (facial) expression

びょうどう・平等 **1** *adj* びょうどう (な) equal **2** *adv* びょうどうに fairly

ひょうばん・評判 *n* reputation

ひょうめん・表面 *n* surface

ひょうろん・評論 *n* criticism

ひらがな・平仮名 *n* – one of the two **かな**, *the syllabic scripts used in writing Japanese*

ひらく・開く *vb 1* Ⓢ to open; to hold (a party or meeting)

ひりょう・肥料 *n* fertiliser

ひる・昼 *n* (around) noon; daylight hours ▶ おひる

ビル *n* (a) building

ひるごはん・昼ご飯 *n* lunch

ひるね・昼寝 **1** *n* a nap **2** *vb 3* Ⓝ ひるね (を) する to have a nap

ひるま・昼間 *n* daytime

ひるめし ▶ ひるごはん

ひろい・広い *adj* wide; spacious

ひろう・拾う *vb 1* 🄬 to pick up

ひろがる・広がる *vb 1* 🄬 to spread

ひろげる・広げる *vb 2* 🄬 to expand

ひろさ・広さ *n* width; extent

ひろば・広場 *n* (town) square

ひろまる・広まる *vb 1* 🄬 to spread

ひろめる・広める *vb 2* 🄬 to spread

ひん・品 *n* elegance ❗ *as a suffix it means 'item' or 'thing'*

びん・便 *n and suf* flight

びん・瓶 *n* bottle

ピン *n* pin; focus

びんかん(な)・敏感(な) *adj* sensitive

ピンク *n* pink

ひんしつ・品質 *n* quality

ひんしゅ・品種 *n* sort

びんせん・便箋 *n* (letter) writing paper

ヒント *n* hint; clue

ひんぱんに・頻繁に *adv* frequently

びんぼう・貧乏 **1** *n* poverty **2** *adj* びんぼう(な) poor

ふフ

ふ・不 *prf* – negates the following word or element in a way similar to English prefixes such as 'un-' and 'in-'

ぶ・分 *suf* per cent

ぶ・部 *n and suf* section; department

ファイト n fighting spirit

ファクシミリ n fax; fax machine

ファスナー n zipper

ファックス n fax

ファックスき・ファックス機 ▶ ファックスきかい

ふあん・不安 1 n anxiety **2** adj ふあん(な) anxious; worried; ふあんが ある to feel anxious

ファン n fan

ふあんてい(な)・不安定(な) adj unstable

ふいに・不意に adv unexpectedly

フイルム n (photographic) film

ふう・風 suf style; appearance

ふうけい・風景 n scenery

ふうせん・風船 n balloon

ブーツ n boots

ふうとう・封筒 n envelope

ふうふ・夫婦 n (married) couple

ブーム n boom

プール n (swimming) pool

ふうん・不運 n bad luck

ふえ・笛 n whistle; flute

ふえる・増える vb 2 ㉜ to increase

フォーク n fork

ぶか・部下 n staff (who work for/under someone)

ふかい・深い n deep

〜ぶかい suf – adds the meaning of very ...' or 'heavily involved in ...'

ふかさ・深さ n depth

ふかけつ・不可欠 n indispensable

ふかのう(な)・不可能(な) *adj* impossible

ふかまる・深まる *vb 1 か* to deepen

ぶき・武器 *n* weapon

ふきげん(な)・不機嫌(な) *adj* in a bad mood

ふきそく(な)・不規則(な) *adj* irregular

ふきゅう・普及 **1** *n* spread **2** *vb 3 か* ふきゅうする to spread

ふきょう・不況 *n* economic recession

ふきん・付近 *n* neighbourhood

ふきん・布巾 *n* cloth

ふく・拭く *vb 1 を* to wipe

ふく・吹く *vb 1 を か* to blow; to play (a wind instrument etc.)

ふく・服 *n* clothing

ふく・副 *prf* deputy

ふくざつ(な)・複雑(な) *adj* complicated

ふくし・福祉 *n and suf* welfare

ふくしゅう・復習 **1** *n* revision **2** *vb 3 を* ふくしゅうする to review

ふくすう・複数 *n* plural

ふくそう・服装 *n* clothing

ふくむ・含む *vb 1 か を* to be included

ふくめる・含める *vb 2 を* to include

ふくらむ・膨らむ *vb 1 か* to swell

ふくろ・袋 *n* bag

ふけいき・不景気 *n* poor economic conditions

ふけつ(な)・不潔(な) *adj* unclean; dirty

ふける・更ける *vb 2 か* to grow late

ふこう(な)・不幸(な) *adj* unhappy

ふごう・符号 *n* symbol

ふごうかく・不合格 *n* fail (in an exam or interview etc.)

ふこうへい(な)・不公平 (な) *adj* unfair

ふごうり(な)・不合理 (な) *adj* unreasonable

ふさい・夫妻 *suf* Mr and Mrs

ふざける *vb 2㊥* – the basic meaning is 'to play around', 'to mess about' but it can also mean 'to talk nonsense'. Often used in a form such as **ふざけないで** to mean 'stop messing around and behave yourself properly'

ふさわしい・相応しい *adj* appropriate

ふし・節 *n* tune

ぶじ・無事 1 *adj* ぶじ(な) safe **2** *adv* ぶじに safely; ぶじにつく to arrive safely

ふしぎ・不思議 1 *adj* ふしぎ(な) mysterious **2** *adv* ふしぎに mysteriously

ぶしゅ・部首 *n* – the 'radical' of a かんじ character which can be used to look it up or to help explain the meaning

ふじゆう・不自由 1 *adj* ふじゆう(な) inconvenient **2** *vb 3㊥* ふじゆうする to be short of ! used as a euphemism for 'disabled' when describing people

ふじゅうぶん(な)・不十分(な) *adj* insufficient; unsatisfactory

ふしょう(する)・負傷(する) *vb 3㊥* to be wounded; to be injured

ふしょうしゃ・負傷者 *n* injured person

ぶじょく・侮辱 1 *n* insult **2** *vb 3㊥* ぶじょくする to insult

ふじん・婦人 *prf* women's

ふじん・夫人 *suf* – added to names with a meaning similar to 'Mrs' but merely a polite title and not related to marriage status

ふすま・襖 *n* – the paper covered sliding doors inside a Japanese house which divide the space into rooms

ふせい・不正 **1** *n* dishonesty **2** *adj* ふせい(な) dishonest

ふせぐ・防ぐ *vb 1* ㊥ to prevent

ふそく・不足 **1** *n* shortage **2** *vb 3* ㉟ ふそくする to be lacking **!** *also appears as in the form* ～ぶそく *as a suffix meaning 'short of' or 'lacking in'*

ふた・蓋 *n* lid; (bottle) top

ぶた・豚 *n* pig

ぶたい・舞台 *n* stage

ふたご・双子 *n* twin/s

ふたたび・再び *adv* once again

ふたつ・二つ *n* two

ふたつめ・二つ目 *n* (the) second

ぶたにく・豚肉 *n* pork

ふたり・二人 *n* two people

ふたん・負担 *n* burden; cost

ふだん(の)・普段(の) *n and adj* everyday

ふち・縁 *n* edge

ふちゅうい・不注意 **1** *n* carelessness **2** *adj* ふちゅうい(な) careless

ふちゅうい・不注意 *n* carelessness

ぶつ *vb 1* ㊥ to hit

ぶつ・物 *suf* item

ふつう・普通 **1** *adj* ふつう(の) ordinary; usual **2** *adv* ふつう(は) usually

ふつか・二日・2日 *n* the second day of the month; two days

ぶっか・物価 *n* prices; にほんは ぶっかが たかい Japan is expensive

ぶつかる *vb 1* ㉟ に to bang into; to clash with

ぶっきょう・仏教 *n* Buddhism

ぶつける・vb 2 ㊅ to hit; to bump into

ぶっしつ・物質 n substance

ぶっそう (な)・物騒 (な) adj dangerous

ふって ▶ ふる

ぶつぶつ (いう) vb 1 ㊉ to grumble; to mumble

ぶつりがく・物理学 n physics

ふで・筆 n – brush (used for Japanese calligraphy)

ふと adv unexpectedly

ふとい・太い adj thick

ふどうさんや・不動産屋 n estate agent; realtor

ふとる・太る vb 1 ㊉ to put on weight ! used in the form ふとっている it means 'fat'

ふとん・布団 n futon ! a mattress and duvet for sleeping on the floor of a Japanese たたみ room. These have no wooden base, unlike the 'futons' sold in the west

ふなびん・船便 n sea mail

ふね・船・舟 n ship; boat

ぶひん・部品 n component; spare part

ふぶき・吹雪 n blizzard

ぶぶん・部分 n part

ふへい・不平 n complaint

ふべん(な)・不便 (な) adj inconvenient

ふぼ・父母 n parents

ふほう・不法 suf illegal

ふまん・不満 n dissatisfaction

ふみきり・踏み切り n level crossing

ふむ・踏む vb 1 ㊅ to tread on

ふもと・麓 n foot (of a mountain)

ぶもん・部門 n field (of expertise etc.)

ふやす・増やす vb 1 ㊅ to increase

ふゆ・冬 *n* winter

フライパン *n* frying pan

ブラウス *n* blouse

ぶらさげる・ぶら下げる *vb 2* ⊗ to swing; to carry; to wear

ブラシ *n* brush

プラス *n* plus

プラスチック **1** *n* plastic **2** *adj* プラスチックの plastic

ブラック *n* black

ふり・不利 *n* disadvantage

ふり(をする)・振り(をする) *vb 3* ⑰ – following the 〜た form of a verb or a n and particle の it adds the meaning of 'pretending to ...' or 'faking ...' ...

ぶり・振り *suf* – Following time expressions it means 'for the first time since ...', 'for the first time in ...'. Following nouns and verb stems it means 'way of ...

フリー *n* free

ふりがな・振り仮名 *n* – the small かな characters used over or beside かんじ characters to indicate the pronunciation

ふります ▶ ふる

ふりむく・振り向く *vb 1* ⑰ to turn around

ふりょう・不良 **1** *adj* ふりょう(の)defective; bad **2** *n* juvenile delinquent

ふりょうひん・不良品 *n* defective item

プリント *n* print

ブルー *n* blue

ふる・降る *vb 1* ⑰ ふって・ふらない・ふります to fall (rain or snow)

ふる・振る *vb 1* ⑰ to swing

ふる・古 *prf* old

ふるい・古い *adj* old; old fashioned

ふるえる・震える *vb 2 ⑦* to tremble

ふるさと・故郷・古里 *n* hometown; home

ふるまい・振る舞い *n* behaviour

ふるまう・振る舞う *vb 1 ⑦* to behave

ブレーキ *n* brakes

プレゼント *n* present

ふれる・触れる *vb 2 ⑦* に to touch

ふろ・風呂 *n* bath

プロ *n and prf* professional

ブローチ *n* brooch

プログラム *n* programme

ふろしき・風呂敷 *n* – a large cloth used for carrying things in

ふろば・風呂場 *n* bathroom ❗ *not in the sense of 'toilet'*

フロント *n* reception desk of a hotel

ふわふわ (の) *adj* soft and fluffy

ふん・分 *n and counter* minute

ぶん・分 ▶ ふん

ぶん・分 *n* part; share

ぶん・文 *n* writing; sentence

ぷん・分 ▶ ふん

ふんいき・雰囲気 *n* atmosphere

ふんか・噴火 **1** *n* (volcanic) eruption **2** *vb 3 ⑦* ふんかする to erupt

ぶんか・文化 *n* culture

ぶんかい(する)・分解(する) *vb 3 ⑳* to take to pieces

ぶんがく・文学 *n* literature

ぶんかさい・文化祭 *n* – a festival or cultural event, especially at school or university

ぶんげい・文芸 *n* literature

ぶんけん・文献 *n* literature

ぶんしょ・文書 *n* writing; document

ぶんしょう・文章 *n* writing; sentence

ふんすい・噴水 *n* fountain

ぶんせき・分析 **1** *n* analysis **2** *vb* **3** を ぶんせきする to analyse

ふんそう・紛争 *n* conflict

ぶんたい・文体 *n* style (of writing)

ぶんぷ・分布 **1** *n* distribution **2** *vb* **3** に ぶんぷする to be distributed

ぶんぽう・文法 *n* grammar

ぶんぼうぐ・文房具 *n* stationery

ふんまつ・粉末 *n* powder

ぶんめい・文明 *n* civilisation

ぶんや・分野 *n* field (of specialisation)

ぶんりょう・分量 *n* quantity

ぶんるい・分類 **1** *n* classification **2** *vb* **3** を ぶんるいする to classify

ぶんれつ・分裂 **1** *n* division **2** *vb* **3** を ぶんれつする to split up

へい・塀 *n* fence; wall

へいかい・閉会 **1** *n* close of a meeting **2** *vb* **3** を に へいかいする to close

へいき・平気 **1** *n* unconcern **2** *adv* へいきで casually; わたしはなんでも へいき です anything's OK by me

へいきん・平均 *n* average

へいこう・平行 **1** *n* parallel **2** *adv* へいこうして in parallel

へいこうせん・平行線 *n* parallel lines

へいじつ・平日 *n* week day; working day

へいせい・平成 *n* – era name for 1989 onwards and used for dates during that period

へいたい・兵隊 *n* soldier

へいほう・平方 *prf* used to mean 'square' in measurements of area especially へいほうメートル 'square metres'

へいぼん(な)・平凡(な) *adj* ordinary

へいや・平野 *n* plain

へいわ・平和 **1** *n* peace **2** *adv* へいわに in peace **3** *adj* へいわ(な) peaceful

ページ *n* and counter page

へこむ・凹む *vb 1* ⑦ to be dented

ベジタリアン *n* vegetarian

ベスト *n* best

ベストセラー *n* best seller

へた(な)・下手(な) *adj* not very good at; unskilful

へだてる・隔てる *vb 2* ⑧ to separate

べつ・別 **1** *adj* べつ(の・な) another; different **2** *phrase* 〜をべつにして without including ...; べつとして apart from ! *as a suffix* 〜べつ means 'classified by ...'. ▶ べつに

べっそう・別荘 *n* a second house in the country

ペット *n* pet

ベッド *n* bed

ペットボトル *n* plastic bottle

べつに・別に *adv* separately ! sometimes used alone as an abbreviation of べつに + a negative verb meaning 'nothing special' or 'not particularly'

べつべつ・別々 **1** *adj* べつべつ(の・な) separate **2** *adv* べつべつに separately

ベテラン 1 *n* an experienced person **2** *adj* ベテランの experienced

へび・蛇 *n* snake

へや・部屋 *n* room; apartment

へらす・減らす *vb 1* ⓔ to reduce; たいじゅうをへらす to lose weight

ぺらぺら *adv* fluently

ヘリコプター *n* helicopter

へる・減る *vb 1* ⓘ to decrease; おなかが へっている to be hungry

へる・経る *vb 1* ⓔ (time) to pass; (place) to go via

ベル *n* bell (bicycle or door)

ベルト *n* belt

ヘルメット *n* helmet

へん(な)・変(な) *adj* strange; wrong

へん・辺 *n* vicinity

へん・偏 *n* – the left hand element of a かんじ character and which can be used for describing and looking it up in a dictionary

べん・弁 *suf* dialect

べん・便 *n* convenience (for transport)

ペン *n* pen

へんか・変化 1 *n* change **2** *vb 3* ⓘ へんかする to change

へんかん・変換 1 *n* conversion **2** *vb 3* ⓔ に へんかんする to convert

ペンキ *n* paint

べんきょう・勉強 1 *n* studying **2** *vb 3* ⓔ べんきょうする to study

へんけん・偏見 *n* prejudice

べんごし・弁護士 *n* lawyer; solicitor; attorney

へんこう・変更 **1** *n* alteration **2** *vb 3* ㊧ へんこうする
to alter

へんじ・返事 **1** *n* reply; answer **2** *vb 3* ㊙ にへんじ (を)
する to reply; to answer

べんじょ・便所 *n* toilet

ベンチ *n* bench

ペンチ *n* pliers

べんとう・弁当 *n* – a packed lunch

べんり(な)・便利(な) *adj* convenient; useful

ほ ホ

ほ・歩 *counter* step; pace

〜っぽい *suf* – adds the meaning 'a little bit like ...', 'seems ...'.
Similar to the English suffix '-ish' in 'childish' こどもっぽい

ほいくえん・保育園 *n* nursery

ほいくしょ・保育所 *n* nursery

ポイント *n* point

ほう・方 *n* direction; way; one (which is) ‼ *used to make
comparisons in the form* ...のほうが *translatable as 'which is',
'which are', 'which would be' etc. Used after a verb in the 〜た
form in the idiom 〜た ほうが いい meaning 'should ...', 'it
would be best to ...'.

ぼう・棒 *n* stick

ぼう・防 *prf* anti-

ぼうえい・防衛 *n* defence

ぼうえき・貿易 *n* trade

ぼうえきがいしゃ・貿易会社 *n* trading company

ぼうえんきょう・望遠鏡 *n* telescope

ほうかい・崩壊 1 *n* collapse 2 *vb* 3 ㉗ ほうかいする
to collapse

ぼうがい・妨害 1 *n* obstruction 2 *vb* 3 ㊧ ぼうがいする
to obstruct

ほうがく・方角 *n* direction

ほうがく・法学 *n* law (as an academic subject)

ほうき・箒 *n* broom

ほうげん・方言 *n* dialect

ぼうけん・冒険 *n* adventure

ほうこう・方向 *n* direction

ぼうこう・膀胱 *n* bladder

ほうこく・報告 1 *n* report 2 *vb* 3 ㊧ ほうこくする
to report

ぼうさん・坊さん *n* Buddhist priest

ぼうし・帽子 *n* hat; cap

ぼうし・防止 1 *n* prevention 2 *vb* 3 ㊧ ぼうしする
to prevent

ほうしゃ・放射 *prf* radiation

ほうしん・方針 *n* policy

ぼうず・坊主 *n* – literally a (Buddhist) priest it can be used to
refer to closely cropped hair or a youth

ほうせき・宝石 *n* precious stone; jewel

ほうそう・放送 1 *n* broadcast 2 *vb* 3 ㊧ ほうそうする
to broadcast

ほうそう・包装 *n* wrapping

ほうたい・包帯 *n* bandage

ほうだい・放題 *suf* as much as you like/want

ぼうだい(な)・膨大(な) *adj* enormous

ほうちょう・包丁 *n* large kitchen knife; cleaver

ほうてい・法廷 *n* court (of law)

ぼうどう・暴動 *n* riot

ぼうはん・防犯 *suf* crime prevention

ほうび・褒美 *n* reward

ほうふ・豊富 **1** *adj* ほうふ(な) plentiful; rich in **2** *phrase* ほうふにあります to have plenty of

ぼうふう・暴風 *n* gales

ほうほう・方法 *n* method; way

ほうぼう・方々 *adv* all over the place

ほうめん・方面 *n* district

ほうもん・訪問 **1** *n* visit **2** *vb* 3 🈂 ほうもんする to visit

ぼうや・坊や *n* kid

ほうりこむ・放り込む *vb* 1 🈂 to throw into

ほうりつ・法律 *n* law

ぼうりょく・暴力 *n* violence

ぼうりょくだん・暴力団 *n* organised crime

ほうる・放る *vb* 1 🈂 to throw

ほえる・吠える *vb* 2 🈖 to bark; to howl

ほお・頬 *n* cheek

ボーイ *n* waiter

ボーイフレンド *n* boyfriend

ぼうっと *adv* absent mindedly; ぼうっとする to stare vacantly into space

ボート *n* boat

ボーナス *n* – the bonus paid twice yearly as part of the salary package for many Japanese jobs

ホーム *n* platform

ボール *n* ball

ホームステイ *n* home-stay

ほか・他・外 **1** *n* other; another **2** *adj* ほかの other

ほかに・外に・他に *adv* besides; as well as

ほがらか・朗らか **1** *adj* ほがらか(な) cheerful **2** *adv* ほがらかに cheerfully

ぼきん・募金 **1** *n* fund raising **2** *vb* **3** Ⓢ ぼきんする to raise money

ぼく・僕 *n* I **!** *used by males*

ぼくし・牧師 *n* minister of religion

ぼくじょう・牧場 *n* ranch; pasture land

ほくせい・北西 *n* north-west

ぼくちく・牧畜 *n* livestock farming

ほくとう・北東 *n* north-east

ポケット *n* pocket

ほげい・捕鯨 *n* whaling

ほけん・保険 *n* insurance

ほけん・保健 *prf* health

ぼご・母語 *n* mother tongue

ほこうしゃ・歩行者 *n* pedestrian

ぼこく・母国 *n* native country

ぼこくご・母国語 ▸ ぼご

ほこり・誇り *n* pride

ほこり・埃 *n* dust

ほし・星 *n* star

ほしい・欲しい *adj* want; would like **!** *although an adjective in Japanese it is often best translated 'to want'. When following the ～て form of a verb it means 'want you to ...'. When following the ～ない form of a verb + で it means 'don't want you to ...'*

ぼしかてい・母子家庭 *n* single parent family **!** *literally a family consisting of a mother and child|children*

ほしがる・欲しがる *vb* **1** Ⓢ Ⓥ (seems) to want **!** *an equivalent of* ほしい *used when talking about people other than oneself*

ぼしゅう・募集 1 *n* recruitment **2** *vb* **3** 愛 ぼしゅうする
to recruit

ほじょ・補助 1 *n* help **2** *vb* **3** 愛 ほじょする to assist

ほしょう・保証 *n* guarantee

ほしょうにん・保証人 *n* guarantor; sponsor

ほす・干す *vb 1* 愛 to dry (in the sun)

ボス *n* boss

ポスター *n* poster

ホステス *n* – a female 'companion' employed by a bar or night club

ポスト *n* letterbox; mailbox; post-box

ほそい・細い *adj* thin; fine

ほぞん・保存 1 *n* preservation **2** *vb* **3** 愛 ほぞんする
to preserve

ボタン *n* button

ほっきょく・北極 *n* North Pole

ぼっちゃん・坊ちゃん *n* – sometimes used by older people to mean 'boy'. Also used to mean 'spoiled' or 'naive'.

ほっておく *vb 1* 愛 to leave (someone) alone

ポット *n* – a jug for boiling water and keeping it hot for dispensing drinks

ホテル *n* hotel

ほど・程 *n* extent ! used after quantities it is translatable as 'about'. It can also be used to mean 'so ... that ...' and 'almost ...'. Following the plain form of a verb it means 'to the extent that ...'. Commonly used in association with negatives to mean 'not as ... as ...' and following a conditional ending and repeat of the verb or adjective to mean 'the more ... the better', 'the more you (do it) the more ...' etc.

ほどう・歩道 *n* pavement; sidewalk

ほどうきょう・歩道橋 *n* pedestrian bridge

ほどく・解く *vb 1* 愛 to untie; to undo

ボトル *n* bottle

ほとんど *n and adv* most; almost; (*in positive structure*) almost all; (*in negative structure*) almost none

ほね・骨 *n* bone; **ほねを おる** to break a bone

ほのお・炎 *n* flames

ほほ・頬 ▶ ほお

ほぼ *adv* almost; approximately

ほほえむ・微笑む *vb 1* ㋩ to smile

ほめる・褒める *vb 2* ㋫ to praise

ほら *exc* look!

ほり・掘り *n* moat

ポリ *prf* plastic

ほる・掘る *vb 1* ㋫ to dig up/out

ほる・彫る *vb 1* ㋫ to carve

ほん・本 *n* book

ほん・本 *prf* this; real; main

ほん・本 *counter – used to count long, thin or cylindrical things*

ぼん・盆 *n* tray; Buddhist festival ▶ おぼん

ぼん・本 ▶ ほん

ぽん・本 ▶ ほん

ほんき・本気 1 *adj* **ほんき(な)** serious; in earnest **2** *adv* **ほんきに** seriously

ほんじつ・本日 *n* today; this day

ほんしゃ・本社 *n* head office

ぼんち・盆地 *n* basin

ほんど・本土 *n* mainland

ポンド *n* pound

ほんとう・本当 1 *n* truth **2** *adj* **ほんとう(の・な)** true; real **3** *adv* **ほんとうに** really！ *also used as an exclamation to express surprise or disbelief and translatable as 'really?' or 'are you sure?'*

ほんにん・本人 *n* – meaning 'the person in question' it is translatable as 'he' or 'she' according to the context

ほんね・本音 *n* – true feelings and intentions as opposed to ▶たてまえ

ほんの *phrase* just a; merely ! often used with words indicating quantity like すこし and ちょっと to mean 'just a little'

ほんぶ・本部 *n* headquarters

ほんもの・本物 *n* (the) real thing

ほんや・本屋 *n* book shop

ほんやく・翻訳 1 *n* translation **2** *vb* **3** ㊨ ほんやくする to translate

ほんやくしゃ・翻訳者 *n* translator

ぼんやり(と) *adv* absent-mindedly

ほんらい・本来 1 *adv* originally; essentially **2** *adj* ほんらいの original

ま マ

ま・間 *n* interval; time; まに あう to be in time (for); まもなく soon

まあ *exc* well!

マーケティング *n* marketing

まあまあ *adv* so so; fairly; not bad

まい *suf* ! a negative equivalent of でしょう and the volitional form Translatable as 'probably won't', 'shouldn't' 'don't expect that...' etc. depending on context.

まい・毎 *prf* every

まい・枚 *counter* ▶ used for flat things

マイカー *n* (private) car

マイク *n* microphone

まいご・迷子 まいごに なる to get lost

まいしゅう・毎週 *n* every week

まいすう・枚数 *n* number of (pieces of paper) ▶ まい

まいつき・毎月 *n* every month

まいった *phrase* – used as an exclamation to express feelings of defeat and embarrassment. Translatable as 'I am at a loss', 'I feel overwhelmed' and a variety of other things depending on the context.

まいど・毎度 *n* every time

まいとし・毎年 *n* every year

マイナス *n* minus

まいにち・毎日 *n* every day

まいばん・毎晩 *n* every night

マイペース (で) *adv* at one's own pace

マイホーム *n* private house

まいる・参る *vb 1 ㋬* to go; to come ! *humble equivalent of* いく

まえ・前 **1** *n* front; in front **2** *prf* front

まかせる・任せる *vb 2 ㋓* to leave (it) to (somebody) to do; to entrust

まがる・曲がる *vb 1 ㋬* to turn; to bend; to be crooked

まく・幕 *n* curtain

まく・巻く *vb 1 ㋓* to wrap; to coil

まく・蒔く *vb 1 ㋓* to sow (seeds); to sprinkle (water)

まくら・枕 *n* pillow

まけ・負け *n* defeat

まける・負ける *vb 2 ㋬* to be beaten; to give a discount

まげる・曲げる *vb 2 ㋓* to bend

まご・孫 *n* grandchild

まことに・誠に adv sincerely; **まことに ありがとう ございます** thank you most sincerely

まさか adv and exc surely not!; no way!

まさつ・摩擦 1 n friction **2** vb 3 ⑰ ⓔ **まさつする** to rub

まさに adv exactly; be just about to

まざる・混ざる・交ざる vb 1 ⑰ to be mixed

まして adv (with negatives) much less; (with positives) even more (so)

まじめ・真面目 1 adj **まじめ(な)** serious; hard-working **2** adv **まじめに** seriously

まじる・混じる・交じる vb 1 ⑰ to be mixed

ます・増す vb 1 ⑰ to increase

まず・先ず adv first of all; probably

まずい adj tastes awful; wrong

マスク n – a mask worn over the nose and mouth to prevent the spread of colds

マスコミ n the media

まずしい・貧しい adj poor

マスター n proprietor of a bar or restaurant

ますます・益々 adv (with positives) more and more; (with negatives) less and less

まぜる・混ぜる・交ぜる vb 2 ⓔ to mix

また・又 adv again; **または** or; **またね** see you soon

まだ・未だ adv still; (with a negative) (not) yet; **まだです** not yet

または・又は ▶ また

まち・町 n town **!** also a subdivision of addresses in Japanese towns and cities ▶ ちょう

まち・街 n town centre; city centre

まちあいしつ・待合室 n waiting room

まちあわせ・待ち合わせ n meeting; rendezvous

まちあわせる・待ち合わせる *vb 2* 🖝 に to meet

まちがい・間違い *n* mistake

まちがう・間違う *vb 1* 🖝 to be mistaken

まちがえる・間違える *vb 2* 🖝 to mistake

まちがって ▶ まちがう

まちかど・町角 *n* street corner; (in the) street

まちかねる・待ちかねる *vb 2* 🖝 to wait impatiently

まちます ▶ まつ

まちまち **1** *adj* まちまち(の) various **2** *adv* まちまちに variously

まつ・待つ *vb 1* 🖝 まって・またない・まちます to wait; to wait for

まつ・松 *n* pine tree

まつげ・睫 *n* eyebrow

まっか(な)・真っ赤(な) *adj* bright red

まっくら(な)・真っ暗(な) *adj* very dark

まっくろ(な)・真っ黒(な) *adj* pitch-black

マッサージ **1** *n* massage **2** *vb 3* 🖝 マッサージする to massage

マッサージ *n* massage

まっさお(な)・真っ青(な) *adj* deep blue; かおが まっさおになる face turns white as a sheet

まっさきに・真っ先に *adv* immediately

まっしろ(な)・真っ白(な) *adj* brilliant white

まっすぐ・真っ直ぐ **1** *adj* まっすぐ(な) straight **2** *adv* まっすぐに straight

まったく・全く *adv* (with negative expressions) utterly (not) ❗ also used as an exclamation to express annoyance

マッチ *n* match

まって ▶ まつ

まつり・祭り *n* festival

まで・迄 *pt* as far as; until; to; even; までも ない・ なく to be unnecessary to

までに・迄に *pt* by; before

まど・窓 *n* window

まどぐち・窓口 *n* (ticket) window; enquiry point

まとまる *vb 1* ㊙ to be gathered together; to be sorted out

まとめる *vb 2* ㊥ to gather together; to put into shape

マナー *n* manners; behaviour

まなぶ・学ぶ *vb 1* ㊥ to learn

まにあう・間に合う ▶ま

まねき・招き *n* invitation

まねく・招く *vb 1* ㊥ to invite; to bring about

まねる・真似る *vb 2* ㊥ to imitate

まぶしい・眩しい *adj* dazzling

マフラー *n* (warm) scarf

ママ *n* mother

まま *n* – the basic meaning is 'as it is', 'in an unchanged condition'. It can be used after the plain forms of verbs and adjectives and この・その・あの to mean 'without change' and 'as (you were told etc.)'.

ママさん *n* – female proprietor of a bar

まめ・豆 *n* beans

まめ **1** *adj* まめ(な) hardworking **2** *adv* まめに carefully

まもなく・間も無く ▶ま

まもる・守る *vb 1* ㊥ to protect; to defend

まやく・麻薬 *n* (illegal) drugs

まよう・迷う *vb 1* ㊙ to be lost; to be at a loss to know what to do; みちにまよう to be lost

マラソン *n* marathon; long race

まる・丸 **1** *n* circle **2** *prf* fully; whole

まるい・丸い *adj* round

まるで　adv utterly (not); as if

まれ・希 **1** adj まれ(な) rare **2** adv まれに rarely

まわす・回す　vb 1 Ⓔ to turn; to forward (a letter); to transfer (a phone call)

まわり・周り・回り　n area around; circulation

まわりみち・回り道　n detour

まわる・回る　vb 1 Ⓝ to turn; to go around

まん・万　counter ten thousand

まんいち・万一　phrase in case (of emergency etc.)

まんがいち・万が一 ▶ まんいち

まんいん・満員　n being full to capacity

まんいんでんしゃ・満員電車　n a crowded train

まんが・漫画・マンガ　n cartoons; comic books; animations; manga

マンション　n apartment; apartment block

まんせき・満席　n having all seats filled

まんぞく・満足 **1** n satisfaction **2** vb 3 Ⓝ に まんぞくする to be satisfied

満タン まんタンに する to fill the car's tank up with petrol/gasoline

まんてん・満点　n full marks

まんなか・真ん中　n middle; centre

み ミ

み・身　n body; みにつける to wear to acquire

み・実　n fruit; nut

み・未　prf incomplete

み・味 *suf* flavour

みあげる・見上げる *vb 2* 🤸 to look up

みあい・見合い *n* – an arranged meeting with a view to marriage ▶ おみあい

みえる・見える *vb 2* 🤸 に to be visible; to seem

みおくり・見送り *n* (a) send off

みおくる・見送る *vb 1* 🤸 to see someone off

みおぼえ・見覚え *n* recollection

みがく・磨く *vb 1* 🤸 to polish; to brush (the teeth); うでを みがく to practice

みかけ・見かけ *n* appearance

みかける・見かける *vb 2* 🤸 to catch sight of

みかた・味方 *n* ally; supporter

みかた・見方 *n* point of view

みかん *n* mandarin orange

みぎ・右 *n* right

みぎがわ・右側 *n* the right hand side

みぎきき・右利き *n* right handed person

ミキサー *n* mixer

みぎて・右手 *n* right hand

みごと・見事 **1** *adj* みごと(な) wonderful **2** *adv* みごとに skilfully

みこみ・見込み *n* prospect; expectation

みじかい・短い *adj* short

みじめ・惨め **1** *adj* みじめ(な) miserable **2** *adv* みじめ に miserably

ミシン *n* sewing machine

ミス *n* error

みず・水 *n* (cold) water

みずうみ・湖 *n* lake

みずから・自ら *adv* on one's own initiative; in person

みずぎ・水着 *n* swimming costume

みずわり・水割り *n* – whiskey|whisky or other spirit diluted with water or tea

みせ・店 *n* shop

みせいねん・未成年 *n* – someone who is under the legal age of adulthood (which is twenty in Japan)

みせる・見せる *vb 2 ⓔ* to show

みそ・味噌 *n* – a paste made from fermented soy beans and which forms the basis of miso soup

みぞ・溝 *n* ditch

みたい *suf* – following the plain forms of verbs and adjectives it means 'looks like', 'is similar to' or '(it) seems (that)'. It can also be translated as 'such as ...'.

みだし・見出し *n* headline

>**みち・道** *n* street; road; way (to somewhere)

みぢか・身近 1 *adj* close; familiar **2** *adv* みぢかに close at hand

みちじゅん・道順 *n* route

みちる・満ちる *vb 2 ⓝ* to be full

みつに・密に *adv* densely

みっか・三日・3日 *n* the third day of the month; three days

みつかる・見つかる *vb 1 ⓝ* to be found

みつける・見つける *vb 2 ⓔ* to find

みっつ・三つ・3つ *n* three

みて ▶ みる

みっともない *adj* disgraceful

みつめる・見つめる *vb 2 ⓔ* to stare

みとおし・見通し *n* prospect

みとめる・認める *vb 2 ⓔ* to admit; to approve

みどり・緑 *n* green; greenery

みどりのひ・緑の日 *n* – Greenery Day (April 29) – *a Japanese public holiday*

みな・皆 *n* everyone; everything

みなおす・見直す *vb 1* ㊡ to look at again

みなさま・皆様 ▶みなさん

みなさん・皆さん *n* everyone; ladies and gentlemen

みなと・港 *n* harbour; port

みなみ・南 *n* south

みにくい・醜い *adj* ugly

みのる・実る *vb 1* ㉗ to bear fruit

みぶん・身分 *n* position; status

みほん・見本 *n* sample

みまい・見舞い ▶おみまい

みまう・見舞う *vb 1* ㊡ to visit (someone who is not well)

みます▶みる

みまん・未満 *suf* less than; under

みみ・耳 *n* ear

みやげ(もの)・土産(物) ▶おみやげ

みやこ・都 *n* capital; large city

みょう・妙 **1** *adj* みょう(な) strange **2** *adv* みょうに strangely

みょうじ・名字 *n* surname

みょうにち・明日 *n* tomorrow

みらい・未来 *n* future

ミリ *n* millimetres

みりょく・魅力 *n* attractiveness

みりょくてき(な)・魅力的(な) *adj* attractive

みる・見る *vb 2* 👁 みて みない みます to see; to watch; to look at ! *following the 〜て form of a verb it adds the meaning 'try ... and see', 'have a go at (doing)'*

ミルク *n* milk

みんかん・民間 *prf* civil

みんしゅ・民主 *prf* democratic

みんしゅしゅぎ・民主主義 *n* democracy

みんな ▶ みな

みんぞく・民族 *n and prf* people; tribe

みんよう・民謡 *n* folk songs

む ム

む・無 *prf* – gives the meaning 'not' and similar to English prefix 'un-'

むいか・六日・6日 *n* the sixth day of the month; six days

ムード *n* atmosphere; ambience

むかい・向かい *n* opposite side

むかう・向かう *vb 1* 👁 to face; to head for

むかえ・迎え ▶ むかえる むかえに いく to go and meet

むかえる・迎える *vb 2* 👁 to meet; to welcome; to greet

むかし・昔 *n* long ago

むかしむかし・昔々 *n* once upon a time

むき・向き **1** *n* direction **2** *suf* aimed at

むく・向く *vb 1* に to turn; to face; to be suited to

むく・剥く *vb 1* 👁 to peel

むけ・向け *suf* for

むける・向ける　*vb 2* Ⓢ to turn towards; to aim towards

むげん・無限　*n* without limits; むげんの endless

むこ・婿　*n* bridegroom ❗ can also mean 'son-in-law' where the husband joins the wife's family and changes his name to hers

むこう・向こう　*n* the opposite side; over there ❗ often used to refer to a foreigner's country and translatable as 'your country'

むこうがわ・向こう側　*n* the other side; they

むし・虫　*n* insect

むし(する)・無視(する)　*vb 3* Ⓢ to ignore

むじ(の)・無地(の)　*adj* plain (without pattern)

むしあつい・蒸し暑い　*adj* humid

むしば・虫歯　*n* a bad (decayed) tooth; a filling

むじゅん・矛盾　*n* contradiction

むしろ・寧ろ　*adv* rather (than)

むす・蒸す　*vb 1* Ⓢ to steam

むすう(の)・無数(の)　*adj* countless

むずかしい・難しい　*adj* difficult

むすこ・息子　*n* son

むすぶ・結ぶ　*vb 1* Ⓢ to tie; to connect

むすめ・娘　*n* daughter

むだ・無駄　**1** *n* waste **2** *adj* むだ(な) futile **3** *adv* むだに uselessly

むだづかい・無駄遣い　*n* (a) waste

むだん・無断　*n and prf* without permission

むちゅう・夢中　**1** *n* being absorbed in (doing something) **2** *adv* むちゅうに intently

むっつ・六つ・6つ　*n* six

むね・胸　*n* chest

むら・村　*n* village

むらさき・紫　*n* purple

むり・無理 **1** *n* impossibility **2** *adj* むり(な) impossible; unreasonable **3** *vb* 3 ㉚ むり(を)する to overdo it; to work too hard

むりょう・無料 *adj* free

むれ・群れ *n* – used to refer to a group of animals so the translation will be words like 'herd', 'pack' or 'swarm' etc. according to the type of creature

めメ

め・目 *n* eye; めに つく to notice; めに かかる to see to meet; めを とおす to look through; めが さめる to wake up

め・芽 *n* bud; shoot

め・目 *suf* number; place

めい・姪 *n* niece

めい・名 **1** *prf* famous **2** *counter* people

めいかく・明確 **1** *adj* めいかく(な) clear; accurate **2** *adv* めいかくに accurately

めいさく・名作 *n* masterpiece

めいし・名刺 *n* business card

めいし・名詞 *n* noun

めいじ・明治 *n* – era name for 1868–1912 and used for dates during that period

めいしょ・名所 *n* (the) sights; famous places

めいじる・命じる *vb* 1 ㊦ to order

めいしん・迷信 *n* superstition

めいじん・名人 *n* (an) expert

めいずる・命ずる ▶めいじる

めいはく(な)・明白(な) *adj* evident

めいぶつ・名物 *n* speciality

めいぼ・名簿 *n* register (of names)

めいる・滅入る *vb 1㋑* to be depressed

めいれい・命令 *n* order

めいわく・迷惑 *n* nuisance; trouble; めいわくを かける to cause trouble

めうえ・目上 *n* one's superior (at work)

メーカー *n* manufacturer

メートル *n* metre *!* sometimes written with the Chinese character 米

めがね・眼鏡・メガネ *n* glasses; spectacles

めがねや・眼鏡屋 *n* optician

めぐまれる・恵まれる *vb 2㋑* に to be blessed (with)

めくる *vb 1㋺* to turn (a page)

めぐる・巡る *vb 1㋺* to travel around; to come around

めざす・目指す *vb 1㋺* to aim for

めざまし・目覚し *n* awakening

めざましどけい・目覚し時計 *n* alarm clock

めざめる・目覚める *vb 2㋑* to wake up

めし・飯 *n* (cooked) rice; meal

めしあがる・召し上がる *vb 1㋺* to eat; to drink *!* an honorific equivalent of たべる and のむ

めした・目下 *n* one's junior (at work)

めじるし・目印 *n* sign; landmark

めす・雌 *n* female

めずらしい・珍しい *adj* rare

めだつ・目立つ *vb 1㋺* to stand out

めちゃくちゃ(な) *adj* messy; disorganised

メッセージ *n* message

めったに・滅多に *adv* (with negative) rarely

めでたい *adj* auspicious; fortunate

めど・目処 *n* aim; めどが たたない there is no prospect of ...

メニュー *n* menu

めまい *n* dizziness

メモ *n* memo

メモ帳 *n* notebook

めやす・目安 *n* standard; target

メリット *n* advantage

めん・面 *n* aspect; surface; mask

めん・綿 *n* cotton

めん・麺 *n* noodles

めんきょ・免許 *n* licence

めんぜいてん・免税店 *n* duty free store

めんせき・面積 *n* area

めんせつ・面接 *n* interview

めんどう(な)・面倒 (な) *adj* troublesome; めんどうを みる to look after (somebody)

めんどうくさい・面倒くさい *adj* troublesome

メンバー *n* member

も モ

も *pt* also; even ! *used to emphasis negatives, quantities and examples. When in the pattern 〜も〜も it means 'both ... and ...', 'either ... or ...', 'neither ... nor ...'.*

もう *adv* already; yet; any more; もう いちど once more; もう すぐ soon; もう いい です that's OK; no thank you

もうかる・儲かる *vb 1* ㉗ to be profitable

もうける・儲ける *vb 2* Ⓢ to make a profit

もうける・設ける *vb 2* Ⓢ to establish

もうしあげる・申し上げる *vb 2* Ⓢ to say ! *humble equivalent of* いう

もうしこみ・申込み・申込 *n* application

もうしこみしょ・申込書 *n* application form

もうしこむ・申し込む *vb 1* に to apply for

もうしわけ・申し訳 *n* apology; excuse; もうしわけありません (I am) extremely sorry

もうしわけない・申し訳ない ▶もうしわけ

もうす・申す *vb 1* Ⓢ to say; to be called ! *a humble form of* いう: こいどともうします My name is Koido

もうふ・毛布 *n* blanket

もえないゴミ・燃えないゴミ *n –* rubbish|garbage which is not for incineration

もえる・燃える *vb 2* Ⓜ to burn

もえるゴミ・燃えるゴミ *n –* rubbish|garbage which is for incineration

モーター *n* motor

もくざい・木材 *n* wood; timber

もくじ・目次 *n* (table of) contents

もくてき・目的 *n* objective

もくひょう・目標 *n* objective; target

もくようび・木曜日 *n* Thursday

もぐる・潜る *vb 1* Ⓜ to dive

もし・若し *adv* if

もじ・文字 *n* letter (of the alphabet); script

もしかして ▶もしかしたら

もしかしたら *adv* perhaps; possibly

もしかすると ▶もしかしたら

もしくは・若しくは *conj* or

もじばけ・文字化け *n* – Japanese text which has been garbled by a computer programme into a series of unreadable symbols. Usually translated as 'gibberish'

もしも ▶ もし

もしもし *phrase* (on telephone) hello; excuse me

もたらす *vb 1* ⓔ to bring about

もたれる *vb 2* ⓥ に to lean

モダン(な) *adj* modern

もち・餅 *n* – blocks or 'cakes' of pounded cooked rice

もち・持ち *suf* having

もちあげる・持ち上げる *vb 2* ⓔ to lift up

もちいる・用いる *vb 2* ⓔ to use

もちかえり・持ち帰り *n and prf* take away (food etc.)

もちかえる・持ち帰る *vb 1* ⓔ to take home; to bring home

もちぬし・持ち主 *n* owner

もちます ▶ もつ

もちろん・勿論 *adv* of course

もつ・持つ *vb 1* ⓔ もって・もたない・もちます
to hold; to own; to have; to carry; to keep

もったいない *adj* wasteful; too good (for person, place or task);
　もったいない what a waste!

もって ▶ もつ

もっていきます ▶ もっていく

もっていく・持っていく *vb 1* ⓔ もっていって・
　もっていかない・もっていきます to take

もっていって ▶ もっていく

もってきて ▶ もってくる

もってきます ▶ もってくる

もってくる・持ってくる *vb 3* ⓔ もってきて・もっ
　てこない・もってきます to bring

もっと *adv* more

もっとも・最も *adv* most

もっとも **1** *conj* however **2** *adj* もっとも(な) reasonable; natural

もてなし *n* hospitality

もてなす *vb 1* ㊰ to treat somebody (to food etc.)

もてる *vb 2* ㊰ に to be popular (especially with the opposite sex)

モデム *n* modem

モデル *n* model

もと・元・基・素 *n* origin; cause; beginning

もと・元 *prf* former

もどす・戻す *vb 1* ㊰ to put back

もとづく・基づく *vb 1* ㊰ に to be based on

もとめる・求める *vb 2* ㊰ to ask for; to demand; to look for

もともと・元々 *adv* from the beginning; by nature

もどり・戻り *n* return

もどる・戻る *vb 1* ㊰ to return; to go back; to come back

モニター *n* monitor

もの・物 **1** *n* thing **2** *suf* item

もの・者 *n* – a humble equivalent of ひと meaning 'person'

もの *pt* – Used after past tenses to mean 'used to ...' and after non-past structures to mean that something 'is only natural' or to express obligation. In the latter use it is translatable as 'should'.

ものおき・物置 *n* closet; storeroom

ものおと・物音 *n* sound

ものがたり・物語 *n* story; tale

ものがたる・物語る *vb 1* ㊰ to tell

ものごと・物事 *n* things

ものさし・物差し *n* ruler

ものすごい・物凄い *adj* tremendous

ものだ・物だ ▶ もの

ものです・物です ▶ もの

もみじ・紅葉 *n* maple tree; autumn change in the colour of leaves

もむ・揉む *vb 1* Ⓔ to massage

もめん・木綿 *n* cotton

もやす・燃やす *vb 1* Ⓔ to burn

もよう・模様 *n* pattern

もよおし・催し *n* meeting; function

もよおす・催す *vb 1* Ⓔ to hold (a meeting etc.)

もらいます ▶ もらう

もらう・貰う *vb 1* Ⓔ にもらって・もらわない・もらいます to receive ❗ following the ～て form of another verb it means to receive the favour of someone doing something for you or 'get (somebody) to (do something)'. This usage is often not reproduced in translation.

もらって ▶ もらう

もり・森 *n* forest

もりあがる・盛り上がる *vb 1* Ⓘ to grow lively

もりあわせ・盛り合わせ *n* assortment

もれ・漏れ *n* leak

もれる・漏れる *vb 2* Ⓘ to leak

もん・門 *n* gate

もん・問 *suf* question

もん – a reduced form of the particle もの and also used in speech (especially by women) as an emphatic particle at the end of sentences ▶ もの

もんく・文句 *n* complaint; もんくを いう to complain

もんだい・問題 *n* problem; issue; question

もんどう・問答 *n* question and answer

や ヤ

や *pt* and **!** *joins a list of nouns which is not complete and although translatable as 'and' it carries the meaning of 'among other things'*

や・屋 *suf* shop **!** *also used to mean 'person who does ...'*

や・夜 *suf* night

〜やいなや *phrase* as soon as

やおや・八百屋 *n* greengrocer

やがて *adv* after a while

やかましい *adj* noisy; fussy

やかん・夜間 *n* night time

やかん・薬缶 *n* non-electric kettle

やき・焼き *prf* – cooked by grilling or roasting ▶ やく

やきとり・焼き鳥 *n* – kebabs of grilled chicken

やきゅう・野球 *n* baseball

やく・焼く *vb 1* ㊟ to burn; to tan; to grill; to roast; to toast

やく・約 *adv* about; approximately

やく・役 *n and suf* role; job; やくに たつ to be useful

やく・訳 **1** *n and suf* translation **2** *vb 3* ㊟ やくする to translate

やくしゃ・役者 *n* actor; actress

やくしょ・役所 *n* – an office of local government ▶ やくば

やくす・訳す ▶ やくする

やくする・訳する *vb 1* ㊟ に to translate

やくそく・約束 **1** *n* promise; arrangement **2** *vb 3* ㊟ に やくそくする to promise; やくそくを まもる to keep a promise; やくそくを やぶる to break a promise

やくだつ・役立つ *vb 1* ⑰ to be useful

やくにん・役人 *n* (an) official

やくば・役場 *n* local government office ❗ *similar to 'town hall' or 'city hall'*

やくひん・薬品 *n* medicines; chemicals

やくぶつ・薬物 *n* chemicals

やくめ・役目 *n* role

やくわり・役割 *n* role

やけ やけに なる to become desperate

やけい・夜景 *n* – the view by night over an area of a city with bright lights

やけど・火傷 **1** *n* burn **2** *vb 3* ⑰ やけどする to get burned; to get scalded

やける・焼ける *vb 1* ⑰ to be burned; to be tanned; to be grilled; to be roasted; to be toasted

やこう・夜行 *prf* night time

やさい・野菜 *n* vegetables

やさしい・優しい *adj* kind

やさしい・易しい *adj* easy

やじるし・矢印 *n* arrows (indicating directions)

やしん・野心 *n* ambition

やすい・安い *adj* cheap

やすい・易い *suf* easy to (do)

やすっぽい・安っぽい *adj* cheap-looking

やすみ・休み *n* holiday; rest; day off

やすみます ▶ やすむ

やすむ・休む *vb 1* ㊗ やすんで・やすまない・やすみます to take time off work or school; to have a break; to have a rest

やすんで ▶ やすむ

やせる・痩せる *vb 2 他* to get thin; to lose weight

やたらに *adv* indiscriminately; irresponsibly

やちん・家賃 *n* rent

やつ・奴 *n* person; thing ! *a rough term used when the proper name of the item has been momentarily forgotten or of someone with whom one is angry*

やっかい・厄介 **1** *n* trouble **2** *adj* やっかい(な) burdensome

やっきょく・薬局 *n* pharmacy; chemist

やっつ・八つ・8つ *counter* eight

やっつける *vb 2 他* to criticise; to beat up

やっと *adv* eventually; barely

やっぱり *adv* – *a more emphatic version of* やはり

やとう・雇う *vb 1 他* to employ

やぬし・家主 *n* – *meaning 'house owner' it could be translated as 'landlord' or 'landlady' according to the context*

やばい *n* – *used to describe a state of danger or a feeling of risk especially as an exclamation when something important has been just remembered in time etc. As an exclamation it often means something like 'Oh no! (I've just realised/remembered that I have to ..)'*

やはり *adv* as expected; nevertheless

やぶる・破る *vb 1 他* to rip; to defeat; to break (a promise etc.)

やぶれる・破れる *vb 2 他* to be ripped

やぶれる・敗れる *vb 2 他* に to be defeated

やま・山 *n* mountain; a pile of ... ► さん

やまあるき・山歩き *n* mountain/hill walking

やまと・大和 *n* – *an old word for Japan*

やまとことば・大和言葉 *n* – words not derived from Chinese characters but of original Japanese stock

やまのて・山の手 *n* – the part of a town built on the hills (and as such a prosperous residential area) especially in Tokyo and often used to mean the rail network that circles Tokyo called the やまのてせん

やまのぼり・山登り *n* mountain climbing

やむ・止む *vb 1* ㉗ to stop (raining)

やむをえない・やむを得ない *adj* unavoidable

やめる・止める *vb 2* Ⓔ to stop; to give up

やめる・辞める *vb 2* Ⓔ to resign

やや *adv* a little bit

ややこしい *adj* complicated and annoying

やりとり・やり取り *n* exchange

やりなおす・やり直す *vb 1* Ⓔ to redo

やりにくい *adj* difficult to do

やりやすい *adj* easy to do

やる・遣る *vb 1* Ⓔ to do; to give ! *A more informal version of* する. *In the meaning 'to give' it is used among friends or by older people to younger. When used after a verb in the* 〜て *form it means 'do for you (as a favour)' and carries strong overtones of social superiority or seniority*

やるき・やる気 *n* will; drive

やろう・野郎 *n* – used as a substitute for ひと meaning 'person' it is highly insulting and somewhat similar to the English 'bastard' as a term of abuse

やわらかい・柔らかい・軟らかい *adj* soft

ヤンキー *n* – refers to youths with their hair dyed (usually blonde) which is seen as a sign of rebelliousness.

ゆユ

ゆ・湯 *n* hot water

ゆいいつ(の)・唯一(の) *adj* one and only; sole

ゆう *vb 3 ㋕* – an alternative pronunciation of いう

ゆうえんち・遊園地 *n* amusement park

ゆうがた・夕方 *n* (early) evening

ゆうき・勇気 *n* bravery

ゆうこう・有効 *n* validity; ゆうこうきげん valid until

ゆうこう・友好 *n* friendship

ゆうしゅう(な)・優秀(な) *adj* excellent

ゆうしょう・優勝 **1** *n* victory **2** *vb 3 ㋕* ゆうしょうする
to win

ゆうじん・友人 *n* friend

ゆうそう(する)・郵送(する) *vb 3 ㋘* to send by post

ゆうそうりょう・郵送料 *n* (cost of) postage

ゆうだち・夕立 *n* a brief shower (of rain)

ゆうのう(な)・有能(な) *adj* capable

ゆうはん・夕飯 *n* evening meal

ゆうびん・郵便 *n and prf* mail

ゆうびんきょく・郵便局 *n* post office

ゆうびんぶつ・郵便物 *n* (items of) mail

ゆうべ・夕べ *n* evening; last night

ゆうめい・有名 **1** *n* fame **2** *adj* ゆうめい(な) famous

ユーモア *n* humour

ゆうりょう・有料 *n* charge; requiring payment

ゆか・床 *n* floor

ゆかい(な)・愉快(な) *adj* pleasant

ゆかた・浴衣 *n* – a light, summer-weight きもの worn especially at festivals and hot spring resorts

ゆき・雪 *n* snow

ゆき・行き *n and suf* – an alternative form of いき attached to the names of train or flight destinations etc. to mean 'bound for ...'

ゆく・行く *vb 1* ⑳ – an alternative form of いく

ゆくえ・行方 *n* whereabouts

ゆくえふめい・行方不明 *n* missing; lost

ゆげ・湯気 *n* steam

ゆけつ・輸血 *n* blood transfusion

ゆしゅつ・輸出 **1** *n* export **2** *vb 3* ㊦ ゆしゅつする to export

ゆずる・譲る *vb 1* ㊦ to hand over; to offer

ゆそう・輸送 **1** *n* transportation **2** *vb 3* ㊦ ゆそうする to transport

ゆたか(な)・豊か(な) *adj* abundant; affluent

ゆだん・油断 **1** *n* carelessness **2** *vb 3* ⑳ ゆだんする to be negligent

ゆっくり(と) *adv* slowly

ゆでる・茹でる *vb 2* ㊦ to boil

ゆにゅう・輸入 **1** *n* import **2** *vb 3* ㊦ ゆにゅうする to import

ゆのみ・湯飲み *n* – a small Japanese style cup without handles

ゆび・指 *n* finger ! also used as あしの ゆび to mean 'toe'

ゆびわ・指輪 *n* ring

ゆめ・夢 *n* dream; ゆめを みる to have a dream

ゆるい・緩い *adj* loose

ゆるす・許す *vb 1* ㊦ to forgive; to allow

ゆれる・揺れる *vb 2* ⑳ to shake

よ ヨ

よ・世 *n* world

よ・夜 *n* night

よ・四 *prf* four

よ *pt* – a particle used at the end of sentences for emphasis and which expresses emotion, enthusiasm or rebuke etc.

よあけ・夜明け *n* dawn

よい・良い *adj* good – an alternative form of いい used in some parts of Japan, in formal speech and which is the base of the negative and past forms ▶ いい

よう・用 *n* something to do ! also used (especially as a suffix) with the meaning 'use' or 'for the use of'.

よう・様 *n* – the basic meaning is 'appearance' and it is used in expressions where it is often translatable as 'look' or 'seem' or 'be similar'. It can also mean 'something like that'. ▶ ように

よう・洋 *prf* – the meaning is 'western' as opposed to Asian or Japanese ▶ わ

よう・酔う *vb 1* ㉝ に to be drunk

ようい・用意 **1** *n* preparation **2** *vb 3* ㊦ よういする to prepare

ようい・容易 **1** *adj* ようい (な) easy **2** *adv* よういに easily

ようか・八日・8日 *n* the eighth day of the month; eight days

ようき・容器 *n* container

ようき・陽気 **1** *adj* ようき (な) cheerful **2** *adv* ようきに cheerfully

ようきゅう・要求 **1** *n* demand **2** *vb 3* ㊦ ようきゅうする to demand

ようご・用語 *n* terminology

ようこそ *phrase* welcome (to 〜)

ようし・用紙 *n and suf* – 'paper' especially in compounds to do with exam and answer papers or referring to the squared paper used for writing Japanese called げんこうようし

ようし・養子 *n* adopted child; foster child

ようじ・用事 *n* business; something to do

ようじ・幼児 *n* infant

ようしつ・洋室 *n* – a western style room as opposed to a traditional Japanese style one ▶ わしつ

ようじん・用心 **1** *n* precautions **2** *vb* **3** 𫝆 に ようじんする to take precautions

ようす・様子 *n* appearance; condition

ようするに・要するに *adv* essentially

ようそ・要素 *n* element

ようち(な)・幼稚(な) *adj* immature

ようちえん・幼稚園 *n* kindergarten

ようてん・要点 *n* point

ようと・用途 *n* use

ように *adv* so that; as; 〜ように なる reach the point when to become able to ...; 〜ように する make a point of (doing something) ▶ よう

ようび・曜日 *n and suf* day of the week

ようふう・洋風 *n* Western style (especially of cookery)

ようふく・洋服 *n* clothing ! sometimes meaning 'western style' clothing as opposed to わふく but also clothing in general

ようもう・羊毛 *n* wool

ようやく・漸く *adv* at last

ようりょう・要領 *n* essential point

ヨーロッパ *n* Europe

よき・予期 **1** *n* expectation **2** *vb* **3** 𫝆 よきする to expect

よきん・預金 *n* savings

よく *adv* often; well; hard; kindly

よく・翌 *prf* the next

よくじつ・翌日 *n* the next day

よくばり(な)・欲張り(な) *adj* greedy

よけい・余計 1 *adj* よけい(な) unnecessary **2** *adv* よけいに all the more

よこ・横 1 *n* width; side **2** *adv* よこに sideways; across; よこになる to lie down

よこぎる・横切る *vb 1* ⊛ to cross

よこす・寄越す *vb 1* ⑰ to come close

よごす・汚す *vb 1* ⊛ to make dirty

よごれ・汚れ *n* dirt

よごれる・汚れる *vb 2* ⑰ to be dirty

よさん・予算 *n* budget

よしゅう・予習 *n* – studying in advance as preparation for a class and translatable as 'preparation', 'revision' or 'review' depending on the context

よす *vb 1* ⊛ to stop

よせる・寄せる *vb 2* ⊛ to deliver; to hand over

よそ・余所 *n* somewhere else; another place; よその ひと stranger; よそに する to put on one side; ignoring

よそく・予測 1 *n* estimate **2** *vb 3* ⊛ よそくする to predict

よち・余地 *n* room; space

よっか・四日・4日 *n* the fourth day of the month; four days

よつかど・四つ角 *n* crossroads

よっつ・四つ *n* four

よって ▶ によって ▶ よる

ヨット *n* yacht

よっぱらい・酔っ払い *n* a drunk

よっぱらう・酔っ払う *vb 1 ㉑* to be drunk

よてい・予定 *n* plan; schedule *! following the dictionary form of a verb +* です *it means that the action is planned*

よなか・夜中 *n* the middle of the night

よび(の)・予備(の) *adj* spare; extra

よびかける・呼びかける *vb 2 ㉓* に to call out (to someone)

よびだす・呼び出す *vb 1 ㉓* to summon; to call

よぶ・呼ぶ *vb 1 ㉓* to call; to invite

よぶん・余分 **1** *adj* よぶん(な) additional; extra **2** *adv* よぶんに additionally

よほう・予報 *n* forecast

よぼう・予防 **1** *n* prevention **2** *vb 3 ㉓* よぼうする to prevent

よぼうちゅうしゃ・予防注射 *n* vaccination

よみ・読み *n* – the pronunciation or 'reading' of かんじ characters ▶ おんよみ ▶ くんよみ

よみあげる・読み上げる *vb 2 ㉓* to read aloud

よみがえる・蘇る・甦る *vb 1 ㉑* to revive

よみがな・読みがな *n* – another word for ふりがな

よみます ▶ よむ

よむ・読む *vb 1 ㉓* よんで・よまない・よみます to read

よめ・嫁 *n* bride *!* can mean daughter-in-law

よやく・予約 **1** *n* booking; reservation **2** *vb 3 ㉓* よやくする to book; to make a reservation

よゆう・余裕 *n* leeway

より *pt* than; from; rather than; アメリカは にほんより おおきいです America is larger than Japan

よりかかる・寄りかかる *vb 1 ㉑* に to lean on

よる・夜 *n* night; evening

よる・寄る *vb 1* ㉗ に to come close; to drop in and visit (en route to somewhere else)

よる・因る *vb 1* ㉗ to depend ! *in the form* 〜による *it means 'according to' or 'due to'*

よろこび・喜び *n* joy

よろこぶ・喜ぶ *vb 1* ㉗ to be delighted

よろしい・宜しい *adj* – a more formal version of いい *meaning 'good' or 'ok'*

よろしく・宜しく *adv* – used alone or in phrases such as よろしくおねがい します *and* どうぞよろしくおねがいいたします *when asking for favourable treatment or consideration. It is difficult to translate as contexts will vary widely but the meaning ranges from 'please' to 'I humbly request that …'. It is also used in phrases like* 〜に よろしく おつたえください *to mean 'please send my best wishes to …'*

よわい・弱い *adj* weak

よん・四 *n* four

よんで ▶ よむ ▶ よぶ

らラ

ら・等 *suf* – adds the meaning of 'more than one'

らい・来 *prf* next

らいげつ・来月 *n* next month

らいしゅう・来週 *n* next week

ライス *n* (cooked) rice ! *used when the rice is served western style on a plate*

ライター *n* cigarette lighter

らいにち(する)・来日(する) *vb 3* ㉗ to come to Japan

らいねん・来年 *n* next year

らく・楽 **1** *adj* らく（な）easy **2** *adv* らくに easily; comfortably

ラケット *n* racket

らしい *suf* appears (that), apparently ! conjugates as an い adjective

ラジオ *n* radio

らっかんてき・楽観的 **1** *adj* らっかんてき（な） optimistic **2** *adv* らっかんてきに optimistically

ラッシュ *n* rush hour

ラッシュアワー ▶ ラッシュ

ラボ *n* (language) laboratory

らん・欄 *n* column

ランチ *n* lunch

ランニング *n* running

らんぼう・乱暴 **1** *n* violence **2** *adj* らんぼう（な）violent **3** *adv* らんぼうに roughly **4** *vb* 3 ⓝ に らんぼうする to use violence against

らんよう・乱用 **1** *n* misuse **2** *vb* 3 ⓦ らんようする to misuse

り リ

リアル（な）*adj* realistic

りえき・利益 *n* profit

りか・理科 *n* science

りかい・理解 **1** *n* understanding **2** *vb* 3 ⓦ りかいする to understand

りく・陸 *n* land

りくぐん・陸軍 *n* army

りくじょうきょうぎ・陸上競技 *n* athletics

りこう(な)・利口(な) *adj* clever

りこん・離婚 **1** *n* divorce **2** *vb 3* ㉞ りこんする to get divorced

りし・利子 *n* interest

りじ・理事 *n* director

りじかい・理事会 *n* board of directors

リストラ *n* restructuring (of a company)

リズム *n* rhythm

りそう・理想 *n* (an) ideal

りそうてき・理想的 **1** *adj* りそうてき(な) idealistic **2** *adv* りそうてき(な) idealistically

りつ・率 *suf* rate

リットル *n* litre

りっぱ(な)・立派(な) *adj* splendid

りっぽう・立方 *prf* cubic (metres etc.)

りてん・利点 *n* advantage

りふじん(な)・理不尽(な) *adj* unreasonable

りゃく・略 *n* abbreviation

りゃくす・略す *vb 1* ㊈ to abbreviate

りゆう・理由 *n* reason

りゅうがく・留学 **1** *n* studying abroad **2** *vb 3* ㉞ りゅうがくする to study overseas

りゅうがくせい・留学生 *n* – a student studying overseas

りゅうこう・流行 **1** *n* trend **2** *adj* りゅうこう(な) fashionable

りゅうちょう・流暢 **1** *adj* りゅうちょう(な) fluent **2** *adv* りゅうちょうに fluently

りょう・利用 **1** *n* use **2** *vb 3* ㊁ りょうする to use

りょう・量 *n* amount

りょう・寮 *n* dormitory; university residence

りょう・両 *prf* both

りょう・料 *suf* charge

りょうがえ・両替 **1** *n* money changing **2** *vb 3* ㊁ りょうがえする to change money

りょうがえじょ・両替所 *n* money changer; bureau de change

りょうがわ・両側 *n* both sides

りょうきん・料金 *n and suf* charge; fee

りょうし・漁師 *n* fisherman

りょうしゅうしょ・領収書 *n* receipt

りょうしん・両親 *n* parents

りょうしん・良心 *n* conscience

りょうて・両手 *n* both hands

りょうほう・両方 *n* both

りょうり・料理 **1** *n* cooking **2** *vb 3* ㊁ りょうりする to cook

りょうりや・料理屋 *n* restaurant

りょかん・旅館 *n – a small hotel offering Japanese style accommodation*

りょけん・旅券 *n – the official term for a passport*

りょこう・旅行 **1** *n* trip **2** *vb 3* ㊃ りょこうする to travel; to go on a trip

りょこうあんないじょ・旅行案内所 *n* tourist information office

りょこうしゃ・旅行者 *n* traveller; tourist

りれきしょ・履歴書 *n* resume; CV

りんご *n* apple

りんじ・臨時 *prf* extraordinary

るル

るい・類 *n* type; sort
るいじ(する)・類似(する) *vb 3* か に to be similar
ルーズ(な) *adj* disorganised; careless
ルール *n* rules
るす・留守 *n* absence
るすでん・留守電 ▶ るすばんでんわ
るすばん・留守番 *n* – taking care of somewhere while the owner|s are absent (for either short and long periods)
るすばんでんわ・留守番電話 *n* (telephone) answering machine
ルビ *n* – another term for ふりがな

れレ

れい・例 *n* example
れい・礼 *n* thanks; bow; reward; れいをする to bow ▶ おれい
れい・零 *n* zero
れいがい・例外 *n* exception
れいぎ・礼儀 *n* politeness
れいぎただしい・礼儀正しい *adj* polite
れいせい・冷静 **1** *adj* れいせい(な) calm **2** *adv* れいせいに calmly
れいぞうこ・冷蔵庫 *n* refrigerator

れいてん・零点 *n* zero marks

れいとう・冷凍 **1** *n* freezing **2** *vb* **3** ⊗ れいとうする
to freeze

れいとうこ・冷凍庫 *n* freezer

れいとうしょくひん・冷凍食品 *n* frozen foods

れいはい・礼拝 **1** *n* worship **2** *vb* **3** ⊗ れいはいする
to worship

れいぶん・例文 *n* example sentence

れいぼう・冷房 *n* air-conditioning

レインコート *n* raincoat

れきし・歴史 *n* history

レクリエーション *n* recreation

レジ *n* cash register

レジャー *n* leisure

レストラン *n* restaurant

れつ・列 *n* line; row; queue

れっしゃ・列車 *n* train

れっとう・列島 *n and suf* chain of islands

レベル *n* level

レポート *n* essay; (academic) paper

れんが・煉瓦 *n* bricks

れんきゅう・連休 *n* – holidays occurring or taken in a row

れんごう・連合 *n and suf* alliance

レンジ *n* oven; microwave oven

れんしゅう・練習 **1** *n* practice; training **2** *vb* **3** ⊗ れんし
ゅうする to practise; to train

レンズ *n* lens

れんそう(させる)・連想(させる) *vb* **2** ⊗ to be
reminded of

れんぞく・連続 1 *n and prf* succession; in succession **2** *vb 3㋐* れんぞくする to occur in succession; れんぞくドラマ drama serial

レンタカー *n* car rental

れんだく・連濁 *n* – the changes in sounds which occur when certain combinations of syllables are combined in words such as in the family name やまだ when the character usually pronounced た becomes pronounced as だ

レントゲン *n* X ray; レントゲンしゃしんを とる to have an X ray

れんらく・連絡 1 *n* contact; connection **2** *vb 3㋐* と れんらくする to connect with

れんらくさき・連絡先 *n* contact address

ろ ロ

ろうか・廊下 *n* corridor

ろうじん・老人 *n* old person

ろうじんホーム・老人ホーム *n* old people's home

ろうそく *n* candle

ろうどう・労働 *n and suf* labour

ろうどうしゃ・労働者 *n* labourer

ろうひ・浪費 1 *n* waste **2** *vb 3㋐* ろうひする to waste

ロープウエイ *n* cable car

ローマじ・ローマ字 *n* – the roman (western) alphabet and especially Japanese words written in that script

ろく・六 *n* six

ろくおん・録音 1 *n* (sound) recording **2** *vb 3㋐* ろくおんする to tape (record sounds)

ろくが・録画 1 n video recording **2** vb 3 ⍟ ろくがする to videotape

ろくがつ・六月 n June

ろくじゅう・六十 n sixty

ロッカー n locker

ロビー n hotel lobby

ロマンチック(な) adj romantic

ろん・論 n and suf explanation; theory

ろんじる・論じる vb 2 ⍟ to argue

ろんそう・論争 n dispute

ろんぶん・論文 n paper; thesis; dissertation

ろんりてき・論理的 1 adj ろんりてき(な) logical **2** adv ろんりてきに logically

わワ

WA pt ! note that the topic particle is written with ひらがな character は 'ha' or (very occasionally) with the かたかな character ハ ▶ は

わ・輪 n ring

わ・和 n harmony ! as a prefix or abbreviation it means 'Japanese' as opposed to western or 'Japanese (language)'

わ・羽 counter birds

わ pt – used at the end of sentences to give emphasis and a distinctive marker of women's speech although also used by men in some areas of Japan

ワイシャツ n shirt

ワイン n wine

わえい・和英 n Japanese and English language ▶ **dictionary**

わえいじてん・和英辞典 *n* Japanese-English dictionary

わが・我が・我 *prf* my; our

わかい・若い *adj* young

わかす・沸かす *vb 1 ⊛* to boil

わがまま(な) *adj* selfish

わかります ▶ わかる

わかる・分かる *vb 1 ⊛* わかって・わからない・わかります to understand ! *often used in situations where the most natural English would be 'to know'*

わかれ・別れ *n* parting

わかれる・別れる *vb 2 ⊛* と to separate

わかれる・分かれる *vb 2 ⊛* to divide

わき・脇 *n* under the arm; side

わきのした・脇の下 *n* armpit

わく・枠 *n* frame

わく・沸く・湧く *vb 1 ⊛* to boil

わけ・訳 *n* reason; meaning; circumstances; 〜わけではありません it isn't that ...; it doesn't mean that ...; 〜わけにはいかない cannot; 〜わけはない it can't be the case ! *the expression 〜わけには いかない is translatable as 'must' (following negatives) and 'must not' (following positives)*

わける・分ける *vb 2 ⊛* to divide; to distribute

わゴム・輪ゴム *n* elastic band

わざと *adv* deliberately

わしつ・和室 *n* Japanese style room

わしょく・和食 *n* Japanese food

わずか・僅か 1 *adv* merely **2** *adj* わずか(な) slight; a few

わすれて ▶ わすれる

わすれます ▶ わすれる

わすれもの・忘れ物 *n* – things which are left behind or forgotten. Often used so that a translation along the lines of 'I've

*forgotten something!' or 'I'm afraid I left my ...' is most natural.
Can be used as verb in the form* わすれものを する *'to forget
something'*

わすれる・忘れる *vb 2* ⊗ わすれて・わすれない・
わすれます to forget

わた・綿 *n* cotton

わだい・話題 *n* topic (of conversation)

わたくし・私 *n – a more formal version of* わたし

わたくしども・私ども *n – a humble equivalent of* わた
したち

わたし・私 *n* I

わたしたち・私たち・私達 *n* we; us

わたしの *adj* my

わたしたちの *adj* our

わたす・渡す *vb 1* ⊗ to hand over

わたる・渡る *vb 1* ⊘ to cross over

わびる・詫びる *vb 2* ⊗ to apologise

わふう・和風 *n – Japanese style (as opposed to Western
style)*

わふく・和服 *n – traditional Japanese style clothing*

わらい・笑い *n* a laugh; laughter

わらう・笑う *vb 1* ⊗ わらって・わらわない・わら
います to laugh; to smile

わり・割り *n* ratio ! *as a suffix with numbers it indicates
multiples of 10% so* さんわり *is 30%*

わりあい・割合 1 *n* rate **2** *adv* comparatively

わりかん・割り勘 *n – splitting a bill so that everyone pays
for their own food and/or drinks*

わりざん・割り算 *n* division

わりに・割に *adv* fairly; in proportion to

わりびき・割引 *n* discount

わる・割る vb 1 ㊊ to split; to smash; to divide by (a number)

わるい・悪い adj bad

わるぐち・悪口 n speaking ill of people

われる・割れる vb 2 ㊐ to be broken; to be divided

われわれ・我々 n we

わん・湾 n bay

わん・椀・碗 n bowl

ワンピース n dress

....

ん ン

ん an abbreviated form of **の**

んだ ▸ のだ

んです ▸ のです

....

を ヲ

を pt ❗ marks the direct object of a verb or the space through which an action moves. When used in telegrams etc. **かたかな** symbol ヲ is used to represent this particle. Pronounced as **お** but often represented in romanised text as 'wo' although 'o' is also used. Some Japanese do pronounce it as 'wo', usually in very formal situations.

Aa

a, an _det_ ! Not used in Japanese.

able _adj_ to be able to... use the potential form of the verb or the dictionary form of the verb + ことが できる; to be able to swim およげる・泳げる; I am able to read hiragana ひらがなを よむ ことが できます。・ ひらがなを 読む ことが できます。

about ! Often about occurs in combinations with verbs, for example: bring about, run about etc. To find the correct translations for this type of verb, look up the separate dictionary entries at bring, run etc. **1** _prep_ ～について(の); it's a book about Japan にほんに ついての ほんです。・ 日本に ついての 本です。; I want some information about this town この まちについて、じょうほうが ほしいです。・ この 町について、情報が ほしいです。 **2** _adv_ ～ぐらい; I have about 2000 yen left にせんえんぐらい のっています。・ 二千円ぐらい 残っています。; Kyoto is about 40km from here きょうとは、ここから よんじゅっキロぐらいです。・ 京都は、ここから 四十キロぐらいです。 **3** _adv_ ～ごろ; (approximate times) We arrived at about 9 o'clock くじごろ、つきました。・ 九時頃、着きました。 **4** to be about to ～ところ use verb in dictionary form + ところ; I was about to go out でかける ところでした。・ 出かける ところでした。

above **1** _prep_ ～の うえ・～の 上; their apartment is above the shop かれらの アパートは みせのうえです。・ 彼らの アパートは 店の 上です。; there is a shelf above the door ドアの うえに たなが あります。・ ドアの 上に 棚が あります。 **2** above all まず だいいちに・まず 第一に

abroad _adv_ がいこく・外国; _n_ to go abroad がいこくに いく・外国に 行く

absent _adj_ けっせき・欠席; to be absent けっせきする・欠席する

accent n (way of speaking) なまり; (stressed part) アクセント

accept vb (a gift, invitation) うけとる・受け取る

accident n (causing injury or damage) じこ・事故; car accident こうつうじこ・交通事故; (by chance) I heard about it by accident ぐうぜん それを ききました。・偶然 それを 聞きました。

accommodation n to look for accommodation とまる ところをさがす・泊まる 所を 探す

accompany vb to accompany someone だれかと いっしょにいく・誰かと 一緒に 行く

account n (in a bank or post office) こうざ・口座; there's money in my bank account ぎんこうこうざに おかねが あります。・銀行口座に お金が あります。

accountant n かいけいし・会計士

accuse vb (legal term) うったえる・訴える; to be accused of cheating カンニングしたと いわれる・カンニングしたと 言われる

across prep to go across the street みちを わたる・道を 渡る; to go across a bridge はしを わたる・橋を 渡る; a journey across the desert さばくを おうだんする たび・砂漠を 横断する 旅; (on the other side of) 〜の むこうがわに〜・〜の 向こう側に〜; he lives across the street かれは みちの むこうがわに すんでいます。・彼は 道の 向こう側に 住んでいます。

act vb (to do something) こうどうする・行動する; (to play a role) えんじる・演じる

activity n かつどう・活動; sports activities スポーツかつどう・スポーツ活動

actor n はいゆう・俳優

actress n じょゆう・女優

actually adv actually, he's a very good tennis player じつは、かれは とても じょうずな テニスプレーヤーです。・実は、彼は とても 上手な テニスプレーヤーです。; what actually happened? じっさい、なにが ありましたか。・実際、何が ありましたか。

adapt *vb* (*to become used to*) なれる・慣れる; I have adapted to life in Japan にほんの せいかつに なれました。・日本の 生活に 慣れました。

add *vb* (*to put in*) くわえる・加える; (*in arithmetic*) たす・足す

address *n* じゅうしょ・住所 ! *Note that Japanese addresses do not usually include street names and are given in reverse order*

admit *vb* みとめる・認める; I admitted that I'd stolen the money おかねを ぬすんだ ことを みとめました。・お金を 盗んだ ことを 認めました。; to be admitted to (the) hospital にゅういんする・入院する

adolescent *n* ティーンエージャー

adopt *vb* (*a child*) ようしに する・養子に する

adult *n* おとな・大人 ! *Irregular kanji reading*

advantage *n* (*a positive point*) りてん・利点; to take advantage of a someone だれかを りようする・誰かを 利用する; to take advantage of an opportunity チャンスを つかむ

adventure *n* ぼうけん・冒険

advertisement *n* こうこく・広告; job advertisements きゅうじん・求人

advertising *n* こうこくぎょう・広告業

advice *n* アドバイス

advise *vb* to politely offer advice in Japanese you can use the ～た form of the verb + ほうがいい; I've been advised not to go there あそこに いかない ほうが いいと、いわれました。・あそこに 行かない 方が いいと、言われました。

aerial *n* アンテナ

aerobics *n* エアロビクス

affect *vb* えいきょうを あたえる・影響を 与える; the war will affect tourism せんそうは かんこうぎょうに えいきょうをあたえます。・戦争は 観光業に 影響を 与えます。

afford *vb* to be able to afford a car くるまを かう よゆうが ある・車を 買う 余裕が ある

afraid *adj* to be afraid こわがる・怖がる; to be afraid of insects むしを こわがる・虫を 怖がる; to be afraid to go out そとに でる ことを こわがる・外に 出る ことを 怖がる

Africa *n* アフリカ

after 1 *prep* あと・後; we'll leave after breakfast あさご はんの あとに、しゅっぱつします。・朝ご飯の 後に、出発します。; the day after tomorrow あさって **2** *conj* after we had eaten, we went for a walk たべた あと、さんぽを しました。・食べた 後、散歩を しました。; I went in after the film had started えいがが はじまってから はい りました。・映画が 始まってから 入りました。 **3** after all さいごに・最後に

afternoon *n* ごご・午後

afterwards, afterward (*US English*) *adv* (*after*) その あと・その 後; (*later*) あとで・後で

again *adv* また; are you going camping again this year? こと し、また キャンプを しますか。・今年、また キャンプ をしますか。

against *prep* はんたい・反対; I'm against animal experimentation どうぶつじっけんにはんたいです。・動物実験に 反対です。

age *n* とし・年; he's my age かれは わたしと おなじ としです。・彼は 私と 同じ 年です。

aged *adj* 〜さい・〜才; a boy aged 13 じゅうさんさいの おとこのこ・十三才の 男の 子

ago *adv* まえ・前; two weeks ago にしゅうかん まえ・二週間 前; long ago むかし・昔

agree *vb* (*to have the same opinion*) さんせいする・賛成す る; I don't agree with you あなたに さんせいしません。・あなたに 賛成しません。; (*to reach a decision*) けつろん になる・結論 になる

agriculture *n* のうぎょう・農業

ahead adv to go on ahead さきに いく・先に行く

Aids n エイズ

aim 1 n もくてき・目的 2 vb aimed at むき・向き; a magazine aimed at young women わかい じょせい むきの ざっし・若い 女性 向きの 雑誌

air n くうき・空気; to let the air out of a rubber ring うきぶ くろの くうきを ぬく・浮袋の 空気を 抜く

air force n くうぐん・空軍

airmail n こうくうびん・航空便; to send a letter by airmail こうくうびんで てがみを おくる・航空便で 手紙を 送る

airport n くうこう・空港

alarm clock n めざましどけい・目覚し時計

alcohol n アルコール

alive adj いきている・生きている

all 1 det (for things) ぜんぶの・全部の; (for people) みんな (の)・皆(の); all the people have left みんなが かえりま した。・皆が 帰りました。; I worked all day いちにちじゅ うはたらきました。・一日中 働きました。 2 pron ぜんぶ・全部; that's all それで ぜんぶです。・それで 全部です。 3 adv all alone ひとりぼっち・一人ぼっち

allow vb smoking is not allowed here ここは きんえんです。 ・ここは 禁煙です。

all right adj (when giving your opinion) まあまあ*; the film was all right えいがは まあまあでした。・映画は まあ まあでした。*; (when talking about health) are you all right? だいじょうぶですか。・大丈夫ですか。; (when asking someone's permission) is it all right if I do it later? あとで しても いいですか。・後で しても いいですか。; come at about nine, all right? くじごろ きてくださいね。・九時 頃来てくださいね。; (when agreeing) いいです。

almond n アーモンド

almost adv ほとんど; almost everyone was Japanese ほとんどが にほんじんでした。・ほとんどが 日本人でした。; I ate almost all the cake ケーキを ほとんど たべました。・ケーキを ほとんど 食べました。; There is almost no opportunity to speak Japanese にほんごを はなす きかいが ほとんどありません。・日本語を話す機会がほとんどありません。

alone 1 adj ひとり・一人、独り; I went alone ひとりで いきました。・一人で 行きました。; to be all alone ひとりでいる ・一人でいる; leave me alone! ほっておいてくれ **2** adv to work alone ひとりで はたらく ・一人で 働く; to live alone ひとりで くらす ・一人で 暮らす; to travel alone ひとりで りょこうする・一人で 旅行する

along prep there are cherry trees blooming all along the river かわに そって、さくらが さいています。・川に沿って、桜が 咲いています。

aloud adv to read aloud こえを だして よむ ・声を 出して 読む

already adv もう; it's ten o'clock already もう じゅうじです。・もう 十時です。; have you finished already? もう おわりましたか。・もう 終わりましたか。

also adv Use particle も; I'm also studying Japanese わたしも にほんごを べんきょうしています。・私も 日本語を 勉強しています。

although conj けれども; although Gillian's not Japanese, she speaks Japanese very well ジリアンさんは にほんじんではありません。けれども にほんごが よく はなせます。・ジリアンさんは 日本人ではありません。けれども 日本語が よく 話せます。! Note word order is different to English. ▶ but

always adv いつも; he always wears black clothes かれは いつも くろい ふくを きている。・彼は いつも 黒い 服を 着ている。

amazed adj びっくりしている

amazing adj すばらしい

ambition n もくひょう・目標

ambitious adj やしんてき(な)・野心的(な)

ambulance n きゅうきゅうしゃ・救急車

America n アメリカ

American 1 adj アメリカの **2** n American person アメリカじん・アメリカ人

amount 1 n (quantity) りょう・量; amount of water みずのりょう。・水の 量。; (of money) how much is the total amount? ごうけいで いくらですか。・合計で いくらですか。

amusement arcade n ゲームセンター

amusement park n ゆうえんち・遊園地

an ▶ a

ancestor n そせん・祖先

and conj (when connecting a finite list of nouns) use particle と; there is a pen and a pencil on the desk つくえの うえに、えんぴつと ペンが あります。・机の 上に、鉛筆とペンが あります。*; (when connecting an incomplete list of nouns) use particle や; in the box there are photos and cards, etc. はこの なかに、しゃしんや カードが あります。・箱の 中に、写真や カードが あります。; (to join a series of actions) そして; I ate and then I watched TV たべました。そしてテレビを みました。・食べました。そして テレビを 見ました。

anger n いかり・怒り

angry adj to get angry おこる・怒る; to be angry with someone だれかに おこっている・誰かに 怒っている

animal n どうぶつ・動物

ankle n あしくび・足首

announcement n はっぴょう・発表

annoy vb いらいらさせる

annoyed *adj* to be annoyed with someone だれかに おこっ
ている・誰かに 怒っている

another 1 *det* another もうひとつ・もう一つ; another
cup of coffee? コーヒー、もう いっぱい。・コーヒー、
もう 一杯。; I'll buy another ticket きっぷを もう いちま
い かいます。・切符を もう 一枚 買います。; (*different*)
ほかの・他の; there's another way of doing it ほかの やり
かたが あります。・他の やり方が あります。; another
person (*one more*) もうひとり・もう一人 (*different*) ちが
うひと・違う人 **2** *pron* would you like another? もう ひと
つ どうですか。・もう 一つ どうですか。

answer 1 *n* (*to a question*) こたえ・答え、かいとう・
解答; what is the answer? こたえは なんですか。・答え
は 何ですか。; (*to a letter*) へんじ・返事; there was no
answer (*at the door*) だれも いませんでした。・誰も い
ませんでした。; (*on the phone*) だれも でんわにでませ
んでした。・誰も 電話に 出ませんでした。 **2** *vb* to
answer a question しつもんに こたえる・質問に 答え
る; to answer the phone でんわに でる・電話に 出る;
answer back くちごたえをする・口答えをする

answering machine *n* るすばんでんわ・留守番電話

ant *n* あり

antique *n* (*Western*) アンティーク; (*Japanese*) こっとう
ひん・骨董品

antique shop *n* (*Western*) アンティークショップ;
(*Japanese*) こっとうや・骨董屋

anxious *adj* しんぱいしている・心配している; then I
started to get anxious そして しんぱいに なりました。・
そして 心配に なりました。

any 1 *det* (*in questions*) is there any tea? こうちゃが ありま
すか。・紅茶が ありますか。; is there any juice left? ジュ
ースは のこっていますか。・ジュースは 残っていま
すか。; have you got any money? おかねは もっています
か。・お金を 持っていますか。; (*with the negative*) we
don't have any bread パンは ありません。; I didn't have any

friends ともだちは いませんでした。・友達は いませんでした。; (whatever) choose any book you like すきな ほんを えらんでください。・好きな 本を 選んでください。 **2** pron **!** Note that *any* is not translated in Japanese.

anyone pron (also **anybody**) (in questions) だれか・誰か; is there anyone there? だれか いますか。・誰か いますか。; (with the negative) だれも・誰も; there isn't anyone in the house うちに だれも いません。・家に 誰も いません; (everyone) だれでも・誰でも; anyone could do it だれでも できる。・誰でも できる。

anything pron (in questions) なにか・何か; do you need anything? なにか いりますか。・何か いりますか。; (with the negative) なにも・何も; I didn't say anything なにも いいませんでした。・何も 言いませんでした。; there isn't anything to do here ここには、する ことが ありません。; (everything) なんでも・何でも; I like anything to do with sports スポーツなら なんでも すきです。・スポーツなら 何でも 好きです。

anyway adv it might be difficult but let's try anyway むずかしいかもしれませんが、とにかくやって みましょう。・難しいかもしれませんが、とにかくやって みましょう。

anywhere adv (in questions) どこか; did you go anywhere interesting in the summer holidays? なつやすみに、どこか おもしろい ところへ いきましたか。・夏休みに、どこか おもしろい 所へ 行きましたか。; (with the negative) どこも; I'm not going anywhere tomorrow あした どこも いきません。・明日 どこも 行きません。; (any place) どこでも; we have time so we can go anywhere you like じかんが ありますから、すきな ところ どこでも いけますよ。・時間が ありますから、好きな所 どこでも 行けますよ。

apart 1 adj はなれている・離れている; I don't want to be apart from the children こどもたちと はなれたくないです。・子供達と 離れたくないです。 **2 apart from** 〜のほかに〜・〜の 外に〜、〜の 他に〜

apartment n アパート

apartment block n アパート

apologize vb あやまる・謝る; I apologised to the teacher せんせいに あやまりました。・先生に 謝りました。

appear vb (to seem) she appears to be happy かのじょは しあわせみたいです。・彼女は 幸せみたいです。; (to come into view) あらわれる・現れる

appetite n しょくよく・食欲; to have a good appetite よくたべる・よく 食べる

apple n りんご

apple juice n りんごジュース

appliance n electrical appliance(s) でんきせいひん・電気製品

application n application form(s) もうしこみしょ・申込書

apply vb to apply for a job しごとに おうぼする・仕事に 応募する; to apply for a passport パスポートを もうしこむ・パスポートを 申し込む

appointment n よやく・予約; to make an appointment with the dentist はいしゃに よやくを いれる・歯医者に 予約を 入れる

appreciate vb I appreciate your help てつだって くれて ありがとう。・手伝って くれて ありがとう。

approach vb (a place or time) ちかづく・近づく; (a person) アプローチする

approve vb しょうにんする・承認する; The boss approved my plan かちょうが わたしの あんを しょうにんしました。・課長が 私の案を 承認しました。

apricot n あんず

April n しがつ・四月

Aquarius n みずがめざ・水瓶座

architect n けんちくか・建築家

area n (of a country) ちほう・地方; (of a city) ちく・地区; the area around here このへん

area code n (US English) しがいきょくばん・市外局番

argue vb (to quarrel) くちげんかを する・口げんかを する; to argue about money おかねの ことで、くちげんかを する・お金の ことで、口げんかを する; (to discuss a subject) ぎろんする・議論する; to argue about politics せいじの ことを ぎろんする・政治の ことを 議論する

argument n (quarrel) くちげんか・口げんか; I had an argument with my mother ははと くちげんかを しました。・母と 口げんかを しました。; (debate) ぎろん・議論

Aries n おひつじざ・牡羊座

arm n うで・腕; my arm hurts うでが いたいです。・腕が 痛いです。

armchair n ソファ

armed adj ぶそうした・武装した

arms n ぶき・武器

army n りくぐん・陸軍、ぐんたい・軍隊; to join the army りくぐんに にゅうたいする・陸軍に 入隊する

around ! Often around occurs in combinations with verbs, for example: run around, turn around etc. To find the correct translations for this type of verb, look up the separate dictionary entries at run, turn etc. **1** prep there are trees all around the garden にわの まわりに きが あります。・庭の 周りに 木が あります。; at the party the people around me were speaking Japanese パーティーで、まわりの ひとは にほんごを はなしていました。・パーティーで、周りの 人は 日本語を 話していました。; to go around the world せかいいっしゅうりょこうをする・世界一周旅行をする **2** adv it is around 2000 yen にせんえんぐらいです。・二千円ぐらいです。; I'll arrive there at around one o'clock そこに つきます。・一時頃、そこに 着きます。

arrange vb to arrange a trip to Kyoto きょうとりょこうの じゅんびをする・京都旅行の 準備を する; to arrange to have lunch together いっしょに ひるごはんを たべる やくそくをする・一緒に 昼ご飯を 食べる 約束を する

arrest vb たいほする・逮捕する

arrive vb つく・着く; I arrived at the station at noon じゅうにじに えきに つきました。・十二時に 駅に 着きました。

arrow n (weapon) や・矢; (symbol) やじるし・矢印

art n びじゅつ・美術

art gallery n びじゅつかん・美術館

artificial adj じんこうの・人工の

artist n げいじゅつか・芸術家

arts and crafts n arts and crafts びじゅつと こうげい・美術と工芸

as 1 conj ～ように; as you know, I used to live in Japan しっているように、にほんに すんでいました。・知っているように、日本に 住んでいました。; (at the time when) ～とき; the phone rang as I was getting out of the bath おふろから あがっている ときに、でんわが なりました。・お風呂から あがっている ときに、電話が 鳴りました。; I used to live there as a child こどもの とき、そこにすんでいました。・子供の とき、そこに 住んでいました。; (British English) (because, since) から; as they were out, I left a message るすでしたから、でんごんを のこしておきました。・留守でしたから、伝言を 残しておきました。; (when used with the same) mine is the same as yours わたしのは あなたのと おなじです。・私のはあなたのと 同じです。 2 prep I went to Japan as an English teacher えいごの せんせいと して、にほんにいきました。・英語の 先生と して、日本に 行きました。; I was dressed as Santa サンタの かっこうを しました。・サンタの 格好を しました。 3 adv as white as snow ゆきの ように しろい・雪の ように 白い; go there as fast as you can できるだけ はやく 行ってください。・できるだけ 速く 行ってください。; I have as much money as him かれと おなじくらい おかねが あります。・彼と 同じくらい お金が あります。 4 as usual いつもどおりに・いつも 通りに

ashamed adj はずかしい・恥ずかしい

ashes n はい・灰

ashtray n はいざら・灰皿

Asia n アジア

Asian adj アジアの **1** n Asian person アジアじん・アジア人

ask vb (for information) きく・聞く; he asked me my name かれは わたしの なまえを ききました。・彼は 私の 名前を 聞きました。; (to ask someone a favour) たのむ・頼む; to ask someone to do the shopping だれかに かいものを たのむ・誰かに 買い物を 頼む; I'll ask them if they are going to come かれらが くるか どうか ききます。・彼らが 来るか どうか 聞きます。I asked my parents for money りょうしんに、おかねが ほしいと たのみました。・両親に、お金が 欲しいと 頼みました。; to ask to speak to someone だれかに おねがいする・誰かに お願いする; to ask a question しつもんを する・質問を する; (to invite to your own place) しょうたいする・招待する; (somewhere else) さそう・誘う; to ask some friends to your party ともだちを パーティーに しょうたいする・友達を パーティーに 招待する; he asked her out かれは かのじょを デートに さそいました。・彼は 彼女を デートに 誘いました。; (to look for information) きく・聞く; did you ask about the tickets? きっぷの ことを ききましたか。・切符の ことを 聞きましたか。

asleep adj to be asleep ねむっている・眠っている; to fall asleep ねむる・眠る

assemble vb (parts of a model, etc) くみたてる・組み立てる; (people gathering) あつまる・集まる

assignment n school assignment しゅくだい・宿題

assistant n アシスタント

at prep ! There are many verbs which involve the use of at, like look at, laugh at, point at etc. For translations, look up the entries at look, laugh, point etc.; (when talking about a position or place of action) で; we met at a concert コンサートで あいました。・コンサートで 会いました。I saw her at the cinema えいがかんで かのじょを みました。・映画館で 彼女

を 見ました。; (when talking about a position or place of existence) に; she's at home かのじょは いえに います。・ 彼女は 家に います。; he's not at his desk いま、かれは せきを はずしております。・ 今、彼は 席を 外しております。; they're at the clinic かれらは びょういんに います。・ 彼らは 病院に います。; (when talking about time) に; the film starts at nine o'clock えいがは くじに はじまります。・ 映画は 九時に 始まります。; (when talking about age) 〜とき・〜才; I was able to read at four (years old) よんさいの とき、ほんを よむ ことが できました。・ 四才の とき、本を 読む ことが できました。

athlete n スポーツせんしゅ・スポーツ選手

athletics n (in Britain) りくじょうきょうぎ・陸上競技; (in the US) うんどうきょうぎ・運動競技

Atlantic n the Atlantic Ocean たいせいよう・大西洋

atmosphere n (the air) くうき・空気; (a mood, a feeling) ふんいき・雰囲気

attach vb つける・付ける; to be attached to the wall かべに はって ある・壁に 貼って ある

attack vb to attack a town まちを こうげきする・町を 攻撃する; to attack someone in the street だれかに おそいかかる・誰かに 襲いかかる

attempt 1 vb Use 〜て form of verb + みる; **2** n ちょうせん・挑戦

attend vb to attend the village school むらの がっこうに かよう・村の 学校に 通う; to attend a lecture こうぎに しゅっせきする・講義に 出席する

attention n to pay attention to the teacher せんせいの いうことを きく・先生の 言う ことを 聞く

attic n やねうら・屋根裏

attitude n たいど・態度; he has a bad attitude かれは たいどが わるいです。・彼は 態度が 悪いです。

attract vb ひきつける・引き付ける

attractive adj すてき(な)・素敵(な)

audience *n* かんきゃく・観客

August *n* はちがつ・八月

aunt *n* (*one's own*) おば・叔母、伯母; (*someone else's*) おばさん

au pair *n* オーペア

Australia *n* オーストラリア

Australian 1 *adj* オーストラリアの **2** *n* Australian people オーストラリアじん・オーストラリア人

author *n* さっか・作家

automatic *adj* じどうの・自動の

autumn *n* あき・秋; in (the) autumn あきに・秋に

available *adj* (*on sale*) tickets for the concert are still available コンサートの チケットは まだあります。; (*free*) あいている・空いている; are you available on Thursday? もくようびは あいていますか・木曜日は 空いていますか

average *adj* へいきんの・平均の; the average teenager ふつうのティーンエージャー・普通の ティーンエージャー

avoid *vb* (*to prevent*) to avoid spending money おかねを つかわないようにする・お金を 使わない ように する; (*to stay away from*) さける・避ける

awake *adj* to be awake (*having slept*) めが さめている・目が 覚めている; to stay awake おきたままでいる・起きたままでいる; the neighbours kept me awake となりのひとの せいで、ねむれませんでした。・隣の 人の せいで、眠れませんでした。

award *n* しょう・賞; she got the award for best actress かのじょは、さいゆうしゅうじょゆうしょうをじゅしょうしました。・彼女は、最優秀女優賞を 受賞しました。

aware *adj* to be aware of the danger きけんだと わかっている・危険だと 分かっている

away *adv* (*absent*) to be away けっせきする・欠席する; she's away on business かのじょは しゅっちょうしてい

ます。・彼女は 出張しています。; (when talking about distances) to be far away とおくにいる・遠くに いる; Osaka is 40 km away おおさかは ここから よんじゅっキ ロです。・大阪は ここから 四十キロです。

awful adj (no good) ひどい; the film was awful あの えいが はひどかったです。・あの 映画は ひどかったです。; (causing shock) すさまじい; I feel awful きもちが わるい です。・気持ちが 悪いです。

awkward adj (describing a situation, a problem) pre ます form + にくい; I feel awkward about telling him かれには いいにくいです。・彼には 言いにくいです。

axe, ax (US English) n おの

Bb

baby n あかちゃん・赤ちゃん

babysit vb ベビーシッターを する

back ! Often back occurs in combinations with verbs, for example: come back, get back, give back etc. To find the correct translations for this type of verb, look up the separate dictionary entries at come, get, give etc. **1** n (part of the body) せなか・ 背中; my back hurts こしが いたいです。・腰が 痛いで す。; (behind) うしろ・後ろ; to sit in the back of the car く るまのうしろに すわる・車の 後ろに 座る; (rear of) うら・裏; at the back of the supermarket スーパーの うら ・スーパーの 裏 **2** adv to be back もどっている・戻っ ている; I'll be back tomorrow あした もどります。・明日 戻ります。; (before in time) back in 1995 せんきゅうひゃ くきゅうじゅうごねんに・千九百九十五年に

back door n うしろの ドア・後ろの ドア

background n (upbringing) そだち・育ち; (career history) けいれき・経歴; (of a picture) はいけい・背景; in the background はいけいに・背景に

backpack *n* リュックサック

back seat *n* こうぶざせき・後部座席

back to front *adv* うしろまえに・後ろ前に; to put a sweater on back to front セーターを うしろまえに きる・セーターを 後ろ前に 着る

backwards, backward *(US English)* *adv* うしろに・後ろに

bacon *n* ベーコン

bad *adj* ! Note that the Japanese prefer to refer to things as "not good" よくない *rather than* "bad"; わるい・悪い; a bad person わるい ひと・悪い 人; a bad idea まちがい・間違い; it was a bad idea to come here ここに きたのは まちがいでした。・ここに 来たのは 間違いでした。; I have some bad news あまり いい はなし じゃない ですが...。・あまりいい話 じゃないですが...。; I'm bad at maths すうがくが にがてです。・数学が 苦手です。; 'was the film good?'—'not bad' 「えいがは よかったですか。」「まあまあ でした。」・「映画は 良かったですか。」「まあまあ でした。」; smoking is bad for you たばこは からだによくないです。・煙草は 体に よくないです。; *(serious)* ひどい; a bad accident ひどい じこ・ひどい 事故; *(when talking about food)* まずい; *(not kind, not honest)* わるい・悪い; to feel bad きぶんが わるい・気分が 悪い; *(severe)* ひどい; I have a bad cold ひどい かぜを ひきました。・ひどい 風邪を ひきました

badger *n* あなぐま・穴熊

badly *adv* *(not well)* to think badly of someone だれかを わるくおもう・誰かを 悪く 思う; she slept badly かのじょは よく ねむれませんでした。・彼女は よく 眠れませんでした。; he did badly in the test かれは テストの せいせきがわるかったです。・彼は 成績が 悪かったです。; *(seriously)* ひどく; I was badly injured ひどい けがを しました。・酷い 怪我を しました。

badminton *n* バドミントン

bad-tempered *adj* おこりやすい・怒りやすい

bag n (with fastener) かばん; plastic bag ビニールぶくろ・ビニール袋; paper bag かみぶくろ・紙袋

baggage n にもつ・荷物

bake vb オーブンで やく・オーブンで 焼く

baker n パンや・パン屋

bakery n パンや・パン屋

balance n バランス; to lose one's balance バランスを うしなう・バランスを 失う

balcony n バルコニー

bald adj はげている

ball n ボール; to play ball ボールあそびを する・ボール遊びを する

ballet n バレエ

balloon n ふうせん・風船

ban vb きんしする・禁止する

banana n バナナ

band n バンド

bandage n ほうたい・包帯

bang 1 n (US English) (a fringe) bangs まえがみ・前髪 **2** vb (to close with a bang) ばたんと しめる・ばたんと 閉める; (to hurt) to bang one's head on the wall かべに あたまを ぶつける・壁に 頭を ぶつける

bank n ぎんこう・銀行

bank account n ぎんこうこうざ・銀行口座

bank holiday n (British English) さいじつ・祭日

bank manager n my mother is a bank manager ははは ぎんこうの してんちょうです。・母は 銀行の 支店長です。! Note that the Japanese do not usually refer to their job title but just the name or type of company they work for

bar n (a place) バー; to go to a bar バーに いく・バーに 行く; (a piece of metal) ぼう・棒; (on a cage or window) a bar てつごうし・鉄格子; (other uses) a bar of soap せっけん; a bar of chocolate チョコレート

barbecue *n* バーベキュー

bargain *n* かいどく・買い得

bark *vb* ほえる・吠える

barrel *n* (of wine or beer) たる・樽; (of oil) バレル

base *vb* based in London ロンドンきょてん・ロンドン拠点; based on a true story じじつに もとづいた・事実に 基づいた

baseball *n* やきゅう・野球

basement *n* ちか・地下

basically *adv* きほんてきに・基本的に

basin *n* せんめんき・洗面器

basket *n* かご

basketball *n* バスケットボール

bat *n* (in cricket or baseball) バット; (an animal) こうもり

bath *n* to have a bath おふろに はいる・お風呂に 入る; he's in the bath かれは おふろに はいっています。・彼は お風呂に 入っています。; (a bathtub) ふろおけ・風呂おけ

bathroom *n* ふろば・風呂場; (US English) (the toilet) to go to the bathroom トイレに いく・トイレに 行く

battery *n* (for a torch etc.) でんち・電池; (for a car) バッテリー

battle *n* たたかい・戦い

bay *n* わん・湾

be *vb* ! There is no exact equivalent of this verb in Japanese; (when describing) ! Note that you can usually use adjective or noun + です。; he is intelligent かれは あたまが いいです。・彼は 頭が いいです。; I am tall わたしは せがたかい です。・私は 背が 高いです。; it's a girl おんなの こです。・女の 子です。; it's Monday げつようびです。・月曜日です。; it's late おそいです。・遅いです。; I am 18 years old じゅうはっさいです。・十八歳です。; my feet are cold あしが つめたいです。・足が 冷たいです。; (when talking about location) (of people and animals) いる;

there are 3 pupils in the classroom きょうしつに せいとが さんにん います。・教室に 生徒が 三人 います。; (of things) ある; the dictionary is on the table じしょは テーブルのうえに あります。・辞書は テーブルの 上に あります。; (when talking about jobs) job title + です。; I am a lawyer べんごしです。・弁護士です。; (when describing the weather) it's not very warm あまり あたたかくないです。・あまり 暖かくないです。; it's raining あめが ふっています。・雨が 降っています。; (when talking about experiences) ! Use the 〜た form of the verb + ことが ある to describe experiences; I've never been to Tokyo とうきょうに いった ことが ありません。・東京に 行った ことが ありません。; have you ever been to Japan? にほんに いった ことが ありますか。・日本に 行った ことが ありますか。; (when talking about health) how are you? おげんきですか。・お元気ですか。; I'm well げんきです。・元気です。; how is your mother? おかあさんは おげんきですか。・お母さんは お元気ですか。; (in continuous tenses) ► ! Use the 〜て form of the verb + いる; I'm reading よんでいます。・読んでいます。; it was snowing ゆきが ふっていました。・雪が 降っていました。; he is playing かれは あそんでいます。・彼は 遊んでいます。; (in questions and short answers) use particle ね; it's hot, isn't it? あついですね。・暑いですね。; (become) なる; he'll be famous かれは ゆうめいに なります。・彼は 有名に なります。; (making a request) please be quiet! しずかに してください。・静かに してください。

beach n すなはま・砂浜; to go to the beach かいがんに いく・海岸に 行く

beak n くちばし

bean n まめ・豆

bear 1 n くま・熊 2 vb がまんする・我慢する; I can't bear it がまんできません。・我慢できません。

beard n ひげ

beat vb (to win against) 〜に かつ・〜に 勝つ; Scotland beat England two nil スコットランドは イングランドに

にたい ゼロで かちました。・スコットランドは イングランドに 二対ゼロで 勝ちました。; **beat up** なぐる・殴る; I was beaten up yesterday きのう なぐられました。・ 昨日 殴られました。

beautiful adj きれい(な); beautiful girl きれいな おんなのこ・きれいな 女の 子; beautiful place きれいな ところ・きれいな 所

beauty n うつくしさ・美しさ

because 1 conj から！Note that word order is different to English. Note that there are also other ways of expressing cause and effect in Japanese; I was late for school because I overslept ねぼうしましたから、がっこうに ちこくしました。・寝坊しましたから、学校に 遅刻しました。**2 because of** 〜の ため; I didn't go because of the rain あめの ため いきませんでした。・雨の ため 行きませんでした。

become vb なる; to become an adult おとなに なる・大人に なる; to become cold さむく なる・寒く なる

bed n ベッド; to go to bed ねる・寝る

bedroom n しんしつ・寝室！Japanese people tend to say わたしの へや rather than わたしの しんしつ

bee n はち・蜂

beef n ぎゅうにく・牛肉; roast beef ローストビーフ

beer n (the product) ビール; (a glass of beer) ビールいっぱい・ビール一杯

before 1 prep まえ・前; before the holidays やすみの まえ・休みの 前; the day before yesterday おととい; the day before the exam しけんの ぜんじつ・試験の 前日 **2** adj まえの・前の; the week before まえの しゅう・前の 週; the day before まえの ひ・前の 日 **3** adv まえ・前; two months before にかげつまえ・二ケ月前; have you been to Paris before? まえに パリに いった ことが ありますか。・前に パリに 行った ことが ありますか。**4** conj I'd like to see him before I go いく まえに、かれに あいたいです。・行く 前に、彼に 会いたいです。; I'd like to see him before he goes かれが いく まえに、あいたいです。・彼が 行く 前に、会いたいです。

beg vb ものごいを する・物乞いを する

beggar n こじき

begin vb (something starts) はじまる・始まる; (to start something) はじめる・始める; to begin working はたらき はじめる・働き始める

beginner n しょしんしゃ・初心者

beginning n (relating to time) はじめ・初め; (relating to an action) はじめ・始め; at the beginning of May ごがつの はじめ・五月の 初めに; the beginning of the race きょ うそうの はじめ・競争の 始め

behave vb I behaved badly わるいことを しました。・ 悪いことを しました。; behave yourself! ちゃんとしな さい。

behaviour (British English), **behavior** (US English) n こう どう・行動

behind prep うしろ・後ろ; I looked behind me うしろを ふりかえりました。・後ろを 振り返りました。

Belgium n ベルギー

believe vb しんじる・信じる

bell n (in a church) かね・鐘; (on a door or bicycle) ベル

belong vb (to be the property of) that book belongs to me あのほんは わたしの です。・あの 本は 私の です。; (to be a member of) to belong to a club クラブに はいって いる・クラブに 入っている

belongings n もちもの・持ち物

below prep 〜のした・〜の 下; the kitchen is below my room だいどころは わたしの へやの したです。・台所 は 私の 部屋の 下です。

belt n ベルト

bench n ベンチ

bend 1 vb (to lean, to move, to make crooked) まげる・曲げ る; to bend one's knees ひざをまげる ・ひざを 曲げる **2** n カーブ; to bend down かがむ

beneath *prep* 〜の した・〜の 下

beside *prep* 〜の そば・〜の 側; he is sitting beside me かれは わたしの そばに すわって います。・彼は 私の 側に 座って います。; to live beside the sea うみの そばに すむ・海の そばに 住む

best 1 *n* ! *This isn't used as much in Japanese as in English*; いちばん・一番; to do one's best がんばる・頑張る **2** *adj* いちばん・一番; the best hotel in town この まちの いちばんいい ホテル・この 町の 一番いい ホテル; best friend しんゆう・親友; the best thing to do would be to phone him かれに でんわした ほうが いいです。・彼に 電話した 方が いいです。**3** *adv* I like tennis best テニスが いちばん すきです。・テニスが 一番 好きです。

better 1 *adj* he is better at sports than me かれは わたしより スポーツが じょうずです。・彼は 私より スポーツが 上手です。; the weather is going to get better てんきは よく なります。・天気は 良く なります。; I was ill but now I'm better びょうきでしたが げんきに なりました。・病気でしたが 元気に なりました。**2** *adv* we'd better go いった ほうが いいです。・行った ほうが いいです。

between 1 *prep* 〜の あいだ・〜の 間; between the post office and the flower shop there is a bank ゆうびんきょくと はなやの あいだに ぎんこうが あります。・郵便局と 花屋の 間に 銀行が あります。

beyond *prep* 〜の むこう・〜の 向こう; beyond the village むらの むこう・村の 向こう

bicycle *n* じてんしゃ・自転車

big *adj* (large) おおきい・大きい; big party おおきい パーティー・大きい パーティー; big car おおきい くるま・大きい 車; big parcel おおきい にもつ・大きい 荷物; (area) ひろい・広い; big garden ひろい にわ・広い 庭; big room ひろい へや・広い 部屋; (heavy, thick) あつい・厚い; big book あつい ほん・厚い 本

bike *n* じてんしゃ・自転車 (motorbike) オートバイ

bill *n* (general household) せいきゅうしょ・請求書; gas bill ガスだい・ガス代; electricity bill でんきだい・電気代;

telephone bill でんわだい・電話代; (in a restaurant) かいけい・会計; could we have the bill please? かいけいおねがいします。・会計お願いします。; (in a hotel) せいさん・精算; (US English) (money) おさつ・お札; 1000 yen bill せんえんさつ・千円札

billiards n ビリヤード

bin n (British English) ごみばこ・ごみ箱

biology n せいぶつがく・生物学

bird n とり・鳥

biro® n (British English) ボールペン

birth n しゅっさん・出産; date of birth せいねんがっぴ・生年月日

birthday n たんじょうび・誕生日; Happy birthday! おたんじょうびおめでとうございます。・お誕生日おめでとうございます。

biscuit n (British English) ビスケット

bit 1 n (a small quantity of rice, bread, wood, string, etc) すこし・少し; there's a bit of rice ごはんが すこし あります。・ご飯が少しあります。 **2 a bit** (British English) ちょっと; a bit odd ちょっと へん・ちょっと 変

bite vb かむ; to bite one's nails つめを かむ

bitter adj にがい・苦い

black adj くろい・黒い

blackboard n こくばん・黒板

blade n (of a knife, a sword) は・刃

blame 1 vb 〜の せいに する 2 n to take the blame せきにんをとる・責任を とる ! It is better to express this using "responsibility" or "fault"

blank adj (describing a page) くうはく(の)・空白(の); (describing a cassette) から(の)・空(の)

blanket n もうふ・毛布

blaze n かじ・火事

bleed vb しゅっけつする・出血する; to have a nose bleed はなちが でている・鼻血が 出ている

blind 1 adj めの みえない・目の 見えない 2 n a blind ブラインド

blister n みずぶくれ・水脹れ

block 1 n (a building) a block of apartments アパート; (a group of houses) ! Not used in Japan. Japanese abroad may use ブロック; (a large piece) a block ブロック

blond, blonde adj きんぱつ(の)・金髪(の); I have blond hair かみは きんぱつです。・髪は 金髪です。; my older sister's blonde あねは きんぱつです。・姉は 金髪です

blood n ち・血; blood test けつえきけんさ・血液検査

blood-type n けつえきがた・血液型

blouse n ブラウス

blow vb (if it's the wind) ふく・吹く; the wind blows かぜが ふきます。・風が 吹きます。; (to blow one's nose) はなを かむ・鼻を かむ; (if it's a light bulb) きれる・切れる

blue adj あおい・青い

blush vb かおが あかく なる・顔が 赤くなる

board 1 n (a piece of wood) a board いた・板; (for games) a board ボード; (a blackboard) こくばん・黒板 2 vb to board a ship ふねに のる・船に 乗る 3 on board のって いる・乗っている

boarding school n ぜんりょうせいの がっこう・全寮制の 学校 ! Extremely unusual in Japan

boast vb じまんする・自慢する

boat n ボート

body n からだ・体; a dead body したい・死体

boil vb (if it's a person boiling something) to boil water おゆを わかす・お湯を 沸かす; to boil an egg たまごを ゆでる・卵を ゆでる; (if it's water, milk) わく・沸く; the water is boiling おゆが わいています。・お湯が 沸いています。; (if it's vegetables) ゆでる

boiled egg n ゆでたまご・ゆで卵

boiler n ボイラー

bomb 1 n ばくだん・爆弾 **2** vb (from the air) ばくだんを とうかする・爆弾を 投下する; (to be blown up) ばくはされる・爆破 される

bone n ほね・骨

bonnet n (British English) (in a car) ボンネット

book 1 n ほん・本 **2** vb よやくする・予約する; to book a room へやを よやくする・部屋を 予約する; this flight is fully booked この ひこうきは まんせきです。・ この 飛行機は 満席です。

booking n よやく・予約

bookshop, bookstore n ほんや・本屋

boot n (worn on the feet) ブーツ; (British English) (of a car) トランク

border n さかい・境; to cross an international border こっきょうをこえる・国境を 越える

bored adj つまらない

boring adj つまらない

born adj to be born うまれる・生まれる; I was born in February にがつに うまれました。・二月に 生まれました。; I was born in Italy イタリアで うまれました。・イタリアで 生まれました。

borrow vb かりる・借りる; to borrow some money from someone だれかに おかねを かりる・誰かに お金を 借りる

boss n ボス

both 1 det both are blonde りょうほうとも きんぱつです。・両方とも 金髪です。; both Anne and Brian came アンも ブライアンも きました。・アンも ブライアンも 来ました。 **2** pron りょうほうとも・両方とも; you are both wrong, both of you are wrong りょうほうとも まちがっています。・両方とも 間違っています。

bother *vb* (to take the trouble) don't go to any bother おかまいなく; (to worry, to upset) しんぱいさせる・心配させる; (in polite apologies) I'm sorry to bother you, but... すみませんが、...

bottle *n* びん・瓶

bottle-opener *n* せんぬき・栓抜き

bottom 1 *n* (the lowest part) the bottom of the mountain やまのふもと・山の ふもと; the bottom of the page ページのした・ページの 下; the bottom of the lake みずうみのそこ・湖の 底; (at the lowest level) bottom of the class クラスで いちばんした・クラスで 一番下; (part of the body) おしり **2** *adj* the bottom drawer いちばんしたの ひきだし・一番下の 引き出し

bound: to be bound to *vb* it's bound to create problems かならずもんだいに なるでしょう。・必ず 問題に なるでしょう。

bow¹ *n* (a knot) ちょうむすび・ちょう結び; (a weapon) ゆみ・弓

bow² *vb* おじぎする

bowl *n* ボール; (for rice) ちゃわん・茶碗

bowling *n* ボーリング

box *n* はこ・箱; (cardboard box) だんボール・段ボール

boxing *n* ボクシング

boy *n* おとこの こ・男の 子

boyfriend *n* ボーイフレンド

bra *n* ブラ

bracelet *n* ブレスレット

braid *n* (US English) みつあみ・三つ編み

brain *n* のう・脳

brake *n* ブレーキ

branch *n* (of tree) えだ・枝; (of company) してん・支店

brand-new *adj* しんぴん(の)・新品(の); brand new computer しんぴんの コンピューター・新品の コンピューター; (new car) しんしゃ・新車

brandy n ブランデー

brave adj ゆうきがある・勇気がある

bread n パン

break 1 vb (to be damaged) こわれる・壊れる; the chair broke いすが こわれました・椅子が 壊れました; (to crack or smash) わる・割る; to break an egg たまごを わる・卵を 割る; (bones) おる・折る; to break one's leg あしのほねを おる・足の 骨を 折る; I broke my arm うでのほねを おりました・腕の 骨を 折りました; (to not keep) やぶる・破る; to break a promise やくそくを やぶる・約束を 破る; to break the rules ルールを やぶる・ルールを 破る **2** n a break (a short rest) きゅうけい・休憩; (at school) やすみじかん・休み時間; to take a break きゅうけいする・休憩する; (a holiday) やすみ・休み; **break down** (if it's a machine) こしょうする・故障する; **break in** (to be broken into) どろぼうに はいられる・泥棒に入られる; **break up** (a couple) わかれる・別れる; to break up with someone だれかと わかれる・誰かと 別れる

breakfast n あさごはん・朝ご飯; to have breakfast あさごはんをたべる・朝ご飯を 食べる A more formal word which is often used in hotels is ちょうしょく

breast n むね・胸

breath n いき・息; to be out of breath いきが きれる・息が 切れる; to hold one's breath いきを とめる・息を 止める

breathe vb いきを する・息を する; to breathe in すいこむ・吸い込む; to breathe out いきを はく・息を 吐く

breeze n そよかぜ・そよ風

brick n れんが・煉瓦

bride n はなよめ(さん)・花嫁(さん)

bridegroom n はなむこ(さん)・花婿(さん)

bridge n はし・橋

brief adj みじかい・短い

bright adj ! Not usually used with colours; (describing light) あかるい・明るい; this room is not very bright この へや は あまり 明るくないです。・この 部屋は あまり 明るくないです。; to get brighter あかるく なる・明るく なる; (intelligent) あたまが いい・頭が いい

brilliant adj (used for emphasis) すごい

bring vb to bring もって くる・持って 来る; (to be accompanied by) つれて くる・連れて 来る; I brought my younger sister to the party いもうとを パーティーに つれて いきました。・妹を パーティーに 連れて 行きました。; **bring back** もって かえる・持って 帰る; I brought back some souvenirs おみやげを もって かえりました。・お土産を 持って 帰りました。; **bring up** そだてる・育てる; to bring up a child こどもを そだてる・子供を 育てる

Britain n イギリス; えいこく・英国 is also used

British 1 adj イギリスの **2** n British person イギリスじん・イギリス人

broad adj ひろい・広い

broadcast vb ほうそうする・放送する; live broadcast なまほうそう・生放送

brochure n パンフレット

broke adj おかねが ない・お金が ない

broken adj こわれている・壊れている

bronze n ブロンズ

brother ! Remember there are two sets of words for family members; n (your own older brother) あに・兄; (your own younger brother) おとうと・弟; (someone else's older brother) おにいさん・お兄さん; (someone else's younger brother) おとうとさん・弟さん

brother-in-law n ぎりの + word for brother ▶ **brother**

brown adj (in colour) ちゃいろい・茶色い; brown eyes ちゃいろいめ・茶色い 目

brush 1 n (for hair, clothes or shoes) ブラシ; toothbrush はブラシ・歯ブラシ; (for sweeping up) ほうき; (for painting)

(for pictures) えふで・絵筆; (for walls etc.) ブラシ **2** vb to brush one's hair かみのけを とかす・髪の毛を とかす; to brush one's teeth はを みがく・歯を 磨く

bucket n バケツ

build vb たてる・建てる; to build a house いえを たてる・家を 建てる

building n たてもの・建; (offices/apartments) ビル

bully vb いじめる

bump vb to bump one's head あたまを ぶつける・頭を ぶつける; **bump into** (to hit) ぶつかる; (to meet) ぐうぜん にあう・偶然に 会う

bunch n a bunch of flowers はなたば・花束; a bunch of grapes ぶどう; a bunch of keys かぎ・鍵

burger n ハンバーガー

burglar n どろぼう・泥棒

burglar alarm n ぼうはんアラーム・防犯アラーム

burglary n we had a burglary どろぼうに はいられました。・泥棒に 入られました。

burn 1 vb (to destroy, to get rid of) もやす・燃やす; to burn rubbish ごみを もやす・ごみを 燃やす; (to injure) to burn oneself やけどを する; to burn one's finger ゆびを やけど する・指を やけどする; (to be on fire) もえている・燃えている; (when cooking) こげる・焦げる **2** n a burn やけど

burst vb (if it's a balloon or pipe) はれつする・破裂する; **burst into** to burst into tears なきだす・泣き出す; **burst out** to burst out laughing わらいだす・笑い出す

bury vb うめる・埋める

bus n バス

bus driver n バスの うんてんしゅ・バスの 運転手

business n (commercial activities) ビジネス; to go to Tokyo on business とうきょうに しゅっちょうする・東京に 出張する; (a company) かいしゃ・会社; (when protecting

one's privacy) it's none of your business あなたとは かんけいありません。・ あなたとは 関係 ありません。

bus station *n* バスのりば・バス乗り場

bus stop *n* バスてい・バス停

busy *adj* いそがしい・忙しい

but *conj* が; that restaurant is good but expensive あの レストランは おいしいですが、たかいです。・ あの レストランは おいしいですが、高いです。**!** *There are a number of other expressions similar in meaning.* ▶**however**

butcher *n* にくや・肉屋

butter *n* バター

butterfly *n* ちょうちょう

button *n* ボタン

buy *vb* かう・買う; to buy a present (for someone) (だれかに)プレゼントを かって あげる・(誰かに)プレゼントを買って あげる

by *prep* *(on one's own)* by oneself ひとりで・一人で; *(using)* use particle で; to travel by bus バスで いく・バスで 行く; we went there by bicycle じてんしゃで いきました。・自転車で行きました。; to pay by credit card クレジットカードではらう・クレジットカードで 払う; to book by phone でんわで よやくする・電話で 予約する; *(as a result of)* I passed the exam by studying hard **!** *Note word order;* いっしょうけんめい べんきょうした けっか、しけんにうかりました。・ 一生懸命 勉強した結果、試験に 受かりました。; *(beside)* そば・側; by the sea うみのそば・海の 側; *(indicating the author or painter)* use particle の; a book by Soseki Natsume なつめそうせきのほん・夏目漱石の 本; a song by The Beatles ビートルズのうた・ビートルズの 歌; *(when talking about time)* までに; by next Thursday らいしゅうの もくようび までに・来週の 木曜日 までに; *(with passive verbs)* に; I was bitten by a dog いぬに かまれました。・犬に 噛まれました。; *(other cases)* by chance ぐうぜん・偶然; by mistake まちがって・間違って; one by one ひとつずつ・一つずつ

Cc

cab *n* タクシー

cabbage *n* キャベツ

cable car *n* ケーブルカー

café *n* きっさてん・喫茶店

cake *n* (western style) ケーキ; (Japanese style) おかし・お菓子

cake shop *n* (Japanese style) わがしや・和菓子屋; (western style) ケーキや・ケーキ屋

calculator *n* でんたく・電卓

calendar *n* カレンダー

calf *n* (the animal) こうし・子牛; (part of the leg) ふくらはぎ

call *vb* (to name) to say 'I'm called Michiko Tanaka', you should say たなか みちこです。 or to be more formal you can say たなか みちこと もうします。; her boyfriend is called Michael かのじょの ボーイフレンドは マイケルと いいます。・彼女の ボーイフレンドは マイケルと 言います。; it's called hako in Japanese にほんごで 箱と いいます。・日本語で 箱と 言います。; somebody called Tanaka telephoned たなかと いうひとから でんわが ありました。・田中と いう 人から 電話が ありました。; (to call out to) よぶ・呼ぶ; the teacher is calling us せんせいは よんでいます。・先生は 呼んでいます。; to call the register (British English) しゅっせきを とる・出席を 取る; (to phone) でんわする・電話する; who's calling? どちらさまですか。・どちら 様ですか。; (to get to come) よぶ・呼ぶ; to call the doctor いしゃを よぶ・医者を 呼ぶ; (to wake) おこす・起こす; (to pay a visit) たずねる・訪ねる; I called yesterday きのう たずねました。・昨日訪ねました。; **call back** (to come back) また くる・ま

た 来る; (to phone back) また でんわする・また 電話する; call up (American English) でんわする・電話する

calm 1 adj しずか(な)・静か(な); **calm down** おちつく・落ち着く

camcorder n ビデオカメラ

camera n (for taking photos) カメラ; (in a studio, for videos) えいがの カメラ・映画の カメラ

camp 1 n a summer camp サマーキャンプ **2** vb to go camping キャンプする

campsite n キャンプじょう・キャンプ場

can¹ vb (to have the possibility) use the potential form of the verb Note that there are a number of other structures which also express potential such as using the dictionary form of the verb + ことが できる; can you come? こられますか。・来られ ますか。; where can I buy stamps? きっては どこで かえ ますか。; 切手は どこで 買えますか。; he can't sleep when it's hot かれは あつい とき、ねむれません。・彼は 暑い とき、眠れません。; (to know how to) use the potential form of the verb Note that there are a number of other structures which also express potential such as using the dictionary form of the verb + ことが できる; she can swim かのじょは およげます。・彼女は 泳げます。; he can't drive yet かれは まだ うんてんが できません。・彼は まだ 運転が できません。; can you speak French? フラン スごが はなせますか。・フランス語が 話せますか。; I can read hiragana ひらがなを よむ ことが できます。・ ひらがなを 読む ことが できます。; (seeing, hearing) See and hear have two potential forms depending on context; (when involuntary) can see みえる・見える; can hear きこ える・聞こえる; I can see mountains from my room. へや から やまが みえます。・部屋から 山が 見えます。; I can hear music おんがくが きこえます。・音楽が 聞こ えます。; (when effort is required) can see みられる・見ら れる; can hear きける・聴ける; you can see Kabuki theatre if you go to Japan にほんに いけば、かぶきが み られます。・日本に 行けば、歌舞伎が 見られます。;

I bought a radio so now I can hear the news every night ラジオ を かいました から、いま まいばん ニュース が きけます。・ ラジオ を 買いました から、今 毎晩 ニュース が 聴けます。; I can understand Japanese にほんご が わかります。・ 日本語 が わかります。; (when giving and receiving permission, offering or suggesting) use the 〜て form of the verb + も いい; can we borrow your car? くるま を かりても いいですか。・ 車 を 借りても いいですか。; can I help you? (in a shop) いらっしゃいませ。; can I smoke? たばこ を すっても いいですか。・ たばこ を 吸っても いいですか。; you can use a dictionary じしょ を つかっても いいですよ。・ 辞書 を 使っても いいですよ。; (when refusing permission) use the 〜て form of the verb + は いけない; you can't put san after your own name じぶん の なまえ に さん を つけては いけません。・ 自分 の 名前 に さん を つけては いけません。; you can't use a dictionary じしょ を つかっては いけません。・ 辞書 を 使っては いけません。

can² *n* かん・缶

Canada *n* カナダ

Canadian 1 *adj* カナダの **2** *n* カナダじん・カナダ人

canal *n* うんが・運河

cancel *vb* キャンセルする

cancer *n* がん・癌

candle *n* ろうそく

candy *n* (US English) あめ

canoe *n* カヌー

can-opener *n* かんきり・缶切り

canteen *n* しょくどう・食堂

cap *n* ぼうし・帽子; baseball cap やきゅうぼう・野球帽

capital 1 *n* しゅと・首都; Tokyo is the capital of Japan とうきょう は にほん の しゅと です。・ 東京 は 日本 の 首都 です。 **2** *adj* capital letter おおもじ・大文字

captain *n* キャプテン

car n くるま・車

caravan n *(British English)* キャンピングカー

card n *(for sending to someone)* カード; *(for playing games)* トランプ; to play cards トランプする; *(business card)* めいし・名刺

care 1 n *(to take care)* きを つける・気を つける; to take care when crossing the street みちを わたる とき、きを つける・道を 渡る とき、気を つける; to take care of someone だれかの めんどうを みる・誰かの 面倒を 見る **2** vb I don't care かまいません。; to care about the environment かんきょうの ことを きに する・環境の ことを 気に する

career n キャリア

careful adj to be careful きを つける・気を つける; please be careful きを つけてください。・気を つけてください。

careless adj ふちゅうい(な)・不注意(な)

car ferry n カーフェリー

carnival n *(British English) (a festival)* まつり・祭り; *(US English) (a fair)* カーニバル

car park n *(British English)* ちゅうしゃじょう・駐車場

carpet n じゅうたん

carrot n にんじん・人参

carry vb *(to hold)* もつ・持つ; I can't carry heavy things おもい ものが もてません。・重い 物が 持てません。; *(to move)* はこぶ・運ぶ; to carry the baggage にもつを はこぶ・荷物を 運ぶ; **carry on** つづく・続く; **carry (something) on** *(なにかを)* つづける・*(何かを)* 続ける

cartoon n まんが・漫画; *(pictures)* まんが・漫画; *(animation)* アニメ

case¹ *in case* conj ねんの ため・念の ため; I took my umbrella just in case ねんの ため、かさを もって でかけました。・念の ため、傘を 持って 出かけました。

case² n ケース

cash 1 n げんきん・現金; I don't have any cash げんきん がありません。・現金が ありません。; to pay in cash げんきんではらう・現金で 払う **2** vb げんきんに する・現金を する

cash dispenser n ATM ! *This is pronounced* エーティー エム; *Note that there are a number of terms in use, but this is perhaps the most general.*

cassette n カセットテープ

cassette player n カセットプレーヤー

castle n おしろ・お城

cat n ねこ・猫

catch vb (*to capture*) とる・採る; to catch a fish さかなを とる・魚を 採る; (*to take hold of*) つかむ・掴む; (*to pinch, to stick*) I caught my finger in the door ドアに ゆびが はさまりました。・ドアに 指が 挟まりました。; my shirt got caught on the thorns シャツが とげに ひっかかり ました。・シャツが とげに 引っかかりました。; (*to get*) まにあう・間に合う; I was running to catch the train でんしゃに まにあう ように、はしっていました。 ・電車に 間に合う ように、走っていました。; (*to take by surprise*) つかまえる・捕まえる; to catch a pupil shoplifting まんびきしている せいとを つかまえる・ 万引きしている 生徒を 捕まえる; to get caught つかま えられる・捕まえられる; (*to become ill with*) to catch flu かぜをひく・風邪を ひく; to catch a cold かぜを ひく ・風邪を ひく; to catch fire もえだす・燃え出す; **catch up** to catch up (with someone) (だれかに) おいつく・ (誰かに)追いつく

caterpillar n けむし・毛虫

cathedral n だいせいどう・大聖堂

Catholic adj カトリックきょう(の)・カトリック教(の)

cauliflower n カリフラワー

cause vb ひきおこす・引き起こす *The causative form of the verb can often be used*; the storm will cause damage あら

しは ひがいを もたらします。・ 嵐は 被害を もたらします。; it has caused us a lot of problems たくさん もんだいを ひきおこしました。・ たくさん 問題を 引き起こしました。; it's going to cause delays おくらせます。・ 遅らせます。

cautious adj ちゅういぶかい・注意深い

cave n ほらあな・洞穴

CD n CD This is pronounced シーディー

CD player n CDプレーヤー This is pronounced シーディープレーヤー

ceiling n てんじょう・天井

celebrate vb いわう・祝う; to celebrate someone's birthday だれかの たんじょうびを いわう・だれかの 誕生日を 祝う

celery n セロリ

cell n さいぼう・細胞

cellar n ちかしつ・地下室

cello n チェロ

cement n セメント

cemetery n ぼち・墓地

centigrade adj thirty degrees centigrade さんじゅうど・三十度

centimetre (British English), **centimeter** (US English) n センチ

central heating n セントラルヒーティング

centre (British English), **center** (US English) n (a place for activities, meetings) センター; a leisure centre スポーツセンター; (the middle) ちゅうしん・中心; the centre of Sapporo さっぽろの ちゅうしんち・札幌の 中心地

century n せいき・世紀

certain adj (definite) たしか(な)・確か(な); (particular) ある

certainly adv もちろん

chain *n* くさり・鎖

chair *n* いす・椅子

chalk *n* チョーク

champagne *n* シャンペン

champion *n* チャンピオン; tennis champion テニスの チャンピオン

chance *n* (when talking about a possibility) かのうせい・ 可能性; there is a chance that she'll get a job in Osaka かの じょは おおさかで しごとが できる かのうせいが あります。・ 彼女は 大阪で 仕事が できる 可能性が あります。; (an opportunity) きかい・機会; to have a chance to meet people ひとに あう きかいが ある・人に 会う 機会が ある; by chance ぐうぜんに・偶然に

change **1** *n* へんか・変化; (cash) small change こぜに・ 小銭; (money returned) おつり・お釣 **2** *vb* (to become different, to make different) かわる・変わる; this town has changed a lot この まちは かなりかわりました。・ この 町は かなり変わりました。; I've changed my mind きが かわりました。・ 気が 変わりました。; (to replace, exchange) とりかえる・取り替える; to change a tyre タイヤをとりかえる・タイヤを 取り替える; to change a shirt for a different colour シャツを べつな いろ にとりかえる・シャツを 別な 色に 取り替える; to change dollars into yen ドルを えんに かえる・ドルを 円に 替える; (to switch) かえる・代える; to change places with someone だれかと ばしょを かえる・誰かと 場所 を 代える; she keeps changing channels かのじょは いつ も チャンネルを かえています。・ 彼女は いつも チャ ンネルを 代えています。; (when talking about one's clothes) to get changed きがえる・着替える; (when using transport) のりかえる・乗り換える

changing room *n* こういしつ・更衣室

channel *n* チャンネル

Channel *n* (English) Channel イギリスかいきょう・イギ リス海峡

chapter n しょう・章

charge 1 vb せいきゅうする・請求する; to charge for the breakage はそんだいを せいきゅうする・破損代を 請求する **2** n (a price, a fee) りょうきん・料金; there's no charge むりょうです。・無料です。 **3** in charge たんとうしている・担当している; to be in charge of the money おかねを たんとうしています。・お金を 担当 しています。

charming adj みりょくてき(な)・魅力的(な)

chase vb おいかける・追いかける; chase away おいは らう・追い払う

chat 1 vb おしゃべりする **2** n おしゃべり; chat up (British English) なんぱする

cheap adj (not expensive) やすい・安い; it's cheap やすい です。・安いです。; the bus is cheaper バスの ほうが やすいです。・バスの 方が 安いです。; (of poor quality) やすっぽい・安っぽい

cheat vb カンニングする

check 1 vb (to make sure) かくにんする・確認する; you should check whether it's true ほんとうか どうか、かくに んした ほうが いいです。・本当か どうか、確認した 方が いいです。; (to inspect (tickets)) (きっぷを)かいさつ する・(切符を)改札する; our tickets weren't checked きっぷは かいさつされませんでした。・切符は 改札 されませんでした。 **2** n (US English) (a bill) かんじょう・ 勘定; (US English) (a cheque) こぎって・小切手; to check in チェックインする; to check out チェックアウトする

checkbook n (US English) こぎってちょう・小切手帳

check-in n チェックイン

checkout n (in a shop) レジ; (in a hotel) チェックアウト; checkout time is 11:00 チェックアウトじかんは じゅう いちじです。・チェックアウト時間は 十一時です。

cheek n ほお

cheeky adj なまいき(な)・生意気(な)

cheerful adj きげんが いい・機嫌が いい

cheese n チーズ

chef n りょうりちょう・料理長

chemist n (in a shop) やくざいし・薬剤師; (in a laboratory) かがくしゃ・化学者; chemist's shop くすりや・薬屋

chemistry n かがく・化学

cheque n (British English) こぎって・小切手; to write a cheque for £50 ごじゅっポンドの こぎってを かく・五十ポンドの 小切手を 書く

cheque book n (British English) こぎってちょう・小切手帳

cherry n さくらんぼ

cherry tree n さくら・桜

chess n チェス

chest n むね・胸

chestnut 1 n くり・栗 **2** adj くりいろ(の)・栗色(の)

chew vb かむ・噛む

chewing gum n ガム

chicken n (the bird) にわとり・鶏; (the meat) とりにく・鳥肉; year of the chicken とりどし・酉年

child n こども・子供

chilly adj it's chilly ちょっと さむいです。・ちょっと 寒いです。

chimney n えんとつ・煙突

chin n あご

China n ちゅうごく・中国

chips n (British English) (French fries) フライドポテト; (US English) (crisps) ポテトチップス

chocolate n チョコレート

choice n せんたく・選択; I had no choice せんたくの よちが ありませんでした。・選択の 余地が ありませんでした。

choir n (church) せいかたい・聖歌隊; (choral music) がっしょうだん・合唱団

choke vb I was choking with the smoke けむりで むせていました。・煙で 咽ていました。; I choked on the rice cake もちがのどに つまりました。・餅が 喉に 詰まりました。

choose vb えらぶ・選ぶ

chopsticks n おはし

chore n (housework) かじ・家事; (other work) ざつよう・雑用

Christian adj キリストきょう(の)・キリスト教(の)

Christian name n ファーストネーム

Christmas n クリスマス; Merry Christmas!, Happy Christmas! メリークリスマス

Christmas Eve n クリスマスイブ

Christmas tree n クリスマスツリー

church n きょうかい・教会

cider n りんごしゅ・りんご酒

cigar n はまき・葉巻

cigarette n たばこ・煙草

cigarette lighter n ライター

cinema n (British English) えいがかん・映画館

circle n えん・円

circus n サーカス

citizen n (of a country) こくみん・国民; (of a city or town) しみん・市民

city n とし・都市

city centre (British English), **city center** (US English) n まちのちゅうしん・町の 中心

civilized adj ぶんめいの すすんだ・文明の 進んだ

civil servant n こうむいん・公務員

clap *vb* はくしゅする・拍手する

clarinet *n* クラリネット

class *n* (*a group of students*) クラス; (*a lesson*) じゅぎょう・授業; history class れきしの じゅぎょう・歴史の 授業; (*a social group*) かいきゅう・階級

classical music *n* クラシックおんがく・クラシック音楽

classmate *n* クラスメート

classroom *n* きょうしつ・教室

clean 1 *adj* (*not dirty*) きれい(な); my hands are clean てはきれいです。・手は きれいです。; to keep the house clean うちを きれいに する・家を きれいにする; (*not polluted*) きれい (な house) そうじする; to clean a room へやを そうじする・部屋を 掃除する; (*teeth, shoes*) みがく・磨く; to have a jacket cleaned ジャケットを クリーニングに だす・ジャケットを クリーニングに 出す

clear 1 *adj* (*easy to understand, making sense*) わかりやすい・分かりやすい; is that clear? わかりますか。・分かりますか。; (*obvious*) あきらか・明らか; it is clear that everyone is dissatisfied みんなが ふまんなのは あきらかです。・皆が 不満なのは 明らかです。; (*easy to see or hear, distinct*) a clear voice きれいな こえ・きれいな 声; clear writing きれいな じ・きれいな 字; (*with no rain or cloud*) はれている・晴れている; a clear day はれているひ・晴れている 日 2 *vb* (*to empty, to remove from*) to clear the table テーブルの うえを かたづける・テーブルの 上を 片づける; to clear the snow じょせつする・除雪する; (*if it's rain*) あがる・上がる

clever *adj* (*intelligent*) あたまが いい・頭が いい; clever at mathematics すうがくが とくい・数学が 得意

cliff *n* がけ・崖

climate *n* きこう・気候

climb *vb* to climb (up) a tree きに のぼる・木に 登る; to climb a mountain やまに のぼる・山に 登る; to climb over

a wall へいを のりこえる・塀を 乗り越える; (to rise
higher) あがる・上がる

climbing n とざん・登山

clinic n しんりょうじょ・診療所

cloakroom n (for coats) クローク; (toilet) トイレ A more
polite word is おてあらい

clock n とけい・時計

close¹ adj (near) ちかい・近い; the station is close えき
は ちかいです。・駅は 近いです。; is the house close to
the school? いえは がっこうに ちかいですか。・家は
学校に 近いですか。; (as a friend or relation) したしい・
親しい **2** adv to be living close (by) ちかくに すんでいる
・近くに 住んでいる; to come closer ちかづく・近づく

close² vb (to close something) (eyes) とじる・閉じる;
(doors, windows) しめる・閉める; (to be closed) (buildings,
doors, windows) しまる・閉まる; the shop closes at noon
みせはじゅうにじに しまります。・店は 十二時に
閉まります。; the door closed ドアが しまりました。・
ドアが 閉まりました。 **close down** しまう

closed adj (eyes) とじている・閉じている; (doors,
windows) しまっている・閉まっている; (buildings) しま
っている

cloth n (material) ぬの・布; (for cleaning or dusting) ふきん

clothes n ふく・服; to put on one's clothes ふくを きる・
服を着る; to take off one's clothes ふくを ぬぐ・服を
脱ぐ; he had no clothes on かれは はだかでした。・彼は
裸でした。

cloud n くも・雲

clown n ピエロ

club n クラブ; a tennis club テニスクラブ; to be in a club
クラブにはいっている・クラブに 入っている For
after school club activities, the suffix ぶ can be added to the
name of the sport; (a nightclub) ナイトクラブ

clue n (in an investigation) てがかり・手がかり; (in a
crossword) ヒント

clumsy adj ぶきよう(な)・不器用(な)

coach 1 n (British English) (a bus) バス; (of a train) きゃくしゃ・客車 **2** vb コーチする

coach station n バスステーション; (for long distance coaches) ちょうきょりバスのりば・長距離バス乗り場

coal n せきたん・石炭

coast n かいがん・海岸

coat n コート; (of an animal) け・毛

coat hanger n ハンガー

cobweb n くものす・くもの巣

cock n おんどり・雄鳥

cocoa n ココア

coconut n ココナッツ

cod n たら

coffee n コーヒー; would you like a coffee? コーヒーはいかがですか。

coffee machine n コーヒーメーカー

coin n コイン; ten yen coin じゅうえんだま・十円玉

coincidence n ぐうぜん・偶然

cold 1 adj (air temperature) さむい・寒い; it's very cold とてもさむいです。・とても寒いです。; it's cold in the classroom きょうしつはさむいです。・教室は寒いです。; it's going to get cold さむくなります。・寒くなります。; (food, drink) to go cold さめる・冷める; the soup is getting cold スープがさめています。・スープが冷めています。 **2** n (the lack of heat) さむさ・寒さ; (common illness) かぜ・風邪

collapse vb (if it's a building, a chair) くずれる・崩れる; (if it's a wall) たおれる・倒れる

collar n (on a shirt or jacket) えり・襟; (for a pet) くびわ・首輪

colleague n どうりょう・同僚

collect vb (to gather or make a collection of) あつめる・集める; to collect the exercise books ノートをあつめる・

ノートを集める; I collect stamps きってを あつめています。・ 切手を 集めています。; (to take away) しゅうしゅうする・収集する; to collect the rubbish ごみを しゅうしゅうする・ごみを 収集する

collection n (a set) しゅうしゅう・収集; (money collected) ぼきん・募金

college n だいがく・大学; to go to college, to be at college だいがくに かよっている・大学に 通っている

colour (British English), **color** (US English) **1** n いろ・色; what colour is the car? くるまは なにいろですか。 車は 何色ですか; **2** vb to colour the drawings (in) えに いろをぬる・絵に 色を 塗る

colourful (British English) **colorful** (US English) adj はで(な)・派手(な)

comb 1 n くし **2** vb to comb one's hair かみを くしで とかす・髪を くしで とかす

come vb to come くる・来る; she's coming today かのじょは きょう きます。・ 彼女は 今日 来ます。; please come to Paris with us パリに いっしょに いってください・パリに 一緒に 行ってください; I came by bike じてんしゃで きました。・ 自転車で 来ました。; come and see! みに きてください。・ 見に 来てください。; I'm coming! いきます。・ 行きます。; is the bus coming? バスは きていますか。・ バスは 来ていますか。; please be careful when you come down the stairs かいだんを おりるとき、きを つけてください。・ 階段を 降りるとき、気を 付けてください。; to come through the city centre まちの ちゅうしんを とおる・町の 中心を 通る; (to call around) たずねる・訪ねる; (to reach) turn left when you come to the traffic lights しんごうを ひだりに まがってください。・ 信号を 左に 曲がってください。; (to attend) さんかする・参加する; will you be able to come to the meeting? かいぎに さんか できますか。・ 会議に 参加 できますか。; (to be a native or a product of) I come from Britain イギリスから きています。・ イギリスから 来ています。Note that you could also say イギリスしゅっ

しんです。; the strawberries all come from Spain いちごは ぜんぶ スペインさんです。・ いちごは 全部 スペイン 産です。; (in a contest) to come first いちいに なる・一位 に なる; **come around ▸ come round; come back** もどる ・ 戻る; to come back home かえる・帰る; **come in** (to enter) はいる・入る; (if it's a plane, a train) つく・着く; the tide's coming in しおが みちる・汐が 満ちる; **come off** とれる・取れる; **come on** (to start to work) つく・ 点く; (when encouraging someone) come on! がんばって・ 頑張って; **come on to** (US English) to come on to someone だれかを なんぱする・誰かを なんぱする*; **come out** (to leave a place) でる・出る; I saw him as I came out of the shop みせから でた ときに かれを みました。・ 店か ら 出た ときに 彼を 見ました。; (to become available) (if it's a film) じょうえいする・上映する; (if it's a book) しゅっぱんされる・出版される; (if it's a photo) the photo didn't come out しゃしんは だめでした。・ 写真は だめでした。; (if it's smoke, fire) there are flames coming out of the windows ほのおが まどから でています。・ 炎が 窓から 出ています。; **come round** (to visit) たずねる・ 訪ねる; (after fainting) いしきが もどる・意識が 戻る; **come to** the bill came to 7500 yen かんじょうは ななせん ごひゃくえんに なりました。・ 勘定は 七千五百円に なりました。; how much does it come to? いくらに なり ますか。; **come up** (to be discussed) to come up in conversation はなしに でて くる・話しに 出て 来る; (if it's the sun) のぼる・昇る

comfortable adj (if it's a chair) すわりごこちが いい・ 座り心地が いい; (if it's a bed) ねごこちが いい・寝心 地が いい; are you comfortable? だいじょうぶですか。・ 大丈夫ですか。; (relaxed) かんじの いい・感じの いい; (having enough money) くらしに こまらない・暮らしに 困らない

comforter n (US English) もうふ・毛布

comic strip n まんが・漫画

---

commercial 1 adj しょうぎょう(の)・商業(の) **2** n こうこく・広告

commit vb to commit a crime はんざいを おかす・犯罪を 犯す; to commit suicide じさつする・自殺する

common adj ふつうの・普通の

communicate vb つたえる・伝える

community n しゃかい・社会

company n (a business) かいしゃ・会社; (a group of actors) theatre company げきだん・劇団; (other people) to keep someone company だれかの あいてを する・誰かの 相手を する; to keep bad company わるい つきあいを する・悪い 付き合いを する

company secretary n そうむぶちょう・総務部長

compare vb くらべる・比べる; to compare France with Italy フランスを イタリアと くらべる・フランスを イタリアと比べる; I am always compared to my older sister いつも あねと くらべられます。・いつも 姉と 比べられます。

compass n コンパス

competition n きょうそう・競争; there's competition between the schools がっこうと がっこうで きょうそう があります。・学校と 学校で 競争が あります。; (a contest) コンクール; a drawing competition えの コンクール・絵の コンクール

competitive adj (person) きょうそうしんが ある・競争心が ある; (situation) きょうそうてき(な)・競争的(な)

complain vb もんくを いう・文句を 言う; to complain about the food たべものに ついて もんくを いう・食べ物について 文句を 言う

complete 1 adj かんぜん(な)・完全(な); it was a complete disaster かんぜんな しっぱいでした。・完全な 失敗でした。; this is a complete waste of time これは じかんの むだです。・これは 時間の 無駄です。 **2** vb (a form) きにゅうする・記入する; (a course) しゅうりょうする・終了する; (to finish something) おえる・終える

completely *adv* かんぜんに・完全に

complicate *vb* ふくざつに する・複雑に する

complicated *adj* ふくざつ(な)・複雑(な)

compliment 1 *n* ほめことば・ほめ言葉 **2** *vb* to compliment someone だれかを ほめる・誰かを ほめる

comprehensive *n* (British English) comprehensive school そうごうちゅうとうがっこう・総合中等学校！ Note that the Japanese education system does not follow this pattern.

compulsory *adj* ぎむてき(な)・義務的(な); compulsory education ぎむきょういく・義務教育

computer *n* コンピュータ

computer game *n* (the game) コンピューターゲーム; (the software) ゲームソフト

computer programmer *n* プログラマー

computer scientist *n* コンピュータかがくしゃ・ コンピュータ科学者

computer studies *n* コンピューター

concentrate *vb* しゅうちゅうする・集中する

concert *n* コンサート

concert hall *n* コンサートホール

concrete *n* コンクリート

condemn *vb* to condemn to death しけいを いいわたす・ 死刑を 言い渡す

condition 1 *n* じょうたい・状態; a terrible condition じょうたいがわるい・状態が 悪い; the engine is in good condition エンジンのちょうしが いいです・ エンジンの調子が いいです。 **2 on condition that** ～と いう じょうけんで・～と 言う 条件で; you can go on condition that you're back by 10 o'clock じゅうじまでに かえるという じょうけんで いっても いいです。・ 十時までに帰ると いう 条件で 行っても いいです。

condom *n* コンドーム

conductor *n* しきしゃ・指揮者

conference *n* かいぎ・会議

confidence *n* じしん・自信; (*trust*) to have confidence in someone だれかを しんようしている・誰かを 信用している

confident *adj* じしんの ある・自信の ある; she's a confident person かのじょは じしんの ある ひとです.・彼女は 自信の ある 人です.

confidential *adj* ひみつ(の)・秘密(の)

confiscate *vb* ぼっしゅうする・没収する

conflict *n* ろんそう・論争

confused *adj* to get confused とうわくする・当惑する

congratulate *vb* おいわいを いう・お祝いを 言う

congratulations *n* (*also exclamation*) おめでとうございます

connection *n* かんけい・関係; it has no connection with the strike ストライキとは かんけい ありません.・ストライキとは 関係 ありません.

conscientious *adj* りょうしんてき(な)・良心的(な)

conscious *adj* (*aware*) きが ついている・気が 付いている; (*after an operation*) めが さめている・目が 覚めている

construct *vb* たてる・建てる

consult *vb* そうだんする・相談する

contact 1 *n* to be in contact with someone だれかと れんらくをとりあっている・誰かと 連絡を 取り合っている; to lose contact with someone だれかと れんらくを しなくなる・誰かと 連絡を しなくなる **2** *vb* れんらくする・連絡する

contact lens *n* コンタクトレンズ

contain *vb* はいっている・入っている; this contains sugar さとうが はいっています.・砂糖が 入っています.

content *adj* まんぞくしている・満足している

contents *n* ないよう・内容

contest n コンクール

continent n (a large mass of land) たいりく・大陸; (British English) (Europe) ヨーロッパたいりく・ヨーロッパ大陸

continental quilt n (British English) かけぶとん・掛け布団

continue vb to continue つづく・続く; to continue something なにかを つづける・何かを 続ける; to continue to talk, to continue talking はなしを つづける・話を続ける

continuous adj たえまない・絶え間ない; continuous effort たえまない どりょく・絶え間ない 努力

contraception n ひにん・避妊

contract n けいやく・契約; two-year contract にねんけいやく・二年契約

contradict vb むじゅんする・矛盾する; (deny) ひていする・否定する

contradiction n むじゅん・矛盾

contrast n コントラスト

contribute vb (to give money) きふする・寄付する; to contribute to a discussion いけんを いう・意見を 言う

control 1 n (of a situation) to be in control しょうあくしている・掌握している **2** vb (country, organisation) しはいする・支配する; (to regulate) きせいする・規制する

convenient adj (useful, practical) べんり(な)・便利(な); it's more convenient to take the bus バスの ほうが べんりです。・バスの 方が 便利です。; (suitable) いい; it's a convenient place to meet まちあわせに いい ところです。・待ち合わせに いい 所です。; it's not convenient for me わたしには ふべんです。・私には 不便です。

conversation n かいわ・会話; to have a conversation かいわをする・会話を する

convince vb なっとくさせる・納得させる

cook 1 vb (to prepare food) りょうりする・料理する; to cook a meal しょくじを つくる。・食事を 作る; to cook

rice ごはんを たく・ご飯を 炊く; (to be cooked in the oven) オーブンで やく・オーブンで 焼く **2** *n* コック

cooker *n* (British English) レンジ

cookie *n* (US English) クッキー

cooking *n* りょうりする こと・料理する こと; to do the cooking りょうりする・料理する

cool *adj* (air temperature) すずしい・涼しい; it's cool today きょうは すずしいです。・今日は 涼しいです。; (drinks) つめたい・冷たい; a cool drink つめたい のみもの・冷たい 飲み物; (calm) おちついている・落ち着いている; (fashionable) すてき(な)・素敵(な); (relaxed) へいき(な)・平気(な); **cool down** (to get colder) さめる・冷める; (to calm down) おちつく・落ち着く

cooperate *vb* きょうりょくする・協力する

cope *vb* (to manage) たいおうする・対応する; I can't cope with this job この しごとに たいおう できません。・この 仕事に 対応 できません。

copper *n* どう・銅

copy 1 *n* コピー **2** *vb* ふくしゃする・複写する; to copy in an exam カンニングする; **copy down, copy out** うつす・写す

cork *n* コルク

corkscrew *n* せんぬき・栓抜き

corner *n* (of a street, a building) かど・角; the shop on the corner かどの みせ・角の 店; to go around the corner かどを まがる・角を 曲がる; (in football) コーナーキック

correct 1 *adj* ただしい・正しい; that is correct それは ただしいです。それは 正しいです。; correct answer せいかい・正解 **2** *vb* なおす・直す

correction *n* しゅうせい・修正

corridor *n* ろうか・廊下

cost *vb* how much does it cost? いくらですか。; it will cost a lot of money おかねが たくさん かかります。・お金が

たくさん 掛かります。; it cost a lot of money たかった
です。・ 高かったです。

costume n いしょう・衣装

cosy adj (British English) cosy room ここちよい へや・心地
良い 部屋

cot n (British English) ベビーベッド

cottage n コテージ

cotton n (the material) コットン; (the thread) ぬいいと・
縫い糸

cotton wool n (British English) だっしめん・脱脂綿

couch n ソファー

cough vb せきを する

could vb (had the ability) use the past potential form of the verb
Note that there are a number of other structures which also
express potential such as using the dictionary form of the verb +
ことが できる; I couldn't move うごけませんでした。・
動けませんでした。; he couldn't sleep well for weeks かれ
はなんしゅうかん ねむれませんでした。・ 彼は 何週
間 眠れませんでした。; (knew how to) use the past potential
form of the verb Note that there are a number of other structures
which also express potential such as using the dictionary form of
the verb + ことが できる; I couldn't speak Japanese にほん
ごが はなせませんでした。・ 日本語が 話せませんで
した。; he couldn't type かれは タイプが できませんで
した。・ 彼は タイプが できませんでした。; he couldn't
read hiragana ひらがなを よむ ことが できませんでし
た。・ ひらがなを 読む ことが できませんでした。;
(seeing, hearing) See and hear have two potential forms
depending on context; (when involuntary) I could see みえまし
た。・ 見えました。; I could hear きこえました。・ 聞こ
えました。; I could see mountains from my room. へやから
やまがみえました。・ 部屋から 山が 見えました。;
I couldn't hear the teacher's voice せんせいの こえが きこ
えませんでした。・ 先生の 声が 聞こえませんでし
た。。; (when effort is required) I could see みられました。・

見られました。; I could hear きけました。・ 聞けました。; I could understand a little Japanese にほんごがすこしわかります。・ 日本語が 少し 分かります。; (when implying that something did not happen) she could have passed if she'd studied more かのじょは もっと べんきょうすればうかりました。・ 彼女は もっと 勉強すれば 受かりました。; (when indicating a possibility) I could be wrong まちがっている かもしれません。・ 間違っている かもしれません。; a bike could be useful じてんしゃは べんりかもしれません。・ 自転車は 便利 かもしれません。; (when asking, offering or suggesting) could I speak to Nobumi? のぶみさんは いらっしゃいますか。・ 暢美さんは いらっしゃいますか。; could you take a message? メッセージを おねがいします。・ メッセージを お願いします。; we could ask John ジョンさんに きいたら どうですか。・ ジョンさんに 聞いたら どうですか。

count vb かぞえる・ 数える; **count on** to count on someone だれかを しんらいする・ 誰かを 信頼する

counter n カウンター

country n (a state) くに・ 国; (the countryside) いなか・ 田舎; to live in the country いなかで くらす・ 田舎で 暮らす

countryside n いなか・ 田舎

couple n a couple of days (two days) ふつかかん・ 二日間; (a few days) に、 さんにち・ 二、 三日; (two people) カップル; (if married) ふうふ・ 夫婦

courage n ゆうき・ 勇気

courageous adj ゆうかん(な)・ 勇敢(な)

course 1 n (a series of lessons or lectures) コース; a Japanese course にほんごの コース・ 日本語の コース; (part of a meal) コース; main course メイン **2** of course もちろん; of course not もちろん + negative

court n (of law) ほうてい・ 法廷; to go to court さいばんにいく・ 裁判に 行く; (for playing sports) コート

court case n さいばん・ 裁判

cousin n (one's own) いとこ; (someone else's) いとこさん

cover 1 *vb* to cover おおう・覆う; the car is covered in mud くるまは どろだらけです。・車は 泥だらけです。**2** *n* (*a lid*) ふた; (*for a cushion, a quilt*) カバー; (*a blanket*) もうふ・毛布; (*on a book, a magazine, an exercise book*) ひょうし・表紙

cow *n* うし・牛

coward *n* おくびょうもの・臆病者

cowboy *n* カウボーイ

cozy *adj* (*US English*) cozy room ここちの よい へや・心地の 良い 部屋

crab *n* かに

crack *vb* (*to damage*) わる・割る; (*to get damaged*) ひびが はいる・ひびが 入る; (*to get broken*) われる・割れる

cradle *n* ゆりかご・揺りかご

cramp *n* けいれん

crash 1 *n* しょうとつ・衝突; car crash こうつうじこ・交通事故 **2** *vb* to crash into a tree きに しょうとつする・木に 衝突する; the plane crashed ひこうきが ついらく しました。・飛行機が 墜落しました。

crayon *n* クレヨン

crazy *adj* (*insane person*) くるっている・狂っている; (*idea*) ばか(な)

cream *n* クリーム

create *vb* つくる・作る; to create employment しごとを つくる・仕事を 作る

credit *n* (*academic*) たんい・単位

credit card *n* クレジットカード

cricket *n* クリケット

crime *n* はんざい・犯罪

criminal 1 *n* はんざいしゃ・犯罪者 **2** *adj* いほう(の)・違法(の)

crisis *n* きき・危機

crisps n (British English) ポテトチップ

critical adj (person) ひはんてき(な)・批判的(な);
(illness) きとく(の)・危篤(の)

criticize vb ひなんする・非難する

crocodile n わに

crooked adj crooked line まがった せん・曲がった 線;
the picture is crooked えが まがっています。・絵が 曲が
っています

cross 1 vb (to go across) to cross the road みちを おうだん
する・道を 横断する; to cross an international border こ
っきょうをこえる・国境を 越える; to cross a bridge
はしをわたる・橋を 渡る; (other uses) to cross one's
legs あしをくむ・足を 組む; our letters crossed てがみ
はいきちがいに なりました。・手紙は 行き違いに
なりました。 **2** n (X mark) ばつ; (Christian symbol) じゅう
じか・十字架 **3** adj ふきげん(な)・不機嫌(な); to get
cross おこる・起こる; cross out せんを ひいて けす・
線を 引いて 消す

crossroads n じゅうじろ・十字路

crossword puzzle n クロスワードパズル

crow n からす

crowd n (a large number of people) ぐんしゅう・群集;
crowds of people ひとごみ・人込み; (watching a game)
かんきゃく・観客

crown n おうかん・王冠

cruel adj ざんこく(な)・残酷(な)

cruelty n ざんこくさ・残酷さ

cruise n ふなたび・船旅

crush vb おしつぶす・押しつぶす

crutch n まつばづえ・松葉づえ

cry 1 vb なく・泣く **2** n なきごえ・泣き声

cucumber n きゅうり

cuddle vb だきしめる・抱き締める

culprit n はんざいにん・犯罪人

cultural adj ぶんかぶんめいの・文化文明の

culture n ぶんか・文化

cunning adj こうかつ(な)

cup n カップ; a cup of coffee コーヒー いっぱい・コーヒー 一杯; (in sport) カップ

cupboard n とだな・戸棚

curb n (US English) ほどう・歩道

cure 1 vb なおす・治す 2 n ちりょうほう・治療法

curious adj こうきしんが ある・好奇心がある

curly adj I have curly hair まきげです。・巻き毛です。

currency n つうか・通貨; foreign currency がいか・外貨

curry n カレー

curtain n カーテン; to draw the curtains カーテンを しめる・カーテンを 閉める

cushion n (on floor) ざぶとん・座布団; (on sofa) クッション

custard n (British English) カスタード

custom n しゅうかん・習慣

customer n きゃく・客

customs n ぜいかん・税関; to go through customs ぜいかんを とおる・税関を 通る

customs officer n ぜいかんり・税関吏

cut 1 vb きる・切る; to cut an apple in half りんごを はんぶんにきる・りんごを 半分に 切る; to cut one's fingers ゆびをきる・指を 切る; to have one's hair cut かみをきる・髪を 切る 2 n (injury) きりきず・切り傷; **cut down** きりたおす・切り倒す; **cut out** to cut a photo out of a magazine ざっしから しゃしんを きりぬく・雑誌から 写真を 切り抜く; **cut up** きざむ・刻む

cute adj かわいい

CV n りれきしょ・履歴書

cycle *vb* to cycle to school がっこうに じてんしゃで いく・ 学校に 自転車で 行く; to go cycling サイクリングする

cycling *n* サイクリング

cyclist *n* サイクリスト

cynical *adj* ひにく(な)・皮肉(な)

Dd

dad, Dad *n* (one's own) ちち・ 父; (someone else's) おとうさん・お父さん！ Japanese children will address their father as おとうさん or パパ

daffodil *n* すいせん・水仙

daisy *n* ひなぎく・ひな菊

damage 1 *vb* to damage そんがいを あたえる・損害を 与える; to be damaged ひがいを うける・被害を 受ける; the building was damaged by the fire たてものは かじで ひがいをうけました。・ 建物は 火事で 被害を 受けました。; (to harm) it can damage your health けんこうに わるいです。・ 健康に 悪いです。**2** *n* ひがい・被害

damp *adj* しめっぽい・湿っぽい

dance 1 *vb* おどる・踊る **2** *n* ダンス

dancer *n* ダンサー

dancing *n* ダンス

danger *n* きけん・危険; she is in danger かのじょは あぶないです。・彼女は 危ないです。

dangerous *adj* あぶない・危ない

dare *vb* I didn't dare to say こわくて いえませんでした。・ 恐くて 言えませんでした。

dark 1 *adj* (lacking light) くらい・暗い; it has got dark くらくなりました。・暗く なりました。; (describing a

colour, clothes) I always wear dark coloured clothes いつも くらいいろの ふくを きています。・ いつも 暗い 色の服を 着ています。; dark blue こんいろ(の)・ 紺色 (の); (describing a person's character) せいかくが くらい・ 性格が暗い 2 n くらやみ・ 暗闇

darts n ダーツ

date n (in a calendar) ひにち・ 日にち; what date is today? きょうは なんにちですか。・ 今日は 何日ですか。; (with a friend) デート; to go out on a date with someone だれ かとデートを する・ 誰かと デートを する

daughter n (your own) むすめ・ 娘; (someone else's) おじ ょうさん・ お嬢さん

daughter-in-law n (your own) よめ・ 嫁; (someone else's) およめさん・ お嫁さん

dawn n よあけ・ 夜明け; at dawn よあけに・ 夜明けに

day n one day いちにち・ 一日; what day is it today? きょう は なんようびですか。・ 今日は 何曜日ですか。; daytime ひるま・ 昼間; we had a very nice day たのしい いちにち でした。・ 楽しい 一日でした。; the next day, the day after つぎのひ・ 次の 日; the day before まえのひ・ 前の 日

daylight n にっちゅう・ 日中

dazzling adj まぶしい・ 眩しい

dead adj しんでいる・ 死んでいる; he is dead かれは しんでいます。・ 彼は 死んでいます。

deaf adj みみの きこえない・ 耳の 聞こえない

deal 1 n (in business) とりひき・ 取引; (with a friend) やく そく・ 約束; a great deal of money たくさんの おかね・ たくさんの お金 2 vb to deal the cards トランプを くば る・ トランプを 配る; deal with しょりする・ 処理す る; to deal with a problem もんだいを しょりする・ 問題 を 処理する

dear 1 adj! Not used in Japanese letters. Usually a general greeting such as はいけい, without the addressee's name, is used at the beginning of the letter and it is finished with けいぐ; (expensive) たかい・ 高い 2 exc oh dear! おやおや

death _n_ し・死

death penalty _n_ しけい・死刑

debate _n_ とうろん・討論

debt _n_ しゃっきん・借金; to be in debt しゃっきんが ある・借金が ある

decade _n_ じゅうねんかん・十年間

decaffeinated _adj_ カフェインの ない

deceive _vb_ だます

December _n_ じゅうにがつ・十二月

decide _vb_ きめる・決める; I decided to go いく ことに きめました。・行く ことに 決めました。

decision _n_ けってい・決定; to make a decision けってい する・決定する

deck _n_ デッキ

deckchair _n_ デッキチェア

decorate _vb_ (with ornaments) かざる・飾る; (with wallpaper or paint) かいそうする・改装する

decoration _n_ かざりもの・飾り物

deep _adj_ ふかい・深い; how deep is the lake? みずうみは どのくらい ふかいですか。・湖は どのくらい 深いで すか。; the hole is three metres deep あなは さんメートル のふかさです。・穴は 三メートルの 深さです。

deer _n_ しか・鹿

defeat 1 _vb_ to defeat an enemy てきを やぶる・敵を 破る; the team was defeated チームが まけました。・ チームが 負けました。 2 _n_ まけ・負け

defence (British English), **defense** (US English) _n_ (military) ぼうえい・防衛; (sport) ぼうぎょ・防御

defend _vb_ (military, sport) まもる・守る; (legal) べんごする・弁護する

definite _adj_ かくじつ(な)・確実(な); nothing is definite なにも きまっていません。・何も 決っていません。; (obvious, visible) あきらか(な)・明らか(な)

definitely adv ぜったい・絶対; they're definitely lying か
れらはぜったい うそを ついています。・彼らは 絶対
嘘をついています。; I'm definitely coming ぜったい いき
ます。・絶対 行きます。; 'definitely!' ぜったい・絶対

degree n (from a university) がくい・学位; (in measurements)
ど・度

delay 1 vb おくらせる・遅らせる 2 n おくれ・遅れ

deliberate adj わざと

deliberately adv わざと; He did it deliberately わざと
しました。

delicious adj おいしい

delighted adj うれしい; I was delighted to receive a present
プレゼントを もらって うれしかったです。

deliver vb とどける・届ける; to deliver newspapers しん
ぶんを はいたつする・新聞を 配達する; to deliver mail
ゆうびんを とどける・郵便を 届ける; to be delivered
とどく・届く

demand vb ようきゅうする・要求する

demolish vb とりこわす・取り壊す

demonstration n デモンストレーション

denim adj デニム(の)

dentist n はいしゃ・歯医者

deny vb ひていする・否定する

department n (in a firm) ぶ・部; (in a large store) うりば・
売り場; shoe department くつうりば・靴売り場; (in a
school) か・課; (in a university) がっか・学科

department store n デパート

depend vb to depend on someone だれかに たよる・誰か
に 頼る; it depends on you あなた しだいです。・あなた
次第です。

depressed adj おちこんでいる・落ち込んでいる

depressing adj ゆううつ(な)・憂うつ(な)

depth n ふかさ・深さ

describe vb びょうしゃする・描写する; please describe what happened なにが おこったかを せつめい して ください。・何が起こったかを 説明して下さい。

description n びょうしゃ・描写

desert n さばく・砂漠

deserve vb あたいする・値する

design 1 vb (to plan) せっけいする・設計する; this house is designed for a hot climate この いえは あつい きこうに あうように せっけいされています。・この 家は 暑い 気候に 合う ように 設計されています。; (in fashion) to design clothes ふくを デザインする・服を デザインする 2 n (a subject of study) (fashion) design デザイン; (a pattern) もよう・模様

desk n つくえ・机

desperate adj ひっし(の)・必死(の)

dessert n デザート

destroy vb はかいする・破壊する

detail n しょうさい・詳細; to go into details くわしく いう・詳しく 言う

detective n たんてい・探偵; private detective しりつたんてい・私立探偵

detective story n すいりしょうせつ・推理小説

determined adj いしの つよい・意思の強い; to be determined to become a doctor ぜったい いしゃに なると けっしんしている・絶対 医者に なると 決心している

develop vb はってんする・発展する

development n はってん・発展

diagram n ず・図

dial vb ダイヤルする

dialling code n (British English) しがいきょくばん・市外局番

dialling tone (British English), **dial tone** (US English) n
はっしんおん・発信音

diamond n ダイヤモンド

diary n (for personal thoughts) にっき・日記; (for appointments) てちょう・手帳

dice n さいころ

dictionary n じしょ・辞書! Note that an English-Japanese dictionary is called a えいわじてん and a Japanese-English dictionary is called a わえいじてん. As Chinese characters are used in Japanese, separate dictionaries for looking these up are necessary. A dictionary which translates Chinese characters into English is called a かんえいじてん

die vb しぬ・死ぬ a more polite expression is なくなる; he died at the age of 65 かれは ろくじゅうごさいで なくなりました。・彼は 六十五歳で 亡くなりました。; to die of cancer がんで しぬ・がんで 死ぬ; (used for emphasis) I'm dying to go on holiday りょこうを ほんとうに たのしみに しています。・旅行を 本当に 楽しみに しています。・I'm dying to go to the toilet トイレに いきたいです。・トイレに 行きたいです。

diet n (way of eating) しょくせいかつ・食生活; (to lose weight) ダイエット; to go on a diet ダイエットする

difference n ちがい・違い; I can't tell the difference ちがいが わかりません。・違いが わかりません。it won't make any difference どうやっても かわりません。・どうやっても 変わりません。

different adj ちがう・違う! Note that ちがう is a verb

difficult adj むずかしい・難しい; Japanese is not difficult にほんごは むずかしくないです。・日本語は 難しくないです。; difficult to get along with つきあいにくい・付き合いにくい

difficulty n もんだい・問題; I have difficulty concentrating しゅうちゅうしにくいです。・集中しにくいです。

dig vb ほる・掘る; **dig up** (to find what was buried) ほりだす・掘り出す

dim adj (describing a light) うすぐらい・薄暗い; (describing a room) くらい・暗い

diner n (US English) レストラン

dinghy n ボート

dining room n しょくどう・食堂

dinner n (at home) ばんごはん・晩ご飯; ゆうごはん・夕ご飯 is also used; (at a restaurant) ゆうしょく・夕食; dinner's ready! ゆうごはんですよ。・夕ご飯ですよ。

dip vb (food) つける

direct 1 adj ちょくせつ(な)・直接(な) 2 vb (when talking about directions) could you direct me to the station? えきは どちらですか。・駅は どちらですか。; (in cinema or theatre) to direct a film えいがを かんとくする・映画を 監督する; to direct a play げきを えんしゅつする・劇を 演出する

direction n ほうこう・方向; is this the right direction? これは ただしい ほうこうですか。・これは 正しい 方向ですか。; they were going in the other direction かれらは はんたいの ほうこうに いきました。・彼らは 反対 の 方向に 行きました。

directions n to give someone directions だれかに みちを おしえる・誰かに 道を 教える; to ask someone for directions だれかに みちを きく・誰かに 道を 聞く

director n (of a film or play) かんとく・監督; (of a company) とりしまりやく・取締役

dirt n よごれ・汚れ

dirty 1 adj きたない・汚い; to get dirty きたなく なる・ 汚くなる 2 vb よごす・汚す

disabled adj a disabled person しんたいしょうがいしゃ ・ 身体障害者！ When a person has a disability, it is more usual in Japanese to refer to it specifically rather than use the general word しょうがいしゃ which means a registered disabled person.

disadvantage n ふりな てん・不利な 点

disagree *vb* いっちしない・一致しない; I disagree わたしははんたいです。・私は 反対です。

disappear *vb* きえる・消える

disappoint *vb* がっかりさせる

disappointed *adj* がっかりしている

disappointing *adj* きたいはずれ(の)・期待はずれ(の)

disappointment *n* きたいはずれ・期待はずれ

disapprove *vb* 〜が わるいと おもう・〜が 悪いと 思う; to disapprove of someone's behaviour だれかの こうどうがわるいと おもう・誰かの 行動が 悪いと 思う

disaster *n* さいがい・災害

discipline *n* しつけ

disco *n* ディスコ

disconnect *vb* きる・切る

discouraged *adj* (*disheartened*) to be discouraged やるきがなくなった・やる 気が なくなった

discover *vb* はっけんする・発見する

discovery *n* はっけん・発見

discrimination *n* さべつ・差別

discuss *vb* (*talk about*) はなしあう・話し合う; to talk about a trip りょこうに ついて はなしあう・旅行について 話し合う; (*discuss seriously*) とうろんする・討論する; to discuss politics せいじに ついて とうろんする・政治について 討論する

discussion *n* とうろん・討論

disease *n* びょうき・病気

disguise 1 *n* へんそう・変装; to wear a disguise へんそうする・変装する 2 *vb* to disguise oneself as a police officer けいさつかんにへんそうする・警察官に 変装する

disgusting *adj* いや(な)・嫌(な); (*food*) まずい

dish *n* (*food*) りょうり・料理; しょっき・食器; to wash the dishes しょっきをあらう・食器を 洗う

dishonest *adj* ふせい(な)・不正(な)

dishwasher *n* しょっきあらいき・食器洗い機

dislike *vb* きらう・嫌う; I dislike him かれが きらいです。・彼が 嫌いです。

dismiss *vb* (a worker) かいこする・解雇する

disobedient *adj* いう ことを きかない・言う ことを 聞かない

disobey *vb* to disobey the teacher せんせいの いう ことを きかない・先生の 言う ことを 聞かない

display *n* てんじ・展示

dispute *n* けんか

disqualify *vb* しかくを とりあげる・資格を 取り上げる

disrupt *vb* じゃまする・邪魔する

dissatisfied *adj* ふまん(な)・不満(な)

distance *n* きょり・距離; in the distance ずっとむこうに・ずっと 向こうに; to keep one's distance はなれる・離れる

distinct *adj* (easy to see, to hear) はっきりした・(definite) あきらか(な)・明らか(な)

distinguish *vb* くべつする・区別する; to distinguish between truth and lies ほんとうか うそか くべつする・本当か 嘘か 区別する

distract *vb* きを ちらす・気を 散らす; to distract someone from working だれかの しごとの じゃまを する・誰かの 仕事の 邪魔を する

distribute *vb* くばる・配る

disturb *vb* じゃまする・邪魔する

disturbing *adj* どうてんさせる・動転させる

dive *vb* とびこむ・飛び込む; to go diving ダイビングする

divide *vb* (in arithmetic) わる・割る; (to share) わける・分ける

diving board *n* とびこみだい・飛び込み台

divorce 1 n りこん・離婚 **2** vb りこんする・離婚する

DIY n (British English) にちようだいく・日曜大工

dizzy adj to feel dizzy めまいが する

do vb ! Note that do or its related forms are not used when forming tenses as they are in English; する; to do the cooking りょうりする・料理する; to do one's homework しゅくだいをする・宿題を する; what has she done to her hair? かのじょはかみを どう しましたか。・彼女は 髪を どうしましたか。; please do as you're told いわれた ように してください。・言われた ように してください。; (in questions, negatives) Questions can be made in Japanese by adding particle か to the end of any statement. To make negative statements, change the final verb to a negative form; do you like cats? ねこが すきですか。・猫が 好きですか。; I don't like cats ねこが すきではありません。・猫が 好きではありません。; I didn't do anything なにも しませんでした。・何も しませんでした。; please don't go いかないでください。・行かないでください。; (in short answers and tag questions) The particle ね can be used as a tag question; he lives in London, doesn't he? かれは ロンドンにすんでいますね。・彼は ロンドンに 住んでいますね。; Yuko didn't phone, did she? ゆうこさんは でんわをしませんでしたね。・祐子さんは でんわを しませんでしたね。; 'do you like strawberries?'—'yes, I do' 「いちごがすきですか。」「はい、すきです。」・「いちごが 好きですか。」「はい、好きです。」; 'I love chocolate'—'so do I!' 「チョコレートが だいすきです。」「わたしも。」・「チョコレートが 大好きです。」「私も。」; 'who wrote it?'—'I did' 「だれが かきましたか。」「わたしが かきました。」・「誰が 書きましたか。」「私が 書きました。」; 'may I sit down?'—'yes, please do' 「すわっても いいですか。」「はい、どうぞ。」・「座っても いいですか。」「はい、どうぞ。」; (to be enough) たりる・足りる; ten pounds will do じゅっポンドで たります。・十ポンドで 足ります。; (to perform) he did well かれは よく できました。・彼は よく できました。; he did badly かれは よく できませんでした。・彼は よく できませんでした。;

do up (*British English*) (*buttons*) かける; (*laces*) むすぶ・結ぶ; (*dress*) しめる; (*house*) かいそうする・改装する; **do with** it's to do with computers コンピューターかんけいです。・コンピューター関係です。; it has nothing to do with him かれと かんけい が ありません。・彼と 関係 が ありません。; **do without** いらない・要らない; I can do without a television テレビが いりません。・テレビは 要りません。

dock *n* がんぺき・岸壁

doctor *n* (*medical*) いしゃ・医者; (*PhD*) はかせ・博士 Note that せんせい *is used to address a doctor and can be added to family names*; Doctor Takahashi たかはしせんせい・高橋先生

document *n* しょるい・書類

documentary *n* ドキュメンタリー

dog *n* いぬ・犬; year of the dog いぬどし・戌年

doll *n* にんぎょう・人形

dollar *n* ドル

dolphin *n* いるか

dominoes *n* ドミノ

donkey *n* ろば

donut ▶ *doughnut*

door *n* ドア; (*sliding door*) とびら・扉

doorbell *n* よびりん・呼び鈴

dormitory *n* きょうどうしんしつ・共同寝室; (*in a university or school*) りょう・寮

dose *n* いっかいりょう・一回量

double 1 *adj* (*of an amount*) にばい(の)・二倍(の); (*when giving a number*) three double five (*British English*) さんごご・三 五 五 **2** *vb* にばいに なる・二倍になる; the population doubled じんこうは にばいに なりました。・人口は二倍に なりました。

double bass *n* コントラバス

double bed n ダブルベッド

double-decker n にかいだてバス・二階建てバス

double room n ダブルベッドの ある へや・ダブルベッドの ある 部屋 Note that these are unusual in Japan.

doubt 1 n there's no doubt that he is innocent かれは むざい にちがい ありません。・彼は 無罪に 違い ありません。2 vb (to suspect) うたがう・疑う; I doubt if she'll come かのじょは こないかもしれません。・彼女は 来ないかもしれません。

dough n きじ・生地

doughnut, donut (US English) n ドーナツ

down ! Often down occurs in combinations with verbs, for example: calm down, let down, slow down etc. To find the correct translations for this type of verb, look up the separate dictionary entries at calm, let, slow etc. **1** prep to walk down the street みちを あるく・道を 歩く; he ran down the hill かれは さかを はしって くだりました。・彼は 坂を 走って 下りました。; the office is down the stairs じむしつは かいだんの したです。・事務室は 階段の 下です。 **2** adv she's down in the cellar かのじょは ちかしつに います。・彼女は 地下室に います。; to go down (prices) さがる・下がる; (the sun) しずむ・沈む; (to climb down) おりる・下りる; (to descend a slope) くだる・下る; to fall down (people) ころぶ・転ぶ; (things) おちる・落ちる

downstairs adv したの かい・下の 階; to go downstairs したの かいに いく・下の 階に 行く; to take the boxes downstairs したの かいに はこを もって いく・下の 階に 箱を 持って 行く

dozen n いちダース・一ダース; a dozen bottles of beer ビール いちダース・ビール 一ダース

draft n (US English) すきまかぜ・隙間風

drag vb ひきずる・引きずる

dragon n year of the dragon たつどし・辰年

drain vb (when cooking) みずきりをする・水切りを する; (if it's water) to drain (away) ながれる・流れる

drama n げき・劇

dramatic adj げきてき(な)・劇的(な)

drapes n (US English) カーテン

draught n (British English) すきまかぜ・隙間風

draughts n (British English) チェッカー

draw 1 vb (with a pen or pencil) かく・描く; to draw a rabbit うさぎをかく・うさぎを描く; to draw a picture えをかく・絵を描く; to draw a line せんをひく・線を引く; (to pull) to draw the curtains カーテンをしめる・カーテンを閉める; (to take out) to draw a knife ナイフをとりだす・ナイフを取り出す; (in a lottery) to draw a ticket くじをひく・くじを引く; (British English) (in sport) ひきわけになる・引き分けになる; winter is drawing near ふゆがちかづいています。・冬が近づいています。 **2** n (in sport) ひきわけ・引き分け; (in a lottery) くじびき・くじ引き; **draw back** to draw back the curtains カーテンをあける・カーテンを開ける; **draw up** to draw up a list リストをかく・リストを書く

drawer n ひきだし・引き出し

drawing n え・絵

dread vb おそれる・恐れる

dreadful adj ひどい・酷い

dream 1 n ゆめ・夢; to have a dream ゆめをみる・夢を見る **2** vb ゆめをみる・夢を見る

dress 1 n ドレス **2** vb (to put one's own clothes on) ふくをきる・服を着る; (to put clothes on someone) だれかにふくをきせる・誰かに服を着せる; **dress up** (in good clothes) せいそうする・盛装する; (in a disguise) かそうする・仮装する; I dressed up as a clown ピエロのかそうをしました。・ピエロの仮装をしました。

dressing gown n ガウン

drill 1 n ドリル **2** vb to drill a hole ドリルであなをあける・ドリルで穴を空ける

drink 1 vb のむ・飲む **2** n のみもの・飲み物; a drink of water みず・水

drive 1 vb (in a car) うんてんする・運転する; to learn to drive うんてんを ならう・運転を 習う; I drive to work くるまでしごとに いきます。・車で 仕事に 行きます。; to drive someone home だれかを くるまで いえに おくる・誰かを 車で 家に 送る; (to make) to drive someone mad だれかを いらいらさせる・誰かを いらいらさせる **2** n ドライブ; to go for a drive ドライブする; **drive away** (in a car) くるまでさって いく・車で 去って 行く; (to chase away) おいはらう・追い払う

driver n うんてんしゅ・運転手

driver's license (US English), **driving licence** (British English) n うんてんめんきょ・運転免許

drizzle n きりさめ・霧雨

drop 1 vb (to come down) さがる・下がる; the temperature has dropped きおんが さがりました。・気温が 下がりました。; (to let fall) おとす・落とす; she dropped her suitcase かのじょは スーツケースを おとしました。・彼女は スーツケースを 落としました。; (to fall) おちる・落ちる **2** n (a fall) a drop in temperature おんどが さがる・温度が 下がる; a drop in prices ねだんが さがる・値段が 下がる; (of liquid) しずく・滴; **drop in** he dropped in to see me かれは あそびに きました。・彼は 遊びに 来ました。; I'll drop in tomorrow あした あそびに いきます。・明日 遊びに 行きます。; **drop off** おろす・降ろす; please drop me off at the station? えきで おろしてください。・駅で 降ろしてください。; **drop out** to drop out of school がっこうを ちゅうたいする・学校を 中退する; to drop out of a race きょうそうから だったいする・競争から 脱退する

drought n かんばつ・干ばつ

drown vb すいしする・水死する

drug 1 n (for illegal use) ドラッグ; to use drugs ドラッグを らんようする・ドラッグを 乱用する; (for medical use)

くすり・薬; to take drugs くすりを のむ・薬を 飲む
2 *vb* to drug someone だれかを くすりで ねむらせる・
誰かを 薬で 眠らせる

drug addict *n* まやくじょうしゅうしゃ・麻薬常習者

drum *n* ドラム; to play drums ドラムを うつ・ドラムを
打つ

drunk *adj* よっぱらった・酔っ払った

dry 1 *adj* かわいている・乾いている; the washing is dry
せんたくものが かわいています。・洗濯物が 乾いて
います。・洗濯物が 乾いて **2** *vb* (*in air*) ほす・干す; to dry the washing せんたくも
のを ほす・洗濯物を 干す; (*with a towel*) ふく・拭く; to
dry oneself からだを ふく・体を 拭く; he dried his hands
かれは てを ふきました。・彼は 手を 拭きました。;
to dry the dishes しょっきを ふく・食器を 拭く; (*using
heat*) かわかす・乾かす; I dried my hair かみを かわかし
ました。・髪を 乾かしました。

duck 1 *n* あひる **2** *vb* かがむ

due 1 due to 〜の ため; yesterday's game was cancelled due
to bad weather あくてんこうの ため、きのうの しあい
は ちゅうしに なりました。・悪天候の ため、昨日の
試合は 中止に なりました。 **2** *adj* (*expected*) the train is
due (*in*) at two o'clock でんしゃは にじに つく よていで
す。・電車は 二時に 着く 予定です。

dull *adj* (*describing a person or book*) つまらない; (*describing
a colour*) にごった・濁った; (*describing the weather*) うっ
とうしい

dumb *adj* (*unable to speak*) はなせない・話せない;
(*stupid*) ばか(な)

dump 1 *vb* すてる・捨てる **2** *n* ごみすてば・ごみ捨て場

during *prep* 〜の あいだ(に)・〜の 間(に); during the
summer なつの あいだ(に)・夏の 間(に)

dust 1 *n* ほこり **2** *vb* ほこりを ふく・ほこりを 拭く

dustbin *n* (*British English*) ごみばこ・ごみ箱

dustman n (British English) ごみ しゅうしゅうにん・ごみ 収集人

dustpan n ちりとり・ちり取り

duty n (a task, part of one's job) しごと・仕事; to take up one's duties ちゃくにんする・着任する; (of a soldier, a nurse) to be on duty とうばんで・当番で; (what one must do) ぎむ・義務; it's my duty わたしの ぎむです。・私の 義務です。; (a tax) customs duties ぜいきん・税金

dye vb そめる・染める; to dye one's hair かみを そめる・髪を染める

Ee

each 1 det each time いつも 2 pron each of the students それ ぞれの がくせい・それぞれの 学生; each of them has a car, they each have a car かれらは それぞれ、くるまを もって います。・彼らは それぞれ、車を 持っています。

each other pron おたがい(に)・お互い(に); they know each other かれらは おたがいに しっています。・彼ら はお互いに 知っています。; we write to each other every year まいとしてがみを だしあっています。・毎年 手 紙を出し合っています。

eager adj ねっしん(な)・熱心(な)

eagle n わし

ear n みみ・耳

early 1 adj はやい・早い 2 adv はやく・早く; to get up early はやく おきる・早く 起きる; early in the morning あさはやく・朝 早く; to arrive early はやく つく・ 早く着く

earn vb I earn a lot of money きゅうりょうは たかいです。 ・給料は 高いです。; how much do you earn? きゅうりょう はいくらですか。・給料は いくらですか。

earring n (for pierced ears) ピアス; (clip-on) イヤリング

earth n (the planet) ちきゅう・地球; (soil) つち・土

easily adv かんたんに・簡単に

east 1 n ひがし・東; in the east of Japan ひがしにほんに・東日本に 2 adv to go east ひがしに いく・東に 行く 3 adj ひがし・東; to work in east London ひがしロンドンではたらく・東ロンドンで 働く

Easter n ふっかつさい・復活祭! not generally celebrated in Japan (British English); Easter holiday はるやすみ・春休み

easy adj かんたん(な)・簡単(な); it's easy to fix なおすのは かんたんです。・直すのは 簡単です。; it's not easy to find work here ここで しごとを みつけるのは かんたんではありません。・ここで 仕事を 見つけるのは 簡単ではありません。; easy to..... verb in pre ます form + やすい

eat vb たべる・食べる; (soup) のむ・飲む! There are various honorific and humble ways of expressing this verb; eat out がいしょくする・外食する

EC n ▶ EU

echo n こだま

economic adj けいざいてき(な)・経済的(な)

economics n けいざいがく・経済学

economy n けいざい・経済

edge n (of a road, table, an object) はし・端; the edge of the lake こはん・湖畔; at the edge of the town まちの はしに・町の 端に

educate vb きょういくする・教育する; I was educated in Paris パリで きょういくを うけました。・パリで 教育を 受けました。

education n きょういく・教育; to get a good education いいきょういくを うける・良い 教育を 受ける

effect n けっか・結果

effective adj こうかてき(な)・効果的(な)

efficient *adj* のうりつてき(な)・能率的(な)

effort *n* どりょく・努力; to make an effort どりょくする・努力する

egg *n* たまご・卵

eggcup *n* ゆでたまごおき・ゆで卵置き

eight *num* (on its own) やっつ・八つ; (with a counter) はち・八; eight books ほん はっさつ・本 八冊; I've got eight やっつ あります。・八つ あります。

eighteen *num* じゅうはち・十八

eighteenth *num* (in a series) じゅうはちばん(め)・十八番(目); the eighteenth of August はちがつじゅうはちにち・八月十八日

eighth *num* (in a series) はちばん(め)・八番(目); (in dates) ようか・八日; the eighth of August はちがつようか・八月八日

eighty *num* はちじゅう・八十

either 1 *conj* they're coming on either Tuesday or Wednesday かれらは かようびか すいようびに きます。・彼らは 火曜日か水曜日に 来ます。; I didn't contact either Helen or Paul ヘレンさんにも ポールさんにも れんらくしませんでした。・ヘレンさんにも ポールさんにも 連絡しませんでした。 **2** *pron* either one is OK どちらでも いいです。; I don't know either どちらも しりません。・どちらも 知りません。 **3** *det* I don't want to do either どちらもしたくないです。 **4** *adv* I can't do it either わたしも できません。・私も できません。

elbow *n* ひじ

elder *adj* としうえ(の)・年上(の)

elderly *adj* ねんぱい(の)・年配(の)

eldest *adj* いちばんとしうえ(の)・一番年上(の); eldest daughter ちょうじょ・長女; eldest son ちょうなん・長男

elect *vb* せんきょする・選挙する

election *n* せんきょ・選挙: to win an election とうせん する・当選する

electric *adj* でんき(の)・電気(の)

electrician *n* でんきやさん・電気屋さん

electricity *n* でんき・電気

electronic *adj* でんし(の)・電子(の); electronic organiser でんしてちょう・電子手帳

elegant *adj* じょうひん(な)・上品(な)

elephant *n* ぞう・象

elevator *n* (US English) エレベーター

eleven *num* じゅういち・十一

eleventh *num* (in a series) じゅういちばん(め)・十一番 (目); (in dates) じゅういちにち・十一日; the eleventh of May ごがつじゅういちにち・五月十一日

else 1 *adv* someone else (additional person) もう ひとり・ もう 一人; (different person) ちがう ひと・違う 人; there is nothing else ほかに ありません。・外に ありません。; what else did he say? かれは ほかに なんと いいました か。・彼は 外に 何と 言いましたか。; something else (object) ほかの もの・外の 物; (topic) ほかの こと・ 外の こと; everything else ほかの ぜんぶ・外の 全部
2 or else *num* be quiet or else I'll get angry しずかに しないと おこりますよ。・静かに しないと 怒りますよ。

elsewhere *adv* べつの ばしょ・別の 場所

embarrassed *adj* はずかしい・恥ずかしい

embarrassing *adj* はずかしい・恥ずかしい

embassy *n* たいしかん・大使館

emergency *n* きゅうきゅう・救急; in an emergency きゅうきゅうのときに・救急の ときに

emergency exit *n* ひじょうぐち・非常口

emigrate *vb* いじゅうする・移住する

emotion *n* かんじょう・感情

emotional adj (describing a scene or moment) かんどうてき(な)・感動的(な); (describing a person) かんじょうてき(な)・感情的(な)

emperor n こうてい・皇帝; (of Japan) てんのう・天皇

employ vb やとう・雇う

employed adj to be employed (taken on) やとわれる・雇われる; I am working for Sony ソニーに つとめています。・ソニーに 勤めています。

employee n しょくいん・職員 ! There are various terms depending on the institution for which people work

employer n (company) かいしゃ・会社; (individual) ボス A more formal word for written Japanese is こうしゃ

employment n しごと・仕事

empty 1 adj (container) から(の)・空(の); (house) あき(の)・空き(の); the room is empty (no people) へやに だれも いません。・部屋に 誰も いません。**2** vb からにする・空に する

encourage vb はげます・励ます

end 1 n (the final part) おわり・終わり; at the end of the film えいがの おわりに・映画の 終わりに; at the end of May ごがつの おわりに・五月の 終わりに; in the end おわりに・終わりに; (the furthest part) おわり・終わり **2** vb (to come to an end) おわる・終わる; (to put an end to) おえる・終える; to end the war せんそうを おえる・戦争を終える

ending n (story) けつまつ・結末

enemy n てき・敵

energetic adj げんき(な)・元気(な)

energy n エネルギー

engaged adj to get engaged こんやくする・婚約する; to be engaged こんやくしている・婚約している; (British English) (describing a phone) はなしちゅう・話し中; (describing a toilet) しようちゅう・使用中

engine n エンジン

engineer n ぎし・技師

England n イギリス

English 1 adj イギリスの **2** n (the people) イギリスじん・イギリス人; (the language) えいご・英語

enjoy vb (to like) たのしむ・楽しむ; I enjoy fishing つりをたのしみます。・釣りを 楽しみます。; did you enjoy your trip? りょこうは どうでしたか。・旅行は どうでしたか。; (to have a good time) to enjoy oneself たのしむ・楽しむ

enjoyable adj たのしい・楽しい

enormous adj きょだい(な)・巨大(な)

enough 1 det I don't have enough money おかねが たりません。・お金が 足りません。; I have enough time じかんが たります。・時間が 足ります。; there's enough room for everyone みんなが はいれます。・皆が 入れます。 **2** adv! enough is not usually translated; is it good enough? いいですか。; he's not old enough (by law) かれは みせいねんしゃです。・彼は 未成年者です。 **3** pron have you had enough? たりましたか。・足りましたか。; I've had enough もう いいです。

enquire vb きく・聞く; I'll enquire about the price ねだんを ききます。・値段を 聞きます。

enquiry n といあわせ・問い合わせ

enter vb (to go into) はいる・入る; (to take part in) さんかする・参加する; to enter a competition きょうぎに さんかする・競技に 参加する

entertain vb (a client) せったいする・接待する; (at home) もてなす・持て成す

entertaining adj おもしろい・面白い

entertainment n (organised) ショー

enthusiasm n ねっしん・熱心

enthusiastic adj ねっしん(な)・熱心(な)

entrance n いりぐち・入り口; the entrance to the museum はくぶつかんの いりぐち・博物館の 入り口

envelope n ふうとう・封筒

environment n かんきょう・環境

envy 1 n しっと **2** vb うらやむ

episode n (of story) episode 1 だいいちわ・第一話; last week's episode of "Friends" せんしゅうの「フレンズ」・先週の「フレンズ」; final episode さいしゅうかい・最終回; (incident) できごと・出来事

equal 1 adj びょうどう(な)・平等(な); equal opportunities きかいきんとう・機会均等 **2** vb six plus four equals ten ろくたす よんは じゅうです。・六 足す 四は 十です。

equality n びょうどう・平等; gender equality だんじょ びょうどう・男女平等

equator n せきどう・赤道

equipment n (in an office, a laboratory, a factory) せつび・設備; (for an activity) どうぐ・道具

eraser n けしゴム・消しゴム

escalator n エスカレーター

escape vb (to get away) にげだす・逃げ出す; I escaped from prison けいむしょから にげだしました。・刑務所 から 逃げ出しました。; (to avoid) さける・避ける; to escape death しを まぬがれる・死を 免れる

especially adv とくに・特に

essay n (by a pupil) さくぶん・作文; (by a student) レポート

essential adj ひつよう(な)・必要(な)

ethnic adj ethnic minority しょうすうみんぞく・少数民族

EU ▶ European Union

euro n ユーロ

Europe n ヨーロッパ

European adj ヨーロッパの

European Union n おうしゅうれんごう・欧州連合

evacuate vb ひなんする・避難する

even¹ 1 adv (when expressing surprise) さえ; I didn't even phone でんわさえ しませんでした。 電話さえ しませんでした。; I even work at weekends しゅうまつさえ はたらきます。・ 週末さえ 働きます。; (in comparisons) もっと; it's even colder today きょうは もっと さむいです。・ 今日は もっと 寒いです。 **2 even though** でも！ or use form of verb + も; he's bored even though he has lots of toys かれは おもちゃが たくさん あっても たいくつしています。・ 彼は おもちゃが たくさん あっても 退屈しています。

even² adj (flat, smooth) たいら(な)・ 平ら(な); (when talking about numbers) even number ぐうすう・ 偶数

evening n よる・ 夜; at eight o'clock in the evening よる はちじに・ 夜 八時に; to spend the evening at home よるを いえで すごす・ 夜を 家で 過ごす; this evening こんばん・ 今晩

event n イベント

eventually adv けっきょく・ 結局

ever adv (at any time) ！ Not usually translated; no-one will ever know だれも しりません。・ 誰も 知りません。; have you ever been to Japan にほんに いった ことが ありますか。・ 日本に 行った ことが ありますか。; I hardly ever go there ほとんど そこに いきません。・ ほとんど そこに 行きません。; (always) he's as lazy as ever かれは あいかわらずなまけものです。・ 彼は 相変わらず 怠け者です。

every det ！ Often not translated. Sometimes まい + counter can be used; every day まいにち・ 毎日; every time I meet her かのじょに あう たびに・ 彼女に 会う たびに; every second day, every other day いちにちおき・ 一日おき; two out of every three people さんにんに ふたり・ 三人に 二人

everyone pron (also **everybody**) みんな・ 皆 Note that on more formal occasions みな is used; everyone else ほかの みんな・ 外の 皆

everything pron ぜんぶ・ 全部

everywhere adv どこでも; everywhere else place + いがい; everywhere except that place

evidence n piece of evidence しょうこ・証拠; to give evidence しょうげんする・証言する

evil adj わるい・悪い

exact adj せいかく(な)・正確(な)

exactly adv せいかくに・正確に

exaggerate vb おおげさに いう・大げさに 言う

exam n しけん・試験; to pass an exam しけんにごうかくする・試験に 合格する; to take an exam しけんをうける・試験を 受ける

examine vb (a candidate) しけんする・試験する; (inspect) しらべる・調べる; (a patient) しんさつする・診察する

example n れい・例; for example たとえば・例えば

excellent adj すばらしい

except prep 〜いがい・〜以外; all except apples りんごいがい・りんご 以外

exchange vb こうかんする・交換する; to exchange money おかねを かえる・お金を 替える

exchange rate n こうかんレート・交換レート

excited adj こうふんしている・興奮している

exciting adj どきどきさせる

exclude vb to be excluded from school たいがくさせられる・退学させられる

excuse 1 n いいわけ・言い訳; to make excuses いいわけをする・言い訳をする 2 vb ゆるす・許す; excuse me! すみません。

exercise n (to keep fit) うんどう・運動; to take exercise, to do exercise うんどうを する・運動を する; (a piece of work) れんしゅう・練習

exercise book n ノート

exhausted adj つかれている・疲れている

exhibition *n* てんらんかい・展覧会

exit *n* でぐち・出口

expect *vb* (*to be prepared for something bad*) かくごする・覚悟する; I'm expecting bad news わるい しらせを かくごしています。・悪い 知らせを 覚悟しています。; (*general expectation*) はず; I expect to win かつ はずです。・勝つ はずです。; (*to wait for*) まつ・待つ; I'm expecting visitors おきゃくさんを まっています。・お客さんを 待っています。; (*to want*) use verb in the ～て form + ほしい for your own expectations and て form + ほしい という for reporting those of other people; I expect you to arrive by five ごじまでに ついて ほしいです。・五時までに 着いて ほしいです。; my boss expects me to do overtime ボスは ざんぎょうして ほしいと いいました。・ボスは 残業 して ほしいと 言いました。

expenses *n* けいひ・経費

expensive *adj* たかい・高い

experience *n* けいけん・経験

experienced *adj* けいけんの ある・経験の ある

experiment 1 *n* じっけん・実験 2 *vb* じっけんする・実験する

expert *n* エキスパート; computer expert コンピューター・エキスパート

explain *vb* せつめいする・説明する; to explain a rule to someone だれかに ルールを せつめいする・誰かに ルールを説明する

explanation *n* せつめい・説明

explode *vb* ばくはつする・爆発する

exploit *vb* りようする・利用する

explosion *n* ばくはつ・爆発

export *vb* ゆしゅつする・輸出する

express 1 *vb* ひょうげんする・表現する 2 *adv* to send a letter express てがみを そくたつで おくる・手紙を速達で送る

expression *n* ひょうげん・表現; facial expression かお
のひょうじょう・顔の 表情

express train *n* とっきゅうれっしゃ・特急列車

extinct *adj* (*describing an animal*) ぜつめつした・絶滅し
た; extinct volcano しかざん・死火山

extra 1 *adj* よぶん(の)・余分(の); an extra bed よぶんの
ベッド・余分の ベッド **2** *adv* to pay extra よけいに
はらう・余計に 払う

extraordinary *adj* いじょう(な)・異常(な)

extreme *adj* ひじょう(な)・非常(な)

extremely *adv* ひじょうに・非常に

eye *n* め・目; my eyes are blue めが あおいです。・目が
青いです。

eyebrow *n* まゆげ・眉毛

eyelash *n* まつげ・まつ毛

eyelid *n* まぶた

eye shadow *n* アイシャドー

eyesight *n* しりょく・視力; to have good eyesight めが
いい・目が いい

Ff

face 1 *n* かお・顔; to make a face かおを しかめる・
顔を しかめる **2** *vb* (*to have to deal with*) 〜に むきあわな
ければ ならない・〜に 向き合わなければ ならない;
I can't face seeing them again もう かれらに あいたくな
いです。・もう 彼らに 会いたくないです。; (*to look
toward(s)*) my room faces the sea わたしの へやは うみに
めんしています。・私の 部屋は 海に 面しています。

fact 1 *n* じじつ・事実 **2** in fact じつは・実は

factory n こうじょう・工場

fade vb (if it's a colour) あせる

fail vb しっぱいする・失敗する; to fail an exam しけんに おちる・試験に 落ちる

failure n (an event, an attempt) しっぱい・失敗; (a person) しっぱいしゃ・失敗者; (in exam) ふごうかく・不合格

faint vb きぜつする・気絶する

fair 1 adj (just) こうへい(な)・公平(な); it's not fair ふこうへいです。・不公平です。; (in colour) fair hair きんぱつ・金髪; fair skin いろじろな はだ・色白な 肌 **2** n (British English) (a funfair) いどうゆうえんち・移動遊園地; rare in Japan; (a display of goods) (trade) fair (トレード)フェアー

fairly adv まあまあ

faith n to have faith (in someone) (だれかを) しんらいする・(誰かを) 信頼する

faithful adj ちゅうじつ(な)・忠実(な)

fall 1 vb (if it's a person) たおれる・倒れる; (to come down, to be reduced) さがる・下がる; (other uses) to fall asleep ねむる・眠る; to fall ill びょうきに なる・病気に なる; to fall in love with someone だれかと こいに おちる・誰かと 恋に 落ちる **2** n ていか・低下; (US English) (autumn) あき・秋; **fall down** たおれる・倒れる; **fall off** おちる・落ちる; to fall off a chair いすから おちる・椅子から 落ちる; **fall out** (from somewhere) おちる・落ちる; the letter fell out of my pocket てがみが ポケットから おちました。・手紙が ポケットから 落ちました。; (to quarrel) けんかする・喧嘩する; **fall over** (if it's a person) ころぶ・転ぶ; (if it's a thing) たおれる・倒れる; **fall through** だめに なる

false adj (facts) ただしくない・正しくない; true or false? まるですか、ばつですか。・○ですか、×ですか。

false teeth n いれば・入歯

familiar adj しっている・知っている

family n (your own) かぞく・家族; (someone else's) ごかぞく・ご家族

famous *adj* ゆうめい(な)・有名(な)

fan *n* (of a pop star, an actor, a sport) ファン; (for cooling)
(electrical) せんぷうき・扇風機; (hand-held) うちわ

fancy dress party *n* (British English) かそうパーティー
・仮装パーティー

fantastic *adj* すばらしい・素晴らしい

far 1 *adv* how far is it to London? ロンドンまで、きょりは
どのくらいですか。・ロンドンまで、距離は どのくら
いですか。; how far is Tokyo from London? とうきょう
とロンドンの きょりは どのくらいですか。・東京と
ロンドンの距離は どのくらいですか。; we went as far
as the coast かいがんまで いきました。・海岸まで
行きました。 **2** *adj* とおい・遠い; at the far side of the
room へやの むこうがわに・部屋の 向こう側に
3 so far いままで・今まで

fare *n* (on a bus, a train or the underground) うんちん・運賃;
(on a plane) りょうきん・料金

farm *n* のうじょう・農場

farmer *n* のうか・農家

fascinating *adj* おもしろい・面白い

fashion *n* ファッション; to be in fashion はやっている・
流行っている; to be out of fashion はやっていない・
流行っていない

fashionable *adj* りゅうこう(の)・流行(の)

fast 1 *adj* (describing movement) はやい・速い; to be fast
すすんでいる・進んでいる; my watch is ten minutes fast
わたしの とけいは じゅっぷん すすんでいます。・
私の 時計は 十分 進んでいます。 **2** *adv* はやく・速く

fasten *vb* to fasten a seatbelt シートベルトを しめる・
シートベルトを締める

fast-forward *vb* to fast-forward a cassette カセットを
さきおくりする・カセットを 先送りする

fat *adj* ふとっている・太っている; to get fat ふとる・太る

fatal *adj* ちめいてき(な)・致命的(な)

father n (your own) ちち・父; (someone else's) おとうさん・お父さん

Father Christmas n (British English) サンタクロース

father-in-law n (one's own) ぎりの ちち・義理の 父

faucet n (US English) じゃぐち・蛇口

fault n せい; it's not my fault わたしの せいでは ありません。・私の せいでは ありません。; whose fault was it? だれの せいでしたか。・誰の せいでしたか。

favour (British English), **favor** (US English) **1** n おねがい・お願い; I have a favour to ask おねがいが あります。・お願いが あります。; to do someone a favour ! no direct equivalent; to ask someone a favour だれかに たのむ・誰かに 頼む **2** in favour of to be in favour of that plan その けいかくに さんせいしている・その 計画に 賛成している

favourite (British English), **favorite** (US English) adj いちばんすき(な)・一番好き(な); this is my favourite film これが わたしの いちばんすきな えいがです。・これが 私の 一番好きな 映画です。

fax n ファックス

fear vb しんぱいする・心配する

feather n はね・羽根

February n にがつ・二月

fed up adj うんざりしている

fee n (to attend an event, a show) にゅうじょうりょうきん・入場料金; (to join a club, a union) にゅうかいきん・入会金

feeble adj よわい・弱い

feed vb (people) ごはんを あげる・ご飯を あげる; (animals) えさを あげる・餌を あげる; I must feed the dog いぬに えさを あげなければ なりません。・犬に 餌を あげなければ なりません。

feel vb かんじる・感じる ! Japanese is very different to English when describing feelings, it is often best to translate with an adjective + です when referring to yourself; (referring to an

emotion, an impression or a physical feeling); I feel lonely さびしいです。・ 寂しいです。; it feels cold さむい です。; I feel tired つかれました。・ 疲れました。; it feels nice きもちいいです。・ 気持ち いいです。; (*to touch*) さわる・ 触る; to feel like... use the pre ます form of the verb + たい for yourself and the pre ます form of the verb + たがる for others; I feel like eating pizza ピザが たべたいです。・ ピザが 食べたいです。; I don't feel like it したくないです。

feeling n (*emotional*) きもち・ 気持ち; to hurt someone's feelings だれかの きもちを きずつける・ 誰かの 気持ちを 傷付ける; (*physical*) かんじ・ 感じ; I have a feeling he's right かれが ただしいと いう きが します。・ 彼が 正しいという 気が します。

felt-tip pen n サインペン

female adj (*in biology*) めす(の)・ 雌(の); (*relating to women*) おんな(の)・ 女(の)

fence n フェンス

fencing n フェンシング; (*Japanese traditional*) けんどう・ 剣道

festival n おまつり・ お祭り

fetch vb もって くる・ 持って くる; please fetch some water みずを もって きてください。・ 水を 持って きてください。

fever n to have a fever ねつが ある・ 熱が ある

few adj に、 さん + counter・ 二、三 + counter ! *Usage very different to English*; a few people に、さんにん・ 二、三人; a few books ほん に、さんさつ・ 本二、三冊; (*not many*) あまり + negative; few people came あまり ひとが きませんでした。・ あまり 人が 来ませんでした。; (*several*) すう + counter・ 数 + counter; the first few weeks はじめの すうしゅうかん・ 初めの 数週間

field n のはら・ 野原; (*of crops*) はたけ・ 畑

fifteen num じゅうご・ 十五

fifteenth num (in a series) じゅうごばん(め)・十五番
(目); (in dates) じゅうごにち・十五日; the fifteenth of
May ごがつじゅうごにち・五月十五日

fifth num (in a series) ごばん(め)・五番(目); (in dates) い
つか・五日; the fifth of June ろくがついつか・六月五日

fifty num ごじゅう・五十

fight 1 vb (in war) たたかう・戦う; to fight the enemy
てきとたたかう・敵と戦う; (physically) けんかする;
(to quarrel) くちげんかを する・口げんかを する 2 n
(physical) けんか

figure n (a number) すうじ・数字; (physical) すがた・姿

file n ファイル; single file ひとり ひとり・一人 一人

fill vb (to make full) いっぱいにする; (to become full) いっぱ
いになる; fill in (form) きにゅうする・記入する

film 1 n (in cinema or on TV) えいが・映画; (for a camera)
フィルム 2 vb さつえいする・撮影する

filthy adj きたない・汚い

final 1 adj さいご(の)・最後(の) 2 n けっしょうせん・
決勝戦

finally adv さいごに・最後に

find vb みつける・見つける; find out to find out the truth
しんじつをはっけんする・真実を発見する

fine 1 adj (weather) はれ(の)・晴れ(の); the weather will
probably be fine てんきは はれでしょう。・天気は 晴れ
でしょう。; (in good health) I feel fine げんきです。・元気
です。; (expressing agreement) (that's) fine いいです。 2 n
ばっきん・罰金

finger n ゆび・指

finish 1 vb (to end) おえる・終える; to finish writing a letter
てがみをかきおえる・手紙を 書き終える; (to come to
an end) おわる・終わる 2 n (in a race) ゴールライン

fire 1 n (to burn) かじ・火事; (open fire) だんろ・暖炉;
ストーブ; (gas/electric) かじ・火事; to catch fire かじ
になる・火事に なる; to be on fire もえている・燃え

ている **2** vb (to shoot) はっぽうする・発砲する; (to dismiss) くびにする・首にする

fire alarm n かさいけいほうき・火災警報機

fire engine n しょうぼうしゃ・消防車

firefighter n しょうぼうし・消防士

fire station n しょうぼうしょ・消防署

fireworks n はなび・花火

firm 1 n かいしゃ・会社 **2** adj かたい・固い

first 1 adj さいしょ(の)・最初(の); the first time だいいっかい・第一回; the first three weeks さいしょの さんしゅうかん・最初の 三週間 **2** adv (to begin with) さいしょに・最初に; first of all さいしょに・最初に; (for the first time) はじめて・初めて; to arrive first さいしょにつく・最初に着く **3** n (in a series or group) the first いちばんめ・一番目; (in dates) ついたち・一日; the first of June ろくがつついたち・六月一日 **4** at first さいしょに・最初に

first aid n おうきゅうてあて・応急手当

first class adv to travel first class ファーストクラスでいく・ファーストクラスで 行く

first floor n the first floor (in Britain) にかい・二階; (in the US) いっかい・一階

first name n ファーストネーム Note that Japanese names are given in the order of family name then given name.

fish 1 n さかな・魚 **2** vb to go fishing つりにいく・釣りに行く

fisherman n りょうし・漁師

fishing n つり・釣り

fishing rod n つりざお・釣り竿

fist n こぶし

fit 1 vb these shoes don't fit me この くつは あしに あいません。・この 靴は 足に 合いません。; this photo won't fit into the envelope この しゃしんは ふうとうに はいりません。・この 写真は 封筒に 入りません。 **2** adj (healthy)

げんき(な)・元気(な); **fit in** (in a room or car) はいる・入る; (in a group or team) とけこむ・溶け込む

fitness n (physical) fitness けんこう・健康

five num (on its own) いつつ・五つ; (with a counter) ご・五; five books ほん ごさつ・本 五冊; I've got five いつつ あります。・五つ あります。

fix vb (to decide on, to set) きめる・決める; (to be decided on, to be set) きまる・決まる; (to repair) なおす・直す; to get a watch fixed とけいを なおして もらう・時計を直して もらう; (to prepare) つくる; to fix dinner ゆうごはんをつくる・夕ご飯を 作る

flag n はた・旗; (national flag) こっき・国旗

flame n ほのお・炎; to go up in flames もえる・燃える

flash 1 n (for a camera) フラッシュ **2** vb to flash (on and off) てんめつする・点滅する

flashlight n かいちゅうでんとう・懐中電灯

flask n (water bottle) すいとう・水筒; (vacuum flask) まほうびん・魔法瓶

flat 1 n (British English) アパート **2** adj たいら(な)・平ら(な); flat tyre パンク

flavour (British English), **flavor** (US English) n あじ・味

flea n のみ

flight n フライト; (flight number 147) ひゃくよんじゅうななびん・百四七便

flight attendant n きゃくしつじょうむいん・客室乗務員

float vb うかぶ・浮かぶ

flood n こうずい・洪水

floor n (a surface) ゆか・床; to sit on the floor ゆかに すわる・床に 座る; (a storey) かい・階

florist n はなや・花屋

flour n こむぎこ・小麦粉

flow vb ながれる・流れる

flower 1 *n* はな・花 **2** *vb* さく・咲く

flu *n* かぜ・風邪

fluent *adj* her Japanese is fluent かのじょの にほんごは ぺらぺらです。・彼女の 日本語は ぺらぺらです。

flush *vb* to flush the toilet トイレを ながす・トイレを 流す

flute *n* フルート

fly 1 *n* はえ **2** *vb* (*if it's a bird, a kite, a plane, an insect*) とぶ・飛ぶ; (*if it's a passenger*) ひこうきで いく・飛行機で 行く; to fly from London to Tokyo ロンドンから とうきょう まで ひこうきで いく・ロンドンから 東京まで 飛行機で 行く; to fly a plane ひこうきを そうじゅうする・飛行機を 操縦する; (*if it's a flag*) かかげる・掲げる; **fly away** とんで いく・飛んで 行く

fog *n* きり・霧

fold *vb* to fold a shirt シャツを おりたたむ・シャツを 折りたたむ; to fold one's arms うでを くむ・腕を 組む

folder *n* (*for work, school*) ファイル; (*in computing*) フォルダー

follow *vb* (*to go or come after*) あとに ついて いく・後に ついて 行く; (*to use, to look at*) したがう・従う; I followed the instructions せつめいどおりに しました。・説明通 りに しました。

following *adj* つぎ(の)・次(の)

fond *adj* I'm very fond of you あなたが すきです。・あなた が 好きです。

food *n* たべもの・食べ物

fool *vb* だます・騙す

foot *n* (*part of the leg*) あし・足; on foot あるいて・歩い て; I go to school on foot がっこうに あるいて いきます。 ・学校に 歩いて 行きます。; (*in measurements*) フィート ! Note that a foot 30.48 cm.

football *n* (*soccer*) サッカー; (*American football*) アメリカ ンフットボール; (*a ball*) サッカーボール

footballer (*British English*), **football player** (*US English*)
n サッカーせんしゅ・サッカー選手

footprint n あしあと・足跡

footstep n あしおと・足音

for prep ❗ *not usually translated*; a letter has come for you あなたにてがみが きました。・あなたに 手紙が 来ました。; to work for a company かいしゃにつとめる・会社に 勤める; he cooked dinner for me かれは わたしに ゆうごはんをつくって くれました。・彼は 私に 夕ご飯を 作ってくれました。❗ *doing favours for people is usually expressed using the 〜て form of the verb plus a verb of giving or receiving*; (*when talking about time*) ❗ *not usually translated*; I've been living here for two years にねんかん ここに すんでいます。・二年間 ここに 住んでいます。; he's going to Paris for a year かれは パリに いちねんかん いきます。・彼は パリに 一年間 行きます。; (*when talking about distance*) ❗ *not translated*; I drove for 80 kilometres はちじゅっキロ うんてんしました。・八十キロ 運転しました。; (*when talking about money*) I bought it for ¥500 ごひゃくえんで 買いました。・五百円で 買いました。; a cheque for £20 にじゅっポンドの こぎって・二十ポンドの小切手; (*be in favour (of)*) (〜に)さんせいする・(〜に)賛成する; (*other uses*) say hello to her for me かのじょによろしく つたえてください。・彼女に よろしく 伝えてください。; T for Tom トムの T; the Minister for Education もんぶだいじん・文部大臣; what is the Japanese for 'book'? 'book' はにほんごで なんですか。・'book' は 日本語で 何ですか。; I went for a swim およぎにいきました。・泳ぎに 行きました。❗ *use* pre ます *form* + に + *verb of motion*

forbid vb きんしする・禁止する; smoking is forbidden here ここは きんえんです。・ここは 禁煙です。; going out is forbidden がいしゅつきんしです。・外出禁止です。

force 1 vb きょうせいする・強制する; to force someone to work だれかを はたらかせる・誰かを 働かせる; ▶ *use causative form* **2** n force ちから・力; by force ちからで・力で

forecast n weather forecast てんきよほう・天気予報

forehead n ひたい・額

foreign adj がいこく(の)・外国(の)

foreigner n がいこくじん・外国人！ usually refers to non-Japanese people

forest n もり・森

forever, for ever adv いつまでも

forget vb わすれる・忘れる; to forget about someone だれかの ことを わすれる・誰かの ことを 忘れる; to forget to call でんわするのを わすれる・電話するのを 忘れる！ the pre ます form + わすれる can often be used

forgive vb to forgive someone だれかを ゆるす・誰かを 許す

fork n フォーク

form 1 n (a shape) かたち・形; (a document) ようし・用紙; (British English) (a class) **2** vb (to start (a band, business, group)) つくる・作る

formal adj (describing language) せいしき(な)・正式(な); formal clothes せいそう・正装; (official) こうしき(の)・公式(の)

former adj (a former) まえの・前の; (the former) もと・元

fortnight n (British English) にしゅうかん・二週間

fortunately adv うんよく・運良く

fortune n (money) たいきん・大金; to make a fortune ざいさんをつくる・財産を 作る; to tell fortunes うらなう・占う

forty num よんじゅう・四十

forward 1 adv まえへ・前へ; to take a step forward まえにでる・前に 出る **2** vb to forward a letter to someone だれかにてがみを てんそうする・誰かに 手紙を 転送する

found vb せつりつする・設立する

fountain n ふんすい・噴水

four num (on its own) よっつ・四つ; (with a counter) よん、
し・四; four books ほん よんさつ・本 四冊; I've got four
よっつ あります。・四つ あります。; it's four o'clock
よじです。・四時です。

fourteen num じゅうよん・十四

fourteenth num (in a series) じゅうよんばん(め)・十四
番(目); (in dates) じゅうよっか・十四日; the fourteenth
of July しちがつじゅうよっか・七月十四日

fourth num (in a series) よんばん(め)・四番(目); (in
dates) よっか・四日; the fourth of July しちがつよっか・
七月四日

fox n きつね

fragile adj こわれやすい・壊れやすい

frame n (picture) わく・枠

France n フランス

frank adj そっちょく(な)・率直(な)

freckle n そばかす

free 1 adj (costing nothing) むりょう(の)・無料(の);
▶ただ is often used in conversation; (independent, able to
come and go) じゆう(な)・自由(な); (not occupied,
available) あいている・空いている; ▶ひま is often used
between friends; are you free on Monday? げつようびは
あいていますか。・月曜日は 空いていますか。;
is this seat free この せきは あいていますか。・この
席は 空いていますか。2 vb (person) かいほうする・
解放する; (animal) にがす・逃がす 3 adv むりょうで・
無料で

freedom n じゆう・自由

freeway n (US English) こうそくどうろ・高速道路

freeze vb (in cold weather) こおる・凍る; the river froze
かわが こおりました。・川が 凍りました。; the ground
was frozen つちが こおっていました。・土が 凍ってい
ました。; (in a freezer) れいとうする・冷凍する; to
freeze to death とうしする・凍死する

freezer n れいとうこ・冷凍庫

freezing adj it's freezing さむいです。・寒いです。; this room is freezing この へやは さむいです。・この 部屋は 寒いです。

French 1 adj フランスの **2** n (the people) フランスじん・フランス人; (the language) フランスご・フランス語

French fries n ポテトフライ

fresh adj しんせん(な)・新鮮(な)

Friday n きんようび・金曜日

fridge n れいぞうこ・冷蔵庫

fried adj いためた・炒めた; deep-fried あげた・揚げた

fried egg n めだまやき・目玉焼き

friend n ともだち・友達; to make friends ともだちに なる・友達に なる; to make friends with someone だれかと ともだちに なる・誰かと 友達に なる

friendly adj (people) あいそうが いい・愛想が いい; (animals) ひと なつっこい・人 なつっこい

fright n to get a fright びっくりする; to give someone a fright だれかを びっくりさせる・誰かを びっくりさせる

frightened adj to be frightened こわがる・怖がる; I'm frightened こわいです。・怖いです。

fringe n (British English) まえがみ・前髪

frog n かえる

from prep **!** There are many verbs which involve the use of from, like borrow from, escape from etc. For translations, look up the entries at borrow, escape etc.; から; I'm from Tokyo とうきょうから きました。・東京から 来ました。 **!** Japanese often say where they're from using place name + しゅっしん eg ロンドンしゅっしんです。 I'm from London; where is she from? かのじょは どこからですか。・彼女は どこからですか。; to come back from the office しごとから かえる・仕事から 帰る; to return from a holiday りょこうから かえる・旅行から 帰る; there's a message from

Paul ポールからの メッセージが あります。; the train from Kyoto is late きょうとからの でんしゃは おくれて います。; 京都からの 電車は 遅れています。; we live ten minutes from the city centre まちの ちゅうしんから じゅっぷんの ところに すんでいます。; 町の 中心から 10分の 所に 住んでいます。; (*when talking about time*) から; the shop is open from ten to six みせは じゅうじから ろくじまであいています。; 店は 十時から 六時まで 開いています。; from Monday to Saturday げつようびから どようびまで; 月曜日から 土曜日まで; from April on しがつから・四月から; from then on それから; in fifty years from now これから ごじゅうねんご・これから 五十年後; (*British English*) (*in arithmetic*) 5 from 8 leaves 3 はちひく ごは さんです。; 八 引く 五は 三です。

front 1 *n* in front of ...のまえ・...の前; (*of a car, a train or queue*) the front of the bus バスの まえの ほう・バスの 前の 方; the front of the queue れつの あたま・列 の 頭 **2** in front of まえに・前に

front door *n* げんかん・玄関

front page *n* だいいちめん・第一面

front seat *n* ぜんぶざせき・前部座席

frost *n* しも・霜

frozen *adj* こおっている・凍っている; frozen food れいとうしょくひん・冷凍食品

fruit *n* くだもの・果物; ▶フルーツ is becoming increasingly common; a piece of fruit くだもの・果物; I like fruit くだものが すきです。果物が 好きです。

frustrated *adj* ふまんが ある・不満が ある

fry *vb* いためる・炒める; to fry onions たまねぎを いためる・玉ねぎを 炒める; (*to deep fry*) あげる・揚げる

frying pan *n* (*British English*) フライパン

full *adj* (*not empty*) いっぱい; the streets were full of people みちは ひとで いっぱいでした。・道は 人で いっぱいでした。; (*describing a flight*) まんせき・満席; (*describing*

a hotel まんしつ ・ 満室; (describing a carpark) まんしゃ ・ 満車; (maximum) to travel at full speed ぜんそくりょくで いく ・ 全速力で 行く; to get full marks まんてんを とる ・ 満点を 取る

full-time adv ! not usually expressed as all jobs are full-time unless otherwise stated; ▶ part-time

fumes n ガス; exhaust fumes はいきガス ・ 排気ガス

fun n it's fun たのしいです。・ 楽しいです。; skiing is fun スキーは たのしいです。・ スキーは 楽しいです。; to have fun たのしむ ・ 楽しむ; she's fun かのじょは おも しろいひとです。・ 彼女は 面白い 人です。

function n (of a person) やくわり ・ 役割; (of a machine) きのう ・ 機能

funeral n おそうしき ・ お葬式

funfair n (British English) いどうゆうえんち ・ 移動遊園地 ! rare in Japan

funny adj (amusing) おもしろい ・ 面白い; (odd) へん(な) ・ 変(な)

fur n (an animal's coat) け ・ 毛; (on a garment) けがわ ・ 毛皮

furious adj ひじょうに おこっている ・ 非常に 怒って いる

furniture n かぐ ・ 家具

further adv もっと とおくに ・ もっと 遠くに; how much further is it? あと どのくらいですか。・ 後 どのくらい ですか。

fuss n おおさわぎ ・ 大騒ぎ to make a fuss (complain) もん くをいう ・ 文句を 言う

fussy adj うるさい; he's a fussy eater かれは すききらい がおおいです。・ 彼は 好き嫌いが 多いです。

future 1 n (general) みらい ・ 未来; (person's) しょうらい ・ 将来; in the future みらいに ・ 未来に **2** adj しょうらい の ・ 将来の

Gg

gallery *n* ギャラリー ▶びじゅつかん

game *n* ゲーム、しあい・試合; a game of football サッカーのしあい・サッカーの試合; a game of tennis テニスのしあい・テニスの試合

games *n* (British English) たいいく・体育

game show *n* ゲームショー

gang *n* (a group of friends, young people) なかま・仲間; (of criminals) ギャング

gap *n* (in between things) すきま・隙間; (a period of time) くうはく・空白

garage *n* (place to keep car) しゃこ・車庫 (British English) (petrol station) ガソリンスタンド; (place for car repairs) じどうしゃしゅうりこうじょう・自動車修理工場

garbage *n* (US English) ごみ

garden 1 *n* にわ・庭 **2** *vb* にわしごとをする・庭仕事をする

gardener *n* にわし・庭師

gardening *n* にわいじり・庭弄り

garlic *n* にんにく

gas *n* (for cooking, heating) ガス; (US English) (gasoline) ガソリン

gas station *n* (US English) ガソリンスタンド

gate *n* もん・門; (at an airport) ゲート

gather *vb* (to come together) あつまる・集まる; (to collect) あつめる・集める

gay *adj* どうせいあい(の)・同性愛(の)

gear *n* (in a car or bus, on a bike) ギア; (equipment) どうぐ・道具; fishing gear つりどうぐ・釣り道具; (clothes)

football gear サッカーの ユニフォーム; swimming gear みずぎ・水着

Gemini *n* ふたござ・双子座

general 1 *n* たいしょう・大将 **2** *adj* いっぱん(の)・一般(の) **3 in general** ふつう・普通

generation *n* せだい・世代

generous *adj* かんだい(な)・寛大(な)

genius *n* てんさい・天才

gentle *adj* やさしい・優しい

gentleman *n* しんし・紳士

geography *n* ちり・地理

germ *n* ばいきん・ばい菌

German 1 *adj* ドイツの **2** *n* (the people) ドイツじん・ドイツ人; (the language) ドイツご・ドイツ語

Germany *n* ドイツ

get *vb* **get away** (to escape) にげる・逃げる; he won't get away with it かれは ただで すまないでしょう。・彼は ただで 済まないでしょう。; **get back** (to arrive back) かえる・帰る; (to have something returned) かえして もらう・返して もらう; (when something is returned) かえってくる・返ってくる; I got my bike back じてんしゃを かえして もらいました。・自転車を 返して もらいました。; the money will be returned おかねは かえって きます。・お金は 返って きます。・**get down** (to come or go down) おりる・下りる; (to take down) おろす・下ろす; I got the box down from the shelf はこを たなから おろしました。・箱を 棚から 下ろしました。・**get in** (car or taxi) のる・乗る; **get off** (to leave a bus or train) おりる・降りる; I'm getting off at the next stop つぎの バスていで おります。・次の バス停で 降ります。; (to remove) to get a stain off しみを とる・染みを 取る; **get on** (to climb on board a bus or train) のる・乗る; to get on the bus バスに のる・バスに 乗る; to get on well きが あう・気が 合う; I get on well with her かのじょと きが あいます。・彼女と

気が合います。; (in polite enquiries) how did you get on?
どうでしたか。; how are you getting on at school? がっこ
うは どうですか。・学校は どうですか。; **get out** (to
leave) でる・出る; I got out of the building ビルを でまし
た。・ビルを 出しました。; (to take out) だす・出す; to get
the furniture out of the house うちから かぐをだす・家
から家具を 出す; **get over** to get over an illness びょうき
が なおる・病気が 治る; **get through to** to get through
(to someone) (だれかに)れんらくする・(誰かに)連絡
する; **get together** あう・会う; **get up** おきる・起きる

ghost n おばけ・お化け; ghost story かいだん・怪談

gift n (a present) プレゼント; (a present from a trip) おみやげ
・お土産; (an ability) さいのう・才能; he has a gift for
languages かれは ごがくが とくいです。・彼は 語学が
得意です。

ginger adj ginger hair (British English) あかげ・赤毛 n しょ
うが

girl n おんなの こ・女の 子

girlfriend n (in a couple) ガールフレンド; (a female friend)
おんなの ともだち・女の 友達

give vb ! For translations of expressions like to give someone a
lift, to give someone an injection, to give someone a fright etc,
look up the entries lift, injection, fright; (to someone else) あげ
る; (to you) くれる; to give a book (to someone) (だれかに)
ほんを あげる・(誰かに)本を あげる; he gave me the
photos かれは わたしに しゃしんを くれました。・
彼は 私に 写真を くれました。; give me the newspaper
しんぶんを ください。・新聞を ください。; give that to
me それを ください。; to give one's seat (to someone)
(だれかに)せきを ゆずる・(誰かに)席を 譲る; to give
someone a message でんごんをつたえる・伝言を 伝え
る! Expressions of giving and receiving are dependant on the
relationship between giver and receiver; **give away** (to make a
present of) あげる; to give away a secret ひみつを いって
しまう・秘密を 言って しまう; **give back** かえす・
返す; **give in** あきらめる・諦める; **give off** to give off a

smell においが する・臭いが する; **give out** くばる・配る; to give out paper かみを くばる・紙を 配る; **give up** (to stop) やめる; to give up smoking たばこを やめる; (to abandon) あきらめる・諦める; to give up the idea of working abroad がいこくで はたらく ことを あきらめる・外国で 働く ことを 諦める; to give oneself up to the police けいさつに じしゅする・警察に 自首する

glad adj うれしい

glass n (substance) ガラス; (for wine, spirits) グラス; (for water, soft drinks) コップ

glasses n めがね

glove n てぶくろ・手袋

glue 1 n (paper glue) のり・糊; (strong glue) せっちゃくざい・接着剤 **2** vb せっちゃくする・接着する

go vb **go across** わたる・渡る; **go ahead** (if it's an event) おこなう・行う; the concert's going ahead コンサートを おこないます。・コンサートを 行います。; (if it's a person) please go ahead どうぞ; **go around go round; go around with go round with**; go どこかに いく・どこかに 行く; **go away!** でて いけ・出て 行け。 **!** this should be used with extreme caution; **go back** (home, hometown) かえる・帰る; (somewhere else) もどる・戻る; to go back to work しごとに もどる・仕事に 戻る; to go back to sleep ねなおす・寝なおす; **go by** (people, cars) とおる・通る; (time) たつ・経つ; **go down** (quality, a price, a salary) さがる・下がる; (person) おりる・下りる; I went down the stairs かいだんを おりました。・階段を 下りました。 I went down the mountain やまを くだりました。・山を 下りました。; (the sun) しずむ・沈む; (a computer) うごかなくなる・動かなくなる; **go in** (to enter) はいる・入る; **go off** (to explode) ばくはつする・爆発する; (to ring) なる・鳴る; (to rot) くさる・腐る; (lights) きえる・消える; **go on** (to continue) つづく・続く; (to be switched on) つく・点く; **go out** (to leave the house) でかける・出かける; are you going out this evening? こんばん でかけますか。・今晩 出かけます

か。; (as a boyfriend, a girlfriend) (single date) デートする; (long term) つきあう・付き合う; (to be switched off, to stop burning) きえる・消える; the tide's going out しおが ひき ます。・潮が 引きます。; **go over** (to check) チェックする; (to revise) ふくしゅうする・復習する; **go round** (British English) (to call on) たずねる・訪ねる; to go round to see a friend ともだちの うちへ あそびに いく・友達 の 家へ 遊びに 行く; (to walk around, to visit) みて まわる ・見て 回る; to go round the museum はくぶつかんを みて まわる・博物館を 見て 回る; (to be enough) たり る・足りる; is there enough bread to go round? パンが たりますか。・パンが 足りますか。; **go round with** (British English) (to spend time with) つきあう・付き合う; **go through** (to have, to live through) to go through a difficult time たいへんな じきを のりこえる・大変な 時期を 乗り越える; I don't want to go through that again にどとし たくないです。・二度と したくないです。; (to search) さがす・探す; (to check) チェックする; **go together** あ う・合う; the skirt and shoes go well together あの スカー トとくつは よく あいます。・あの スカートと 靴は よく 合います。; **go up** (if it's a person) I went up the stairs かいだんを あがりました。・階段を 上がりました。; to go up the mountain やまを のぼる・山を 登る; (if it's a price, a salary) あがる・上がる; **go well** うまく いく・ うまく 行く; **go with** (if it's clothes) あう・合う; the trousers don't really go with the jacket あの ズボンは あの ジャケットに あ いません。・あの ズボンは あの ジャケットに 合いま せん。

goal n (sports) ゴール; (aim) もくひょう・目標

goalkeeper n ゴールキーパー

goat n やぎ

god n かみ・神; God かみさま・神様

goddaughter n なづけむすめ・名づけ娘! this relationship is not common in Japan

godfather n なづけおや・名付け親! this relationship is not common in Japan. You could try to explain the situation with

せんれいをうけた ときの だいふです。; (*crime underworld*) おやぶん・親分

godmother *n* なづけおや・名付け親 **!** *this relationship is not common in Japan. You could try to explain the situation with* せんれいをうけた ときの だいぼです。

godson *n* なづけむすこ・名づけ息子 **!** *this relationship is not common in Japan*

going: to be going to I'm going to go to Kobe こうべ に いきます。・神戸に 行きます。; I was going to phone you but I didn't have time でんわを する つもりでしたが、じかんが ありませんでした。・電話を する つもりでしたが、時間が ありませんでした。**!** *There is no specific future tense in Japanese. Use the non-past tense.*

gold 1 *n* きん・金 **2** *adj* きん(の)・金(の); gold ring きんの ゆびわ・金の 指輪

goldfish *n* きんぎょ・金魚

golf *n* ゴルフ

golf course *n* ゴルフコース

good 1 *adj* いい・いい **!** *is the only irregular adjective in Japanese. To make past and negative forms the stem changes to* よ; a good book いいほん・いい 本; we've got some good news いい しらせが あります。・いい 知らせが あります。; good eyesight めが いい・目が いい; good at maths すうがくが とくい・数学が 得意; it's a good time to visit Japan にほんに いくには いい じきです。・日本に 行くには いい 時期です。; exercise is good for you うんどうは からだに いいです。・運動は 体に いいです。; to look good (*healthy*) she looks good かのじょは げんきそうです。・彼女は 元気そうです。; I had a good time たのしかったです。・楽しかったです。; (*talking about food*) おいしい; (*obedient*) いい; good child いい こ・いい子; (*kind*) it's very good of you to let me know おしらせ ありがとうございます。・お知らせ ありがとうございます。**2** *n* it's no good shouting おおきい こえで いっても しょうが ありません。・大きい 声で 言っても しょうが ありません。; I am not good at French フランス

ごが とくいではありません。・フランス語が 得意で
はありません。**3** *exc* (when pleased or relieved) good よか
ったですね。; (when praising) good!; よく できました。
4 for good ずっと

good afternoon *n* (also *exclamation*) (when meeting) こん
にちは・今日は

goodbye *n* (also *exclamation*) さようなら

good evening *n* (also *exclamation*) こんばんは・今晩は

good-looking *adj* かっこういい・格好いい

good morning *n* (also *exclamation*) (when meeting) おはよ
うございます

goodnight *n* (also *exclamation*) おやすみなさい・お休み
なさい

goods *n* しょうひん・商品

goose *n* がちょう・鵞鳥

gossip *vb* (to chat) しゃべる・喋る; (to talk in a harmful way)
ゴシップを する

got: to have got *vb* (to have) ▶have; have you got any
money? おかねが ありますか。・お金が ありますか。;
I've got a cold かぜを ひいています。・風邪を ひいてい
ます。; I've got a dog いぬを かっています。・犬を 飼っ
ています。; I've got two children こどもが ふたりいます。
・子供が 二人います。; (to be obliged to) to have got to
! Use the ない form of the verb minus the last い＋ければ な
りません; I've got to go いかなければ なりません。・
行かなければ なりません。; I've got to do my homework
しゅくだいを しなければ なりません。・宿題を しな
ければ なりません。

government *n* せいふ・政府

GP *n* (British English) **!** The system is different and GPs do not
exist in Japan. A general word for doctor は いしゃ

grab *vb* to grab (someone) by the arm (だれかの)うでを
つかむ・(誰かの)腕を 掴む; he tried to grab my handbag
かれは わたしの ハンドバッグを ひったくろうと

しました。・彼は 私の ハンドバッグを 引っ手繰ろう
としました。

grade n (a mark) せいせき ・ 成績; (US English) (a class)
ねんせい ・ 年生; I'm in the first grade いちねんせいで
す。・一年生です。

grade school n (US English) しょうがっこう ・ 小学校

gradually adv すこしずつ ・ 少しずつ

graduate vb そつぎょうする ・ 卒業する

gram(me) n グラム

grammar n ぶんぽう ・ 文法

grandchild n (your own) まご ・ 孫; (someone else's) おま
ごさん ・ お孫さん

granddaughter n ! Japanese prefer to use the word
grandchild, まご

grandfather n (your own) そふ ・ 祖父; (someone else's)
おじいさん ・ お祖父さん

grandmother n (your own) そぼ ・ 祖母; (someone else's)
おばあさん ・ お祖母さん

grandparents n (your own) そふぼ ・ 祖父母; (someone
else's) おじいさんと おばあさん ・ お祖父さんと お祖
母さん

grandson n ! Japanese prefer to use the word grandchild, まご

grapefruit n グレープフルーツ

grapes n ぶどう

grass n くさ ・ 草; (in gardens) しばふ ・ 芝生; to cut the
grass しばかりを する ・ 芝刈りを する

grasshopper n ばった

grateful adj ありがたい; I would be grateful if you could let
me know おしえて くださって ありがたく おもいま
す。・ 教えて くださって ありがたく 思います。

grave n おはか ・ お墓

gray (US English) ▶ grey

greasy adj あぶらっぽい ・ 油っぽい

great adj (stressing size, amount, importance) たいへん・大変; a great improvement たいへんな じょうたつ・大変な 上達; to have great difficulty reading よむのに たいへん くろうする・読むのに 大変 苦労する; the guide book was a great help ガイドブックは たいへん やくに たちました。・ ガイドブックは 大変 役に 立ちました。; (showing enthusiasm) that's great! すごいですね。・ I had a great time たのしかったです。・ 楽しかったです。

Great Britain n えいこく・英国; イギリス is also used

great grandfather n (your own) そうそふ・そう祖父; (someone else's) ひいおじいさん・ひいお爺さん

great grandmother n (your own) そうそぼ・そう祖母; (someone else's) ひいおばあさん・ひいお婆さん

greedy adj どんよく(な)・貪欲(な)

green adj みどり・緑! Note that the green of vegetation and traffic lights is usually expressed using あおい

greengrocer n やおや・八百屋

greenhouse n おんしつ・温室

grey (British English), **gray** (US English) adj はいいろ(の)・灰色(の); grey hair しらが・白髪

grill vb やく・焼く

grin vb にやにや わらう・にやにや 笑う

groceries n しょくりょうひん・食料品

ground n じめん・地面; (land used for sports) グランド

ground floor n (British English) いっかい・一階

group n (a number of people) あつまり・集まり; a group of Japanese people にほんじんの あつまり・日本人の 集まり; (a band) グループ

grow vb (to get big) おおきく なる・大きく なる; (as a gardener, a farmer) そだてる・育てる; to grow vegetables やさいを そだてる・野菜を 育てる; (to get long (hair)) のびる・伸びる; I decided to let my hair grow かみを のばすことに しました。・髪を 伸ばす ことに しました。; (to let grow (a beard)) to grow a beard ひげを はやす・

ひげを 生やす; (to become) なる; to grow old としを とる・年を とる; (to increase in size) ふえる・増える; the population will grow じんこうが ふえます。・人口が 増えます。 **grow up** おとなに なる・大人に なる; when I grow up, I want to be a doctor おとなに なったら、いしゃに なりたいです。・大人に なったら、医者に なりたいです。

grumble vb もんくを いう・文句を 言う

guard n (at a bank) けいびいん・警備員; (in a prison) しゅえい・守衛; to be on guard けいかいする・警戒する

guard dog n ばんけん・番犬

guardian n ほごしゃ・保護者

guess vb すいていする・推定する; (US English) I guess...~とおもいます。・~と 思います。

guest n (a person invited to stay) おきゃくさん・お客さん; (at a hotel) とまりきゃく・泊まり客

guesthouse n みんしゅく・民宿

guide 1 n (on a tour or holiday) ガイド; (a person showing the way) あんないにん・案内人; (British English) (Girl Guide) ガールスカウト **2** vb あんないする・案内する

guide book n ガイドブック

guided tour n ガイドつきの ツアー・ガイド付きの ツアー

guilty adj ゆうざい(の)・有罪(の); I feel guilty りょうしんが いたいです。良心が 痛いです。

guinea pig n モルモット; (figuratively in an experiment) じっけんだい・実験台

guitar n ギター

gum n はぐき・歯茎; chewing gum ガム

gun n じゅう・銃; (handgun) けんじゅう・拳銃

gym n たいいくかん・体育館

gymnasium n たいいくかん・体育館

gymnastics n たいそう・体操

gypsy n ジプシー

Hh

habit n しゅうかん・習慣

hail n あられ

hair n (on the head) かみの け・髪の毛

hairbrush n くし

hairdresser n とこや・床屋

hairdryer n ヘアードライヤー

hairstyle n かみがた・髪型

half 1 n はんぶん・半分; to cut a melon in half メロンを はんぶんにきる・メロンを 半分に 切る; (in a game) the first half ぜんはん・前半 **2** adj half a litre ごひゃく CC・五百 CC CC is pronounced シーシー **3** pron (when talking about quantities, numbers) to spend half of one's pocket money こづかいを はんぶん つかう・小遣いを 半分 使う; half the pupils speak French せいとの はんすうは フランスごが はなせます。・生徒の 半数は フランス 語が 話せます。; an hour and a half いちじかんはん・一時間半; he's three and a half かれは さんさいと ろっかげつです。・彼は 三才と 六ヶ 月です。Note that in Japanese age is only usually expressed in full years, even with small babies and children; it's half (past) three (British English) さんじはんです。・三時半です。 **4** adv Toshihide's half Japanese half Chinese としひでさん は にほんじんと ちゅうごくじんの ハーフです。・ 俊英さんは 日本人と 中国人の ハーフです。

half hour n さんじゅっぷん・三十分

half term n (British English) ちゅうかんきゅうか・中間 休暇！Note that there is no half-term holiday in Japanese schools.

hall n (by the front door in a house or apartment) げんかん・ 玄関; (for public events) ホール

ham n ハム

hamburger n ハンバーガー

hammer n かなづち・金づち

hamster n ハムスター

hand n (the part of the body) て・手; I had a pencil in my hand えんぴつをてに もっていました。・鉛筆を 手に 持っていました。; to hold hands てを つなぐ・手を つなぐ; (help) please give me a hand てつだってください。・手伝ってください。; (on a clock or watch) とけいの はり・時計の針; (when judging a situation or subject) on the other... いっぽう・一方

handbag n ハンドバッグ

handball n ハンドボール

handicapped adj a handicapped person しょうがいしゃ・障害者！When a person has a disability, it is more usual in Japanese to refer to it specifically rather than use the general word しょうがいしゃ which means a registered disabled person.

handkerchief n ハンカチ

handle n とって・取っ手

handsome adj ハンサム(な); a handsome man ハンサムなひと・ハンサムな 人

handwritten n てがき(の)・手書き(の)

handy adj べんり(な)・便利(な)

hang vb (on a hook, a coat hanger, a line) to hang a picture (up) on the wall かべに えをかける・壁に 絵を 掛ける; to hang clothes (up) in a wardrobe ふくを ようふくだんすに しまう・服を 洋服だんすに しまう; to hang washing on a line せんたくものを ほす・洗濯物を 干す; (to be attached) the picture hangs over the piano えは ピアノの うえのかべに かかっています。・絵は ピアノの 上の壁に 掛かっています。; to be hanging from the ceiling てんじょうから つるしている・天井から 吊るしている; (to kill as capital punishment) こうしゅけいに する・絞首

刑に する; (as suicide) くびつりじさつを する・首吊り
自殺を する; **hang around** (to wait) まつ・待つ; (to waste
time, to do nothing) ぶらぶらする; **hang on to** つかむ; she
was hanging on to the rope かのじょは ロープを つかん
でいました。・彼女は ロープを つかんでいました。;
hang up (on a hook, a coat hanger, a line) to hang up one's
coat コートを かける・コートを 掛ける; to hang
washing up to dry outside そとに せんたくものを ほす・
外に 洗濯物を 干す; (when phoning) じゅわきを おく・
受話器を 置く

hang-gliding n ハンググライダーを する こと

happen vb (to occur) おこる・起こる; what happened?
なにが おこりましたか。・何が 起こりましたか。; that
accident happened last week その じこは せんしゅう お
きました。・その 事故は 先週 起きました。; to happen
again また おこる・また 起こる; (to affect someone)
what happened to you? どうしましたか。; something odd
happened yesterday きのう ふしぎな ことが ありまし
た。・昨日 不思議な ことが ありました。

happy adj (content) しあわせ(な)・幸せ(な); to make
happy しあわせに する・幸せに する; I'm happy with this
language school この ごがくがっこうに まんぞくして
います。・この 語学学校に 満足しています。; (in
greetings) Happy birthday! おたんじょうび おめでとう。・
お誕生日 おめでとう。; Happy New Year! あけまして おめ
でとうございます。・明けまして おめでとうございま
す。

hard 1 adj (firm, stiff) かたい; the ground is hard じめんが か
たいです。・地面が かたいです。; (difficult) むずかしい
・難しい; a hard question むずかしい しつもん・難しい
質問; it's not hard to change a light bulb でんきゅうを かえ
るのは むずかしくないです。・電球を 替えるのは 難
しくないです。; it's hard to understand わかりにくいで
す。・集中しにくいです。; (harsh, tough) a hard winter
きびしいふゆ・厳しい 冬; I'm having a hard time at the
moment いまたいへんです。・今 大変です。; (severe)

きびしい・厳しい **2** adv to work hard いっしょうけんめいはたらく・一生懸命 働く; he hit me hard かれはつよくわたしを ぶちました。・彼は 強く 私を ぶちました; to try hard to concentrate がんばって しゅうちゅうする・頑張って 集中する

hardly adv ほとんど + negative; she hardly ate anything かのじょは ほとんど たべませんでした。・彼女は ほとんど 食べませんでした。

hardware n (for computers) ハードウェア

hard-working adj (at work) しごとねっしん(な)・仕事熱心(な); (at school) べんきょうねっしん(な)・勉強熱心(な)

harm vb to harm someone だれかに きずを つける・誰かに 傷を つける; to harm the environment かんきょうに わるいえいきょうを あたえる・環境に 悪い 影響を 与える

harmful adj ゆうがい(な)・有害(な)

harmless adj むがい(な)・無害(な)

harvest n しゅうかく・収穫

hat n ぼうし・帽子

hate vb (to feel a strong dislike for) I hate mice ねずみが きらいです。・ねずみが 嫌いです。; (to feel hatred for) にくむ・憎む; to hate someone だれかを にくむ・誰かを 憎む

hatred n けんお・嫌悪

have 1 vb (to eat, to drink) to have a sandwich サンドイッチをたべる・サンドイッチを 食べる; to have a glass of wine ワインを のむ・ワインを 飲む; to have dinner ゆうごはんをたべる・夕ご飯を 食べる; (to get) I had a letter from Dennis yesterday きのう、デニスさんから てがみをもらいました。・昨日、デニスさんから 手紙をもらいました。; (to hold or organize) to have a party パーティーをする; to have a competition コンクールを する; (to spend) we had a nice day at the beach すなはまで いいいちにちをすごしました。・砂浜で いい 一日を 過ごしました。; I had a good time in Kyoto きょうとの たびは

たのしかったです。・京都の 旅は 楽しかったです。；
(to suffer) to have flu かぜを ひく・ 風邪を ひく; to have a
headache ずつうが する・ 頭痛が する; I have toothache
はが いたいです。・ 歯が 痛いです。; (to get something
done) to have a pizza delivered ピザを はいたつして もら
う・ ピザを 配達して もらう; she had her hair cut かの
じょは かみを きりました。・ 彼女は 髪を 切りまし
た。; to have a baby こどもを うむ・ 子供を 産む 2 aux
vb you've seen her, haven't you? かのじょを みましたね。
・ 彼女を 見ましたね。; he hasn't called, has he? かれは
でんわしていませんね。・ 彼は 電話していませんね。
3 to have to 〜ない form of the verb without the last いい＋ け
れば ならない; I have to study べんきょうしなければ な
りません。・ 勉強しなければ なりません。; I have to pay
はらわなければ なりません。・ 払わなければ なりま
せん。; I have to go home かえらなければ なりません。・
帰らなければ なりません。; you don't have to work on
Saturday どようびは はたらかなくても いいです。・
土曜日は 働かなくても いいです。

hay n わら

hazelnut n ヘーゼルナッツ

he pron かれ・ 彼 Note that Japanese prefer to use a name
rather than a pronoun; he's coming next week かれは らいし
ゅうきます。・ 彼は 来週 来ます。; there he is かれは
あそこです。・ 彼は あそこです。

head 1 n (the part of the body) あたま・ 頭; (the person in
charge) たんとうしゃ・ 担当者 2 vb (to be in charge of)
ひきいる・ 率いる; (in soccer) to head the ball ボールを
ヘディングする; **head for** むかう・ 向かう

headache n to have a headache ずつうが する・ 頭痛が
する; my headache's gone ずつうが なおりました。・
頭痛が 治りました。

headlamp, headlight n ヘッドランプ

headline n みだし・ 見出し; to hit the headlines みだしに
なる・ 見出しに なる; the news headlines おもな ニュ
ース・ 主な ニュース

headquarters n (of a company, a business) ほんぶ・本部; (of an army) しれいぶ・司令部

headteacher n こうちょうせんせい・校長先生

health n けんこう・健康

healthy adj (in good health) けんこうてき(な)・健康的 (な); (good for the health) けんこうにいい・健康にいい

hear vb to hear きこえる・聞こえる; he can't hear anything かれは なにも きこえません。・彼は 何も 聞こえません。; I heard someone's footsteps だれかの あしおとが きこえました。・誰かの 足音が 聞こえました。; you can hear him practising the piano かれが ピアノの れんしゅう をしているのが きこえます。・彼が ピアノの 練習を しているのが 聞こえます。; (to learn, to discover) to hear the news ニュースを きく・ニュースを 聞く; I heard about that school's reputation あの がっこうの ひょうば んをききました。・あの 学校の 評判を 聞きました。; we've heard a lot about you いろいろ うかがっています。 ・色々 伺っています。; (to listen to) きく・聞く; to listen to the radio ラジオを きく・ラジオを 聞く; **hear from** れんらくが ある・連絡が ある; have you heard from Joyce? ジョイスさんから れんらくが きましたか。・ ジョイスさんから 連絡が 来ましたか。; **hear of** きく・ 聞く

heart n (part of the body) しんぞう・心臓; (the centre) right in the heart of London ロンドンの ちゅうしんに・ロン ドンの 中心に; to learn by heart あんきする・暗記する

heart attack n しんぞうほっさ・心臓発作

heat 1 vb (to heat a room, part of body) あたためる・暖め る; (to heat food, liquid) あたためる・温める **2** n あつさ・ 暑さ; I can't stand the heat あつくて たえられません。・ 暑くて 耐えられません。; (on a cooker) at a low heat よわ びで・弱火で; (in a sporting contest) よせん・予選; **heat up** (to cool food) あたためる・温める; (to warm up again) あた ためなおす・温め直す

heater n だんぼうき・暖房機

heating n だんぼう・暖房

heatwave n ねっぱ・熱波

heaven n てんごく・天国

heavy adj (in weight) おもい・重い; (in quantity, intensity) the traffic is very heavy くるまが おおいです。・車が 多いです。; heavy smoker ヘビースモーカー; to have a heavy cold ひどい かぜを ひいている・ひどい 風邪を ひいている; (describing food) おもい・重い

hedge n いけがき・生け垣

hedgehog n はりねずみ

heel n かかと

height n (of a person) せ・背; (of a building, a tree) たかさ・高さ; fear of heights こうしょきょうふしょう・高所恐怖症

helicopter n ヘリコプター

hell n じごく・地獄

hello n (when greeting someone) こんにちは・今日は You can also use greetings appropriate to the time of day Not usually used between family members; (on the phone) もしもし

helmet n ヘルメット

help 1 vb The idea of helping someone is often expressed using the auxiliary verbs あげる、くれる and もらう after the ～て form of the verb; たすける・助ける; to help each other おたがいに たすけあう・お互いに 助け合う; to help with the housework かじを てつだう・家事を 手伝う; (at a meal) to help oneself じぶんで よそう・自分で よそう; please help yourselves! ごじゆうに おとり ください。・ご自由に お取り ください。; I can't help thinking about it どうしても それを かんがえて しまいます。・どうしても それを 考えて しまいます。 **2** exc help! たすけて！・助けて！ **3** n help (a helping hand) てつだい・手伝い; (urgent assistance) きゅうじょ・救助; to ask someone for help だれかに てつだいを たのむ・誰かに 手伝いを 頼む; to shout for help たすけを もとめる・助けを 求める; **help out** てを かす・手を 貸す

helpful *adj* (*useful*) やくに たつ・役に 立つ

helping *n* second helping おかわり・お代わり

helpless *adj* (*defenceless*) むぼうび(の)・無防備(の);
(*because of weakness, ill health*) むりょく(の)・無力(の)

hen *n* めんどり・めん鳥

her 1 *pron* かのじょ・彼女 *Note that Japanese prefer to use
a name rather than a pronoun;* I know her かのじょを しって
います。・彼女を 知っています。; I don't know her かの
じょを しりません。・彼女を 知りません。; he's seen
her かれは かのじょを みました。・彼は 彼女を 見ま
した。; please help her! かのじょを たすけてください。・
彼女を 助けてください。; I gave the book to her かのじょ
に ほんを あげました。・彼女に 本を あげました。
2 *det* かのじょの・彼女の; I hate her dog かのじょの
いぬが きらいです。・彼女の 犬が 嫌いです。; she
broke her leg かのじょは あしを おりました。・彼女は
足を 折りました。

herd *n* むれ・群れ

here *adv* (*when talking about location*) ここ; is it far from here?
ここから とおいですか。・ここから 遠いですか。; I'm
up here うえに います。・上に います。; (*when drawing
attention*) here's the post office ここは ゆうびんきょくで
す。・ここは 郵便局です。; here comes the train でんし
ゃが きました。・電車が 来ました。; (*when offering
something*) here you are どうぞ; (*in general statements*)
please say I'm not here いないと いってください。・
いないと 言ってください。

hers *pron* かのじょ・彼女の！ *Note that Japanese prefer
to use a name rather than a pronoun;* the red pen is hers あか
いペンは かのじょのです。・赤い ペンは 彼女ので
す。; which bag is hers? どの かばんが かのじょのです
か。・どの かばんが 彼女のですか。; my jacket is red
but hers is green わたしの ジャケットは あかいですが、
かのじょのは みどりです。・私の ジャケットは 赤い
ですが、彼女のは 緑です。

herself *pron* Not used as a reflexive pronoun in Japanese; she wants to enjoy herself かのじょは たのしみたいです。・ 彼女は 楽しみたいです。; she's hurt herself かのじょは けがをしました。・ 彼女は 怪我を しました。; (when used for emphasis) she did it all by herself かのじょは ぜんぶじぶんで しました。・ 彼女は 全部自分でしました。

hesitate *vb* ためらう

hi *exc* こんにちは・今日は

hiccups *n* to have hiccups しゃっくりする

hidden *adj* かくれている・隠れている

hide *vb* (to avoid showing) かくす・隠す; to hide the present プレゼントをかくす・プレゼントを 隠す; (to avoid being seen) かくれる・隠れる

hi-fi *n* ステレオ

high 1 *adj* (having a great height, describing a level, a price, a standard, grades, a voice) たかい・高い; the mountains are high やまは たかいです。・ 山は 高いです。; prices are high ねだんが たかいです。・ 値段が 高いです。; the standard is high レベルが たかいです。・ レベルが 高いです。; to get high grades いい せいせきを とる・いい 成績を 取る; (describing a speed) high speed train こうそくでんしゃ・高速電車 **2** *adv* たかく・高く; to climb higher もっと たかく のぼる・もっと 高く 登る

high rise block *n* (skyscraper) まてんろう・摩天楼; (apartment block) 高層住宅; (offices) こうそうオフィスビル・高層オフィスビル

high school *n* (in the US) こうとうがっこう・高等学校 This is generally shortened to こうこう

hijack *vb* ハイジャックする

hike *vb* to go hiking ハイキングする

hiking *n* ハイキング

hill *n* おか・丘・(a rise in the road) さか・坂

him *pron* かれ・彼 Note that Japanese prefer to use a name rather than a pronoun; I know him かれを しっています。・

彼を 知っています。・I don't know him かれを しりませ
ん。・彼を 知りません。・she's seen him かのじょは か
れをみました。・彼女は 彼を 見ました。・please help
him! かれをたすけてください。・彼を 助けてください。・I gave the book to him かれに ほんを あげました。・
彼に 本を あげました。

himself pron Not used as a reflexive pronoun in Japanese; he
wants to enjoy himself かれは たのしみたいです。・彼は
楽しみたいです。・he's hurt himself かれは けがを しま
した。・彼は 怪我を しました。; (when used for emphasis)
he did it all by himself かれは ぜんぶ じぶんで しました。
・彼は 全部 自分で しました。

hippopotamus, hippo n かば

hire vb (to employ) やとう・雇う; (British English) (to rent)
かりる・借りる; to hire a car くるまを かりる・車を
借りる; (to lend for a fee) かす・貸す; they hire (out) the
skates スケートを かします。・スケートを 貸します。

his 1 det かれの・彼の Note that Japanese prefer to use a
name rather than a pronoun; I hate his dog かれの いぬが
きらいです。・彼の 犬が 嫌いです。; he broke his leg
かれは あしを おりました。・彼は 足を 折りました。
2 pron the red pen is his あかい ペンは かれの です。・
赤い ペンは 彼の です。; which house is his? どの いえが
かれの ですか。・どの 家が 彼の ですか。; my shirt is
white but his is yellow わたしの シャツは しろですが、
かれの は きいろです。・私の シャツは 白ですが、
彼の は 黄色です。

history n れきし・歴史

hit 1 vb (to strike something) うつ・打つ; (to strike a person)
ぶつ; (to crash into) to hit a wall かべに ぶつかる・壁に
ぶつかる; to hit one's head on a chair いすに あたまを ぶ
つける・椅子に 頭を ぶつける; to hit a pedestrian ほこ
うしゃを ひく・歩行者を ひく **2** n (a song, film) ヒット;
hit back なぐりかえす・殴り返す; to hit someone back
だれかを なぐりかえす・誰かを 殴り返す

hitchhike vb ヒッチハイクを する

hitchhiker n ヒッチハイクをする ひと・ヒッチハイクをする 人

hoarse adj しわがれた

hobby n しゅみ・趣味

hockey n ホッケー

hold 1 vb もつ・持つ; I held some money in my right hand みぎてにおかねを もちました。・右手に お金を 持ちました。; (to arrange) to hold a competition コンクールをする; the party will be held in the school パーティーは がっこうで あります。・パーティーは 学校で あります。; (to keep or hide) to be held hostage ひとじちに とられる・人質に 取られる; (to keep back) とって おく・取って おく; to hold a seat for someone だれかに せきをとって おく・誰かに 席を 取って おく; (other uses) to hold the world record せかいきろくを もっている・世界記録を 持っている; please hold the line (telephone) しょうしょうおまちください。・少々 お待ち ください。**2** n to get hold of someone (to find) だれかを みつける・誰かを 見つける; (by phone) だれかに れんらくする・誰かに 連絡する; **hold on** (to wait) まつ・待つ; (to grasp) つかむ・掴む please hold on tight! しっかり つかんでください。・しっかり 掴んでください。**hold up** (to raise) あげる・上げる; to hold up one's hand てをあげる・手を 上げる; (to delay) to hold someone up だれかを おくらせる・誰かを 遅らせる; to hold up the traffic こうつうを おくらせる・交通を 遅らせる; (to rob) おそう・襲う

hole n あな・穴

holiday n (British English) (a vacation) りょこう・旅行; to go on holiday りょこうする・旅行する; (a national or religious festival) a (public) holiday しゅくじつ・祝日; (British English) (time taken off work) to take a day's holiday いちにち ねんきゅうをとる・一日 年休を 取る

Holland n オランダ

holly n ひいらぎ

home 1 n いえ・家 うち is also used in conversation; to leave home いえを でる・家を 出る; to work from home

いえでしごとを する・家で 仕事を する; (for elderly, ill or disabled people) a home for handicapped children ようごしせつ・養護施設; an old people's home ろうじんホーム・老人ホーム **2** adv to go home いえに かえる・家に 帰る; on my way home かえる とちゅうで・帰る 途中で; to be home (after school, work) かえっている・帰っている; I will take you home うちまで おくります。・家まで 送ります。 **3 at home** (in one's house) I'm working at home うちで しごとを しています。・家で 仕事を しています。; I live at home りょうしんと いっしょに すんでいます。・両親と 一緒に 住んでいます。; to feel at home リラックスする; please make yourselves at home どうぞ 寛いでください。・どうぞ 寛いでください。; (when talking about a sports team) じもと(の)・地元(の)

homeless adj いえの ない・家の ない

homesick adj ホームシック(の); I am homesick ホームシックになっている。

homework n しゅくだい・宿題

homosexual n どうせいあいしゃ・同性愛者

honest adj しょうじき(な)・正直(な); to be honest, I'd rather go home しょうじきに いうと うちに かえりたいです。・正直に 言うと 家に 帰りたいです。; (frank, sincere) そっちょく(な)・率直(な)

honestly adv しょうじきに・正直に

honey n はちみつ・蜂蜜

honeymoon n しんこんりょこう・新婚旅行

hood n (to cover the head) フード; (US English) (of a car) ボンネット

hoof n ひづめ

hook n (for hanging clothes, pictures) フック; (for fishing) つりばり・釣り針

hooligan n ちんぴら

hoover vb (British English) to hoover the carpet じゅうたんに そうじきを かける・絨毯に 掃除機を 掛ける

hope 1 vb I hope you don't mind but I borrowed your book すみませんが、ほんをかりました。・すみませんが、本を借りました。; we hope to meet lots of people たくさんのひとにあいたいです。・たくさんの人に会いたいです。; I hope it's sunny tomorrow あしたははれだといいです。・明日は晴れだといいです。; I hope so そうだといいですね。; I'm hoping for a good result いいけっかをきたいしています。・いい結果を期待しています。**2** n きぼう・希望

hopeless adj (without hope of success) ぜつぼうてき（な）・絶望的（な）; (without any ability) へた（な）・下手（な）; I am hopeless at cooking りょうりがへたです。・料理が下手です。

horn n (on a car, a bus) クラクション; to sound a horn クラクションをならす・クラクションを鳴らす; (of an animal) つの・角; (an instrument) ホルン

horoscope n ほしうらない・星占い

horrible adj ひどい・酷い; (of food) まずい

horror film n ホラーえいが・ホラー映画

horse n うま・馬; he likes horses かれはうまがすきです。・彼は馬が好きです。; year of the horse うまどし・午年

horseracing n けいば・競馬

horseriding n じょうば・乗馬

hospital n びょういん・病院; he's still in (the) hospital かれはまだにゅういんしています。・彼はまだ入院しています。; to be taken to (the) hospital びょういんにはこばれる・病院に運ばれる

host family n ホストファミリー

hostage n ひとじち・人質

hostel n (for homeless) しゅうようじょ・収容所; youth hostel ユースホステル

hostess n ホステス

hot adj (very warm) (air temperature) あつい・暑い; (food, liquid, etc) あつい・熱い; It's hot today きょうはあつい

です。・今日は　暑いです。; hot soup　あつい　スープ・熱いスープ; it's too hot in this room　この　へやは　あつすぎます。・この　部屋は　暑すぎます。; a hot meal あたたかいしょくじ・温かい　食事; (strong, with a lot of spices) からい・辛い; this mustard is hot この　からしは　からいです。・このからしは　辛いです。; a hot curry からいカレー・辛い　カレー

hot air balloon n ききゅう・気球

hot dog n ホットドッグ

hotel n ホテル

hour n an hour いちじかん・一時間; I earn four pounds an hour じきゅうは　よんポンドです。・時給は　四ポンドです。

house n いえ・家 うち is also used in conversation; to go to someone's house だれかの　いえに　いく・誰かの　家に行く; the bike is at my house じてんしゃは　うちにあります。・自転車は　家に　あります。

housewife n せんぎょうしゅふ・専業主婦

housework n かじ・家事; to do the housework かじをする・家事を　する

housing estate (British English), **housing development** (US English) n じゅうたくだんち・住宅団地

hovercraft n ホバークラフト

how adv (in what way) どうやって; how did you find us? どうやって　みつけましたか。・どうやって　見つけましたか。; (when talking about ability) use the potential form of the verb There are a number of other structures which also express ability such as using the dictionary form of the verb + ことができる; I know how to swim およげます。・泳げます。I know how to ski スキーが　できます。I know how to make a curry カレーが　つくれます。・カレーが　作れます。; (in polite questions) how are you? おげんきですか。・お元気ですか。; how is your father? おとうさんは　おげんきですか。・お父さんは　お元気ですか。; how was your

holiday? りょこうは どうでしたか。・ 旅行は どうでしたか。; (in questions requiring specific information) how long will it take? どのくらい かかりますか。; how tall are you? しんちょうは いくつですか。・ 身長は いくつですか。; how old is he? かれは なんさいですか。・ 彼は 何才ですか。; how much is this これは いくらですか。; (when making a suggestion) how would you like to eat out? がいしょくするのは どうですか。・ 外食するのは どうですか。; how about going to the cinema tonight? こんばん えいがをみに いくのは どうですか。・ 今晩 映画を 見に 行くのは どうですか。

however adv (nevertheless) しかし; however hard I study, I can't pass the exam いくら べんきょうしても、しけん に うかりません。・ いくら 勉強しても、試験に 受か りません。

how many 1 pron (general) いくつ; (with a counter) なん + counter; how many are there? いくつですか。; how many people? なんにんですか。・ 何人ですか。; how many books? ほんは なんさつですか。・ 本は 何冊ですか。; how many CDs did you buy? CDを なんまい かいました か。・ CDを 何枚 買いましたか。

how much 1 pron いくら; how much does it come to? ごう けいは いくらですか。・ 合計は いくらですか。; how much is that jacket? その ジャケットは いくらですか。 2 det how much money do you have left? おかねは どのく らいのこっていますか。・ お金は どのくらい 残って いますか。

huge adj おおきい・ 大きい

human being n にんげん・ 人間

humour (British English), **humor** (US English) n ユーモア; to have a sense of humour ユーモアの センスが ある

hundred num one hundred, a hundred ひゃく・ 百; three hundred さんびゃく ・ 三百; eight hundred and fifty yen は っぴゃくごじゅうえん・ 八百五十円; about a hundred people ひゃくにんくらい・ 百人くらい

hungry *adj* おなかが すいた・お腹が 空いた; I'm very hungry おなかが すいています。・お腹が 空いています。

hunt *vb* to go hunting かりに いく・狩りに 行く

hurdles *n* ハードル

hurrah, hurray *n* (also *exclamation*) ばんざい・万歳

hurry **1** *vb* いそぐ・急ぐ; please hurry home! いそいで かえってください。・急いで 帰ってください。; to hurry someone だれかを いそがせる・誰かを 急がせる **2** *n* to be in a hurry いそいでいる・急いでいる; there's no hurry いそいでいません。・急いでいません。; hurry up いそいでください。・急いで下さい。

hurt *vb* (*to injure*) to hurt oneself けがを する・怪我を する; to hurt one's leg あしを けがする・足を 怪我する; (*to be painful*) my throat hurts のどが いたいです。・喉が 痛いです。; that hurts いたいです。・痛いです。; (*to upset*) きずを つける・傷を つける; to hurt someone's feelings だれかに きずつける・誰かに 傷つける

husband *n* (*one's own*) おっと・夫; (*someone else's*) ごしゅじん・ご主人

Ii

I *pron* わたし・私 When you are talking about yourself, わたし can often be left out if it is obvious; I've got to go いかなければ なりません。・行かなければ なりません。; I didn't do it わたしが やりませんでした。・私が やりませんでした。; I'M the one who has to do it わたしが しなければ なりません。・私が しなければ なりません。; she can drive but I can't かのじょは うんてんできますが、わたしは できません。・彼女は 運転できますが、私は できません。

ice _n_ こおり・氷

ice cream _n_ アイスクリーム

ice hockey _n_ アイスホッケー

ice rink _n_ スケートリンク

ice-skate _n_ アイススケート

ice-skating _n_ アイススケート

icing _n_ アイシング

idea _n_ かんがえ・考え; what a good idea! いい かんがえ ですね・いい 考え ですね・I've no idea そうぞうが つきません・想像が つきません。

identity card _n_ みぶんしょうめいしょ・身分証明書

idiot _n_ ばか

if _conj_ ❗ There are several different ways of expressing the conditional in Japanese, a common one is to use the ～た form of the verb + ら for the conditional clause; if it rains, we won't go あめがふったら、いきません。・雨が 降ったら、行きません。; if I were rich, I would travel おかねもちだったら、りょこうをします。・お金持ちだったら、旅行をします。; if I were you, I'd refuse わたしだったら、ことわります。・私だったら、断ります。; I wonder if they'll come かれらは きますかね。・彼らは 来ますかね。

ignore _vb_ むしする・無視する

ill _adj_ びょうき(の)・病気(の)

illegal _adj_ ふほう(な)・不法(な)

illness _n_ びょうき・病気

imagination _n_ そうぞう・想像: to have imagination そうぞうりょくがある・想像力が ある

imagine _vb_ そうぞうする・想像する

imitate _vb_ まねをする

immediately _adv_ すぐに

impatient _adj_ to be impatient まちきれない・待ちきれない; impatient person せっかちな ひと・せっかちな 人

import vb ゆにゅうする・輸入する

important adj じゅうよう(な)・重要(な); it is important to eat well ちゃんと たべる ことは たいせつです。・ちゃんと 食べる ことは 大切です。

impossible adj むり(な)・無理(な); it's impossible to finish all that work today きょう その しごとを ぜんぶする ことは むりです。・今日 その 仕事を 全部する ことは 無理です。

impressed adj かんどうした・感動した; I was impressed by that film その えいがは とても いいと おもいました。・その 映画は とても いいと 思いました。

impression n いんしょう・印象; to make a good impression いい いんしょうを あたえる・いい 印象を 与える

improve vb (to make better) よくする・良くする; to improve living conditions せいかつを よくする・生活を 良くする; my Japanese has improved にほんごが じょうたつしました。・日本語が 上達しました。; (to get better) よくなる・良くなる

improvement n かいぜん・改善

in ! Often in occurs in combinations with verbs, for example: drop in, fit in, move in etc. To find the correct translations for this type of verb, look up the separate dictionary entries at drop, fit, move etc. **1** prep (inside) use particle に; in the house いえに・家に; there's a letter in the envelope ふうとうに てがみが あります。・封筒に 手紙が あります。; there is a woman in the photograph しゃしんに おんなの ひとが うつっています。・写真に 女の 人が 写っています。; (at) use particle で; I learned Japanese in school がっこうで にほんごを ならいました。・学校で 日本語を 習いました。; in the countryside いなかで さんぽする・田舎で 散歩する; (when talking about countries or cities) use particle に; to live in Japan にほんに すむ・日本に 住む; my elder sister lives in New York あねは ニューヨークに すんでいます。・姉は ニューヨークに 住んでいます。; (dressed in) she was in a skirt かのじょは スカートを はいていました。

・ 彼女 は スカート を はいていました。; to be dressed in black くろい ふくを きる・黒い 服を 着る; (showing the way in which something is done) Use particle で; written in Japanese にほんごで かいてある・日本語で 書いてある; we paid in cash げんきんで はらいました。・現金 で払いました。; in pencil えんぴつで・鉛筆で; (during) in October じゅうがつに・十月に; in the night よなか (に)・夜中(に); in the morning ごぜんちゅう(に)・午前中(に); (within) in ten minutes じゅっぷんご・十分後; in three years さんねんご・三年後; (other uses) she's in her twenties かのじょは にじゅうだいです。・彼女は 二十代です。; one in ten じゅうぶんの いち・十分の 一; to cut an apple in two りんごを ふたつに きる・りんごを 二つに 切る **2** adv (at home, available) いえに いる・家にいる

inch n インチ! Note that an inch 2.54 cm.

include vb ふくむ・含む; breakfast is included ちょうしょくは ふくまれています。・朝食は 含まれています。

including prep ふくんで・含んで; including the children, there were eight people こどもを ふくんで、はちにんでした。・子供を 含んで、八人でした。

income n しゅうにゅう・収入

income tax n しょとくぜい・所得税

inconvenient adj ふべん(な)・不便(な); it's an inconvenient time for me つごうが わるいです。・都合が 悪いです。

increase 1 vb (numbers) あがる・上がる; to increase in value かちが あがる・価値が 上がる; (volume) ふえる・増える; it increased by 20% にじゅっパーセント ふえました。・二十パーセント 増えました。 **2** n ぞうか・増加

increasingly adv ますます・益々

incredible adj (unbelievable) しんじられない・信じられない; (astonishing) すごい

independent adj (person) どくりつした・独立した; (school) しりつ(の)・私立(の)! In conversation, this is *sometimes pronounced* わたくしりつ(の) *to avoid confusion with* しりつ(の)・**市立** *municipal*

India *n* インド

Indian 1 *adj* インド(の) **2** *n (person from India)* インドじん・インド人; *(person from North America)* アメリカンインディアン

indicate *vb* しめす・示す

indifferent *adj* むかんしん(な)・無関心(な)

indigestion *n* しょうかふりょう・消化不良

individual 1 *adj* こせいてき(な)・個性的(な) **2** *n* こじん・個人

indoor *adj* しつない(の)・室内(の); an indoor swimming pool しつないプール・室内プール

indoors *adv* しつないで・室内で

industrial *adj* こうぎょう(の)・工業(の); Industrial Revolution さんぎょうかくめい・産業革命

industry *n* さんぎょう・産業

inevitable *adj* さけられない・避けられない

infant school *n (British English)* しょうがっこう・小学校

infection *n* かんせん・感染

influence 1 *n* えいきょう・影響 **2** *vb (to persuade)* さゆうする・左右する; *(to make a strong impression on)* to influence (someone) (だれかに) えいきょうを あたえる・(誰かに)影響を 与える

inform *vb* しらせる・知らせる; to inform the police of an accident けいさつに じこを しらせる・警察に 事故を 知らせる; to keep informed しらせる・知らせる

informal *adj (describing a person, a person's manner)* カジュアル(な); *(describing a word, a language)* くだけた・砕けた; *(describing a discussion or an interview)* ひこうしき(の)・非公式(の)

information *n* じょうほう・情報

information desk *n* あんないじょ・案内所

information technology *n* じょうほうこうがく・情報工学

ingredient *n* ざいりょう・材料

inhabitant *n* じゅうみん・住民

injection *n* ちゅうしゃ・注射; to give (someone) an injection (だれかに)ちゅうしゃを する・(誰かに)注射をする

injured *adj* けがを した・怪我を した

injury *n* けが・怪我

ink *n* インク

innocent *adj* (not guilty of crime) むざい(の)・無罪(の); (without ill intent) むじゃき(な)・無邪気(な)

inquiry *n* といあわせ・問い合わせ

insect *n* むし・虫

inside **1** *prep* ～の なか・～の 中; inside the house うちの なか・家の 中 **2** *adv* なか・中; he's inside かれは なかに います・彼は 中に います; let's play inside なかで あそびましょう・中で 遊びましょう; I looked inside なかを みました・中を 見ました; let's bring the chairs inside いすを なかに いれましょう・椅子を 中に 入れましょう。**3** *n* なか・中; the inside of the palace きゅうでんの なか・宮殿の 中 **4** *adj* なか(の)・中(の) **5** inside out うらがえしに・裏返しに; to put one's shirt on inside out シャツを うらがえしに きる・シャツを 裏返しに 着る

inspect *vb* (if it's an official) しらべる・調べる; (if it's a conductor) けんさつする・検札する

inspector *n* (of a school) けんさかん・検査官; (on a bus, a train) しゃしょう・車掌; (in the police) けいぶ・警部

instantly *adv* あっというまに・あっという間に
❗ Not usually used in very formal language. In this case すぐ is preferred.

instead **1** instead of ～の かわり(に)・～の 代わり(に); I hired a van instead of a car くるまの かわりに バン

をかりました。・車の代わりにバンを借りました。; use oil instead of butter バターの かわりに あぶらを つかう・バターの 代わりに 油を 使う; his wife came instead of him かれの かわりに おくさんが きました。・彼の 代わりに 奥さんが 来ました。

instruction n せつめい・説明; way of using つかいかた・使い方; instruction booklet せつめいしょ・説明書

instrument n がっき・楽器

insult vb ぶじょくする・侮辱する

insurance n ほけん・保険

insure vb ほけんをかける・保険を 掛ける; to insure a car くるまに ほけんを かける・車に 保険を 掛ける

intelligent adj あたまが いい・頭が いい

intend vb use a verb in dictionary form + つもり; I intend to study Japanese にほんごを べんきょうする つもりです。・日本語を 勉強する つもりです。! Note that there are several ways of expressing intention in Japanese

intense adj もうれつ(な)・猛烈(な)! not used in formal Japanese

intensive care unit n しゅうちゅうちりょうしつ・集中治療室

interest 1 n (enthusiasm) きょうみ・興味; to have an interest in music おんがくに きょうみが ある・音楽に 興味が ある; (financial) りそく・利息 2 vb きょうみを そそる・興味を そそる

interested adj to be interested in sports スポーツに きょうみが ある・スポーツに 興味が ある; are you interested? きょうみが ありますか。・興味が ありますか。

interesting adj おもしろい

interfere vb (to get involved in) かんしょうする・干渉する; (to have a bad effect on) じゃまする・邪魔する; it's going to interfere with my work しごとの じゃまに なります・仕事の 邪魔に なります。

intermission n きゅうけいじかん・休憩時間

international adj こくさいてき(な)・国際的(な);
international relations こくさいかんけい・国際関係! こくさい is often used as a prefix element to form a new noun such as こくさいこうりゅう for international exchange

internet n インターネット

interpreter n つうやくしゃ・通訳者

interrupt vb じゃまをする・邪魔をする

interval n (in time or at a location) at intervals ときどき・時々; (British English) (during a play, a show) きゅうけいじかん・休憩時間

interview 1 n (for a job) めんせつ・面接; (with a journalist) インタビュー **2** vb (if it's an employer) めんせつする・面接する; (if it's a journalist) インタビューする

intimidate vb おどす・脅す

into prep (when talking about a location) に; to go into the garden にわにはいる・庭に入る; to get into a car くるまにのる・車に乗る; to get into bed ベッドにはいる・ベッドに入る; (indicating a change) に; to translate a letter into Japanese てがみを にほんごに ほんやくする・手紙を日本語に 翻訳する

introduce vb (to bring in) どうにゅうする・導入する; to introduce a new machine あたらしい きかいを どうにゅうする・新しい 機械を 導入する; (when people meet) しょうかいする・紹介する; I introduced him to Ms Yamada かれにやまださんを しょうかいしました。・彼に山田さんを 紹介しました。; introduce oneself じこしょうかいする・自己紹介する; (on radio or television) しょうかいする・紹介する; to introduce a programme ばんぐみを しょうかいする・番組を 紹介する

invade vb しんりゃくする・侵略する

invent vb はつめいする・発明する

invention n はつめい・発明

investigate vb とりしらべる・取り調べる

investigation n とりしらべ・取り調べ

invisible adj めに みえない・目に 見えない

invitation *n* しょうたい・招待

invite *vb* しょうたいする・招待する; to invite (someone) to a party パーティーに (だれかを)しょうたいする・パーティーに (誰かを)招待する

involved *adj* to be involved in an accident じこに まきこまれる・事故に 巻き込まれる

Ireland *n* アイルランド

Irish 1 *adj* アイルランドの 2 *n* (the people) アイルランドじん・アイルランド人; (the language) アイルランドご・アイルランド語

iron 1 *n* (metal) てつ・鉄; (for clothes) アイロン 2 *vb* アイロンをかける

island *n* しま・島

it *pron* ! Not used or translated in Japanese; where is it? どこですか。who is it? だれですか。・誰ですか。it's me わたしです。・私です。it's a nice house いい いえです。・いい家です。it is difficult むずかしいです。・難しいです。it's easy to make a mistake まちがいやすいです。・間違いやすいです。it's cold さむいです。・寒いです。I've heard about it ききました。・聞きました。did you go to it? いきましたか。・行きましたか。

itchy *adj* かゆい・痒い

its *det* ! Not used or translated in Japanese; its nose はな・鼻; its tail しっぽ・尻尾; its ear みみ・耳; its eyes め・目; my little sister has a rabbit, its ears are long いもうとは うさぎを かっています。みみは ながいです。・妹は うさぎを 飼っています。耳は 長いです。

itself *pron* ! Not used as a pronoun in Japanese; (when used as a reflexive pronoun) the cat's going to hurt itself ねこが けがをします。・猫が 怪我を します。; (when used for emphasis) the car itself was not damaged くるまじたいは ダメージを うけていません。・車自体は ダメージを 受けていません。; the heating comes on by itself だんぼうは じどうてきに はいります。・暖房は 自動的に はいります。

Jj

jacket *n* ジャケット

jail *n* けいむしょ・刑務所

jam *n* (British English) ジャム

Jamaica *n* ジャマイカ

January *n* いちがつ・一月

Japan *n* にほん・日本! In formal speech or documents Japan is often called にっぽん

Japanese 1 *adj* にほんの・日本の **2** *n* (the people) にほんじん・日本人; (the language) にほんご・日本語

jaw *n* あご

jazz *n* ジャズ

jealous *adj* うらやましい; I am jealous of her new shoes かのじょの あたらしい くつが うらやましいです。・彼女の 新しい靴が うらやましいです。

jeans *n* ジーパン

jeer *vb* to jeer ばかにする

jelly *n* (US English) (jam) ジャム; (British English) (a dessert) ゼリー

Jesus *n* (Jesus Christ) イエス キリスト

jet *n* ジェットき・ジェット機

jewellery (British English), **jewelry** (US English) *n* ほうせき・宝石

Jewish *adj* ユダヤ(の); (Jewish person) ユダヤじん・ユダヤ人

jigsaw puzzle *n* ジグソーパズル

job *n* (work) しごと・仕事; to look for a job しごとを さがす・仕事を 探す

jogging n ジョギング

join vb (meet up with) あう・会う; I'll join you at eight o'clock はちじに いきます。・八時に 行きます。; (become a member of) はいる・入る; to join a club クラブに 入る・クラブに はいる; to join a company かいしゃに はいる・会社に 入る; **join in** さんかする・参加する; to join in a game ゲームに さんかする・ゲームに 参加する

joke 1 n じょうだん・冗談 2 vb じょうだんを いう・冗談を言う

journalist n きしゃ・記者

journey n たび・旅; to go on a journey たびを する・旅を する; I hate my journey to work かいしゃに かようのは いやです。・会社に 通うのは いやです。

joy n よろこび・喜び

judge 1 n さいばんかん・裁判官 2 vb はんだんする・判断する

judo n じゅうどう・柔道

jug n みずさし・水差し

juice n ジュース; fruit juice フルーツジュース

jujitsu n じゅうじゅつ・柔術

July n しちがつ・七月

jump vb とぶ・飛ぶ; the children were jumping on the bed こどもたちが ベッドの うえで とびはねていました。・子供達が ベッドの 上で 飛び跳ねていました。; to jump across the river かわを とびこえる・川を 飛び越える; to jump out of the window まどから とびおりる・窓から 飛び降りる; to jump the queue (British English) れつに わりこむ・列に 割り込む

jumper n (British English) セーター

June n ろくがつ・六月

junior high school n (US English) ちゅうがっこう・中学校

junior school n (British English) しょうがっこう・小学校

jury n ばいしんいん・陪審員

just¹ adv (very recently) use the 〜た form of verb + ところ;
I have just received the letter いま、てがみを もらった ところです。; I'm just, 今、手紙を もらった ところです。; I had just turned on the TV テレビを つけた ところでした。; (at this or that very moment) use the dictionary form of verb + ところ; I was just about to phone you でんわする ところ でした。・電話する ところでした。; I arrived just as he was leaving かれが うちを でる ところに わたしは つきました。・彼が 家を 出る ところに 私は 着きました。; (only) だけ; it was just 1000 yen せんえん だけでした。・千円 だけでした。; there are only two left ふたつ だけ のこっています。・二つ だけ 残っています。; (barely) I got there just in time ちょうど まにあいました。・ちょうど 間に合いました。; (when comparing) it takes just as long by train as by car でんしゃはくるまと おなじ くらい じかんが かかります。・電車は 車と 同じ くらい 時間が かかります。; (immediately) just before ちょくぜん・直前; just after ちょくご・直後

just² adj こうへい(な)・公平(な)

justice n せいぎ; legal system of justice しほう・司法

Kk

kangaroo n カンガルー

karate n からて・空手

keen adj ねっしん(な)・熱心(な); a keen student ねっしんながくせい・熱心な 学生; she is keen on dancing かのじょは ダンスが すきです。・彼女は ダンスが 好きです。

keep vb we keep the wine in the cellar ちかに ワインが おいてあります。・地下に ワインが 置いて あります。; to keep (someone) waiting (だれかを)またせる・(誰か

を待たせる; (to delay) what kept you? どうして おくれました か。・どうして 遅れましたか。; I won't keep you long ながく かかりません。・長く かかりません。; (to put) where do you keep the cups? カップは どこに ありますか。; (not to break, not to reveal) to keep a promise やくそくをまもる・約束を 守る; (to continue) pre ます form + つづける; to keep walking あるきつづける・歩き続ける; to keep calm おちつく・落ち着く; (if it's food) もつ・持つ; **keep away** keep away from the fire! ひから はなれなさい!・火から 離れなさい!; **keep out** to keep out of the sun にっこうを さける・日光を 避ける; **keep up** ついていく・ついて 行く; I can't keep up ついて いけません。・ついて 行けません。

kettle n やかん

key n かぎ・鍵

keyhole n かぎあな・鍵穴

kick vb ける; I kicked the ball ボールを けりました。; **kick off** しあいを かいしする・試合を 開始する; **kick out** おいだす・追い出す

kid n (a child) こども・子供

kidnap n ゆうかい・誘拐

kill vb ころす・殺す; to kill oneself じさつする・自殺する

kilo n キロ

kilogram(me) n キログラム

kilometre (British English), **kilometer** (US English) n キロメートル

kind 1 n it's a kind of... 〜の いっしゅです。・〜の 一種 です。; it's a kind of fish さかなの いっしゅです。・魚の 一種です。; what kind どんな; what kind of film is it? どんな えいがですか。・どんな 映画ですか。; what kind of car is it? どんなくるまですか。・どんな 車ですか。 **2** adj しんせつ(な)・親切(な)

king n こくおう・国王

kingdom n おうこく・王国

kiss 1 vb キスする; to kiss (each other) キスする **2** n キス

kitchen n だいどころ・台所

kite n たこ

kitten n こねこ・子猫

knee n ひざ・膝

kneel down vb ひざまずく

knife n ナイフ

knit vb あむ・編む

knock 1 vb ノックする; to knock on the door ドアを ノックする **2** n to get a knock on the head あたまを ぶつける; **knock down** (in a traffic accident) くるまに はねられる・車に 跳ねられる; (to demolish) とりこわす・取り壊す; **knock out** (to make unconscious) ノックアウトする; **knock over** (in a traffic accident) はねる・跳ねる; (a drink) こぼす

knot n むすびめ・結び目

know vb (understand) わかる・分かる; I know why he phoned かれが どうして でんわしたか わかります。・彼が どうして 電話したか 分かります。; (be informed about) しる・知る; I don't know the Japanese word for it にほんごでなんと いうか しりません。・日本語で 何というか 知りません。; he knows everything かれは なんでも しっています。・彼は 何でも 知っています。; to know all about films えいがの ことを なんでも しっている・映画の ことを 何でも 知っている; to get to know (someone) (だれかと) しりあいに なる・(誰かと) 知り合いに なる; let me know しらせてください・知らせてください。! Note that when positive, しる is only used in the present or past progressive forms しっている and しっていた but when negative it becomes either しらない or しらなかった。

knowledge n ちしき・知識

LI

laboratory *n* (institution) けんきゅうじょ・研究所; (room) じっけんしつ・実験室; (school laboratory) りかしつ・理科室

lace *n* (the material) レース; (for shoes) ひも・紐; to tie one's laces ひもを むすぶ・紐を 結ぶ

lack 1 *n* lack of food たべものが ない・食べ物が ない; lack of money おかねが ない・お金が ない **2** *vb* ない; he lacks confidence かれは じしんが ありません。・彼は 自信が ありません。

ladder *n* はしご

lady *n* じょせい・女性

lake *n* みずうみ・湖

lamb *n* (animal) こひつじ・子羊; (meat) ラム

lamp *n* ランプ; (desk-lamp) スタンド

lampshade *n* ランプの かさ

land 1 *n* (as opposed to the sea) りく・陸; (property) とち・土地; to own land とちを もつ・土地を 持つ **2** *vb* (to fall) おちる・落ちる; (if it's a plane) ちゃくりくする・着陸する

landscape *n* けしき・景色

language *n* げんご・言語; foreign language がいこくご・外国語; bad language げひんな ことば・下品な 言葉

language laboratory *n* ランゲージラボラトリー

large *adj* (big) おおきい・大きい; (large in area) ひろい・広い; large garden ひろい にわ・広い 庭; large room ひろい へや・広い 部屋

last 1 *adj* まえの・前の; my last place of work まえの しょくば・前の 職場; last week せんしゅう・先週; last

month せんげつ・先月; last year きょねん・去年 **2** *adv* (*most recently*) この あいだ・この 間 *not used in formal Japanese*; when I last came here この あいだ ここに きた とき・この 間 ここに 来た とき; (*at the end*) さいご (に)・最後(に); I'll do the dishes last (of all) さいごに しょっきを あらいます。・最後に 食器を 洗います。; (*in final position*) he came last in the race かれは いちばん さいごでした。・彼は 一番 最後でした。**3** *pron* the last さいご・最後; they were the last to arrive かれらは さいごに つきました。・彼らは 最後に 着きました。; the night before last おとといの よる・おとといの 夜 **4** *vb* つづく・続く; the film lasts two hours えいがは にじかん つづきます。・映画は 二時間 続きます。

late 1 *adv* (*far into the day or night*) おそい・遅い; late in the afternoon ゆうがた・夕方; it's getting late おそく なっています。・遅く なっています。; (*not on time*) to arrive half an hour late さんじゅっぷん おくれる・三十分 遅れる **2** *adj* おくれている・遅れている; to be late for work しごとに おくれている・仕事に 遅れている; the train was two hours late でんしゃは にじかん おくれました。・電車は 二時間 遅れました。; to make (someone) late (だれかを)おくらせる・(誰かを)遅らせる

later *adv* あとで・後で; I'll call back later あとで また でんわします。・後で また 電話します。; see you later! また あとで。・また 後で。

latest 1 *adj* さいきん(の)・最近(の); the latest news さいきんの ニュース・最近の ニュース **2** **at the latest** おそくとも・遅くとも

Latin *n* ラテンご・ラテン語

laugh 1 *vb* わらう・笑う; to laugh at a joke じょうだんに わらう・冗談に 笑う; to make (someone) laugh (だれかを)わらわせる・(誰かを) 笑わせる; to laugh at (someone) (だれかを) ばかに する・(誰かを) ばかに する

laundry *n* せんたくもの・洗濯物; to do the laundry せんたくする・洗濯する

law n (a set of rules in a country) ほうりつ・法律; to obey the law ほうりつを まもる・法律を 守る; it's against the law ふほうです。・不法です。; (a rule) the law of gravity じゅうりょくのほうそく・重力の 法則; (as a subject) ほうがく・法学

lawn n しばふ・芝生

lawnmower n しばかりき・芝刈機

lawyer n べんごし・弁護士

lay vb (to put) おく・置く; lay some newspapers on the floor しんぶんを ゆかに おく・新聞を 床に置く; (to spread) しく・敷く; to lay a carpet じゅうたんを しく・絨毯を 敷く; to lay the table テーブルに しょっきを ならべる・テーブルに 食器を 並べる; (of a chicken) to lay an egg たまごを うむ・卵を 産む; **lay down** おく・置く; I laid the tray down on the table おぼんを テーブルの うえに おきました。・お盆を テーブルの 上に 置きました。; **lay off** かいこする・解雇する

lazy adj lazy person なまけもの・怠け者

lead¹ vb (to guide) いく・行く; this road will lead you to the village この みちは むらに いきます。・この 道は 村に 行きます。; (in sport) せんとうに たつ・先頭に 立つ; to lead a busy life いそがしい せいかつを おくる・忙しい 生活を 送る; (to have as a result) to lead to an accident じこになる・事故に なる

lead² n (metal) なまり・鉛; (in a pencil) しん・芯

leader n リーダー

leaf n individual leaf は・葉; leaves はっぱ・葉っぱ

leak vb もれる・漏れる; water is leaking from the pipe パイプから みずが もれています。・パイプから 水が 漏れています。; in Japanese pipes don't leak, the water leaks (from the pipe)

lean 1 vb (to support oneself) to lean against the wall かべに よりかかる・壁に よりかかる; (to put) to lean a bicycle against the wall じてんしゃを かべに もたせかける・自転車を 壁に もたせかける; to lean out of the window

まどからのりだす・窓から 乗り出す **2** *adj* (person)
やせた; (meat) あかみ(の)・赤身(の); lean back うし
ろへ もたれる・後ろへ もたれる; lean forward まえに
かがむ・前に かがむ; lean on よりかかる

learn *vb* ならう・習う; to learn how to drive くるまの
うんてんをならう・車の 運転を 習う

leash *n* ひも・紐

least 1 *det* the least いちばんすくない・一番少ない;
I have the least money わたしの もっている おかねが い
ちばんすくないです。・私の 持っている お金が 一番
少ないです。**2** *pron* it was the least I could do! たいした
おかまいもしていません。・たいした お構いも して
いません。**3** *adv* the least いちばん + opposite adjective;
the least expensive shop いちばんやすい みせ・一番安
い店; the least difficult question いちばんかんたんな
しつもん・一番簡単な 質問 **4** at least (at the minimum)
すくなくとも・少なくとも; he's at least thirty かれは す
くなくともさんじゅっさいです。・彼は 少なくとも
三十才です。; (when expressing some doubt) he's gone
out—at least, I think so かれは でかけたと おもいます。・
彼は 出かけたと 思います。

leather *n* かわ・革

leave *vb* (to go away) でる・出る; to leave school (graduate)
そつぎょうする・卒業する; to leave school (go home)
がっこうからかえる・学校から 帰る; she left her
husband かのじょは うちを でました。・彼女は 家を
出ました。; I left the next day つぎの ひ、でました。・
次の日、出ました。; (to go out of) でる・出る; I left the
room へやを でました。・部屋を 出ました。; (to allow to
remain) おいて おく・置いて おく; leave your coat here
ここにコートを おいて おいてください。・ここに
コートを置いて おいてください。; I left the window open
(deliberately) まどを あけて おきました。・窓を 開けて
おきました。; I left the window open (by accident) まどを あ
けっぱなしにしました。・窓を 開けっ放しに しまし
た。; (to put, to give) のこす・残す; I didn't leave a message

メッセージをのこしませんでした。・メッセージを残しませんでした。; I left him some money かれに おかねをのこして あげました。・彼に お金を 残して あげました。; (to put off) のばす・延ばす; let's leave it until tomorrow あしたまでのばしましょう。・明日まで延ばしましょう。; (to remain) のこる・残る; there's nothing left なにも のこっていません。・何も 残っていません。; we've got ten minutes left あと じゅっぷん あります。・後 十分 あります。; (other uses) I left it up to them かれらに まかせました。・彼らに 任せました。; **leave behind** おきわすれる・置き忘れる; I left my bag behind かばんを おきわすれました。・かばんを 置き忘れました。; **leave out** (not to show or talk about) (by accident) pre ます form + わすれる; (deliberately) 〜ない + ように する; (to exclude (a person)) なかまはずれにする; to feel left out なかまはずれに なっている・仲間はずれに なっている; **leave over** there was not much left over あまり のこっていませんでした。・あまり 残っていませんでした。; there is some food left over たべものが のこっています・食べ物が 残っています。

lecture n (to students) こうぎ・講義; (to the public) こうえん・講演

left 1 n ひだり・左; please take the first street on the left さいしょの みちを ひだりに はいってください。・最初の 道を 左に 入ってください。 **2** adj ひだり(の)・左(の); left hand ひだりて・左手; left handed ひだりきき・左利き **3** adv ひだりに・左に; to turn left ひだりに まがる・左に 曲がる

leg n (of a person or animal) あし・足; (of meat) もも

legal adj ほうてき(な)・法的(な)

leisure n レジャー

leisure centre (British English), **leisure center** (US English) n レジャーセンター

lemon n レモン

lemonade n レモネード

lend *vb* かす・貸す; to lend (someone) money (だれかに) おかねを かす・(誰かに) お金を 貸す

length *n* ながさ・長さ

leopard *n* ひょう・豹

less 1 *det* もっと すくない・もっと 少ない; less money もっとすくない おかね・もっと 少ない お金; I have less work than he does かれより しごとが すくないで す・彼より 仕事が 少ないです。**2** *pron* it costs less もっとやすいです。・もっと 安いです。; he reads less than she does かのじょは かれより おおく よんでいま す・彼女は 彼より 多く 読んでいます。; my book is less useful than his book わたしの ほんは かれの ほど やくにたちません。・私の 本は 彼の ほど 役に 立ち ません。**3** *adv* we travel less in winter ふゆは あまり りょ こうしません。・冬は あまり 旅行しません。**4** *prep* (minus) ひく **5** less and less だんだん すくなく・だん だん 少なく; there is less and less time だんだん じかん がすくなく なります。・だんだん 時間が 少なくな ります。**1** less than 〜いか・〜以下; less than 1000 yen せんえんいか・千円以下; in less than half an hour さん じゅっぷんいか・三十分以内

lesson *n* じゅぎょう・授業; Japanese lesson にほんご のじゅぎょう・日本語の 授業

let¹ *vb* (when making suggestions) let's go home かえりまし ょう。・帰りましょう。; let's go! いきましょう。・行き ましょう。; (to allow) Let often can be expressed using the causative form of the verb; my father let me go to and study abroad ちちは りゅうがく させて くれました。・父は 留学させて くれました。; I let him do what he likes かれは すきなままに させています。・彼を 好きな ままに させています。; I'm letting my hair grow かみのけを のばし っぱなしにしています。・髪の毛を 伸ばしっぱな しにしています。; **let down** がっかりさせる; **let go** (to stop holding) はなす・放す; please let go of me はなして ください。・放して ください。; (to release (animal)) かい ほうする・解放する; (to release (prisoner)) しゃくほう

する・釈放する; **let in** (to a room or house) いれる・入れる; he let me in かれは わたしを いれて くれました。・彼は 私を 入れて くれました。; the roof lets in the rain やねが あまもりする・屋根が 雨漏りする; **let out** (to let the air out of a tyre) タイヤの くうきを ぬく・タイヤの 空気を 抜く; let me out! だしてください。・出してください。; to let out a scream ひめいを あげる・悲鳴をあげる; **let through** to let (someone) through (だれかを)とおしてあげる・(誰かを)通して あげる

let² vb (British English) かす・貸す

letter n てがみ・手紙; (of the alphabet) もじ・文字

letter box n (British English) ゆうびんうけ・郵便受け

lettuce n レタス

level 1 n レベル **2** adj たいら(な)・平ら(な)

liar n うそつき・嘘つき

library n としょかん・図書館

licence (British English), **license** (US English) n めんきょ・免許; driving licence うんてんめんきょしょう・運転免許証

license plate n (US English) ナンバープレート

lick vb なめる

lid n ふた

lie 1 vb (on the ground, on a bed) よこに なる・横に なる; I lay down on the sofa ソファーに よこに なりました。・ソファーに 横に なりました。; (to be situated) ある; (not to tell the truth) うそを つく・嘘を つく **2** n うそ・嘘; to tell a lie うそを つく・嘘を つく; **lie around** my children leave their toys lying around うちの こどもは おもちゃを あちこちに おきっぱなしに します。・家の 子供は おもちゃを あちこちに 置きっぱなしに します。; **lie down** よこに なる・横に なる

life n (human life in general) じんせい・人生; (state of being alive) いのち・命; (lifespan) いっしょう・一生; (life expectancy) じゅみょう・寿命; (everyday life) せいかつ・生活

lifestyle n ライフスタイル

lift 1 vb あげる・上げる; to lift one's arm うでを あげる・腕を 上げる; to lift a lid ふたを あげる・ふたを 上げる **2** n (British English) (an elevator) エレベーター; (in a car) to give (someone) a lift to the station (だれかを) えきに おくってあげる・(誰かを) 駅に 送って あげる; **lift up** もちあげる・持ち上げる

light 1 n (from the sun, moon) ひかり・光; (in a room, on a machine) でんき・電気; to switch on a light でんきを つける・電気を 点ける; (for traffic) the lights are green しんごうは あおです。・信号は 青です。; (in a street) a light あかり・明かり; have you got a light? ライターを おもちですか。・ライターを お持ちですか。 **2** adj (not dark) not usually used to describe colours; it's still light outside そとは まだ あかるいです。・外は まだ 明るいです。; (not heavy) かるい・軽い **3** vb ひを つける・火を 点ける; I lit a cigarette たばこに ひを つけました。・たばこに 火を 点けました。; to light a fire ひを たく・火を たく

light bulb n でんきゅう・電球

lighthouse n とうだい・燈台

lightning n いなずま・稲妻

like¹ prep people us like us わたしたちの ような ひと・私達の ような 人; what's it like? どうですか。

like² vb (when expressing an interest) すき・好き not a verb in Japanese; I like dancing ダンスが すきです。・ダンスが 好きです。; I like it! すきです。・好きです。; how do you like America? アメリカは どうですか。; (when expressing a wish) pre ます form of the verb + たい; I'd like to live here ここに すみたいです。・ここに 住みたいです。; (when ordering food and drink) 〜を ください; I'd like coffee please コーヒーを ください。

limit n かぎり・限り

line n せん・線; straight line まっすぐの せん・真っ直ぐの 線; (US English) (a queue) れつ・列; to stand in line れつにならぶ・列に 並ぶ; (a row) れつ・列; (lines in

play|film) せりふ; (line of writing) ぎょう・行; (telephone line) でんせん・電話線 the line is engaged はなしちゅうです。・話し中です。 **2** vb to be lined with trees きがならんでいる・木が並んでいる

link vb (by train) むすぶ・結ぶ; to link Paris to London パリとロンドンをむすぶ・パリ と ロンドン を 結ぶ; (to make a connection between) れんけつする・連結する; the two murders are linked ふたつの さつじんじけんは かんれんしています。・二つの 殺人事件は 関連して います。

lion n ライオン

lip n くちびる・唇

lipstick n くちべに・口紅

liquid 1 n えき・液 **2** adj えきたい(の)・液体(の)

list n リスト

listen vb きく・聞く; to listen to someone だれかに きく・誰かに 聞く

litre (British English), **liter** (US English) n リットル

little¹ 1 det すこし(の)・少し(の); little wine ワイン・少しの ワイン; there is very little time じかんが あまりありません。・時間が あまり ありません。 **2** pron a little すこし だけ・少し だけ; I only ate a little すこしだけ たべました。・少し だけ 食べました。 **3** adv すこし・少し **4** a little (bit) ちょっと **5** little by little すこしずつ・少しずつ

little² adj ちいさい・小さい

live¹ vb (to have one's home) すむ・住む; I live in London ロンドンにすんでいます。・ロンドンに 住んでいます。; (to be alive) いきる・生きる; (to lead a life) くらす・暮らす; that's not enough to live on せいかつ できる ほど ではありません。・生活 できる ほどではありません。

live² adj (alive) いきている・生きている; (of a match, a show) なま(の)・生(の)

lively adj (person) げんき(な)・元気(な); (town, party) にぎやか(な)

living room n (Japanese style) ちゃ の ま・茶 の 間; (Western style) リビング

load n (on a truck, being carried) かもつ・貨物; loads of money たくさん の おかね・たくさん の お金

loaf n パン

loan n ローン

lobster n ロブスター

local adj じもと(の)・地元(の); a local newspaper ちほう の しんぶん・地方の 新聞; the local people じもと との ひと・地元の 人

lock 1 vb かぎ を かける・鍵 を かける; I locked the door ドア の かぎ を かけました。・ドア の 鍵 を かけました。2 n かぎ・鍵; a bicycle lock じてんしゃ の ロック・自転車 の ロック; lock in to lock (someone) in (だれか を) とじこめる・(誰かを)閉じ込める

locker n ロッカー

logical adj ろんりてき(な)・論理的(な)

London n ロンドン

lonely adj さびしい・寂しい

long 1 adj ながい・長い; a long letter ながい てがみ・長い手紙; long hair ちょうはつ・長髪; the film is two hours long えいが は にじかん です。・映画 は 二時間 です。; I haven't seen him for a long time かれに ながい あいだ あっていません。・彼に 長い 間 会っていません。2 adv ながく・長く; long ago むかし・昔; please stay as long as you like すき な だけ とまって ください。・好き な だけ 泊まって ください。; I won't be long ながく かかりません。・長く かかりません。3 as long as Use a conditional form of the verb; as long as the weather is nice てんき が よければ・天気 が 良ければ; as long as you ring me でんわ さえ すれば・電話 さえ すれば

look 1 vb みる・見る; to look at a picture え を みる・絵 を 見る; to look out of the window まど から みる・窓 から 見る; (to appear) to look tired つかれている ように み

える・疲れている ように 見え; to look well げんきに
みえる・元気に 見える; he looks young かれは わかく
みえる。彼は 若く 見えます。; she looks like her
mother かのじょは おかあさんに にています。彼女
は お母さんに 似ています。; what does it look like? どの
ような ものですか。・どの ような 物ですか。; **look
after** めんどうをみる・面倒を 見る; to look after a child
こどものめんどうをみる・子供の 面倒を 見る; **look
down** (to lower one's eyes) めを ふせる・目を 伏せる; to
look down on someone だれかを けいべつする・誰かを
軽蔑する; **look for** さがす・探す; I am looking for a job
しごとをさがしています。・仕事を 探しています。;
look forward to I am looking forward to meeting her かのじょ
にあうのを たのしみに しています。・彼女に 会う
のを 楽しみに しています。; **look onto** ながめる・
眺める; my room looks onto the garden わたしの へやは
にわにめんしています。・私の 部屋は 庭に 面してい
ます。; **look out** ちゅういする・注意する; **look up to**
look up a word in a dictionary じしょでことばを しらべる
・辞書で 言葉を 調べる; (to raise one's eyes) みあげる・
見上げる

loose adj (describing clothes) ゆったりした; (describing a
screw) ゆるい・緩い

lorry n (British English) トラック

lose vb なくす

lost adj to get lost みちに まよう・道に 迷う; lost property
おとしもの・落とし物; lost property office いしつぶつ
とりあつかいじょ・遺失物取扱所

lot pron a lot たくさん; I eat a lot たくさん たべます。・
たくさん 食べます。; a lot of money たくさんの おかね・
たくさんのお金; there's not a lot left たくさんは のこって
いません。・たくさんは 残っていません。

lottery n たからくじ・宝くじ

loud adj (too noisy) うるさい; to talk in a loud voice おおきい
こえではなす・大きい 声で 話す

loudspeaker *n* スピーカー

lounge *n* (*Japanese style*) いま・居間; (*Western style*) リビング; (*in a hotel*) ラウンジ

love 1 *vb* (*when talking about people*) あいする・愛する; to love each other おたがいに あいしあう・お互いに 愛し合う; (*when talking about things, activities*) だいすき・大好き; I love reading どくしょが だいすきです。・読書が大好きです。 **2** *n* あい・愛; to be in love あいしている・愛している; to make love セックスする

lovely *adj* (*beautiful*) きれい(な); a lovely apartment きれいな アパート; you've got lovely eyes めが きれいです。・目が きれいです。; (*very nice, kind*) すてき(な)・素敵(な)

low 1 *adj* ひくい・低い; to speak in a low voice ひくい こえではなす・低い 声で 話す **2** *adv* to turn the music down low おんがくの おとを ちいさく する・音楽の音を小さくする

lower *vb* さげる・下げる

loyal *adj* ちゅうじつ(な)・忠実(な)

luck *n* うん・運; good luck! がんばってください。・頑張ってください。; to bring someone (good) luck だれかにこううんをまねく・誰かに 幸運を 招く

lucky *adj* to be lucky ラッキー(な)

luggage *n* にもつ・荷物

lunch *n* ひるごはん・昼ご飯

lunchbreak *n* ひるやすみ・昼休み

lung *n* はい・肺

luxurious *adj* ぜいたく(な)・贅沢(な)

luxury 1 *n* せいたく・贅沢 **2** *adj* luxury hotel ごうかなホテル・豪華な ホテル

lyric *n* かし・歌詞

Mm

machine *n* きかい・機械

mad *adj* (crazy) きちがい(の)・気違い(の); (very angry)
ひどくおこっている・ひどく怒っている; mad about
(someone) (だれかに)むちゅう・(誰かに)夢中

magazine *n* ざっし・雑誌

magic *adj* まほう(の)・魔法(の)

maiden name *n* きゅうせい・旧姓

mail 1 *n* (the postal system) ゆうびん・郵便; (letters) ゆう
びんぶつ・郵便物 **2** *vb* (US English) to mail a letter (to
someone) (だれかに)てがみを だす・(誰かに)手紙を
出す

mailbox *n* (US English) ポスト

mailman *n* (US English) ゆうびんや・郵便屋

main *adj* おも(な)・主(な)

main course *n* (western-style meal) メイン

major 1 *adj* じゅうよう(な)・重要(な) a major event
じゅうようなできごと・重要な 出来事 **2** *n* しょうさ
・少佐

majority *n* かはんすう・過半数

make *vb* **!** Note that the word make can often be translated by
つくる. This entry covers the most frequent uses of make but to
find translations for other expressions like to make a mess, to
make a mistake, to make sure etc, look up the entries at mess,
mistake, sure etc.; to make つくる・作る; to make a film え
いがを とる・映画を 撮る; to make some coffee コーヒ
ーをいれる・コーヒーを 入れる; to make a phone call
でんわをかける・電話を かける; to make friends とも
だちができる・友達が できる; to make friends with
someone だれかと ともだちに なる・誰かと 友達に

なる; to make breakfast あさごはんを つくる ・ 朝ご飯を作る; to be made of gold きんで できている ・ 金でできている; to be made in Japan にほんせい ・ 日本製; to be made in Canada カナダせい ・ カナダ製; (to cause a particular reaction) Use the causative form of the verb; to make (someone) happy (だれかを)よろこばせる ・ (誰かを)喜ばせる; to make (someone) jealous (だれかを)しっとさせる ・ (誰かを)嫉妬させる; to make (someone) annoyed (だれかを)いらいらさせる ・ (誰かを)食べさせる; to make (someone) cry (だれかを)なかせる ・ (誰かを)泣かせる; to make (someone) eat (だれかを)たべさせる ・ (誰かを)食べさせる; to make (someone) laugh (だれかを)わらわせる ・ (誰かを)笑わせる Note that often it is preferred in Japanese to use the expression to become... rather than to make...For example in English we might say "The medicine made him sleepy", in Japanese it would be preferable to say "He took some medicine and became sleepy"; to make (someone) wait (だれかを)またせる ・ (誰かを)待たせる; (to earn) to make a lot of money たくさん おかねを かせぐ ・ たくさん お金を稼ぐ; to make a profit りえきを える ・ 利益を得る; **make do** まにあわせる ・ 間に合わせる; **make out** to make out a list リストを つくる ・ リストを作る; **make up** (to be friends again) なかなおりを する ・ 仲直りをする; to make up an excuse いいわけを かんがえる ・ 言い訳を考える; to make up a parcel にづくりする ・ 荷造りする

make-up n けしょうひん ・ 化粧品; to wear make-up けしょうする ・ 化粧する

male adj (in biology) おす(の) ・ 雄(の); (relating to men) おとこ(の) ・ 男(の)

man n おとこのひと ・ 男の人; (as a species) じんるい ・ 人類

manage vb (to run) けいえいする ・ 経営する; to manage to finish one's homework なんとか しゅくだいを おわらせる ・ 何とか 宿題を 終わらせる

manager n (of a project, a hotel) しはいにん ・ 支配人; (of a shop, a bank) てんちょう ・ 店長; (of a football team) マネ

ージャー; (senior manager in large company) ぶちょう・部長; (line manager) かちょう・課長

manners n マナー; good manners マナーが いい; bad manners マナーが わるい・マナーが 悪い

manufacture vb せいぞうする・製造する

many 1 det (a lot of) たくさん; were there many tourists? たくさん かんこうきゃくが いましたか。・たくさん 観光客が いましたか。; not many あまり + negative verb; there weren't many people there あまり ひとが いませんでした。・あまり 人が いませんでした。; (when used with how, too, so, as) how many? いくつ or なん + counter; how many books have you got? ほんが なんさつ あります か。・本が 何冊 ありますか。; too many pre ます form of the verb + すぎる; you eat too many chips ポテトフライを たべすぎます。・ポテトフライを 食べ過ぎます。; there are so many things to do たくさん する ことが あり ます。; I got as many presents as you did あなたと おなじ ぐらい プレゼントを もらいました。・あなたと 同じ ぐらい プレゼントを もらいました。**2** pron are there many left? たくさん のこっていますか。・たくさん 残 っていますか。; I've got too many ありすぎます。・あり 過ぎます。; take as many as you like すきなだけ いくら でもとってください。・好きなだけ 取っ てください。; many (of them) speak English えいごの はな せるひとが おおいです。・英語の 話せる 人が 多い です。

map n ちず・地図

marble n だいりせき・大理石

marbles n ビーだま・ビー玉

march vb (in the army) こうしんする・行進する; (in a demonstration) デモこうしんを する・デモ行進を する

March n さんがつ・三月

margarine n マーガリン

mark 1 n (on clothes) しみ・染み; (to indicate something) しるし・印; (damage to a surface) きず・傷; to leave

coffee cup marks on the table テーブルに コーヒーカップ のあとを つける ・ テーブルに コーヒーカップの 跡をつける; (British English) (a grade) せいせき ・ 成績; to get good marks いい せいせきを とる ・ いい 成績を とる 2 vb (to stain) しみをつける ・ 染みを 付ける; to mark the homework しゅくだいを チェックする ・ 宿題 をチェックする; to mark an exam しけんを さいてんす る ・ 試験を 採点する; (to indicate) しめす ・ 示す

market n (the place) いちば ・ 市場; a flea market のみの いち ・ 蚤の 市; (the system) しじょう ・ 市場; the stock market かぶしきしじょう ・ 株式市場

marketing n マーケティング

marmalade n マーマレード

marriage n けっこん ・ 結婚

married adj けっこんしている ・ 結婚している; to be married (to someone) (だれかと) けっこんしている ・ (誰かと)結婚している

marry vb to marry (someone) (だれかと) けっこんする ・ (誰かと)結婚する

marsh n ぬまち ・ 沼地

mashed potatoes n マッシュポテト

mask n マスク

mat n マット

match 1 n (British English) (a game) しあい ・ 試合; a football match サッカーの しあい ・ サッカーの 試合; (a matchstick) マッチ 2 vb the shoes match the belt くつは ベルトにあいます。・ 靴は ベルトに 合います。

mate n (British English) なかま ・ 仲間; workmate しごとな かま ・ 仕事仲間

material n きじ ・ 生地

math (US English), **maths** (British English) n すうがく ・ 数学

mathematics n (school subject) すうがく ・ 数学; (calculations) さんすう ・ 算数

matter 1 *n* what's the matter? どうしましたか。 *A more emotive way to ask is* どうしたんですか。; what's the matter with her? かのじょは どうしましたか。・彼女は どう しましたか。 **2** *vb* it doesn't matter たいした ことではあ りません。・大した ことではありません。

maximum 1 *adj* the maximum price さいこうかかく・ 最高価格; a maximum temperature of 30 degrees (weather) さいこうきおんさんじゅうど・最高気温 三十度 **2** *n* さいだいげん・最大限

may *vb* (when talking about a possibility) plain form + かもしれ ない; they may be able to come かれらは これる かも しれません。・彼らは 来られる かもしれません。; she may not have seen him かのじょは かれを みなかった かもしれません。・彼女は 彼を 見なかった かもし れません。; it may rain あめが ふる かもしれません。・ 雨が 降る かもしれません。; (when asking for or giving permission) 〜て form of the verb + も いいです(か)。; may I come in? はいっても いいですか。・入っても いいで すか。; you may sit down すわっても いいです。・座っ ても いいです。

May *n* ごがつ・五月

maybe *adv* たぶん・多分 ! Note that たぶん often indicates a higher probability than 'maybe' does in English and is more similar to 'probably'

mayor *n* (of a city) しちょう・市長 (of a town) ちょうち ょう・町長 (of a village) そんちょう・村長

me *pron* Note that わたし can often be left out if it is obvious. わたし・私; they asked me かれらは わたしに ききま した。・彼らは 私に 聞きました。; he hit me かれは わたしを ぶちました。・彼は 私を ぶちました。; please help me! たすけてください。・助けてください。; please don't bother me! じゃまを しないでください。・ 邪魔を しないでください。; she gave the book to me かの じょは ほんを くれました。・彼女は 本を くれまし た。; please show it to me! みせてください。・見せてく ださい。; in front of me わたしの まえ・私の 前

meal n しょくじ・食事

mean 1 vb to mean いみする・意味する; what does that
mean? それは どう いう いみですか。・それは どう
いう 意味ですか。; what does じしょ mean? じしょは
どう いう いみですか。・辞書は どう いう 意味ですか。; (to have as a result) it means giving up my job しごとを
やめる ことに なります。・仕事を 辞める ことに な
ります。; (to intend) I meant to order a pizza ピザを ちゅう
もんする つもりでした。・ピザを 注文する つもりで
した。; I didn't mean to say that そう いう つもりではあ
りませんでした。・そう 言う つもりではありません
でした。; I meant it as a joke じょうだんの つもりでした。・
冗談の つもりでした。; (to intend to say) what do you
mean? どう いう ことですか。; her work means a lot to her
かのじょにとって しごとは たいせつです。・彼女に
とって 仕事は 大切です。; money doesn't mean much to
him おかねは かれに たいせつではありません。・お
金は 彼に 大切ではありません。**2** adj (British English)
(not generous) けち(な); to be mean to someone
だれかを いじめる・誰かを いじめる

meaning n いみ・意味

means n ほうほう・方法; a means of earning money おか
ねを かせぐ ほうほう・お金を 稼ぐ 方法; a means of
transport こうつうしゅだん・交通手段

meant to be meant to vb I'm meant to be at my parents'
house ほんとうは りょうしんの うちに いる はずで
す。・本当は 両親の 家に いる はずです。; it's meant to
be difficult むずかしい はずです。・難しい はずです。

meanwhile adv その あいだに・その 間に

measles n はしか

measure vb はかる・測る

meat n にく・肉

mechanic n じどうしゃせいびし・自動車整備士

medal n メダル; gold medal きんメダル・金メダル

media n マスメディア

medical adj いがくてき(な)・医学的(な); to have medical treatment ちりょうを うける・治療を 受ける

medicine n くすり・薬

Mediterranean n ちちゅうかい・地中海

medium adj ちゅうくらい(の)・中くらい(の)

meet vb (by accident or appointment) あう・会う; I met him at the supermarket かれに スーパーで あいました。・彼に スーパーで 会いました。; can we meet (up) next week? らいしゅう また あいませんか。・来週 また 会いませんか。; to meet again また あう・また 会う; (to be introduced to) しりあいに なる・知り合いに なる; I met him at a wedding かれと けっこんしきで しりあいに なりました。・彼と 結婚式で 知り合いに なりました。; (to fetch) むかえに いく・迎えに 行く; I can meet you at the station えきに むかえに いけます。・駅に 迎えに 行けます。; can you meet me at the station? えきに むかえに こられますか。・駅に 迎えに 来られますか。; (to have a meeting) かいぎする・会議する

meeting n かいぎ・会議

melon n メロン

melt vb the snow is melting ゆきが とけています。・雪が 溶けています。; the salt will melt the ice しおは こおりを とかします。・塩は 氷を 溶かします。

member n かいいん・会員; a member of staff (in a school) きょういん・教員; (in a bank) ぎんこういん・銀行員; (in a company) かいしゃいん・会社員

memory n きおく・記憶; good memory きおくが いい・記憶が いい; he's got a bad memory かれは きおくが わるいです。・彼は 記憶が 悪いです。; (of a person, a place or time) おもいで・思い出

mend vb (to fix) しゅうりする・修理する; (by sewing) つくろう・繕う

mental adj せいしんてき(な)・精神的(な); mental illness せいしんびょう・精神病

menu n メニュー

mess *n* my room is in a mess へやが ちらかっています。・部屋が 散らかっています。; to make a mess in the kitchen だいどころを ちらかす・台所を 散らかす

message *n* メッセージ

metal *n* きんぞく・金属

method *n* ほうほう・方法

metre (*British English*), **meter** (*US English*) *n* メートル

Mexico *n* メキシコ

microphone *n* マイク

microwave oven *n* でんしレンジ・電子レンジ

midday *n* おひる・お昼; at midday おひるに・お昼に

middle *n* まんなか・真ん中; in the middle of the road みちの まんなかに・道の 真ん中に; I'm in the middle of cooking a meal りょうりの とちゅうです。・料理の 途中です。; she's in the middle of writing a letter かのじょは てがみを かいている ところです。・彼女は 手紙を 書いている ところです。

middle-aged *adj* ちゅうねん(の)・中年(の)

midnight *n* よる じゅうにじ・夜 十二時; at midnight よるじゅうにじに・夜 十二時に

might *vb* (*when talking about a possibility*) plain form + かもしれない; her answer might be right かのじょの こたえが あっているかもしれません。・彼女の 答えが 合っているかもしれません。; they might have got lost かれらは みちに まよった かもしれません。・彼らは 道に 迷ったかもしれません。; 'will you come?'—'I might' 「きますか。」「いくかもしれません。」・「来ますか。」「行くかもしれません。」; we might miss the plane ひこうきに まにあわない かもしれません。・飛行機に 間に合わないかもしれません。; he said he might not come かれはたぶん いけないと いいました。・彼は 多分 行けないと 言いました。; (*when implying something didn't happen*) you might have been killed! しんだ かもしれません。・死んだかもしれません。; you might have warned us なにかいってくれれば よかったのに。・何か 言って くれれ

ば 良かった のに。; (when making suggestions) you might try leaving a message メッセージ を のこす のは どうです か。・ メッセージ を 残す のは どうですか。; it might be better to wait まつ のは どうですか。・ 待つ のは どうで すか。

mild adj おだやか（な）・ 穏やか（な）; the weather's mild, it's mild おだやか な てんきです。・ 穏やか な 天気です。

mile n マイル！ Note that a mile 1609 m.

military adj ぐんたい（の）・ 軍隊（の）

milk 1 n ぎゅうにゅう・ 牛乳

milkman n ぎゅうにゅうはいたつにん・ 牛乳配達人
❗ note that milk delivery is rare in Japan

million num ひゃくまん・ 百万; three million dollars さん びゃくまんドル・ 三百万ドル; a million inhabitants ひゃ くまんにんのじんこう・ 百万人の 人口

mind 1 n かんがえ・ 考え; I have a lot on my mind かんが える ことが いっぱいです。考える ことが いっぱい です。; to make up one's mind きめる・ 決める; I changed my mind きが かわりました。・ 気が 変わりました。
2 vb (when expressing an opinion) I don't mind かまいませ ん。; 'where shall we go?'—'I don't mind' 「どこに いきま しょうか。」「どこでも いいです。」・「どこに 行きま しょうか。」「どこでも いいです。」; I don't mind the heat あつくても かまいません。・ 暑くても かまいませ ん。; (in polite questions or requests) do you mind if I smoke? たばこを すっても いいですか。・ たばこを 吸っても いいですか。; would you mind closing the door? ドアを し めてください。・ ドアを 閉めてください。; (to be careful) mind the steps! だんさに ちゅういしてくださ い。・ 段差に 注意してください。; mind you don't break the glass グラスを わらない ように きを つけてくださ い。・ グラスを 割らない ように 気を つけてくださ い。; (to take care of) めんどうを みる・ 面倒を 見る; never mind, I'll get the next train しんぱいしないでくださ い。つぎの でんしゃに のります。・ 心配しないでく ださい。次の 電車に 乗ります。

mine¹ *pron* わたしの ・ 私の; the red pen is mine あかい ペンはわたしのです。・ 赤い ペンは 私のです。

mine² *n* こうざん ・ 鉱山

miner *n* こうざんろうどうしゃ ・ 鉱山労働者

mineral water *n* ミネラルウォーター

minimum 1 *adj* さいてい ・ 最低; the minimum temperature will be 15 degrees さいてい きおんは じゅう ごどです。・ 最低 気温は 十五度です。**2** *n* さいてい ・ 最低

minister *n* (in government) だいじん ・ 大臣; the minister for Education もんぶだいじん ・ 文部大臣; (in religion) ぼくし ・ 牧師

minor *adj* じゅうようではない ・ 重要ではない; minor injury けいしょう ・ 軽症

minority *n* しょうすう ・ 少数; ethnic minority しょうすう みんぞく ・ 少数民族

minus *prep* four minus three is one よん ひく さんは いち です。・ 四 引く 三は 一です。; it's minus four outside そ とはマイナスよんどです。・ 外は マイナス四度です。

minute *n* ふん ・ 分; they'll be here any minute now かれらは もうすぐつきます。・ 彼らは もう すぐ 着きます。

mirror *n* (on a wall) かがみ ・ 鏡; (on a car) ミラー

miserable *adj* かなしい ・ 悲しい; I feel miserable かなし いです。・ 悲しいです。

miss *vb* (to fail to hit) use the negative of あたる ・ 当たる to hit; to miss the target まと にあたらない ・ 的に 当たら ない; (to fail to see) みそこなう ・ 見損なう; I missed the TV news テレビニュースをみそこないました。・ テレ ビニュースを見損ないました。; you can't miss it すぐ わかります。; (to fail to take) to miss an opportunity きかい をのがす ・ 機会を逃す; (to feel sad not to see) I miss you あなたがいなくて さびしいです。; I miss Japanese food にほんのたべものが こいしいです。・ 日本の 食べ物 が 恋しいです。; (other uses) don't miss this film この えい がをぜったい みてください。・ この 映画を 絶対 見

てください。; I missed her plane ひこうきに まにあいませんでした。・飛行機に 間に合いませんでした。; to miss school (due to illness) がっこうを やすむ・学校を 休む; (by skipping classes) がっこうを さぼる・学校を さぼる

Miss n 〜さん

missing adj to be missing みつからない・見つからない; there's a book missing ほんが みつかりません。・本が 見つかりません。

mist n きり・霧

mistake n まちがい・間違い; a spelling mistake つづり のまちがい・つづりの 間違い; to make a mistake まちがいをする・間違いを する

mistletoe n やどりぎ・宿り木

mix vb (to put together) まぜる・混ぜる; (to go together) まざる・混ざる; to mix with the other students ほかの がくせいとまじわる・外の 学生と 交わる; mix up まざる・混ざる; to get French and Japanese mixed up フランスご とにほんごが まざっている・フランス語と 日本語 が混ざっている

mobile phone n けいたいでんわ・携帯電話

model n (of a train, a car, a building) もけい・模型; (fashion) model モデル

modern adj げんだいてき(な)・現代的(な)

Mohammed n マホメット

mole n (spot) ほくろ; (animal) もぐら

mom, Mom n (US English) (someone else's) おかあさん・お母さん; (your own) はは・母! Japanese children will address their mother as おかあさん or ママ

moment n ちょっとの あいだ・ちょっとの 間; at the moment いま・今; wait a moment ちょっとまってください。・ちょっと 待ってください。

Monday n げつようび・月曜日

money n おかね・お金

monkey *n* さる・猿; year of the monkey さるどし・申年

month *n* (period of one month) いっかげつ・一ヶ月; I'll be back in two months' time にかげつご もどります。・二ヶ月後戻ります。

monument *n* してきねんぶつ・史的記念物

mood *n* I'm in a good mood きぶんが いいです。・気分が いいです。; I'm in a bad mood きぶんが わるいです。・気分が悪いです。

moon *n* つき・月

moped *n* スクーター

moral *adj* モラル(の)

more 1 *det* I have more work than him かれより しごとが あります。・彼より 仕事が あります。; there's no more bread もう パンが ありません。・もう パンが ありません。; there's more tea コーヒーは まだ あります。; would you like more coffee? コーヒーを もういっぱい どうですか。・コーヒーを もう一杯 どうですか。; he bought two more tickets かれは きっぷを もう にまい かいました。・彼は 切符を もう 二枚 買いました。 **2** *pron* もっと; to cost more もっと おかねが かかる・もっとお金が かかる; I got more than her かのじょより もっともらいました。・彼女より もっと もらいました。; I can't tell you any more これ いじょう いえません。・これ 以上 言えません。; we need more もっと ひつようです。・もっと 必要です。 **3** *adv* (when comparing) 〜より〜; it's more complicated than that それより ふくざつ です。・それより 複雑です。; Kyoto is more beautiful than Tokyo きょうとは とうきょうより きれいです。・京都 は 東京より きれいです。; (when talking about time) he doesn't live there any more かれは もう そこに すんでい ません。・彼は もう そこに 住んでいません。 **4** more and more もっともっと; more and more expensive もっと もっとたかい・もっともっと 高い **5** more or less だ いたい もう 〜いじょう・〜以上; there were more than 20 people there そこに にじゅうにんいじょう いました。・そこに 二十人以上 いました。

morning n あさ・朝; at three o'clock in the morning ごぜんさんじに・午前三時に; (during) the morning ごぜんちゅう・午前中

mosquito n か・蚊

most 1 det (the majority of) ほとんど(の); most schools will be closed ほとんどの がっこうは しまります。・ほとんどの 学校は 閉まります。; (in superlatives) the most いちばん・一番; who has the most money? だれが いちばんおかねを もっていますか。・誰が 一番お金を 持っていますか。 **2** pron ほとんど; most (of them) can speak Japanese ほとんどは にほんごが はなせます。・ほとんどは 日本語が 話せます。 **3** adv いちばん・一番; the most expensive shop in Tokyo とうきょうの いちばんたかいみせ・東京の 一番高い 店; the most beautiful town in Japan にほんで いちばんきれいなまち・日本で 一番きれいな 町 **4** at (the) most せいぜい **5** most of all とくに・特に

mostly adv ほとんど

mother n (someone else's) おかあさん・お母さん; (your own) はは・母! Japanese children will address their mother as おかあさん or ママ

mother-in-law n (someone else's) ぎりの おかあさん・義理の お母さん; (your own) ぎりの はは・義理の 母

motor n モーター

motorbike n オートバイ

motorcyclist n オートバイに のるひと・オートバイに 乗る 人

motorist n うんてんしゃ・運転者

motor racing n カーレース

motorway n (British English) こうそくどうろ・高速道路

mountain n やま・山; to go camping in the mountains やまで キャンプする・山で キャンプする

mountain bike n マウンテンバイク

mountain climbing n とざん・登山

mouse n ねずみ

moustache, mustache (US English) n くちひげ

mouth n (of a person, animal) くち・口; (of a river) かこう・河口

move vb (to make a movement) うごく・動く; please don't move! うごかないでください。・動かないでください。; the train's started to move でんしゃが うごきはじめました。・電車が 動きはじめました。; (to put elsewhere) いどうする・移動する; to move the car くるまを いどうする・車を 移動する; to move a chair (out of the way) いすをどかす・椅子を 退かす; to move (house) ひっこす・引っ越す; to move to Gunma ぐんまに ひっこす・群馬に 引っ越す; **move away** (to live elsewhere) ひっこす・引っ越す; (to make a movement away) はなれる・離れる; to move away from the window まどから はなれる・窓から 離れる; **move back** もどる・戻る; **move forward** すすむ・進む; **move into** to move into university accomodation だいがくの りょうに はいる・大学の 寮に入る; **move out** でる・出る; **move over** どく・退く; move over please どいてください。・退いてください。

movement n うごき・動き

movie n (US English) えいが・映画

movies n (US English) えいが・映画

movie theater n (US English) えいがかん・映画館

moving adj うごいている・動いている

mow vb to mow the lawn しばかりをする・芝刈りをする

MP n (British English) こっかいぎいん・国会議員

Mr n ~さん

Mrs n ~さん

Ms n ~さん

much 1 adv (a lot) もっと; this bag is much more expensive このかばんは もっと たかいです。・この かばんは もっと 高いです。; (not a lot) あまり + negative; he doesn't read much かれは あまり よみません。・彼は あまり

読みません。; (not often) あまり + negative; they don't eat out much かれらは あまり がいしょくしません。・彼らは あまり 外食しません。; (when used with very, too or so); I like it very much だいすきです。・大好きです。; I ate too much たべすぎました。・食べ過ぎました。; She drank too much かのじょは のみすぎました。・彼女は 飲みすぎました。; I want to go so much とても いきたい です。・とても 行きたいです。 **2** pron (in questions) たくさん; is there much to be done? する ことは たくさん ありますか。 **3** det (not a lot of) あまり + negative; I haven't got much time じかんが あまり ありません。・時間が あまり ありません。; (a lot of) たくさん; do you have much homework? しゅくだいが たくさん ありますか。・宿題が たくさん ありますか。; (when used with how, very, too, so or as) how much money have you got? おかねが どのくらい ありますか。・お金が どのくらい あります か。; she doesn't eat very much meat かのじょは にくを あまり たべません。・彼女は 肉を あまり 食べませ ん。; I spent too much money おかねを つかいすぎまし た。・お金を 使い過ぎました。; please don't put so much salt on しおを そんなに かけないでください。・塩を そん なに かけないでください。; she has as much work as me かのじょは わたしと おなじ くらい しごとが ありま す。・彼女は 私と 同じ くらい 仕事が あります。

mud n どろ・泥

mug 1 n マグカップ

multiply vb (increase) ふえる・増える; (in maths) かける

mum, Mum n (British English) (someone else's) おかあさん ・お母さん; (your own) はは・母! Japanese children will address their mother as おかあさん or ママ

mumps n おたふくかぜ・おたふく風邪

murder 1 n さつじん・殺人 **2** vb ころす・殺す

murderer n ひとごろし・人殺し

muscle n きんにく・筋肉

museum n はくぶつかん・博物館

mushroom n きのこ

music n おんがく・音楽

musical n ミュージカル

musical instrument n がっき・楽器

musician n ミュージシャン

Muslim adj イスラムきょう(の)・イスラム教(の)

mussel n ムールがい・ムール貝

must vb (when stressing the importance of something) you must go to hospital びょういんに いかなければ なりません。・病院に 行かなければ なりません。; we mustn't tell the teacher せんせいに いっては いけません。・先生に 言っては いけません。; (when talking about a rule) she must take the exam in June かのじょは ろくがつに しけんを うけなければなりません。・彼女は 六月に 試験を 受けなければなりません。; (when assuming that something is true) it must be nice to live there あそこに すむのは いいでしょう。・あそこに 住むのは いいでしょう。you must be Mr Yamamoto's younger sister やまもとさんの いもうとさんでしょう。・山本さんの 妹さんでしょう。it must have been boring つまらなかったでしょう。

mustard n からし

mutton n マトン

my det わたしの・私の Not always used if the owner is obvious. うちの can also mean my; they hate my dog かれらは うちの いぬが きらいです。・彼らは 家の 犬が 嫌いです。; what do you think of my car? (わたしの)くるまは どうですか。・(私の) 車は どうですか。; I sold all my CDs CDを ぜんぶ うりました。・CDを 全部 売りました。; I broke my leg あしの ほねを おりました。・足の 骨を 折りました。

myself pron Not used as a reflexive pronoun in Japanese; I want to enjoy myself たのしみたいです。・楽しみたいです。; I didn't hurt myself けがを しませんでした。・怪我を しませんでした。; (when used for emphasis) I did it all by myself ぜんぶ じぶんで しました。・全部 自分で しました。

mystery n なぞ・謎

Nn

nail *n* (for use in attaching, repairing) くぎ; (on the fingers or toes) つめ

nail polish *n* マニキュア

naked *adj* はだか(の)・裸(の)

name *n* (of a person) なまえ・名前; what's your name? おなまえは なんですか。・お名前は 何ですか。; my name is Michiko みちこです。・美智子です。; (of a book, a play or film) タイトル

narrow *adj* せまい・狭い

nasty *adj* いや(な)・嫌(な)

national *adj* くにの・国の

native *adj* native language ぼこくご・母国語; a native French speaker フランスごが ぼこくごの ひと・フランス語が 母国語の 人

natural *adj* しぜん(な)・自然(な)

naturally *adv* (of nature) しぜんに・自然に; (of course) とうぜん・当然

nature *n* しぜん・自然

naughty *adj* わんぱく(な)・腕白(な)

navy *n* かいぐん・海軍

navy blue *adj* こん(の)・紺(の)

near 1 *prep* ちかくに・近くに; he was sitting near us かれは ちかくに すわっていました。・彼は 近くに 座っていました。**2** *adv* they live near かれらは ちかくに すんでいます。・彼らは 近くに 住んでいます。**3** *adj* ちかい・近い; the school is quite near がっこうは けっこう ちかいです。・学校は 結構 近いです。; the nearest shops are several kilometres away いちばんちかい みせは

すうキロ はなれています。・一番近い 店は 数キロ
離れています。

nearby *adv* ちかく・近く

nearly *adv* we're nearly there あと もう すこしです。・
後 もう 少しです。; nearly all (of them) ほとんど; nearly
5% ごパーセント ちかく・五パーセント 近く; I nearly
forgot わすれる ところでした。・忘れる ところでし
た。

neat *adj* (*in how one looks*) きちんとした; (*describing work,*
handwriting) きれい(な)

necessary *adj* ひつよう(な)・必要(な)

neck *n* くび・首

necklace *n* ネックレス

need *vb* ((*to*) *have to*) you don't need to get permission きょか
を えなくても いいです。・許可を 得なくても いいで
す。; they'll need to come early かれらは はやく こなけれ
ばなりません。・彼らは 早く 来なければ なりませ
ん。; (*to want*) いる・要る; I need money おかねが いりま
す。・お金が 要ります。; we need to know by Tuesday か
ようびまでに しりたいです。・火曜日までに 知りた
いです。; everything you need ひつような もの ぜんぶ・
必要な 物 全部

needle *n* はり・針

negative 1 *adj* ひていてき(な)・否定的(な);
(*pessimistic*) ひかんてき(な)・悲観的(な) **2** *n* しゃしん
の ネガ・写真の ネガ

neighbour (*British English*), **neighbor** (*US English*) *n*
(*living next-door*) となりの ひと・隣の 人; (*living close by*)
きんじょの ひと・近所の 人

neither 1 *conj* (*in neither... nor sentences*) she can speak
neither French nor English かのじょは フランスごも えい
ごも はなせません。・彼女は フランス語も 英語も 話
せません。; (*nor*) 'I can't sleep'—'neither can I' 「ねむれま
せん。」「わたしも。」・「眠れません。」「私も。」**2** *det*
どちらも; neither answered どちらも こたえませんでし

た。・どちらも 答えませんでした。**3** *pron* どちらも;
neither of them is coming どちらも きません。・どちらも
来ません。

nephew *n* おい・甥

nerves *n* しんけい・神経; to get on someone's nerves
だれかを いらいらさせる・誰かを いらいらさせる

nervous *adj* (frightened) こわい・怖い; (anxious) ふあん
(な)・不安(な); nervous feeling ふあんな きもち・不
安な 気持ち; nervous disposition しんけいしつ・神経質

nest *n* す・巣

net *n* (for fishing) あみ・網; (in sport) ネット

Netherlands *n* オランダ

network *n* ネットワーク

neutral *adj* ちゅうりつ(の)・中立(の)

never *adv* (not ever) they never come here かれらは ぜんぜ
んここに きません。・彼らは 全然 ここに 来ませ
ん。; she has never been to the opera かのじょは オペラ
にいった ことがありません。・彼女は オペラに 行った
ことがありません。; I'll never go back there again にどと
そこに いきません。・二度と そこに 行きません。;
(when used for emphasis) she never contacted us かのじ
ょはれんらく さえ しませんでした。・彼女は 連絡
さえしませんでした。

nevertheless *adv* それにもかかわらず

new *adj* あたらしい・新しい; new bike あたらしい じて
んしゃ・新しい 自転車; new car しんしゃ・新車; new
computer あたらしい コンピューター・新しい コンピ
ューター; new clothes あたらしい ふく・新しい 服

newborn baby *n* うまれた ばかりの あかちゃん・
生まれた ばかりの 赤ちゃん

news *n* a piece of news じょうほう・情報; have you heard
the news? ききましたか。・聞きましたか。; that's good
news よかったですね。・良かったですね。; have you
any news of John? ジョンさんの こと、なにか ききま

したか。・ ジョンさんの こと、 何か 聞きましたか。; (on radio, TV) ニュース

newsagent's n (British English) **!** No direct equivalent in Japan, but there are stands in stations and elsewhere where you can buy newspapers, magazines, cigarettes and sweets. These are called キオスク

newspaper n しんぶん・新聞

New Year n しんねん・新年; Happy New Year! あけま して おめでとうございます

New Year's Day, New Year's (US English) n がんじつ・元日

New Year's Eve n おおみそか・大晦日

New Zealand n ニュージーランド

next 1 adj (when talking about what is still to come) つぎ(の)・次(の); I'll take the next train つぎの でんしゃにのります。・次の 電車に 乗ります。; the next day つぎの ひ・次の 日; next week らいしゅう・来週; the next week つ ぎの しゅう・次の 週; next month らいげつ・来月; the next month つぎの つき・次の 月; next year らいねん・来年; the next year つぎの とし・次の 年 **2** adv (in the past) what did you do next? つぎに なにを しましたか。・ 次に 何を しましたか。; (now) what'll we do next? つぎは なにをしましょうか。・次は 何を しましょうか。; (in the future) when you next come to Niigata, please give me a call こんど にいがたに きたら、 れんらくしてくださ い。・今度 新潟に 来たら、 連絡してください。 **3** next to 〜の となり・〜の 隣

next door adv となり・隣

nice adj (enjoyable) たのしい・楽しい; we had a nice time たのしかったです。・楽しかったです。; (kind, friendly) しんせつ(な)・親切(な); everyone was very nice to me みんなは わたしに とても しんせつでした。・皆は 私 にとても 親切でした。; (of weather, place) いい

nickname n ニックネーム

niece n めい・姪

night n (as opposed to day) よる・夜; I didn't sleep last night きのうのよる、ねむれませんでした。・昨日の夜、眠れませんでした。; he studied all night かれは ひとばん じゅう べんきょうしました。・彼は 一晩中 勉強しました。(evening) ばん・晩 last night きのうの ばん・昨日の晩

nightclub n ナイトクラブ

nightdress n ねまき・寝巻き

nightmare n あくむ・悪夢; to have a nightmare あくむを みる・悪夢を 見る

nil n ゼロ

nine num (on its own) ここのつ・九つ; (with a counter) きゅう・九; nine books ほん きゅうさつ・本九冊; I've got nine ここのつ あります。・九つ あります。; nine o'clock くじ・九時

nineteen num じゅうきゅう・十九

nineteenth num (in a series) じゅうきゅうばん(め)・十九番(目); (in dates) the nineteenth of July しちがつじゅうくにち・七月十九日

ninety num きゅうじゅう・九十

ninth num (in a series) きゅうばん(め)・九番(目); (in dates) the ninth of December じゅうにがつここのか・十二月九日

no 1 adv いいえ Note that when a question is asked in the negative and the answer would be "no" in English, it would be はい in Japanese to mean that that is correct e.g. 「それを しませんでしたか。」「はい、しませんでした。」; no thanks いいえ、けっこうです。・いいえ、結構です。; he no longer works here かれは もう ここで はたらいていません。・彼は もう ここで 働いていません。2 det (not any) we have no money おかねが ありません。・お金が ありません。; there are no trains でんしゃが ありません。・電車が ありません。; (when refusing permission) no smoking! きんえん、禁煙; (when used for emphasis) it's no problem だいじょうぶです。・大丈夫です。

nobody ▶ no-one

noise n (sound) おと・音; (disturbance) そうおん・騒音;
to make noise さわぐ・騒ぐ

noisy adj うるさい

none pron none of them went to the class だれも クラスに
いきませんでした。・誰も クラスに 行きませんでし
た。; none of us can speak Chinese だれも ちゅうごくご
が はなせません。・誰も 中国語が 話せません。; none
of the answers were right こたえは ひとつも あっていま
せん。・答えは 一つも 合っていません。; there's none
left もう ありません。; I've got none, I have none ありませ
ん。

nonsense n that's nonsense! ばかばかしいです。

noodle n めん・麺

noon n しょうご・正午; at noon しょうごに・正午に

no-one pron (also **nobody**); no-one だれも + negative;
no-one tells me anything だれも おしえて くれません。・
誰も 教えて くれません。; no-one saw him だれも かれ
を みませんでした。・誰も 彼を 見ませんでした。;
there's no-one else in the office but me わたし いがい、
オフィスに だれも いません。・私 以外、オフィスに
誰も いません。

nor conj ! For translations of nor when used in combination with
neither, look at the entry for neither in this dictionary; 'I don't like
him'—'nor do I' 「かれが すきじゃ ありません。」「わた
しも。」・「彼が 好きじゃ ありません。」「私も。」

normal adj ふつう(の)・普通(の)

normally adv ふつうに・普通に

north 1 n きた・北; in the north of Japan にほんの きたに
・日本の 北に 2 adv to go north きたに いく・北に 行く
3 adj きた(の)・北(の); to work in north London きた ロ
ンドンではたらく・北ロンドンで 働く

North America n ほくべい・北米

northeast n ほくとう・北東

Northern Ireland *n* きたアイルランド・北アイルランド

northwest *n* ほくせい・北西

nose *n* はな・鼻

not 1 *adv* **!** *Note that there is no translation in Japanese for not. The verb, adjective or noun in question must be made into a negative form;* she's not at home かのじょは うちに いません。・彼女は 家に いません。; hasn't he phoned you? かれが でんわを しませんでしたか。・彼が 電話を しませんでしたか。; we're going to go out whether it rains or not あめが ふっても でかけます。・雨が 降っても 出かけます。; not everyone likes football みんな サッカーが すきだとは かぎりません。・皆 サッカーが 好きだとは 限りません。**2 not at all** (*in no way*) he's not at all worried かれは ぜんぜん しんぱいしていません。・彼は 全然 心配していません。; 'thanks a lot'—'not at all' 「どうもありがとう。」「どういたしまして。」

note 1 *n* (*to remind oneself*) メモ; (*a message*) メッセージ; I left you a note メッセージを のこしました。・メッセージを 残しました。; (*British English*) (*money*) さつ・札; a 5000 yen note ごせんえんさつ・五千円札; (*in music*) おんぷ・音符 **2** *vb* to note (down) かいて おく・書いて おく

notebook *n* ノート

nothing *pron* なにも + negative; nothing has changed なにも かわっていません。・何も 変わっていません。; there's nothing left なにも のこっていません。・何も 残っていません。; she said nothing かのじょは なにも いいませんでした。・彼女は 何も 言いませんでした。; I knew nothing about it それに ついては なにも しりませんでした。・それに ついては 何も 知りませんでした。; there's nothing we can do about it なにも できません。・何も できません。; I had nothing to do with it! わたしとは かんけい ありません。・私とは 関係 ありません。; for nothing ただで

notice 1 vb きづく・気付く **2** n (a written sign) おしらせ・お知らせ; notice board けいじばん・掲示板; (warning people) よこく・予告; at short notice きゅうに・急に; don't take any notice, take no notice きに しないでください・気に しないでください。

novel n しょうせつ・小説

November n じゅういちがつ・十一月

now 1 adv いま・今; we have to do it now いま しなければ なりません。・今 しなければ なりません。; I'm phoning her now いま かのじょに でんわを かけています。・今 彼女に 電話を かけています。; please do it right now いま してください。・今 してください。; now is the time to contact them いますぐ かれらに でんわした ほうが いいです。・今すぐ 彼らに 電話した 方が いいです。; I should have told you before now まえ いえば よかったです。・前 言えば よかったです。; it hasn't been a problem until now いままでは もんだいではありません でした。・今までは 問題ではありませんでした。; between now and next Monday いまから らいしゅうの げつようびまでに・今から 来週の 月曜日 までに; from now on いまから・今から **2** now and again, now and then ときどき・時々

nowhere adv どこも + negative; I went nowhere yesterday きのうどこも いきませんでした。・昨日 どこも 行き ませんでした。; there's nowhere to sit すわる ところが ありません。・座る ところが ありません。

nuclear adj nuclear power げんしりょく・原子力; nuclear weapon かくへいき・核兵器

nuisance n to be a nuisance じゃまを する・邪魔を する; it's a nuisance paying in cash げんきんで はらうの は めんどうです。・現金で 払うの は 面倒です。

numb adj to go numb しびれる; my hands are numb てが しびれました。・手が しびれました。

number 1 n (a figure) すうじ・数字; (of a house, a bus, a telephone, a passport) ばんごう・番号; wrong number まちがいでんわ・間違い電話; (when talking about

quantities) a number of すう + counter; a number of people すうにん・数人; a number of times すうかい・数回; a small number of tourists しょうすうの りょこうしゃ・少数の 旅行者 **2** *vb* ばんごうを つける・番号を 付ける

numberplate *n* (*British English*) ナンバープレート

nun *n* しゅうどうじょ・修道女

nurse *n* かんごふ・看護婦

nursery *n* (*child care establishment*) たくじしょ・託児所

nursery school *n* ほいくえん・保育園

nut *n* ナッツ; walnut くるみ

nylon *n* ナイロン

Oo

oar *n* オール

obedient *adj* よく いう ことを きく・よく 言う こと を 聞く

obey *vb* したがう・従う; to obey someone だれかに したがう・誰かに 従う; to obey the law ほうりつを まもる・法律を 守る

object 1 *n* もの・物 **2** *vb* はんたいする・反対する

objective *adj* きゃっかんてき(な)・客観的(な)

obligation *n* ぎり・義理

oblige *vb* to be obliged to leave a job しごとを やめざるを えない・仕事を 辞めざるを 得ない

obtain *vb* てに いれる・手に 入れる

obvious *adj* あきらか(な)・明らか(な)

obviously *adv* あきらかに・明らかに

occasion *n* on special occasions とくべつな ときに・特別な ときに

occasionally *adv* たまに

occupy *vb* (*to take over*) せんりょうする・占領する; (*to keep busy*) to keep oneself occupied いそがしく する・忙しくする

occupied *adj* (*room, toilet*) しようちゅう・使用中

occupation *n* しょくぎょう・職業

occur *vb* (*happen*) おこる・起こる; (*think*) a plan occurred to me けいかくを おもいつきました。・計画を 思いつきました。

ocean *n* うみ・海 ▶Atlantic ▶Pacific

o'clock *adv* it's five o'clock ごじです。・五時です。; at one o'clock いちじに・一時に

October *n* じゅうがつ・十月

octopus *n* たこ

odd *adj* (*strange*) へん(な)・変(な); (*one of a pair*) かたほう(の)・片方(の); (*when talking about numbers*) odd number きすう(の)・奇数(の)

odour (*British English*), **odor** (*US English*) *n* におい・臭い

of *prep* use particle の; the sound of an engine エンジンの おと・エンジンの 音; it's in the centre of Kobe こうべの ちゅうしんにあります。・神戸の 中心に あります。; a photo of the dog いぬの しゃしん・犬の 写真; half of the salad サラダの はんぶん・サラダの 半分; the names of the pupils せいとの なまえ・生徒の 名前; (*when talking about quantities*) a kilo of potatoes じゃがいも いちキロ・じゃがいも 一キロ; a bottle of wine ワイン いっぽん・ワイン一本; two bottles of cola コーラ にほん・コーラ 二本; have you heard of it? きいた ことが ありますか。・聞いた ことが ありますか。; there are six of us in the family かぞくは ろくにんです。・家族は 六人です。

off ! *Often off occurs in combinations with verbs, for example: get off, go off, take off etc. To find the correct translations for this type of verb, look up the separate dictionary entries at get, go, take etc.* **1** *adv* (*leaving*) I'm off (*British English*) いきます。・行きます。; I'm off to Italy tomorrow あした イタリアに

いきます。・明日 イタリアに 行きます。; (away) the coast is a long way off かいがんは とおいです。・海岸は 遠いです。; we could see them from a long way off とおくか ら かれらが みえました。・遠くから 彼らが 見えまし た。; (free) to take a day off やすむ・休む; today's my day off きょうは やすみです。・今日は 休みです。; (not working, switched off) the lights are all off でんきは ぜんぶ きえています。・電気は 全部 消えています。**2** adj the milk is off ぎゅうにゅうが わるく なりました。・牛乳 が 悪く なりました。

offence (British English), **offense** (US English) n (a crime) はんざい・犯罪; to take offence おこる・怒る

offend vb おこらせる・怒らせる

offer vb to offer someone a job だれかに しごとを てい きょうする・誰かに 仕事を 提供する; I offered to help Miyoko with her homework みよこさんに しゅくだいを てつだって あげると いいました。・美代子さんに 宿 題を 手伝って あげると 言いました。When offering to do something for someone, use the ～て form of the verb + あげ る; Miyoko offered to help me with my homework みよこさ んは わたしの しゅくだいを てつだって くれると い いました。・美代子さんは 私に 宿題を 手伝って く れると 言いました。When someone offers to do something for you, use the ～て form of the verb + くれる.

office n じむしょ・事務所; head office ほんしゃ・本社; branch office ししゃ・支社

office block n (British English) オフィスビル

officer n (in the army or navy) しょうこう・将校; (in the police) けいかん・警官

office worker n じむいん・事務員! かいしゃいん can also be used

official adj こうしき(の)・公式(の)

often adv よく; I often go there そこに よく いきます。・ そこに よく 行きます。; not often あまり + negative; I don't go there often そこに あまり いきません。・そこ に あまり 行きません。

oil n (for energy) せきゆ・石油; oil company せきゆがいしゃ・石油会社; (for a car) オイル; (for cooking) あぶら・油; oil painting あぶらえ・油絵

okay, OK **1** adj (when asking or giving opinions) is it okay if I come back later? あとで また きても いいですか・後でまた 来ても いいですか。; it's okay to invite them かれらを しょうたいしても いいです・彼らを 招待しても いいです。; (when talking about health) I feel okay げんきです・元気です。; are you okay? (general greeting) おげんきですか・お元気ですか。; are you OK? (when concerned) だいじょうぶですか・大丈夫ですか。

old adj (not new) ふるい・古い; an old chest of drawers ふるいたんす・古い たんす; old houses ふるい いえ・古い 家; (not young) おとしより(の)・お年寄り(の); an old woman おばあさん・お婆さん; an old man おじいさん・お爺さん; old people ろうじん・老人; (when talking about a person's age) how old are you? なんさいですか・何歳ですか; a three-year old girl さんさいの おんなのこ・三才の 女の 子; a ten year old car じゅうねんものの くるま・十年物の 車; I'm as old as he is かれと おなじ としです・彼と 同い年です。; she's eight years older than her brother かのじょは おとうとさんより はっさい うえです・彼女は 弟さんより 八才 上です。; I am the oldest いちばんとしうえです・一番年上です。; I'm now old enough to drink いま アルコールが のめるとしに なりました・今 アルコールが 飲める歳に なりました。; (previous) まえ(の)・前(の); that's my old address それは まえの じゅうしょです・それは 前の 住所です。; in the old days むかし・昔

old-fashioned adj (describing attitudes, ideas) ふるくさい・古臭い; (describing people) あたまが ふるい・頭が 古い

olive **1** n オリーブ **2** adj オリーブいろ(の)・オリーブ色(の)

olive oil n オリーブゆ・オリーブ油

Olympics n オリンピック

omelette *n* オムレツ

on ! *Often* on *occurs in combinations with verbs, for example:* count on, get on, keep on *etc. To find the correct translations for this type of verb, look up the separate dictionary entries for* count, get, keep *etc.* **1** *prep or* use particle に; you've got a spot on your nose はなに にきびが あります。・ 鼻に きびが あります。; there's a stain on the jacket ジャケット に しみが あります。・ ジャケット に 染みが あります。; there is a poster on the wall かべに ポスターが はってあります。・ 壁に ポスターが 貼って あります。; to live on the third floor さんがいに 住む・ 三階に 住む; *(on top of)* 〜の うえ・ 〜の 上; it's on the table テーブル のうえに あります。・ テーブルの 上に あります。; it's on top of the drawers たんすの うえに あります・ たんすの 上に あります。; *(when talking about transport)* to go on the bus バスで いく・ バスで 行く; I came on my bike today きょうは じてんしゃで きました。・ 今日は 自転車で 来ました。; to get on the train でんしゃに のる・ 電車に 乗る; *(about)* 〜に ついて; it's a book on Africa アフリカに ついての ほんです。・ アフリカに ついての 本です。; a programme on dinosaurs きょうりゅうに ついての ばんぐみ・ 恐竜に ついての 番組; *(when talking about time)* I was born on the sixth of December じゅうにがつ むいかに うまれました。・ 十二月 六日に 生まれました。; I'll be there on Saturday どようびに いきます。・ 土曜日に 行きます。; we went there on my birthday わたしの たんじょうびに いきました。・ 私の 誕生日に 行きました。; *(when talking about the media)* on television テレビで; I saw it on the news ニュースで みました。・ ニュースで 見ました。; is this film out on video? この えいがは もう ビデオに でていますか。・ この 映画は もう ビデオに 出ていますか。; *(using)* to be on drugs やくを つかっている・ 麻薬を 使っている **2** *adv (when talking about what one wears)* to have a sweater on セーターを きている・ セーターを 着ている; to have make-up on けしょうしている・ 化粧している; *(working, switched on)* why are all the lights on? なぜ でんきが ぜんぶ ついていますか。・ なぜ 電気が 全部 点いていますか。; the radio was

on all day ラジオ は いちにちじゅう ついていました。・ラジオ は 一日中 点いていました。; (*showing*) what's on? (*on TV*) テレビで; (*in the cinema*) えいがかんで・映画館で; (*when talking about time*) from Tuesday on, I'll be here かようびから ここに います。・火曜日から ここに います。; a little later on あとで・後で

once 1 *adv* (*one time*) いっかい・一回; once a day いちにちいっかい・一日一回; (*in the old days*) むかし・昔 **2** *conj* いったん + conditional form of verb; it'll be easier once we've found a house いったん いえを みつけたら あとは かんたんです。・いったん 家を 見つけたら 後は 簡単です。**3 at once** いますぐ・今すぐ **4 once more** もう いちど・もう一度

one 1 *num* (*on its own*) ひとつ・一つ; (*with a counter*) いち・一; one book ほん いっさつ・本 一冊 I've got one ひとつ あります。・一つ あります。; one child こどもひとり・子供一人; one of my colleagues どうりょうの ひとり・同僚の 一人; one hundred ひゃく・百 **2** *det* (*the only*) Mauriceis the one person who can help Zoe ゾイさんを たすけられる ひとは モリスさんだけです。・ゾイさん を 助けられる 人は モリスさんだけです。; it's the one thing that annoys me それだけが いらいらさせます。; (*the same*) to take three exams in the one day いちにちに しけんをみっつも うける・一日に 試験を 三つも 受ける **3** *pron* (*when referring to something generally*) I need an dictionary—have you got one? じしょが ひつようです。ありますか。・辞書が 必要です。ありますか。; (*when referring to a specific person or thing*) I like the new one あたらしいのが すきです。・新しいのが 好きです。; the one who got sacked is Geoffrey くびに なったのは ジェフリーさんです。・首に なったのは ジェフリーさんです。; which one? どれですか。・どれですか。; this one これです。・これですか。; (*when used to mean 'you' or 'people'*) this pronoun is not used in Japanese **4 one by one** ひとつずつ・一つずつ

one another *pron* to love one another おたがいに あいしあう・お互いに 愛し合う; we can't bear being apart from one another いっしょに いないと たえられません。・一緒に いないと 耐えられません。

oneself *pron* じぶん・自分; to enjoy oneself たのしむ・楽しむ; by oneself ひとりで・一人で

onion *n* たまねぎ・玉ねぎ

only 1 *adv* only 〜だけ; it's only a game ゲームだけです。; they've only met once かれらは いっかいだけ あいました。・彼らは 一回だけ 会いました。**2** *adj* she was the only one who couldn't speak Japanese かのじょだけは にほんごが はなせませんでした。・彼女だけは 日本語が 話せませんでした。; the only problem is that I can't drive もんだいは、うんてんが できない ことです。・問題は 運転が できない ことです。; an only child ひとりっこ・一人っ子 **3** only just use the 〜た form of verb + ところ; I've only just arrived いま ついた ところです。・今 着いた ところです。; I've only just heard いま 聞いた ところです。・今 聞いた ところです。; I've only just moved house ひっこした ところです。・引っ越した ところです。

onto *prep* use particle に; to get onto a train でんしゃに のる・電車に 乗る

open 1 *vb* ! *Note that there are two ways of expressing the action to open in Japanese depending on what is being opened*; *(to open (something))* to open an umbrella かさを ひらく・傘を 開く; to open a book ほんを ひらく・本を 開く; to open a meeting かいぎを ひらく・会議を 開く; to open a gate もんを ひらく・門を 開く; to open an envolope ふうとうを あける・封筒を 開ける; to open a package こづつみを あける・小包を 開ける; to open one's eyes めを あける・目を 開ける; to open a shop みせを あける・店を 開ける; to open a window まどを あける・窓を 開ける; *(to become open)* what time do you open? なんじに あきますか。・何時に 開きますか。; the shop opens at eight みせは くじに あきます。・店は 九時に 開きます。; the flowers opened はなが ひらきました。・花が 開きました。; *(to start)* はじまる・始まる **2** *adj (not closed)* あいている・開いている; the pool isn't open プールは あいていません。・プールは 開いていません。; leave the door open ドアを あけて おいてください。・ドアを

開けて おいてください。; (frank) そっちょく(な)・率直(な) **3** n out in the open そとで・外で

opener n (for bottles) せんぬき・栓抜き; (for cans) かんきり・缶切り

open-minded adj へんけんの ない・偏見の ない

opera n オペラ

operate vb (to make something work) そうさする・操作する; (to carry out an operation) しゅじゅつを する・手術を する; to operate on someone だれかの しゅじゅつを する・誰かの 手術を する; to operate on Mr Kitamura's leg きたむらさんの あしの しゅじゅつを する・喜多村さんの 足の 手術を する

operation n しゅじゅつ・手術; to have an operation しゅじゅつを うける・手術を 受ける

operator n オペレーター

opinion n いけん・意見; in my opinion, they're lying かれらは うそを ついていると おもいます。・彼らは 嘘を ついていると 思います。

opponent n (in sport) あいて・相手

opportunity n きかい・機会; I took the opportunity to visit Nagasaki きかいを りようして ながさきへ いきました。・機会を 利用して 長崎へ 行きました。

oppose vb to oppose a plan けいかくに はんたいする・計画に反対する; to be opposed to nuclear weapons かくへいきに はんたいする・核兵器に 反対する

opposite 1 prep むかいがわ・向かい側; she was sitting opposite me かのじょは むかいがわにすわっていました。・彼女は 向かい側に 座っていました。**2** adj the opposite sex いせい・異性; he was walking in the opposite direction かれは はんたいの ほうがへ あるいていました。・彼は 反対の 方角へ 歩いていました。; opposite effect ぎゃくこうか・逆効果 **3** adv むかいがわに・向かい側に **4** n はんたい・反対; it's the exact opposite せいはんたいです。・正反対です。

optician n めがねや・眼鏡屋

optimist n らくてんか・楽天家

optimistic adj らっかんてき(な)・楽観的(な)

or conj ! *There is no one word equivalent to 'or' in Japanese. See below for expressions in various contexts;* (when there's a choice between two or more things or options) Aか Bか; once or twice a week しゅう いっかいか にかい・週 一回か 二回; is this Chinese or Japanese? これは ちゅうごくご ですか、にほんごですか。これは 中国語ですか、日本語ですか。; do you have any brothers or sisters? きょうだいがいますか。; (in negative sentences with only one verb) 〜も〜も; I can't do it today or tomorrow きょうも、あしたも、できません。・今日も、明日も、できません。; I don't like meat or fish にくも、さかなも、すきではありません。・肉も、魚も、好きではありません。; (otherwise) そうでなければ; please be careful or the plates will get broken きを つけてください。そうで なければ さらが われます。・気を つけてください。そうで なければ 皿が 割れます。

oral adj こうとう(の)・口頭(の)

orange 1 n オレンジ **2** adj オレンジ(の)

orange juice n オレンジジュース

orchard n かじゅえん・果樹園

orchestra n オーケストラ

order 1 vb (to tell) めいずる・命ずる; (to ask for) ちゅうもんする・注文する; to order goods from a magazine ざっしからしなものを ちゅうもんする・雑誌から 品物を 注文する **2** n (an instruction) めいれい・命令; to give orders めいれいする・命令する; the right order ただしい じゅんばん・正しい 順番; the list is in alphabetical order リストは アルファベットじゅんです。・リストは アルファベット順です。 **3 in order to** 〜(の)ために; I phoned in order to change the date ひにちを かえる ために でんわを しました。・日にちを 変えるために 電話を しました。

ordinary adj (not unusual) ふつう(の)・普通(の); an ordinary family ふつうの かぞく・普通の 家族; (average) へいぼん(な)・平凡(な)

organ n (the musical instrument) オルガン; (a part of the body) ぞうき・臓器

organic adj (food) むのうやく(の)・無農薬(の)

organization n そしき・組織

organize vb きかくする・企画する; to be organized きちんとする

original adj (first) さいしょ(の)・最初(の); (true, real) ほんもの(の)・本物(の); (new, fresh) どくそうてき(な)・独創的(な)

ornament n かざりもの・飾り物

orphan n こじ・孤児

ostrich n だちょう

other 1 adj ! Note that other is not used in the same way as in English. If the other item has been previously mentioned, it will be referred to as "the previous one", "the one we saw before" etc rather than "the other one"; not that dress, the other one we saw before その ドレスではありません。さきに みた ほうです。・その ドレスではありません。先に 見た 方です。; they sold the other car かれらは もう ひとつの くるまを うりました。・彼らは もう 一つの 車を 売りました。; to interrupt the other pupils ほかの せいとの じゃまをする・外の 生徒の 邪魔を する; every other day いちにちおき・一日おき 2 pron Haruki made the others laugh はるきさんは ほかの ひとを わらわせました。・治樹さんは 外の 人を 笑わせました。; some students remember Japanese words easily, others have problems いちぶの がくせいは にほんごの たんごを すぐ おぼえますが、そうじゃないがくせいも います。・一部の 学生は 日本語の 単語を すぐ 覚えますが、そうじゃない学生も います。; they came in one after the other かれらは かわるがわる はいって きました。・彼らは かわるがわる 入って 来ました。

otherwise *conj* そうでななければ; it's safe, otherwise I wouldn't go あんぜんです。 そうでなければ わたしは いきません。・ 安全です。 そうでなければ 私は 行き ません。

otter *n* かわうそ

ought *vb* (when talking about what should be done) use a plain form of the verb + べき; you ought not to do that それを する べきではありません。; you ought do your homework before watching TV テレビを みるまえに しゅくだいを する べきです。・ テレビを 見る前に 宿題を する べきで す。; (when making a polite suggestion) Use the 〜た form of the verb + ほうが いい for positive suggestions and the 〜な い form of the verb + ほうが いい for negative suggestions; you ought to go to bed ねた ほうが いいです。・ 寝た 方 が いいです。; you ought not to smoke たばこを すわない ほうが いいです。・ たばこを 吸わない 方が いいで す。; (when saying something may happen) Use plain form of the verb + はず; they ought to arrive tomorrow かれらは あ したつく はずです。・ 彼らは 明日 着く はずです。; it ought not to be finished before three o'clock さんじまえに はおわらない はずです。・ 三時前には 終わらない はずです。; (when saying something should happen); (when expressing personal regret) Use the 〜ば conditional form + よかった; I ought to have gone いけば よかったです。・ 行けば 良かったです。; (when expressing obligation in the past) Use plain form of verb + べきだった; I ought to have gone with them わたしが かれらと いっしょに いく べ きでした。・ 私が 彼らと 一緒に 行く べきでした。

our *det* Not always used if the owners are obvious. うちの can also mean our; わたしたちの ・ 私達の; that's our dog それ はうちの いぬです。・ それは 家の 犬です。; what do you think of our new house? あたらしい うちを どう おも いますか。・ 新しい 家を どう 思いますか。; all our CDs have been stolen わたしたちの CDは ぜんぶ ぬすまれ ました。・ 私達の CDは 全部 盗まれました。

ours *pron* うちの can also mean ours; わたしたちの ・ 私達 の; the grey car is ours はいろの くるまは わたしたち

のです。・ 灰色の 車は 私達のです。; which case is ours?
どの ケースが わたしたちのですか。・ どの ケースが
私達のですか。; their car is bigger than ours かれらの くる
まは わたしたちのより おおきいです。・ 彼らの
車は 私達のより 大きいです。

ourselves *pron (when used as a reflexive pronoun) not used
as a pronoun in Japanese*; we want to enjoy ourselves たのし
みたいです。・ 楽しみたいです。; we didn't hurt ourselves
けがを しませんでした。・ 怪我を しませんでした。;
(when used for emphasis) we did everything ourselves じぶん
たちでぜんぶ しました。・ 自分達で 全部 しました。;
we like to be by ourselves ふたりきりが すきです。・
二人きりが 好きです。

out ! *Often occurs in combinations with verbs, for example:
blow out, come out, find out, give out etc. To find the correct
translations for this type of verb, look up the separate dictionary
entries at blow, come, find, give etc.* **1** *adv (outside)* she's out in
the garden かのじょは にわに います。・ 彼女は 庭に
います。; I'm looking for the way out でぐちを さがしてい
ます。・ 出口を 探しています。; *(absent)* to be out でか
けている・ 出かけている; someone telephoned while you
were out でかけた とき、 だれかが でんわを しました。
・ 出かけた とき、 誰かが 電話を しました。; *(not
lighting, not on)* to be out きえている・ 消えている; all the
lights were out でんきが ぜんぶ きえていました。・
電気が 全部 消えていました。 **2 out of** to go out of the
building たてものを でる・ 建物を 出る; to get out of the
city まちを でる・ 町を 出る; to take a pencil out of the
drawer えんぴつを ひきだしから とりだす・ 鉛筆を
引き出しから 取り出す

outdoor *adj* おくがい(の)・屋外(の); outdoor sport おく
がいスポーツ・屋外スポーツ

outdoors *adv* そと(で)・外(で)

outer space *n* うちゅうくうかん・宇宙空間

outside 1 *prep (in front of)* 〜のまえ・〜の 前; to wait
outside the school がっこうの まえでまつ・ 学校の

前で 待つ; (beyond) outside the city しがい・市外 **2** adv そと・外; let's go outside そとに いきましょう。・外に 行きましょう。; let's play outside そとで あそびましょ う。・外で 遊びましょう。; please take the chairs outside いすを そとに もって いって ください。・椅子を 外に 持って 行って ください。**3** n そと・外; outside of the building ビルの そと・ビルの 外 **4** adj そとがわ(の)・ 外側(の)

oven n オーブン

over ! Often over occurs in combinations with verbs, for example: get over, move over etc. To find the correct translations for this type of verb, look up the separate dictionary entries at get, move etc. **1** prep to climb over a wall へいを のりこえる・塀を 乗り越える; to jump over a puddle みずたまりを とびこ える・水溜まりを 飛び越える; (across) it's over there むこうに あります。・向こうに あります。; please come over here ここに きてください。・ここに 来て く ださい。; (above) 〜の うえ・〜の 上; the picture over the piano ピアノの うえのえ・ピアノの 上の 絵; people over 18 じゅうはっさいいじょうの ひと・十八歳以上 の 人; (during) we saw them over the weekend しゅうまつ の あいだに かれらに あいました。・週末の 間に 彼らに 会いました。; (everywhere) I've searched all over for my keys かぎを あっちこっち さがしました。・鍵を あっちこっち 探しました。**2** adv (finished) おわってい る・終わっている; the term is over がっきが おわって います。・学期が 終わっています。; is the film over? え いがは おわりましたか。・映画は 終わりましたか。; (to one's home) to ask someone over だれかを うちに しょ うたいする・誰かを 家に 招待する; to start (something) over again (なにかを)やりなおす・(何かを) やり直す

overtake vb おいこす・追い越す

overweight adj ふとりすぎ(の)・太りすぎ(の)

owe vb I owe money to Ann アンさんに おかねを かりて います。・アンさんに お金を 借りています。

owl n ふくろう

own 1 *adj* じぶんの・自分の; you should clean your own room じぶんの へやを そうじする べきです。・自分の 部屋を 掃除する べきです。; he'd like his own car かれは じぶんの くるまを ほしがっています。・彼は 自分の 車を 欲しがっています。 **2** *pron* I didn't use his pencil—I used my own かれの えんぴつを つかいませんでした。 じぶんのを つかいました。・彼の 鉛筆を 使いません でした。自分のを 使いました。; they have a house of their own かれらは じぶんたちの いえが あります。・ 彼らは 自分達の 家が あります。 *Note that in Japanese, ownership is often expressed by implication using* ～が ある. *The verb* もつ *can also be used in the present progressive form*; he owns a restaurant かれは レストラン を もっています。・彼は レストランを 持っていま す。; I own three cars わたしは くるまが さんだい あり ます。・私は 車が 三台 あります。; Ms Sato owns her own business さとうさんは じぶんの かいしゃを もっ ています。・佐藤さんは 自分の 会社を 持っています。 **4 on one's own** ひとりで・一人で; **own up** じはくする ・自白する

owner *n* もちぬし・持ち主

ox *n* おうし・牡牛; year of the ox うしどし・丑年

oxygen *n* さんそ・酸素

oyster *n* かき

Pp

Pacific *n* the Pacific Ocean たいへいよう・太平洋

pack 1 *vb* にづくりする・荷造りする; I've got to pack my suitcase にづくりを しなければ なりません。・荷造り をしなければ なりません。 **2** *n* a pack of cigarettes たば こ ひとはこ・たばこ 一箱; a pack of cards トランプ;

pack up にもつを まとめる・荷物を まとめる; to pack up one's belongings もちものを まとめる・持ち物を まとめる

package n (large) にもつ・荷物; (small) こづつみ・小包

package holiday n パックりょこう・パック旅行

packed adj こんでいる・混んでいる

page n ページ; on page six ろくページに・六ページに

pain n いたみ・痛み; I've got a pain in my back せなかが いたいです。・背中が 痛いです。

painful adj いたい・痛い

paint 1 n ペンキ 2 vb ペンキを ぬる・ペンキを 塗る; to paint a picture えを かく・絵を 描く

paintbrush n ブラシ

painter n (decorator) ペンキや・ペンキ屋; (artist) がか・画家

painting n (a picture) え・絵; (the activity) (decorating) ペンキを ぬる こと・ペンキを 塗る こと; (art) かいが・絵画

pair n the English expression 'a pair of' is not usually expressed in Japanese unless there is more than one pair; two pairs of shoes くつ にそく・靴 二足

pajamas n (US English) パジャマ

Pakistan n パキスタン

palace n きゅうでん・宮殿; Japanese Imperial Palace こうきょ・皇居

pale adj しろっぽい・白っぽい; (face) あおじろい・青白い; to go pale with fear きょうふで あおざめる・恐怖で 青ざめる

pancake n ホットケーキ

panic vb パニックじょうたいになる・パニック状態 になる

pants n (British English) (underwear) women's underwear パンティー; men's underwear パンツ; (US English) (trousers) ズボン

pantyhose n (US English) パンティーストッキング

paper n (for writing or drawing on) かみ・紙; a piece of paper かみ いちまい・紙 一枚; (a newspaper) しんぶん・新聞

parachuting n パラシュート

parade n パレード

paralysed (British English), **paralyzed** (US English) adj まひする・麻痺する

parcel n にもつ・荷物

parent n (one's own) おや・親; parent or guardian ほごしゃ・保護者

parents n (one's own) りょうしん・両親; (someone else's) ごりょうしん・ご両親

Paris n パリ

park 1 n こうえん・公園 **2** vb to park a car くるまを ちゅうしゃする・車を 駐車する; to park near the office かいしゃのちかくに ちゅうしゃする・会社の 近くに 駐車する; no parking ちゅうしゃきんし・駐車禁止

parking lot n (US English) ちゅうしゃじょう・駐車場

parking meter n パーキングメーター

parliament n ぎかい・議会

parrot n おうむ

part いちぶ・一部; part of the film えいがの いちぶ・映画の一部; it's part of the job しごとの いちぶです。・仕事の一部です。; this part of the country この ちほう・この 地方; (a piece for a machine, a car) ぶひん・部品; (in a series) part four だいよんぶ・第四部; (a role) やく・役; to play the part of Tommy トミーの やくを えんじる・トミーの役を 演じる

participate vb さんかする・参加する

particular in particular とくに・特に

partner n (in a relationship) あいて・相手; (in dancing, sport) パートナー

part-time *adv* パートタイム(の); to work part-time (on a permanent basis) パートタイムではたらく・パートタイムで働く; to work part-time (on a temporary basis) アルバイトする

party *n* (a social event) パーティー; a birthday party たんじょうびパーティー・誕生日パーティー; (formal) welcome party かんげいかい・歓迎会; (formal) farewell party そうべつかい・送別会; have a party パーティーをひらく・パーティーを 開く; a political party せいとう・政党

pass *vb* (to go past) とおる・通る; to let (someone) pass (だれかを)とおす・(誰かを)通す; to pass the school がっこうをとおる・学校を 通る; to pass a car くるまをおいこす・車を追い越す; to pass (someone) in the street (だれかと)みちで すれちがう・(誰かと)道で すれ違う; (to give) わたす・渡す; pass me the salt, please しおをとってください・塩を 取ってください; to pass the ball (to someone) (だれかに)ボールを わたす・(誰かに)ボールを 渡す; (to spend) すごす・過ごす; to pass the time listening to the radio ラジオを きいてじかんをすごす・ラジオを 聞いて 時間を 過ごす; (to succeed in an exam) ごうかくする・合格する; to pass an exam しけんにごうかくする・試験に 合格する; **pass around** to pass around the photos しゃしんを まわる・写真を 回す; **pass on** つたえる・伝える; to pass on a message (to someone) (だれかに)メッセージを つたえる・(誰かに)メッセージを 伝える

passage *n* (indoors) ろうか・廊下; (outdoors) つうろ・通路

passenger *n* じょうきゃく・乗客

passport *n* パスポート

past **1** *n* (when talking about time) かこ・過去; in the past かこに・過去に **2** *adj* かこ(の)・過去(の); the past few days have been difficult ここに、さんにち たいへんでした・ここ ニ、三日 大変でした。 **3** *prep* (when talking about time) it's twenty past four よじ にじゅっぷんです・四時 二十分です。; it's

past midnight よなかの じゅうにじすぎです。・ 夜中の 十二時過ぎです。(beyond) むこう・向こう; it's past the traffic lights しんごうの むこうです。・ 信号の 向こう です。**4** adv to go past, to walk past とおる・通る

pasta n パスタ

pastry n (for baking) パイきじ・パイ生地; to make pastry パイきじをつくる ・ パイ生地を作る; (a cake) ペストリー

patch n (on a garment) つぎ・継ぎ; (on a tyre) つぎはぎ・継ぎはぎ

path n こみち・小道

patience n にんたい・忍耐; to lose patience かんにんぶくろのおが きれる・堪忍袋の 緒が 切れる

patient 1 n かんじゃ・患者 **2** adj にんたいづよい・忍耐強い

patrol car n パトカー

pattern n (a design) もよう・模様; (when making garments) (for knitting) あみものの パターン・編み物の パターン; (for sewing) かたがみ・型紙

pavement n (British English) ほどう・歩道

paw n あし・足

pay 1 vb to pay はらう・払う; to pay the bill かんじょうをはらう・勘定を 払う; to pay for the shopping かいものの だいきんを はらう・買い物の 代金を 払う; Dennis paid for my meal デニスさんは ごちそうして くれました。; (when talking about wages) this work doesn't pay very well ここの しごとは きゅうりょうが よくないです。・ここの 仕事は 給料が 良くないです。; I'm paid eight pounds an hour じきゅう はちポンドです。・ 時給 八ポンドです。; (to give) to pay attention to the teacher せんせいの いうことを よく きく・先生の 言うことを よく 聞く; to pay (someone) a visit (だれかを)ほうもんする・(誰かを)訪問する; to pay (someone) a compliment (だれかを)ほめる・(誰かを)誉める **2** n pay きゅうりょう・

給料; the pay is good きゅうりょうが いいです。・給料
が いいです。; **pay back** かえす・返す

PE n たいいく・体育

pea n えんどうまめ・えんどう豆

peace n へいわ・平和

peach n もも・桃

peacock n くじゃく

peanut n ピーナツ

pear n せいようなし・西洋梨

pearl n パール

pebble n こいし・小石

pedestrian n ほこうしゃ・歩行者

pedestrian crossing n おうだんほどう・横断歩道

peel vb かわをむく・皮をむく

pen n ペン

penalty n (for offence) しょばつ・処罰; (in sport) ペナル
ティー; **penalty kick** ペナルティーキック

pence n ペンス

pencil n えんぴつ・鉛筆

pencil case n ふでばこ・筆箱

pencil sharpener n えんぴつけずり・鉛筆削り

penfriend (British English), **penpal** ペンフレンド

penguin n ペンギン

penknife n ペンナイフ

pensioner n (someone living on a pension) ねんきんぐらし
のひと・年金暮らしの人; (old person) ろうじん・老人

people n (in general) ひとびと・人々 ▶ **person**; (if
counting) ～にん・～人 note that two people is ふたり
when counting. As Japanese has no real plural forms, ひと can
be used for both person and people in most cases; we met very
nice people いいひとたちに あいました。・いい人達
に 会いました。; most people don't know what's going on ほ

とんどの ひとは なにが おこって いるか わかりません。・ほとんどの 人は 何が 起こって いるか わかりません。; there were three people at the meeting かいぎには さんにん いました。・会議には 三人 いました。; there are too many people here ここは ひとが おおすぎます。・ここは 人が 多すぎます。; to help other people ひとを てつだう・人を 手伝う

pepper n (the spice) こしょう; (the vegetable) ピーマン

per prep per person ひとりに つき・一人に つき

per cent, percent (US English) n パーセント

perfect adj かんぺき(な)・完璧(な); to speak perfect Japanese かんぺきな にほんごを はなす・完璧な 日本語を 話す; it's the perfect place for a picnic ピクニックには ちょうど いい ばしょです。・ピクニックには ちょうど いい 場所です。

perform vb (to do) おこなう・行う; (to act, to play) じょうえんする・上演する

perfume n こうすい・香水; to wear perfume こうすいを つける・香水を つける

perhaps adv たぶん・多分

period n (in time) きかん・期間; a trial period しようきかん・試用期間; (in history) じだい・時代; (for women) せいり・生理; to have one's period せいりに なる・生理に なる; (a school lesson) じげん・時限 This is often shortened to げん; first period いちじげん・一時限; I have 3 periods of maths a week すうがくの じゅぎょうは しゅうさんかい あります。・数学の 授業は 週 三回 あります。

permanent adj えいきゅうてき(な)・永久的(な)

permission n きょか・許可; to get permission to go to a party パーティーに いく きょかを もらう・パーティーに 行く 許可を もらう

person n ひと・人; an old person ろうじん・老人; kind person しんせつな ひと・親切な 人

personal adj こじん(の)・個人(の)

personality *n* せいかく・性格

perspire *vb* あせを かく・汗を かく

persuade *vb* せっとくする・説得する; to persuade (someone) to buy a car (だれかに)くるまを かう ように ときふせる・(誰かに)車を 買う ように 説き伏せる

pessimist *n* ひかんろんしゃ・悲観論者

pessimistic *adj* ひかんてき(な)・悲観的(な)

pet *n* ペット; do you have any pets? ペットを かっていますか。・ペットを 飼っていますか。

petrol *n* (British English) ガソリン; to run out of petrol ガソリンが なくなる・ガソリンが なくなる

petrol station *n* (British English) ガソリンスタンド

pet shop *n* ペットショップ

phone 1 *n* でんわ・電話; the phone's ringing でんわが なっています。・電話が 鳴っています。; to answer the phone でんわに でる・電話に 出る; he's on the phone かれは でんわちゅうです。・彼は 電話中です。**2** *vb* でんわする・電話する; to phone someone だれかに でんわする・誰かに 電話する

phone book *n* でんわちょう・電話帳

phone booth *n* でんわボックス・電話ボックス

phone call *n* でんわ・電話; to receive a phone call でんわを もらう・電話を もらう; to make a phone call でんわを かける・電話を かける

phone card *n* テレホンカード

phone number *n* でんわばんごう・電話番号

photo *n* しゃしん・写真

photocopier *n* コピーき・コピー機

photocopy *n* コピー

photograph *n* しゃしん・写真; to take a photograph しゃしんをとる・写真を 撮る

photographer *n* カメラマン

physics *n* ぶつり・物理; (*academic subject*) ぶつりがく・物理学

piano *n* ピアノ

pick *vb* (*to choose*) えらぶ・選ぶ; to pick a number ばんごうをえらぶ・番号を選ぶ; (*to collect*) つむ・摘む; to pick apples りんごを つむ・りんごを 摘む; (*to take*) とる・取る; to pick a book off the shelf たなから ほんを とる・棚から 本を 取る; **pick on** いじめる; he's always picking on me かれは いつも わたしを いじめています。・彼は いつも 私を いじめています。; **pick out** えらぶ・選ぶ; **pick up** (*to lift*) to pick the clothes up off the floor ゆかから ふくを ひろう・床から 服を 拾う; to pick a baby up あかちゃんを だきあげる・赤ちゃんを 抱き上げる; to pick up the phone でんわに でる・電話に 出る; (*to collect*) to pick up passengers じょうきゃくを のせる・乗客を 乗せる; my father's coming to pick me up from school ちちが がっこうに むかえに きます。・父が 学校に 迎えに 来ます。; (*to buy*) かう・買う; I stopped to pick up a newspaper しんぶんを かう ために たちどまりました。・新聞を 買う ために 立ち止まりました。; (*to learn*) おぼえる・覚える

picnic *n* ピクニック; to go on a picnic ピクニックに いく・ピクニックに 行く

picture *n* え・絵; to paint a picture of someone だれかの えをかく・誰かの 絵を 描く; (*a photograph*) しゃしん・写真

piece *n* (*a bit*) not usually used in Japanese; a piece of cheese チーズ; a piece of string ひも・紐; (*a part of a machine*) ぶひん・部品; (*a broken part*) はへん・破片; (*a coin*) a 50 yen piece ごじゅうえんだま・五十円玉; (*other uses*) not usually used in Japanese; a piece of furniture かぐ・家具; a piece of information じょうほう・情報; a piece of advice アドバイス

pierce *vb* あなを あける・穴を 開ける

pig *n* ぶた; year of the pig いのししどし・亥年

pigeon *n* はと

pile n やま・山; a pile of rubbish ごみの やま・ごみの 山;
(lots) piles of toys たくさんの おもちゃ

pill n (a tablet) じょうざい・錠剤; (a method of contraception)
ピル

pillow n まくら・枕

pilot n パイロット

pin 1 n ピン **2** vb ピンで とめる・ピンで 止める

pinball n スマートボール

pinch vb つねる; he pinched my arm, he pinched me on the
arm かれは わたしの うでを つねりました。・彼は
私の 腕を つねりました。; (to hurt by being too tight) my
shoes pinch くつが きついです。・靴が きついです。

pineapple n パイナップル

pine tree n まつ・松

pink adj ピンクいろ(の)・ピンク色(の)

pint n (the quantity) ごひゃく cc・五百 cc Note that cc is
pronounced シーシー in Japanese ! Note that a pint 0.57 l in
Britain and 0.47 l in the US; a pint of milk ぎゅうにゅう ごひ
ゃく cc・牛乳 五百 cc; (British English) (a drink) to go
for a pint いっぱい のみに いく・一杯 飲みに 行く

pipe n (for gas, water) かん・管; (for smoking) パイプ

pirate n かいぞく・海賊

Pisces n うおざ・魚座

pitch n (British English) a football pitch サッカーの グランド

pity 1 n なさけ・情け; (when expressing regret) what a pity!
ざんねんです。・残念です。; it's a pity you can't come こ
られないのは ざんねんです。・来られないのは 残念
です。**2** vb かわいそうに おもう・かわいそうに 思う

pizza n ピザ

place n ところ・所; it's the best place to buy clothes ふく
を かうには いちばんいい ところです。・服を 買うに
は 一番いい 所です。; Akita is a nice place あきたは いい
ところです。・秋田は いい 所です。; they come from all

over the place かれらは いろいろな ところから きています。・ 彼らは 色々な 所から 来ています。; this place is dirty ここは きたないです。・ ここは 汚いです。; (a home) at Alison's place アリソンさんの いえで・ アリソンさんの 家で; I'd like a place of my own じぶんの うちが ほしいです。・ 自分の 家が 欲しいです。; (on public transport, in a car park, at table) is this place free? この せきは あいていますか。・ この 席は 空いていますか。; to save a place for someone だれかに せきを とって おく・ 誰かに 席を 取って おく; to find a place to park ちゅうしゃできる スペースを みつける・ 駐車できる スペースを 見つける; (on a team, a course) to get a place on a team チームには いる・ チームに 入る; to get a place on a course コースに はいる・ コースに 入る; (in a contest) to win first place だいいちいに なる・ 第一位に なる

plain 1 adj (simple) しっそ(な)・ 質素(な); a plain dress しっそな ドレス・ 質素な ドレス; (not good-looking) ぶきりょう(な)・ 不器量(な) **2** n へいげん・ 平原

plait n (British English) みつあみ・ 三つ編

plan 1 n (what one intends to do) けいかく・ 計画; we need a plan けいかくが ひつようです。・ 計画が 必要です。; do you have any plans for the future? しょうらいは なにを しますか。・ 将来は 何を しますか。; (what one has arranged to do) よてい・ 予定; I don't have any plans for tonight こんばんは なんの よていも ありません。・ 今晩は 何の 予定も ありません。 **2** vb (to prepare, to organize) けいかくを する・ 計画を する; to plan a trip りょこうの けいかくを する・ 旅行の 計画を する; to plan a meeting かいぎの けいかくを する・ 会議の 計画を する; (to intend) use verb in dictionary form + つもり; I'm planning to go to Scotland スコットランドに いく つもりです。・ スコットランドに 行く つもりです。

plane n ひこうき・ 飛行機

planet n わくせい・ 惑星

plant 1 n しょくぶつ・ 植物 **2** vb うえる・ 植える

plaster n (British English) ばんそうこう

plastic 1 *n* プラスチック **2** *adj* プラスチックせい（の）・プラスチック製（の）

plate *n* さら・皿

platform *n* ホーム; on platform 4 よんばんせんに・四番線に

play 1 *vb* (to have fun) あそぶ・遊ぶ; to play with friends ともだちとあそぶ・友達と遊ぶ; to play a trick on someone だれかに いたずらを しかける・誰かに いたずらを しかける; to play cards トランプをする; (when talking about sports) する; to play football サッカーを する; France is playing (against) Ireland フランスは アイルランドとたいせんしています。・フランスは アイルランドと対戦しています。; (when talking about music) (piano, guitar, instruments played with fingers) ひく・弾く; (flute, trumpet, instruments played by blowing) ふく・吹く; (drums and percussion instruments) たたく・叩く; (to put on) かける・掛ける; to play a CD CD を かける・CD を 掛ける Note that CD is pronounced シーディー; (when talking about theatre, cinema) えんじる・演じる; to play the role of Romeo ロミオの やくを えんじる・ロミオの 役を 演じる; the film will be playing next week えいがは らいしゅうじょうえいします。・映画は 来週 上映します。 **2** *n* げき・劇; **play around** あそぶ・遊ぶ; **play back** to play back a tape テープを さいせいする・テープを 再生する

player *n* せんしゅ・選手; a tennis player テニスの せんしゅ・テニスの 選手

playground *n* あそびば・遊び場; the school playground こうてい・校庭

please *adv* (polite request) おねがいします。・お願いします。; (please do....) use the 〜て form of the verb + ください; please come in どうぞ はいってください。・どうぞ 入ってください。; please wait a moment ちょっと まってください。・ちょっと 待ってください。; (please don't....) use the ない form of the verb + でください; please don't smoke たばこを すわないでください。・たばこを

吸わないでください。; (when accepting food and drink) い
ただきます。; 'more cake?'—'yes please' 「ケーキは いか
がですか。」「いただきます。」; (polite acceptance of a
favour) おねがいします。・ お願いします。

pleased adj うれしい; I was pleased to receive the letter
てがみを もらって うれしかったです。・ 手紙を もら
ってうれしかったです。; pleased to meet you はじめま
して。

plenty pron to have plenty of time じかんが いっぱい ある
・ 時間が いっぱい ある

plot n (a plan) けいかく・ 計画; (the story in a film, a novel, a
play) プロット

plug n (on an appliance) コンセント; to pull out the plug コン
セントをひきぬく・ コンセントを 引き抜く; (in a sink
or bath) せん・ 栓; **plug in** コンセントをさしこむ・
コンセントを差し込む

plum n うめ・ 梅

plumber n すいどうや・ 水道屋

plus prep プラス; three plus three are six さん たす さんは
ろくです。・ 三 足す 三は 六です。

pocket n ポケット

pocketbook n (US English) さいふ・ 財布

pocket money n こづかい・ 小遣い

poem n し・ 詩

point 1 n (a statement in a discussion) しゅちょう・ 主張;
(the most important idea) ようてん・ 要点: that's not the
point それは ちがいます。・ それは 違います。; (use)
there's no point in shouting どなっても しかたが ありま
せん。・ 怒鳴っても 仕方が ありません。; (when talking
about time) to be on the point of..... volitional form + と した
ところ; I am on the point of moving ひっこそうと したと
ころです。・ 引っ越そうと した とこです。; I was on the
point of selling the house いえを うろうと した ところで
した。・ 家を 売ろうと した ところでした。; (the sharp

end) とがった ところ・尖った 所; the point of a pencil えんぴつの さき・鉛筆の 先; (*in a contest, a game*) てん・点 **2** *vb* (*to indicate*) to point (one's finger) at someone だれ かを してきする・誰かを 指摘する; (*to aim*) to point a gun at someone だれかに じゅうを むける・誰かに 銃を 向ける; **point out** してきする・指摘する; please point the mistakes out to me まちがいを してきしてくだ さい。間違いを 指摘してください。

poison 1 *n* どく・毒 **2** *vb* どくを のませる・毒を 飲ま せる

pole *n* ぼう・棒; North Pole ほっきょく・北極; South Pole なんきょく・南極

police *n* けいさつ・警察

policeman *n* けいかん・警官

police station *n* けいさつしょ・警察署

policewoman *n* ふじんけいかん・婦人警官

polish *vb* to polish shoes くつを みがく・靴を 磨く; to polish the car くるまを みがく・車を 磨く

polite *adj* ていねい(な)・丁寧(な)

political *adj* せいじてき(な)・政治的(な)

politician *n* せいじか・政治家

politics *n* せいじ・政治

pollute *vb* おせんする・汚染する

pollution *n* おせん・汚染; environmental pollution かんき ょうおせん・環境汚染

pond *n* いけ・池

pony *n* ポニー

ponytail *n* ポニーテール

pool *n* (*a swimming pool*) プール; (*on the ground, the floor*) みずたまり・水溜まり; (*the game*) ビリヤード

poor *adj* (*not wealthy*) びんぼう(な)・貧乏(な); (*not satisfactory*) へた(な)・下手(な); I am poor at sports スポーツが へたです・スポーツが 下手です。; (*expressing sympathy*) かわいそう(な)

popular adj a popular sport りゅうこうの スポーツ・ 流行の スポーツ; she's very popular かのじょは にんき ものです。・ 彼女は 人気者です。; to be popular with the girls おんなの こに にんきが ある・ 女の子に 人気が ある

population n じんこう・ 人口

pork n ぶたにく・ 豚肉

port n みなと・ 港

portrait n ポートレート

positive adj せっきょくてき(な)・ 積極的(な)

possibility n かのうせい・ 可能性

possible adj かのう(な)・ 可能(な); they came as quickly as possible かれらは できるだけ はやく きました。・ 彼らは できるだけ 早く 来ました。; I did as much as possible できるだけ しました。

post (British English) **1** n the post (the system) ゆうびん・ 郵便; (the letters) ゆうびんぶつ・ 郵便物; has the post come yet? ゆうびんは もう きましたか。・ 郵便は もう 来ましたか。 **2** vb to post a letter てがみを だす・ 手紙 を出す

postbox n (British English) ポスト

postcard n はがき・ 葉書

postcode n (British English) ゆうびんばんごう・ 郵便番号

poster n ポスター

postman n (British English) ゆうびんや・ 郵便屋

post office n ゆうびんきょく・ 郵便局

postpone vb to postpone a concert コンサートを えんき する・ コンサートを 延期する; let's postpone the party until next week パーティーを らいしゅうまでえんきし ましょう。・ パーティーを 来週まで 延期しましょう。

pot n (a container) びん・ 瓶; to make a pot of tea こうちゃ をいれる・ 紅茶を 入れる; (for plants) うえきばち・ 植木鉢; (a saucepan) なべ

potato n じゃがいも

pottery n とうき・陶器

pound n (the currency) ポンド; (the measurement) ポンド;
! Note that a pound 453.6 g; two pounds of apples りんご いちキロ・りんご 一キロ

pour vb (from a container) つぐ; to pour milk into a bowl ミルクをボールに つぐ; (to serve) ついであげる; someone poured me some sake だれかが おさけを ついで くれました。・誰かが お酒を ついで くれました。; (to flow) ながれる・流れる; (to escape) smoke poured out of the window まどから けむりが でて いきました。・窓から 煙が 出て 行きました。; (to rain) it's pouring (with rain) どしゃぶりです。・どしゃ降りです。; (to enter or leave in large numbers) to pour into the city まちに さっとうする・町に 殺到する; people poured out of the stadium ひとが スタジアムからどっと でて きました。・人が スタジアムからどっと 出て 来ました。

powder n こな・粉

power n (control) けんりょく・権力; to be in power けんりょくをにぎっている・権力を 握っている; (influence) Joyce has great power ジョイスさんは えいきょうりょくがつよいです。・ジョイスさんは 影響力が 強いです。; (electricity) でんりょく・電力; power cut ていでん・停電

practical adj じつようてき(な)・実用的(な)

practise (British English), **practice** (US English) vb れんしゅうする・練習する; to practise the violin バイオリンをれんしゅうする・バイオリンを 練習する

praise vb to praise someone だれかを ほめる・誰かを 誉める

prawn n (British English) えび・海老

prayer n いのり・祈り

precaution n ようじん・用心

precious adj きちょう(な)・貴重(な)

precise adj せいかく(な)・正確(な)

prefer vb ～の ほうが すき・～の 方が 好き: I prefer chocolate to vanilla バニラより チョコレートが すきです・バニラより チョコレートが 好きです・I'd prefer to phone でんわした ほうが いいです・電話した 方が いいです。

pregnant adj にんしんしている・妊娠している

prejudice n へんけん・偏見

prepare vb (to get ready) じゅんびする・準備する; to prepare for a trip りょこうの じゅんびを する・旅行の 準備を する; the pupils are preparing for the exam せいとは じゅけんべんきょうを しています・生徒は 受験勉強を しています。; (to get something ready) よういする・用意する; to prepare the paperwork しょるいを よういする・書類を 用意する

prepared adj (willing) I'm prepared to wait まっても かまいません・待っても かまいません。; (ready) to be prepared for an exam しけんの じゅんびが できている・試験の 準備が できている

prescription n しょほうせん・処方箋

present 1 n (a gift) プレゼント; to give (someone) a present (だれかに)プレゼントを あげる・(誰かに)プレゼントを あげる; (now) げんざい・現在; I'll be here for the present しばらく ここに います。 2 vb (to give) to present a prize to someone だれかに しょうを おくる・誰かに 賞を 贈る; (on radio or TV) to present a programme ばんぐみを ていきょうする・番組を 提供する

president n だいとうりょう・大統領

press 1 vb おす・押す; to press the bell ベルを おす・ベルを 押す 2 n ほうどうきかん・報道機関

pressure n あつりょく・圧力; to put pressure on someone だれかに あつりょくを かける・誰かに 圧力を かける

pretend vb ～ふりを する; Mr Ueda's pretending to be annoyed うえださんは おこっている ふりを しています・上田さんは 怒っている ふりを しています。

pretty 1 adj かわいい **2** adv かなり; that's pretty good それ は かなり いいです。

prevent vb ふせぐ・防ぐ; to prevent a war せんそうを ふせぐ・戦争を 防ぐ

previous adj まえ(の)・前(の)

price n ねだん・値段

pride n ほこり・誇り; (self-respect) じそんしん・自尊心

priest n しさい・司祭

primary school n しょうがっこう・小学校

primary school teacher n しょうがっこうの せん せい・小学校の 先生

prime minister n (in Japan) そうりだいじん・総理大 臣; (in other countries) しゅしょう・首相

prince n おうじ・王子

princess n おうじょ・王女

principal n (US English) こうちょう・校長

print 1 vb いんさつする・印刷する; to print a book ほん を いんさつする・本を 印刷する **2** n (of a photo) プリ ント; (of a finger) しもん・指紋; (of a foot) あしあと・ 足跡

printer n プリンター

priority n ゆうせん・優先

prison n けいむしょ・刑務所

prisoner n しゅうじん・囚人; prisoner of war ほりょ・ 捕虜

private 1 adj (personal) こじん(の)・個人(の); my private life しせいかつ・私生活; (not run by the state) しりつ(の) ・私立(の); a private school しりつ がっこう・私立 学 校 **2 in private** ひとの みえない ところで・人の 見え ない 所で

prize n しょう・賞

probably adv たぶん・多分

problem *n* もんだい・問題; to cause a problem もんだいをおこす・問題を起こす

process *n* かてい・過程; I am in the process of writing a letter てがみを かいている とちゅうです。・手紙を書いている 途中です。

produce 1 *vb* (to make) つくる・作る; (to create) to produce a film えいがを せいさくする・映画を 制作する; to produce a play げきを えんじゅつする・劇を 演出する 2 *n* agricultural produce のうさんぶつ・農産物

product *n* さんぶつ・産物

production *n* せいさん・生産

profession *n* しょくぎょう・職業

professional *adj* プロ(の)

professor *n* きょうじゅ・教授

profit *n* りえき・利益

program 1 *n* (for a computer) プログラム; (US English) ▶ programme 2 *vb* プログラミングする

programme (British English), **program** (US English) 1 *n* (on radio, TV) ばんぐみ・番組; a programme about China ちゅうごくについての ばんぐみ・中国 についての 番組; (for a play, a concert) プログラム

progress *n* しんぽ・進歩; to make progress しんぽする・進歩する

project *n* (at school) けんきゅうテーマ・研究テーマ

promise 1 *vb* やくそくする・約束する; we promised to finish by January いちがつまでに おわると やくそくしました。・一月までに 終わると 約束しました。2 *n* やくそく・約束

pronounce *vb* はつおんする・発音する

proof *n* しょうこ・証拠

properly *adv* ちゃんと; please do it properly ちゃんと してください。

property *n* しょゆうぶつ・所有物

protect vb まもる・守る; to protect oneself じぶんを まもる・自分を 守る

protest vb (to complain) もんくを いう・文句を 言う; (to demonstrate) こうぎする・抗議する

protester n こうぎしゃ・抗議者

proud adj ほこりに おもう・誇りに 思う; she's proud of her work かのじょは しごとを ほこりに おもっています。・彼女は 仕事を 誇りに 思っています。

prove vb りっしょうする・立証する

provided conj I'll lend you my car provided you pay for the petrol ガソリンだいを はらうなら くるまを かして あげます。・ガソリン代を 払うなら 車を 貸して あげます。

psychiatrist n せいしんかい・精神科医

psychologist n しんりがくしゃ・心理学者

pub n (British English) パブ

public 1 n こうしゅう・公衆 **2** adj a public park こうえん・公園; a public library こうりつとしょかん・公立図書館 **3 in public** ひとまえで・人前で

public holiday n きゅうじつ・休日; (for celebration) さいじつ・祭日

public transport n こうきょうゆそうきかん・公共輸送機関

pudding n (British English) デザート

puddle n みずたまり・水たまり

pull vb ひく・引く; to pull (on) a rope ロープを ひく・ロープを 引く; to pull someone's hair だれかの かみを ひっぱる・誰かの 髪を 引っ張る; (to move by dragging) to pull the table into the kitchen だいどころに テーブルを ひきずる・台所に テーブルを 引きずる; (to take out) to pull a handkerchief out of one's pocket ハンカチを ポケットからとりだす・ハンカチを ポケットから 取り出す; to pull a face (British English) へんな かおを する・変な 顔を する; **pull down** (to knock down) こわす・

壊す; (to lower) ひきさげる・引き下げる; **pull out** to pull a tooth out はを ひきぬく・歯を 引き抜く; **pull up** (to stop) とまる・止まる; (to remove) to pull up the weeds くさを ねこそぎに する・草を 根こそぎに する; to pull up one's socks くつしたを ひきあげる・靴下を 引き上げる

pullover *n* セーター

pump *n* ポンプ; a bicycle pump じてんしゃの くうきいれ・自転車の 空気入れ; **pump up** ポンプで ふくらます・ポンプで 膨らます

pumpkin *n* かぼちゃ

punch *n* パンチ

puncture *n* パンク

punish *vb* ばっする・罰する

pupil *n* せいと・生徒

puppet *n* あやつりにんぎょう・操り人形; puppet show にんぎょうげき・人形劇

puppy *n* こいぬ・小犬

pure *adj* じゅんすい(な)・純粋(な)

purple *adj* むらさきいろ(の)・紫色(の)

purpose **1** *n* もくてき・目的 **2 on purpose** わざと; you did it on purpose, didn't you! わざと しましたね。

purse *n* (for money) さいふ・財布; (US English) (a handbag) ハンドバッグ

push *vb* おす・押す; to push a car くるまを おす・車を 押す; to push the door open ドアを おしあける・ドアを 押し開ける; to push someone out of the way だれかを おしのける・誰かを 押しのける; (to sell) せんでんする・宣伝する; to push drugs ドラッグを うる・ドラッグを 売る

pushchair *n* (British English) ベビーカー

pusher *n* ばいにん・売人

put *vb* おく・置く; to put the cards on the table カードを テーブルの うえに おく・カードを テーブルの 上に

置く; to put sugar in coffee さとうを コーヒーに いれる・砂糖を コーヒーに 入れる; to put someone in prison だれかを けいむしょに いれる・誰かを 刑務所に 入れる; to put someone in a bad mood だれかを いやな きもちにさせる・誰かを 嫌な 気持ちに させる; **put away** かたづける・片付ける; **put back** (to return to its place) もどす・戻す; to put a book back on a shelf ほんを たなにもどす・本を 棚に 戻す; (to change the time) to put the clocks back とけいを もどす・時計を 戻す; **put down** (on a surface) おく・置く; please put your bag down here ここに かばんを おいてください。・ここに かばんを 置いてください。; (when phoning) to put the phone down でんわをきる・電話を 切る; (British English) (to give an injection to) あんらくしさせる・安楽死させる; we had to put our dog down いぬを あんらくしさせなければ なりませんでした。・犬を 安楽死させなければ なりませんでした。; **put forward** to put the clocks forward とけいをすすめる・時計を 進める; **put off** (to delay) we have to put the party off until next week パーティーを らいしゅうまでえんきしなければ なりません。・パーティーを来週まで延期しなければ なりません。; (to switch off) けす・消す; **put on** (when dressing) (shirts, dresses) きる・着る; (hats) かぶる; (shoes, trousers, skirts, socks) はく; (makeup) つける; (spectacles) かける; (to switch on) to put the heating on だんぼうを つける・暖房を つける; to put the kettle on おゆを わかす・お湯を 沸かす; to put a CD on CD を かける Note that CD is pronounced シーディー; (to put on weight) ふとる・太る; (to organize, to produce) じょうえんする・上演する; to put on a play げきをじょうえんする・劇を 上演する; **put out** to put out a cigarette たばこを けす・たばこを 消す; (to take out) to put the bins out ごみばこを だす・ごみ箱を 出す; **put up** (to lift) to put one's hair up かみを もちあげる・髪を持ち上げる; to put up one's hand (in class) ≈ てを あげる・手を 上げる; (to attach) to put a poster up ポスターを はる・ポスターを 貼る; (when camping) to put up a tent テントをはる・テントを 張る; (British English) (to raise) あげる・上げる; to put the rent up やちんを あげる・家賃を

上げる; (to give someone a place to stay) とめる・泊める;
put up with がまんする・我慢する

puzzle n (mysterious thing) なぞ・謎; (game) パズル

pyjamas n (British English) パジャマ

....

Qq

qualified adj (having studied) しかくが ある・資格が
ある; (having experience, skills) のうりょくが ある・能力
が ある

quality n ひんしつ・品質

quantity n (amount) りょう・量; (number) かず・数

quarrel 1 n けんか 2 vb くちげんかする・口げんかする

quarter 1 n よんぶんの いち・四分の一; a quarter of an
hour じゅうごふん・十五分; to cut the tomatoes in quarters
トマトを よっつに きる・トマトを 四つに 切る
2 pron (when talking about quantities, numbers) a quarter of the
population can't read じんこうの よんぶんの いちは よ
めません。・人口の 四分の 一は 読めません。; (when
talking about time) an hour and a quarter いちじかんじゅう
ごふん・一時間十五分; it's (a) quarter past five ごじゅう
ごふんです。・五時十五分です。; it's (a) quarter to nine
はちじよんじゅうごふんです。・八時四十五分です。

quay n ふとう・埠頭

queen n じょおう・女王

question 1 n (a request for information) しつもん・質問;
to ask someone a question だれかに しつもんを する・
誰かに 質問を する; (a problem, a matter) もんだい・
問題 2 vb the police questioned the suspect けいさつは
ようぎしゃを とりしらべました。・警察は 容疑者を
取り調べました。; (to suspect) うたがう・疑う

questionnaire n アンケート

queue (*British English*) **1** n れつ・列; to join the queue れつ
にならぶ・列に並ぶ **2** vb れつを つくる・列を 作る

quick adj はやい・速い; a quick answer すばやい こたえ
・素早い 答え; it's quicker to go by train でんしゃで いっ
たほうが はやいです。・電車で 行った 方が 速いで
す。; quickest いちばんはやい・一番速い

quickly adv はやく・速く; Chris's Japanese progressed
quickly クリスさんの にほんごは はやく じょうたつし
ました。・クリスさんの 日本語は 速く 上達しました。

quiet 1 adj (*silent*) しずか(な)・静か(な); to keep quiet
しずかにする・静かに する; to go quiet しずかに なる
・静かに なる; please be quiet! しずかに してください。
・静かに してください。; (*not talkative*) おとなしい; (*calm*)
おだやか(な)・穏やか(な); a quiet life へいおんな せい
かつ・平穏な 生活 **2** n しずけさ・静けさ; to speak in a
quiet voice ちいさい こえで はなす・小さい 声で 話す

quietly adv しずかに・静かに; to speak quietly しずかに
はなす・静かに 話す; to read quietly しずかに よむ・
静かに 読む

quit vb (*to resign*) やめる・辞める; (*US English*) (*to give up*)
やめる; to quit smoking たばこを やめる

quite adv (*rather*) かなり; they go back to France quite often
かれらは かなり ひんぱんに フランスへ もどります。
・彼らは かなり 頻繁に フランスへ 戻ります。; I quite
like Chinese food ちゅうかりょうりが かなり すきです
・中華料理が かなり 好きです。; she earns quite a lot of
money かのじょは おかねを かなり かせぎます。・彼
女は お金を かなり 稼ぎます。; (*completely*) かんぜんに
・完全に; it isn't quite ready yet まだ かんぜんに できて
いません。・まだ 完全に できていません。; you're quite
right まったく あなたの いうとおりです。・全く あな
たの 言うとおりです。; (*exactly*) I don't quite know what Mr
Murakami does むらかみさんが なにを しているかは は
っきりとは わかりません。・村上さんが 何を している
かはっきりとは 知りません。

quiz n クイズ

Rr

rabbit *n* うさぎ; year of the rabbit うさぎどし・卯年

race 1 *n* (*ethnic group*) じんしゅ・人種; (*a contest*) きょうそう・競争; to have a race きょうそうする・競争する; (*for horse-racing*) けいば・競馬 **2** *vb* (*to compete with*) to race (against) someone だれかと きそう・誰かと 競う; let's race to the car くるまの ところまで きょうそうしましょう。・車の 所まで 競争しましょう。

racehorse *n* きょうそうば・競走馬

racetrack *n* (*for horses*) けいばじょう・競馬場; (*for cars*) サーキット

racism *n* じんしゅさべつ・人種差別

racket, racquet *n* ラケット

radiator *n* ヒーター

radio *n* ラジオ; on the radio ラジオで

radio station *n* ラジオほうそうきょく・ラジオ放送局

rage *n* げきど・激怒; to fly into a rage いかりくるう・怒り狂う

raid *vb* to raid a bank ぎんこうを しゅうげきする・銀行を 襲撃する; the police raided the building けいさつは ビルの ていれを しました。・警察は ビルの 手入れを しました。

rail *n* (*for holding on to*) てすり・手すり; (*for trains*) by rail でんしゃで・電車で

railway (*British English*), **railroad** (*US English*) *n* (*a track*) せんろ・線路; (*the rail system*) てつどう・鉄道

railway line *n* (*British English*) てつどう・鉄道! Note that Japanese railway lines have names with the suffix せん e.g. the やまのてせん in Tokyo

railway station n (British English) えき・駅

rain 1 n あめ・雨 **2** vb あめが ふる・雨が 降る; it's raining あめが ふっている・雨が 降っている

rainbow n にじ・虹

raincoat n レインコート

raise vb (to lift) もちあげる・持ち上げる; (to increase) あげる・上げる; to raise prices ねだんを あげる・値段を 上げる; (in anger) to raise one's voice こえを おおきくする・声を 大きくする; (to talk about) to raise a subject ぎだいに とりあげる・議題に 取り上げる; (to bring up) to raise children こどもを そだてる・子供を 育てる

ram n year of the ram ひつじどし・未年

range n (a selection) there is a range of activities いろいろな かつどうが あります。・色々な 活動が あります。; (of mountains) さんみゃく・山脈; (US English) (for cooking) レンジ

rare adj (not common) まれ(な); (very slightly cooked) レア(の)

rarely adv めったに + negative; we rarely meet めったに あいません。・めったに 会いません。

raspberry n ラズベリー

rat n ねずみ; year of the rat ねずみどし・子年

rather adv (when saying what one would prefer) むしろ + verb in 〜たい form; I'd rather go home むしろ かえりたいです。・むしろ 帰りたいです。; I'd rather be here むしろ ここに いたいです。; I'd rather read the paper むしろ しんぶんをよみたいです。・むしろ 新聞を 読みたいです。; I'd rather you didn't do that そんなことを しないでください。; (quite) かなり; I think it's rather valuable これは かなりねうちが あるとおもいます。・これはかなり 値打ちがあると 思います。

raw adj なま(の)・生(の)

razor n かみそり

razor blade n かみそりの は・かみそりの 刃

reach *vb* (*to arrive at*) つく・着く; we reached the town at midnight よる じゅうにじに まちに つきました。・夜十二時に 町に 着きました。; (*to be delivered to*) とどく・届く; the letter never reached him てがみは かれに とどきませんでした。・手紙は 彼に 届きませんでした。; (*by stretching*) to reach up てを のばす・手を 伸ばす; I can't reach the shelf たなに てが とどきません。・棚に 手が 届きません。; (*to come to*) たっする・達する; to reach a decision けつろんに たっする・結論に 達する; (*to contact by phone*) I can be reached at this number この でんわばんごうに います。・この 電話番号に います。; **reach out** てを のばす・手を 伸ばす

react *vb* はんのうする・反応する

read *vb* よむ・読む; difficult to read よみにくい・読みにくい; to read to someone だれかに よみあげる・誰かに 読み上げる; **read out** to read out the names なまえを よみあげる・名前を 読み上げる; **read through** よみとおす・読み通す

reading *n* どくしょ・読書

ready *adj* (*prepared*) よういが できている・用意が できている; to get ready じゅんびする・準備する; to get a meal ready りょうりする・料理する; (*happy*) I'm ready to help at anytime いつでも よろこんで てつだいます。・いつでも 喜んで 手伝います。

real *adj* (*not imagined*) ほんとう(の)・本当(の); (*not artificial*) ほんもの(の)・本物(の); are they real diamonds? その ダイヤは ほんものですか。・その ダイヤは 本物ですか。; it's a real shame ほんとうに ざんねんです。・本当に 残念です。

reality *n* じじつ・事実

realize *vb* きが つく・気が 付く; I didn't realize (that) Mr Lindsay was your boss リンジーさんが あなたの ボスとは しりませんでした。・リンジーさんが あなたの ボスとは 知りませんでした。

really *adv* とても; it's really easy to make とても つくりやすいです。・とても 作りやすいです。; what really

happened? じっさいは どうしましたか。・ 実際は どう
しましたか。; really? ほんとうですか。・ 本当ですか。

rear 1 *n* うしろ・後ろ 2 *vb* そだてる・育てる

reason *n* りゆう・理由; tell me the reason why どうして
か おしえてください。・ どうしてか 教えてください。

reassure *vb* あんしんさせる・安心させる

receipt *n* りょうしゅうしょ・領収書; a till receipt レシ
ート

receive *vb* (to get) もらう; we received a letter from the
teacher せんせいから てがみを もらいました。・ 先生
から手紙を もらいました。; (to meet) むかえる・迎え
る; to be well received かんげいを うける・歓迎を 受け
る

recent *adj* さいきん(の)・最近(の)

recently *adv* さいきん・最近

reception *n* (in a hotel, a hospital, a company) うけつけ・
受付; ask at (the) reception うけつけで きいてください。
・受付で 聞いてください。; (a formal event) かんげいか
い・歓迎会

receptionist *n* うけつけの ひと・受付の 人

recipe *n* りょうりの つくりかた・料理の 作り方

recognize *vb* わかる・分かる

recommend *vb* すいせんする・推薦する

record 1 *n* (information) (historical, public) きろく・記録;
(personal, career) けいれき・経歴; medical records カル
テ; (for playing music) レコード; (in sport) きろく・記録;
to break the world record せかいきろくを やぶる・世界
記録を破る 2 *vb* (information) きろくを とる・記録を
とる; (audio) ろくおんする・録音する; (video) ろくがす
る・録画する

recorder *n* リコーダー

recover *vb* かいふくする・回復する; to recover from an
illness びょうきが なおる・病気が 治る

recycle vb リサイクルする

red adj あかい・赤い; to go red, to turn red あかく なる・赤く なる; red hair あかげ・赤毛

red-haired adj あかげ(の)・赤毛(の)

reduce vb to reduce prices ねだんを さげる・値段を 下げる; to reduce the number of employees しょくいんを へらす・職員を 減らす; to reduce speed スピードを おとす・スピードを 落とす

reduction n (in prices) ねさげ・値下げ; (in numbers) げんしょう・減少

redundant adj (British English) to be made redundant かいこ される・解雇される

referee n (in sports) しんぱんいん・審判員; (when applying for a job) すいせんしゃ・推薦者

reflection n はんしゃ・反射

refreshed adj すっきりした

refrigerator n れいぞうこ・冷蔵庫

refugee n なんみん・難民

refuse¹ vb ことわる・断る; to refuse to do ..... volitional form of verb + と; to refuse to listen きこうと しない・聞こうと しない; to refuse to stop とまろうと しない・止まろうと しない; to refuse to pay はらおうと しない・払おうと しない

refuse² n (British English) ごみ

regards n please give Monica my regards モニカさんに よろしく つたえてください。・モニカさんに よろしく 伝えてください。

region n ちほう・地方

regional adj ちほう(の)・地方(の)

register n しゅっせきぼ・出席簿; to take the register しゅっせきを とる・出席を とる

regret vb こうかいする・後悔する; I regret changing my mind きが かわった ことを こうかいしています。・

気が 変わった ことを 後悔 しています。 I regret that I won't be able to take part ざんねんですが、 さんか できません。・ 残念ですが、 参加 できません。

regular *adj* きそくてき(な)・ 規則的(な)

regularly *adv* きそくてきに・ 規則的に

rehearsal *n* リハーサル

rehearse *vb* リハーサルを する

reject *vb* ことわる・ 断る; to reject advice アドバイスを ことわる・ アドバイスを 断る; to reject a candidate りっこうほしゃを みとめない・ 立候補者を 認めない

relationship *n* かんけい・ 関係; to have a good relationship いい かんけいに ある・ いい 関係に ある; she has a good relationship with her parents かのじょは ごりょうしんと いい かんけいに あります。・ 彼女は ご両親と いい 関係に あります。

relative *n* しんせき・ 親戚

relax *vb* くつろぐ

relaxed *adj* くつろいだ

relay race *n* リレー

release *vb* (*person*) じゆうにする・ 自由に する; (*information*) こうひょうする・ 公表する

reliable *adj* a reliable person しんらいできる ひと・ 信頼できる 人; a reliable car たよりに なる くるま・ 頼りに なる 車

relieved *adj* あんしんした・ 安心した

religion *n* しゅうきょう・ 宗教

religious education, RE (*British English*) *n* しゅうきょうの べんきょう・ 宗教の 勉強

rely *vb* (*to depend on*) たよる・ 頼る; (*to count on*) しんらいする・ 信頼する; we can rely on him かれは しんらい できます。・ 彼は 信頼 できます。

remain *vb* のこる・ 残る

remark *n* はつげん・ 発言

remarkable *adj* いちじるしい・著しい

remember *vb* おぼえる・覚える; do you remember her? かのじょをおぼえていますか。・彼女を 覚えていますか。; I remember writing down the address じゅうしょをかいたのをおぼえています。・住所を 書いたのを覚えています。; to remember to... わすれずに...・忘れずに...; to remember to post the letter わすれずに てがみをだす・忘れずに 手紙を 出す; to remember to turn off the lights わすれずに でんきを けす・忘れずに 電気を 消す

remind *vb* (to remind to do something) わすれない ようにいう・忘れない ように 言う; to remind someone to buy stamps だれかに きってを かう ことを わすれない ように いう・誰かに 切手を 買う ことを 忘れない ように 言う; (to bring something from the past to mind) おもいだす・思い出す; that reminds me of home それは うちをおもいださせます。・それは 家を 思い出させます。

remote control *n* リモコン

remove *vb* (object) とりのぞく・取り除く; (clothing) ぬぐ・脱ぐ

rent 1 *vb* かりる・借りる; to rent an apartment アパートをかりる・アパートを 借りる 2 *n* やちん・家賃; rent out かす・貸す

repair *vb* なおす・直す; to have a bicycle repaired じてんしゃをなおして もらう・自転車を 直して もらう

repeat *vb* (to say again) くりかえす・繰り返す; to repeat a year りゅうねんする・留年する

replace *vb* かえる・代える・換える

reply 1 *vb* へんじする・返事する 2 *n* へんじ・返事; to write a reply へんじを かく・返事を 書く

report 1 *vb* (to tell about) ほうこくする・報告する; (to police, emergency services) つうほうする・通報する; to report an accident じこを つうほうする・事故を 通報する; (in the news) to report on an event できごとを ほうどうする・出来事を 報道する; (to complain about) to report

the noise そうおんを うったえる・騒音を 訴える **2** *n*
(*in the news*) ほうどう・報道; (*an official document*) ほうこ
くしょ・報告書; (*British English*) (*from school*) つうちひょ
う・通知表

report card *n* (*US English*) つうちひょう・通知表

reporter *n* きしゃ・記者

represent *vb* だいひょうする・代表する

representative *n* だいひょう・代表

republic *n* きょうわこく・共和国

request *n* おねがい・お願い

rescue *vb* (*from danger*) すくう・救う

resemble *vb* にている・似ている; to resemble each other
おたがいに にている・お互いに 似ている

resentment *n* うらみ・恨み

reservation *n* よやく・予約

reserve *vb* よやくする・予約する

resign *vb* じにんする・辞任する

resist *vb* ていこうする・抵抗する

respect 1 *vb* そんけいする・尊敬する **2** *n* そんけい・
尊敬

responsibility *n* せきにん・責任

responsible *adj* (*trustworthy*) せきにんかんが ある・
責任感が ある; (*the cause of*) he is responsible for the
accident じこは かれの せいです。・事故は 彼の せい
です。; (*in charge*) I am responsible for the school timetable
がっこうの じかんわりを たんとうしています。・
学校の 時間割を 担当しています。

rest 1 *n* (*what is left*) のこり・残り; we spent the rest of the
time in the garden のこりの じかんを にわで すごしまし
た。・残りの 時間を 庭で 過ごしました。; (*a break*) き
ゅうけい・休憩; to have a rest きゅうけいする・休憩
する **2** *vb* やすむ・休む

restaurant *n* レストラン

result n けっか・結果; the exam results しけんの けっか・試験の 結果; as a result of an accident じこの ため・事故の ため

résumé n (US English) a résumé りれきしょ・履歴書

retire vb たいしょくする・退職する! Note that this can also refer to giving up ones job at any point even well before retirement age

return vb (to go|come back) もどる・戻る; (from abroad, to one's home) かえる・帰る; (to give|take back) かえす・返す; can you return my book? ほんを かえしてください。・本を 返してください。; (to send back) おくりかえす・送り返す; to return faulty goods (by post) (ゆうびんで)ふりょうひんを おくりかえす・(郵便で)不良品を 送り返す; to return to work しごとに もどる・仕事に 戻る; to return to school (after a holiday) (やすみの あと)がっこうが また はじまる・(休みの 後)学校が また 始まる

return ticket n おうふく(きっぷ)・往復(切符)

revenge n ふくしゅう・復讐; to get one's revenge ふくしゅうする・復讐する

revolution n かくめい・革命

reward 1 n ほうび・褒美 2 vb ほうびを あたえる・褒美を 与える

rewind vb まきもどす・巻戻す

rhinoceros, rhino n さい

rhythm n リズム

rib n ろっこつ・肋骨

rice n (uncooked) こめ・米; (cooked) ごはん・ご飯! Rice which is served on a plate is often referred to as ライス

rice field n たんぼ・田んぼ

rich adj かねもち(の)・金持(の); to get rich かねもちに なる・金持ちに なる

rid: to get rid of vb とりのぞく・取り除く

ride 1 *vb* to ride, to go riding じょうばを する・乗馬を する; to ride a horse じょうばを する・乗馬を する; to be riding a bike じてんしゃに のっている・自転車に 乗っている **2** *n* to go for a ride (*in a car*) ドライブに いく・ドライブに 行く; (*on a bicycle*) サイクリングに いく・サイクリングに 行く; (*on a horse*) じょうばに でかける・乗馬に でかける

ridiculous *adj* ばかげた

rifle *n* ライフル

right 1 *adj* (*not left*) みぎ(の)・右(の); right hand みぎて・右手; right handed みぎきき・右利き; (*honest, good*) いい; it's not right to steal ぬすみは よくないです。・盗みは 良くないです。; to do the right thing いい ことを する; (*correct*) ただしい・正しい; the right answer ただしい こたえ・正しい 答え; is this the right direction? このほうこうは ただしいですか。・この 方向は 正しいですか。; what's the right time? いま なんじですか。・今 何時ですか。; she's right かのじょの いう とおりです。・彼女の 言う とおりです。; that's right その とおりです。 **2** *n* (*the direction*) the right みぎ・右; please take the first street on the right さいしょの みちを みぎにはいってください。・最初の 道を 右に 入ってください。; (*what one is entitled to*) a right けんり・権利; to have a right to be educated きょういくを うけるけんりが ある・教育を 受ける権利が ある; human rights じんけん・人権 **3** *adv* みぎに・右に; to turn right みぎに まがる・右に 曲がる

ring 1 *vb* (*British English*) (*to phone*) でんわする・電話する; to ring for a taxi でんわで タクシーを よぶ・電話で タクシーを 呼ぶ; (*to make a sound*) ならす・鳴らす; to ring the bell ベルを ならす・ベルを 鳴らす; the doorbell rang ベルが なりました。・ベルが 鳴りました。 **2** *n* (*a piece of jewellery*) ゆびわ・指輪; wedding ring けっこんゆびわ・結婚指輪; engagement ring こんやくゆびわ・婚約指輪; (*a circle*) えん・円; (*in a circus*) リング; **ring up** (*British English*) でんわする・電話する

rinse *vb* すすぐ

ripe *adj* じゅくした・熟した

rise *vb* (if it's smoke, water, a price) あがる・上がる; (if it's a plane) じょうしょうする・上昇する; (if it's the sun) のぼる・昇る

risk **1** *n* (danger) きけん・危険; the business is at risk かいしゃは きけんに さらされています。・会社は 危険に さらされています。

river *n* かわ・川; (flowing into the sea) かこう・河口

riverbank *n* かわぎし・川岸

road *n* どうろ・道路

road sign *n* どうろひょうしき・道路標識

roadworks *n* どうろこうじ・道路工事

roar *n* (if it's a lion) ほえごえ・吠え声; (if it's a crowd) どよめき; (if it's an engine) とどろき

roast **1** *vb* オーブンで やく・オーブンで 焼く **2** *adj* to eat roast beef ローストビーフを たべる・ローストビーフを 食べる

rob *vb* ぬすむ・盗む

robbery *n* ごうとう・強盗

robin *n* こまどり

robot *n* ロボット

rock *n* (the material) がんせき・岩石; (a large stone) いわ・岩; (music) ロック

rock climbing *n* ロッククライミング

rocket *n* ロケット

role *n* やく・役

roll **1** *vb* ころがる・転がる; the ball rolled under a car ボールはくるまの したに ころがりました。・ボールは 車の 下に 転がりました。 **2** *n* (of paper, cloth, plastic) まき・巻; a roll of film フィルム いっぽん・フィルム 一本; (bread) ロールパン; (US English) (at school) to call the roll

しゅっせきをとる・出席を取る; roll about, roll
around (if it's an object) ころがる・転がる; roll over she
rolled over (in bed) かのじょは（ベッドで）ねがえりをう
ちました。・彼女は（ベッドで）寝返りをうちました。;
roll up まく・巻く; to roll up a newspaper しんぶんを ま
く・新聞を 巻く

roller coaster n ジェットコースター

roller-skate n ローラースケートの くつ・ローラー
スケートの靴

roller-skating n ローラースケート

romantic adj ロマンチック（な）

roof n やね・屋根; (if used for activity) おくじょう・屋上

room n へや・部屋; (for sleeping) しんしつ・寝室; (for
teaching) きょうしつ・教室; (for meetings) かいぎしつ・
会議室; (space) ばしょ・場所; to make room ばしょを
あける・場所を 空ける

rooster n year of the rooster とりどし・酉年

root n ね・根

rope n ロープ

rose n ばら

rotten adj くさった・腐った

rough adj (not smooth) あらい・粗い; (not gentle) あらっぽ
い・荒っぽい; (tough) ちあんの わるい・治安の 悪い;
to live in a rough area ちあんの わるい ちいきに すむ・
治安の 悪い 地域に 住む; (not exact, precise) a rough
figure おおまかな すうじ・大まかな 数字; (difficult) た
いへん（な）・大変（な）; I had a rough time yesterday きの
うは たいへんでした。・昨日は 大変でした。; (caused
by bad weather) a rough sea あれた うみ・荒れた 海

round ! Often round occurs in combinations with verbs. For more
information, see the note at around. **1** prep to be sitting round a
table テーブルの まわりに すわっている・テーブルの
周りに 座っている; to sail round the world せかいいっし
ゅうの こうかいを する・世界一周の 航海を する;

to go round Oxford オックスフォードめぐりを する・オックスフォード巡りを する **2** *adv* to go round and round ぐるぐるまわる・ぐるぐる 回る; to go round to John's house ジョンさんの うちへ 行く; to invite someone round だれかを うちに よぶ・誰かを 家に 呼ぶ **3** *n* (*in a quiz, sports*) ラウンド **4** *adj* まるい・丸い

roundabout *n* (*British English*) (*in a fair*) メリーゴーラウンド; (*for traffic*) Roundabouts are often referred to as ロータリー or ラウンドアバウト but there is no real Japanese equivalent.

route *n* ルート; a bus route バスの ろせん・バスの 路線

routine *n* daily routine にっか・日課

row¹ 1 *n* れつ・列; the pupils were sitting in rows せいとは れつに なって すわっていました。・生徒は 列に なって 座っていました。; (*when talking about frequency*) to be absent five days in a row つづけて いつか やすむ・続けて 五日 休む **2** *vb* こぐ・漕ぐ; (*as a sport*) ボートレースを する

row² *n* (*British English*) けんか; to have a row (with someone) (だれかと) けんかを する・(誰かと) けんかを する

rowing *n* ボートレース

rowing boat (*British English*), **rowboat** (*US English*) *n* ボート

royal *adj* (*of the Japanese royal family*) こうしつ(の)・皇室(の); (*of other royal families*) おうしつ(の)・王室(の)

rub *vb* to rub one's eyes めを こする・目を こする; **rub out** (*British English*) けす・消す; to rub out a mistake まちがいをけす・間違いを 消す

rubber *n* (*the material*) ゴム; (*British English*) (*an eraser*) けしゴム・消しゴム

rubbish *n* (*British English*) (*refuse*) ごみ; (*poor quality goods*) がらくた

rubbish bin *n* (*British English*) ごみばこ・ごみ箱

rucksack n リュックサック

rude adj (not polite) しつれい(な)・失礼(な); she was rude
to the teacher かのじょは せんせいに しつれいでした。
・彼女は 先生に 失礼でした。; (vulgar) げひん(な)・
下品(な); a rude word げひんな ことば・下品な 言葉

rug n じゅうたん

rugby n ラグビー

ruin 1 vb (to spoil) だいなしに する・台無しに する; to
ruin a meal しょくじを だいなしに する・食事を 台無
しにする; Geoffrey ruined the atmosphere ジェフリーさ
んのせいで ざが しらけました。・ジェフリーさんの
せいで座が しらけました。; (to damage) だめに する;
you'll ruin your shoes くつを だめに します。・靴を だ
めにします。; to be ruined だめに なる **2** n はいきょ・
廃虚

rule 1 n (of a game) ルール; (in a school, an organization)
きそく・規則; it's against the rules きそくいはんです。・
規則違反です。 **2** vb (if it's a leader) しはいする・支配す
る; (if it's a king, queen) くんりんする・君臨する

ruler n じょうぎ・定規

rumour (British English), **rumor** (US English) n うわさ・噂

run 1 vb to run はしる・走る; to run after someone だれか
のあとを おいかける・誰かの 後を 追いかける; to
run across the street みちを はしって わたる・道を 走
って 渡る; to run in a race きょうそうに さんかする・
競争に 参加する; (from danger) にげる・逃げる; (to
manage) けいえいする・経営する; (to work, to operate) さ
どうする・作動する; the car runs on unleaded petrol この
くるまはむえんガソリンで はしります。・この 車は
無鉛ガソリンで走ります。; the system is running well シ
ステムはうまく いっています。・システムは うまく
行っています。; (to organize) おこなう・行う; to run a
competition コンクールを おこなう・コンクールを 行
う; (when talking about transport) うごく・動く; the buses
don't run after midnight よる じゅうにじいこうはバスが
うごきません。・夜 十二時以降は バスが 動きませ

ん。; (to flow) ながれる・流れる; (to fill with water) to run a bath おふろに おゆを いれる・お風呂に お湯を 入れる; (to come off) おちる・落ちる; (in an election) りっこうほする・立候補する; to run for president だいとうりょうせんに しゅっぱする・大統領選に 出馬する; (other uses) to be running late おくれている・遅れている; to be running a temperature ねつがある・熱が ある **2** n ランニング; to go for a run はしる・走る; **run about, run around** はしゃぎまわる・はしゃぎ回る; **run away** にげる・逃げる; **run off** にげる・逃げる

runner n ランナー

rush 1 vb (to hurry) いそぐ・急ぐ; to rush to finish one's homework しゅくだいを いそいで すます・宿題を 急いで 済ます; to rush out of the house いえから ころがりでる・家から 転がり出る; to be rushed to the hospital びょういんにいそいで はこばれる・病院に 急いで 運ばれる; (to put pressure on) to be in a rush いそいでいる・急いでいる; to do one's homework in a rush いそいで しゅくだいを する・急いで 宿題を する

rush hour n ラッシュアワー

Russia n ロシア

rusty adj さびた

Ss

sad adj かなしい・悲しい; she looks sad かのじょは かなしそうです。・彼女は 悲しそうです。

saddle n (for horse) くら・鞍; (for bicycle) サドル

safe 1 adj (without risk) あんぜんな(な)・安全(な); a safe place あんぜんな ばしょ・安全な 場所; it's not safe for children こどもには あぶないです。・子供には 危ない

です。; is it safe to go there? あそこの ちあんは いいです か。・ あそこの 治安は いいですか。; *(free from danger)* to feel safe あんしん できる ・ 安心 できる; your car is safe here くるまは ここだと 安全です。・ 車は こ こだと 安全です。; *(out of danger)* I'm glad you're safe ぶじ でよかったです。・ 無事で 良かったです。 **2** *n* きんこ ・ 金庫

safety *n* あんぜん ・ 安全

Sagittarius *n* いてざ ・ 射手座

sail 1 *n* ほ ・ 帆; to set sail こうかいする ・ 航海する **2** *vb* to sail around the world せかい いっしゅうの ふなたびに でる ・ 世界 一周の 船旅に 出る; to go sailing ヨットあ そびする ・ ヨット遊びする

sailing *n* ヨットあそび ・ ヨット遊び

sailing boat *(British English)*, **sailboat** *(US English)* *n* ヨット

sailor *n* *(general)* ふなのり ・ 船乗り; *(naval)* すいへい ・ 水兵

saint *n* せいじん ・ 聖人

salad *n* サラダ

salary *n* きゅうりょう ・ 給料

sale *n* on sale *(available)* はつばいちゅう ・ 発売中; *(special offer)* やすうり ・ 安売り; for sale うりもの ・ 売り物; the sales セール

sales assistant *(British English)* てんいん ・ 店員

salmon *n* さけ ・ 鮭

salt *n* しお ・ 塩

same 1 *adj* おなじ ・ 同じ; she's got the same coat as me かのじょはわたしと おなじ コートを もっています。 ・ 彼女は 私と 同じ コートを 持っています。; they go to the same school かれらは おなじ がっこうに かよって います。 ・ 彼らは 同じ 学校に 通っています。; it's the same as the car I had before まえ もっていた くるまと お なじです。 ・ 前 持っていた 車と 同じです。; it's all the

same to me かまいません。; the houses all look the same ぜんぶの いえが おなじに みえます。・ 全部の 家が 同じに 見えます。; people are the same everywhere ひとは どこでも おなじです。・ 人は どこでも 同じです。; it's the same as ever いつもと おなじです。・ いつもと 同じです。**2** *pron* the same おなじ・ 同じ; I'll have the same わたしも おなじに します。・ 私も 同じに します。; to do the same as the others ほかの ひとと おなじに する・ 外の 人と 同じに する

sand *n* すな・ 砂

sandal *n* サンダル

sandwich *n* サンドイッチ; a ham sandwich ハムサンド

Santa (Claus) *n* サンタクロース *Children often call Santa* サンタさん

sardine *n* いわし

satellite TV *n* えいせいほうそう・ 衛星放送

satisfactory *adj* いい

satisfied *adj* まんぞくしている・ 満足している

Saturday *n* どようび・ 土曜日

sauce *n* ソース

saucepan *n* なべ

saucer *n* うけざら・ 受け皿

sausage *n* ソーセージ

save *vb* (to rescue) すくう・ 救う; I saved his life かれの いのちを たすけました。・ 彼の 命を 助けました。; (to avoid spending) to save せつやくする・ 節約する; to save money ちょきんする・ 貯金する; (to avoid wasting) to save time じかんを せつやくする・ 時間を 節約する; (to keep) とって おく・ 取って おく; to save a piece of cake (for someone) (だれかに)ケーキを とって おく・ (誰かに)ケーキを 取って おく; to save a file ファイル をセーブする

savings *n* ちょきん・ 貯金

saw *n* のこぎり

saxophone *n* サキソホーン

say *vb* いう・言う; to say goodbye さよならと いう・さよならと 言う; she says (that) she can't go out tonight かのじょは こんばん でかけられないと いいました。・彼女は 今晩 出かけられないと 言いました。; he said to wait here かれは ここに いてと いいました。・彼は ここに いてと 言いました。; they say she's very rich かのじょは おかねもちだと いわれています。・彼女は お金持ちだと 言われています。; I can't say who did it 誰が やったか いえません。・誰が やったか 言えません。; she wouldn't say かのじょは いって くれませんでした。・彼女は 言って くれませんでした。; what does the message say? メッセージは なんですか。・メッセージは 何ですか。; it says here that smoking is not allowed きんえんと ここに かいて あります。・禁煙と ここに 書いてあります。; I'd say she was forty かのじょは よんじゅっさい くらいだと おもいます。・彼女は 四十才 くらいだと 思います。; let's say there are twenty people come to the party にじゅうにん くらい パーティーに くると して かんがえましょう。・二十人 くらい パーティーに 来ると して 考えましょう。

scandal *n* スキャンダル

scare *vb* こわがらす・怖がらす; you scared me! びっくりしました。; scare away おどかして おいはらう・おどかして 追い払う

scared *adj* こわい・恐い

scarf *n* (*long, for warmth*) マフラー; (*square, as fashion accessory*) スカーフ

scenery *n* けしき・景色

school ! *Note that the Japanese school system is different* **1** *n* がっこう・学校; to be at school がっこうに かよっている・学校に 通っている **2** *adj* がっこうの・学校の; a school bus スクールバス

schoolbag *n* かばん *Japanese children at elementary school carry a regulation satchel called a* ランドセル

schoolboy n だんしせいと・男子生徒

schoolgirl n じょしせいと・女子生徒

schoolwork n がっこうの べんきょう・学校の 勉強

science n (at university) かがく・科学; to study science かがくをべんきょうする・科学を 勉強する; (in school) りか・理科

scientist n かがくしゃ・科学者

scissors n はさみ

score vb to score a goal とくてんする・得点する

Scorpio n さそりざ・さそり座

Scotland n スコットランド

scratch 1 vb (when itchy) かく; to scratch one's arm うでを かく・腕を かく; (with nails) ひっかく・引っかく; (on a bush, thorns) ひっかかる・引っかかる; (to mark, to damage) きずつける・傷つける 2 n すりきず・擦り傷

scream vb ひめいを あげる・悲鳴を あげる

screen n (at cinema) スクリーン; (on TV, computer) がめん・画面

screw n ねじ

sea n うみ・海; beside the sea, by the sea うみぞいで・海沿いで

seagull n かもめ

seal n とど

search vb さがす・探す; to search for someone だれかを さがす・誰かを 探す; (to examine a place) そうさくする・捜索する; I was searched at the airport くうこうで しんたいけんさされました。・空港で 身体検査されました。

seashell n かいがら・貝殻

seasick adj to be seasick, to get seasick ふなよいに なる・船酔いに なる

seaside n at the seaside かいがんで・海岸で; to go to the seaside うみにいく・海に 行く

season n きせつ・季節

seat n (a chair, a bench) いす・椅子; to have a seat すわる・座る; (on transport, in a theatre) せき・席

seatbelt n シートベルト

second 1 adj (in a sequence) にばん(め)・二番(め); (of a number of items) ふたつめ・二つ目; (of a number of times) にかいめ・二回目; this is the second time I've called この でんわは にかいめです。・この 電話は 二回目です。; the second Monday of each month まいつき だいに げつよ うび・毎月 第二 月曜日 **2** n (in a series) にばんめ・二 番目; (in time) a second いちびょう・一秒; (a very short time) しゅんかん・瞬間; (in dates) ふつか・二日; the second of May ごがつふつか・五月二日 **3** adv to come second にいに なる・二位に なる

secondary school n (British English) ちゅうとうこうと うがっこう・中等高等学校 The general word がっこう is more often used unless you have to be really specific.

second-hand adj ちゅうこ(の)・中古(の); second hand car ちゅうこしゃ・中古車; second hand goods ちゅうこひん・中古品

secret 1 adj ひみつ(の)・秘密(の) **2** n ひみつ・秘密; to tell someone a secret だれかに ひみつを いう・誰か に秘密を 言う **3** in secret ないしょで・内緒で

secretary n ひしょ・秘書

see vb みる・見る; what can you see? なにが みえます か。・何が 見えますか。; I can't see みえません。・見え ません。; he saw the people running かれは ひとびとが はしっているのをみました。・彼は 人々が 走っている のを見ました。; do they see each other often? かれらは よくあいますか。・彼らは よく 会いますか。; see you tomorrow! また あした。・また 明日。; I'll go and see みに いきます。・見に 行きます。; (to accompany) I'll see you home うちまで おくります。・家まで 送ります。

seem vb (to appear) she seems happy かのじょは しあわ せみたいです。・彼女は 幸せ みたいです。; Zoe seems

annoyed ゾイさんは いらいらしている みたいです。; he seems tired かれは つかれている みたいです。; 彼は 疲れている みたいです。; they seem to be looking for someone かれらは だれかを さがしている みたいです。・彼らは 誰かを 捜している みたいです。; (when talking about one's impressions) 〜と おもう・〜と 思う; it seems (that) there are a lot of problems もんだいが たくさん あると おもいます。・問題が たくさん あると 思います。; it seems strange (to me) へんだと おもいます。・変だと 思います。! Note that there are also several other ways to say 'seems' in Japanese.

seldom adv めったに + negative; I seldom drive めったに うんてんしません。・めったに 運転しません。

self-confident ▶ confident

selfish adj わがまま(な)

sell vb うる・売る; to sell books to the students がくせい に ほんを うる・学生に 本を 売る; he sold me his car かれは わたしに くるまを うりました。・彼は 私に 車を 売りました。; water is sold in bottles みずは びんで うられています。・水は 瓶で 売られています。; do you sell bread? パンを うっていますか。・パンを 売っていますか。

send vb おくる・送る; to send a package to someone だれ かにこづつみを おくる・誰かに 小包を 送る; he sent her a letter かれは かのじょに てがみを おくりました。・彼は 彼女に 手紙を 送りました。; to send a pupil home from school せいとを がっこうから うちに かえす・生徒を 学校から 家に 返す; send back おくりかえす・送り返す; send for to send for the doctor おいしゃさんを よぶ・お医者さんを 呼ぶ; to send for some goods しな ものをたのむ・品物を 頼む; send on to send on post ゆうびんぶつを てんそうする・郵便物を 転送する

senior high school (US English), **senior school** (British English) n こうとうがっこう・高等学校 ! Note that this is often abbreviated to こうこう

sense n (common) sense じょうしき・常識; (allowing one to see, hear, smell etc) かんかく・感覚; (a meaning) いみ・意味; it doesn't make sense わかりません。・分かりません。; it makes sense to prepare properly ちゃんと じゅんびした ほうが いいです。・ちゃんと 準備した 方が いいです。

sensible adj (describing a person) しっかりした; (describing a decision, suggestion) けんめい(な)・懸命(な)

sensitive adj (describing a person) びんかん(な)・敏感(な); (describing a situation) きわどい・際どい

sentence 1 n (in grammar) ぶん・文; (for a crime) a (prison) sentence せんこく・宣告 **2** vb to sentence to one year in prison ちょうえきいちねんの はんけつを いいわたす・懲役一年の 判決を 言い渡す

separate 1 adj a separate room べつの へや・別の 部屋; that is a separate problem それは べつの もんだいです。・それは 別の 問題です。 **2** vb to separate わける・分ける; (if it's a couple) わかれる・別れる

separated adj わかれている・別れている

separately adv べつべつに・別々に

September n くがつ・九月

serial n a TV serial れんぞくドラマ・連続ドラマ

series n シリーズ

serious adj (causing worry) たいへん(な)・大変(な); a serious accident だいじこ・大事故; a serious illness おもいびょうき・重い 病気; (describing a personality) しんけん(な)・真剣(な); to be serious about going to university しんけんに だいがくに いく ことを かんがえている・真剣に 大学に 行く ことを 考えている

serve vb (in a shop) are you being served? いらっしゃいませ。; (food) だす・出す; (in sport) サーブする

service n (in a shop, a restaurant) サービス; (in a church) れいはい・礼拝

service station n サービスエリア

set 1 n (a collection) a set of keys かぎ・鍵; a set of stamps きってのセット・切手のセット; (in tennis) セット **2** vb (to decide on) きめる・決める; to set a date ひにちをきめる・日にちを きめる; (for a particular time) セットする; to set an alarm clock めざましどけいをセットする・目覚し時計をセットする; to set a video (British English) ビデオをセットする; (in school) to set homework しゅくだいをだす・宿題を出す; to set an exam しけんをつくる・試験を作る; (to establish) to set a record きろくをつくる・記録を作る; (when talking about a story, a film) the film is set in Nagoya なごやのえいがです。・名古屋の映画です。; (when talking about the sun) しずむ・沈む; (other uses) to set the table しょくたくのようい をする・食卓の用意をする; to set fire to a house いえにひをつける・家に火を付ける; to set someone free だれかをじゆうにする・誰かを自由にする; **set off** (to leave) しゅっぱつする・出発する; (to cause to go off) to set off fireworks はなびをうちあげる・花火を打ち上げる; to set off a bomb ばくはつさせる・爆発させる; to set off a burglar alarm ぼうはんアラームをならす・防犯アラームを鳴らす; **set up** せつりつする・設立する; to set up a company かいしゃをせつりつする・会社を設立する

settle vb (to decide on) きめる・決める; nothing is settled yet まだ なにも きめていません。・まだ 何も 決めていません。; (to make one's home) すみつく・住み着く; **settle down** (to calm down) おちつく・落ち着く; (to marry) けっこんする・結婚する

seven num (on its own) ななつ・七つ; (with a counter) なな・七 しち is also used; seven books ほん ななさつ・本 七冊 I've got seven ななつ あります。・七つ あります。

seventeen num じゅうなな・十七; じゅうしち is also used

seventeenth num (in a series) じゅうななばんめ(の)・十七番目(の); (in dates) じゅうしちにち・十七日; the seventeenth of May ごがつじゅうしちにち・五月十七日

seventh num (in a series) ななばんめ(の)・七番目(の); (in dates) なのか・七日; the seventh of July しちがつなのか・七月七日

seventy num ななじゅう・七十

several det いくつかの

severe adj (serious) はげしい・激しい; (harsh) きびしい・厳しい

sew vb ぬう・縫う

sewing n さいほう・裁縫

sewing machine n ミシン

sex n (gender) せいべつ・性別; (love-making) セックス; to have sex セックスする

shade n (out of the sun) ひかげ・日陰; to sit in the shade ひかげにすわる・日陰に座る; (a colour) a shade いろあい・色合; (for a lamp) ランプの かさ

shadow n かげ・陰

shake vb (to tremble) ゆれる・揺れる; the building shook with the earthquake じしんで たてものが ゆれました。・地震で 建物が 揺れました。; (to shake something) ふる・振る; (to shake a bottle) びんを ふる・瓶を 振る; to shake hands with someone だれかと あくしゅを する・誰かと 握手をする; (when saying no) to shake one's head あたまを ふる・頭を 振る; (with cold, fear, shock) ふるえる・震える; his hands were shaking かれは てが ふるえていました。・彼は 手が 震えていました。

shall vb Note that there is no true future tense in Japanese; (when talking about the future) I shall see you next Tuesday らいしゅうの かようびに あいましょう。・来週の 火曜日に 会いましょう。; (when making suggestions) shall I help you? てつだいましょうか。・手伝いましょうか。; shall we eat out? がいしょくしましょうか。・外食しましょうか。

shame n はじ・恥; (when expressing regret) that's a shame ざんねんです。・残念です。

shampoo n シャンプー

shape n (a form) かたち・形; a square shape しかくい かたち・四角い 形; in the shape of a square しかくの かたち・四角の 形; (when talking about health) he's in good shape かれは げんきです。・彼は 元気です。; to get in shape うんどうする・運動する

share 1 vb きょうようする・共用する; to share a house いえを きょうようする・家を 共用する 2 n わけまえ・分け前; to pay one's share じぶんの ぶんを はらう・自分の 分を 払う; **share out** (British English) (amongst others) わける・分ける

shark n さめ

sharp adj (used for cutting) よくきれる・よく 切れる; (with a point) するどい・鋭い; (sudden) きゅう(な)・急(な); a sharp bend きゅうな カーブ・急な カーブ; (intelligent) ぬけめの ない・抜け目の ない; (in taste) したをさす よう(な)・舌を 刺す よう(な)

shave vb そる

she pron かのじょ・彼女 Note that Japanese prefer to use a name rather than a pronoun; she'll be there too かのじょも います。・彼女も います。; she's intelligent かのじょは あたまが いいです。・彼女は 頭が いいです。

sheep n ひつじ・羊

sheet n (for a bed) シーツ; (a piece) (of paper) かみ いちまい・紙 一枚; (of glass) ガラス いちまい・ガラス 一枚

shelf n たな・棚

shell n (of an egg, a nut, a crab, a tortoise, a snail) から・殻; (on the beach) かいがら・貝殻

shelter 1 n (from rain) あまやどり・雨宿り; (for homeless people) しゅうようじょ・収容所 2 vb (to take shelter) ひなんする・避難する

shin n むこうずね・向うずね

shine vb (to give out light) ひかる・光る; (the sun) てる・照る; (to point) to shine a torch at someone だれかを かい

ちゅうでんとうでてらす・誰かを 懐中電灯で 照らす; (to reflect light) かがやく・輝く

ship n ふね・船; a passenger ship きゃくせん・客船

shirt n シャツ

shiver vb ふるえる・震える

shock n (an upsetting experience) ショック; to get a shock ショックを うける・ショックを 受ける; to give someone a shock だれかに ショックを あたえる・誰かに ショックを 与える; (the medical state) ショック; (from electricity) かんでん・感電; to get a shock かんでんする・感電する **2** vb (to upset) ショックを あたえる・ショックを 与える

shoe n (for a person) くつ・靴; (for a horse) ていてつ・てい鉄

shoot vb (using a weapon) うつ・撃つ; to shoot someone だれかを うつ・誰かを 撃つ; to shoot someone dead だれかを うちころす・誰かを 撃ち殺す; (to make) to shoot a film さつえいする・撮影する

shop **1** n みせ・店 **2** vb to go shopping かいものに いく・買い物に 行く

shop assistant n (British English) てんいん・店員 **!** Often respectfully referred to as てんいんさん

shopkeeper n てんしゅ・店主

shopping n かいもの・買い物; to do the shopping かいものする・買い物する

shopping cart n (US English) カート

shopping centre (British English), **shopping mall** (US English) n ショッピングセンター

shopping trolley n (British English) カート

shop window n ショーウインドー

shore n (the edge of the sea) きし・岸; (dry land) りく・陸

short **1** adj (not long) みじかい・短い; a short skirt みじかいスカート・短い スカート; I have short hair かみが み

じかいです。・髪が 短いです。; the days are getting shorter ひがみじかく なっています。・日が 短く なっています。; (not tall) せが ひくい・背が 低い; to be short of money おかねが たりない・お金が 足りない 2 in short ようするに・要するに

short cut n ちかみち・近道

shortly adv (soon) まも なく・間も なく; (not long) shortly before we left でる ちょくぜん・出る 直前

shorts n はんズボン・半ズボン

shot n (from a gun) はっぽう・発砲; (in sports) (in football) シュート

should vb (when talking about what is right, what one ought to do) ▶ must; she should learn to drive かのじょは うんてん を ならう べきです。・彼女は 運転を 習う べきです。; shouldn't he be at school? かれは がっこうに いる べきでしょうか。・彼は 学校に いる べきでしょうか。; (when saying something may happen) we should be there by midday おひるまでに そこに つく はずです。・お昼 までに そこに 着く はずです。; it shouldn't be too difficult そんなに むずかしくない はずです。・そんなに 難しくない はずです。; (when implying that something, though likely, didn't happen) the letter should have arrived yesterday てがみは きのう きた はずです。・手紙は 昨日 来た はずです。; (when asking for advice or permission) should I call the doctor? いしゃを よんだ ほうが いいですか。・医者を 呼んだ 方が いいですか。

shoulder n かた・肩

shout 1 vb (general) おおごえで いう・大声で 言う; (in anger) どなる 2 n さけびごえ・叫び声; shout out さけぶ・叫ぶ

shovel n スコップ

show 1 vb (to let someone see) みせる・見せる; to show someone a photo だれかに しゃしんを みせる・誰かに 写真を 見せる; I'll show you how to make it つくりかたを みせます。・作り方を 見せます。; (to go with) I'll show

you to your room へやを あんないします。・ 部屋を 案内します。; (to point to, to indicate) しめす・ 示す; (to be on TV, at the cinema) where is that film showing? その えいがは どこで じょうえいしていますか。・ その 映画は どこで 上映していますか。; to be shown (on TV) (テレビ) で ほうそうする。・ (テレビ) で 放送する 2 n (on a stage) ショー; (on TV, radio) ばんぐみ・ 番組; (an exhibition) てんじかい・ 展示会; **show off** きどる・ 気取る; **show round** to show around the town まちを あんないする・ 町を 案内する; **show up** あらわれる・ 現れる

shower n (for washing) シャワー; to have a shower シャワーをあびる・ シャワーを 浴びる; (rain) にわかあめ・ にわか雨

shrimp n えび

shrink vb to shrink ちぢむ・ 縮む; to shrink something なにかをちぢめる・ 何かを 縮める

shut 1 adj (eyes) とじている・ 閉じている; (doors, windows) しまっている・ 閉まっている; (buildings) しまっている・ 閉まっている; my eyes were shut めを とじていました。・ 目を 閉じていました。2 vb (door, window) しめる・ 閉める; to shut the windows まどをしめる・ 窓を 閉める; I can't shut the door properly ドアをちゃんとしめられません。・ ドアを ちゃんと 閉められません。; (eyes) とじる・ 閉じる; please close your eyes めをとじてください。・ 目を 閉じてください。; (shop) しまう; **shut down** へいさする・ 閉鎖する; the factory shut down in May こうじょうは ごがつに へいさしました。・ 工場は 五月に 閉鎖しました。; **shut up** (to be quiet) だまる・ 黙る; please shut up! だまってください。・ 黙ってください。

shy adj うちき(な)・ 内気(な)

sick adj (ill) びょうき(の)・ 病気(の); to get sick びょうきになる・ 病気に なる; to feel sick むかつく; to be sick (British English) (to vomit) はく・ 吐く; (fed up) うんざりしている; I'm sick of it! もう うんざりしています。

sickness n びょうき・ 病気

side *n* がわ・側; on both sides りょうがわに・両側に; left hand side ひだりがわ・左側; right hand side みぎがわ・右側; the side of the river かわぞい・川沿い; (of a person's body) わきばら・脇腹; on my right (side) わたしのみぎがわに・私の右側に; (in a conflict, a contest) がわ・側; (a team) チーム; **side with someone** だれかにみかたする・誰かに 味方する

sidewalk *n* (US English) ほどう・歩道

sigh *n* ためいき・ため息

sight *n* しかく・視覚; I have good sight めが いいです。・目が いいです。; out of sight みえない ところに・見えない 所に

sightseeing go sightseeing けんぶつ する・見物 する

sign 1 *n* (a symbol) しるし・印; (for traffic, for advertising) かんばん・看板; (a notice) はりがみ・張り紙 **2** *vb* サインする; **sign on** (British English) しつぎょうてあてを せいきゅうする・失業手当を 請求する

signal 1 *n* しんごう・信号 **2** *vb* (to make signs) あいずを する・合図を する; to signal to someone to come だれかに くるように あいずを する・誰かに 来るように 合図をする; (when driving) to signal left ひだりに ウインカーをだす・左に ウインカーを 出す

signature *n* サイン

signpost *n* あんないひょうしき・案内標識

silence *n* (of person) ちんもく・沈黙; (of place) しずけさ・静けさ

silent *adj* (person) だまっている・黙っている; (place) しんとした

silk *n* きぬ・絹

silly *adj* ばか(な)

silver 1 *n* ぎん・銀 **2** *adj* ぎん(の)・銀(の); a silver ring ぎんの ゆびわ・銀の 指輪

simple *adj* かんたん(な)・簡単(な)

since 1 prep 〜いらい・〜以来: I haven't seen him since yesterday きのうのいらい かれを みていません。・昨日 以来彼を 見ていません。; I haven't been feeling well since Monday げつようびいらい ぐあいが よくないです。・ 月曜日以来具合が 良くないです。; she has been living in Japan since April かのじょは しがついらい にほんに すんでいます。・彼女は 四月以来 日本に 住んでいます。 **2** conj (from the time when) 〜て form of the verb + いらい: since she left かのじょが でていらい・彼女が 出て以 来: I've lived here since I was ten じゅっさいの ときから ここにすんでいます。・ 十才の ときから ここに 住ん でいます。; it's ten years since she died かのじょが なく なってからじゅうねんです。・彼女が 亡くなってか ら十年です。; (because) から; since she was ill, she couldn't go かのじょは びょうき でしたから いけませ んでした。・彼女は 病気 でしたから 行けませんでし た。 **3** adv それいらい・それ以来

sincere adj せいじつ(な)・誠実(な)

sincerely adv せいじつに・誠実に; Yours sincerely; Sincerely yours Not used in Japanese letters. Usually a general greeting けいぐ is used at the end of the letter. ▶ dear

sing vb うたう・歌う

singer n かしゅ・歌手

singing adj n うたごえ・歌声

single adj (one) いち + counter counter; we did it three times in a single day いちにちに さんかいしました。・ 一日に 三回しました。; (when used for emphasis) every single day まいにち・毎日; I didn't see a single person ひとりも み ませんでした。・ 一人も 見ませんでした。; (without a partner) どくしん・独身

single bed n シングルベッド

single room n シングルべや・シングル部屋

single ticket n (British English) かたみち(じょうしゃけ ん)・片道(乗車券)

sink 1 n ながし・流し **2** vb ちんぼつする・沈没する

sister n ! Note that there are two sets of words for family members; (your own older sister) あね・姉; (your own younger sister) いもうと ・ 妹; (someone else's older sister) おねえさん・お姉さん; (someone else's younger sister) いもうとさん・妹さん

sister-in-law n ぎり + word for sister

sit vb (to take a seat) すわる・座る; to be sitting on the floor ゆかに すわっている・床に 座っている; (British English) (to take) to sit an exam しけんを うける・試験を 受ける; **sit down** すわる ・ 座る; to be sitting down すわっている ・ 座っている; **sit up** please sit up straight! きちんと すわってください。・ きちんと 座ってください。

sitting room n (Japanese style) ちゃのま・茶の 間; (Western style) リビング

situated adj situated near the town centre まちの ちゅうしんの ちかくに ある・町の 中心の 近くに ある

situation n じょうきょう・状況

six num (on its own) むっつ・六つ; (with a counter) ろく・ 六; six books ほん ろくさつ・本 六冊; I've got six むっつ あります。・六つ あります。

sixteen num じゅうろく・十六

sixteenth num (in a series) じゅうろくばんめ(の)・ 十六番目(の); (in dates) じゅうろくにち・十六日; the sixteenth of July しちがつじゅうろくにち・七月十六日

sixth num (in a series) ろくばんめ(の)・六番目(の); (in dates) むいか・六日; the sixth of February にがつむいか ・二月六日

sixty num ろくじゅう・六十

size n (when talking about clothes, shoes) サイズ; do you have this in a smaller size? もっと ちいさいのが ありますか。 ・ もっと 小さいのが ありますか。; what size do you take? サイズは (in clothes) いくつですか・ (in shoes) なんセンチですか・何センチですか。; (when talking about how big something is) おおきさ・大きさ

skateboard n スケートボード

skating n スケート

skating rink n スケートリンク

sketch n (a drawing) スケッチ; (a funny scene) スキット

ski 1 n スキー 2 vb to go skiing スキーに いく・スキーに 行く

skiing n スキー

skilful (British English), **skillful** (US English) adj じょうず (な)・上手(な)

skill n ぎじゅつ・技術

skin n ひふ・皮膚

skinny adj やせた

skip vb (to give little jumps) スキップする; (with a rope) なわ とびする・縄跳びする; to skip classes じゅぎょうを さぼる・授業を さぼる

ski resort n スキーじょう・スキー場

skirt n スカート

sky n そら・空; blue sky あおぞら・青空

skydiving n スカイダイビング

slap vb to slap someone だれかを ぴしゃりと うつ・ 誰かを ぴしゃりと 打つ

sled, sledge (British English) 1 n そり

sleep 1 n すいみん・睡眠; to go to sleep ねむる・眠る; to go back to sleep ねなおす・寝直す; to put someone to sleep だれかを ねかす・誰かを 寝かす 2 vb (to be asleep) ねむっている・眠っている; to sleep with someone だれかと ねる・誰かと 寝る; **sleep in** ねぼう する・寝坊する

sleeping bag n ねぶくろ・寝袋

sleepy adj ねむい・眠い

sleet n みぞれ

sleeve n そで・袖; to roll up one's sleeves そでを めくる ・袖を めくる; short sleeves はんそで・半袖

slice 1 n スライス **2** vb to slice bread パン を スライス する

slide 1 vb すべる・滑る **2** n (an image) スライド; (in a playground) すべりだい・滑り台

slim 1 adj スマート **2** vb (British English) やせる・痩せる

slip vb (to slide) すべる・滑る

slipper n スリッパ

slippery adj すべりやすい・滑りやすい

slot machine n スロットマシーン

slow adj (journey, music) ゆっくりした; (service, speed) おそい・遅い; (not bright) ものおぼえがわるい・物覚えが悪い; (describing a watch, a clock) to be slow おくれている・遅れている; that clock is 20 minutes slow そのとけいは にじゅっぷん おくれています。・その 時計は 二十分 遅れています。; slow down スピードを おとす・スピードを 落とす

slowly adv ゆっくり; to walk slowly ゆっくり あるく・ゆっくり 歩く

sly adj ずるい

small adj ちいさい・小さい; a small house ちいさい いえ・小さい 家; a small quantity すこしの りょう・少しの 量

small ad n (British English) ぶんるいこうこく・分類広告

smart adj (British English) (elegant) おしゃれ(な); (intelligent) あたまがいい・頭が いい; (expensive) こうきゅう(な)・高級(な)

smash vb (to break) めちゃめちゃに こわす・めちゃめちゃに 壊す; (to get broken) めちゃめちゃに こわれる・めちゃめちゃに 壊れる; smash up めちゃめちゃに こわす・めちゃめちゃに 壊す

smell 1 n (an odour) において; (the sense) the sense of smell きゅうかく・嗅覚 **2** vb におう; that smells nice いい においです。; I can smell burning こげた においが します。・焦げた においが します。

smile 1 *vb* ほほえむ・微笑む; to smile at someone だれか
にほほえむ・誰かに 微笑む **2** *n* ほほえみ・微笑み

smoke 1 *n* けむり・煙 **2** *vb* たばこを すう・煙草を
吸う

smooth *adj* (not rough) なめらか(な)・滑らか(な)

smother *vb* ちっそくさせる・窒息させる

snack *n* けいしょく・軽食

snail *n* かたつむり

snake *n* へび; year of the snake みどし・巳年

snapshot *n* しゃしん・写真

sneaker *n* スニーカー

sneeze *vb* くしゃみを する

snobbish *adj* (about people) おうへい(な)・横柄(な)

snooker *n* ビリヤード

snore *vb* いびきを かく

snow 1 *n* ゆき・雪 **2** *vb* ゆきが ふる・雪が 降る; it's
snowing ゆきが ふっています。・雪が 降っています。

snowball *n* ゆきだま・雪玉

snowman *n* ゆきだるま・雪だるま

so 1 *adv* とても; I'm so happy とても しあわせです。・と
ても 幸せです。; she's so smart かのじょは とても あたま
が いいです。・彼女は とても 頭が いいです。; I've
so much work to do しごとが たくさん あります。・仕
事が たくさん あります。; she speaks so fast that I can't
understand her かのじょは わからない ほど はやく は
なします。・彼女は 分からない ほど 速く 話します。;
(also) I'm fifteen and so is he わたしは かれも じゅうごさ
いです。・私も 彼も 十五才です。; if you go, so will I あ
なたが いくなら、わたしも 行きます。・あなたが 行
くなら、私も 行きます。; (other uses) I think so わたしも
そう おもいます。・私も そう 思います。; I'm afraid so
そうです。・そうです。; I told you so わたしの いった とおりです。・
私の 言った 通りです。; who says so? だれが そう いい
ましたか。・誰が そう 言いましたか。; and so on など

2 so (that) から; it's cold so please close the window さむい ですから、まどを しめてください。・ 寒いですから、窓を 閉めてください。 **3 so as** ～ように; we left home early so as not to miss the train でんしゃに おくれない ようには やく うち を でました。・ 電車に 遅れない ように 早く 家を 出ました。 *Note that the word order is different in Japanese in this type of sentence.*

soap *n* (for washing) せっけん・石けん; (on TV) ドラマ

soccer *n* サッカー

social *adj* (history, background) しゃかい(の)・社会(の); (life, event) しゃこうてき(な)・社交的(な)

social studies *n* しゃかいがく・社会学

social worker *n* ソーシャルワーカー

sock *n* くつした・靴下

sofa *n* ソファー

soft *adj* (not hard or tough) やわらかい・柔らかい; soft toy ぬいぐるみ; (not harsh, strict or severe) やさしい・優しい

software *n* ソフト

soldier *n* へいたい・兵隊

sole *n* あしの うら・足の 裏; (of a shoe) くつの そこ・靴の 底

solicitor *n* (British English) べんごし・弁護士

solution *n* かいけつ・解決

solve *vb* かいけつする・解決する; to solve a problem もんだいを かいけつする・問題を 解決する

some 1 *det* (an amount or a number of) ! *Not used in this way in Japanese*; I have to buy some bread パンを かわなければ なりません。・パンを 買わなければ なりません。; could I have some water? みずを ください。・水を ください。; she ate some strawberries かのじょは いちごを たべました。・彼女は いちごを 食べました。; (certain) ある; there are some people who don't like travelling by plane ひこうきの たびが きらいな ひとも います。・飛行機の 旅が 嫌いな 人も います。 **2** *pron* (an amount or a number

of) ! *Not used in this way in Japanese*; I made some yesterday きのう つくりました。・ 昨日 作りました。; (*certain people or things*) some are quite expensive たかいのも あります。・ 高いの も あります。; some (of them) are Japanese-speakers にほんごが はなせる ひとも います。・ 日本語が 話せる 人も います。

someone *pron* (*also* **somebody**) だれか・誰か; someone telephoned だれかが でんわしました。・ 誰か が 電話しました。

something *pron* なにか・何か; I'll show you something interesting なにか おもしろい ものを みせます。・ 何か 面白いものを 見せます。

sometimes *adv* ときどき・時々

somewhere *adv* どこか; they live somewhere in Ireland か れらは アイルランドの どこかに すんでいます。彼ら は アイルランドの どこかに 住んでいます。; let's go somewhere else どこか ほかの ところに いきましょう。 ・ どこか 外の 所に 行きましょう。

son *n* (*one's own*) むすこ・息子; (*someone else's*) むすこさ ん・息子さん

song *n* うた・歌

son-in-law *n* ぎりの むすこ・義理の 息子

soon *adv* (*in a short time*) もうすぐ; see you soon! またね。; (*early*) はやい・早い; the sooner the better はやければ は やいほど いいです。・ 早ければ 早い ほど いいです 。; as soon as possible できるだけ はやく・できるだ け 早く; come as soon as you can できるだけ はやく き てください。・ できるだけ 早く 来てください。

sore *adj* いたい・痛い; I have a sore throat のどが いたい です。・ 喉が 痛いです。; I have a sore leg あしが いたい です。・ 足が 痛いです。; I have a sore back せなかが い たいです。・ 背中が 痛いです。; it's very sore とても い たいです。・ とても 痛いです。

sorry 1 *exc* (*when apologizing*) sorry! すみません。; (*when asking someone to repeat*) sorry? はい？ **2** *adj* (*when*

apologizing) すみません。; I'm sorry I'm late おそくなって すみません。・ 遅くなって すみません。 Note that word order is different in Japanese; to say sorry あやまる ・ 謝る; (when expressing regret) ざんねん ・ 残念; I'm sorry he can't come かれが こられなくて ざんねんです。・ 彼が 来られなくて 残念です。; (to feel pity for) to feel sorry for someone だれかを かわいそうに おもう ・ 誰かを かわ いそうに 思う

sort 1 *n* it's a sort of bird とりの いっしゅです。・ 鳥の 一 種です。; it's a sort of computer コンピューターの いっし ゅです。・ コンピューターの 一種です。; I don't like that sort of thing そう いう ことが すきではありません。・ そういう ことが 好きではありません。; he's not that sort of person かれは そういう ひとではありません。 ・ 彼は そういう 人ではありません。 2 *vb* ぶんるいす る ・ 分類する; to sort the documents しょるいを ぶんる いする ・ 書類を 分類する; **sort out** (to solve) かいけつ する ・ 解決する; to sort out a problem もんだいを かい けつする ・ 問題を 解決する; (to deal with) する; I'll sort it out わたしが それを します。・ 私が それを します。; (to organize) よりわける ・ より分ける; to sort out the washing せんたくものを よりわける ・ 洗濯物を より 分ける

sound 1 *n* おと ・ 音; I like the sound of waves なみの おと がすきです。・ 波の 音が 好きです。; (of a radio, a television) おんりょう ・ 音量; to turn the sound up おんり ょうをあげる ・ 音量を 上げる 2 *vb* Use い adjective minus last い + そうです; Use な adjective (or noun) + みたい です; it sounds dangerous あぶなそうです。・ 危なそう です。; it sounds interesting おもしろそうです。; it sounds like a piano ピアノ みたいです。

soup *n* (Western style) スープ; (Japanese style) しる ・ 汁; miso soup みそしる ・ みそ汁

sour *adj* すっぱい ・ 酸っぱい; to go sour すっぱく なる ・ 酸っぱくなる

south 1 *n* みなみ ・ 南; in the south of England イギリスの みなみに ・ イギリスの 南に 2 *adv* to go south みなみに

いく・南に 行く **3** *adj* みなみ・南: to work in south London みなみロンドンで はたらく・南ロンドンで 働く

South Africa *n* みなみアフリカ・南アフリカ

South America *n* みなみアメリカ・南アメリカ

southeast *n* なんとう・南東

southwest *n* なんせい・南西

souvenir *n* きねんひん・記念品

space *n* (room) くうかん・空間; to take up space ばしょ をとる・場所を 取る; (an area of land) an open space ひらけたばしょ・開けた 場所; (outer space) うちゅう・宇宙; (a gap) すきま・隙間

Spain *n* スペイン

spare *adj* (extra) よぶん(な)・余分(な); (available) のこ っている・残っている; are there any spare seats? のこ っている せきが ありますか。・残っている 席が あり ますか。

spare part *n* こうかんようぶひん・交換用部品

spare room *n* おきゃくさんようのしんしつ・お客さ ん用の寝室

spare time *n* ひまな とき・暇な とき

speak *vb* はなす・話す: to speak Japanese にほんごを はなす・日本語を 話す; who's speaking, please? どちら さまですか。・どちら 様ですか。; generally speaking いっぱんてきにいうと・一般的に 言うと; **speak up** おおきいこえで はなす・大きい 声で 話す

special *adj* とくべつ(な)・特別(な): a special offer とく ばいひん・特売品; Elena's a special friend エレナさんは とくべつなともだちです。・エレナさんは 特別な 友 達です。

speciality (British English), **specialty** (US English) *n* めいぶつ・名物

specially *adv* とくべつに・特別に

spectator *n* かんきゃく・観客

speech n スピーチ

speed 1 n スピード **2** vb (to drive too fast) スピードを だしすぎる・スピードを 出しすぎる; **speed up** スピードをあげる・スピードを 上げる

speed limit n そくどせいげん・速度制限

spell vb (when speaking) つづりをいう・綴りを 言う; (when writing) つづる・綴る; how do you spell it? つづりはなんですか。・綴りは 何ですか。

spelling n つづり・綴り

spend vb (to pay money) つかう・使う; (to pass) すごす・過ごす; to spend time reading ほんを よんで すごす・本を読んで 過ごす; to spend time writing letters てがみをかいてすごす・手紙を 書いて 過ごす

spider n くも

spill vb (if it's a person) こぼす; please don't spill the juiceジュースをこぼさないでください。; (if it's a liquid)こぼれる

spinach n ほうれんそう

spit vb つばを はく・つばを 吐く

spite: in spite of prep 〜(な)のに; we went out in spite ofthe bad weather てんきがわるいのに でました。・天気が悪いのに 出ました。

spiteful adj いじわる(な)・意地悪(な)

spoil vb (to damage) だいなしに する・台なしに する;(as a parent) あまやかす・甘やかす; to spoil a child こどもをあまやかす・子供を 甘やかす

sponge n スポンジ

spoon n スプーン

sport n スポーツ; I am good at sports スポーツが とくくです。・スポーツが 得意です。

sports centre (British English), **sports center**(US English) n スポーツセンター

sports club n スポーツクラブ

spot 1 *n* (*on an animal*) はんてん・斑点; (*British English*) (*on the face or body*) にきび; (*a place*) ところ・所; on the spot (*there and then*) げんばに・現場に **2** *vb* (*to see*) みる・見る; (*to recognize*) きが つく・気が 付く

sprain *vb* to sprain one's wrist てくびを ねんざする・手首を ねんざする

spring *n* はる・春; in spring はるに・春に

spy *n* スパイ

square 1 *n* (*the shape*) しかく・四角; (*in a town*) ひろば・広場 **2** *adj* しかくい・四角い

squash 1 *n* スカッシュ **2** *vb* つぶす・潰す

squeak *vb* きしむ

squeeze *vb* to squeeze a lemon レモンを しぼる・レモンを 搾る; to squeeze someone's hand だれかの てを にぎる・誰かの 手を 握る

squirrel *n* りす

stable *n* うまごや・馬小屋

stadium *n* スタジアム

staff *n* (*of a company*) しゃいん・社員; (*of a bank*) ぎんこういん・銀行員; (*of a school, a college*) しょくいん・職員

stage *n* ステージ

stain 1 *n* しみ・染み **2** *vb* よごす・汚す

stairs *n* かいだん・階段; to fall down the stairs かいだんで ころぶ・階段で 転ぶ

stamp *n* (*for an envelope*) きって・切手; a hundred and ten yen stamp ひゃくじゅうえん きって・百十円 切手; (*on a document, a passport*) スタンプ

stamp-collecting *n* きってしゅうしゅう・切手収集

stand *vb* to be standing たっている・立っている; to be able to stand たつ ことが できる・立つ ことが できる; you're standing in my way じゃまです。・邪魔です。(*to put*) to stand a vase on a table かびんを テーブルの

うえにおく・花瓶をテーブルの 上に 置く; (to step) to stand on a nail くぎを ふむ・くぎを 踏む; (to bear) I can't stand the cold さむさに たえられません。・寒さ に耐えられません。; I can't stand his selfishness かれの わがままは がまん できません。・彼の わがままは 我慢 できません。; (other uses) to stand for election (British English) せんきょに りっこうほする・選挙に 立候補 する; **stand back** さがる・下がる; **stand for** (to represent) だいひょうする・代表する; (to mean) いみす る・意味する; **stand out** めだつ・目立つ; **stand up** たちあがる・立ち上がる; **stand up for** まもる・守る; to stand up for oneself じぶんを まもる・自分を 守る; **stand up to** たちむかう・立ち向かう; to stand up to someone だれかに たちむかう・誰かに 立ち向かう

star n (in space) ほし・星; (a famous person) スター

stare vb to stare at someone だれかを じろじろ みる・ 誰かを じろじろ 見る

start 1 vb (to begin) はじめる・始める You can use the pre ます form of the verb + はじめる to indicate the start of an action; to start working はたらきはじめる・働き始める; to start writing かきはじめる・書き始める; to start running はしりはじめる・走り始める; you should start by phoning them まず かれらに でんわした ほうが いい です。・まず 彼らに 電話した 方が いいです。; (to set up) せつりつする・設立する; to start a company かいし ゃを せつりつする・会社を 設立する; (to cause) ひき おこす・引き起こす; to start a war せんそうを ひき おこす・戦争を 引き起こす; (to begin working) うごきだす ・動き出す; the engine won't start エンジンが かかりませ ん。・エンジンが かかりません。; (to put into action) to start a car engine くるまの エン ジンを かける・車の エンジンを かける; to start a machine きかいの スイッチを いれる・機械の スイッ チを入れる **2** n (time) はじめ・初め; at the start of the week しゅうの はじめに・週の 初めに; (matter) はじま り・始まり; the start of married life けっこんせいかつの はじまり・結婚生活の 始まり; **start off** はじめる・始 める; **start over** (US English) やりなおす・やり直す

starter n (British English) ぜんさい・前菜

state n (a country) くに・国; (part of a country) しゅう・州; (a government) くに・国; (a condition) じょうたい・状態; this house is in a bad state (of repair) この うちは わるいじょうたいです。・この 家は 悪い 状態です。she's in no state to work かのじょは はたらける ような じょうたいではありません。・彼女は 働ける ような 状態ではありません。

station n (for trains) えき・駅; (on TV) テレビきょく・テレビ局; (for buses) バス のりば・バス乗り場

statue n ぞう・像

stay 1 vb (to remain) いる; we stayed there for a week そこに いっしゅうかん いました。・そこに 一週間 いました。; (to have accommodation) とまる・泊まる; to stay at a friend's house ともだちの うちに とまる・友達の 家に 泊まる **2** n たいざい・滞在; stay away from to stay away from school がっこうに いかない・学校に 行かない; stay in いえに いる・家に いる; stay up (to go to bed late) おそくねる・遅く寝る

steady adj (continuous) to make steady progress ちゃくじつ なじょうたつを する・着実な 上達を する; (not likely to move) あんていしている・安定している

steak n ステーキ

steal vb ぬすむ・盗む; to steal someone's money だれか の おかねを ぬすむ・誰かの お金を 盗む

steam n すいじょうき・水蒸気

steel n こうてつ・鋼鉄

steep adj けわしい・険しい

steering wheel n ハンドル

step 1 n (when walking) いっぽ・一歩; to take a step ふみ だす・踏み出す; (in stairs, at a door) だん・段; (a series of actions) to take steps てを うつ・手を 打つ **2** vb to step on someone's foot だれかの あしを ふむ・誰かの 足を 踏む; step aside わきに よる・脇に 寄る

stepbrother n No distinction is usually made between step- and blood-relatives. ▶ **brother**

stepfather n (one's own) ままちち・まま父 No distinction is usually made between step- and blood relatives. ▶ **father**

stepmother n (one's own) ままはは・まま母 No distinction is usually made between step- and blood-relatives. ▶ **mother**

stepsister n No distinction is usually made between step- and blood relatives. ▶ **sister**

stereo n ステレオ

stick 1 vb (using glue or tape) はる・貼る; (to become attached) くっつく; (to get blocked) ひっかかる・引っかかる; the door is stuck ドアが ひっかかっています。・ドアが引っかかっています。**2** n (a piece of wood) ぼう・棒; (for walking) つえ・杖; **stick at** to stick at something なにかをさいごまで する・何かを 最後まで する; **stick out** でっぱる・出っ張る; there's a nail sticking out くぎが でっぱっています。・くぎが 出っ張っています。

sticky tape n (British English) セロテープ

stiff adj (not soft, not supple) かたい; (after sport, walking) to have stiff legs あしが きんにくつうに なっている・足が 筋肉痛に なっている; (not easy to use) かたい・硬い

still¹ adv (when there has been no change) まだ; does she still learn the piano? かのじょは まだ ピアノを ならっていますか。・彼女は まだ ピアノを 習っていますか。I still don't understand why he did that なんで かれが それを したか まだ わかりません。・何で 彼が それを した か まだ 分かりません。(when referring to the future) まだ; she still has a chance of winning かのじょには まだ かつ かのうせいが あります。・彼女には まだ 勝つ 可能性が あります。

still² **1** adv to sit still じっと すわる・じっと 座る **2** adj うごかない・動かない

sting vb さす・刺す

stir vb かきまぜる・かき混ぜる

stomach n い・胃; I have a pain in my stomach いが いたいです。・胃が 痛いです。

stone n いし・石; (a pebble) こいし・小石

stop 1 vb (to put an end to) やめる; to stop smoking たばこ をやめる・煙草を やめる; to stop laughing わらうのを やめる・笑うのを やめる; to stop working はたらくの をやめる・働くのを やめる; please stop it! やめてくだ さい。; (to prevent) to stop someone from going だれかが い くのをやめさせる・誰かが 行くのを やめさせる; (to come to a halt) とまる・止まる; the bus didn't stop バスが とまりませんでした。・バスが 止まりませんでした。; (when talking about machines, noise, weather) やむ; suddenly the noise stopped きゅうに おとが やみました。・急に 音がやみました。; the rain stopped あめが やみました。 ・雨が やみました。 **2** n a (bus) stop バスてい・バス停; to miss one's stop のりこす・乗り越す

store n みせ・店

storey (British English), **story** (US English) n かい・階

storm n あらし・嵐

story n ものがたり・物語; a true story ほんとうの もの がたり・本当の 物語; a ghost story かいだん・怪談; (in a newspaper) きじ・記事; (a rumour) うわさ・噂; (US English) (of a house) ▶ **storey**

stove n (US English) オーブン

straight 1 adj まっすぐ(の)・真っ直ぐ(の); a straight line ちょくせん・直線; straight hair まっすぐのかみ・ 真っ直ぐの髪; (in the right position) the picture isn't straight えがまがっています。・絵が 曲がっています。; (honest) しょうじき(な)・正直(な) **2** adv まっすぐに・ 真っ直ぐに; to stand up straight ちゃんと たつ・ちゃん と立つ; to go straight ahead まっすぐ いく・真っ直ぐ 行く; (without delay) すぐ; to go straight home すぐ かえる ・すぐ 帰る

strange adj (odd) へん(な)・変(な); it's strange that she doesn't come here any more かのじょが もう ここに こな

いのは へんです。・彼女が もう ここに 来ないのは
変です。; (unknown) みち(の)・未知(の)

stranger n (unknown person) しらない ひと・知らない 人;
(outsider) よその ひと・よその 人

straw n (for feeding animals) わら; (for drinking) ストロー

strawberry n いちご

stream n おがわ・小川

street n みち・道

streetlamp n がいとう・街灯

strength n たいりょく・体力

stressful adj ストレスが かかる

stretch vb のばす・伸ばす; to stretch one's arms てを
のばす・手を 伸ばす

strict adj きびしい・厳しい

strike n ストライキ; to go on strike ストライキに はいる
・ストライキに 入る

string n ひも・紐

striped adj しまもよう(の)・縞模様(の)

stroke vb なでる

stroller n (US English) うばぐるま・乳母車

strong adj (having physical, mental strength) つよい・強い;
she's strong かのじょは つよいです。・彼女は 強いで
す。; (not easily damaged) じょうぶ(な)・丈夫(な);
(having force, power) つよい・強い; a strong wind つよい
かぜ・強い 風; (tea, coffee) こい・濃い; strong tea こい
こうちゃ・濃い 紅茶; (obvious, noticeable) きょうれつ
(な)・強烈(な); a strong smell of garlic きょうれつな に
んにくの におい・強烈な にんにくの 臭い; a strong
German accent つよい ドイツごの なまり・強い ドイ
ツ語の 訛り; (having military power) つよい・強い

stubborn adj がんこ(な)・頑固(な)

student n (at university) がくせい・学生; (at school) せいと
・生徒

study 1 vb べんきょうする・勉強する; to study history れきしをべんきょうする・歴史を 勉強する; to study to be a teacher せんせいに なるために べんきょうする・先生に なるために 勉強する; to study for an exam しけんべんきょうする・試験勉強する **2** n べんきょう・勉強; (room) しょさい・書斎

stuff 1 n (things) もの・物; (belongings) もちもの・持ち物; I have a lot of stuff to do たくさん する ことが あります。 **2** vb つめる・詰める; to stuff a suitcase with clothes スーツケースをふくで つめる・スーツケースを 服で詰める

stuffing n つめもの・詰め物

stupid adj ばか(な)

style n (a way of dressing, behaving) ゆうがさ・優雅さ; to have style ゆうがさが ある・優雅さが ある; (a design, a type) (of garment) スタイル; (of building) ようしき・様式; (a fashion) はやり

stylish adj ゆうが(な)・優雅(な)

subject n (of a conversation) わだい・話題; to change the subject わだいを かえる・話題を 変える; (being studied) (at school, college) がっか・学課; (for an essay, a report) テーマ

suburb n こうがい・郊外

subway n (US English) (the underground) ちかてつ・地下鉄; (British English) (an underground passage) ちかどう・地下道

succeed vb せいこうする・成功する

success n せいこう・成功; to be a success (if it's a party) せいこうする・成功する; (if it's a film, a book) だいヒットになる・大ヒットに なる

successful adj to be successful (in an attempt) せいこうする・成功する; (describing a film, a book) だいヒットに なる・大ヒットに なる

such 1 det there's no such thing; (when referring to a physical thing) そう いう ことが ありません。; (when referring to a

concept) そう いう ことが ありません。**2** adv they have such a lot of money かれらは おかねが たくさん あります。**・** 彼らは お金が たくさん あります。**;** she's such a strange person かのじょは とても へんな ひとです。**・** 彼女は とても 変な 人です。

suddenly adv とつぜん **・** 突然

suffer vb (put up with) がまんする **・** 我慢する

sugar n さとう **・** 砂糖

suggestion n ていあん **・** 提案

suicide n to commit suicide じさつする **・** 自殺する

suit 1 n (a man's) せびろ **・** 背広; (a woman's) スーツ **2** vb (to be convenient) つごうが いい **・** 都合が いい; that suits me それは つごうが いいです。**・** それは 都合が いい です。; does Friday suit you? きんようびは つごうが いいですか。**・** 金曜日は 都合が いいですか。; (to look well on) that hat suits you その ぼうしは にあいます。**・** その 帽子は 似合います。

suitable adj てきとう(な) **・** 適当(な); a suitable present てきとうな プレゼント **・** 適当な プレゼント; it is unsuitable for children こどもに ふさわしくないです。**・** 子供に ふさわしくないです。; (time) つごうが いい **・** 都合が いい

suitcase n スーツケース

sum n (amount of money) きんがく **・** 金額; (total) ごうけい **・** 合計; けいさん **・** 計算; **sum up** ようやくする **・** 要約 する

summer n なつ **・** 夏; in summer なつに **・** 夏に

summer holiday (British English), **summer vacation** (US English) n (a trip) なつの りょこう **・** 夏の 旅行; (from school) なつやすみ **・** 夏休み

sun n たいよう **・** 太陽; to sit in the sun ひなたに すわる **・** 日向に 座る

sunbathe vb ひなたぼっこする **・** 日向ぼっこする

sunburn n ひやけ **・** 日焼け

sunburned *adj* to get sunburned ひに やける・日に 焼ける

Sunday *n* にちようび・日曜日

sunglasses *n* サングラス

sunny *adj* はれた・晴れた; it's going to be sunny tomorrow あした はれます。・明日 晴れます。

sunrise *n* ひの で・日の 出

sunset *n* にちぼつ・日没

sunshade *n* パラソル

sunshine *n* にっこう・日光

suntan *n* ひやけ・日焼け; to get a suntan ひやけする・日焼けする

suntan oil *n* サンタンオイル

supermarket *n* スーパー

supper *n* (an evening meal) ゆうしょく・夕食

support *vb* (to agree with, to help) しえんする・支援する; to support the strike ストライキを しえんする・ストライキを 支援する; (to keep) やしなう・養う; to support a family かぞくを やしなう・家族を 養う; (to hold, to help physically) ささえる・支える

supporter *n* (of a sports team) ファン; (of a political party) しえんしゃ・支援者

suppose *vb* (to imagine) そうぞうする・想像する; I don't suppose you know yet まだ しらないでしょう。・まだ 知らないでしょう。; (to be meant to) to be supposed to verb in dictionary form + ことに なっている; I'm supposed to go to London ロンドンへいく ことに なっています。・ロンドンへ 行く ことに なっています。

sure *adj* たしか(な)・確か(な); I'm sure he said nine o'clock たしかに かれは くじだと いいました。・確かに 彼は 九時だと 言いました。; are you sure? ほんとうですか。・本当ですか。; I'm not sure if Emily's coming エミリさんがくるか どうか わかりません。・エミリさんが 来るか どうか わかりません。; to make sure た

しかめる・確かめる; (bound) he's sure to win きっと
かれは かつでしょう。・きっと 彼は 勝つでしょう。;
sure of oneself じしんが ある・自信が ある

surf vb to go surfing サーフィンに いく・サーフィンに
行く

surface n ひょうめん・表面

surface mail n ふなびん・船便; to send by surface mail
ふなびんで おくる・船便で 送る

surfboard n サーフボード

surgeon n げかい・外科医

surgery n to have surgery しゅじゅつを うける・手術を
受ける; (British English) (the place) びょういん・病院

surname n みょうじ・名字

surprise 1 n (an event, a gift) おもいがけない もの・
思い掛けない 物; (being amazed) おどろき・驚き **2** vb
おどろかす・驚かす; to surprise someone だれかを お
どろかす・誰かを 驚かす

surprised adj びっくりした; I'm not surprised びっくり
していません。

surrender vb こうふくする・降伏する

surround vb かこむ・囲む; to be surrounded by trees
きにかこまれている・木に 囲まれている

surroundings n しゅうへん・周辺

survey n アンケート

survive vb いきのこる・生き残る

suspect 1 vb うたがう・疑う; she's suspected of having
stolen money かのじょは おかねを ぬすんだうたがい
があります。・彼女は お金を 盗んだ 疑いが ありま
す。**2** n ようぎしゃ・容疑者

suspicious adj (having suspicions) うたがわしい・疑わ
しい; (causing suspicion) あやしい・怪しい; a suspicious
person あやしい じんぶつ・怪しい 人物

swan n はくちょう・白鳥

swap vb こうかんする・交換する

sweat vb あせを かく・汗を かく

sweater n セーター

sweatshirt n トレーナー

Sweden n スウェーデン

sweep vb はく・掃く

sweet 1 adj あまい・甘い; I have a sweet tooth あまい ものが すきです。・甘い 物が 好きです。; (kind, gentle) しんせつ(な)・親切(な); (cute) かわいい **2** n (British English) (candy) あめ; (dessert) デザート

swim 1 vb およぐ・泳ぐ; to swim in a lake みずうみで およぐ・湖で 泳ぐ **2** n to go for a swim およぎに いく・泳ぎに行く

swimming n すいえい・水泳

swimming pool n プール

swimsuit n みずぎ・水着

swing 1 vb (to move back and forth) ふる・振る; (to move something back and forth) ふる・振る; to swing one's legs あしをふる・足を 振る **2** n ぶらんこ

switch 1 n スイッチ **2** vb とりかえる・取り替える; to switch seats せきを とりかえる ・席を 取り替える; **switch off** けす・消す; to switch off the light でんきを けす・電気を 消す; **switch on** つける; to switch the radio on ラジオを つける

Switzerland n スイス

sympathetic adj (showing pity) おもいやりの ある・思いやりの ある; (showing understanding) どうじょうてき(な)・同情的(な)

syringe n ちゅうしゃき・注射器

system n (organisation) そしき・組織; (method) やりかた・やり方

Tt

table *n* テーブル

tablet *n* じょうざい・錠剤

table tennis *n* たっきゅう・卓球

tail *n* しっぽ・尻尾

take *vb* (*to take hold of*) とる・取る; to take someone's hand だれかのてを とる・誰かの 手を 取る; (*to carry with one*) もって いく・持って 行く; I took my umbrella かさを もって いきました。・傘を 持って 行きました; I'll take the letters to Sharon シャロンさんに てがみを もっていきます。・シャロンさんに 手紙を 持って 行きます; (*to accompany, to bring*) つれて いく・連れて 行く; to take the children for a walk こどもたちを さんぽに つれていく・子供たちを 散歩に 連れて 行く; to take someone home (だれかを)いえに おくる・(誰かを)家に 送る; (*to remove*) とる・取る; to take a book off the shelf ほんを たなから とる・本を 棚から 取る; (*to steal*) ぬすむ・盗む; (*to cope with, to bear*) がまんする・我慢する; he can't take the pain かれは いたみを がまんできません。・彼は 痛みを 我慢できません。; I can't take any more もう がまんできません。・もう 我慢できません。; (*when talking about what is necessary*) it takes time じかんが かかります。・時間が かかります。; it takes two hours to get to Matsue まつえまで にじかん かかります。・松江まで 二時間 かかります。; to take time to do homework しゅくだいに じかんが かかる・宿題に 時間が かかる; it won't take long ながく かかりません。・長く かかりません。; it takes courage ゆうきが いる・勇気が 要る; (*to accept*) うけとる・受け取る; (*to use when travelling*) いく・行く; to take a taxi タクシーで いく・タクシーで 行く; take the first turn on the right さいしょを みぎに まがってください。・最初を 右に 曲が

ってください。; (*to do*) to take exams しけんを うける・試験を受ける; (*to have*) to take a vacation りょこうする・旅行する; to take a shower シャワーを あびる・シャワーを浴びる; to take driving lessons くるまの レッスンをうける・車の レッスンを受ける; I don't take sugar さとうをいれません。・砂糖を 入れません。; (*to wear*) I take a size 10; (*in clothes*) ようふくの サイズは じゅうです。・洋服の サイズは 十です。; I take a size 5; (*in shoes*) くつの サイズは ごです。・靴の サイズは 5です。; **take apart** ぶんかいする・分解する; **take away** to take away the rubbish ごみを もって いく・ごみを 持って行く; a pizza to take away もちかえりの ピザ・持ち帰りの ピザ; **take back** かえす・返す; I had to take the coat back コートを かえさなければ なりませんでした。・コートを 返さなければ なりませんでした。;

take down (*to remove*) to take a box down off a shelf たなからはこを おろす・棚から 箱を 降ろす; to take a poster down ポスターを はがす; to take down a tent テントをかいたいする・テントを 解体する; (*to write down*) かきとる・書き取る; **take hold of** つかむ・掴む; **take off** (*from an airport*) りりくする・離陸する; (*to remove clothing*) ぬぐ・脱ぐ; I took off my shoes くつを ぬぎました。・靴を 脱ぎました。; to take off one's clothes ふくをぬぐ・服を 脱ぐ; **take out** (*from a box, a pocket, a bag*) とりだす・取り出す; I took a pen out of my pocket ポケットからペンを とりだしました。・ポケットから ペンを取り出しました。; (*from a bank account*) ひきだす・引き出す; to take money out おかねを ひきだす・お金を 引き出す; **take part** to take part in a game ゲームに さんかする・ゲームに 参加する; **take place** おこなう・行う; **take up** (*as a hobby*) to take up golf ゴルフをはじめる・ゴルフを 始める; (*to use up*) to take up space ばしょをとる・場所を 取る; to take up time じかんが かかる・時間がかかる

talented *adj* じょうず(な)・上手(な)

talk 1 *vb* (*to speak*) はなす・話す; to talk on the phone でんわではなす・電話で 話す; to talk in Japanese にほんご

ではなす・日本語で 話す; to talk to someone だれかと はなす・誰かと 話す; I talked about the trip りょこうに ついてはなしました。・旅行について 話しました。; they were talking about you かれらは あなたの ことを は なしていました。・彼らは あなたの ことを 話してい ました。; to talk to oneself ひとりごとを いう・ 独り言 を言う; (to chat) しゃべる・ 喋る 2 n (a conversation) は なし・話; (about an academic subject) はっぴょう・ 発 表; give a talk は はっぴょうする・発表する; (discussions) talks かいだん・会談

talkative adj おしゃべり(な)・ お喋り(な)

tall adj (describing a person) せが たかい・背が 高い; (describing a building, a tree) たかい・ 高い; I am six feet tall しんちょうは ひゃくはちじゅうセンチです。・身長は 百八十センチです。; to get tall せが たかく なる・背が 高くなる

tan n ひやけ・日焼け; to get a tan ひに やける・ 日に 焼ける

tanned adj ひに やけた・ 日に 焼けた

tap 1 n (British English) じゃぐち・ 蛇口; to turn the tap on みずをだす・ 水を 出す; to turn the tap off みずを とめ る・ 水を 止める 2 vb to tap on the door ドアを かるく たたく・ ドアを 軽く たたく

tape 1 n テープ; (for repairs, for sticking) セロテープ 2 vb (audio) ろくおんする・ 録音する; (video) ろくがする・ 録画する

tape recorder n テープレコーダー

target 1 n (for arrows) まと・ 的; (aim) もくてき・ 目的 2 vb もくひょうをたっせいする・ 目標を達成する

tart n (British English) タルト; apple tart アップルパイ

task n しごと・ 仕事

taste 1 n (when eating, drinking) あじ・ 味; (when talking about preferences) このみ・ 好み; it's not to my taste わた しの このみではありません。・私の 好みではありま せん。; Yukiko has good taste ゆきこは しゅみが いいで

す。・ 幸子は 趣味が いいです。**2** vb (when describing a flavour) it tastes good おいしいです。; it tastes awful まずい です。; it tastes of cinnamon シナモンの あじが します。 ・ シナモンの 味が します。; (when eating, drinking) あじ わう ・ 味わう

Taurus n おうしざ ・ 牡牛座

tax n ぜいきん ・ 税金

taxi n タクシー

taxi rank (British English), **taxi stand** (US English) n タクシーのりば ・ タクシー乗り場

tea n (as drunk in the west) こうちゃ ・ 紅茶; (as drunk in Japan) おちゃ ・ お茶; (British English) (a meal) ばんごはん ・ 晩ご飯(ゆうしょく is also used.)

tea ceremony n さどう ・ 茶道

teach vb おしえる ・ 教える; to teach Japanese にほんご を おしえる ・ 日本語を 教える

teacher n せんせい ・ 先生

team n チーム

teapot n (for Japanese tea) きゅうす; (for English tea) ティーポット

tear¹ vb (to cause damage to) やぶる ・ 破る; to tear pages out of a book ほんの ページを やぶりとる ・ 本の ページを 破り取る; (to get damaged) やぶれる ・ 破れる; **tear off** ひきさく ・ 引き裂く; **tear up** ずたずたに やぶる ・ ずたずたに破る

tear² n なみだ ・ 涙; to burst into tears なきだす ・ 泣き出す

tease vb からかう

teaspoon n (cutlery) ティースプーン; (measurement) こさじ ・ 小さじ

technical adj ぎじゅつてき(な) ・ 技術的(な)

teenager n ティーンエージャー

telephone n でんわ ・ 電話

telephone directory *n* でんわちょう ・ 電話帳

telescope *n* ぼうえんきょう ・ 望遠鏡

television *n* テレビ; I saw that film on television あの えいがを テレビで みました。 ・ あの 映画を テレビで 見ました。

tell *vb (to say to)* いう ・ 言う; did you tell your parents? ごりょうしんに いいましたか。 ・ ご両親に 言いましたか。; to tell someone about a problem だれかに もんだいをうちあける ・ 誰かに 問題を 打ち明ける; to tell jokes じょうだんをいう ・ 冗談を 言う; *(when giving information)* おしえる ・ 教える; to tell someone your address だれかにじゅうしょをおしえる ・ 誰かに 住所を 教える; to tell someone the way だれかに みちを おしえる ・ 誰かに道を 教える; *(to work out, to know)* I can tell (that) she's disappointed かのじょは がっかりした ようです。 ・ 彼女は がっかりした ようです。; you can tell he's lying かれは うそを ついているのが わかるでしょう。 ・ 彼は 嘘をついているのが 分かるでしょう。; *(when making distinctions)* to tell the twins apart ふたごをみわける ・ 双子を 見分ける; I can't tell which is which みわけがつきません。 ・ 見分けが つきません。; *(to reveal)* いう ・ 言う; please don't tell anyone だれにも いわないでください。 ・ 誰にも 言わないでください。; **tell off** to tell someone off だれかをしかる ・ 誰かを 叱る

temper *n* to be in a temper おこっている ・ 怒っている; to lose one's temper おこる ・ 怒る

temperature *n* おんど ・ 温度; to have a temperature ねつがある ・ 熱が ある

temporary *adj* いちじてき(な) ・ 一時的(な); *(describing a job)* りんじ(の) ・ 臨時(の)

ten *num (on its own)* とお ・ 十; *(with a counter)* じゅう ・ 十; ten books ほん じゅっさつ ・ 本 十冊; I've got ten とおあ ります。・ 十 あります。

tennis *n* テニス

tennis court *n* テニスコート

tense adj きんちょうしている・緊張している

tent n テント

tenth num (in a series) じゅうばん(め)・十番(目); (in dates) the tenth of December じゅうにがつとおか・十二月十日

term n がっき・学期

terrible adj (expressing shock) ひどい; (used for emphasis) すごい

terrified adj おそれを した・恐れを した

terror n きょうふ・恐怖

terrorist n テロリスト

test 1 vb (to try out) ためして みる・試して みる; (in exams) テストする **2** n テスト; (in school, college) しけん・試験: a driving test うんてんめんきょの しけん・運転免許の 試験; to have an eye test しりょくけんさを うける・視力検査を 受ける

than 1 prep Note that the word order is different to English in sentences expressing comparison; (in comparisons) 〜より〜; stronger than... 〜より つよい・〜より 強い; more intelligent than... 〜より あたまが いい・〜より 頭が いい; faster than... 〜より はやい・〜より 速い; I've got more money than you わたしは あなたより もっと お金が あります・私は あなたより もっと お金が あります。; (when talking about quantities) more than 〜いじょう・〜以上; more than half of the pupils were absent はんぶんいじょうの せいとが けっせきしました・半分以上の 生徒が 欠席しました。; more than £100 ひゃくポンドいじょう・百ポンド以上; less than 〜いか・〜以下; less than 2% にパーセントいか・二パーセント以下 **2** conj 〜より〜; he's older than I am かれは わたしより としうえです・彼は 私より 年上です。

thank vb かんしゃする・感謝する

thanks 1 adv ありがとう。**2 thanks to** 〜の おかげで

thank you adv ありがとうございます。; thank you for coming きてくれて ありがとうございます・来て く

れて ありがとう ございます。; (when accepting food and drink) 'more wine?'—'thank you' 「ワインは いかがです か。」「いただきます。」

that pron what's that? それは なんですか。・ それは 何で すか。; who's that? その ひとは だれですか。・ その 人 は 誰ですか。; is that Lewis? あの ひとは ルイスさん ですか。・ あの 人は ルイスさんですか。; that's how jam is made そうやって ジャムが つくられます。・ そうやっ て ジャムが 作られます。; that's not true それは ほんと うではありません。・ それは 本当ではありません。; that's the kitchen そこは だいどころです。・ そこは 台 所です。

the det ! Not used in Japanese.

theatre (British English), **theater** (US English) n げきじょ う・劇場

their det かれらの・彼らの Not used if obvious. If you know their names, it is better to use these rather than かれら; I don't like their house かれらの いえが すきではありません。・ 彼らの 家が 好きではありません。

theirs pron かれらの・彼らの If you know their names, it is better to use these rather than かれら; that new house is theirs あの あたらしい いえは かれらのです。・ あの 新しい 家は 彼らのです。; which car is theirs? かれらの くるま は どれですか。・ 彼らの 車は どれですか。

themselves pron Not used as a reflexive pronoun in Japanese; they want to enjoy themselves かれらは たのし みたいです。・ 彼らは 楽しみたいです。; they didn't hurt themselves かれらは けがを しませんでした。・ 彼らは 怪我を しませんでした。; (when used for emphasis) they did it all by themselves かれらは じぶんたちで しまし た。・ 彼らは 自分達で しました。

then adv (at that point in time) その とき; I was living in Paris then その とき、パリに すんでいました。・ その とき、 パリに 住んでいました。; we saw each other a lot then そ の とき、よく あいました。・ その とき、よく 会いま した。; from then on その ときから; (after, next) そして;

I had breakfast and then I went to work あさごはんを たべ ました。そしてかいしゃに いきました。・ 朝ご飯を 食べました。そして会社に 行きました。; The 〜て form of the verb can also be used when describing a chronological sequence of actions; I watched a film, drank some beer, then went home. えいがを みて、ビールを のんで、かえりました。・ 映画を 見て、ビールを 飲んで、帰りました。

there 1 pron there is a problem もんだいが あります・ 問 題があります。; there aren't any shops みせが ありませ ん。・ 店が ありません。; there was no room よゆうが あ りませんでした。余裕が ありませんでした。; there are a lot of people ひとが たくさん います。・ 人が たくさ ん います。**2** adv (when talking about location) the train wasn't there でんしゃが ありませんでした。・ 電車が ありませんでした。; please go over there あそこに いっ てください。・ あそこに 行ってください。; when do we get there? いつ つきますか。・ いつ 着きますか。; I don't go there very often そこに あまり いきません。・ そこに あまり 行きません。; (when drawing attention) there's the sea うみです。・ 海です。; (when offering something) there you are, there you go どうぞ。

therefore adv ですから

these 1 det この; these books aren't mine この ほんは わ たしのではありません。・ この 本は 私のではありま せん。**2** pron これ; what are these? これは なんですか。 ・ これは 何ですか。; these are my bags これは わたしの かばんです。・ これは 私の かばんです。; I prefer these これのほうが いいです。・ これの 方が いいです。; (when referring to people) この ひとたち・ この 人達; these are my friends from Manchester この ひとたちは マ ンチェスターの ともだちです。・ この 人たちは マンチェスターからの友達です。

they pron かれら・ 彼ら Not used if obvious. If you know their names, it is better to use these rather than かれら; they'll be there too かれらも います。・ 彼らも います。; they're intelligent かれらは あたまが いいです。・ 彼らは 頭が

いいです。; that's how they make tofu それは とうふの つくりかたです。・ それは 豆腐の 作り方です。

thick *adj* あつい・厚い

thief *n* どろぼう・泥棒

thigh *n* ふともも・太もも

thin *adj* (line) ほそい・細い; (person, animal) やせた・痩せた: to get thin やせる・痩せる

thing *n* (physical object) もの・物; (abstract entity) こと; please take the things off the chair いすから ものを どかしてください。・ 椅子から 物を 退かしてください。: I've got things to do する ことが あります。; that is a stupid thing to do それは ばかな ことです。; the best thing would be to call him かれに でんわした ほうが いいです。・ 彼に 電話した 方が いいです。: I can't hear a thing なにも きこえません。・ 何も 聞こえません。; (belongings) もちもの・持ち物

think *vb* (when talking about opinions) use a plain form + と おもう; what do you think of it? どう おもいますか。・ どう 思いますか。; I think it's unfair ふこうへいだと おもいます。・ 不公平だと 思います。; who do you think will win? だれが かつと おもいますか。・ 誰が 勝つと 思いますか。; (to concentrate on an idea) かんがえる・考える; please think hard before answering こたえるまえに よく かんがえてください。・ 答える 前に よく 考えてください。; (to remember) おもいだす・思い出す; I can't think of his name かれの なまえが おもいだせません。・ 彼の 名前が 思い出せません。; (to take into account, to have in mind) to think about someone だれかの ことを かんがえる・ 誰かの ことを 考える; I thought of you when I saw the dress あの ドレスをみた とき、あなたの ことを おもいだしました。・ あの ドレスを 見た とき、あなたの ことを 思い出しました。; (to have vague plans to) to be thinking of going to America アメリカに いく ことを かんがえている・ アメリカに 行く ことを 考えている; (to have an idea about) to think of a solution かいけつほうを おもいつく・ 解決法を 思いつく

third 1 adj さんばん(め) ・ 三番(目) **2** n (in a series) さんばんめ(の) ・ 三番目(の); (in dates) the third of June ろくがつみっか ・ 六月三日; (when talking about quantities) さんぶんのいち ・ 三分の 一; a third of the population じんこうのさんぶんのいち ・ 人口の 三分の 一 **3** adv to come third さんいに なる ・ 三位に なる

thirsty adj to be thirsty のどが かわいている ・ 喉が 渇いている

thirteen num じゅうさん ・ 十三

thirteenth num (in a series) じゅうさんばん(め) ・ 十三番(目); (in dates) Friday the thirteenth じゅうさんにちの きんようび ・ 十三日の 金曜日

thirty num さんじゅう ・ 三十

this 1 det この; I like this garden この にわが すきです。 ・ この 庭が 好きです。; do you know this place? この ばしょを しっていますか。 ・ この 場所を 知っていますか。; who is this woman? この おんなの ひとは だれですか。 ・ この 女の 人は 誰ですか。; I prefer this hotel この ホテルの ほうが いいです。 ・ この ホテルの 方が いいです。 **2** pron what's this? これは なんですか。 ・ これは 何ですか。; who's this? この ひとは だれですか。 ・ この 人は 誰ですか。; this is the kitchen ここは だいどころです。 ・ ここは 台所です。; this is my older sister こちらは あねです。 ・ こちらは 姉です。; this isn't the right address これは ただしい じゅうしょではありません。 ・ これは 正しい 住所ではありません。; how much is this? これは いくらですか。

thorn n とげ

those 1 det (referring to things near the listener) その; (referring to things not close to either speaker or listener) あの; those books are his その ほんは かれのです。 ・ その 本は 彼のです。 **2** pron (referring to things near the listener) それ; (referring to things not close to either speaker or listener) あれ; what are those? あれは なんですか。 ・ あれは 何ですか。; those are my letters それは わたしの てがみです。 ・ それは 私の 手紙です。; I prefer those あれの ほうが

いいです。・あれの 方が いいです。; (when referring to people) その ひとたち・その 人達; those are my cousins そのひとたちは いとこです。・その 人達は いとこで す。

though conj けれども; though it's expensive, I'll buy it たか いけれども かいます。・高い けれども 買います。

thought n (idea) かんがえ・考え

thousand num せん・千; three thousand pounds さんぜ んポンド・三千ポンド; about a thousand people せんに んぐらい・千人ぐらい

thread n いと・糸

threat n おどし・脅し

threaten ・ vb おどす・脅す

three num (on its own) みっつ・三つ; (with a counter) さん・ 三; three books ほん さんさつ・本 三冊; I've got three み っつあります。・三つ あります。

throat n のど・喉

through ! Often through occurs in combinations with verbs, for example: go through, let through, read through etc. To find the correct translations for this type of verb, look up the separate dictionary entries at go, let, read etc.; prep (from one side to the other) to drive through the desert さばくを とおりぬける・ 砂漠を 通り抜ける; I ran through the park こうえんを は しりました。・公園を 走りました。; (via, by way of) to go through the town centre まちなかを とおって いく・町 中を 通って 行く; to look through a window まどから み る・窓から 見る; (past) to go through a red light あかしん ごうを とおる・赤信号を 通る; to go through customs ぜいかんを とおる・税関を 通る; (when talking about time) right through the day いちにちじゅう・一日中; from Friday through to Sunday きんようびから にちようびま で・金曜日から 日曜日まで; it's open April through September (US English) しがつから くがつまで あいてい ます。・四月から 九月まで 開いています。

throw vb なげる・投げる; to throw stones at someone だれかに いしを なげる・誰かに 石を 投げる; please throw me the ball ボールを わたしに なげてください。・ボールを 私に 投げてください。; **throw away, throw out** すてる・捨てる

thumb n おやゆび・親指

thunder n かみなり・雷

thunderstorm n らいう・雷雨

Thursday n もくようび・木曜日

ticket n きっぷ・切符

tickle vb くすぐる

tide n しお・潮; high tide まんちょう・満潮; low tide かんちょう・干潮

tidy adj (describing a place, a desk) きちんとした; (describing a person) きれいずき(な)・きれい好き(な); **tidy up** かたづける・片づける

tie 1 vb むすぶ・結ぶ; to tie a dog to a tree いぬを きに つなぐ・犬を 木に つなぐ; to tie a parcel (up) with string に もつを ひもで しばる・荷物を 紐で 縛る **2** n (worn with a shirt) ネクタイ; (in sport) どうてん・同点

tiger n とら・虎; year of the tiger とらどし・寅年

tight adj (too small) きつい; (closely fitting) ぴったりした

tights n (British English) タイツ

till¹ ▶ until

till² n レジ

timber n もくざい・木材

time n じかん・時間; I don't have time to go there そこに いくじかんが ありません。・そこに 行く 時間が あ りません。; we haven't seen them for some time しばらく かれらに あっていません。・しばらく 彼らに 会って いません。; a long time ago むかし・昔; (when talking about a specific hour or period of time) the time when... ～と き; what's the time?, what time is it? なんじですか。・何時 ですか。; what time does the film start? えいがは なんじに

はじまりますか。・ 映画は 何時に 始まりますか。; to arrive on time じかんどおりにつく・ 時間通りに 着く; in five days' time いつかごに・ 五日後に; in a week's time いっしゅうかんごに・ 一週間後に; this time last year きょねんのいまごろ・ 去年の 今ごろ; by this time next week らいしゅうの いまごろまでに・ 来週の 今ごろ までに; it's time we left そろそろ しつれいします。・ そろそろ 失礼します。; (a moment) at times ときどき・ 時々; this is no time to argue けんかしている ばあいでは ありません。・ けんかしている 場合ではありません。; any time now もう すぐ; for the time being いまの ところ・ 今の ところ; (a period in the past) とき; we didn't know each other at the time その ときは おたがいに しりませんで した。・ その ときは お互いに 知りませんでした。; (an experience) to have a good time たのしむ・ 楽しむ; to have a hard time くろうする・ 苦労する; (an occasion) the first time we met はじめて あった とき・ 初めて 会った とき; from time to time ときどき・ 時々; (when comparing) three times more expensive さんばい たかい・ 三倍 高い; ten times quicker じゅうばい はやい・ 十倍 早い

timetable n (for trains, buses) じこくひょう・ 時刻表; (in school, at work) じかんわり・ 時間割

tin n (the metal) すず; (British English) (a can) かん・ 缶; tinned tomatoes かんづめの トマト・ 缶詰の トマト

tin opener n (British English) かんきり・ 缶切り

tiny adj ちいさ(な)・ 小さ(な)

tip n (the point, the end) せんたん・ 先端; to stand on tiptoe つまさきで たつ・ 爪先で 立つ; (given in a hotel, a restaurant) チップ; (a piece of advice) じょげん・ 助言

tire n (US English) タイヤ

tired adj (needing rest) つかれている・ 疲れている; to get tired つかれる・ 疲れる; (needing a change) I'm tired of this job この しごとに あきています。・ この 仕事に 飽き ています。; I'm tired of computer games コンピューター ゲームに あきています。・ コンピューターゲームに 飽きています。

tiring *adj* つかれさせる・疲れさせる

tissue *n* ティッシュ

to *prep* ! *There are many adjectives like* mean, nice, rude *etc and verbs like* belong, write *etc which involve the use of* to. *For translations, look up the adjective entries at* mean, nice, rude *or the verb entries at* belong, write.

toast *n* トースト; a piece of toast トースト いちまい・トースト一枚

toaster *n* トースター

today *adv* きょう・今日

toe *n* あしの ゆび・足の指

together *adv* いっしょに・一緒に

toilet *n* トイレ *A more polite word is* おてあらい

toilet paper *n* トイレットペーパー

tomato *n* トマト

tomorrow *adv* あした・明日

tongue *n* した・舌

tonight *adv* (this evening) こんばん・今晩; (during the night) よなかに・夜中に

too *adv* (also) use particle も; I'm going too わたしも いきます。・私も 行きます。; (more than is necessary or desirable) use い adjective without the final い + すぎる or the pre ます form of the verb + すぎる; too big おおきすぎる・大きすぎる; too expensive たかすぎる・高すぎる; too far とおすぎる・遠すぎる; there were too many people ひとが おおすぎました。・人が 多すぎました。; I ate too much たべすぎました。・食べ過ぎました。

tool *n* どうぐ・道具

tooth *n* は・歯; false teeth いれば・入れ歯

toothache *n* I have toothache はが いたいです。・歯が 痛いです。

toothbrush *n* はブラシ・歯ブラシ

toothpaste n はみがきこ・歯磨き粉

top 1 n (the highest part) the top of the mountain やまの ちょうじょう・山の 頂上; the top of the stairs かいだんの うえ・階段の 上; top of the page ページの あたま・ページの 頭; (a cover, a lid) (on a bottle, pan) ふた; (on a pen) キャップ; (the highest level) to be at the top of the class クラスのなかで いちばん できる・クラスの 中で 一番 できる **2** adj いちばんうえ(の)・一番上(の); the top shelf いちばんうえの たな・一番上の 棚

torch n (British English) かいちゅうでんとう・懐中電灯

torn adj やぶれている・破れている

tortoise n かめ・亀

total 1 n ごうけい・合計 **2** adj ぜんたい(の)・全体(の)

touch 1 vb (with one's hand) さわる・触る; (to interfere with) いじる **2** n to get in touch れんらくする・連絡する

tough adj (not soft, not sensitive) かたい; (rough) this is a tough area この へんは ちあんが わるいです。・この 辺は 治安が 悪いです。; (difficult) むずかしい・難しい; (severe) a tough law きびしい ほうりつ・厳しい 法律

tour 1 n to go on a tour of the castle おしろの ツアーをする・お城の ツアー を する **2** vb to go touring かんこうりょこうする・観光旅行する

tourism n かんこうぎょう・観光業

tourist n かんこうきゃく・観光客

tourist information office n かんこうあんないじょ・観光案内所

toward(s) prep (when talking about place, time) use particle へ; towards the east ひがしへ・東へ; towards evening ゆうがたごろ・夕方ごろ; (when talking about attitudes) 〜にたいして・〜に 対して; he has a bad attitude towards his work かれは しごとに たいして たいどが わるいです。・彼は 仕事に 対して 態度が 悪いです。

towel n タオル

tower n とう・塔

tower block n (British English) (residential) こうそうじゅうたく・高層住宅; (commercial) こうそうビル・高層ビル

town n まち・町; to go into town まちへいく・町へ行く

town hall n しやくしょ・市役所; (for a small town) やくば・役場

toy n おもちゃ

track n (a path) みち・道; (for sports) トラック; (the rails) せんろ・線路; (left by a person, an animal, a car) あと・跡

tracksuit n トレーニングウエア

trade n ぼうえき・貿易; (skill) to learn a trade ぎじゅつをならう・技術を習う

tradition n でんとう・伝統

traditional adj でんとうてき(な)・伝統的(な)

traffic n こうつう・交通

traffic jam n こうつうじゅうたい・交通渋滞

traffic lights n しんごう・信号

train 1 n でんしゃ・電車; the train to Hiroshima ひろしまゆきのでんしゃ・広島行きの 電車 **2** vb (to teach, to prepare) to train employees けんしゅうさせる・研修させる; to train athletes くんれんさせる・訓練させる; to train a dog いぬを しつける・犬を 躾る; (to learn a job) to train as a doctor いしゃのしかくをとる・医者の 資格を 取る; she trained as a teacher かのじょは きょういんめんきょをもっています。・彼女は 教員免許を 持っています。; (for a sporting event) トレーニングする

trainer n (British English) (shoe) スニーカー; (sports coach) コーチ

training course n トレーニングコース

tramp n ふろうしゃ・浮浪者

translate vb やくす・訳す

translator n ほんやくしゃ・翻訳者

transport, transportation (*US English*) *n* ゆそう・輸送; a means of transport ゆそうきかん・輸送機関

trap *n* わな; to set a trap for someone だれかに わなを しかける・誰かに わなを 仕掛ける

trash *n* (*US English*) ごみ

trash can *n* (*US English*) ごみばこ・ごみ箱

travel *vb* (*to travel to work or school*) かよう・通う; (*to take a holiday*) りょこうする・旅行する; (*to travel on business*) しゅっちょうする・出張する; to travel abroad がいこく りょこうする・外国旅行する

travel agency *n* りょこうがいしゃ・旅行会社

traveller (*British English*), **traveler** (*US English*) *n* りょこうしゃ・旅行者

traveller's cheque (*British English*), **traveler's check** (*US English*) *n* トラベラーズチェック

tray *n* おぼん・お盆

treat *vb* (*to deal with, to behave with*) あつかう・扱う; to treat someone badly だれかを わるく あつかう・誰かを 悪く扱う; (*to pay for*) おごる; to treat someone to a meal だれかに ごはんを おごる・誰かに ご飯を おごる

treatment *n* ちりょう・治療; to receive treatment ちりょうをうける・治療を 受ける

tree *n* き・木

tremble *vb* (*person*) ふるえる・震える; (*ground*) ゆれる・揺れる

trendy *adj* トレンディ(な)

trial *n* (*test*) テスト; (*in law*) さいばん・裁判; to go on trial さいばんにかけられる・裁判に かけられる

triangle *n* さんかく・三角; (*musical instrument*) トライアングル

trick 1 *n* (*a joke*) いたずら; to play a trick on someone だれかにいたずらを する・誰かに いたずらを する; (*a clever way of doing something*) こつ; (*to entertain*) てじな・手品 **2** *vb* だます

trip 1 n (holiday) りょこう・旅行; (a day out) ひがえりりょこう・日帰り旅行; (business trip) しゅっちょう・出張; (school day trip) えんそく・遠足 **2** vb to trip (up) つまずく・躓く; to trip someone (up) だれかを つまずかせる・誰かを 躓かせる

trouble n (difficulties) こんなん・困難; to be in trouble こまっている・困っている; to get someone into trouble だれかをこまらせる・誰かを 困らせる; to make trouble もんだいをおこす・問題を 起こす; (an effort) to go to a lot of trouble to... わざわざ ～する

trousers n ズボン

trout n ます

truck n トラック

truck driver n トラックの うんてんしゅ・トラックの 運転手

true adj ほんとう(の)・本当(の); is it true that he's coming? かれが くるのは ほんとうですか。・彼が 来るのは 本当ですか。; to come true じつげんする・実現する

trumpet n トランペット

trunk n (of a tree) みき・幹; (of an elephant) はな・鼻; (US English) (in a car) トランク

trunks n (for swimming) みずぎ・水着

trust vb (to believe) しんようする・信用する; to trust a friend ともだちを しんようする・友達を 信用する; I don't trust them かれらを しんようしません。・彼らを 信用しません。; (to rely on) しんらいする・信頼する; I can't trust him かれを しんらいできません。・彼を 信頼できません。

truth n しんじつ・真実

try 1 vb (to try to do something) use the volitional form of the verb + と する; to try to go いこうと する・行こうと する; to try to forget わすれようと する・忘れようと する; (to try it and see) use the ～て form of the verb + みる;

please try phoning him かれに でんわして みてください。・彼に 電話して みてください。I tried writing my name in katakana じぶんの なまえを カタカナで かいて みました。・自分の 名前を カタカナで 書いて みました。; (to test) use the 〜て form of the verb + みる; to try (out) a new restaurant あたらしい レストランに いって みる・新しい レストランに 行って みる; to try (on) a pair of trousers ズボンを はいて みる; (to taste) あじわう・味わう; (in court) さいばんに かける・裁判に かける; to try hard がんばる **2** n (in rugby) トライ

T-shirt n Tシャツ

tube n くだ・管; (British English) (the underground) ちかてつ・地下鉄

Tuesday n かようび・火曜日

tuna (in fish) まぐろ・鮪; (in can, sandwich) ツナ

tunnel n トンネル

turkey n しちめんちょう・七面鳥

turn 1 vb (to move one's body) むける・向ける; to turn one's face toward(s) the sun たいように かおを むける・太陽に 顔を 向ける; (to change direction) to turn right みぎに まがる・右に 曲がる; to turn the corner かどを まがる・角を曲がる; (to twist) まわす・回す; to turn the handle ハンドルを まわす・ハンドルを 回す; (to change) to turn the bedroom into an office しんしつを オフィスに かえる・寝室を オフィスに 変える; to turn into a frog かえるに なる・蛙に なる; (to become) なる; to turn into a butterfly ちょうに なる・蝶に なる; to turn red あかく なる・赤く なる **2** n (in a bend) カーブ; (in games) ばん・番; whose turn is it? だれの ばんですか・誰の 番ですか; **turn around, turn round** (to face the opposite way) (if it's a person) せなかを むける・背中を 向ける; (if it's a car) むきを かえる・向きを 変える; to turn the table around テーブルを まわす・テーブルを 回す; (to go round and round) まわる・回る; to turn something round and round なにかを まわす・何かを 回す; **turn back** ひきかえす・引き返す; **turn down** (to lower) よわく する・弱く する; to

turn down the heater ヒーターを よわくする・ヒーター を 弱く する; (to reject) ことわる・断る; to turn someone down だれかを ことわる・誰かを 断る; **turn off** to turn the oven off オーブンを けす・オーブンを 消す; to turn off the light でんきを けす・電気を 消す; to turn the tap off みずを とめる・水を 止める; **turn on** つける; to turn on the TV テレビを つける; to turn the tap on みずを だす・水を 出す; **turn out** it turned out to be easier than expected おもったより かんたんでした。・思ったより 簡単で した。; **turn over** (to roll over) ねがえりを うつ・寝返り を 打つ; to turn over the page ページを めくる; **turn up** (to show up) あらわれる・現れる; (to increase) to turn up the heater ヒーターを つよくする・ヒーターを 強く する; to turn the music up おんがくの ボリュームを あげ る・音楽の ボリュームを 上げる

turtle n がめ・亀

TV n テレビ

twelfth num (in a series) じゅうにばんめ（の）・十二番目 （の）; (in dates) じゅうににち・十二日; the twelfth of July しちがつじゅうににち・七月十二日

twelve num じゅうに・十二; twelve pupils せいと じゅ うににん・生徒 十二人; I've got twelve じゅうに あります。・十二 あります。

twenty num にじゅう・二十

twice adv にばい（の）・二倍（の）; twice as many people にばいのひと・二倍の 人; twice as much time にばいの じかん・二倍の 時間; (two times) にかい・二回

twin 1 n ふたご・双子 **2** adj a twin brother ▶ brother; a twin sister ▶ sister

twist vb (to bend out of shape) ひねる; (to injure) to twist one's ankle あしくびを ねんざする・足首を ねんざする

two num (on its own) ふたつ・二つ; (with a counter) に・二; two books ほん にさつ・本 二冊; I've got two ふたつ あ ります。・二つ あります。